Epithelial and Neuronal Cell Polarity and Differentiation

FRONT COVER
SV exocytosis in a rat hippocampal neuron developing in isolation in primary culture. From the paper
by Cameron et al., pp. 93-100.
Inset (top): localization of Na$^+$,K$^+$-ATPase in Fischer rat thyroid epithelial cells by laser scanning
confocal microscopy. Courtesy of E. Rodriguez-Boulan.

Epithelial and Neuronal Cell Polarity and Differentiation

Edited by

E. Rodriguez-Boulan and W. J. Nelson

SUPPLEMENT 17   1993

JOURNAL OF CELL SCIENCE

Published by THE COMPANY OF BIOLOGISTS LIMITED, Cambridge

The Company of Biologists Limited is a non-profit-making organization whose directors are active professional biologists. The Company, which was founded in 1925, is the owner and publisher of this and *The Journal of Experimental Biology* and *Development* (formerly *Journal of Embryology and Experimental Morphology*).

Journal of Cell Science is devoted to the study of cell organization. Papers will be published dealing with the structure and function of plant and animal cells and their extracellular products, and with such topics as cell growth and division, cell movements and interactions, and cell genetics. Accounts of advances in the relevant techniques will also be published. Contributions concerned with morphogenesis at the cellular and sub-cellular level will be acceptable, as will studies of micro-organisms and viruses, in so far as they are relevant to an understanding of cell organization. Theoretical articles and occasional review articles will be published.

Subscriptions

Journal of Cell Science is published monthly and in 1994 will have 12 normal issues and 1 casebound supplement. The 12 normal issues will be in the form of 1 volume (107). In 1994 the Supplement will be 'Cell Biology of Cancer' edited by David Glover, Alan Hall and Nick Hastie.
Supplements may be purchased individually – prices on application to The Company of Biologists Ltd.

Subscription rates 1994 (for volume 107 plus Supplement 18)

USA, Canada and Mexico: Institutional US$1050; Individual US$150.
Rest of the World: Institutional £595; Individual £95.
(All prices include post and packaging).

Orders

Orders for 1994, which can be in £ Sterling/Dollars or using Access/Visa credit cards, should be sent to Subscription Administrator, The Company of Biologists Ltd, Bidder Building, 140 Cowley Road, Cambridge CB4 4DL, UK (telephone 0223 426164; 24 hour ordering by Fax 0223 423353) or to your normal agent or bookseller. Individual rates apply only when payment is made by personal cheque or credit card and is sent direct to the Company, not by way of an agent.
Orders must be accompanied by payment. Please contact the above address for prices of back volumes.

Back numbers

Back numbers of the *Journal of Cell Science* may be ordered through The Company of Biologists Ltd. This journal is the successor to the *Quarterly Journal of Microscopical Science*, back numbers of which are obtainable from Messers William Dawson & Sons, Cannon House, Park Farm Road, Folkestone, Kent CT19 5EE, UK.

Journal of Cell Science
Supplement 17
December 1993

Typeset, Printed and Published by
THE COMPANY OF BIOLOGISTS LIMITED
Bidder Building, 140 Cowley Road, Cambridge CB4 4DL, UK
© The Company of Biologists Limited 1993

ISBN: 0 948601 40 X

Preface

The search for mechanisms involved in generating and maintaining cell polarity has attracted a wide variety of scientific disciplines, including cell biologists, neurobiologists, developmental biologists, biochemists and clinicians. There are few areas of research that can draw upon this broad foundation of information and expertise. The purpose of the Keystone Meeting on Epithelial and Neuronal Cell Polarity and Differentiation, held at Tamarron, Colorado (February 4-10, 1993) was to bring together these diverse groups to discuss the latest advances in our knowledge of epithelial and neuronal polarity. The research presented at this meeting, recorded in the papers in this volume, covered a wide variety of topics: recent findings that have identified biogenic pathways, sorting signals and extracellular cues involved in the organization of polarized cell surfaces in epithelial and neuronal cells; important roles of cell adhesion proteins, the submembrane cytoskeleton, growth factors and proto-oncogenes in regulating the development of cell surface polarity; and new insights into mechanisms involved in abnormal organization of epithelial cells in a variety of disease processes. One of the exciting aspects of the meeting was to see the integration of information presented in these diverse areas and how this integration is leading to the rapid advance in our understanding of cell polarity.

The success of the meeting was aided considerably by financial support from the *Journal of Cell Science* and Dr Hank Lane, Costar Corporation. Through this generous support, we were able to subsidize the travel and accomodation of not only an international group of speakers, but also a large number of postdoctoral fellows and graduate students who presented posters during the afternoon sessions.

We hope that the papers presented in this volume convey the excitement of the participants of this meeting, and that they serve to attract new investigators who can bring further ideas and diversity to this important area of research.

Enrique Rodriguez-Boulan
Cornell University Medical College, New York

W. James Nelson
Stanford University School of Medicine, Stanford

CONTENTS

Supplement 17   December 1993

Journal of Cell Science, Supplement 17, 1-7 (1993)
Printed in Great Britain © The Company of Biologists Limited 1993

Molecular sorting in polarized and non-polarized cells:

common problems, common solutions

Ira Mellman, Ellen Yamamoto, J. Andrew Whitney, Min Kim, Walter Hunziker* and Karl Matter

Department of Cell Biology, Yale University School of Medicine, 333 Cedar Street, PO Box 3333, New Haven, Connecticut 06510, USA

*Present address: Institute of Biochemistry, University of Lausanne, CH-1066, Epalinges, Switzerland

SUMMARY

We have been interested in determining how epithelial cells generate and maintain their characteristically polarized distributions of membrane proteins. Our efforts to date strongly indicate that the polarized transport in MDCK cells may be due to a set of discrete targeting determinants often found on a membrane protein's cytoplasmic domain. Surprisingly, these determinants are widely distributed and are not specific to proteins expressed in polarized cells. They also appear to function in controlling polarized transport along both the biosynthetic and the endocytic (or transcytotic) pathways. Signals for basolateral transport have been characterized and, like the cytoplasmic domain signal used by plasma membrane receptors for accumulation at clathrin-coated pits, they often involve a critical tyrosine residue. Although the basolateral and coated pit signals may also be co-linear, they are not identical. The basolateral and apical transport determinants are also hierarchically arranged. Although a single protein may contain one or more signals specifying basolateral transport, inactivation of these signals appears to reveal a determinant that directs efficient apical transport. Given that the sequence determinants responsible for polarized transport are not restricted to epithelial cells and are related to determinants commonly utilized in all cells, it is possible that non-polarized cells contain cognate apical and basolateral pathways that are responsible for 'constitutive' transport from the Golgi to the plasma membrane. The presence of two cognate pathways might confer a high degree of plasticity to pre-differentiated cells, allowing them rapidly to begin assuming a polarized phenotype in response to extracellular stimuli without requiring the synthesis of epithelial cell-specific transport machinery.

Key words: epithelial cells, polarization, Golgi, plasma membrane, apical transport, basolateral transport

INTRODUCTION

Understanding how polarized cells generate distinct plasma membrane domains within a continuous lipid bilayer has emerged as one of the central fundamental problems in molecular cell biology. Since many functions of epithelial cells, neuronal cells and certain cells of the immune system depend on the maintenance of characteristically polarized phenotypes, polarity is also a problem fundamental to understanding embryonic development, tissue morphogenesis, neural transmission and aspects of the immune response.

Over the past several years, excellent work from a number of laboratories (most of which are represented in this monograph) has described the general features that define polarity in cultured (MDCK, Caco-2) and primary (heptocytes, intestine) epithelial cells. The majority of plasma membrane proteins in these cells can be distinguished by being distributed primarily either to the apical or to the basolateral plasma membrane domains; relatively few proteins have been identified that are equally distributed on both surfaces. In addition, it is clear that the sorting of most newly synthesized plasma membrane proteins to either the apical or basolateral surfaces can occur either in the trans-Golgi network, after delivery to the basolateral surface, or at both locations. Still other proteins may be sorted by an ex post facto mechanism involving their selective removal following delivery to both plasma membrane domains.

Defining the molecular mechanisms responsible for the sorting of proteins in epithelial cells, however, has been another matter. Our situation has proved roughly analogous to the plight of quantum physicists searching for a Grand Unified Theory of the universe: every time a series of equations begins to come close to a simple explanation, a new sub-atomic particle is discovered that sends everyone clamoring back to their drawing boards and supercomputers. Until recently, it was becoming increasingly apparent that targeting in polarized cells could be explained by a single general paradigm which was simple, elegant, and - best of all - made sense. This paradigm held that delivery of membrane proteins to the apical surface of epithelial cells was the only transport event that required the involvement of a specific sorting signal. Transport to the basolateral membrane, on the other hand, was thought to occur in the absence of a specific apical signal, i.e. by 'default'.

Such an arrangment is inherently attractive for two reasons. First, the apical surface of most epithelia represents the plasma membrane domain that is differentiated for epithelial-cell-specific functions, such as nutrient adsorption or resorption. Accordingly, most epithelial-cell-specific proteins are localized to the apical plasma membrane. The basolateral surface, on the other hand, is functionally analogous to the plasma membrane of non-polarized cells, containing those membrane proteins and receptors involved in constitutive or 'housekeeping' functions. Thus, it is reasonable to presume that the requirement for transporting proteins to a differentiated apical domain reflects the development of transport machinery and targeting signals that facilitate this unique transport event. This view is also consistent with the long-standing belief that transport through the biosynthetic pathway to the plasma membrane in non-polarized cells occurs by 'bulk flow', i.e. in the absence of any signals specifying forward transport (Mellman and Simons, 1992). However, to date, no specific apical targeting determinant has been identified, although there is evidence suggesting that the structural information that directs transport to the apical surface must be found in a membrane protein's extracellular and/or membrane spanning domain.

CYTOPLASMIC DOMAINS AND POLARIZED TRANSPORT

Problems with the prevailing simple, unified view of polarized transport began to emerge with a series of observations demonstrating that the cytoplasmic domain of at least some membrane proteins determined whether newly synthesized proteins would be targeted to the apical or basolateral surfaces. This was first apparent in the case of the polymeric immunoglobulin receptor (pIg-R), when Mostov and colleagues (see this monograph) found a clear role for the pIg-R cytoplasmic tail in allowing the receptor to reach the basolateral surface prior to mediating transcytosis to the apical surface. This observation could be rationalized by the fact that the pIg-R was an epithelial-cell-specific protein whose cytoplasmic domain might simply make use of yet another differentiated feature of polarized cells.

Coated pit localization and basolateral targeting

More difficult to accommodate, however, were observations showing that the mouse IgG Fc receptor (FcRII) exhibited distinct polarities in transfected MDCK cells, depending on the structure of the receptor's cytoplasmic domain (Hunziker and Mellman, 1989). Although expressed in certain epithelia (placental syncytiotrophoblasts) (Stuart et al., 1989), FcRII is more characteristic of macrophages, granulocytes and lympocytes where it

exists in multiple isoforms due to alternative mRNA splicing. The two major splice products, FcRII-B1 and -B2, differ from each other only by the presence of a 47-residue in-frame insertion found proximal to the membrane in the cytoplasmic domain of FcRII-B1. Interestingly, this insertion completely prevents the ability of FcRII-B1 to enter clathrin-coated pits, explaining why Fc-receptor-positive lymphocytes (which express only FcRII-B1) bind but cannot internalize receptor-bound ligands (Amigorena et al., 1992; Miettinen et al., 1992; Miettinen et al., 1989).

When expressed in MDCK cells, the two Fc receptor isoforms were found to have entirely different polarities. FcRII-B2 was found predominantly (>80%) on the basolateral surface while FcRII-B1 was concentrated on the apical domain. Moreover, deletion mutants of FcRII-B2 that either did or did not remove the receptor's coated pit localization domain (Miettinen et al., 1992) also exhibited different distributions: receptor mutants capable of coated pit localization were found basolaterally, and those unable to accumulate at coated pits were found apically (Hunziker and Mellman, 1989). Interestingly, the small fraction of FcRII-B2 that appeared on the apical plasma membrane was also capable of apical-to-basolateral transcytosis; the likely significance of this observation will be considered below.

Shortly thereafter, the polarized distribution of a number of other receptors and non-receptor membrane proteins were found to correlate with the endocytosis phenotype, with those proteins capable of rapid endocytosis generally being found basolaterally. Examples included wild type and mutant forms of the influenza virus hemagglutinin (Brewer and Roth, 1991), lgp120 (Hunziker et al., 1991a), lysosomal acid phosphatase (Prill et al., 1992), nerve growth factor receptor (Le Bivic et al., 1991) and VSV G protein (D. Sabatini et al., unpublished). Importantly, the polarized distributions of each of these proteins reflected polarized sorting of newly synthesized proteins in the TGN, not the redistribution due to transcytosis following insertion into a single plasma membrane domain. This was true even for FcRII which, as mentioned above, is capable of apical-to-basolateral transcytosis, as long as the apically expressed receptor is capable of being internalized (Hunziker et al., 1991a).

Taken together, these results strongly suggested that the cytoplasmic domains of a variety of membrane proteins, many of which were not epithelial-cell-specific, contained a determinant which was required for efficient basolateral transport. Moreover, removal or inactivation of this determinant resulted in transport to the apical surface. The results also suggested that there was a correlation between basolateral transport and the presence of a functional internalization signal. Such a correlation further suggested that there may be a mechanistic relationship between sorting in the Golgi and localization at clathrin-coated pits.

Sorting signals in the LDL receptor cytoplasmic domain

One important exception to the correlation between coated pit localization and basolateral targeting was the human low density lipoprotein (LDL) receptor. While expression of the full length wild-type receptor resulted in its expectedly efficient transport to the basolateral surface, we found that

proximal signal   distal signal   *basolateral targeting*

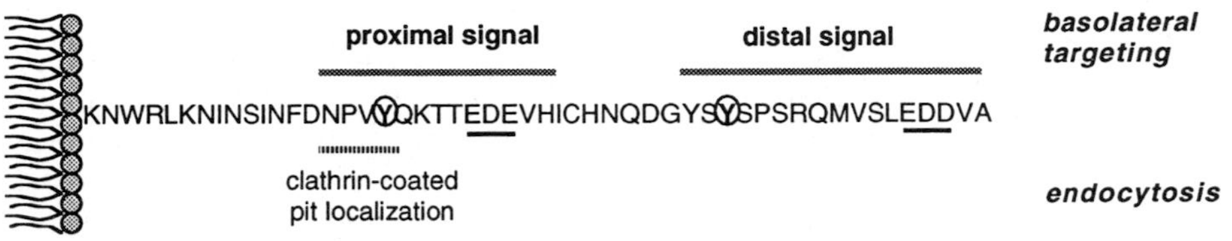

KNWRLKNINSINFDNPVYQKTTEDEVHICHNQDGYSYSPSRQMVSLEDDVA

clathrin-coated pit localization   *endocytosis*

Fig. 1. Domain organization of the LDL receptor cytoplasmic tail. Adapted from Matter et al. (1992).

mutation of tyrosine-18 - well known to be a critical element of the receptor's coated pit localization signal - had absolutely no effect on basolateral targeting (Hunziker et al., 1991a). Deletion of the entire cytoplasmic domain did, however, result in apical transport, demonstrating that the LDL receptor cytoplasmic tail did contain information required to reach the basolateral surface.

Very recently, this apparent discrepancy was solved by the observation that the LDL receptor cytoplasmic domain contains not one but two determinants for basolateral targeting (Matter et al., 1992). One of these mapped to the distal region of the tail, and the second was in a more membrane-proximal location and, in fact, was co-linear with the receptor's coated pit localization signal (Fig. 1). Importantly, upon inactivation of the distal determinant by COOH-terminal deletion, basolateral transport of the truncated receptors was found to be completely dependent on the critical tyrosine residue at position 18. Thus, even in LDL receptor, a coated pit-like signal can play a role in mediating transport from the TGN to the basolateral surface; in the full length receptor, however, this role is normally 'masked' by the existence of a second basolateral targeting determinant.

Next we further defined the features of the two basolateral targeting determinants. Importantly, both were shown to act independently from each other and separately to direct the basolateral transport of a heterologous receptor (FcRII) when used to substitute for the FcRII cytoplasmic tail. The two signals were not identical, however, but differed in their relative efficiencies at mediating basolateral targeting. Although both were equivalent at low expression levels (<50,000 receptors/cell), at high expression the proximal signal proved to be progressively less capable of targeting receptor transport to the basolateral domain. Instead, an increasing fraction of the receptor was transported from the Golgi directly to the apical plasma membrane (Matter et al., 1992). To continue our analogy with quantum physics, the proximal signal can thus be considered as a 'weak force' and the distal signal as a 'strong force' for polarized transport.

The two signals were related in other ways, however. As already mentioned, the proximal signal was found to depend critically on tyrosine-18 for basolateral targeting activity. Although this tyrosine is also a critical determinant for LDL receptor endocytosis, the proximal basolateral signal was not identical to the coated pit signal (Matter et al., 1992). This was demonstrated by the fact that COOH-terminal deletions up to tail residue-22 - a deletion that has no effect on receptor endocytosis - was found to completely inactivate the proximal determinant's ability to mediate receptor transport to the basolateral plasma membrane (Fig. 1). Thus, the basolateral targeting signal requires the amino acid residues on the COOH-terminal side of tyrosine-18 that are not required for endocytosis.

Surprisingly, the strong distal determinant was also found to be tyrosine-dependent, preferentially requiring the tyrosine at position 35 (Matter et al., 1992). No other single amino acid residue in the region was found to be essential. Although neither tyrosine-35 nor the tyrosine at position 37 were able to support internalization of the receptor from the plasma membrane, this finding suggests that tyrosines may form part of a common recognition motif, or at least serve as critical elements of two distinct motifs, important for at least two types of molecular sorting events: basolateral transport and coated pit localization. Like the coated pit signal, basolateral targeting via the distal determinant - at least under some conditions - also required amino acids on the COOH-terminal side of the critical tyrosine residue. This requirement was not absolute since it was abrogated by mutations that brought the distal determinant to a position closer to the membrane. For example, if the proximal region of the receptor cytoplasmic domain was deleted, or if the distal determinant was spliced directly to the membrane anchoring domain of FcRII, the requirement for these additional amino acids disappeared. Nevertheless, basolateral targeting activity remained tyrosine-dependent (Matter et al., 1993).

The only other receptor which has thus far been analyzed in detail is the pIg-R for which a distinct basolateral targeting determinant has also been characterized (Casanova et al., 1991). While a superficial sequence similarity between this region and the distal region of the LDL receptor tail exists (Yokode et al., 1992), none of the conserved residues are in fact required for basolateral targeting of the LDL receptor (Matter et al., 1992). At present, there is still insufficient information available to know whether the pIg-R determinant is tyrosine-dependent or, more importantly, whether the pIg-R similarly contains more than one basolateral targeting signal. The existence of a second signal might well explain the lack of effect of mutations affecting pIg-R tyrosines known to be involved in internalization (Mostov, this monograph). In any event, it is conceivable that - as is true even for coated pit signals - there will be considerable sequence diversity in a putative motif specifying basolateral targeting.

Generalized distribution and hierarchical arrangment of targeting determinants

Results from the LDL receptor, as well as from other membrane proteins, indicates several important principles governing the polarized transport in epithelial cells.

First, since distinct basolateral targeting signals exist, it is clear that transport to the basolateral surface can no longer be considered to occur by 'default'.

Second, since inactivation of the basolateral signal(s) invariably results in efficient apical targeting as opposed to random appearance on both surfaces, apical targeting signals must also exist, but they must be recessive to the baso-

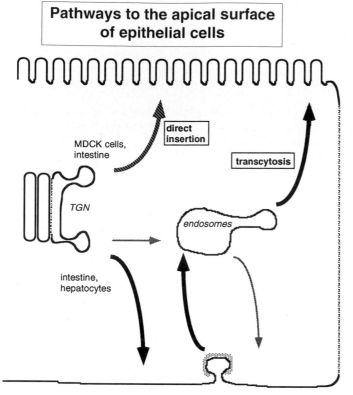

Pathways to the apical surface of epithelial cells

direct insertion

transcytosis

MDCK cells, intestine

TGN

endosomes

intestine, hepatocytes

Fig. 2. Pathways of apical and basolateral transport in epithelial cells.

lateral signal. In other words, the basolateral and apical targeting determinants are hierarchically arranged. Since apical transport occurs in the absence of a cytoplasmic domain, apical signals must be localized in either the membrane-spanning or extracellular domains, as suggested previously. It is likely, however, that accumulation in apically targeted transport vesicles does not reflect the presence of distinct amino acid sequences but rather a less well-defined physical feature of membrane proteins; thus, apical targeting may not be strictly 'signal-dependent', but occurs when there is no longer a signal that specifies accumulation in basolateral vesicles.

Third, and most intriguing, it is obvious that the determinants specifying polarized transport in epithelial cells are not limited to proteins expressed only in polarized cells, but are far more generally distributed. Thus, somewhat paradoxically, signals specifying polarized transport are not unique features of polarized cells. Rather, the induction of polarity in non-polarized cells may reflect the reorganization of pre-existing transport machinery. The implications of this possibility will be discussed further, below.

TRANSCYTOSIS AND POLARIZED TRANSPORT

In MDCK cells, pathways leading to the apical or basolateral surfaces are thought to diverge in the Golgi; in other words, apical and basolateral proteins are sorted in the TGN and transported directly to their final destinations. In other epithelial cells, however, these transport pathways can be indirect, with apical transport occurring after delivery to the basolateral plasma membrane. Consequently, basolateral-

to-apical transcytosis can play an important role in the biosynthetic transport of the same proteins that are sorted directly in the TGN of MDCK cells (Fig. 2). While it is reasonable to propose that the same sorting signals would be active in both direct and indirect transport to the apical surface, this possibility presents a conceptual problem since the sorting of proteins on the transcytotic pathway occurs not in the Golgi but in endosomes. At present, there is no evidence that endosomes are capable of decoding sorting signals used on the biosynthetic pathway. On the contrary, extensive work from Mostov and co-workers has suggested that basolateral-to-apical transcytosis, at least of pIg-R, depends on a unique phosphoserine-dependent signal that has no clear role in Golgi sorting.

Our own recent observations, however, suggest that the signals specifying direct and indirect transport may be fundamentally similar, and possibly identical. Thus, transcytosis in MDCK cells is not an activity limited to a small subset of highly specialized proteins, but is seemingly determined by the relative activities of the same ubiquitously distributed basolateral and apical targeting determinants that control polarized transport from the TGN.

Transcytosis of LDL receptors and LDL receptor chimera

While LDL receptors are not usually capable of mediating transcytosis from their normal site of residence on the basolateral plasma membrane, we have found that transcytosis is induced by mutations that remove or inactivate the receptor's distal basolateral targeting determinant. Moreover, LDL-receptor-mediated transcytosis was found to be comparable in both rate and efficiency to the basolateral-to-apical transcytosis of dIgA by the pIg-R (Matter et al., 1993). Like dIgA transcytosis (Hunziker et al., 1991b), transcytosis via these mutant LDL receptors was also found to be markedly reduced by treatment with the brefeldin A and nocodazole.

LDL receptor transcytosis was measured using two types of constructs. First, chimeric receptors were prepared bearing the extracellular and membrane anchor domains of FcRII spliced to the cytoplasmic tail harboring the deletion or tyrosine mutations that inactivated the receptor's basolateral targeting domain (Matter et al., 1992). In this case, transcytosis was easily measured by determining the transport of ^{125}I-Fab fragments of the anti-FcRII monoclonal antibody 2.4G2. Neither LDL nor the anti-LDL receptor antibody C7 could be used to measure transcytosis, since both rapidly dissociate after delivery to acidic endosomes. To ensure that non-chimeric LDL receptor mutants also mediated transcytosis, we also used a biotinylation protocol to visualize movement of receptors from the basolateral to the apical surfaces. Both assays gave qualitatively equivalent results.

It is virtually impossible that the LDL receptor could have acquired a specific transcytotic signal as a consequence of eliminating a domain involved in basolateral targeting. No new sequence was added, and neither the mutant nor wild-type forms of the receptor were phosphorylated. Rather, it appears far more likely that LDL receptor transcytosis reflects the sorting activity of the pre-existing apical targeting signal. Following internalization and delivery to basolateral endosomes, LDL receptor is normally sorted with high fidelity into recycling vesicles directed back to the basolateral plasma membrane. Without a strong distal targeting domain, recycling might be rendered less efficient and a greatly increased fraction of the receptor sorted into nascent transcytotic vesicles via the apical signal. This scheme predicts that, even in endosomes, the apical signal would be able to compete more effectively with the relatively weak proximal basolateral targeting domain. After the LDL receptor reaches the apical plasma membrane, it would still contain a partially active proximal basolateral targeting domain which, in principle, might initiate receptor transcytosis in the reverse direction. Interestingly, this is precisely what happens, and in a fashion that is completely dependent on the basolateral targeting activity of the remaining proximal determinant. LDL receptor chimera bearing deletions up to the basolateral targeting signal (CT27, cytoplasmic tail 27 residues in length; see Fig. 1) mediate rapid internalization and efficient apical-to-basolateral transcytosis of 2.4G2 Fab fragments. Deletions into this signal, however (CT22), while not blocking rapid endocytosis, do completely prevent transcytosis. In other words, there is a correlation between the region of proximal determinant required for basolateral targeting and the region that is required for apical-to-basolateral transcytosis. Together, these results further emphasize the possibility that common, widely distributed determinants may control virtually all post-Golgi sorting events that occur in polarized epithelial cells.

MECHANISMS OF POLARIZED TRANSPORT ON THE ENDOCYTIC AND BIOSYNTHETIC PATHWAYS

The possibility that common determinants direct basolateral and/or apical targeting on both the biosynthetic and transcytotic pathways suggest that the sorting machinery associated with the TGN, apical endosomes and basolateral endosomes may be fundamentally similar, if not identical. While the tyrosine dependence of basolateral targeting of LDL receptor and other membrane proteins suggests a superficial relationship to the type of recognition event responsible for receptor localization at clathrin-coated pits, this is little more than one of several interesting possibilities.

One hint has been offered by the effect of brefeldin A (BFA). We have previously found that BFA greatly inhibits basolateral-to-apical transcytosis of dIgA bound to pIg-R (Hunziker et al., 1991b). LDL receptor transcytosis is similarly affected. This inhibition occurs at a very early step on the pathway, probably corresponding to the sorting of pIg-R into transcytotic vesicles at the level of basolateral endosomes.

The BFA effect is most easily interpreted as a block in transcytotic vesicle formation. By analogy to conventional wisdom regarding BFA's effects on the Golgi, one tends to think in terms of the drug blocking the formation of COP-coated vesicles that are required for transport. However, it is interesting to note that the drug does not completely block dIgA transcytosis, but reduces it down to a basal level. Moreover, BFA has little or no effect on the basolateral-to-apical transcytosis of other probes. Sandvig and co-workers, for example, have shown that the low level of fluid transcytosis that occurs across MDCK cells is almost completely unaffected by BFA (Sandvig et al., 1991). Similarly, we have found that the low level of lgp120 transcytosis is also BFA-resistant - occurring at an efficiency similar to that exhibited by dIgA-bound pIg-R in the presence of the drug. These results suggest either that a second BFA resistant pathway of transcytosis exists (or is induced by drug treatment), or that the drug acts not to block vesicle formation but to interfere with the ability of endosomes to selectivly include and/or exclude specific proteins; i.e. that BFA causes a block in molecular sorting. If so, the drug would appear to increase the relative strength of the basolateral targeting determinant (which favors recycling to the basolateral membrane) over the apical determinant (which favors transcytosis). For several reasons, we have begun to favor the second possibility.

First, the efficient apical-to-basolateral transcytosis of LDL receptor mutants or FcRII-B2 is not blocked by BFA. In fact, it is slightly (but significantly) stimulated. Thus, this pathway is clearly not abrogated by the drug, and the ability of apical endosomes to return normal fractions of internalized receptor back to the apical surface has been decreased.

Second, and perhaps more interestingly, is the effect of BFA on polarized sorting in the Golgi. Like its effect on transcytosis, BFA does not block transport from the TGN to the plasma membrane, but renders the sorting efficiency of the process much less efficient. This was dramatically demonstrated for LDL receptor and LDL receptor mutants targeted either to the basolateral or apical domains. Whereas sorting to either surface is normally 90-95% accurate, BFA randomized the appearance of both apically and basally directed receptors.

Do endosomes have coats?

BFA is known to block the ARF-dependent assembly of COP-containing coats on Golgi membranes in vitro and in intact cells. Although the actual function of the coat remains somewhat contravorsial, it is clear that its assembly is required for normal membrane traffic between the ER and the Golgi, and perhaps beyond. In the absence of the COP coat, Golgi membranes tubulate extensively and at least in part fuse with elements of the ER. In the TGN, it is known that γ-adaptin (and probably β-COP) binding is blocked by BFA, and that the TGN tubulates to form a network that interacts with the plasma membrane and perhaps endosomes.

It is conceivable that BFA has an analogous effect on endosomes. In addition to blocking transcytosis, it is well established that the drug induces extensive tubulation of endosomal elements, even in non-polarized cells (Hunziker et al., 1991b). Accordingly, we reasoned that endosomes might also be associated with a BFA-sensitive coat, possibly related to the Golgi coat. While various electron micrographs have suggested the existence of coat material on endosomes, these structures have never been confirmed or characterized. We thus have undertaken an in vitro biochemical approach to the problem which has already yielded a surprising suggestion.

Endosomes were purified from CHO cells and MDCK cells by free flow electrophoresis under conditions minimizing contamination even by trans-Golgi markers. The enriched membranes were then incubated in the presence of ^{35}S-labeled cytosol in the presence of GTPγS and/or BFA, washed, and analyzed by SDS-PAGE. A series of proteins were identified whose binding was stimulated by GTPγS and blocked by BFA. Since many of these had a molecular mass similar to those expected for the Golgi coat complex, we next asked whether any of them might be reactive with antibodies to COP proteins. In fact, our evidence thus far suggests that we can detect significant binding of a major COP protein, β-COP, to highly purified endosomes from both CHO and MDCK cells. Based on the purity of the fractions used and the high degree of in vitro binding obtained, it is unlikely that this binding represents contamination by Golgi membranes. Moreover, unlike binding to Golgi membranes from the same cells, we have found that AlFn⁻, which will stimulate β-COP binding to the Golgi, has no effect on β-COP binding to endosomes.

Although a variety of critical control experiments need to be performed - including identifying the binding protein as β-COP as opposed to a related cross-reacting species - this finding is consistent with the picture that has begun to emerge, emphasizing a commonality of mechanisms involved in sorting events on both the endocytic and secretory pathways.

IMPLICATIONS FOR THE ROLE OF BIOLOGICAL ASYMMETRY IN POLARITY

The possibility that polarized transport of membrane proteins in epithelial cells relies on sorting signals that are ubiquitously distributed among proteins expressed in both polarized and non-polarized cells has a number of important implications for understanding the mechanism of polarity induction in epithelial, embryonic, neuronal or immune cells. Since these signals are not restricted to polarized cells, it must be considered that they not only exist - but may even be active - in non-polarized cells. In other words, transport from the TGN to the plasma membrane in non-polarized cells may not be a constitutive 'bulk flow' event, but may be directed by the same types of sorter, coats, etc. that target transport in polarized cells. In other words, cognate apical and basolateral pathways may exist in non-polarized cells. The two pathways cannot normally be distinguished, however, since both transport their cargo to a common undifferentiated plasma membrane domain.

The pre-existence of apical and basolateral pathways would mean that all cells are, in a sense, polarized cells waiting to happen. In turn, this means that 'pre-differentiated' or 'non-polarized' cells would have the ability respond rapidly to events that signal the onset of a polarized phenotype without having to synthesize transport machinery required for polarized secretion, membrane insertion, or even motility. That cells can rapidly develop polarized phenotypes is illustrated by various events typical of phenomena as diverse as early embryogenesis and target cell killing by cytotoxic T-cells.

All that would be needed to induce polarity, then, is a source of asymmetry and a mechanism to detect its presence. For example, the occurrence of particular cell-cell or cell-substrate interaction might involve interactions between integrin-like molecules that lead to an asymmetric reorganization of specific cytoskeletal elements that, in turn, can distinguish between cognate apical versus cognate basolateral transport vesicles. If the interacting cells can then stabilize their interaction by the formation of junctional complexes, polarized secretion might lead to the development of a polarization of plasma membrane components.

Another attractive feature of this model is the fact that there are few, if any, cells that are truly non-polarized. Even aside from the fact that intracellular organelles generally assume a microtubule-stabilized, non-random distribution in the cytoplasm, the plasma membranes and/or secretory activities of single cells, such as fibroblasts and lymphocytes, may also be at least transiently polarized as a direct consequence of activities such as motility. For example, the leading edge of motile fibroblasts is thought to be a site for vectorial membrane insertion. Conceivably, this asymmetry of secretion may reflect the spatial-temporal asymmetry that is the unavoidable consequence of vectorial movement across a substrate.

Thus, underlying all the perceived complexity of polarity may be a relatively simple, common set of unifying principles. Whether this bodes well for our understanding of the universe is, however, another issue.

REFERENCES

Amigorena, S., Bonnerot, C., Drake, J. R., Choquet, D., Hunziker, W., Guillet, J.-G., Webster, P., Sautes, C., Mellman, I. and Fridman, W. H. (1992). Cytoplasmic domain heterogeneity and functions of IgG Fc receptors in B-lymphocytes. *Science* **256**, 1808-1812.

Brewer, C. B. and Roth, M. G. (1991). A single amino acid change in the cytoplasmic domain alters the polarized delivery of influenza virus hemagglutinin. *J. Cell Biol.* **114**, 413-421.

Casanova, J. E., Apodaca, G. and Mostov, K. E. (1991). An autonomous signal for basolateral sorting in the cytoplasmic domain of the polymeric immunoglobulin receptor. *Cell* **66**, 65-75.

Hunziker, W. and Mellman, I. (1989). Expression of macrophage-lymphocyte Fc receptors in MDCK cells: polarity and transcytosis differ for isoforms with or without coated pit localization domains. *J. Cell Biol.* **109**, 3291-3302.

Hunziker, W., Harter, C., Matter, K. and Mellman, I. (1991a). Basolateral sorting in MDCK cells requires a distinct cytoplasmic domain determinant. *Cell* **66**, 907-920.

Hunziker, W., Whitney, J. A. and Mellman, I. (1991b). Selective inhibition of transcytosis in MDCK cells by brefeldin A. *Cell* **67**, 617-627.

Le Bivic, A., Sambuy, Y., Patzak, A., Patil, N., Chao, M. and Rodriguez-Boulan, E. (1991). An internal deletion in the cytoplasmic tail reverses the apical localization of human NGF receptor in transfected MDCK cells. *J. Cell Biol.* **115**, 607-618.

Matter, K., Hunziker, W. and Mellman, I. (1992). Basolateral sorting of LDL receptor in MDCK cells: the cytoplasmic domain contains two tyrosine-dependent determinants. *Cell* **71**, 741-753.

Matter, K., Whitney, J. A., Yamamoto, E. and Mellman, I. (1993). Common signals control LDL receptor sorting in endosomes and the Golgi complex of MDCK cells. *Cell* **74**, 1053-1064.

Mellman, I. and Simons, K. (1992). The Golgi complex: in vitro veritas? *Cell* **68**, 829-840.

Miettinen, H. M., Matter, K., Hunziker, W., Rose, J. K. and Mellman, I.

(1992). Fc receptors contain a cytoplasmic domain determinant that actively regulates coated pit localization. *J. Cell Biol.* **118**, 875-888.

Miettinen, H. M., Rose, J. K. and Mellman, I. (1989). Fc receptor isoforms exhibit distinct abilities for coated pit localization as a result of cytoplasmic domain heterogeneity. *Cell* **58**, 317-327.

Prill, V., Lehmann, L., von Figura, K. and Peters, C. (1993). The cytoplasmic tail of lysosomal acid phosphatase contains overlapping but distinct signals for basolateral sorting andapid internalization in polarized MDCK cells. *EMBO J.* **12**, 2181-2193.

Sandvig, K., Prydz, K., Hansen, S. H. and van Deurs, B. (1991). Ricin

transport in brefeldin A-treated cells: correlation between Golgi structure and toxic effect. *J. Cell Biol.* **115**, 971-981.

Stuart, S., Simister, N. E., Clarkson, S. B., Kacinski, B. M., Shapiro, M. and Mellman, I. (1989). Human IgG Fc receptor (hFcRII; CD32) exists as multiple isoforms in macrophages, lymphocytes and IgG-transporting placental epithelium. *EMBO J.* **8**, 3657-3666.

Yokode, M., Pathak, R. K., Hammer, R. E., Brown, M. S., Goldstein, J. L. and Anderson, R. G. W. (1992). Cytoplasmic sequences required for basolateral targeting of LDL receptor in livers of transgenic mice. *J. Cell Biol.* **117**, 39-46.

Journal of Cell Science, Supplement 17, 9-12 (1993)
Printed in Great Britain © The Company of Biologists Limited 1993

Polarity signals in epithelial cells

Enrique Rodriguez-Boulan* and Chiara Zurzolo†

Department of Cell Biology, Cornell University Medical College, 1300 York Ave, New York, NY 10021, USA

*Author for correspondence
†Present address: Dipartimento di Biologia e Patologia Cellulare e Molecolare, CEOS, CNR, II Policlinico, Via Pansini 5, 80131 Napoli, Italy

SUMMARY

In simple epithelia, specialized vectorial functions such as transport and secretion are made possible by the segregation of proteins and lipids into opposite surface domains. This polarized distribution results from selective delivery to and retention at the appropriate domain. In the case of direct delivery, the sorting site for apical and basolateral proteins is the *trans*-Golgi network (TGN) where they are incorporated into distinct apical and basolateral vesicles that are targeted to the respective surfaces. The machinery that controls this simple process is in fact rather complicated. It involves many different steps from the recognition event (between 'sorting signal(s)' and 'sorting receptor(s)') to the formation of the vesicles, their budding, and the docking to the specialized plasma membrane domain. Here we summarize the latest developments in the sorting of apical and basolateral proteins, focusing in particular on the signals that are involved in this process and the current hypotheses about the mechanisms responsible for it, in both epithelia and in non-polarized cells.

Key words: epithelial polarity, sorting signals, *trans*-Golgi network, GPI-anchored proteins

INTRODUCTION

Work in the past decade has greatly increased our knowledge of the mechanisms responsible for epithelial cell polarity. These mechanisms fall into three groups: intracellular sorting and polarized delivery of proteins and lipids to the cell surface (Rodriguez-Boulan and Powell, 1992; van Meer and Burger, 1992), retention by domain-specific cytoskeletal interactions (Nelson, 1991) and diffusive restriction by the tight junctional fence (Cerejido et al., 1980; Gumbiner, 1990). One of the principal intracellular sorting sites for both proteins and lipids is the *trans*-Golgi network (TGN).

THE TGN: CROSSROADS OF ENDOCYTIC AND EXOCYTIC TRAFFIC

Intense research has demonstrated the crucial role of the TGN in the sorting of proteins to lysosomes, secretory granules and the cell surface. Lysosomal hydrolases are segregated into clathrin-coated vesicles via specific interaction of mannose 6-phosphate residues with a receptor that recycles between the TGN and a prelysosomal compartment; the cytoplasmic domain of this receptor carries a determinant that is recognized by Golgi-specific adaptor molecules (Pearse and Robinson, 1990; Robinson, 1992) that induce the formation of a clathrin-coated bud (Griffiths et al., 1988). Aggregation, presumably triggered by the ionic conditions in the TGN, is presumed to promote the incorporation of regulated secretory proteins into secretory granules.

In epithelial cells, proteins destined to the apical and to the basolateral surface follow a similar pathway through the ER and the Golgi apparatus until, in the TGN, they are incorporated into distinct apical and basolateral vesicles, which are targeted to the respective surface (Rodriguez-Boulan and Powell, 1992; Simons and Wandinger-Ness, 1990). The mechanisms that direct the budding of these vesicles and the docking into and fusion with specific surface domains are still unknown.

Clear progress has been made in the identification of features in the proteins and lipids that direct them apically or basolaterally. We will analyze these features separately for apical and basolateral sorting.

APICAL SORTING IN EPITHELIA

Unlike basolateral proteins, no discrete protein features have been identified in apical proteins that promote apical sorting. The hypothesis by van Meer and Simons (van Meer and Simons, 1988), that partition into hydrogen-bonded glycolipid rafts serves to recruit apical proteins into apical targeted vesicles, is, prima facie, supported by the remarkable apical localization of proteins anchored to the cell surface by glycosylphosphatidyl inositol (GPI) (Ali and Evans, 1990; Lisanti et al., 1988, 1990). In GPI-anchored proteins, the C-terminal amino acid is linked by an amide bond to ethanolamine, which in turn is linked by a phosphodiester bond to a mannosyl-glycosaminyl core glycan anchored to the membrane by phosphatidylinositol (Cross, 1990; Fer-

Table 1. Localization of GPI-anchored proteins in epithelial cells

GPI-anchored protein	Localization	Cell type
5′ Nucleotidase	apical	intestine, kidney[1]
Trehalase	apical	intestine, kidney[1]
Alkaline phosphatase	apical	intestine, kidney, MDCK*[1]
Renal dipeptidase	apical	kidney[1]
N-CAM (GPI-anchored)	apical	MDCK*[2]
Thy-1	apical	MDCK*[2]
Carcinoembryonic antigen (CEA)	apical	intestine, Caco-2, SKCO15[3]
Decay accelerating factor (DAF)	apical	MDCK*, Caco-2, SKCO-15[3]
Decay accelerating factor (DAF)	unpolarized	FRT*[4]
gD1-DAF	apical	MDCK*[5]
gD1-DAF	Basolateral	FRT*[4]
VSV G-PLAP	apical	MDCK*[6]
PLAP	apical	MDCK*[7]

*Transfected GPI-anchored proteins.
[1]Hooper et al. (1988); [2]Powell et al. (1991); [3]Lisanti et al. (1990); [4]Zurzolo et al. (1993); [5]Lisanti et al. (1989); [6]Brown et al. (1989); [7]Brown and Rose (1992).

guson and Williams, 1988; Low and Saltiel, 1988). The addition of GPI to the protein is a transamidation event in the lumen of the RER directed by a transient C-terminal hydrophobic signal (Berger et al., 1988; Caras et al., 1989; Gerber et al., 1992). GPI-anchored proteins are usually identified by their sensitivity to cleavage by PI-specific phospholipase C; considerable variability of the GPI structure can be generated by substitutions of the glycan with ethanolamine phosphate or by sugars (aGal, aMan or bGalNAc) (Deeg et al., 1992; Ferguson and Williams, 1988). Table 1 shows a list of endogenous and exogenous GPI-anchored proteins that, with few exceptions (see below), have been found in the apical surface of diverse epithelia.

Evidence for the apical sorting role of GPI was provided by the transfection of cDNAs encoding transmembrane and GPI-anchored isoforms of a protein (Powell et al., 1991), and by the apical localization of GPI-anchored fusion proteins of basolateral viral glycoproteins VSV G and *Herpes simplex* gD1 (Brown et al., 1989; Lisanti et al., 1989).

The 'cluster hypothesis' for apical targeting is supported by the observation that GPI-anchored proteins and GSLs show resistance to dissociation by certain mild non-ionic detergents (TX-100, TX-114) at low temperature (Hoessli and Rungger-Brandle, 1985; Hooper and Turner, 1988). This resistance is acquired at, or just before, arrival to the Golgi apparatus of the GPI-anchored protein (Brown, 1992). Since GSLs are produced in the Golgi apparatus, these experiments suggest that clusters of GPI-anchored proteins and GSLs are formed in the Golgi apparatus.

Hannan et al. (1993), using fluorescence energy tranfer and fluorescence recovery after photobleaching, observed that a fusion GPI-anchored protein, gD1-DAF, was clustered and immobile at the moment of arriving to the surface of wild-type (Con A-resistant MDCK) MDCK cells but was mobile in a mutant MDCK cell line that failed to sort gD1-DAF. After long periods of residence at the cell surface, the new surface molecule population acquired char-

acteristics of the stable population in that their mobility increased to high levels (R=90% as detected by FRAP). These experiments suggest the existence of a transmembrane 'sorting receptor' that may be involved in linking the GSL-GPI-protein aggregates in the luminal leaflet of the TGN to the vesicle-forming machinery on the cytoplasmic side; the reason for the slow dissociation of this immobilizing mechanism at the cell surface is unknown.

Recent experiments with the Fischer Rat Thyroid (FRT) cell line have shown that, unlike in other epithelial cell lines, GPI-anchored proteins are mainly basolateral (Table 1); gD1-DAF is targeted basolaterally whereas exogenous DAF is unpolarized (Zurzolo et al., 1993a). Interestingly, GPI-anchored proteins fail to become detergent-unextractable during passage through the Golgi complex of these cells (Zurzolo et al., 1993b). Since GSLs are as poorly extractable as in MDCK cells, it is that GPI has structural differences in FRT cells that prevent it from associating with GSL patches. On the other hand we found that VIP21/caveolin (Rothberg et al., 1992; Kurzchalia et al., 1992), suggesting an important role of this factor in the clustering of GSLs and GPI-anchored proteins, is absent in FRT cells (Zurzolo et al., 1993b). Study of the mechanisms responsible for the alternative sorting of GPI-anchored proteins in FRT cells and ConA resistant MDCK cells may help elucidate the molecular basis of apical sorting in epithelial cells.

BASOLATERAL SORTING SIGNALS

Discrete cytoplasmic signals, partially resembling endocytic signals, have been discovered in several basolateral proteins (Table 2) (Brewer and Roth, 1991; Casanova et al., 1991; Dagermont et al., 1993; Hunziker et al., 1991; Le Bivic et al., 1991; Matter et al., 1992; Prill et al., 1993; Yokode et al., 1992). Whereas in some cases a tyrosine residue is a critical part of the signal, other basolateral signals do not exhibit such a requirement. Two mechanisms may be invoked for the role of such signals in basolateal sorting. They may facilitate incorporation of proteins carrying such

Table 2. Signals for basolateral sorting

Protein	Sequence
Basolateral signals overlapping with coated pit localization domain:	
p75 NGF receptor	FKRTNSLYSSLP[1]
Influenza HA (Tyr mut.)	CSNGSLQYRICI[2]
Lgp 120	RKRSHAGYQTI[3]
Fc Receptor	EAENTITYSLLKH[3]
Lysosomal acid phosphatase (LAP)	RMQAQPPGYRHV[4]
LDL Receptor	FNDPVY[5]
Basolateral signals distinct from coated pit localization domain:	
LDL Receptor	HICRNQDGYSYPS
Poly IgA Receptor	RHRNVDRVSIGSY[6]
Transferrin Receptor*	---[7]

Y=Tyr required for coated pit localization.
[1]Le Bivic et al. (1991); [2]Brewer and Roth (1991); [3]Hunziker et al. (1991); [4]Prill et al. (1993); [5]Matter et al. (1992), Yokode et al. (1992); [6]Casanova et al. (1991); [7]Dargermont et al. (1993).
*Basolateral sequence still undefined but distinct from YTRF coated pit localization motif.

Polarized cell   **Unpolarized cell**

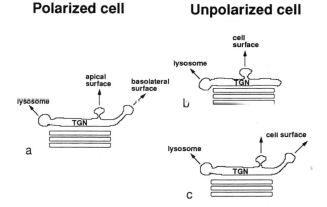

Fig. 1. Vesicular sorting in the TGN of polarized and unpolarized cells. In polarized MDCK cells, at least two different vesicle populations transport apical and basolateral proteins to the respective surface (model a). It is still unclear whether any of these vesicles is specific to epithelial cells; therefore, it is not known yet whether only one type of vesicle (model b) or both types of vesicles (b and c) are found in unpolarized cells.

signals into preformed coated areas, as is believed to occur in plasma membrane coated vesicles. Alternatively, they may be an essential part of the vesicle-forming mechanism, i.e. constituent molecules of a basolateral vesicle-specific coat may be recruited into the TGN membrane by interaction with the tails of the receptors. Why would such interaction take place only in the TGN and not during transit through the ER and the Golgi apparatus? Changes in the ionic microenvironment of the TGN (e.g. lower pH) might cause conformational changes in the basolateral proteins that favor their interaction with the coat elements. Current evidence does not support clathrin coated vesicles or coatomer proteins as constituents of such coats (Griffiths and Simons, 1986), but this point must be checked experimentally.

ARE TGN SORTING MECHANISMS EPITHELIAL-SPECIFIC?

A prevalent model (Simons and Wandinger-Ness, 1990) proposes that a major difference between epithelial cells and non-polarized cells may be the existence of additional sorting mechanisms in the TGN of epithelial cells. More specifically, epithelial cells would express a new 'apical pathway' that might not exist in non-polarized cells. This concept is based on the 'special nature' of the apical surface and the general nature of basolateral proteins, which are also present and reach normally the cell surface in non-polarized cells. However, an alternative model (Rodriguez-Boulan et al., 1992) (Fig. 1) proposes that the main difference between epithelial cells and non-polarized cells might lie in their ability to set up polarized surface domains upon interaction with other cells or with the cell substrate. According to this view, non-polarized (unpolarized) cells would have 'apical' and 'basolateral' sorting mechanisms in the TGN, but the two classes of vesicles produced cannot be discriminated by the cell surface or by the surface targeting machinery. These two models can be tested by study-

ing the in vitro production of vesicles by polarized and non polarized cells. In vitro TGN budding systems have been developed (de Curtis et al., 1988; Tooze and Huttner, 1990; Wandinger-Ness et al., 1990) and will play an important role in analyzing the molecular basis of protein sorting in epithelial cells.

This work was supported by grants from NIH and New York Heart Association.

REFERENCES

Ali, N. and Evans, W. H. (1990). Priority targeting of GPI-anchored proteins to the bile-conalicular (apical) plasma membrane of hepatocytes. *Biochem. J.* **271**, 193-199.

Berger, J., Howard, A. D., Brink, L., Gerber, L., Haubert, J., Cullen, B. R. and Udenfriend, S. (1988). COOH-terminal requirements for the correct processing of a phosphatidyl-inositol-glycan anchored membrane protein. *J. Biol. Chem.* **263**, 10016-10021.

Brewer, C. B. and Roth, M. G. (1991). A single amino acid change in the cytoplasmic domain alters the polarized delivery of Influenza Viral Hemagglutin. *J. Cell Biol.* **114**, 413-421.

Brown, D. A. (1992). Interactions between GPI-anchored proteins and membrane lipids. *Trends Cell Biol.* **2**, 338-343.

Brown, D. A., Crise, B. and Rose, J. K. (1989). Mechanism of membrane anchoring affects polarized expression of two proteins in MDCK cells. *Science* **245**, 1499-1501.

Caras, I. W., Weddell, G. N. and Williams, S. R. (1989). Analysis of the signal for attachment of a glycosylphospholipid membrane anchor. *J. Cell Biol.* **108**, 1387-1396.

Casanova, J. E., Apodaca, G. and Mostov, K. E. (1991). An autonomous signal for basolateral sorting in the cytoplasmic domain of the polymeric immunoglobulin receptor. *Cell* **66**, 65-75.

Cerejido, M., Stefani, E. and Palomo, A. M. (1980). Occluding junctions in a cultured transporting epithelium: Structural and functional hererogeneity. *J. Membr. Biol.* **53**, 19-32.

Cross, G. A. M. (1990). Glycolipid anchoring of plasma membrane proteins. *Annu. Rev. Cell Biol.* **6**, 1-39.

Dagermont, C., Le Bivic, A., Rothemberger, S., Iacopetta, B. and Kuhn, L. C. (1993). The internalization signal and the phosphorylation site of transferrin receptor are distinct from the main basolateral sorting information. *EMBO J.* **12**, 1713-1721.

de Curtis, I., Howell, K. E. and Simons, K. (1988). Isolation of a fraction enriched in the *trans*-Golgi network from baby hamster kidney cells. *Exp. Cell Res.* **175**, 248-265.

Deeg, M. A., Humphrey, D. R., Yang, S. H., Ferguson, T. R., Reinhold, V. N. and Rosenberry, T. L. (1992). Glycan components in the glycoinositol phospholipid anchor of human erythrocyte acetylcholinesterase. *J. Biol. Chem.* **267**, 18573-18580.

Ferguson, M. A. J. and Williams, A. F. (1988). Cell-surface anchoring of proteins via glycosyl-phosphatidylinositol structures. *Annu. Rev. Biochem.* **57**, 285-320.

Gerber, L. D., Kodukula, K. and Udenfriend, S. (1992). Phosphatidylinositol glycan (PI-G) anchored membrane proteins. *J. Biol. Chem.* **267**, 12168-12173.

Griffiths, G., Hoflack, B., Simons, K., Mellman, I. and Kornfeld, S. (1988). The mannose 6-phosphate receptor and the biogenesis of lysosomes. *Cell* **52**, 329-341.

Griffiths, G. and Simons, K. (1986). The *trans* Golgi network: sorting at the exit site of the Golgi complex. *Science* **234**, 438-443.

Gumbiner, B. (1990). Generation and maintenance of epithelial cell polarity. *Curr. Opin. Cell Biol.* **2**, 881-887.

Hannan, L. A., Lisanti, M. P., Rodriguez-Boulan, E. and Edidin, M. (1993). Correctly sorted molecules of a GPI-anchored protein are clustered and immobile when they arrive at the apical surface of MDCK cells. *J. Cell Biol.* **120**, 353-358.

Hoessli, D. and Rungger-Brandle, E. (1985). Association of specific cell-surface glycoproteins with a Triton X-100 resistant complex of plasma membrane proteins isolated from T-lymphoma cells (P1798). *Exp. Cell Res.* **156**, 239-250.

Hooper, N. M. and Turner, A. J. (1988). Ectoenzymes of the kidney microvillar membrane. *Biochem. J.* **250**, 865-869.

Hunziker, W., Harter, C., Matter, K. and Mellman, I. (1991). Basolateral sorting in MDCK cells requires a distinct cytoplasmic domain determinant. *Cell* **66**, 907-920.

Kurzchalia, T. V., Dupree, P., Parton, R. G., Kellner, R., Virta, H., Lehnert, M. and Simons, K. (1992). VIP21, a 21 kD membrane protein is an integral component of trans-Golgi-network-derived transport vesicles. *J. Cell Biol.* **118**, 1003-1014.

Le Bivic, A., Sambuy, Y., Patzak, A., Patil, N., Chao, M. and Rodriguez-Boulan, E. (1991). An internal deletion in the cytoplasmic tail reverses the apical localization of human NGF receptor in transfected MDCK cells. *J. Cell Biol.* **115**, 607-618.

Lisanti, M., Caras, I. P., Davitz, M. A. and Rodriguez-Boulan, E. (1989). A glycophospholipid membrane anchor acts as an apical targeting signal in polarized epithelial cells. *J. Cell Biol.* **109**, 2145-2156.

Lisanti, M., Sargiacomo, M., Graeve, L., Saltiel, A. and Rodriguez-Boulan, E. (1988). Polarized apical distribution of glycosyl phosphatidylinositol anchored proteins in a renal epithelial line. *Proc. Nat. Acad. Sci. USA.* **85**, 9557-9561.

Lisanti, M. P., Le Bivic, A., Saltiel, A. and Rodriguez-Boulan, E. (1990). Preferred apical distribution of glycosyl-phosphatidylinositol (GPI) anchored proteins: a highly conserved feature of the polarized epithelial cell phenotype. *J. Membr. Biol.* **113**, 155-167.

Low, M. G. and Saltiel, A. R. (1988). Structural and fuctional roles of glycosyl-phosphatidylinositol in membranes. *Science* **239**, 268-275.

Matter, K., Hunziker, W. and Mellman, I. (1992). Basolateral sorting of LDL receptor in MDCK cells: The cytoplasmic domain contains two Tyrosine-dependent targeting determinants. *Cell* **71**, 741-753.

Nelson, W. J. (1991). Cytoskeleton functions in membrane traffic in polarized epithelial cells. *Semin. Cell Biol.* **2**, 375-385.

Pearse, B. M. F. and Robinson, M. S. (1990). Clathrin, adaptors and sorting. *Annu. Rev. Cell Biol.* **6**, 151-171.

Powell, S. K., Cunningham, B. A., Edelman, G. M. and Rodriguez-Boulan, E. (1991). Transmembrane and GPI anchored forms of NCAM are targeted to opposite domains of a polarized epithelial cell. *Nature* **353**, 76-77

Prill, V., Lehmann, L., von Figura, K. and Peters, C. (1993). The cytoplasmic tail of lysosomal acid phosphatase contains overlapping but distinct signals for basolateral sorting and rapid internalization in polarized MDCK cells. *EMBO J.* **12**, 2181-2193.

Robinson, M. S. (1992). Adaptins. *Trends Cell Biol.* **2**, 293-297.

Rodriguez-Boulan, E. and Powell, S. K. (1992). Polarity of epithelial and neuronal cells. *Annu. Rev. Cell Biol.* **8**, 395-427.

Rothberg, K. G., Heuser, J. E., Donzell, W. C., Ying, Y.-S., Glenney, J. R. and Anderson, R. G. W. (1992). Caveolin, a protein component of caveolae membrane coats. *Cell* **68**, 673-682.

Simons, K. and Wandinger-Ness, A. (1990). Polarized sorting in epithelia. *Cell* **62**, 207-210.

Tooze, S. A. and Huttner, W. B. (1990). Cell-free protein sorting to the regulated and constitutive secretory pathways. *Cell* **60**, 837-847.

van Meer, G. and Burger, K. N. J. (1992). Sphingolipid trafficking-sorted out?. *Trends Cell Biol.* **2**, 332-337.

van Meer, G. and Simons, K. (1988). Lipid polarity and sorting in epithelial cells. *J. Cell. Biochem.* **36**, 51-58.

Wandinger-Ness, A., Bennett, M. K., Antony, C. and Simons, K. (1990). Distinct transport vesicles mediate the delivery of plasma membrane proteins to the apical and basolateral domains of MDCK cells. *J. Cell Biol.* **111**, 987-1000.

Yokode, M., Pathak, R. K., Hammer, R. E., Brown, M. S., Goldstein, J. L. and Anderson, R. G. W. (1992). Cytoplasmic sequence required for basolateral targeting of LDL receptor in livers of transgenic mice. *J. Cell Biol.* **117**, 39-46.

Zurzolo, C., Lisanti, M. P., Caras, I. W., Nitsch, L. and Rodriguez-Boulan, E. (1993a). Glycosylphosphatidilinositol-anchored proteins are preferentially targeted to the basolateral surface in Fischer Rat Thyroid epithelial cells. *J. Cell Biol.* **121**, 1031-1039.

Zurzolo, C., van 't Hof, W., van Meer, G. and Rodriguez-Boulan, E. (1993b). VIP21/caveolin, glysphingolipid clusters, and the sorting of glycosylphosphatidylinositol-anchored proteins in epithelial cells. *EMBO J.* **13** (in press).

Journal of Cell Science, Supplement 17, 13-20 (1993)
Printed in Great Britain © The Company of Biologists Limited 1993

Sorting of ion transport proteins in polarized cells

Cara J. Gottardi[1], Grazia Pietrini[1,2], Denise L. Roush[1] and Michael J. Caplan[1]

[1]Department of Cellular and Molecular Physiology, Yale University School of Medicine, 333 Cedar Street, New Haven, CT 06510, USA
[2]CNR Center of Cytopharmacology and Department of Pharmacology, University of Milan, via Vanvitelli 32, 20129 Milan, Italy

SUMMARY

The plasma membranes of polarized epithelial cells and neurons express distinct populations of ion transport proteins in their differentiated plasma membrane domains. In order to understand the mechanisms responsible for this polarity it will be necessary to elucidate the nature both of sorting signals and of the cellular machinery which recognizes and acts upon them. In our efforts to study sorting signals we have taken advantage of two closely related families of ion transport proteins whose members are concentrated in different epithelial plasmalemmal domains. The H^+,K^+-ATPase and the Na^+,K^+-ATPase are closely related members of the E_1-E_2 family of ion transporting ATPases. Despite their high degree of structural and functional homology, they are concentrated on different surfaces of polarized epithelial cells and pursue distinct routes to the cell surface in cells which manifest a regulated delivery pathway. We have transfected cDNAs encoding these pumps' subunit polypeptides, as well as chimeras derived from them, in a variety of epithlial and non-epithelial cell types. Our observations suggest that these pumps encode multiple sorting signals whose relative importance and functions may depend upon the cell type in which they are expressed. Recent evidence suggests that the sorting mechanisms employed by epithelial cells may be similar to those which operate in neurons. We have examined this proposition by studying the distributions of ion pumps and neurotransmitter re-uptake cotransporters expressed endogenously and by transfection in neurons and epithelial cells, respectively. We find that one of the classes of proteins we studied obeys the correlation between neuronal and epithelial sorting while another does not. Our data are consistent with the possibility that sorting signals and sorting mechanisms are extremely plastic and can be adapted to different uses in different cell types or under different physiological conditions.

Key words: epithelia, neurons, polarity, transport proteins

INTRODUCTION

As described in many of the contributions to this volume, the plasma membranes of polarized epithelial cells are divided into structurally and biochemically distinct domains (Simons and Fuller, 1985; Caplan and Matlin, 1989; Rodriguez-Boulan and Nelson, 1989). These domains subserve different purposes and are consequently characterized by unique protein compositions. In order to generate and maintain the anisotropic protein distributions typical of the polarized state, cells must be able distinguish among newly synthesized membrane polypeptides and to concentrate them within the appropriate plasmalemmal subdivisions. The capacity of cells to segregate and target membrane proteins implies the existence of sorting signals. A sorting signal can be considered to encompass any information embedded within the primary, secondary or tertiary structure of a given protein which somehow specifies its appropriate localization (Caplan and Matlin, 1989).

Our efforts to examine the nature of sorting signals have taken advantage of the existence of the E_1-E_2 family of ion transporting ATPases, whose individual members are restricted to distinct subcellular compartments despite their close structural and functional inter-relationships (Pedersen and Carafoli, 1987). By creating chimeras from these highly homologous proteins, we are able to limit our search for sorting information to a relatively few regions of sequence dissimilarity. This approach has allowed us to begin to identify sequence domains which appear to play important roles in pump targeting (Gottardi and Caplan, 1993a). Furthermore, this system allows us to demonstrate quantitatively that our chimeric constructs assume folding patterns compatible with these ion pumps' highly conformation-dependent enzymatic activities (Blostein et al., 1993).

The E_1-E_2 class of ion pumps includes the Na^+,K^+-ATPase, the H^+,K^+-ATPase, the ER and cell surface calcium ATPases and the H-ATPase of the yeast plasmalemma. Each of these transport proteins shares a distinctive reaction mechanism characterized by a ligand-dependent progression through the several conformational states which are referred to in the designation 'E$_1$-E$_2$' (Pedersen and Carafoli, 1987). In the course of their catalytic cycles each of these pumps becomes transiently phosphorylated on an aspartate residue and each is sensitivite to inhibition by vanadate. Within this family, the Na$^+$,K$^+$-ATPase and the H$^+$,K$^+$-ATPase probably constitute the most closely related pair (De Pont et al., 1988). Both of these pumps are composed of ~100 kDa α-subunits and ~55 kDa β-subunits (Jorgensen, 1982; Saccomani et al., 1977; Okamoto et al., 1990). The α-subunits are non-glycosylated, span the membrane several times and appear to carry all of the determinants involved in enzymatic catalysis. The β-subunits are heavily glycosylated, span the membrane once and appear to play an important role in post-synthetic maturation (Caplan, 1990).

The genes encoding both subunits of the H$^+$,K$^+$- and Na$^+$,K$^+$-ATPases have been cloned, revealing ~65% amino acid sequence identity for the α-subunits (Shull and Lingrel, 1986) and ~40% identity for the β-subunits (Reuben et al., 1990; Shull, 1990). Regions of these molecules known to be involved in activities common to all of the E$_1$-E$_2$ ATPases manifest even more dramatic similarity. The sequence of the putative high-affinity ATP binding site, for example, is identical among the two pumps. Several other long stretches are similarly conserved. Hydropathy plots suggest that these proteins' resemblance extends to their tertiary structure as well. The Na$^+$,K$^+$- and H$^+$,K$^+$-ATPases share the same number and distribution of presumed membrane spanning domains, and intervening hydrophilic segments are also closely related in length and topology (Shull and Lingrel, 1986). Thus, within the limits of resolution imposed by these rather crude techniques for predicting structure, these proteins appear to be practically superimposable.

Given this level of compositional and structural homology, it is extremely interesting to note that the Na$^+$,K$^+$-ATPase and the H$^+$,K$^+$-ATPase are concentrated in distinct subcellular locations. The Na$^+$,K$^+$-ATPase occupies the basolateral plasmalemma of almost every polarized epithelial cell (Caplan, 1990). In contrast, the H$^+$,K$^+$-ATPase resides in both the apical membrane and a pre-apical storage compartment of gastric parietal cells (Hirst and Forte, 1985; Smolka et al., 1983; Urushidani and Forte, 1987; Smolka and Weinstein, 1986) (see Fig. 1). Functionally, these two pumps are characterized by different stoichiometries, affinities for different cations and susceptibilities to different inhibitors. It would appear, therefore, that the structures of these two closely related ion pumps encode distinct sorting signals and define individual functional properties. We have prepared molecular chimeras derived from these pumps' subunit polypeptides. By expressing these constructs in polarized epithelial cells we have begun to identify the sequence domains which determine each pump's cell biological and functional properties.

ASSEMBLY REQUIREMENTS OF THE E$_1$-E$_2$ ATPases

In order to study the sorting of pump chimeras in polarized cells we first needed to determine the rules which govern

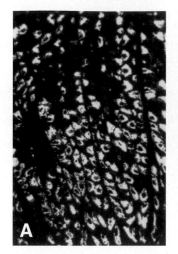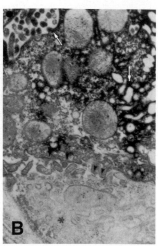

Fig. 1. The H$^+$,K$^+$-ATPase is present at the apical membrane and in tubulovesicular elements in gastric parietal cells. Immunofluorescence (A) and immunoelectron microscopic (B) localization of the H$^+$,K$^+$-ATPase was performed using a polyclonal synthetic peptide antibody directed against the α-subunit. As can be seen in (A), the antibody interacts exclusively with parietal cells, producing a bright cytoplasmic staining pattern. When examined at higher resolution (B), it can be seen that dense HRP reaction product is associated with the membranes of tubulovesicular elements and apical secretory canaliculi (arrows). The parietal cell basolateral membrane (arrowheads) and an adjacent chief cell (asterisk) are devoid of staining). (Fig. taken from Gottardi and Caplan, 1993a; used with permission.)

subunit assembly and cell surface delivery. We chose to study this problem by examining the behavior of Na$^+$,K$^+$-ATPase, H$^+$,K$^+$-ATPase and chimeric α-subunits transiently expressed by transfection in COS cells. By determining which pairs of subunits were able to attain a cell surface distribution we were able to draw conclusions about the sequence domains which specify α- and β-subunit interactions (Gottardi and Caplan, 1993b).

The cDNAs encoding the rat H$^+$,K$^+$-ATPase α- (kindly provided by G. Shull, University of Cincinnati) and the rabbit β-subunit (kindly provided by M. Reuben and G. Sachs, UCLA) have been subcloned into the pCB6 mammalian expression vector (kindly provided by M. Roth, University of Texas at Dallas). We have transiently expressed these cDNAs in COS cells and documented their expression by western blot. Examination of the COS cells by immunofluorescence revealed that transfected cells expressed extremely high levels of the exogenous proteins. Cells transfected with H$^+$,K$^+$ α alone exhibited a cytoplasmic labeling pattern consistent with an ER localization. When co-expressed in concert with the H$^+$,K$^+$ β, a fraction of the H$^+$,K$^+$ α-subunit was apparently able to depart from the ER, as suggested by a superposition of cell surface staining on top of the predominant ER pattern. Surface staining was also observed when these cells were stained with the H$^+$,K$^+$ β antibody. A similar pattern is generated when influenza HA protein expressed in COS cells is immunolabeled in non-permeabilized cells, strongly suggesting that these localizations do indeed represent surface staining. It is interesting to note that a punctate pattern, consistent with an intracellular vesicular compartment, was also found in

Requirements for the Assembly of ATPase Subunits

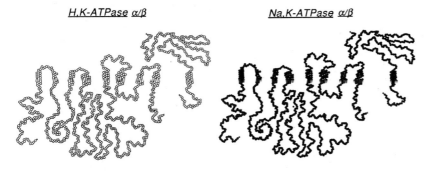

H.K-ATPase α/β   *Na.K-ATPase α/β*

H519N α/ Na.K-ATPase β   *N519H α/ H.K-ATPase β*

Fig. 2. The carboxy-terminal half of the α-subunit determines β-subunit assembly preference. This schematic diagram summarizes our data from transient transfection studies on the assembly preferences of pump subunits and chimeras. We find that each α-subunit prefers to complex with its own β-subunit. Analysis of chimeric α-subunits reveals that these proteins interact preferentially with the β-subunits appropriate to the pump from which the COOH-terminal portion of the chimera is derived.

cells labeled for H^+,K^+ β. No H^+,K^+ or Na^+,K^+ α-subunit labeling was ever seen to co-localize with H^+,K^+ β in these structures. To our surprise, an almost identical distribution was observed in COS cells transfected with H^+,K^+ β alone. Both surface and intracellular vesicle labeling were detected. These studies demonstrate that the H^+,K^+ α requires assembly with the H^+,K^+ β in order to to be delivered to the cell surface. In contrast, the H^+,K^+ β can apparently exit the ER without benefit of H^+,K^+ α assembly and accumulates at the plasmalemma as well as in an intracellular compartment which contains no Na^+,K^+ α-subunit.

Two $H^+,K^+/Na^+,K^+$ α-subunit chimeras have been generated. The construct referred to as H519N encodes the N-terminal half of the H^+,K^+-ATPase coupled to the C-terminal half of the Na^+,K^+-ATPase α-subunits. N519H constitutes the complimentary chimera. Both constructs have as their point of 'in register' fusion a *Nar*I site, which resides in the sequence encoding amino acid 519, a component of the FITC-binding regions of both pumps (Shull and Lingrel, 1986; Shull et al., 1986). A cDNA encoding the rat Na^+,K^+-ATPase α-subunit was kindly provided by E. Benz (Yale University). All chimera construction was carried out in the BlueScript plasmid and products were analyzed by restriction mapping and sequencing. For the purposes of expression studies both constructs were subcloned into pCB6.

Both constructs were expressed by transient transfection in COS cells. Immunofluorescence analysis revealed that a fraction of the expressed H519N polypeptide was able to reach the cell surface. This plasma membrane localization was achieved in the absence of any exogenous H^+,K^+ β-subunit. The situation observed for N519H was somewhat different. When this protein was expressed alone only ER labelling could be detected. Co-transfection with the H^+,K^+

β-subunit, however, enabled a fraction of the N519H protein to attain a cell surface distribution. The H^+,K^+ β in these cells displayed the previously described surface and vesicular pattern. No N519H was detected in association with the vesicles. We interpret these results to indicate that N519H assembles with the H^+,K^+ β-subunit and requires this interaction in order to depart from the ER. We further speculate that H519N assembles with the endogenous Na^+,K^+ β expressed by the COS cells, and thus does not require the addition of an exogenous β protein in order to achieve a surface localization.

Our results (summarized in Fig. 2) strongly suggest that β-subunits assemble with the C-terminal portions of the H^+,K^+- and Na^+,K^+-ATPase α-subunits. These findings are entirely consistent with the observations of Luckie et al. (1992) and Lemas et al. (1992), who studied chimeras generated from portions of the Na^+,K^+- and Ca^{2+}-ATPase α-subunits. These investigators found that α-subunits composed of the C-terminal third of the sodium pump coupled to the N-terminal portions of the Ca^{2+}-ATPase assembled with the Na^+,K^+-ATPase β-subunit and were translocated to the cell surface. The complementary constructs showed no affinity for the β polypeptide and were retained in the ER.

The observations presented above also demonstrate that the process of α/β-subunit assembly is at least somewhat selective and that the molecular basis for this selectivity resides in the C-terminal portion of the α-polypeptide. The H^+,K^+-ATPase α-subunit and the N519H chimera are unable to complex with Na^+,K^+-ATPase β-subunit. In contrast, the H519N chimera, whose C terminus is derived from the sodium pump, readily participates in heterodimers with the Na^+,K^+-ATPase β-subunit. In the context of this apparent capacity for discrimination, it is interesting to note that several investigators have found that the H⁺,K⁺-ATPase β-subunit can form functional complexes with the Na⁺,K⁺-ATPase α subunit. These experiments were performed in yeast (Eakle et al., 1992) and *Xenopus* oocyte (Horisberger et al., 1991; Noguchi et al., 1992) expression systems, which lack endogenous production of Na⁺,K⁺-ATPase β-subunit. As will be discussed below, we have never been able to detect assembly between endogenous Na⁺,K⁺-ATPase α-subunit and H⁺,K⁺-ATPase β-subunit under conditions in which the Na⁺,K⁺-ATPase β-protein is also being synthesized. It would appear, therefore, that the C-terminal portion of the H⁺,K⁺-ATPase α-subunit manifests a high degree of selectivity in choosing a β-subunit partner. The sodium pump's α-polypeptide may be somewhat less selective, although our results suggest that it prefers its own β-subunit to that of the H⁺,K⁺ pump.

Finally, it should be noted that studies performed in collaboration with the laboratory of Dr R. Blostein (McGill University) demonstrate that the H519N chimera is active as a transport protein (Blostein et al., 1993). Measurements of ⁸⁶Rb uptake reveal that this protein mediates an ion flux which is sensitive to inhibition by both ouabain and SCH 28080, inhibitors of the Na⁺,K⁺-ATPase and H⁺,K⁺-ATPase, respectively. It has yet to be determined whether the counter ion for Rb movement is Na or a proton, nor is it known whether the flux is electrogenic or electroneutral. Experiments designed to answer these questions are underway. It is clear, however, that H519N is able to assume a tertiary structure compatible with the extremely conformation-dependent transport mechanism of an E_1-E_2 ATPase. We feel confident, therefore, that this protein's folding has not been adversely affected by chimera construction and that its sub-domain structure is intact.

ION PUMP SORTING IN POLARIZED EPITHELIA

We wished to examine the nature of the sorting information responsible for localizing the H⁺,K⁺-ATPase to the parietal cell apical membrane. For these purposes we stably transfected the polarized LLC-PK1 epithelial cell line with cDNAs encoding the H⁺,K⁺-ATPase subunits. The presence of H⁺,K⁺ subunit polypeptides was confirmed by western blotting. Indirect immunofluorescence performed on the H⁺,K⁺-ATPase-expressing cell line reveals that co-expression with its H⁺,K⁺ β-subunit is required in order for the H⁺,K⁺-ATPase α to reach the cell surface. Confocal analysis confirms that both the H⁺,K⁺ α- and β-subunits immunolocalize predominantly to the apical brush border. Neither α- nor β-subunits of the endogenous Na⁺,K⁺-ATPase appear to be mis-sorted in these cells. This observation strongly suggests that the pump subunits exhibit strict fidelity with respect to assembly when expressed in this system. The observed spatial segregation of H⁺,K⁺ from Na⁺,K⁺ subunit polypeptides argues against the formation of hybrid pump dimers. Clearly, this cell line is able to distinguish the H⁺,K⁺ α/β complex from the Na⁺,K⁺ α/β complex and to target each to its appropriate membrane domain.

A stable cell line expressing only the H⁺,K⁺ β-subunit was generated in order to determine which of the two subunits encoded the apical sorting information. A western blot

Table 1. The polarized distributions of pump subunits and pump chimeras expressed endogenously or by transfection in LLC-PK₁ cells

Cell line	Antibody	Average A/B ratio (±s.d.)
Untransfected	Na,Kα	0.071±0.007
Untransfected	Na,Kβ	0.175±0.012
H⁺,K⁺-ATPase α/β	H,Kα	42.1±4.65
H⁺,K⁺-ATPase α/β	H,Kβ	31.2±3.92
H519N	H,Kα	30.0±3.19
H519N	Na,Kα	0.254±0.013
H519N	Na,Kβ	2.64±0.228

Distributions were determined by quantitative confocal microscopy, as previously described (Gottardi and Caplan, 1993a). As can be seen below, in untransfected cells, the Na⁺,K⁺-ATPase α- and β-subunits are predominantly basolateral. When co-expressed, both the H⁺,K⁺-ATPase α- and β-subunits are essentially limited to the apical surface. The H519N chimera also behaves as an apical protein. It is interesting to note that the Na⁺,K⁺-ATPase α-subunit retains its basolateral polarity in H519N-expressing cells, whereas the sodium pump β-subunit's distribution is markedly altered. (Adapted from Gottardi and Caplan, 1993a; used with permission.)

of this cell line shows that both mature and immature forms of the protein are present. Immunofluorescence analysis reveals that the H⁺,K⁺ β-subunit is localized to the apical brush border as well as to a population of large subapical vesicles. The endogenous Na⁺,K⁺ α-subunit does not appear to escort H⁺,K⁺ β- to the cell surface, as it is found only in its normal basolateral distribution.

The apical localization of the H⁺,K⁺ β-subunit would suggest that it is in fact the β that encodes the sorting information responsible for the polarized cell surface distribution of the H⁺,K⁺-ATPase α/β dimer. In order to test this hypothesis, we have prepared a stably transfected LLC-PK1 cell line which expresses a high level of the H519N chimera. Western blot analysis reveals that this chimeric protein has the same mobility as the full-length H⁺,K⁺-ATPase α-subunit and is not detected with an antibody against the carboxy-terminal half of the H⁺,K⁺-ATPase.

We next used indirect immunofluorescence and confocal microscopy in order to determine the cell surface distribution of this chimera. We find that the H519N chimera is almost exclusively localized to the apical membrane. The endogenous Na⁺,K⁺-ATPase α-subunit maintains its steady-state basolateral distribution, demonstrating that expression of this chimera does not alter the sorting of the endogenous ATPase. Interestingly, the Na⁺,K⁺-ATPase β-subunit co-localizes with the chimera at the apical brush border as well as with the Na⁺,K⁺ α-subunit at the basolateral surface. Quantitative data on the distributions of the H⁺,K⁺-ATPase and H519N are presented in Table 1.

Both the chimera and the Na⁺,K⁺ β are actually components of the apical membrane and are exposed at the apical surface. This fact is demonstrated by incubating the monolayer with the Na⁺,K⁺ β antibody from the apical side before fixation and permeabilization, which results in strong apical staining that is seen only in our chimera transfected cells and not in the control cells. Taken together, these results suggest that cell surface expression of this chimeric α-subunit requires assembly with the Na⁺,K⁺-ATPase β-subunit. They further demonstrate that the Na⁺,K⁺ β-subunit does

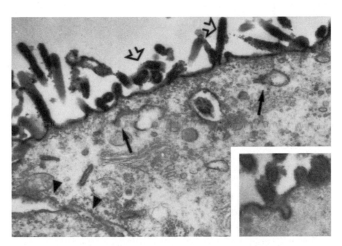

Fig. 3. The H⁺,K⁺-ATPase β-subunit is present at the apical surface and in subapical endosomes in transfected LLC-PK₁ cells. The H⁺,K⁺-ATPase β-subunit was localized in singly transfected LLC-PK₁ cells by immunoelectron microscopy. Dense HRP reaction product can be seen associated with the apical membrane and microvilli (open arrows) as well as with a population of intracellular vesicles whose morphology is characteristic of endosomes (filled arows). Note that the basolateral surface (arrowheads) is not stained. Inset demonstrates staining in a coated pit. (Fig. taken from Gottardi and Caplan, 1993a; used with permission).

not encode dominant sorting information. It would appear that the N-terminal half of the H⁺,K⁺-ATPase must encode an apical signal which is able to function when expressed as part of a chimeric construct. In order to fully test this hypothesis, it will be necessary to evaluate the sorting of the complementary N519H chimera expressed in concert with H⁺,K⁺ β. We have recently succeeded in generating several LLC-PK₁ cells lines which express this combination of subunits and are in the process of establishing these proteins' subcellular distributions.

In light of the preceding evidence that the β-subunit does not encode sorting information, it is surprising that the H⁺,K⁺ β expressed alone is sorted predominantly to the apical membrane. It is also interesting that in addition to its cell surface localization, the H⁺,K⁺ β was detected in a population of subapical vesicles. This distribution has never been observed for the Na⁺,K⁺ β- or α-subunit. In order to better understand the unique behavior of the H⁺,K⁺ β it is necessary to establish the identity of this vesicular compartment. We performed electron microscopy in which the localization of the H⁺,K⁺ β was revealed by the immunoperoxidase technique (see Fig. 3). Dense reaction product can be detected along the microvilli, within the endoplasmic reticulum and within coated pits and compartments that resemble tubular endosomes.

To further characterize these structures, we wished to determine whether this compartment could be loaded with a fluid-phase endocytosis marker such as horseradish peroxidase (HRP) (Stoorvogel et al., 1991). Stably transfected cells expressing solely the H⁺,K⁺ β-subunit were incubated in the presence of both HRP and the H⁺,K⁺ β antibody at 4°C to prebind the H⁺,K⁺ β-subunits at the cell surface. The cells were warmed to 37°C for various lengths of time and subsequently fixed and permeabilized for indirect immuno-

fluorescence. Our results show that even after only 10 minutes both HRP and H⁺,K⁺ β colocalize within the same compartment. They continue to colocalize at 20 minutes and as long as 45 minutes after warming the cells. The structure they occupy is not labeled by antibodies to LGP 120, a lysosomal marker. It seems likely, therefore, that the vesicles seen in H⁺,K⁺ β-expressing cells are derived from the cell surface and represent an endosomal compartment.

These results also raise the interesting possibility that the H⁺,K⁺ β-subunit encodes an endocytosis or coated pit localization signal. Analysis of the H⁺,K⁺ β-subunit's amino acid sequence reveals that its cytoplasmic tail contains a four amino acid motif, YXRF, which has been shown to function as the transferrin receptor's coated pit localization sequence (Collawn et al., 1990; Girones et al., 1991). This motif is not present in the sequence of the Na⁺,K⁺-ATPase β-polypeptide (Gottardi and Caplan, 1993a). In attempting to suggest possible roles for this signal, it is useful to recall that in its native gastric parietal cell the H⁺,K⁺-ATPase α/β complex resides within a pre-apical compartment which rapidly fuses with the apical membrane in response to physiological stimulation. When the stimulatory signal is removed the H⁺,K⁺-ATPase is rapidly endocytosed and returned to its pre-apical compartment. In light of the endosomal localization of the H⁺,K⁺ β in transfected cells, it is tempting to speculate that it is the H⁺,K⁺ β-subunit that encodes the signal for the rapid retrievel of H⁺,K⁺ α/β enzyme from the apical membrane.

Finally, it is interesting to recall that coated pit localization signals have been shown to be sufficient to ensure basolateral targeting of membrane proteins in MDCK cells (Brewer and Roth, 1991; Hunziker et al., 1991; Hunziker and Mellman, 1989; Le Bivic et al., 1991). It is perhaps surprising, therefore, that the H⁺,K⁺ β, which appears to manifest such a signal, behaves as an apical protein in LLC-PK₁ cells. In our attempts to understand this behavior, it has been interesting to consider functional differences between renal cells derived from different portions of the nephron. The LLC-PK₁ cell line was derived from the cortex of the pig kidney and manifests the morphological and physiological properties of proximal tubule cells (Pfaller et al., 1990). The apical membrane of the proximal tubule participates in the recapture and resorption of peptides and proteins which have eluded the glomerular basement membrane and passed into the glomerular filtrate. Electron microscopic examination of this tubule segment reveals that it is well equiped for this task. Coated pits and coated vesicles are associated with the bases of microvilli throughout the proximal brush border (Rodman et al., 1984). In contrast, little or no receptor-mediated endocytosis has been shown to occur from the apical surfaces of the sort of distal tubule cells which gave rise to the MDCK cell line. This comparison has led us to speculate that coated pit localization sequences do not specify sorting to the basolateral surface per se but, rather, cause the proteins bearing them to accumulate in a given cell's most endocytically active domain. According to this model, the relevant sorting signal would mediate targeting to a functionally defined instead of a topographically defined destination. Extrapolating from this model, one would predict that the H⁺,K⁺-ATPase β-subunit expressed in MDCK cells would behave as a basolateral polypeptide. Preliminary experiments suggest that this is, in fact, the case. Future studies with this and other proteins will hopefully determine how endocytosis signals are interpreted by the sorting machinery of diverse epithelial cell types.

COMPARISONS OF EPITHELIAL AND NEURONAL SORTING SIGNALS

Recently, several groups have begun to extend the insights gained through the study of sorting in epithelia to non-epithelial cell types. Elegant studies on cultured hippocampal neurons have led to the suggestion that neuronal sorting mechanisms may be closely related to those employed by epithelial cells. Infection of these cells with enveloped viruses revealed that influenza HA protein accumulates in axonal processes, while the VSV G protein is restricted to the dendrites (Dotti and Simons, 1990). Further experiments indicated that GPI-linked proteins are predominantly axonal in neurons (Dotti et al., 1991). These observations have prompted the speculation that the same signals and machinery involved in sorting to the basolateral and apical domains of epithelia function in neurons to mediate targeting to dendrites and axons, respectively. In order to examine this hypothesis further, we chose to determine the distribution in cultured hippocampal neurons of the Na^+,K^+-ATPase, which, as mentioned above, occupies the basolateral plasmalemmas of most polarized epithelia. The simple equation of basolateral and dendritic membranes would lead to the physiologically unsupportable conclusion that axonal membranes lack Na^+,K^+-ATPase. We wondered whether the sodium pump needs of the axon are met by a neuron-specific isoform of the Na^+,K^+-ATPase, which might be a substrate for apical sorting if expressed in epithelia.

Three isoforms of the Na^+,K^+-ATPase α-subunit have been identified (Shull et al., 1986). While the tissue distribution of α1 is fairly ubiquitous, previous studies of α3 expression suggested that it is found predominantly in neurons (McGrail et al., 1991). Using isoform-specific synthetic peptide antibodies we have shown that hippocampal neurons in culture express both the α1 and α3 subunits of the Na^+,K^+-ATPase (Pietrini et al., 1992). When the distributions of these proteins were compared with those of known dendrite and axon markers (MAP-2 and GAP43, respectively) (Caceres et al., 1986; Goslin et al., 1990), we found that both sodium pump isoforms are found in both types of neuronal process. There would appear to be no polarity present in the distribution of either protein. Since the α3 isoform is not endogenously produced in epithelia, we further wondered whether it would manifest a polarized distribution when expressed by transfection in LLC-PK₁ cells. We found that the distribution of the α3 protein in epithelial cells mirrored precisely that of α1. Thus, while both isoforms are restricted to the basolateral surfaces of at least one polarized epithelial cell line, these two proteins are present in all of the subdomains of the neuronal plasmalemma. In light of these observations, it is interesting to note that the ankyrin-fodrin cytoskeleton underlies only the basolateral surfaces of most epithelial cells, whereas elements of this matrix are present in both the axons and dendrites of neurons (Nelson and Hammerton, 1989; Kordely and Bennett, 1991). The role that the cytoskeleton may play in determining the sodium pump's distribution in neurons and epithelial cells remains to be established.

We have also carried out experiments designed to test the prediction that axonal proteins would be apically sorted when expressed by transfection in epithelial cells. Our initial studies have made use of the Na,Cl-dependent GABA transport system which populates the presynaptic plasma membranes of GABA-ergic nerve terminals (Radian and Kanner, 1983). This protein mediates the re-uptake of neurotransmitter from the synaptic space and is thus responsible for terminating GABA-ergic transmission. Similar transport systems exist for a number of neurotransmitters, including serotonin, norepinephrine and dopamine.

Immunoelectron microscopic examination of the distribution of the GABA transporter in situ reveal that this protein is limited in its distribution to axonal plasmalemma (Radian et al., 1990). We have localized this polypeptide in polarized hippocampal neurons grown in culture and find a similarly axonal localization. We have expressed a cDNA encoding the GABA transporter (gift from B. Kanner) in MDCK cells. Immunofluorescence, cell surface biotinylation and tracer uptake assays all indicate that this protein is predominantly present in the apical surfaces of the epithelial cells (Pietrini et al., 1993). This finding, in contrast to that presented above for the sodium pump, is in keeping with the hypothesis that the axonal and apical sorting pathways are functionally related. Perhaps of greater interest is the recent finding that MDCK cells endogenously express a close cousin of the GABA transporter. The betaine transport system is involved in the osmoregulation of renal epithelial cells and is ~50% identical to the GABA transporter at the amino acid level (Yamauchi et al., 1992; Guastella et al., 1990). Tracer flux studies demonstrate that the betaine transporter is restricted to the MDCK cell's basolateral plasma membrane (Yamauchi et al., 1991). We are in the process of developing chimeras between these transporters in order to identify polypeptide domains which participate in their epithelial as well as their neuronal localizations.

SORTING TO REGULATED COMPARTMENTS

The problem of protein sorting is confronted by a large variety of cell types whose various membranous destinations are somewhat more subtly distinguishable than the dramatically differentiated cell surface domains of epithelial cells and neurons. Even in non-polarized cells, a sorting decision may be required in order to select the route that a secretory or membrane protein follows to the cell surface. Endocrine and exocrine cells, for example, possess both constitutive and regulated pathways to the plasmalemma (Burgess and Kelly, 1987). Proteins with potent biological activities, such as hormones and digestive enzymes, are stored within the cell in secretory granules, whose fusion with the plasmalemma is dependent upon stimulation by secretagogues. Polypeptides which serve non-regulated, house-keeping functions, such as components of the basement membrane, by-pass the storage step and are released from the cell as they are made. There is a large and fascinating of literature describing investigations into the mechanisms and signals which function to target proteins for regulated or constitutive delivery.

The H^+,K^+-ATPase is an example of one of a very few membrane proteins whose surface delivery is regulated by secretagogues. As mentioned above, the H^+,K^+-ATPase resides in a storage compartment composed of tubulovesicular elements in its native gastric parietal cell (Hirst and Forte, 1985; Smolka et al., 1983; Urushidani and Forte, 1987; Smolka and Weinstein, 1986). These vesicles also contain intrinsic factor, an exocrine secretory product involved in cobalamin absorption. Hormonal stimulation by gastrin, acetyl choline or histamine lead to increased gastric acid secretion by inducing the tubulovesicular elements to fuse with the parietal cell apical membrane. Thus, in addition to behaving as an apical plasma membrane protein, the H^+,K^+-ATPase can be thought of as a participant in a regulated pathway for exocytosis.

We wondered whether the information which directs the H^+,K^+-ATPase to its regulated compartment in intercalated cells would also mediate sorting to the regulated pathway in endocrine and exocrine cells. In order to examine this question, we have transfected RINm5AH-T$_2$-B cells with cDNAs encoding subunits of the H^+,K^+ pump and our pump chimeras. This cell line is derived from a rat insulinoma and retains many of the differentiated characteristics of its pancreatic β cell progenitor (Nielsen, 1989). Most relevant among these is the presence of a well-developed regulated secretory pathway characterized by numerous insulin-containing intracellular storage vesicles whose secretion can be mobilized by membrane depolarization. Our preliminary studies suggest that the H^+,K^+-ATPase, as well as one of our pump chimeras, becomes concentrated in the insulin storage compartment. These data suggest that the H^+,K^+ pump carries the sorting information necessary to ensure its diversion to the regulated delivery pathway when it is heterologously expressed in endocrine cells. It also appears that the requisite information may be associated with the H^+,K^+-ATPase β-subunit, since this protein also accumulates in the insulin compartment when expressed individually.

Studies are underway to determine whether information and mechanisms involved in the pump's sorting to the regulated secretory pathway are related to those which drive its apical localization in epithelia. We are especially interested in the role that the H^+,K^+ β-subunit's putative endocytosis signal may play in mediating its diversion into the regulated compartment. If any theme can be detected in our observations on pump and co-transporter sorting, it is that these proteins are endowed with multiple sorting signals whose relative importance and functions appear to depend upon the cell types in which these polypeptides find themselves expressed. According to this formulation, sorting is a plastic phenomenon which can be adapted to the various needs of different tissues or to the various environmental conditions confronted by individual cells. The means by which cell types modify their sorting machinery in order to accommodate their physiological roles remain mysterious and will, in all likelihood, persist as a subject for investigation for quite some time to come.

The authors thank Drs G. Shull, M. Reuben, G. Sachs, J. G. Forte, D. C. Chow, E. Benz, G. Banker, J. Handler and K. Amsler for generously providing reagents, and the members of the Caplan lab for helpful discussions and valuable insights. This work was supported by NIH GM-42136 (M.J.C.) and a fellowship from the David and Lucille Packard Foundation (M.J.C.).

REFERENCES

Brewer, C. B. and Roth, M. G. (1991). A single amino acid change in the cytoplasmic domain alters the polarized delivery of influenza virus hemagglutinin. *J. Cell Biol.* **114**, 413-421.

Blostein, R., Zhang, R., Gottardi, C. J. and Caplan, M. J. (1993). Functional properties of an H^+,K^+-ATPase/Na^+,K^+-ATPase chimera. *J. Biol. Chem.* **268**, 10654-10658.

Burgess, T. L. and Kelly, R. B. (1987). Constitutive and regulated secretion of proteins. *Annu. Rev. Cell Biol.* **3**, 243-293.

Caceres, A., Banker, G. A. and Binder, L. (1986). Immunocytochemical localization of tubulin and microtubule-associated protein 2 during the development of hippocampal neurons in culture. *J. Neurosci.* **6**, 714-722.

Caplan, M. J. (1990). Biosynthesis and sorting of the sodium, potassium-ATPase. In *Regulation of Potassium Transport Across Biological Membranes* (ed. L. Reuss, J. M. Russell and G. Szabo), pp. 77-101. Austin: University of Texas Press.

Caplan, M. J. and Matlin, K. S. (1989). Sorting of membrane and secretory proteins in polarized epithelial cells. In *Functional Epithelial Cells in Culture* (ed. K. S. Matlin and J. D. Valentich), pp. 71-127. New York: Alan R. Liss.

Collawn, J. F., Stangel, M., Kuhn, L. A., Esekogwu, V., Jing, S., Trowbridge, I. S. and Tainer, J. A. (1990). Transferrin receptor internalization sequence YXRF implicates a tight turn as the structural recognition motif for endocytosis. *Cell* **63**, 1061-1072.

De Pont, J. J. H. H. M., Helmich-de Jong, M. L., Skrabanja, A. T. P. and van der Hijden, H. T. W. M. (1988). H^+,K^+-ATPase: Na^+,K^+-ATPase's stepsister. In *The Na⁺,K⁺ Pump* (ed. J. C. Skou, J. G. Norby, A. V. Maunsbach and M. Esmann), pp. 585-602. New York: Alan R. Liss.

Dotti, C. G., Parton, R. G. and Simons, K. (1991). Polarized sorting of glypiated proteins in hippocampal neurons. *Nature* **349**, 158-161.

Dotti, C. G. and Simons, K. (1990). Polarized sorting of viral glycoproteins to the axon and dendrites of hippocampal neurons in culture. *Cell* **62**, 63-72.

Eakle, K. A., Kim, K. S., Kabalin, M. A. and Farley, R. A. (1992). High-affinity Ouabain binding by yeast cells expressing Na^+,K^+-ATPase α-subunits and the gastric H^+,K^+-ATPase β-subunit. *Proc. Nat. Acad. Sci. USA* **89**, 2834-2838.

Girones, N., Alvarez, E., Seth, A., Lin, I. M., Latour, D. A. and Davis, R. J. (1991). Mutational analysis of the cytoplasmic tail of the human transferrin receptor: identification of a sub-domain that is required for rapid endocytosis. *J. Biol. Chem.* **266**, 19006-19012.

Goslin, K., Schreyer, D. J., Skene, H. P. and Banker, G. (1990). Changes in the distribution of GAP-43 during the development of neuronal polarity. *J. Neurosci.* **10**, 588-602.

Gottardi, C. J. and Caplan, M. J. (1993a). An ion transporting ATPase encodes multiple apical localization signals. *J. Cell Biol.* **121**, 283-293.

Gottardi, C. J. and Caplan, M. J. (1993b). Molecular requirements for the cell surface expression of multisubunit ion-transporting ATPases: identification of protein domains that participate in Na^+,K^+-ATPase and H^+,K^+-ATPase subunit assembly. *J. Biol. Chem.* (in press).

Guastella, J., Nelson, N., Nelson, H., Czyzyk, L., Kenyan, S., Miedel, M., Davidson, N., Lester, H. and Kanner, B. (1990). Cloning and expression of a rat brain GABA transporter. *Science* **249**, 1303-1306.

Hirst, B. H. and Forte, J. G. (1985). Redistribution and characterization of H^+,K^+-ATPase membranes from resting and stimulated gastric parietal cells. *Biochem. J.* **231**, 641-649.

Horisberger, J. D., Jaunin, P., Reuben, M. A., Lasater, L. S., Chow, D. C., Forte, J. G., Sachs, G., Rossier, B. C. and Geering, K. (1991). The H^+,K^+-ATPase β-subunit can act as a surrogate for the β-subunit of Na^+,K^+-pumps. *J. Biol. Chem.* **266**, 19131-19134.

Hunziker, W., Harter, C., Matter, K. and Mellman, I. (1991). Basolateral sorting in MDCK cells requires a distinct cytoplasmic domain determinant. *Cell* **66**, 907-920.

Hunziker, W. and Mellman, I. (1989). Expression of macrophage-lymphocyte Fc receptors in MDCK cells: polarity and transcytosis differ for isoforms with or without coated pit localization domains. *J. Cell Biol.* **109**, 3291-3302.

Jorgensen, P. L. (1982). Mechanism of the Na$^+$,K$^+$ pump: protein structure and conformations of the pure Na$^+$,K$^+$-ATPase. *Biochim. Biophys. Acta* **694**, 27-68.

Kordely, E. and Bennett, V. (1991). Distinct ankyrin isoforms at neuron cell bodies and nodes of Ranvier resolved using erythrocyte ankyrin-deficient mice. *J. Cell Biol.* **114**, 1243-1259.

Le Bivic, A., Sambuy, Y., Patzak, A., Patil, N., Chao, M. and Rodriguez-Boulan, E. (1991). An internal deletion in the cytoplasmic tail reverses the apical localization of human NGF receptor in transfected MDCK cells. *J. Cell Biol.* **115**, 607-618.

Lemas, V., Takeyasu, K. and Fambrough, D. M. (1992). The carboxy-terminal 161 amino acids of the Na$^+$,K$^+$-ATPase alpha-subunit are sufficient for assembly with the beta-subunit. *J. Biol. Chem.* **267**, 20987-20991.

Luckie, D. B., Lemas, V., Boyd, K. L., Fambrough, D. M. and Takeyasu, K. (1992). Molecular dissection of functional domains of the E$_1$-E$_2$ ATPase using sodium and calcium pump chimeric molecules. *Biophys. J.* **62**, 220-227.

McGrail, K. M., Phillips, J. M. and Sweadner, K. J. (1991). Immunofluorescent localization of three Na$^+$,K$^+$-ATPase isozymes in the rat central nervous system: both neurons and glia can express more than one Na$^+$,K$^+$-ATPase. *J. Neurosci.* **11**, 381-391.

Nelson, W. J. and Hammerton, R. W. (1989). A membrane-cytoskeletal complex containing Na$^+$,K$^+$-ATPase, ankyrin and fodrin in Madin-Darby canine kidney cells: implications for the biogenesis of epithelial cell polarity. *J. Cell Biol.* **108**, 893-902.

Nielsen, J. H. (1989). Mechanisms of pancreatic β-cell growth and regeneration: studies on rat insulinoma cells. *Exp. Clin. Endocrinol.* **93**, 277-285.

Noguchi, S., Maeda, M., Futai, M. and Kawamura, M. (1992). Assembly of a hybrid from the α-subunit of Na$^+$,K$^+$-ATPase and the β-subunit of H$^+$,K$^+$-ATPase. *Biochem. Biophys. Res. Commun.* **182**, 659-666.

Okamoto, C. T., Karpilow, J. M., Smolka, A. and Forte, J. G. (1990). Isolation and characterization of gastric microsomal glycoproteins: evidence for a glycosylated beta subunit of the H$^+$,K$^+$-ATPase. *Biochim. Biophys. Acta* **1037**, 360-372.

Pedersen, P. L. and Carafoli, E. (1987). Ion motive ATPases: I. ubiquity, properties and significance to cell function. *Trends Biochem. Sci.* **12**, 146-150.

Pfaller, W., Gstraunthalerand, G. and Loidl, P. (1990). Morphology of the differentiation and maturation of LLC-PK$_1$ epithelia. *J. Cell. Physiol.* **142**, 247-254.

Pietrini, G., Matteoli, M., Banker, G. and Caplan, M. J. (1992). Isoforms of the Na$^+$,K$^+$-ATPase are present in both axons and dendrites of hippocampal neurons in culture. *Proc. Nat. Acad. Sci. USA* **89**, 8414-8418.

Pietrini, G., Suh, Y.-J., Edelmann, L., Rudnick, G. and Caplan, M. J. (1993). The axonal GABA transporter is sorted to the apical membranes of polarized epithelial cells. *J. Biol. Chem.* (in press).

Radian, R. and Kanner, B. (1983). Stoichiometry of sodium and chloride-coupled γ-aminobutyric acid transport by synaptic plasma membrane vesicles isolated from rat brain. *Biochemistry* **22**, 1236-1241.

Radian, R., Ottersen, O. P., Storm-Mathisen, J., Castel, M. and Kanner, K. (1990). Immunocytochemical localization of the GABA transporter in rat brain. *J. Neurosci.* **10**, 1319-1330.

Reuben, M. A., Lasater, L. S. and Sachs, G. (1990). Characterization of a beta subunit of the gastric H$^+$,K$^+$-ATPase. *Proc. Nat. Acad. Sci. USA* **87**, 6767-6771.

Rodman, J. S., Kerjaschki, D., Merisko, E. and Farquhar, M. G. (1984). Presence of an extensive clathrin coat on the apical plasmalemma of the rat kidney proximal tubule cell. *J. Cell Biol.* **98**, 1630-1636.

Rodriguez-Boulan, E. and Nelson, W. J. (1989). Morphogenesis of the polarized epithelial cell phenotype. *Science* **245**, 718-725.

Saccomani, G., Stewart, H. B., Shaw, D., Lewin, M. and Sachs, G. (1977). Characterization of gastric mucosal membranes: ix. Fractionation and purification of K$^+$-ATPase-containing vesicles by zonal centrifugation and free-flow electrophoresis technique. *Biochim. Biophys. Acta* **465**, 311-330.

Shull, G. E. (1990). cDNA cloning of the β-Subunit of the rat gastric H$^+$,K$^+$-ATPase. *J. Biol. Chem.* **265**, 12123-12126.

Shull, G. E., Greeb, J. and Lingrel, J. B. (1986). Molecular cloning of three distinct forms of the Na$^+$,K$^+$-ATPase α-subunit from rat brain. *Biochemistry* **25**, 8125-8132.

Shull, G. E. and Lingrel, J. (1986). Molecular cloning of the rat stomach H$^+$,K$^+$-ATPase. *J. Biol. Chem.* **261**, 16788-16791.

Simons, K. and Fuller, S. D. (1985). Cell surface polarity in epithelia. *Annu. Rev. Cell Biol.* **1**, 295-340.

Smolka, A., Helander, H. F. and Sachs, G. (1983). Monoclonal antibodies against gastric H$^+$,K$^+$-ATPase. *Amer. J. Physiol.* **245**, G589-G596.

Smolka, A. and Weinstein, W. A. (1986). Immunoassay of pig and human gastric proton pump. *Gastroenterology* **90**, 532-539.

Stoorvogel, W., Strous, G. J., Geuze, H. J., Oorschot, V. and Schwartz, A. L. (1991). Late endosomes derive from early endosomes by maturation. *Cell* **65**, 417-427.

Urushidani, T. and Forte, J. G. (1987). Stimulation-associated redistribution of H$^+$,K$^+$-ATPase activity in isolated gastric glands. *Amer. J. Physiol.* **252**, G458-G465.

Yamauchi, A., Kwon, H. M., Uchida, S., Preston, A. and Handler, J. S. (1991). Myo-inositol and betaine transporters regulated by tonicity are basolateral in MDCK cells. *Amer. J. Physiol.* **261**, F197-F202.

Yamauchi, A., Uchida, S., Kwon, H. M., Preston, A. S., Robey, R. B., Garcia-Perez, A., Burg, M. B. and Handler, J. S. (1992). Cloning of a Na and Cl-dependent betaine transporter that is regulated by hypertonicity. *J. Biol. Chem.* **267**, 649-652.

Journal of Cell Science, Supplement 17, 21-26 (1993)
Printed in Great Britain © The Company of Biologists Limited 1993

Protein traffic in polarized epithelial cells: the polymeric immunoglobulin receptor as a model system

Keith Mostov

Departments of Anatomy and Biochemistry, and the Cardiovascular Research Institute, University of California at San Francisco, San Francisco, CA 94143, USA

SUMMARY

As a model system to study protein traffic in polarized epithelial cells, we have used the polymeric immunoglobulin receptor. This receptor travels first to the basolateral surface, where it can bind polymeric IgA or IgM. The receptor is then endocytosed and delivered to endosomes. The receptor is sorted into transcytotic vesicles, which are exocytosed at the apical surface. The 103-amino acid cytoplasmic domain of the receptor contains several sorting signals. The 17 residues closest to the membrane are an autonomous signal that is necessary and sufficient for basolateral sorting. For rapid endocytosis there are two independent signals, both of which contain critical tyrosine residues. Finally, transcytosis is signaled by phosphorylation of a particular serine.

Key words: transcytosis, protein sorting, sorting signals

INTRODUCTION

The most basic type of organization of cells into tissues is that of epithelia (Simons and Fuller, 1985; Rodriguez-Boulan and Nelson, 1989). Epithelial cells line a cavity or cover a surface. As such, they can form a selective barrier to the exchange of molecules between the lumen of an organ and an underlying tissue. For many decades physiologists have studied the movements of small molecules such as water, ions or sugars across epithelia. It has become increasingly clear that large molecules, such as proteins, can also cross an epithelial layer. One way that this can occur is by diffusion between cells, i.e. by a paracellular route. However, in many types of epithelia, the cells are closely attached to each other by tight junctions. These tight junctions form an effective seal between cells and usually preclude paracellular transport of macromolecules (Cereijido et al., 1989).

The other, more common transport route is across the cells themselves via vesicular carriers, in a process known as transcytosis (Mostov and Simister, 1985; Bomsel and Mostov, 1991). Macromolecules enter the cell by endocytosis, whereby a small region of the plasma membrane invaginates and pinches off, forming a vesicle. The encapsulated molecules are then transported across the cell. When these vesicles reach the opposite side, they fuse with the plasma membrane and their contents are released by exocytosis. Transcytosis may occur in either direction across a cell, from apical-to-basolateral, or basolateral-to-apical.

Transcytosis is a particularly complex example of the general process of membrane traffic in epithelial cells, and it is useful to consider transcytosis in relation to other protein transport processes that have been studied in polarized cells (Simons and Wandinger-Ness, 1990; Bomsel and Mostov, 1991). One such transport process is the targeting of membrane proteins to different poles of the cell. In most epithelial cells, the apical and basolateral surfaces maintain different protein and lipid compositions. Several mechanisms are involved in establishing and maintaining this compositional asymmetry (Bomsel and Mostov, 1991). First, newly synthesized plasma membrane proteins can be targeted directly to the appropriate membrane domain. In Madin-Darby canine kidney (MDCK) epithelial cells, segregation of apical and basolateral proteins appears to take place in the *trans*-most Golgi compartment or *trans*-Golgi network (TGN) (Griffiths and Simons, 1986). From here, proteins are packaged into vesicles destined for either the apical or basolateral surface, as demonstrated in work on viral coat membrane proteins (Rindler et al., 1984).

A second mechanism for the maintenance of cell polarity is the resorting of membrane proteins following endocytosis from the cell surface (Brown et al., 1983; Bomsel and Mostov, 1991). Internalized proteins can be transported to any of a number of cellular destinations. (1) They can be recycled to the plasma membrane from which they were internalized. Examples of this class of protein include the transferrin and LDL receptors (Brown et al., 1983). (2) They can be transported to lysosomes for degradation (for example, EGF receptor). (3) They can enter the transcytotic pathway for transport to the opposite pole of the cell. In hepatocytes, these three classes of proteins have been shown to segregate in an early endosomal compartment (Geuze et al., 1984). This review focuses on the cellular and molecular mechanisms of IgA transport across epithelial cells, but we can only cover selected aspects of this problem and will concentrate primarily on research done by our laboratory over the last decade.

TRANSCYTOSIS

A wide variety of molecules have been shown to be transcytosed (Mostov and Simister, 1985; Bomsel and Mostov, 1991), and it is likely that transcytosis is ubiquitous in epithelia. The best-studied examples are transport of immunoglobulins that occurs in at least three situations in mammals: transport of IgA and IgM across various mucosa (Childers et al., 1989), transport of IgG across the intestinal epithelium in newborn rats (Rodewald and Kraehenbuhl, 1984) and transport of IgG across the human placenta. The first process is discussed in detail below. Other examples of transcytosis include: insulin and serum albumin across endothelia (King and Johnson, 1985), epidermal growth factor across kidney epithelia (Maratos-Flier et al., 1987), nerve growth factor across intestinal epithelium and transferrin across capillaries in the brain (Bomsel and Mostov, 1991).

In some cases, transcytosis is a quantitatively major pathway. In hepatocytes, for example, newly synthesized apical (bile canalicular) membrane proteins are not delivered directly to the apical surface (Bartles et al., 1987); rather these proteins are first sent to the basolateral (sinusoidal) surface and from there transcytosed to the apical plasma membrane. In these cells, transcytosis is the only way for membrane proteins to reach the apical surface. In the intestinal cell line, CaCo2, a number of apical proteins utilize both the direct TGN-to-apical pathway and the indirect transcytotic pathway (LeBivic et al., 1990; Matter et al., 1990) to reach the apical surface.

TRANSCYTOSIS OF POLYMERIC IMMUNOGLOBULINS

The major class of immunoglobulin found in a wide variety of mucosal secretions, such as gastrointestinal and respiratory secretions, is IgA (Brandtzaeg, 1981; Bienenstock, 1984; Ahnen et al., 1985; Childers et al., 1989). IgA is produced by submucosal plasma cells that are often found in lymphoid aggregates such as gut-associated lymphoid tissue (GALT) and bronchus-associated lymphoid tissue (BALT) (Bienenstock, 1984). After secretion, IgA is taken up by an overlying epithelial cell, transported across the cell and released into external secretions (Brandtzaeg, 1981). Here the IgA forms the first specific immunologic defence against infection. This transport system transports only polymeric immunoglobulins (Brandtzaeg, 1981). Dimers or higher oligomers of IgA are transported, as are pentamers of IgM, although transport of the latter is less efficient. All of these polymers contain the J (joining) chain.

This transport of polymeric immunoglobulins is now known to be a receptor-mediated event. In 1965, Tomasi and associates found that IgA isolated from human saliva contained an extra polypeptide that was a glycoprotein of 70 kDa (Tomasi et al., 1965). This protein, named secre-

tory component (SC), was found to be synthesized by epithelial cells and added to IgA as it was transported across the cell. In 1974, Brandtzaeg examined the cellular location of SC by immunofluorescence (Brandtzaeg, 1974) and reported its presence on the basolateral surface of various epithelial cells. IgA from appropriate secretions could bind to the basolateral cell surface, and antisera to SC could block the binding of IgA. This led to the proposal that SC acted as a receptor mediating the uptake and transport of IgA across cells.

The hypothesis that SC was an IgA receptor presented an interesting paradox that formed the basis for many studies (Brandtzaeg, 1974; Mostov et al., 1980). If SC were a receptor for IgA on the basolateral cell membrane, it would be expected to be an integral membrane protein that could only be solubilized with detergents, yet SC isolated from secretions was water-soluble and had no affinity for membranes. One proposed solution to this paradox was that SC was secreted at the basolateral surface and combined with IgA in the extracellular fluid or blood (Kuhn and Kraehenbuhl, 1979). The SC-IgA complex could then bind to an unidentified receptor on the basolateral cell surface and be transported to the luminal surface. A problem with this model was that no SC could be detected in blood.

An alternative hypothesis was that SC was part of a larger precursor, now known as the polymeric immunoglobulin receptor (pIg-R) (Mostov et al., 1980). The first evidence in support of this model came from cell-free translation of rabbit liver and mammary mRNA (Mostov et al., 1980). SC was found to be synthesized as a large precursor of about 90 kDa. In a cell-free membrane integration system, this precursor was shown to be a membrane-spanning protein, which had a cytoplasmic domain of about 10 to 15 kDa. Moreover, the precursor could specifically bind to IgA, suggesting that it was the true polymeric immunoglobulin receptor (pIg-R).

We next studied the biosynthesis and processing of pIg-R in a human colon carcinoma cell line, HT29, which was known to secrete SC (Mostov and Blobel, 1982). Biosynthetic labelling of these cells revealed that the pIg-R was found initially as a single species of 90 kDa. Its carbohydrate side chains were subsequently modified to the complex type, which increased the apparent size of the protein to about 105 kDa. The pIg-R was then slowly cleaved to SC (70 kDa) and released from the cells. This cleavage is slower than in vivo, probably because the HT29 cells are not well differentiated or polarized. This type of pulse-chase analysis has been carried out by others using rabbit mammary cells in culture and intact rat liver, and the general observations have been confirmed (Solari and Kraehenbuhl, 1984; Sztul et al., 1985a,b).

The current understanding of the general pathways taken by the pIg-receptor is summarized in Fig. 1. An epithelial cell is shown with the apical surface at the top and the basolateral surface at the bottom. In step 1, the pIg-R is synthesized by membrane-bound polysomes of the rough endoplasmic reticulum (RER) as an integral membrane protein. A portion of the molecule extends into the lumen of the RER (open circle), a segment spans the membrane, and a portion is in the cytoplasm (filled circle). After transport through the Golgi apparatus (step 2), the receptor is tar-

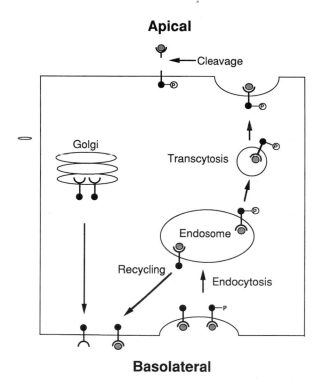

Apical

Basolateral

Fig. 1. The pathway of IgA transcytosis. An epithelial cell is shown, with the apical surface at the top and the basolateral surface at the bottom. Junctional complexes divide the two surfaces and join the cell to its neighbors. For further details see text.

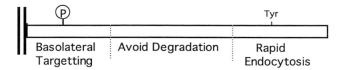

Fig. 2. Arrangement of sorting signals in the cytoplasmic domain of the pIg-R. The membrane is at the left and the carboxy terminus is at the right. The phosphate group is indicated by the P. For further details see text.

most rabbits are heterozygous. However, even in homozygous rabbits, there are two primary translation products, one of 70 to 75 kDa and one of 90 to 95 kDa. The pIg-R mRNA can be alternately spliced to yield a pIg-R protein that lacks the second and third of the five immunoglobulin domains (Deitcher and Mostov, 1986). This alternately spliced form is the 70 to 75 kDa translation product, whereas the form with all five immunoglobulin domains is the 90 to 95 kDa product. Sequencing of a genomic clone revealed that the two immunoglobulin domains involved are encoded by a single large exon. This is a rare example of two immunoglobulin domains encoded on one exon.

EXPRESSION OF pIg-R cDNA

The pathway of the pIg-R is unusual for a membrane protein in polarized cells because it is targeted first to the basolateral surface and then, following endocytosis, to the apical surface, rather than directly to its final destination. Postendocytotic sorting is complicated by the fact that internalized pIg-R enters endosomes that contain a variety of other receptors and ligands (Geuze et al., 1984). The pIg-R is apparently sorted away from this mixture of receptors and ligands in tubular extensions of the endosomes, and is then packaged to carrier vesicles for transcytosis to the apical surface (Geuze et al., 1984). These two features of the pIg-R pathway, sequential targeting to both surfaces and postendocytotic sorting into the transcytotic pathway, offer unique opportunities for the study of membrane trafficking. Our major strategy in studying the sorting of the pIg-R has been to express the cloned rabbit pIg-R cDNA in cultured cell lines, and analyze the function of normal and mutant receptors. For expression we have used a retroviral vector system developed by Mulligan and colleagues (Breitfeld et al., 1989a).

First, the pIg-R cDNA was expressed in the fibroblast line, y2, which is a derivative of the NIH 3T3 mouse fibroblast line (Deitcher et al., 1986). Although these cells have no obvious apical-basolateral polarity, the pIg-R appears to function normally. In a pulse-chase experiment, the receptor was found to be first synthesized as a single species of about 90 kDa. In the subsequent chase, it was converted to a heterogeneous form of about 105 kDa, due to modification of the carbohydrates, and was eventually cleaved to release SC, which was released into the medium. Like authentic SC, the SC released by these cells was heterogeneous. This is apparently due both to heterogeneity in glycosylation and to heterogeneity in the exact site of cleavage from the transmembrane anchor.

geted to the basolateral surface (step 3). Here the portion of the molecule formerly in the RER lumen is outside the cell, where it can bind IgA (step 4). The receptor-ligand complex is then endocytosed in coated vesicles (step 5) and transported by a variety of vesicles and tubules to the apical surface (step 6). At the apical surface (or perhaps during transport), the extracellular portion of the pIg-R is proteolytically cleaved from the transmembrane anchor. This cleaved fragment is the previously identified SC. It remains associated with the IgA in the extracellular secretions, and has the additional function of stabilizing the IgA against denaturation or proteolysis in the harsh external environment.

Our next step was to clone cDNA for pIg-R (Mostov et al., 1984). We used rabbit liver mRNA, an abundant source of pIg-R mRNA. We obtained a full-length cDNA clone that encoded a protein of 755 amino acids (not including the 18-amino acid N-terminal signal sequence). The protein had a single membrane-spanning segment and a cytoplasmic C-terminal domain of 103 amino acids (Fig. 2). The extracellular ligand-binding portion, which is cleaved to generate SC, contains five homologous repeating domains of 10 to 110 residues each. These are members of the immunoglobulin superfamily, and most closely resemble immunoglobulin variable regions (Mostov et al., 1984).

In the rabbit, there appears to be only one gene for pIg-R (Deitcher and Mostov, 1986). However, in many rabbits, there are four primary translation products, two of 70 to 75 kDa and two of 90 to 95 kDa. Part of the heterogeneity is due to the existence of multiple alleles of rabbit SC and

In these fibroblasts, when the pIg-R reaches the cell surface it is not immediately cleaved to SC. This results in a pool of uncleaved receptor on the surface where it is capable of internalizing bound ligand. About 35% of the bound ligand can be internalized. This endocytosed ligand is rapidly recycled back to the surface and then released into the medium, without substantial degradation.

We next expressed the pIg-R in cultured epithelial cells (Mostov and Deitcher, 1986), specifically, the Madin-Darby canine kidney (MDCK) cell line, which has been widely used for studying cell polarity. When grown on porous filter supports, such as a Millipore filter, these cells form a well-polarized, electrically resistant epithelial monolayer (Simons and Fuller, 1985). Tight junctions separate the apical from the basolateral surfaces and, in effect, a simple epithelial tissue is reconstituted in culture. The monolayer is relatively impermeable, especially to macromolecules. Under these culture conditions, one can experimentally access either the apical surface or, through the filter, the basolateral surface. In MDCK cells, as in fibroblasts, pIg-R is synthesized as a single species and then converted to a heterogeneous form due to carbohydrate modification. Proteolytic cleavage also occurs in these cells, and the free SC is released almost exclusively into the apical medium. This is exactly as occurs in vivo: SC is released at the lumenal surface and not into the bloodstream. Moreover, if ^{125}I-labeled dIgA is added to the basolateral medium, it is taken up by the cells and transported into the apical medium. This transcytosis is saturated by a competing excess of unlabeled dIgA, and does not occur in cells that do not express the receptor. Most importantly, the transport of dIgA is unidirectional, occurring only in the basolateral-to-apical direction. This process occurs with a half-time of about 30 minutes (Mostov and Deitcher, 1986).

REGULATION OF SORTING OF pIg-R

We have carried out additional studies to determine why the pathway for transcytosis of pIg-R is unidirectional (Breitfeld et al., 1989c). One possibility is that unidirectionality is conferred by the protease that cleaves the pIg-R to SC at the apical surface. To test this hypothesis, we took advantage of the recent observation that the cleavage of pIg-R to SC is inhibited by the microbial thiol protease inhibitor, leupeptin (Musil and Baenziger, 1987). We found that even though cleavage to SC was inhibited, transcytosis of ligand to the apical surface and its release into the apical medium were unaffected. In the absence of cleavage, ligand simply dissociates from the uncleaved pIg-R at the apical surface. More importantly, if ligand was added to the apical medium, apical-to-basolateral transcytosis was not observed. These results indicate that the unidirectionality of transport is conferred by signals other than proteolytic release of SC.

It appears that transcytosis is imperfect in terms of its efficiency. When a ligand molecule is endocytosed from the basolateral surface, it has three possible fates: transcytosis to the apical surface, recycling to the basolateral surface, or degradation. We have recently developed an assay that allows us to examine the fate of ligand endocytosed at the basolateral surface (Breitfeld et al., 1989c). We found that about 55% of internalized ligand is transcytosed over a 2 hour time course, while about 20% recycles. Very little (3-5%) is degraded. The recycling of receptor to the basolateral surface provides a further opportunity to be re-endocytosed and transcytosed. We also found that ligand could be endocytosed from the apical plasma membrane (Breitfeld et al., 1989c), but that this apically internalized ligand mostly recycles back to the apical surface. Almost none is transcytosed to the basolateral domain. There is thus a clear difference between ligand endocytosed from the basolateral surface, which can go to either surface, and ligand endocytosed apically, which can only return to the apical domain. It appears that once the receptor reaches the apical plasma membrane, it is essentially 'trapped'; it is then either cleaved to SC, or endocytosed and recycled back to the apical surface. The molecular signals that account for these observations are not known.

It is interesting to note that treatment of the MDCK cells with the microtubule-depolymerizing drug nocodazole slows the rate of transcytosis by 60-70%, but does not affect the overall accuracy of delivery (Breitfeld et al., 1990a; Hunziker et al., 1990). This suggests that microtubules may facilitate the process of transcytosis, but are not absolutely required for targeting of vesicles to the appropriate membrane. Importantly, transport of newly synthesized receptor from the Golgi to the basolateral membrane is completely unaffected by nocodazole treatment, suggesting that this process does not involve microtubules.

SORTING SIGNALS IN THE pIg-R

A major goal of our research is to analyze the structural determinants inherent to molecules, such as the pIg-R, that direct them to the appropriate cellular locations. We assume that the pIg-R contains sorting signals that control its transport. The complexity of the pIgR's cellular itinerary suggests that it may contain multiple sorting signals. One obvious location for such signals is the 103-amino acid, C-terminal cytoplasmic domain. Being in the cytoplasm, this receptor 'tail' would be accessible to interact with proteins in the cytoplasm that presumably constitute the cellular sorting machinery.

To address this issue, we first constructed a mutant pIg-R that lacked 101 of the 103 amino acids of the cytoplasmic domain (Mostov et al., 1986) (Fig. 2). Oligonucleotide-directed in vitro mutagenesis was used to insert a stop codon two amino acids after the membrane-spanning segment. This truncated 'tail-minus' receptor was expressed using the retroviral vector system in both nonpolarized fibroblasts and in MDCK cells.

In fibroblasts, the receptor is transported normally to the surface and is cleaved to SC. However, unlike the wild-type pIgR, the tail-minus mutant is not endocytosed, an observation that is not completely surprising. In other systems, notably the low density lipoprotein receptor, the cytoplasmic tail has been shown to be essential for endocytosis (Davis et al., 1987). When expressed in MDCK cells, this tail-minus pIg-R does not appear at the basolateral surface, rather it is sent directly to the apical surface from the

Golgi and is cleaved to SC. This result suggests that the cytoplasmic domain either contains a signal for basolateral targeting or that the cytoplasmic domain is necessary for basolateral targeting to occur. In a separate construction, we further truncated the receptor by deleting both the transmembrane and cytoplasmic domains, producing a soluble receptor (Mostov et al., 1987) (Fig. 2). This 'anchor-minus' receptor was secreted predominantly from the apical pole of MDCK cells. This suggests that the extracellular (or luminal) portion of the pIg-R may contain an apical sorting signal.

Recently we have made a large number of mutations in the cytoplasmic domain of the pIg-R, which indicate that it contains at least four sorting signals (Breitfeld et al., 1989b; Bomsel and Mostov, 1991). The arrangement of these signals is depicted in Fig. 2. Deletion of the carboxy-terminal 30 amino acids, which are encoded by a single exon, produces a receptor that follows the pathway of the wild-type receptor, except that the rate of endocytosis from the basolateral surface is decreased by about 60% (Breitfeld et al., 1990b). Exactly the same phenotype is produced by mutation of a tyrosine residue in this segment to a serine. This result is consistent with previous observations in several other systems, which have shown that tyrosine residues are important for rapid, clathrin-mediated endocytosis (Davis et al., 1987; Jing et al., 1990) and suggests a similar role for tyrosine in the pIgR. Mutation of a second, more membrane-proximal tyrosine reduces the endocytotic rate by only 5-10%. However, mutation of both tyrosines together virtually eliminates endocytosis, suggesting that both residues may play a role in this process.

Deletion of 37 residues from the middle section of the tail produces a pIg-R that is endocytosed normally, but is then degraded (Breitfeld et al., 1990a). It is unlikely that this receptor is simply malfolded, as it is normally delivered to the basolateral cell surface, binds ligand and is endocytosed. Perhaps the receptor has a mechanism to avoid degradation, which has been disrupted by the mutation. Alternatively, a signal for degradation may have been artificially created.

Further mutational analysis indicates that only the 17 amino acids closest to the membrane are needed for basolateral targeting (Casanova et al., 1991). A truncated receptor containing only these residues in the cytoplasmic domain is sorted basolaterally from the TGN, while deletion of these residues, leaving the remainder of the tail intact, produces a receptor that is targeted directly to the apical surface. Moreover, transplantation of this 17-amino acid signal to a heterologous, normally apical protein (placental alkaline phosphatase) is sufficient to redirect the chimeric protein to the basolateral surface.

Finally, the receptor has been shown to be phosphorylated on a serine residue in the cytoplasmic domain (Larkin et al., 1986). Phosphorylation occurs at the basolateral surface and/or shortly after endocytosis. Mutation of this serine to an alanine, which cannot be phosphorylated, produces a receptor that is not efficiently transcytosed, but rather recycles to the basolateral surface (Casanova et al., 1990). In contrast, mutation of this serine to an aspartic acid, whose negative charge may mimic that of the phosphate group, produces a receptor that is transcytosed more efficiently

than wild type. These results indicate that phosphorylation is the signal that directs the segregation of receptor into the transcytotic pathway.

The aspartic acid mutant also allows several indirect conclusions to be drawn. First, if the function of the pIg-R were simply to maximally transcytose IgA, why would the cell use phosphorylation, rather than simply using aspartate at this site? The most likely explanation is that phosphorylation is used to regulate transcytosis, perhaps in response to external cues. Second, many other proteins are transcytosed in epithelial cells. These may not necessarily use a phosphorylation mechanism, but may instead be analogous to the Asp mutant. Third, both the TGN and the basolateral endosome are organelles where apical/basolateral sorting takes place. However, the endosome relies on a negative charge from either phosphate or aspartate at a specific site in the pIg-R to send the molecule to the apical surface. The TGN, in contrast, ignores this charge, and sends even the Asp mutant to the basolateral surface. In other words, the negative charge does not inactivate the signal for TGN to basolateral targeting. Rather, it appears that targeting from the TGN and the endosome use different mechanisms.

Having made substantial progress in defining these sorting signals, the next step is to analyze the cellular machinery that recognizes such signals and is ultimately responsible for sorting processes. A first step in this direction is the work of Sztul and colleagues (Sztul et al., 1991), who have isolated putative transcytotic vesicles from rat liver. These vesicles are enriched in a 108 kDa protein which is apparently bound to the cytoplasmic face of the vesicular membrane. The possibility that this protein may be involved in either docking of the vesicle to its target membrane or in attachment to microtubules for transport is currently under investigation.

CONCLUSION

As this review indicates, substantial progress has been made in understanding the cellular and molecular basis of the transcytosis of immunoglobulins. This knowledge is important for two reasons. First, transcytosis is one of several systems of protein traffic in epithelial cells. Analyzing the sorting signals and cellular machinery that decode these signals will permit elucidation of the general principles that govern protein sorting. Second, transcytosis is important in the overall physiology of an organism. For example, polymeric immunoglobulins form a very early, specific immunologic defence against infection, and their transport is mediated by specific transcytotic events. Although much less is known about the regulation of their transcytosis, many other proteins are carried across epithelia by this mechanism to tissue sites where they are likely to carry out important functions. Analyzing transcytosis is thus an important area of connection between cell and molecular biology and the overall functioning of organs and organ systems.

I thank all members of my laboratory, past and present, for their enormous contributions to this work and stimulating discussions, and Maria Kerschen for manuscript preparation. Work in this laboratory was supported by NIH R01 AI25144, a Searle Scholarship, and the Cancer Research Institute.

REFERENCES

Ahnen, D. J., Brown, W. R. and Kloppel, T. M. (1985). Secretory component: The polymeric immunoglobulin receptor. What's in it for the gastroenterologist and hepatologist? *Gastroenterology* **89**, 667-682.

Bartles, J. R., Ferraci, H. M., Stieger, B. and Hubbard, A. L. (1987). Biogenesis of the rat hepatocyte plasma membrane in vivo: Comparison of the pathways taken by apical and basolateral proteins using subcellular fractionation. *J. Cell Biol.* **105**, 1241-1251.

Bienenstock, J. (1984). The mucosal immunologic network. *Ann. Allergy* **53**, 535-539.

Bomsel, M. and Mostov, K. E. (1991). Sorting of plasma membrane proteins in epithelial cells. *Curr. Opin. Cell. Biol.* **3**, 647-653.

Brandtzaeg, P. (1974). Mucosal and glandular distribution of immunoglobulin components: differential localization of free and bound SC in secretory epithelial cells. *J. Immunol.* **112**, 1553-1559.

Brandtzaeg, P. (1981). Transport models for secretory IgA and secretory IgM. *Clin. Exp. Immunol.* **44**, 221-232.

Breitfeld, P., Casanova, J. E., Harris, J. M., Simister, N. E. and Mostov, K. E. (1989a). Expression and analysis of the polymeric immunoglobulin receptor. *Meth. Cell Biol.* **32**, 329-337.

Breitfeld, P. P., Casanova, J. E., McKinnon, W. C. and Mostov, K. E. (1990a). Deletions in the cytoplasmic domain of the polymeric immunoglobulin receptor differentially affect endocytotic rate and postendocytotic traffic. *J. Biol. Chem.* **265**, 13750-13757.

Breitfeld, P. P., Casanova, J. E., Simister, N. E., Ross, S. A., McKinnon, W. C. and Mostov, K. E. (1989b). Sorting signals. *Curr. Opin. Cell Biol.* **1**, 617-623.

Breitfeld, P. P., Harris, J. M. and Mostov, K. M. (1989c). Postendocytotic sorting of the ligand for the polymeric immunoglobulin receptor in Madin-Darby canine kidney cells. *J. Cell Biol* **109**, 475-486.

Breitfeld, P. P., McKinnon, W. C. and Mostov, K. E. (1990b). Effect of nocodazole on vesicular traffic to the apical and basolateral surfaces of polarized MDCK cells. *J. Cell Biol.* **111**, 2365-2373.

Brown, M. S., Anderson, R. G. W. and Goldstein, J. L. (1983). Recycling receptors: The round-trip itinerary of migrant membrane proteins. *Cell* **32**, 663-667.

Casanova, J. E., Apodaca, G. and Mostov, K. E. (1991). An autonomous signal for basolateral sorting in the cytoplasmic domain of the polymeric immunoglobulin receptor. *Cell* **66**, 65-75.

Casanova, J. E., Breitfeld, P. P., Ross, S. A. and Mostov, K. E. (1990). Phosphorylation of the polymeric immunoglobulin receptor required for its efficient transcytosis. *Science* **248**, 742-745.

Cereijido, M., Ponce, A. and Gonzalez-Marical, L. (1989). Tight junctions and apical/basolateral polarity. *J. Membr. Biol.* **110**, 1-9.

Childers, N. K., Bruce, M. G. and McGhee, J. R. (1989). Molecular mechanisms of immunoglobulin A defense. *Annu. Rev. Microbiol.* **43**, 503-536.

Davis, C. G., van Driel, I. R., Russell, D. W., Brown, M. S. and Goldstein, J. L. (1987). The low density lipoprotein receptor: Identification of amino acids in cytoplasmic domain required for rapid endocytosis. *J. Biol. Chem.* **262**, 4075-4082.

Deitcher, D. L. and Mostov, K. E. (1986). Alternate splicing of rabbit polymeric immunoglobulin receptor. *Mol. Cell. Biol.* **6**, 2712-2715.

Deitcher, D. L., Neutra, M. R. and Mostov, K. E. (1986). Functional expression of the polymeric immunoglobulin receptor from cloned cDNA in fibroblasts. *J. Cell Biol.* **102**, 911-919.

Geuze, H. J., Slot, J. W., Strous, G. J. A. M., Peppard, J., von Figura, K., Hasilik, A. and Schwartz, A. L. (1984). Intracellular receptor sorting during endocytosis: Comparative immunoelectron microscopy of multiple receptors in rat liver. *Cell* **37**, 195-204.

Griffiths, G. and Simons, K. (1986). The *trans*-Golgi network: Sorting at the exit site of the Golgi complex. *Science* **234**, 4381-4443.

Hunziker, W., Mâle, P. and Mellman, I. (1990). Differential microtubule requirements for transcytosis in MDCK cells. *EMBO J.* **9**, 3515-3525.

Jing, S., Spencer, T., Miller, K., Hopkins, C. and Trowbridge, I. S. (1990). Role of the human transferrin receptor cytoplasmic domain in endocytosis: localization of a specific signal sequence for internalization. *J. Cell Biol.* **110**, 283-294.

King, G. L. and Johnson, S. M. (1985). Receptor-mediated transport of insulin across endothelial cells. *Science* **227**, 1583-1586.

Kuhn, L. C. and Kraehenbuhl, J.-P. (1979). Role of secretory component a secreted glycoprotein, in the specific uptake of IgA dimer by epithelial cells. *J. Biol. Chem.* **254**, 11072-22081.

Larkin, J. M., Sztul, E. S. and Palade, G. E. (1986). Phosphorylation of the rat hepatic polymeric IgA receptor. *Proc. Nat. Acad. Sci. USA* **83**, 4759-4763.

LeBivic, A., Quaroni, A., Nichols, B. and Rodriguez-Boulan, E. (1990). Biogenic pathways of plasma membrane proteins in Caco-2, a human intestinal epithelial cell line. *J. Cell Biol.* **111**, 1351-1361.

Maratos-Flier, E., Kao, B. Y., Verdin, E. M. and King, G. L. (1987). Receptor-mediated vectorial transcytosis of epidermal growth factor by Madin-Darby canine kidney cells. *J. Cell Biol.* **105**, 1595-1601.

Matter, K., Brauchbar, M., Bucher, K. and Hauri, H.-P. (1990). Sorting of endogenous plasma membrane proteins occurs from two sites in cultured human intestinal epithelial cells (Caco-2). *Cell* **60**, 429-437.

Mostov, K., Breitfeld, P. and Harris, J. M. (1987). An anchor-minus form of the polymeric immunoglobulin receptor is secreted predominantly apically in Madin-Darby canine kidney cells. *J. Cell Biol.* **105**, 2031-2036.

Mostov, K. E. and Blobel, G. (1982). A transmembrane precursor of secretory component. *J. Biol. Chem.* **257**, 11816-11821.

Mostov, K. E., de Bruyn Kops, A. and Deitcher, D. L. (1986). Deletion of the cytoplasmic domain of the polymeric immunoglobulin receptor prevents basolateral localization and endocytosis. *Cell* **47**, 359-364.

Mostov, K. E. and Deitcher, D. L. (1986). Polymeric immunoglobulin receptor expressed in MDCK cells transcytoses IgA. *Cell* **46**, 613-621.

Mostov, K. E., Friedlander, M. and Blobel, G. (1984). The receptor for transepithelial transport of IgA and IgM contains multiple immunoglobulin-like domains. *Nature* **308**, 37-43.

Mostov, K. E., Kraehenbuhl, J.-P. and Blobel, G. (1980). Receptor-mediated transcellular transport of immunoglobulin: Synthesis of secretory component as multiple and larger transmembrane forms. *Proc. Nat. Acad. Sci. USA* **77**, 7257-7261.

Mostov, K. E. and Simister, N. E. (1985). Transcytosis. *Cell* **43**, 389-390.

Musil, L. and Baenziger, J. (1987). Cleavage of membrane secretory component to soluble secretory component occurs on the cell surface of rat hepatocyte monolayers. *J. Cell Biol.* **104**, 1725-1733.

Rindler, M. J., Ivanov, I. E., Plesken, H., Rodriguez-Boulan, E. and Sabatini, D. D. (1984). Viral glycoproteins destined for apical or basolateral plasma membrane domains transverse the same Golgi apparatus during their intracellular transport in Madin-Darby Canine Kidney cells. *J. Cell Biol.* **98**, 1304-1319.

Rodewald, R. and Kraehenbuhl, J.-P. (1984). Receptor-mediated transport of IgG. *J. Cell Biol.* **99**, 159S-164S.

Rodriguez-Boulan, E. and Nelson, W. J. (1989). Morphogenesis of the polarized epithelial cell phenotype. *Science* **245**, 718-725.

Simons, K. and Fuller, S. D. (1985). Cell surface polarity in epithelia. *Annu. Rev. Cell Biol.* **1**, 243-288.

Simons, K. and Wandinger-Ness, A. (1990). Polarized sorting in epithelia. *Cell* **62**, 207-210.

Solari, R. and Kraehenbuhl, J.-P. (1984). Biosynthesis of the IgA antibody receptor: A model for the transepithelial sorting of a membrane glycoprotein. *Cell* **36**, 61-71.

Sztul, E., Kaplin, A., Saucan, L. and Palade, G. (1991). Protein traffic between distinct plasma membrane domains: Isolation and characterization of vesicular carriers involved in transcytosis. *Cell* **64**, 81-89.

Sztul, E. S., Howell, K. E. and Palade, G. E. (1985a). Biogenesis of the polymeric IgA receptor in rat hepatocytes. I. Kinetic studies of its intracellular forms. *J. Cell Biol.* **100**, 1248-1254.

Sztul, E. S., Howell, K. E. and Palade, G. E. (1985b). Biogenesis of the polymeric IgA receptor in rat hepatocytes. II. Localization of its intracellular forms by cell fractionation studies. *J. Cell Biol.* **100**, 1255-1262.

Tomasi, T. B. Jr, Tan, E. M., Solomon, A. and Prendergast, R. A. (1965). Characteristics of an immune system common to certain external secretions. *J. Exp. Med.* **121**, 101-124.

Journal of Cell Science, Supplement 17, 27-32 (1993)
Printed in Great Britain © The Company of Biologists Limited 1993

Role of heterotrimeric G proteins in polarized membrane transport

Sanjay W. Pimplikar* and Kai Simons

Cell Biology Programme, European Molecular Biology Laboratory, Postfach 102209, 69017 Heidelberg, Germany

*Author for correspondence

SUMMARY

MDCK cells maintain the polarized distribution of surface proteins mainly by sorting the newly synthesized proteins in the *trans*-Golgi network (TGN). In order to identify the components of the putative sorting machinery and to study factors that affect the sorting process, we have developed an in vitro system that reconstitutes the transport of viral glycoproteins from the TGN to the apical or basolateral surface. We have used this system to study effects of membrane impermeable reagents (such as peptides and antibodies) on the polarized transport. We observed that reagents affecting the stimulatory class (Gs) of heterotrimeric GTP binding proteins (G proteins) influenced the apical but not the basolat-

eral transport. In contrast, reagents specific for the inhibitory class of G proteins (Gi) affected the basolateral but not the apical transport. These results show that the heterotrimeric G proteins differentially regulate the two pathways of polarized transport. The G proteins may regulate the process of polarized sorting of proteins in a fashion analogous to their role in signal transduction by providing a communication link with the cytosolic side of the membrane.

Key words: protein sorting, heterotrimeric G proteins, epithelial cells

THE POLARITY PATHWAYS

In polarized epithelial cells, the plasma membrane is divided into two domains, apical and basolateral, which are distinct in their lipid and protein compositions. Most of the early information on polarized sorting and transport of proteins comes from studies on the transport of viral glycoproteins in MDCK cells infected with vesicular stomatitis virus (VSV) or influenza virus (Rodriguez-Boulan and Sabatini, 1978; Simons and Fuller, 1985). Both VSV glycoprotein (VSV-G) and influenza haemagglutinin (HA), like cellular membrane proteins, are inserted in the ER membrane upon synthesis and occupy the same compartments while en route through the Golgi complex to the *trans*-Golgi network (TGN; Rindler et al., 1984; Fuller et al., 1985; Griffiths and Simons, 1986). In the TGN, VSV-G and HA are segregated and packaged in two distinct classes of vesicles and are delivered to basolateral and apical domains, respectively (Wandinger-Ness et al., 1990). Pulse-chase experiments have demonstrated that the endogenous cellular proteins are also transported directly to the desired cell surface. Thus, it appears that MDCK cells sort apical and basolateral proteins in the TGN and deliver them directly to their respective destinations (see Fig. 1; for a review see Rodriguez-Boulan and Powell, 1992).

This is not the strategy adopted by all epithelial cells to achieve polarized distribution of their cell-surface proteins. Hepatocytes, for example, deliver both the apical and basolateral proteins first to the basolateral domain. The

apical proteins are then selectively retrieved and are delivered to the apical domain via a transcytotic pathway (Bartles and Hubbard, 1988). Thus, hepatocytes seem to sort their apical proteins not from the TGN but from the basolateral side. Interestingly, the processes of apical sorting from the TGN (vectorial delivery) and from the basolateral surface (transcytotic delivery) share many characteristics such as microtubule-dependence and sensitivity to the drug brefeldin A, a drug that profoundly affects the membrane traffic in non-polarized cells. Some cells, for example CaCo2, seem to use both the direct and the transcytotic pathway to deliver proteins to the apical surface (Le Bivic et al., 1990; Matter et al., 1990). A third mechanism, that of random delivery of proteins to both surfaces followed by selective removal or retention, may also contribute significantly towards the generation of polarity (Nelson and Hammerton, 1989).

It is not clear why epithelial cells adopt different strategies to attain the polarized distribution of proteins. These differences become more enigmatic if one considers the fact that a vectorially delivered apical protein, when expressed in other epithelial cells, may be delivered to the apical domain by the transcytotic pathway. This suggests that both vectorial and transcytotic apical sorting mechanisms share common features (Simons and Wandinger-Ness, 1990).

THE FACTORS THAT AFFECT POLARIZED TRANSPORT

Although most of the molecules responsible for generat-

Apical membrane

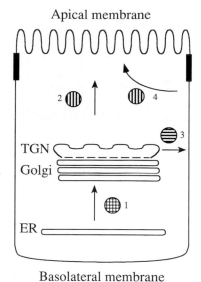

Basolateral membrane

Fig. 1. Schematic representation of exocytic pathways in polarized MDCK cells. Newly synthesized proteins are transported from the ER to the Golgi complex (1). At this stage, the apical and basolateral proteins are not yet sorted from each other and occupy the same compartments. In the TGN, the apical proteins are sorted into apical vesicles and transported directly to the apical membrane (vectorial delivery; 2) wheras the basolateral proteins are delivered directly to the basolateral membrane (3). Apically destined proteins that were delivered to the basolateral membrane (e.g. polymeric Ig receptor) are then retrieved from the surface and transported to the apical surface (transcytotic delivery; 4).

ing and maintaining the polarity in epithelial cells remain unidentified, a wealth of phenomenological information is available on the factors that affect the state of polarity or regulate the polarized delivery of proteins. For example, it is generally observed that both the vectorial (direct) and transcytotic (indirect) delivery of apical proteins is dependent on the presence of intact microtubules, whereas delivery of proteins to the basolateral surface is relatively independent of microtubules (Rindler et al., 1987; Hunziker et al., 1990). Conflicting observations are also reported, however (Salas et al., 1986; van Zeijl and Matlin, 1990). A fungal metabolite, brefeldin A, that has been extensively used to study non-polarized membrane transport, inhibits both the vectorial and the transcytotic pathway to the apical surface but has no effect on the basolateral route (Low et al., 1991; Hunziker et al., 1991). However, we (unpublished data) and others have observed that brefeldin A inhibits both the apical and basolateral pathways (Rodriguez-Boulan and Powell, 1992) and Prydz et al. (1992) have reported that most endocytic and transcytotic events are either unaffected or even stimulated by brefeldin A.

A recent exciting development in the area of membrane traffic has been the appreciation of the role of GTP binding proteins at various steps of intracellular transport. Broadly, the GTP binding proteins can be classified into two families: small, monomeric ras-related proteins (smgp) and the heterotrimeric G proteins (G proteins). In non-polar-

ized cells, the involvement of rab and ARF proteins (two subfamiles of smgp) at various stages of both exocytic and endocytic traffic is well documented (reviewed by Pfeffer, 1992). Recent evidence indicates that rab proteins also play an important role in cell polarity (Luetcke et al., 1993) and polarized protein transport (Huber et al., 1993). Different members of the rab family are localized to specific organelles of the exo- and endocytic pathways (Olkkonen et al., 1993) suggesting that they may be involved in each specific transport step.

INVOLVEMENT OF THE G PROTEINS IN MEMBRANE TRANSPORT

Although the role of G proteins in signal transduction is widely known, their involvement in membrane transport, both in non-polarized and polarized cells, has been recognized only recently (reviewed by Barr et al., 1992; Bomsel and Mostov, 1992). Most of the information about the G proteins comes from studies on their role in signal transduction. These proteins are composed of α, β and γ subunits and it is the α subunit that binds the guanine nucleotides. In the inactive state, the α subunit is bound by GDP, which is replaced by GTP upon activation of an upstream receptor. This activated state of G proteins can also be mimicked by the addition of $AlF_{(3-5)}$ and affected specifically by toxins and other reagents such as mastoparan. These properties have been exploited to investigate the involvement of G proteins in the process of membrane traffic. Overexpression of $Gi\alpha$-3 in LLC-PK1 cells inhibits the secretion of proteoglycans, and this inhibition can be reversed by pertussis toxin (PTX; Stow et al., 1991). In vitro budding of exocytic vesicles from the TGN is shown to be sensitive to reagents that affect the Gi function (Barr et al., 1991). The same reagents affect the binding of ARF and β-COP, proteins known to be involved in membrane traffic, to the Golgi membranes (Donaldson et al., 1991). These reagents also interfere with the action of brefeldin A on the association of these proteins with the Golgi membranes (Ktistakis et al., 1992). These observations suggest that the G proteins play a role in membrane traffic, perhaps in vesicle formation.

There is a tantalizing possibility that G proteins may regulate specific pathways of polarized traffic. For example, the proteoglycans studied by Stow et al. (1991) are secreted to the basolateral but not to the apical surface. Thus, inhibition of proteoglycan secretion by overexpression of $Gi\alpha$-3 may represent regulation of the basolateral route by a Gi class of G proteins. However, the general effect of $Gi\alpha$-3 overexpression on apical or basolateral secretion is not yet known. On the other hand, it seems that the transcytotic pathway from the basolateral to apical direction is regulated by a Gs class of G proteins (K. Mostov, personal communication). Using an in vitro system that reconstitutes budding of polymeric Ig receptor-containing transcytotic vesicles from early endosomes, Bomsel and Mostov (1992) have observed that Gs-specific reagents influence the budding of transcytotic vesicles whereas the Gi-specific reagents do not affect the system.

Basolateral Transport Assay

Apical Transport Assay

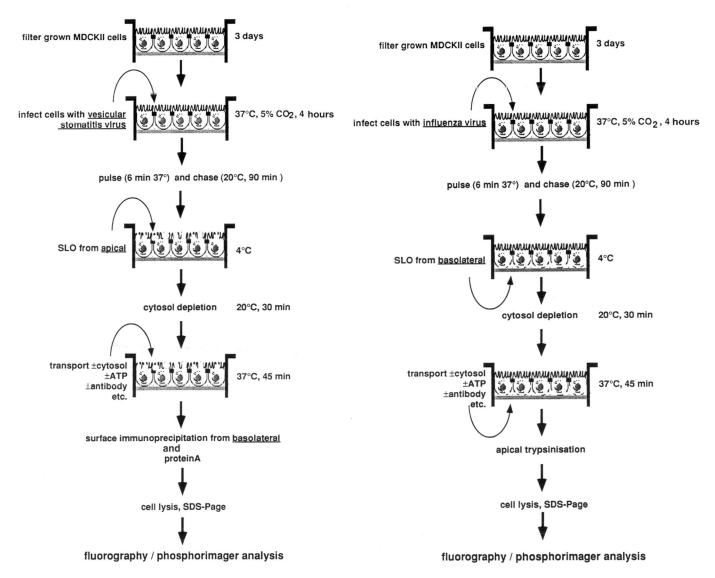

Fig. 2. Schematic representation of the in vitro transport assay in SLO-permeabilized cells. (A) TGN-to-basolateral transport of VSV-G protein. (B) TGN-to-apical transport of HA.

AN IN VITRO SYSTEM TO STUDY POLARIZED TRANSPORT

In order to access the site of polarized sorting directly and to gain a better understanding of the sorting process, we have developed an in vitro system to study the polarized sorting and transport of proteins (Kobayashi et al., 1992; Pimplikar and Simons, 1993). We use the bacterial toxin streptolysin O (SLO) to permeabilise selectively either surface of MDCK monolayers grown on a permeable filter support. The toxin is thought to bind to cholesterol in the cell surface at low temperatures (4°C) but the pores are formed only after raising the temperature (20°C or above). The pores formed are usually in the range of 30 nm and thus large enough to allow leakage of cytosolic proteins but small enough to retain the vesicles. Under these conditions,

transport of proteins between two organelles becomes dependent upon addition of exogenous cytosol and energy. An advantage of the SLO permeabilization procedure is that the integrity of the cellular structure and intercellular junctions is mostly maintained. Thus, the SLO permeabilization procedure has proved useful in reconstructing a number of in vitro membrane transport systems (Gravotta et al., 1990; Tan et al., 1992).

Briefly, MDCK cells are grown on a permeable filter support until a tight monolayer is obtained (Fig. 2). The cells are then infected either with influenza virus to study apical transport of HA glycoprotein, or with vesicular stomatitis virus (VSV) to study basolateral transport of VSV-G glycoprotein. After a short pulse of radioactive methionine, the newly synthesized viral glycoproteins are blocked in the TGN at 20°C. At this stage, the opposite cell surface is per-

Table 1. Effects of G protein-specific reagents on polarized transport in MDCK cells

	Transport step		
Reagents	TGN→apical	TGN→basolateral	Transcytotic vesicles
AlF$_{(3-5)}$	↑	↓	↑
Mastoparan	–	↓	–
PTX	–	↑	–
CTX	↑	–	↑
Gs antibodies	↓	?	↓

↑, stimulation; ↓, inhibition; –, no significant effect; ?, not known. The data for the TGN→apical and TGN→basolateral transport are from Pimplikar and Simons (1993) and those for the production of transcytotic vesicles are from Bomsel and Mostov (1992).

meabilized with SLO and the endogenous cytosol is removed by washing. Upon raising the temperature to 37°C and addition of exogenous cytosol and ATP, the appearance of viral glycoprotein at the intact cell surface is monitored. Under these conditions the transport of viral glycoproteins from the TGN to the cell surface is temperature-, cytosol- and energy-dependent. An additional advantage of the SLO-permeabilized cell system is that besides the polarized transport we can also study ER-to-Golgi transport by monitoring acquisition of Endo H resistance by HA. This non-polarized transport step serves as a control to demonstrate the specificity of reagents that affect the polarized transport steps.

In conjunction with studies on intact cells, we have used the in vitro system to study the roles of Gs and Gi classes of G proteins on the apical and basolateral transport (Pimplikar and Simons, 1993). We observed that the basolateral transport of proteins was inhibited by AlF$_{(3-5)}$ and mastoparan and stimulated by PTX. These observations are consistent with the involvement of Gi in basolateral traffic. Recent studies suggest that the Gi class may also regulate ER to Golgi transport (Schwaninger et al., 1992; Wilson et al., 1993). In contrast to the basolateral transport, the apical transport was stimulated by AlF$_{(3-5)}$ and cholera toxin (CTX) but was unaffected by mastoparan. These data suggested involvement of the Gs class of G proteins in the apical transport. Furthermore, antibodies against Gs inhibited the TGN to apical transport of HA but had no effect on its passage from the ER to Golgi. Therefore, these observations (Table 1) suggest that the basolateral and apical transport pathways are specifically regulated by the Gi and Gs class of G proteins, respectively. It is interesting to note that both the vectorial and the transcytotic apical pathway seem to be regulated by the Gs class of G proteins. This further strengthens the idea that the apical sorting machinery at these two sites (TGN and basolateral surface) may be identical (Simons and Wandinger-Ness, 1990). At the present stage it is not known precisely which step of the transport assay (vesicle budding or vesicle fusion) is regulated by G proteins.

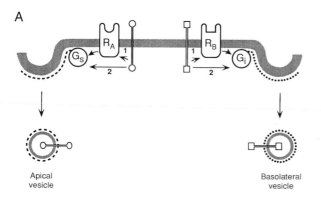

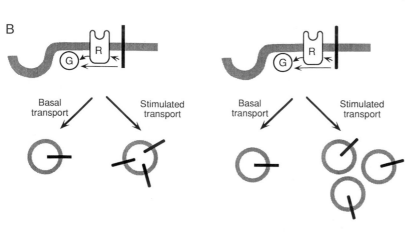

Fig. 3. Proposed role for G proteins in polarized membrane transport. (A) Upon arrival in the TGN, an apical-membrane protein interacts (1) with an apical-specific receptor (R$_A$) or directly with the Gs protein (2). These interactions activate the Gs protein. The activated Gs stimulates the downstream events resulting in increased apical transport. In an analogous way, a basolateral-membrane protein interacts (1) with a basolateral-specific receptor (R$_B$) or directly with the Gi protein (2). These interactions inhibit the Gi protein. The inhibition of Gi results in de-repression of the downstream events resulting in increased basolateral transport. The apical and basolateral vesicles are enclosed in specific coat proteins (shown as broken lines and small dots). In the TGN, the apical- and basolateral-secretory proteins could bind to their putative receptors (not shown in the figure), which either directly or via R$_A$ and R$_B$, will interact with the respective G proteins. (B) There are two ways in which the G proteins can regulate membrane transport. The G proteins could facilitate the *incorporation* of the cargo molecules in vesicles that are being constitutively formed (Entry model). A stimulated transport, therefore, results from the increased number of cargo molecules per vesicle. An alternative possibility is that the G proteins regulate the *formation* of vesicles (Budding model). In this mode of action, a stimulated transport results from the increased number of vesicles. For the sake of simplicity, the coat proteins and the secretory proteins are not shown. Also, the receptors and the G proteins are not specified since this mode of action will be the same for both the apical and basolateral transport.

REGULATION OF POLARIZED TRANSPORT BY TRIMERIC G PROTEINS: A WORKING HYPOTHESIS

What precise role do G proteins play in polarized sorting and transport of membrane proteins? Current evidence from non-polarized and polarized cells favours the idea that G proteins regulate some aspect of vesicle budding (Barr et al., 1991; Bomsel and Mostov, 1992). However, it is possible that the G proteins may also be required for the fusion of vesicles and there is evidence that fusion of secretory granules with the plasma membrane (Gomperts, 1990) and fusion between early endosomes (Colombo et al., 1992) may be regulated by G proteins.

Without excluding the possibility that the G proteins may also be involved in the fusion of apical and basolateral vesicles with the respective domains, we speculate that the G proteins regulate the polarized sorting at the donor site, i.e. in the TGN. Our data suggest that the apical transport is under stimulatory control whereas the basolateral transport is under inhibitory control. We propose that the apical proteins, via an apical-specific receptor or acting alone, stimulate the Gs protein (Fig. 3A). The activated Gs then activates the downstream events resulting in apical transport. In contrast, the basolateral proteins inhibit the Gi protein via a basolateral receptor or acting alone as an antagonist. Inhibition of Gi function results in de-repression of the downstream events resulting in basolateral transport.

There are two possibilities in which the G proteins may control the downstream events and thus regulate the process of polarized transport (Fig. 3B). The G proteins may regulate the efficiency of protein inclusion into the correct vesicles (Entry model). During a given time interval, a constant number of both apical and basolateral vesicles are constitutively released from the TGN. The Gs and Gi class of G proteins could control the entry of newly synthesized apical and basolateral proteins in the respective budding vesicles. Therefore, a treatment that results in the stimulation or inhibition of a given G protein function will result in increased or decreased number of cargo molecules in the budded vesicles. Alternatively, the apical or basolateral proteins may stimulate the formation of vesicles (Budding model; also see Barr et al., 1992; Bomsel and Mostov, 1992). In this case, formation of the apical and basolateral vesicles will be under stimulatory and inhibitory controls, respectively. Stimulation of the Gs by an apical protein will result in an increased number of apical vesicles while inhibition of the Gi by a basolateral protein will increase the budding of the basolateral vesicles.

We assume that the apical and basolateral vesicles are formed by recruiting different cytosolic proteins on the TGN membrane. The nascent apical and basolateral vesicles will be coated with specific coat proteins, which may be released in the cytosol prior to fusion. Consistent with this idea, we have found that a protein associates with VSV-G tail only in the TGN but not in the ER or at the cell surface. Importantly, this protein does not associate with the HA tail in the TGN (unpublished observations). The G proteins could play a part in ensuring that the correct cargo is linked with the correct cytoplasmic coat proteins. It is not yet clear whether inhibiting a given G function results in mis-sorting of the cargo proteins to a 'wrong' pathway or simply in its accumulation in the TGN.

It should be noted that these two models are not mutually exclusive and that the G proteins may regulate both aspects (entry and budding) of vesicle formation. Whatever may be the precise role of G proteins in membrane traffic, it is clear that they play an important role in the polarized membrane transport.

We thank Drs P. Dupree and E. Ikonen for their comments on the manuscript, H. Virta and C. Frederiksen for technical help and Drs L. Huber, P. Riedinger and S. Bednarczyk for their help with the illustrations.

REFERENCES

Barr, F. A., Leyte, A. L., Mollner, S., Pfeuffer, T., Tooze, S. A. and Huttner, W. B. (1991). Trimeric G proteins of the trans-Golgi network are involved in the formation of constitutive secretory vesicles and immature secretory granules. *FEBS Lett.* **293**, 239-243.

Barr, F. A., Leyte, A. and Huttner, W. B. (1992). Trimeric G proteins and vesicle formation. *Trends Cell Biol.* **2**, 91-94.

Bartles, J. R. and Hubbard, A. L. (1988). Plasma membrane protein sorting in epithelial cells: Do secretory proteins hold the key? *Trends Biochem. Sci.* **13**, 181-184.

Bomsel, M. and Mostov, K. (1992). Role of heterotrimeric G proteins in membrane traffic. *Mol. Biol. Cell* **3**, 1317-1328.

Colombo, M. I., Mayorga, L. S., Casey, P. J. and Stahl, P. D. (1992). Evidence for a role for heterotrimeric GTP-binding proteins in endosome fusion. *Science* **255**, 1695-1697.

Donaldson, J. G., Kahn, R. A., Lippincott-Schwartz, J. and Klausner, R. D. (1991). Binding of ARF and β-COP to Golgi membranes:possible regulation by a trimeric G protein. *Science* **254**, 1197-1199.

Fuller, S. D.,Bravo, R. and Simons, K. (1985). An enzymatic assay reveals that proteins destined for the apical or basolateral domains of an epithelial cell line share the same late Golgi compartments. *EMBO J.* **4**, 297-307.

Gravotta, D., Adesnik, M. and Sabatini, D. (1990). Transport of influenza HA from the trans-Golgi network to the apical surface of MDCK cells permeabilized in their basolateral plasma membranes: Energy dependence and involvement of GTP-binding proteins. *J. Cell Biol.* **111**, 2893-2908.

Gomperts, B. D. (1990). G_E: A GTP-binding protein mediating exocytosis. *Annu. Rev. Physiol.* **52**, 591-606.

Griffiths, G. and Simons, K. (1986). The trans Golgi network: sorting at the exit site of the Golgi complex. *Science* **234**, 438-443.

Huber, L. A., Pimplikar, S. W., Parton, R. G., Virta, H., Zerial, M. and Simons, K. (1993). Rab8, a small GTPase involved in vesicular traffic between the TGN and the basolateral plasma membrane. *J. Cell Biol.* **123**, 35-45.

Hunziker, W., Male, P. and Mellman, I. (1990). Differential microtubule requirements for transcytosis in MDCK cells. *EMBO J.* **9**, 3515-3525.

Hunziker, W., Whitney, J. A. and Mellman, I. (1991). Selective inhibition of transcytosis by brefeldin A in MDCK cells. *Cell* **67**, 617-628.

Kobayashi, T., Pimplikar, S. W., Parton, R. G., Bhakdi, S. and Simons, K. (1992). Sphingolipid transport from the trans-Golgi network to the apical surface in permeabilized MDCK cells. *FEBS Lett.* **300**, 227-231.

Ktistakis, N. T., Linder M. E. and Roth, M. G. (1992). Action of brefeldin A blocked by activation of a pertussis-toxin-sensitive G protein. *Nature* **356**, 344-346.

Le Bivic, A., Quaroni, A., Nichols, B. and Rodriguez-Boulan, E. (1990). Biogenetic pathways of plasma membrane proteins in Caco-2, a human intestinal epithelial cell line. *J. Cell Biol.* **111**, 1351-1361.

Low, S. H., Tang, B. L., Wong, S. H. and Hong, W. (1991). Selective inhibition of protein targeting to the apical domain of MDCK cells by brefeldin A. *J. Cell Biol.* **118**, 51-62.

Luetcke, A., Jansson, S., Parton, R. G., Chavrier, P., Valencia, A., Huber, L., Lehtonen, E. and Zerial, M. (1993). Rab17, a novel small GTPase, is specific for epithelial cells and is induced during cell polarization. *J. Cell Biol.* (in press).

Matter, K., Brauchbar, M., Bucher, K. and Hauri, H. P. (1990). Sorting of endogenous plasma membrane proteins occurs from two sites in cultured human intestinal epithelial cells (Caco-2). *Cell* **60**, 429-437.

Nelson, W. J. and Hammerton, R. W. (1989). A membrane-cytoskeletal complex containing Na, K-ATPase, ankyrin, and fodrin in MDCK cells: implications for the biogenesis of epithelial cell polarity. *J. Cell Biol.* **108**, 893-902.

Olkkonen, V., Dupree, P., Huber, L. A., Luetcke, A., Zerial, M. and Simons, K. (1993). Compartmentalization of rab proteins in mammalian cells. In *GTPases in Biology*, vol I (ed. B. Dickey and L. Birnbaumer), pp. 423-445. Heidelberg: Springer-Verlag.

Pfeffer, S. R. (1992). GTP-binding proteins in intracellular transport. *Trends Cell Biol.* **2**, 41-46.

Pimplikar, S. W. and Simons, K. (1993). Regulation of apical transport in epithelial cells by a Gs class of heterotrimeric G protein. *Nature* **362**, 456-458.

Prydz, K., Hansen, S. H., Sandvig, K. and van Deurs, B. (1992). Effects of brefeldin A on endocytosis, transcytosis and transport to the Golgi complex in polarized MDCK cells. *J. Cell Biol.* **119**, 259-272.

Rindler, M. J., Ivanov, I. E., Plesken, H., Rodriguez-Boulan, E. and Sabatini, D. D. (1984). Viral glycoproteins destined for apical or basolateral plasma membrane domains traverse the same Golgi apparatus during their intracellular transport in doubly infected Madin-Darby canine kidney cells. *J. Cell Biol.* **98**, 1304-1319.

Rindler, M. J., Ivanov, I. E. and Sabatini, D. D. (1987). Microtubule-acting drugs lead to the nonpolarized delivery of the influenza hemagglutinin to the cell surface of the polarized MDCK cells. *J. Cell Biol.* **104**, 231-241.

Rodriguez-Boulan, E. and Sabatini, D. D. (1978). Asymmetric budding of viruses in epithelial monolayers: a model system for study of epithelial polarity. *Proc. Nat. Acad. Sci. USA* **75**, 5071-5075.

Rodriguez-Boulan, E. and Powell, S. K. (1992). Polarity of epithelial and neuronal cells. *Annu. Rev. Cell Biol.* **8**, 395-427.

Salas, P. J. I., Misek, D., Vega-Salas, D. E., Gundersen, D., Cereijido, M. and Rodriguez-Boulan, E. (1986). Microtubule and actin filaments are not critically involved in the biogenesis of epithelial polarity. *J. Cell Biol.* **102**, 1853-1857.

Schwaninger, R., Plutner, H., Bokoch, G. M. and Balch, W. E. (1992). Multiple GTP-binding proteins regulate vesicular transport from the ER to Golgi membranes. *J. Cell Biol.* **119**, 1077-1096.

Simons, K. and Fuller, S. D. (1985). Cell surface polarity in epithelia. *Annu. Rev. Cell Biol.* **1**, 243-288.

Simons, K. and Wandinger-Ness, A. (1990). Polarized sorting in epithelia. *Cell* **62**, 207-210.

Stow, J. L, de Almeida, J. B., Narula, N., Holtzman, E. J., Ercoloni, L. and Ausiello, D. A. (1991). A heterotrimeric G protein, Gαi-3, on golgi membranes regulates the secretion of a heparan sulfate proteoglycan in LLC-PK1 epithelial cells. *J. Cell Biol.* **114**, 1113-1124.

Tan, A., Bolscher, J., Feltkamp, C. and Ploegh, H. (1992). Retrograde transport from the golgi region to the endoplasmic reticulum is sensitive to GTPγS. *J. Cell Biol.* **116**, 1357-1367.

van Zeijl, M. J. A. H and Matlin, K. S. (1990). Microtubule perturbation inhibits intracellular transport of an apical membrane glycoprotein in a substrate-dependent manner in polarized MDCK cells. *Cell Regul.* **1**, 921-936.

Wandinger-Ness, A., Bennett, M. K., Antony, C. and Simons, K. (1990). Distinct transport vesicles mediate the delivery of plasma membrane proteins to the apical and basolateral domains of MDCK cells. *J. Cell Biol.* **111**, 987-1000.

Wilson, B. S., Palade, G. and Farquhar, M. (1993). ER-through-Golgi transport assay based on O-glycosylation of native glycophorin in permeabilized erythroleukemia cells: Role for G$_{i3}$. *Proc. Nat. Acad. Sci. USA* **90**, 1681-1685.

Journal of Cell Science, Supplement 17, 33-39 (1993)
Printed in Great Britain © The Company of Biologists Limited 1993

Distribution and role of heterotrimeric G proteins in the secretory pathway of polarized epithelial cells

Jennifer L. Stow and J. Bruno de Almeida

Renal Unit and Department of Pathology, Massachusetts General Hospital and Harvard Medical School, Charlestown, MA 02129, USA

SUMMARY

The movement of newly synthesized proteins in the constitutive secretory pathway, from their site of synthesis in the endoplasmic reticulum to the cell surface or to intracellular destinations, requires an orderly sequence of transport steps between membrane-bound compartments. Until recently, the trafficking and secretion of proteins through this pathway was thought to occur as a relatively automatic, unregulated series of events. Recent studies show that protein trafficking in the constitutive secretory pathway requires GTP hydrolysis by families of GTP-binding proteins (G proteins), which at multiple steps potentially provide regulation and specificity for protein trafficking. Many monomeric G proteins are known to be localized and functional on membrane compartments in the constitutive secretory pathway. Now, members of the heterotrimeric G protein family have also been localized on intracellular membranes and compartments such as the Golgi complex. We have studied the localization and targeting of $G\alpha$ subunits to distinct membrane domains in polarized epithelial cells. The distribution of different $G\alpha$ subunits on very specific membrane domains in cultured epithe-

lial cells and in epithelial cells of the kidney cortex, is highly suggestive of roles for these G proteins in intracellular trafficking pathways. One of these G protein subunits, $G\alpha_{i-3}$, was localized on Golgi membranes. Studies on LLC-PK$_1$ cells overexpressing $G\alpha_{i-3}$ provided evidence for its functional role in regulating the transport of a constitutively secreted heparan sulfate proteoglycan through the Golgi complex. Inhibition or activation of heterotrimeric G proteins by pertussis toxin or by aluminium fluoride respectively, have provided further evidence for regulation of intracellular transport by pertussis toxin-sensitive G proteins. Although the functions of Golgi-associated G proteins are not yet understood at the molecular level, heterotrimeric G proteins have been implicated in the binding of cytosolic coat proteins and vesicle formation on Golgi membranes. Future studies will elucidate how multiple G proteins, of both the heterotrimeric and monomeric families, are involved in the regulation of Golgi function and protein trafficking in the secretory pathway.

Key words: G proteins, secretion, Golgi, vesicle trafficking

INTRODUCTION

The delivery of newly synthesized proteins to different membrane domains results in a geographic segregation of functions within polarized epithelial and neuronal cells. Similarly, the polarized secretion of newly synthesized proteins from distinct sides of epithelial cells enables differentiation and specialization of separate compartments of the extracellular milieu. Many membrane proteins and soluble proteins synthesized in the rough ER are trafficked via the constitutive secretory pathway, through the Golgi complex, to the cell surface or other destinations (Farquhar, 1985; Kelly, 1985; Palade, 1975; Rothman and Orci, 1992). The trafficking of these proteins is believed to occur as a continuous stream of small quantities of proteins that are shuttled between compartments in small vesicles or other membrane-bound carriers. Although the mechanisms governing the sorting and vesicular transport of proteins through this

constitutive pathway have been studied extensively, there is still little understanding of how this dynamic, multi-stage pathway is regulated.

One example of a protein that is secreted in a constitutive and a polarized fashion from many epithelial cells is the heparan sulfate proteoglycan BMHSPG, which is a component of the basement membrane underlying the epithelia. The intracellular processing and secretion of the BMHSPG has been studied in kidney epithelial cell lines (Caplan et al., 1987; de Almeida and Stow, 1991; Stow and Farquhar, 1987; Stow et al., 1989). In polarized monolayers of cultured LLC-PK$_1$ cells and MDCK cells, the BMHSPG is sorted and secreted in a polarized fashion from the basal surface of the cells (Caplan et al., 1987; de Almeida and Stow, 1991). The BMHSPG is secreted relatively abundantly and continuously from LLC-PK$_1$ cells grown on filters and the sequential post-translational modifications of biosynthetically labelled BMHSPG can be used to follow its intracellular trafficking. Thus, assaying the processing and secretion of BMHSPG in LLC-PK₁ cells has provided a useful model in which to study the secretory pathway. Importantly it has enabled us to follow an endogenous protein in intact cells for studies of secretion, particularly with respect to the regulation of secretion by G proteins, as described below.

The use of non-hydrolyzable nucleotide analogs such as GTPγS provided the first clue that GTP-binding proteins were involved in various steps of vesicle trafficking (Balch, 1990; Beckers and Balch, 1989; Melancon et al., 1987; Ruohola et al., 1988; Tooze et al., 1990). Addition of GTPγS to permeabilized cells and or cell-free assays was generally found to block constitutive protein transport between membrane-bound compartments, by inhibiting either fusion or formation of vesicle carriers. The effects of GTPγS were initially attributed to the many examples of monomeric G proteins found throughout the secretory pathway (Balch, 1990). However, it has since become known that members of the heterotrimeric G protein family are also present and functional in the secretory pathway.

DISTRIBUTION OF HETEROTRIMERIC G PROTEINS

Two large gene families of guanine nucleotide-binding (G) proteins have been identified. The ras supergene family consists of several families of small molecular mass, monomeric G proteins, which are found in soluble or membrane-attached forms in yeast and higher cells and are involved in a diverse range of cellular events, including protein trafficking and secretion (Downward, 1990). The other main family of G proteins has long been recognized for its involvement in signal transduction pathways and the regulation of receptors at the cell surface (Gilman, 1987; Stryer and Bourne, 1986). Heterotrimeric G proteins exist as αβγ subunit complexes in which the α subunit is responsible for binding and hydrolysis of GTP. The βγ subunit is complexed to α during the inactive portion of the hydrolysis cycle and more recent studies have shown that βγ may have its own independent signalling functions following dissociation from α (Federman et al., 1992; Tang and Gilman, 1991). The Gα subunits have traditionally been classified by their functional sensitivity to bacterial toxins; Gα$_i$ and α$_o$ are ADP-ribosylated by pertussis toxin, whereas Gα$_s$ is specifically ADP-ribosylated by cholera toxin. The heterotrimeric G proteins exist largely as membrane-associated proteins and the individual subunits have myristoylation or other fatty acyl modifications for membrane attachment (Fukada et al., 1990; Jones et al., 1990; Mumby et al., 1990).

Multiple gene products of each of the α, β and γ subunits associate in distinct combinations generating heterogeneity amongst these G proteins (Simon et al., 1991). Discrete deployment of these heterogeneous G proteins to different sites on membranes throughout the cell then may allow for the simultaneous regulation of many different signal transduction pathways. The cellular distribution and intracellular localization of heterotrimeric G protein subunits is thus important to elucidate. The localization of different G proteins on membranes in cells and tissues has recently been studied in our laboratory and by others. Detection and localization of different G proteins have been made possible by the availability of specific peptide antibodies that can distinguish between the different G protein subunits (Spiegel et al., 1990).

Distinct membrane targeting of Gα$_i$ proteins in LLC-PK₁ cells

The polarized epithelial cell line LLC-PK₁ expresses only two of the known pertussis toxin-sensitive Gα subunits, Gα$_{i-2}$ and Gα$_{i-3}$. Our studies showed that Gα$_{i-2}$ and Gα$_{i-3}$ are localized on distinct membrane domains and have quite separate functions in these polarized cells (Ercolani et al., 1990; Holtzman et al., 1991; Stow et al., 1991a). Gα$_{i-2}$ was found to be associated with the plasma membrane, while Gα$_{i-3}$ was found in a novel position on intracellular Golgi membranes. The immunofluorescence staining of Gα$_{i-2}$ resembles a cobblestone pattern, typical of basolateral plasma membrane staining, in confluent monolayers of LLC-PK₁ cells (Ercolani et al., 1990). The Gα$_{i-2}$ subunit is targeted in a polarized fashion to the basolateral membrane, particularly the lateral membrane, and is not found on the apical membrane of these cells. The localization of Gα$_{i-2}$ on the cell membrane is consistent with its proposed role in regulating adenylyl cyclase in response to hormone receptors (Ercolani et al., 1990). Gα$_{i-2}$ is developmentally expressed in LLC-PK₁ cells. The expression of Gα$_{i-2}$ is under transcriptional control and its appearance on the plasma membrane parallels the gradual development of polarity as the cultures progress from a sparse, non-polar morphology to a confluent, polarized morphology (Holtzman et al., 1991). Due to the lateral membrane localization of Gα$_{i-2}$ and its pattern of expression, it is tempting to speculate that this Gα subunit may actually be involved in the acquisition of functional or morphological polarity in these cells.

In contrast to Gα$_{i-2}$, its highly homologous relative, Gα$_{i-3}$, was found to be localized on the perinuclear Golgi complex in LLC-PK₁ cells (Ercolani et al., 1990; Stow et al., 1991a). It is not currently known how different Gα subunits are targeted to distinct membrane domains. Our recent studies, using expression of chimeric proteins, have identified regions of the Gα proteins that appear to be responsible for their targeting (J. Stow, L. Ercolani, D. Ausiello et al., unpublished data). The targeting or membrane association of Gα subunits in LLC-PK₁ cells appears to be a saturable process. This was also elegantly demonstrated in fibroblasts where the localization of Gα$_{i-3}$ was dependent on its level of overexpression (Hermouet et al., 1992). While LLC-PK₁ cells express Gα$_{i-3}$ only on their Golgi membranes, other cells have Gα$_{i-3}$ associated with additional membranes. In the A6 toad kidney cells, Gα$_{i-3}$ is found on the perinuclear Golgi complex and is also present near the apical cell surface where it is intimately associated with, and regulates, Na⁺ channel activity (Ausiello et al., 1992; Cantiello et al., 1989). In fibroblasts, Gα$_{i-3}$ is present on Golgi membranes and also in some cases at the plasma membrane where it can regulate adenylyl cyclase (Hermouet et al., 1992). The multiple locations and functions

Gαi-3   β-cop

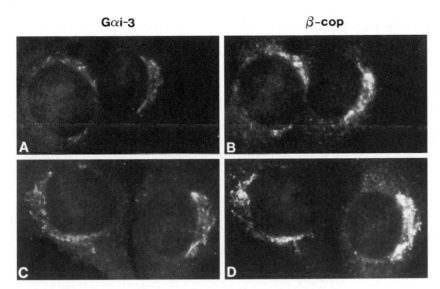

Fig. 1. Immunofluorescence localization of Gα$_{i-3}$ on Golgi membranes. NRK cells were doubled-labelled with antibodies specific for Gα$_{i-3}$ and β-COP, which were then reacted with FITC- and rhodamine-labelled conjugates, respectively. (A and C) Localization of Gα$_{i-3}$ in two sets of cells; (B and D) β-COP staining in the same two sets of cells. Staining for both proteins is over the perinuclear Golgi complexes in these cells. The staining of Gα$_{i-3}$, which is associated with Golgi cisternae, has a more linear appearance. β-COP is believed to be associated with Golgi vesicles, and its staining over the Golgi is more punctate.

for Gα$_{i-3}$ in such cells reinforces the concept that a given G protein subunit may be used promiscuously, for different functions in different cells, and for different functions within the same cell.

Heterotrimeric G proteins on Golgi membranes

At a time when heterotrimeric G proteins were thought to function only at the level of the plasma membrane, several studies provided evidence for the association of pertussis toxin-sensitive G proteins on intracellular membranes such as the rough ER (Audigier et al., 1988), the Golgi complex (Ali et al., 1989; Toki et al., 1989) and endosomes (Ali et al., 1989). However, the functions of these intracellular G proteins and their potential involvement in trafficking pathways, such as the secretory pathway, were not known at that time. It is now clear that Gα$_{i-3}$ and other G protein subunits are fairly universal components of Golgi membranes. Gα$_{i-3}$ has now been specifically detected on the Golgi membranes in different tissues and cells, including different kidney cell lines in our own laboratory (Fig. 1) and in a number of other cell types by other groups (Barr et al., 1991; Hermouet et al., 1992; Ktistakis et al., 1992; Stow et al., 1991a). Gα$_{i-3}$ on Golgi membranes is localized on the cytoplasmic face of Golgi cisternae where it is peripherally, but stably, attached to the membrane (Stow et al., 1991a). While weak cytoplasmic staining of Gα$_{i-3}$ disappears after cycloheximide treatment of cells, the more intense Golgi staining remains, suggesting that Gα$_{i-3}$ is a stable resident of the Golgi membranes and that the cytoplasmic staining may be attributed to a newly synthesized pool of the subunit (Stow et al., 1991a). Gα$_{i-3}$ on the Golgi membranes associates with a βγ complex, as was shown by its ability to be efficiently ADP-ribosylated by pertussis toxin, which requires heterotrimer formation (Sunyer et al., 1989). In isolated rat liver Golgi membranes, Gα$_{i-3}$ is the only pertussis toxin-sensitive protein that can be detected by immunoblotting (Fig. 2) or by ^{32}P-ADP-ribosylation with pertussis toxin (Stow et al., 1991a). Other G protein subunits are however present on these membranes. Immunoblotting confirmed the presence of the β subunit and of the cholera toxin-sensitive Gα$_s$ subunit on rat liver

Golgi membranes (Fig. 2). Golgi membranes from other cells may contain different combinations of Gα subunits. *Trans*-Golgi membranes from PC12 cells contain Gα$_{i-3}$ and other pertussis toxin-sensitive subunits; Gα$_o$ and Gα$_{i-1,2}$, and the Gα$_s$ subunit have also been found on these membranes (Leyte et al., 1992).

The localization of Gα$_i$ subunits on various intracellular membranes, together with functional studies such as those described below, have now established a role for these G proteins in the secretory pathway.

Polarized distribution of Gα subunits in the kidney

The distinct intracellular and intercellular distributions of G proteins found in cultured cells are also found in epithelial cells in tissues and this is graphically demonstrated by the distribution of Gα subunits in the kidney cortex. The renal nephron of the kidney is composed of a large number of morphologically and functionally distinct polarized epithelial cells. The apical or lumenal membranes and the basolateral membranes of these cells host a variety of ion channels and hormone receptors that are known to be coupled to G protein-mediated signal transduction pathways. The distribution of different Gα subunits on membrane domains throughout kidney epithelial cells is therefore potentially important for the segregation of functions associated with these membranes.

Using specific peptide antibodies, the distribution of different Gα subunits in cells along the nephron has been studied by several groups (Brunskill et al., 1991; Gupta et al., 1991; Stow et al., 1991b). There is a heterogeneous distribution of Gα$_i$ and Gα$_s$ subunits in cells from functionally distinct areas of the tubules (Brunskill et al., 1991; Stow et al., 1991b) and examples of Gα$_i$, Gα$_s$ and Gα$_o$ have been found in the renal glomerulus (Gupta et al., 1991). Proximal tubule cells express several different Gα subunits, the largest number appearing to be concentrated in this region of the nephron. Gα$_{i-2}$, Gα$_{i-3}$ and Gα$_s$ are all heavily concentrated in the sub-apical vesicles of proximal tubule cells (Fig. 3). Gα$_{i-3}$ was also found associated with the basolateral membrane of cells in some segments of the proximal tubules (Stow et al., 1991b). Cells of the cortical collecting duct show a highly polarized distribution of Gα_s, which is on the basolateral membranes of the principal and intercalated cells (Fig. 3). The principal cells also contain

Gα_{i-2}, which is restricted to lateral membranes, in a similar localization to that seen in cultured renal LLC-PK_1 cells (Ercolani et al., 1990; Stow et al., 1991a). The distribution of the Gα_{i-1} subunit provides the most dramatic example

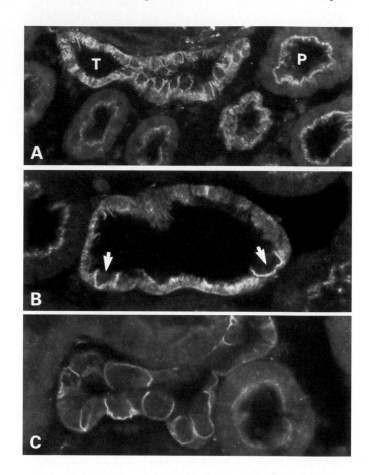

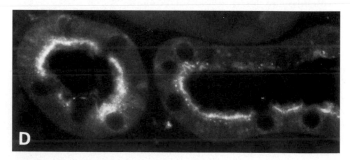

Fig. 2. Immunoblotting of Golgi-associated proteins. (A) Golgi membranes (M) and cytosol (C) were purified from rat liver homogenates and separated by SDS-PAGE on a 5%-15% gradient gel. Proteins were eletrophoretically transferred to membranes and sections of the gels were stained with specific antibodies that were detected by an alkaline phosphatase reaction. Various heterotrimeric G protein subunits, including Gα_{i-3}, Gα_s and Gβ, were detected as bands of the appropriate molecular masses, as indicated. These G protein subunits were found only on the membranes and not in the cytosol. Monomeric G proteins were also detected, rab 6 was found on the Golgi membranes and ARF was found in the cytosol in freshly prepared fractions. The coatomer protein β-COP was found predominantly in the cytosol but was also detected on Golgi membranes. The positions of marker proteins (kDa) are indicated. (B) Immunoblotting with peptide antibodies specific for different Gα subunits showed that Gα_{i-3} (shown in A) is the only pertussis toxin-sensitive G protein present on these membranes. Antibodies against Gα_{i-1 and 2} and Gα_o failed to detect any proteins on these membranes.

Fig. 3. Immunofluorescence localization of Gα subunits in rat kidney cortex. Rat kidney sections were fixed and stained with specific peptide antibodies to detect different G proteins. The polarized distribution of Gα_s in the kidney cortex is shown in (A, B and C). (A) In the thick ascending limb (T) Gα_s was found on the highly infolded basolateral membranes of these cells. In contrast, proximal tubule cells (P) had staining of Gα_s in the subapical invaginations. (B) Basolateral staining of Gα_s was found on the infoldings of the principal cells in the cortical collecting duct and on the basal and lateral domains of the intercalated cells (arrows). (C) An area of cortical collecting duct shows staining of the Gα_s in a highly polarized fashion on the basolateral membranes of intercalated cells. (D) Staining of Gα_{i-3} in the proximal tubule cells, where it is concentrated in the subapical invaginations just below the level of the lumenal brush border.

Fig. 4. Effect of BFA and aluminium fluoride on Golgi membrane localization of p200. The p200 protein was localized in NRK cells by immunofluorescence with a specific antibody. In untreated cells (A), there was staining over the perinuclear Golgi complex (arrow) and weaker staining in the cytoplasm. Following treatment with BFA (5 µM for 30 minutes) (B) the Golgi was no longer stained and there was only weak staining of the cytoplasm (arrow). Pretreatment of the cells with 30 mM NaF + 50 µM AlCl$_3$ (C) prior to addition of BFA under the same conditons, resulted in retention of the Golgi staining (arrow).

of a highly selective and polarized localization of G proteins. Gα_{i-1} is found on the apical membrane of cells in the thick ascending limb of the distal nephron; however in a highly specialized group of cells within this tubule, the macula densa, Gα_{i-1} was found at the basal aspect of the cells (Stow et al., 1991b). The inverted polarity of the Gα_{i-1} protein is perhaps related to the altered morphological polarity of the macula densa cells (Rouiller and Orci, 1969), which are uniquely positioned for their highly specialized roles in the control of glomerular filtration rate and renin secretion. The functional relevance of the polarized localization of Gα_{i-1} in thick ascending limb cells or in macula densa cells is not known.

In general, the functions of these G protein subunits on distinct membrane domains in kidney epithelial cells are not known. However their distributions on specific membrane domains, once again, suggests that geographic segregation of G protein subunits may be important for the control of both membrane protein signalling events and membrane trafficking.

FUNCTION OF HETEROTRIMERIC G PROTEINS IN THE SECRETORY PATHWAY

The localization of Gα_{i-3} on the Golgi membranes provided us with the first suggestion that this G protein might be involved in Golgi trafficking, and subsequent studies in polarized LLC-PK$_1$ cells produced evidence for a functional role of Gα_{i-3} in secretory trafficking (Stow et al., 1991a). The constitutive polarized secretion of BMHSPG in LLC-PK$_1$ cells was used as a model to determine the effects of overexpression of Gα_{i-3}. The overexpression of close-to-physiological amounts of Gα_{i-3} resulted in correct targeting of this protein to Golgi membranes and functionally it produced a significant retardation of the secretion of BMHSPG. The effect of the overexpressed, and presumably activated, Gα_{i-3} was at the level of trafficking through the Golgi complex where precursors of the BMHSPG accumulated. These studies suggested that activated Gα_{i-3} might be imposing a rate-limiting or regulatory step in the transport of proteins, exemplified by BMHSPG, through the Golgi complex. This retardation or block in trafficking

could be relieved by pretreating cells with pertussis toxin which increased the rate of intracellular trafficking and secretion of BMHSPG. Pertussis toxin ADP-ribosylates Gα_{i-3}, functionally uncoupling it from its receptor or activating protein. Since Gα_{i-3} is the only known pertussis toxin substrate on Golgi membranes in LLC-PK$_1$ cells, the effects of the toxin can be attributed directly to Gα_{i-3}. Furthermore, since pertussis toxin also enhanced secretion in cells expressing only endogenous Gα_{i-3}, this G protein can be regarded as a normal, intrinsic regulator in the secretory pathway. Interestingly, either blocking or enhancing the rate of intracellular transport disrupted neither the sequence of post-translational processing of the BMHSPG nor the polarity of its secretion, also supporting the concept that the activation/deactivation of Gα_{i-3} is perhaps a normal regulatory step in this pathway.

The effects of Gα_{i-3} overexpression on constitutive secretion are consistent with the effects of agents that cause a more widespread activation of heterotrimeric G proteins. It has been known for some time that exogenous addition of aluminium fluoride can be used to activate G proteins; in the context of the GDP-binding pocket of Gα, the fluoride ions of this complex mimic the γ phosphate of GTP, prompting activation of the G protein (Higashijima et al., 1991). Recently, aluminium fluoride has been shown to be a more specific activator for heterotrimeric G proteins than for several families of monomeric G proteins (Kahn, 1991) and it has been used specifically to implicate heterotrimeric G proteins in a number of membrane trafficking pathways. For instance, functional assays have shown that heterotrimeric G proteins are involved in regulating several steps of the endocytic pathway (Carter et al., 1993; Columbo et al., 1992). In an earlier study, Melancon and coworkers provided some of the first evidence that heterotrimeric G proteins were required for Golgi trafficking when they showed that both GTPγS and aluminium fluoride blocked in vitro vesicle transport between Golgi compartments (Melancon et al., 1987). Using another cell-free assay, which measures the budding of secretory vesicles and secretory granules off *trans*-Golgi network (TGN) membranes, Barr and coworkers also provided important evidence for the involvement of heterotrimeric G proteins in secretory trafficking (Barr et al., 1991, 1992). Data showing that vesicle budding was blocked by both GTPγS and aluminium fluoride but enhanced by addition of free βγ subunits or by pertussis toxin (Barr et al., 1991), are consistent with similar effects on secretion produced by overexpression of $G\alpha_{i-3}$ and pertussis toxin in intact cells (Stow et al., 1991). Further studies on vesicle budding from TGN membranes have also shown that, in addition to $G\alpha_{i-3}$, there are other pertussis toxin- and cholera toxin-sensitive G proteins on these membranes (Leyte et al., 1992). Cholera toxin, which ADP-ribosylates and activates $G\alpha_s$, also stimulated TGN vesicle budding, suggesting that the $G\alpha_s$ may act in concert with $G\alpha_i$s as an opposing and therefore regulatory partner. Taken together, these studies confirm the requirement for a pertussis toxin-sensitive $G\alpha$ protein in secretory trafficking, although the molecular mechanisms by which it, together with other G proteins, perform this regulation are still unknown.

Molecular mechanisms of G protein regulation

Due to the presence of multiple G protein subunits on Golgi membranes, it is easy to speculate that there is more than one mode of regulation based on GTP-hydrolysis and perhaps more than a single signal transduction pathway involved. The key proteins to which the heterotrimeric G proteins are functionally connected should be, in traditional terms, a receptor and an effector or their equivalents. Neither of these proteins has yet been identified on Golgi membranes. The receptor on the Golgi could fit into the traditional family of G-protein-coupled, seven membrane-spanning domain receptors, or possibly the family of single membrane-spanning domain receptors involved in sorting, or it could defy presumption and be a completely different class of membrane protein. Studies to date have also not identified a likely effector on the Golgi. We were not able to find effects on vesicle trafficking with intermediates in pathways of common effectors such as phospholipase or adenylyl cylcase (J. Stow, unpublished data).

There are several lines of evidence to connect heterotrimeric G proteins to other Golgi-associated proteins involved in vesicle trafficking. One set of proteins that appears to be intimately involved in trafficking is the coatomer, including the β-COP protein (Duden et al., 1991; Serafini et al., 1991). β-COP is a component of a cytosolic complex, which binds to Golgi membranes where it forms a specialized coat that may be responsible for structuring Golgi transport vesicles or other vehicles. β-COP and other cytosolic proteins such as γ-adaptin and the monomeric G protein ARF (ADP-ribosylating factor) have two features in common: their binding to Golgi membranes is prevented by the fungal metabolite brefeldin A (BFA) and enhanced by activation of G proteins (Donaldson et al., 1991b; Ktistakis et al., 1992; Robinson and Kries, 1992). The BFA-induced dissociation of β-COP is prevented by aluminium fluoride or mastoparan, which in turn is also altered by pertussis toxin, implying that a heterotrimeric G protein is responsible for stabilizing its membrane association (Donaldson et al., 1991b; Ktistakis et al., 1992). The binding of β-COP and ARF to Golgi membranes was measured directly, in vitro, to show that a heterotrimeric G protein was involved in this binding (Donaldson et al., 1991a). We have identified a cytosolic protein, p200, which

binds specifically to Golgi membranes (Narula et al., 1992). The binding of p200 to Golgi membranes is regulated in a similar fashion to the coatomer proteins, and its association with the Golgi is influenced by BFA and by activation of G proteins. The dissociation of p200 in the presence of BFA in NRK cells is prevented by activation of heterotrimeric G proteins by aluminium fluoride (Fig. 4). Our recent studies have shown that p200 binding to Golgi membranes is also affected by pertussis toxin (J. Stow, B. de Almeida, unpublished data). These studies have provided evidence that heterotrimeric G proteins, including specifically pertussis toxin-sensitive G proteins, are involved in regulating the dynamic interaction of soluble vesicle coating proteins with Golgi membranes. The effects of G protein activation/inhibition on coat protein binding are not yet reconciled into a ready explanation of how G proteins ultimately regulate secretion. Obviously, other proteins in this molecular network need to be identified in order for us to understand how G proteins are able to provide regulation in constitutive pathways of protein secretion and membrane trafficking.

This work was supported by NIH grants DK 42881 and PODK 38452.

REFERENCES

Ali, N., Milligan, G. and Evans, W. H. (1989). Distribution of G-proteins in rat liver plasma-membrane domains and endocytic pathways. *Biochem. J.* **261**, 905-912.

Audigier, Y., Nigam, S. N. and Blobel, G. (1988). Identification of a G protein in rough endoplasmic reticulum of canine pancreas. *J. Biol. Chem.* **263**, 16352-16357.

Ausiello, D. A., Stow, J. L., Cantiello, H. F. and Benos, D. J. (1992). Purified epithelial Na⁺ channel complex contains the pertussis toxin-sensitive Gαi-3 protein. *J. Biol. Chem.* **267**, 4759-4765.

Balch, W. E. (1990). Small GTP-binding proteins in vesicular transport. *Trends Biochem. Sci.* **15**, 473-7.

Barr, F. A., Leyte, A. and Huttner, W. B. (1992). Trimeric G proteins and vesicle formation. *Trends Cell Biol.* **2**, 91-94.

Barr, F. A., Leyte, A., Molliner, S., Pfeuffer, T., Tooze, S. A. and Huttner, W. B. (1991). Trimeric G-proteins of the trans-Golgi network are involved in the formation of constitutive secretory vesicles and immature secretory granules. *FEBS Lett.* **293**, 1-5.

Beckers, C. J. M. and Balch, W. E. (1989). Calcium and GTP: Essential components in vesicular trafficking between the endoplasmic reticulum and Golgi apparatus. *J. Cell Biol.* **108**, 1245-1256.

Brunskill, N., Bastani, B., Hayes, C., Morrissey, J. and Klahr, S. (1991). Localization and polar distribution of several G-protein subunits along nephron segments. *Kidney Int.* **40**, 997-1006.

Cantiello, H. C., Patenaude, C. R. and Ausiello, D. A. (1989). G protein subunit αi-3 activates a pertussis toxin sensitive Na⁺ channel from the epithelial cell line, A6. *J. Biol. Chem.* **264**, 20867-20870.

Caplan, M. J., Stow, J. L., Newman, A. P., Madri, J., Anderson, H. C., Farquhar, M. G., Palade, G. E. and Jamieson, J. D. (1987). Dependence on pH of polarized sorting of secreted proteins. *Nature* **329**, 632-635.

Carter, L. L., Redelmeier, T. E., Woollenweber, L. A. and Schmid, S. L. (1993). Multiple GTP-binding proteins participate in clathrin-coated vesicle-mediated endocytosis. *J. Cell Biol.* **120**, 37-45.

Columbo, M. I., Mayorga, L. S., Casey, P. J. and Stahl, P. D. (1992). Evidence for a role for heterotrimeric GTP-binding proteins in endosome fusion. *Science* **255**, 1695-1697.

de Almeida, J. B. and Stow, J. L. (1991). Disruption of microtubules alters polarity of basement membrane proteoglycan secretion in epithelial cells. *Amer. J. Physiol.* **260**, C691-C700.

Donaldson, J. G., Kahn, R. A., Lippincott, S. J. and Klausner, R. D.

(1991a). Binding of ARF and beta-COP to Golgi membranes: possible regulation by a trimeric G protein. *Science* **254**, 1197-9.

Donaldson, J. G., Lippincott, S. J. and Klausner, R. D. (1991b). Guanine nucleotides modulate the effects of brefeldin A in semipermeable cells: regulation of the association of a 110-kD peripheral membrane protein with the Golgi apparatus. *J. Cell Biol* **112**, 579-88.

Downward, J. (1990). The ras superfamily of small GTP-binding proteins. *Trends Biochem. Sci.* **15**, 469-472.

Duden, R., Griffiths, G., Frank, R., Argos, P. and Kreis, T. (1991) β-COP, a 110kd protein associated with non-clathrin-coated vesicles and the Golgi complex, shows homology to β-adaptin. *Cell* **64**, 649-664.

Ercolani, L., Stow, J. L., Boyle, J. F., Holtzman, E. J., Lin, H., Grove, J. R. and Ausiello, D. A. (1990). Membrane localization of the pertussis toxin-sensitive G-protein subunits αi-2 and αi-3 and expression of a metallothionein-αi-2 fusion gene in LLC-PK1 cells. *Proc. Nat. Acad. Sci. USA* **87**, 4637-4639.

Farquhar, M. G. (1985). Progress in unraveling pathways of Golgi traffic. *Annu. Rev. Cell. Biol.* **1**, 447-488.

Federman, A. D., Conklin, B. R., Schrader, K. A., Reed, R. A. and Bourne, H. R. (1992). Hormonal stimulation of adenylyl cyclase through Gi-protein βγ subunits. *Nature* **356**, 159-161.

Fukada, Y., Takao, T., Ohguro, H., Yoshizawa, T., Akino, T. and Shimonishi, Y. (1990). Farnesylated γ-subunit of photoreceptor G protein indispensable for GTP binding. *Nature* **346**, 658-660.

Gilman, A. G. (1987). G proteins: transducers of receptor-generated signals. *Annu. Rev. Biochem.* **56**, 615-649.

Gupta, A., Bastani, B., Purcell, H. and Hruska, K. A. (1991). Identification and localization of pertussis toxin-sensitive GTP-binding proteins in bovine kidney glomeruli. *J. Amer. Soc. Nephrol.* **2**, 172-178.

Hermouet, S., de Mazancourt, P., Spiegel, A. M., Farquhar, M. G. and Wilson, B. S. (1992). High level expression of transfected G protein αi3 subunit is required for plasma membrane targeting and adenylyl cyclase inhibition in NIH 3T3 fibroblasts. *FEBS Letts* **312**, 223-228.

Higashijima, T., Graziano, M. P., Suga, H., Kainosho, M. and Gilman, A. G. (1991). ^{19}F and ^{31}P NMR spectroscopy of G protein α subunits. Mechanism of activation by Al^{3+} and F^-. *J. Biol. Chem.* **266**, 3396-3401.

Holtzman, E. J., Soper, B. W., Stow, J. L., Ausiello, D. A. and Ercolani, L. (1991). Regulation of the G-protein αi-2 subunit gene in LLC-PK1 renal cells and isolation of porcine genomic clones encoding the gene promoter. *J. Biol. Chem.* **266**, 1763-1771.

Jones, T. L., Simonds, W. F., Merendino Jr, J. J., Brann, M. R. and Spiegel, A. M. (1990). Myristoylation of an inhibitory GTP-binding protein alpha subunit is essential for its membrane attachment. *Proc. Nat. Acad. Sci. USA* **87**, 568 572.

Kahn, R. A. (1991). Fluoride is not an activator of the smaller (20-25 kDa) GTP-binding proteins. *J. Biol. Chem.* **266**, 15595-15597.

Kelly, R. B. (1985). Pathways of protein secretion in eukaryotes. *Science* **230**, 25-32.

Ktistakis, N. T., Linder, M. E. and Roth, M. G. (1992). Action of brefeldin A blocked by activation of a pertussis-toxin-sensitive G protein. *Nature* **356**, 344-346.

Leyte, A., Barr, F. A., Kehlenbach, R. H. and Huttner, W. B. (1992). Multiple trimeric G-proteins on the trans-Golgi network exert stimulatory and inhibitory effects on secretory vesicle formation. *EMBO J.* **11**, 4795-4804.

Melancon, P., Glick, B. S., Malhotra, V., Weidman, P. J., Serafini, T., Gleason, M. L., Orci, L. and Rothman, J. E. (1987). Involvement of GTP-binding "G" proteins in transport through the Golgi stack. *Cell* **51**, 1053-1062.

Mumby, S. M., Heukeroth, R. O., Gordon, J. I. and Gilman, A. G. (1990). G-protein α-subunit expression, myristoylation, and membrane association in COS cells. *Proc. Nat. Acad. Sci. USA* **87**, 728-732.

Narula, N., McMorrow, I., Plopper, G., Doherty, J., Matlin, K. S., Burke, B. and Stow, J. L. (1992). Identification of a 200-kD, Brefeldin-sensitive protein on Golgi membranes. *J. Cell Biol.* **117**, 27-38.

Palade, G. (1975). Intracellular aspects of the process of protein synthesis. *Science* **189**, 347-358.

Robinson, M. S. and Kries, T. E. (1992). Recruitment of coat proteins onto Golgi membranes in intact and permeabilized cells: Effects of brefeldin A and G protein activators. *Cell* **69**, 129-138.

Rothman, J. E. and Orci, L. (1992). Molecular dissection of the secretory pathway. *Nature* **355**, 409-15.

Rouiller, C. and Orci, L. (1969). *The Kidney: Morphology, Biochemistry, Physiology* (ed. C. R. and A. F. Muller), pp. 1-80. New York: Academic Press.

Ruohola, H., Kabcenell, A. K. and Ferro-Novick, S. (1988). Reconstitution of protein transport from the endoplasmic reticulum to the Golgi complex in yeast: The acceptor Golgi compartment is defective in the sec23 mutant. *J. Cell Biol.* **107**, 1464-1476.

Serafini, T., Stenbeck, G., Brecht, A., Lottspeich, F., Orci, L., Rothman, J. E. and Wieland, F. T. (1991). A coat subunit of Golgi-derived non-clathrin-coated vesicles with homology to the clathrin-coated vesicle coat protein β-adaptin. *Nature* **349**, 215-220.

Simon, M. I., Strathmann, M. P. and Gautman, N. (1991). Diversity of G proteins in signal transduction. *Science* **252**, 802-808.

Spiegel, A. M., Simonds, W. F., Jones, T. L. Z., Goldsmith, P. K. and Unson, C. G. (1990). Antibodies against synthetic peptides as probes of G protein structure and function. In *G Proteins and Signal Transduction* (ed. N. M. Nathanson and T. K. Harden), pp. 185-195. New York: Rockefeller University Press.

Stow, J. L., de Almeida, J. B., Narula, N., Holtzman, E. J., Ercolani, L. and Ausiello, D. A. (1991a). A heterotrimeric G protein, Gαi-3, on Golgi membranes regulates the secretion of a heparan sulfate proteoglycan in LLC-PK1 epithelial cells. *J. Cell Biol.* **114**, 1113-1124.

Stow, J. L. and Farquhar, M. G. (1987). Distinctive populations of basement membrane and cell membrane heparan sulfate proteoglycans are produced by cultured cell lines. *J. Cell Biol.* **105**, 529-539.

Stow, J. L., Sabolic, I. and Brown, D. (1991b). Heterogenous localization of G protein α-subunits in rat kidney. *Amer. J. Physiol.* **261**, F831-F840.

Stow, J. L., Soroka, C., MacKay, K., Striker, L., Striker, G. and Farquhar, M. G. (1989). Basement membrane heparan sulfate proteoglycans are synthesized by glomerular epithelial cells in culture. *Amer. J. Path.* **135**, 637-646.

Stryer, L. and Bourne, H. R. (1986). G proteins: a family of signal transducers. *Annu. Rev. Cell. Biol.* **2**, 391-419.

Sunyer, T., Monastirsky, B., Codina, J. and Birnbaumer, L. (1989). Studies on nucleotide and receptor regulation of Gi proteins: Effects of pertussis toxin. *Mol. Endocrinol.* **3**, 1115-1124.

Tang, W.-J. and Gilman, A. G. (1991). Type-specific regulation of adenylyl cyclase by G protein βγ subunits. *Science* **254**, 1500-1503.

Toki, C., Oda, K. and Ikehara, Y. (1989). Demonstration of GTP-binding and ADP-ribosylated proteins in rat liver Golgi fraction. *Biochem. Biophys. Res. Commun.* **164**, 333-338.

Tooze, S. A., Weiss, U. and Huttner, W. B. (1990). Requirement for GTP hydrolysis in the formation of secretory vesicles. *Nature* **347**, 207-208.

Journal of Cell Science, Supplement 17, 41-47 (1993)
Printed in Great Britain © The Company of Biologists Limited 1993

An electron microscopic study of TGN38/41 dynamics

Mark S. Ladinsky* and Kathryn E. Howell

Department of Cellular and Structural Biology, University of Colorado School of Medicine, Box B-111, Denver, CO 80262, USA

*Present address: Laboratory for 3-D Fine Structure, Department of MCD Biology, Box 347, University of Colorado, Boulder, CO 80309, USA

SUMMARY

We have used electron microscopy to further characterize details of the dynamics of TGN38/41, a protein found to cycle between the *trans*-Golgi network and the plasma membrane. Immunogold-labeling of NRK cells under steady-state conditions shows the majority of TGN38/41 is localized to the *trans*-most Golgi cisternae and the *trans*-Golgi network. Small amounts of this molecule can be detected in early endosomes. Capture of cycling TGN38/41 molecules at the cell surface altered the steady state distribution. This was accomplished by binding TGN38/41 luminal domain antibodies to solid supports (beads), which were introduced to the culture media of cells. As increasing numbers of antigen-antibody complexes formed, the beads were internalized by the 'zippering mechanism' of phagocytosis. This provides a system that can address many questions related to the function of TGN38/41 and the *trans*-Golgi network itself.

Key words: TGN38/41, *trans*-Golgi network, bead internalization, early endosome

INTRODUCTION

TGN38/41 is a type 1, transmembrane heterodimeric protein, which resides primarily in the *trans*-most Golgi cisternae and the *trans*-Golgi network (TGN) (Luzio et al., 1990; Jones et al., 1993; Crosby et al., 1993). Both subunits contain the same luminal and transmembrane domains, but differ in that TGN41 has an extended cytoplasmic domain of 23 amino acids (Reaves et al., 1992). The cytoplasmic domain of TGN38/41 associates with a complex comprising a 62 kDa protein and rab6 or one of two other small GTP-binding proteins; this complex is essential for the budding of exocytic transport vesicles from the TGN (Jones et al., 1993).

Our previous studies (Ladinsky and Howell, 1992) have shown that TGN38/41 cycles to the plasma membrane (PM) and returns to its resident compartment within 30 minutes. This was demonstrated by adding to the media of living cells antibodies that recognize the luminal domains of both TGN38 and 41. This resulted in uptake of the antibodies and labeling of juxtanuclear cisternal structures within 30 minutes, as shown by indirect immunofluorescence microscopy. Incubation of the cells with the antibodies for longer periods (up to three hours) resulted in an increasing signal. Parallel experiments with antibodies against the luminal domain of the lysosomal membrane protein, lgp120, showed no labeling by 60 minutes and only dim staining of a vesicular population by 120 minutes. The cycling of TGN38/41 is not affected by perturbation of the Golgi complex with brefeldin A or depolymerization of

microtubules with nocodazole. Return of TGN38/41 from the plasma membrane occurs via clathrin-coated vesicles and the endocytic pathway.

Recently, three other groups have confirmed that TGN38/41 cycles between the TGN and the cell surface (Humphrey et al., 1993; Reaves et al., 1993; Bos et al., 1993). In addition, an internalization signal of YQRL in the cytoplasmic domain of TGN38 has been identified (Humphrey et al., 1993; Bos et al, 1993).

Since TGN38/41 is difficult to detect at the PM by either light or electron microscopic immunolabeling methods, it is reasonable to assume that at steady state there are few molecules at the PM at any one time, and the residence time of those is very short. However, we show by electron microscopy that at steady state, TGN38/41 can be detected in early endosomes by co-localization with a marker of fluid-phase endocytosis. In order to further demonstrate the cycling of TGN38/41 to the plasma membrane, we altered the steady state by means of capture of the antibody-antigen complex on beads in vivo. Antibodies against the luminal domain of TGN38/41 were linked to beads such that the Fab domain was accessible to the cell surface. These supports were then introduced to the media of living cells, and after incubation for increasing times the cells were fixed and prepared for electron microscopy.

We verify that the TGN38/41 molecule does indeed reach the PM, where its luminal domain is accessible to specific antibodies introduced from the culture medium. When enough antigen-antibody interactions have occurred, the cells are able to selectively internalize the entire solid support.

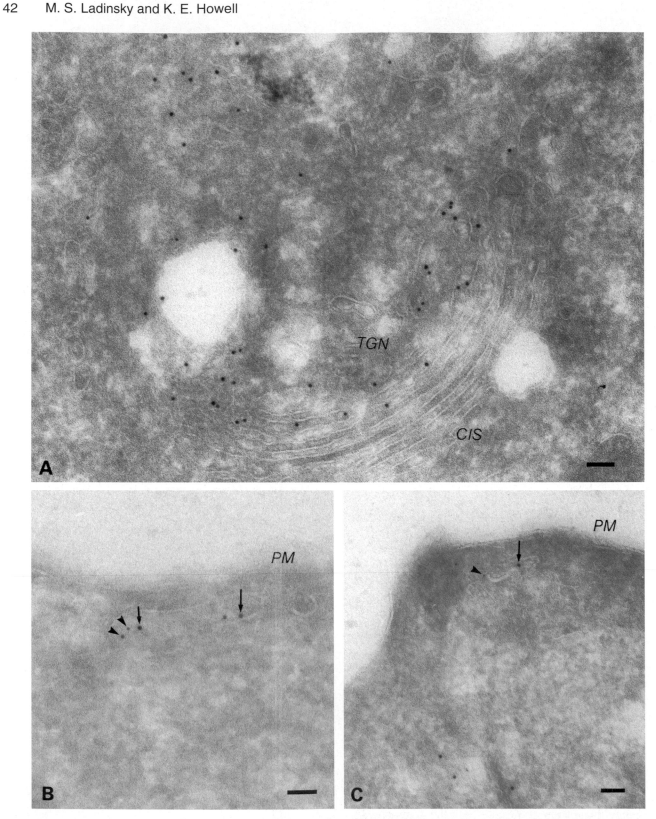

Fig. 1. Immunogold localization of TGN38/41. NRK cells were incubated with HRP for 5 minutes at 37°C to label the early endosome. Cryosections were double-labeled with antibodies to the luminal domain of TGN38/41 (10 nm colloidal gold protein A) and against HRP directly coupled to 5 nm colloidal gold. (A) At steady state, the majority of TGN38/41 is localized to the *trans*-most Golgi cisternae and the TGN. Label is absent from the *cis* and medial cisternae. ×105,800. (B and C) A small amount of TGN38/41 (small arrows) is localized in a tubular compartment near the plasma membrane, which is identified as the early endosome by colocalization with internalized HRP (arrowheads). (B) ×94,500; (C) ×124,200. Bars, 0.1 μm.

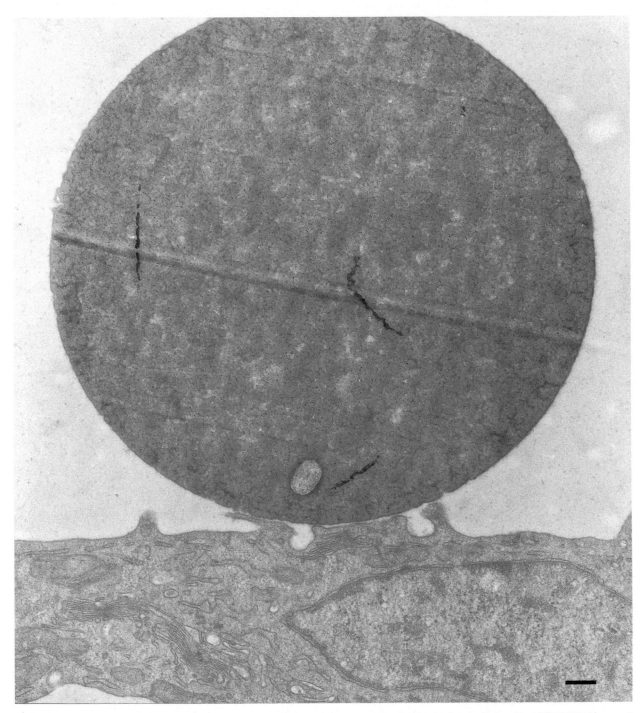

Fig. 2. Capture of TGN38/41 antigen-antibody complexes at the cell surface. Antibodies to the luminal domain of TGN38/41 were bound to the surface of 4 μm beads (via a linker antibody specific for the F_c region of rabbit IgG, which is covalently attached to the bead surface). NRK cells were incubated with the beads for 30 minutes and were then fixed and processed for electron microscopy. At 30 minutes, enough TGN38/41 has been 'trapped' at the cell surface to initiate contact of the bead with the cell; the first step of phagocytosis. ×35,000. Bar, 0.2 μm.

MATERIALS AND METHODS

Cell culture

Normal rat kidney (NRK) cells were cultured in Dulbecco's Modified Eagle's Medium (Sigma) supplemented with 8% fetal calf serum at 37°C and 5% CO_2. Cells were grown in monolayer on #1 thickness 18 mm glass coverslips within sterile 12-well culture plates (Falcon) to a confluency of 75-85%. For the bead-inter-nalization experiments, culture medium was removed from the wells and replaced with 1 ml of fresh medium containing approximately 0.25 mg beads per coverslip. Cells were further incubated at 37°C, fixed at 30, 60 and 180 minute intervals, and prepared for electron microscopy.

Preparation of beads

Magnetic beads (4 μm) were a gift from J. Ugelstadt and R.

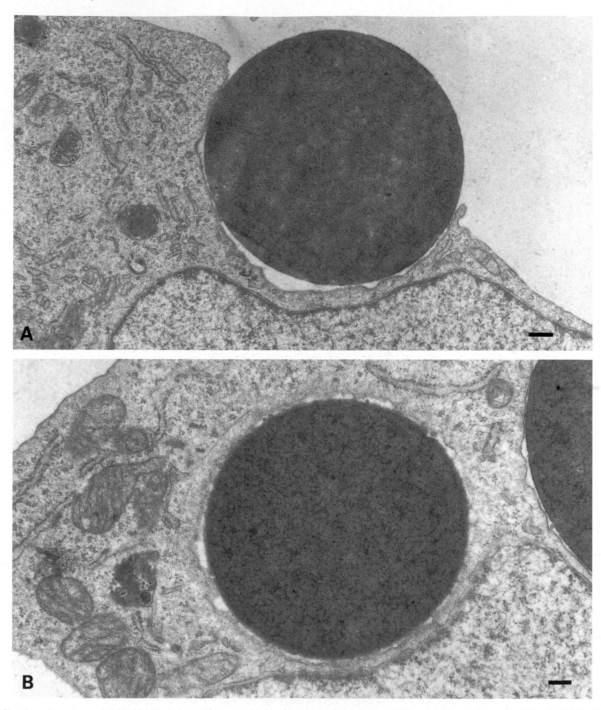

Fig. 3. Continued capture of TGN38/41 at the surface results in phagocytosis of the bead. For details see legend to Fig. 2. (A) At 60 minutes, the bead is partially internalized. (B) By 180 minutes, the bead is fully internalized. The phagophore membrane is in tight association with the bead surface. Note that this cell has internalized two beads. (A) ×18,620; (B) ×26,600. Bars, 0.5 μm.

Schmid, SINTEF, Trondheim, Norway. The free hydroxyl groups on the bead surface were activated, followed by covalent coupling of affinity-purified sheep antibodies against the F_c domain of rabbit IgG (Howell et al., 1989). TGN38/41 luminal domain antibodies then were immuno-bound to the beads and unbound antibodies were removed by repeated washing. The beads were used only as a solid support for the antibodies that could be easily visualized at both the light and EM levels; their magnetic properties were not utilized for any of the experiments.

Electron microscopy

Cells on coverslips were fixed at 37°C with 2% glutaraldehyde, 5% sucrose in 0.1 M cacodylate buffer, pH 7.2, for 30 minutes. Coverslips were then washed with 0.1 M cacodylate buffer and postfixed at room temperature with 2% OsO_4, 0.8% $K_3Fe(CN)_6$, 5% sucrose in 0.1 M cacodylate buffer for 60 minutes. Cells were en bloc stained with 2% aqueous uranyl acetate for 2 hours. then dehydrated into acetone and flat-embedded in Epon-Araldite. Ultrathin sections (40-50 nm) were cut on a Reichert-Jung Ultra-

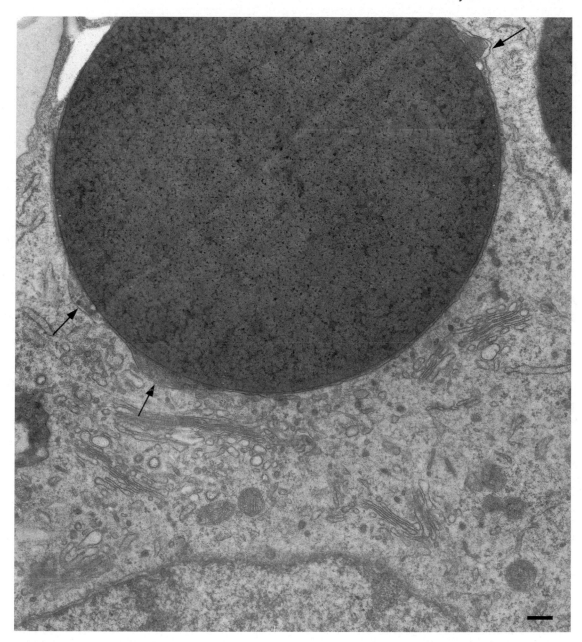

Fig. 4. Complete internalization of the bead. For details see legend to Fig. 2. Once the bead is fully internalized, lysosomes fuse with the phagophore membrane (arrows) in a vain attempt to degrade its contents. The Golgi complex is oriented next to the phagophore membrane ×31,360. Bar, 0.2 μm.

cut E microtome (Leica), transferred to Formvar-coated slot grids, and post-stained with 2% aqueous uranyl acetate and Reynold's lead citrate. Samples were viewed and photographed on a Philips CM-10 transmission electron microscope operating at 80 kV.

Immunolabeling of cryosections

For preparation of cryosections, NRK cells were grown on 100 mm tissue culture dishes to a confluency of ~80%. The cells were removed from the dishes with trypsin-EDTA, transferred to flasks in 30 ml of fresh medium, and allowed to recover in suspension for 90 minutes. The cells were then centrifuged at low speed and the pellets resuspended in 1 ml of medium containing 10 mg/ml horseradish peroxidase (HRP; Serva) and incubated at 37°C for 5 minutes. Following this treatment, the cells were spun again and the pelleted cells fixed overnight in 8% paraformaldehyde, 250 mM HEPES, 5% sucrose, pH 7.4. Pellets were infiltrated into

2.1 M sucrose, transferred to copper specimen stubs, and rapidly frozen in liquid nitrogen. Thin sections (90-100 nm) were cut on a Reichert-Jung Ultracut E microtome equipped with an FC4D cryo-stage, and transferred to Formvar-coated, carbon-coated, glow-discharged grids. Sections were treated with 10% bovine serum in PBS to block nonspecific binding sites, and double-labeled with TGN38/41 luminal domain antibody (10 nm colloidal gold protein-A; EY Laboratories) and rabbit anti-HRP directly coupled to 5 nm colloidal gold (Chemicon).

RESULTS

Steady-state distribution of TGN38/41 in NRK cells

Immunofluorescence microscopy shows that at steady state the majority of TGN38/41 is localized to the Golgi complex (Luzio et al., 1990; Ladinsky and Howell, 1992; Reaves and Banting, 1992). Electron microscopy of cryosections labeled with colloidal gold probes shows TGN38/41 in the *trans*-most cisternae and the TGN (Luzio et al, 1990; Ladinsky and Howell, 1992; Crosby et al., 1993); this is illustrated in Fig. 1A. Consistent with the finding that TGN38/41 cycles to the plasma membrane, a small amount of label was detected in clathrin-coated vesicles (Ladinsky and Howell, 1992) and in tubular compartments close to the plasma membrane. To demonstrate that the tubular compartments are early endosomes, HRP, a marker of fluid-phase endocytosis, was internalized into cells for 5 minutes at 37°C, followed by fixation and double labeling for HRP and TGN38/41 (Fig. 1B and C). Both antigens consistently colocalized to the same tubular compartment, indicating that at steady state sufficient TGN38/41 is present in early endosomes to be distinguished above background. The fact that label can be seen clearly in early endosomes and only rarely at the plasma membrane is further evidence that the residence time of TGN38/41 at the plasma membrane is brief.

Alteration of the steady-state distribution of TGN38/41

We were able to alter the steady-state distribution of TGN38/41 by capture of antigen-antibody complexes at the plasma membrane. Antibodies against the luminal domain of TGN38/41 were bound to the surface of 4 μm beads, which were placed in the culture medium and incubated at 37°C for increasing times. As controls, antibodies against the luminal domains of mannosidase II (a *cis*-medial Golgi membrane protein) and lgp 120 (a lysosomal membrane glycoprotein) were bound to the beads and incubated with the cells, using the same protocol as that for TGN38/41.

As cycling TGN38/41 molecules reach the plasma membrane, they interact with the luminal domain antibodies on the bead. Within 30 minutes, enough antigen-antibody complexes have formed to initiate binding of the bead to the cell surface (Fig. 2). As soon as contact between the bead and the cell surface is established, large invaginations of the plasma membrane form at the zone of interaction. By 60 minutes, the beads are partially internalized (Fig. 3A), and by 180 minutes the beads are fully engulfed within the cells (Fig. 3B). The internalized membrane is tightly apposed to the bead surface. This process is similar to the 'zippering mechanism' demonstrated for phagocytosis (Griffin et al., 1975, 1976). Continuous delivery of antigen and formation of immune complexes must occur to complete the internalization process. Once the bead is fully internalized, lysosomes fuse with the phagophore membrane in an attempt to degrade the contents (Fig. 4). The Golgi complex orients next to the phagophore membrane.

Control experiments, using beads with antibodies to the luminal domain of mannosidase II on their surface, showed no interaction with the cells over a 3 hour time course (Fig. 5 and Table 1). Other control experiments using antibodies to the luminal domain of lgp 120 showed contact of the beads with the cell surface only after 3 hours (Table 1). A similar lysosomal membrane glycoprotein (LEP100) has been shown to cycle to the plasma membrane, but the amounts moving and kinetics of cycling are much slower

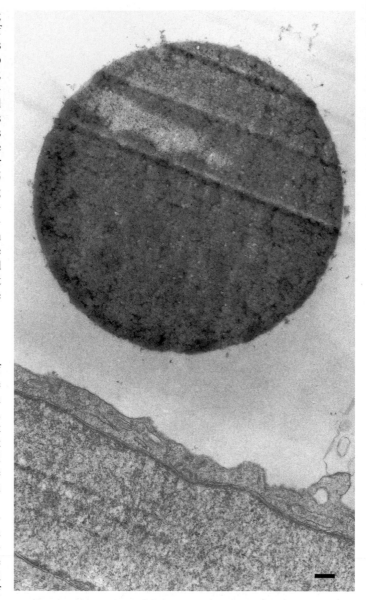

Fig. 5. Control experiment using antibodies against mannosidase II. Antibodies to the luminal domain of mannosidase II were bound to the surface of the beads, and incubated with NRK cells for 180 minutes. No interaction between the cells and the beads occurred during this time. ×28,000. Bar, 0.2 μm.

than for TGN38/41 (Lippincott-Schwartz and Fanbrough, 1987). These controls show that the internalization of beads with TGN38/41 luminal domain antibody is specific and further demonstrates the rapidity of the cycling of TGN38/41.

DISCUSSION

TGN38/41 can now be considered as more than simply a 'marker' of the TGN. Many groups have used TGN38/41 as a 'marker' (Wood et al., 1991; Lippincott-Schwartz et al., 1991; Robinson and Kreis, 1991), since early studies showed it to be predominantly localized to that compartment by both immunofluorescence and immunogold labeling. The dynamic nature of this molecule became apparent through brefeldin A studies (Ladinsky and Howell, 1992;

Table 1. Summary of bead internalization experiments

Antibody bound to beads	Incubation time at 37°C (minutes)		
	30	60	180
Anti-TGN38/41 (luminal domain)	Bead in contact cell surface	Bead partially internalized	Bead fully internalized
Anti-manII (luminal domain)	No contact	No contact	No contact
Anti-Igp120 (luminal domain)	No contact	No contact	Bead in contact with cell surface

Reaves et al., 1993) and studies to elucidate the signals that 'retain' the molecule in the TGN (Humphrey et al, 1993; Bos et al., 1993).

All of these studies provide evidence that once TGN38/41 reaches the plasma membrane, it is rapidly internalized and returns to the TGN via the endocytic pathway. In our immuno-labeling experiments, under steady-state conditions, TGN38/41 is not labeled at the plasma membrane at a level that can be distinguished from background. However, TGN38/41 can be labeled in a tubular compartment just beneath the plasma membrane. We have identified this compartment as the early endosome by colocalization with HRP, internalized for 5 minutes at 37°C. The immunofluorescence studies of several groups, using double-labeling with several different endocytic markers, suggest that TGN38/41 travels through the late endosome on its return route to the TGN. The immunogold labeling presented here shows TGN38/41 within early endosomes, but further electron microscopic data is required to document the complete pathway.

Linkage of TGN38/41 antibodies to beads allows the capture of antigen-antibody complexes at the cell surface, which results in an alteration of the steady-state distribution of TGN38/41. As increasing numbers of TGN38/41 molecules are captured at the surface, the zippering mechanism of phagocytosis is initiated (Griffin et al., 1975, 1976), resulting in the internalization of the bead.

This experimental technique, together with immunolabeling, can be used to answer several questions about the function of TGN38/41 and the dynamics of the TGN itself. Can the TGN be depleted of TGN38/41? If so, does sorting and secretion proceed normally in the absence of TGN38/41 in the TGN? When TGN38/41 is translocated to the plasma membrane or phagophore membrane, does the structure of the TGN or the orientation of the Golgi complex change significantly?

The dynamics of TGN38/41 led to the hypothesis that this molecule plays a role in the vesicular transport process from the TGN to the plasma membrane. In investigating this hypothesis, it was found that the cytoplasmic domain of TGN38/41 acts as a 'receptor' for a cytosolic complex of p62 and rab6 (Jones et al., 1993). Binding of this complex to TGN38/41 is essential for the budding of exocytic transport vesicles. In this process, TGN38/41 buds into the transport vesicle and is transported with it to the plasma membrane. TGN38/41 appears to be a typical endocytic receptor, which has a unique steady-state distribution. After transport to the plasma membrane, it is recycled to its res-

ident compartment for further rounds of budding. These new insights into the function of TGN38/41 can begin to explain the rapid cycling behavior of this molecule.

The authors would like to thank John Ugelstad and Ruth Schmid, SINTEF, Trondheim, Norway for the shell and core magnetic beads and Jeff Crosby for linking the antibodies to the beads. This work was supported by National Institute of Health Grant GM 42629 to K.E.H.

REFERENCES

Bos, K., Wraight, C. and Stanley, K. K. (1993). TGN38 is maintained in the *trans*-Golgi network by a tyrosine-containing motif in the cytoplasmic domain. *EMBO J.* **12**, 2219-2228.

Crosby, J. R., Jones, S. M., Ladinsky, M. S. and Howell, K. E. (1993). TGN38 and small GTP-binding proteins are part of a macromolecular complex in the *trans*-Golgi network. In *Molecular Mechanisms of Membrane Traffic, NATO ASI Series*, Series H, vol. 74, pp. 113-116.

Griffin, F. M. Jr, Griffin, J. A., Leider, J. E. and Silverstein, S. C. (1975). Studies on the Mechanism of Phagocytosis I. Requirements for circumferential attachment of particle-bound ligands to specific receptors on the macrophage plasma membrane. *J. Exp. Med.* **142**, 1263-1282.

Griffin, F. M. Jr, Griffin, J. A. and Silverstein, S. C. (1976). Studies on the Mechanism of Phagocytosis II. The interaction of macrophages with anti-immunoglobulin IgG-coated bone marrow-derived lymphocytes. *J. Exp. Med.* **144**, 788-809.

Howell, K. E., Schmid, R., Ugelstad, J. and Gruenberg, J. (1989). Immunoisolation using magnetic solid supports: subcellular fractionation for cell free functional studies. *Meth. Cell Biol.* **31**, 265-292.

Humphrey, J. S., Peters, P. J., Yuan, L. C. and Bonifacino, J. S. (1993). Localization of TGN38 to the *trans*-Golgi network: involvement of a cytoplasmic tyrosine-containing sequence. *J. Cell Biol.* **120**, 1123-1135.

Jones, S. M., Crosby, J. R., Salamero, J. and Howell, K. E. (1993). A cytosolic complex of p62 and rab6 associates with TGN38/41 and is involved in budding of exocytic vesicles from the *trans*-Golgi network. *J. Cell Biol.* **122**, 775-788.

Ladinsky, M. S. and Howell, K. E. (1992). The *trans*-Golgi network can be dissected structurally and functionally from the cisternae of the Golgi complex by brefeldin A. *Eur. J. Cell Biol.* **59**, 92-105.

Lippincott-Schwartz, J. and Fanbrough, D. M. (1987). Cycling of the integral membrane glycoprotein, LEP100, between plasma membrane and lysosomes: kinetic and morphological analysis. *Cell* **49**, 669-677.

Lippincott-Schwartz, J., Yuan, L., Tipper, C., Amherdt, M., Orci, L., Klausner, R. D. (1991). Brefeldin A's effects on endosomes, lysosomes, and the TGN suggest a general mechanism for regulating organelle structure and membrane traffic. *Cell* **67**, 601-616.

Luzio, J. P., Burke, B., Banting, G., Howell, K. E., Braghetta, P. and Stanley, K. K. (1990). Identification, sequencing and expression of an integral membrane protein of the *trans*-Golgi network (TGN38). *Biochem J.* **270**, 97-192.

Reaves, B., Wilde, A. and Banting, G. (1992). Identification, molecular characterization, and immunolocalization of an isoform of the *trans*-Golgi network (TGN)-specific integral membrane protein TGN38. *Biochem J.* **283**, 313-316

Reaves, B. and Banting, G. (1992). Perturbation of the morphology of the *trans*-Golgi network following brefeldin A treatment: redistribution of a TGN-specific integral membrane protein, TGN38. *J. Cell Biol.* **116**, 85-94.

Reaves, B., Horn, M. and Banting, G. (1993). TGN38/41 recycles between the cell surface and the TGN: brefeldin A affects its rate of return to the TGN. *Mol. Cell Biol.* **4**, 93-105.

Robinson, M. S. and Kreis, T. E. (1992). Recruitment of coat proteins onto Golgi membranes in intact and permeabilized cells: effects of brefeldin A and G protein activators. *Cell* **69**, 129-138.

Wood, S. A, Park, J. E. and Brown, W. J. (1991). Brefeldin A causes a microtubule-mediated fusion of the *trans*-Golgi network and early endosomes. *Cell* **67**, 591-600.

Journal of Cell Science, Supplement 17, 49-59 (1993)
Printed in Great Britain © The Company of Biologists Limited 1993

Endosomal pathways for water channel and proton pump recycling in kidney epithelial cells

Dennis Brown and Ivan Sabolić

Renal Unit and Department of Pathology, Massachusetts General Hospital and Harvard Medical School, Boston, MA, USA

SUMMARY

The plasma membrane composition of virtually all eukaryotic cells is maintained and continually modified by the recycling of specific protein and lipid components. In the kidney collecting duct, urinary acidification and urinary concentration are physiologically regulated at the cellular level by the shuttling of proton pumps and water channels between intracellular vesicles and the plasma membrane of highly specialized cell types. In the intercalated cell, hydrogen ion secretion into the urine is modulated by the recycling of vesicles carrying a proton pumping ATPase to and from the plasma membrane. In the principal cell, the antidiuretic hormone, vasopressin, induces the insertion of vesicles that contain proteinaceous water channels into the apical cell membrane, thus increasing the permeability to water of the epithelial layer. In both cell types, 'coated' carrier vesicles are involved in this process, but whereas clathrin-coated vesicles are involved in the endocytotic phase of water channel recycling, the transporting vesicles in intercalated cells are coated with the cytoplasmic domains of the proton pumping ATPase. By a combination of morphological and functional techniques using FITC-dextran as an endosomal marker, we have shown that recycling endosomes from intercalated cells are acidifying vesicles but that they do not contain water channels. In contrast, principal cell vesicles that recycle water channels do not acidify their lumens in response to ATP. These non-acidic vesicles lack functionally important subunits of the vacuolar proton ATPase, including the 16 kDa proteolipid that forms the transmembrane proton pore. Because these endosomes are directly derived via clathrin-mediated endocytosis, our results indicate that endocytotic clathrin-coated vesicles are non-acidic compartments in principal cells. In contrast, recycling vesicles in intercalated cells contain large numbers of proton pumps, arranged in hexagonally packed arrays on the vesicle membrane. These pumps are inserted into the apical plasma membrane of A-type (acid-secreting) intercalated cells, and the basolateral plasma membrane of B-type (bicarbonate-secreting) cells in the collecting duct. Both apical and basolateral targeting of H+-ATPase-containing vesicles in these cells may be directed by microtubules, because polarized insertion of the pump into both membrane domains is disrupted by microtubule depolymerizing agents. However, the basolateral localization of other transporting proteins in intercalated cells, including the band 3-like anion exchanger and facilitated glucose transporters, is not affected by microtubule disruption.

Key words: kidney, immunocytochemistry, proton pump, water channel, principal cell, intercalated cell, collecting duct

INTRODUCTION

The process of vesicle recycling is involved in establishing, maintaining and modulating the plasma membrane composition of virtually all eukaryotic cells. Because epithelial cells from the kidney must react rapidly to changes in their environment in order to maintain a constant *milieu interieur* for the organism, they have developed highly specialized mechanisms that enable them to modify transepithelial transport processes in response to a variety of stimuli. Thus, specific plasma membrane components are inserted on demand by exocytosis of specific transport vesicles, and are subsequently removed from the cell surface by endocytosis of membrane segments in which particular proteins are concentrated. While such events occur in most, if not all, regions of the kidney tubule, the most remarkable examples of plasma membrane recycling in response to physiological stimuli occur in the collecting duct.

Urinary acidification and urinary concentration are finely regulated in this tubule segment, and occur independently in two distinct cell types, the intercalated cell and the principal cell. In the intercalated cell, hydrogen ion secretion is controlled in response to body acid-base status by the cycling of vesicles carrying a vacuolar type proton pumping ATPase to and from the plasma membrane (Brown, 1989; Brown et al., 1988a; Madsen and Tisher, 1986; Madsen et al., 1991; Schwartz and Al-Awqati, 1985; Schwartz et al., 1985). As will be described below, proton pumps can be inserted into opposite poles of subsets of intercalated cells, and this represents, therefore, an intriguing and unusual example of membrane protein targetting (Brown et al., 1988a; Schwartz et al., 1985). In principal cells, the antidiuretic hormone, vasopressin, induces the insertion of vesicles that contain proteinaceous water channels into the apical cell membrane, thus increasing the permeability to water of the epithelial cell layer (Abramov et al., 1987; Brown, 1989; Handler, 1988; Verkman, 1989).

The polarized insertion of membrane components involves at least two distinct steps once the proteins have been packaged into appropriate transporting vesicles at the level of the Golgi. First, vesicles must move through the cytosol towards their target membrane; and second, a recognition process must take place that results in fusion of the vesicle with the correct membrane domain. Movement through the cytosol involves interaction of vesicles with cytoskeletal elements, including microtubules, via microtubule motors (Schroer and Sheetz, 1991; Vale, 1987) and actin microfilaments, in part via myosin isoforms (Adams and Pollard, 1986; Johnston et al., 1991; Zot et al., 1992). Vesicle recognition and fusion steps are poorly understood, but probably involve a specific interaction between cytoplasmically oriented protein domains that are characteristic of the transported vesicle, the membrane target, or both. A considerable amount of recent work has implicated GTP-binding proteins in vesicle trafficking and targetting, but well-defined roles for these molecules are still lacking (Balch, 1990; Goud and McCaffrey, 1991).

PROTON PUMP RECYCLING IN INTERCALATED CELLS

Whereas principal cells recycle water channels in non-acidic endosomes, the opposite is true of collecting duct intercalated cells. The endosomal pathway in this cell type is specialized to transport proton pumps to and from the plasma membrane, and these endosomes do not contain water channels (Lencer et al., 1990a). Thus, there is a clear-cut division of labor between these two cell types in this segment of the urinary tubule.

During systemic acidosis in vivo, or an increase in pCO_2 at the basolateral pole of isolated tubules in vitro, specialized cytoplasmic vesicles that are enriched in proton pumps, fuse with the apical plasma membrane of intercalated cells (Dorup, 1986; Madsen and Tisher, 1983; Madsen et al., 1991; Schwartz and Al-Awqati, 1985). This process increases the number of proton pumps at the cell surface. Similar carbonic-anhydrase-rich, proton-secreting cells are also found in toad and turtle urinary bladder, and an identical exocytotic process also occurs in these tissues (Dixon et al., 1986; Gluck et al., 1982; Stetson and Steinmetz, 1983). The transporting vesicles are highly characteristic, having a cytoplasmic 'coat' that, by conventional electron microscopy, resembles clathrin. However, morphological and immunocytochemical evidence identified the coating material as the cytoplasmic domain of a vacuolar-type proton pumping ATPase (Brown et al., 1987; Brown and Orci, 1986). Specific antibodies against different subunits of the proton pumping ATPase from bovine kidney medulla were used to show that the vesicle-coating material contained defined subunits of the proton pump (Brown et al.,

1987, 1988b). The 'coat' seen on the cytoplasmic side of the plasma membrane of intercalated cells also contained the same pump subunits.

Rapid-freeze, deep-etch microscopy of vacuolar proton pumps

The structure of the membrane coat was elucidated using the rapid-freeze, deep-etch technique, in which high-resolution microscopic images of proteins can be obtained. In proton-secreting cells from the toad bladder, the membrane-coating material had a structure that was identical to that of immunoaffinity-purified proton pumps, incorporated into phospholipid liposomes, thus confirming its identity as part of the proton pumping ATPase responsible for distal urinary acidification (Brown et al., 1987). Part of the underside of a plasma membrane domain rich in proton pumps is shown in Fig. 1. The pumps are tightly packed into this membrane region, at a density of about 14,000 per μm^2. Vesicles inside the cell with a similar structure were also observed using the deep-etching procedure (Brown et al., 1987).

Opposite polarity of proton pumps in A and B intercalated cells

In the cortical collecting duct (Schwartz et al., 1985) and in the turtle urinary bladder (Stetson and Steinmetz, 1985), morphological variants of carbonic anhydrase-rich cells have been described (Fig. 2), which are believed to be proton-secreting (A-cells) or bicarbonate-secreting (B-cells). Both types co-exist in kidney cortical collecting ducts, in accord with the ability of this tubule segment to secrete either net acid or net base under different physiological conditions of acidosis or alkalosis. Using anti-proton pump antibodies, all medullary intercalated cells were found to have proton pumps associated with their apical plasma membrane, whereas cortical intercalated cells had three patterns of labeling (Fig. 2A): apical, basolateral, and diffuse cytoplasmic or bipolar (Brown et al., 1988a). This finding provided direct support for the idea that different intercalated cells in the cortex are responsible for either proton (apical pumps) or bicarbonate (basolateral pumps) secretion into the tubule lumen. The cells with a diffuse staining might be an intermediate or transitional cell type.

Cellular remodeling in intercalated cells

Provocative data by Schwartz et al. (1985) suggested that A and B cells may be interconvertible, and may change their functional polarity by inserting proton pumps into either apical or basolateral plasma membranes, depending on prevailing acid-base conditions of the animal. However, others have argued that A and B cells do not interconvert during alterations in acid-base status (Verlander et al., 1988; Schuster, 1988) and Schwartz has also concluded that a direct interconversion of A- and B-cells is unlikely to occur at least in an in vitro model of acidification (Koichi et al., 1992). While this question has not yet been clearly resolved, several observations are pertinent. The A cells have a basolateral band-3-like chloride-bicarbonate exchanger, AE1 (Alper et al., 1989; Drenckhahn et al., 1985; Schuster et al., 1986), whereas no band-3-like chloride-bicarbonate

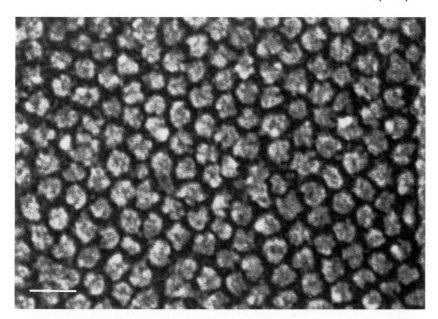

Fig. 1. Rapid-freeze, deep-etch microscopy of a proton-pumping cell from toad urinary bladder, analogous to the kidney intercalated cell. The underside of the apical plasma membrane is coated with the cytoplasmic subunits of a proton-pumping ATPase, arranged into a hexagonally packed paracrystalline array. Each cytoplasmic 'stud' measures 10 nm in diameter. Bar, 20 nm.

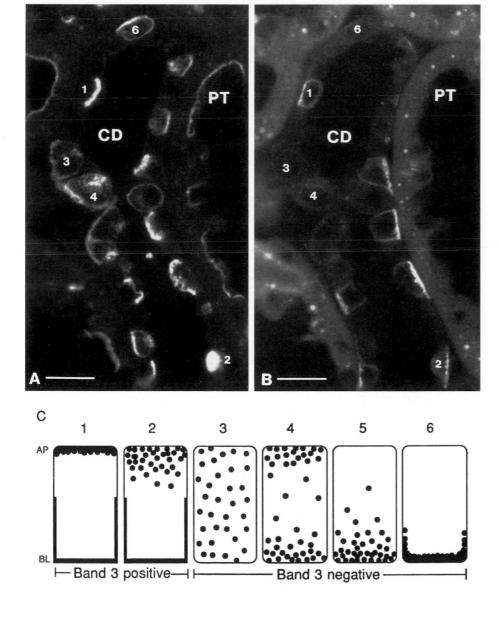

Fig. 2. A 1 μm thick frozen section of rat kidney cortex, double-stained to reveal the proton pumping ATPase (A) and the AE1 band 3-like anion exchanger (B). Intercalated cells in the collecting duct (CD) are all labeled with the proton pump antibody (monoclonal antibody raised against the 31 kDa subunit), but only the A-type intercalated cells show basolateral AE1 staining (e.g. cells 1, 2). The observed patterns of proton pump staining of intercalated cells is complex and is illustrated schematically in (C). Patterns 1 and 2, showing either tight (1) or diffuse (2) apical staining are usually found in A-intercalated cells that have basolateral AE1. The other patterns, diffuse (3), diffuse-bipolar (4), diffuse basal (5) and tight basolateral (6), are characteristic of B-intercalated cells that are AE1-negative. Not all of the staining patterns shown in C are represented in the collecting duct shown in A and B. The classification of intercalated cells based on proton pump distribution is also discussed by Bastani et al. (1991). Cell number 6, showing tight basolateral staining, is sectioned tangentially so that the lateral membrane staining appears as a thin band around the entire cell, the apical membrane is not visible in this section. PT, proximal tubules. Bar, 20 μm.

exchanger has yet been located by immunocytochemistry in type B cells, either in the apical or the basolateral plasma membrane. Double-staining studies show that all B-type intercalated cells with basolateral or diffuse proton pump staining lack detectable AE1, while the vast majority of cells with apical proton pumps show strong basolateral AE1 staining (Fig. 2). However, we consistently found a small (1%) population of cortical intercalated cells with apical proton pumps but no basolateral AE1 (Alper et al., 1989). Whether this cell type is a distinct population or a transitional type of intercalated cell is unknown. The absence of AE1-like antigenicity on the apical surface of all intercalated cells demonstrates that if a simple exchange of transporting molecules from apical to basolateral plasma membrane and vice versa occurs in these cells during adaptation to acid-base loads, then the apical anion exchanger must be modified in some way that renders it undetectable by a range of anti-band 3 antibodies (Schuster, 1988). In acidotic animals, functionally detectable apical anion exchangers appear to be internalized by B-intercalated cells (Satlin and Schwartz, 1989), but whether or not proton pumps are subsequently inserted into the apical membrane of the same cells is still unclear. By immunofluorescence microscopy, a decrease in the number of basolaterally stained intercalated cells is found in the cortex of rats with metabolic aci-

dosis and the number of cells with apical proton pumps increases, both after acute (6 hour) gavage with NH4Cl (Brown, Sabolić and Gluck, unpublished) and after chronic (14-day) NH4Cl treatment (Bastani et al., 1991).

In contrast, immunocytochemically-detectable AE1, as determined by quantitative laser confocal microscopy, significantly diminishes in basolateral plasma membranes of A-type intercalated cells in the cortex after just 6 hours gavage with HCO3$^-$, which induces metabolic alkalosis (Alper et al., 1991). Whether this decrease reflects turnover and degradation of AE1, or a phenomenon of epitope masking is unclear at present. Nevertheless, this decrease would be an expected adaptation to alkalosis, because it would presumably reduce the rate of net acid secretion by the cortical collecting duct by decreasing the H$^+$ secreting capacity of A intercalated cells.

WATER CHANNEL RECYCLING IN PRINCIPAL CELLS

The water permeability of the kidney collecting duct epithelium is regulated by vasopressin-induced recycling of water channels between an intracellular vesicular compartment and the plasma membrane of principal cells (Fig. 3); an

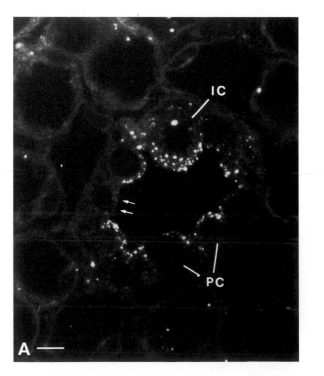

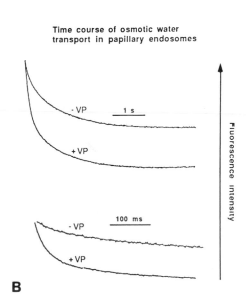

Time course of osmotic water transport in papillary endosomes

Fig. 3. (A) Semithin frozen section of a collecting duct from proximal papilla of a rat that was injected intravenously with FITC-dextran. The FITC-dextran enters the tubule lumen and acts as a marker of fluid-phase endocytosis. Apical endosomes in principal cells (PC) are labeled, and the intercalated cell (IC) shows an even greater degree of endocytosis. Principal cell labeling is heterogeneous; one cell appears to be devoid of staining (arrows). In contrast to the proximal papilla shown here, intercalated cells are absent from the distal two-thirds of the papilla, and endosomes isolated from this kidney region are derived only from principal cells. Bar, 10 μm. (B) Time course of osmotic water transport in isolated papillary endosomes measured by the fluorescence quenching technique. Vesicles loaded with either FITC-dextran or 6-carboxyfluorescein are exposed to a 100 mosM sucrose gradient in a stopped-flow apparatus. As the vesicles shrink, due to water efflux, the concentration of the fluorophore within the vesicles increases, and the decrease in fluorescence signal due to concentration-dependent quenching is followed. Vesicles from vasopressin-treated (+VP), but not control (−VP), Brattleboro rats show an initial rapid rate of quenching (i.e. of water efflux) due to the presence of water channels. The absolute water permeabilities (P_f) of the vesicles can be calculated from the rate of quenching and vesicle size (from electron micrographs).

analogous mechanism exists in other vasopressin-sensitive epithelia such as the toad urinary bladder and the amphibian epidermis (Abramov et al., 1987; Brown, 1989, 1991a,b; Handler, 1988; Harris et al., 1991b; Hays, 1983; Hays et al., 1987; Verkman, 1989). The apically derived endosomes in principal cells are generated via clathrin-mediated endocytosis (Brown and Orci, 1983; Brown et al., 1988; Strange et al., 1988) and they appear to function primarily to recycle membrane components, including water channels, back to the apical membrane during hormonal stimulation (Fig. 3). These vesicles do not, however, acidify their interior. This was shown using FITC-dextran as an in vivo marker of endocytosis and acidification, coupled with co-localization of a lysosomal glycoprotein LGP 120; most of the internalized fluorescent probe did not move into lysosomes and remained in an apical, non-acidic compartment (Lencer et al., 1990b).

Endosomes that contain water channels lack proton pump subunits

These specialized endosomes were purified by differential and density-gradient centrifugation from kidney papilla, and some of their transport characteristics were measured, along with their protein composition (Sabolić et al., 1992b). Fluorescence quenching measurements showed that the isolated vesicles maintained a high, $HgCl_2$-sensitive water permeability, consistent with the presence of vasopressin-sensitive water channels. They did not, however, exhibit ATP-dependent luminal acidification, nor any N-ethyl-maleimide-sensitive ATPase activity, properties that are characteristic of most acidic endosomal compartments (Fig. 4). Western blotting with specific antibodies showed that

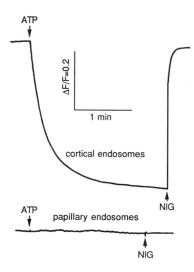

Fig. 4. ATP-dependent acidification in FITC-dextran-loaded vesicles from kidney cortex and papilla. Vesicles loaded with FITC-dextran in vivo were equilibrated with KCl buffer, pH 7.4, and diluted in the same buffer. A 50 μg protein sample from each vesicle preparation was used in the assay. Before addition of ATP, extravesicular fluorescence was quenched with anti-FITC antibodies. Where indicated, nigericin (NIG) was added to dissipate the ΔpH. ATP-driven H^+ uptake is vigorous in cortical endosomes, but is absent from papillary vesicles, indicating that they do not contain a functional proton pumping ATPase.

the 31 kDa and 70 kDa cytoplasmically oriented subunits of the vacuolar proton pump were not present in these apical endosomes from the papilla, whereas they were readily detectable in endosomes prepared in parallel from the cortex. In contrast, the 56 kDa subunit of the proton pump was present in papillary endosomes, and was localized at the apical pole of principal cells by immunocytochemistry.

In addition, an antibody that recognizes the 16 kDa transmembrane subunit of oat tonoplast ATPase (Lai et al., 1988) cross-reacted with a distinct 16 kDa band in cortical endosomes, but no 16 kDa band was detectable in endosomes from the papilla. Therefore, early endosomes derived from the apical plasma membrane of collecting duct principal cells fail to acidify because they lack functionally important subunits of a vacuolar-type proton pumping ATPase, including the 16 kDa transmembrane domain that serves as the proton-conducting channel, and the 70 kDa cytoplasmic subunit that contains the ATPase catalytic site. Interestingly, endosomes that are involved in water channel internalization and recycling in the toad urinary bladder also fail to acidify in response to ATP, and they also lack the 31 and 70 kDa subunits of the proton pump, while retaining the 56 kDa subunit (Harris et al., 1991a).

The specialized nature of apical endosomes in vasopressin-sensitive cells presumably reflects the superficial vesicle-shuttling mechanism that characterizes their physiological response to hormonal stimulation. However, other cell types also use a similar process to recycle functionally important cell surface molecules between cytoplasmic vesicles and the plasma membrane in response to a variety of stimuli. For example, the insulin-sensitive glucose transporter Glut-4 has a similar recycling mechanism (Suzuki and Kono, 1980), as does the H^+,K^+-ATPase in gastric parietal cells (Forte et al., 1977). In the mammalian urinary bladder, sodium channels are inserted into the apical membrane of surface epithelial cells as a result of stretch-induced exocytosis (Lewis and DeMoura, 1984). Whether these and other vesicles involved in specialized recycling processes also lack the capacity to acidify remains to be determined.

Endocytotic clathrin-coated vesicles are not acidic in principal cells

The identification of early endosomes devoid of proton pump subunits suggests that the vesicles that initially pinch off from the apical plasma membrane of collecting duct principal cells also do not acidify. Because, in the case of water channel endocytosis, this is a clathrin-mediated process (Brown and Orci, 1983; Brown et al., 1988; Strange et al., 1988), our results imply that endocytotic clathrin-coated vesicles lack the capability to acidify. However, when total cellular clathrin-coated vesicles are isolated from various sources, including the kidney, proton pump subunits can be detected in these vesicles, and ATP-dependent acidification can be measured in the total vesicle population (Forgac et al., 1983; Stone, 1988; Xie and Stone, 1986). The most likely explanation for these results is that the coated vesicles that are specifically involved in (apical) endocytosis are not acidic vesicles, but that other clathrin-coated vesicles within the cell, that subserve other transport functions, do contain membrane-associated proton

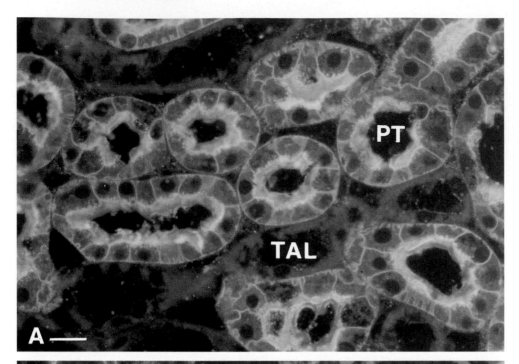

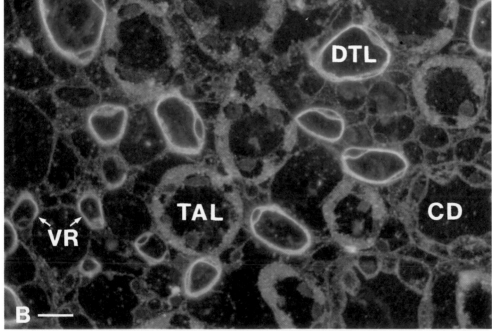

Fig. 5. Immunofluorescence localization of the CHIP28 water channel in 1 μm frozen sections of rat kidney cortex (A) and inner stripe of the medulla (B). Proximal tubules (PT) show a marked apical and basolateral membrane staining, whereas thick ascending limbs of Henle (TAL) are unstained. In (B), TAL are also unstained, but descending thin limbs of Henle (DTL) and some vasa recta profiles (VR) are brightly stained. Collecting ducts (CD) show only a low background level of staining in this region. Sections were counterstained with Evans blue to give a red background coloration. Bar, 20 μm.

pumps, and are capable of generating an internal acidic pH. In support of this, staining of fibroblasts with the morphological pH marker, DAMP, has demonstrated intracellular heterogeneity of coated vesicle labeling (Anderson et al., 1984). In addition, it has been reported that clathrin-coated vesicles involved in endocytosis in other cell types are non-acidifying vesicles (Fuchs et al., 1987).

Identification of a water channel

A recent exciting development in the field of water channel physiology has been the isolation, cloning and functional expression of a 28 kDa integral membrane protein known as CHIP28. First isolated from erythrocytes by Agre

and colleagues (Denker et al., 1988), this member of a family of channel proteins has a kidney homolog (Zhang et al., 1993), and is expressed at high levels in proximal tubule and descending limbs of Henle in both apical and basolateral plasma membranes (Nielsen et al., 1993; Sabolic et al., 1992a) (Fig. 5). However, because these membrane domains are constitutively permeable to water, and because CHIP28 cannot be detected in papillary principal cells (although it cross-reacts weakly with principal cells in the cortex) CHIP28 is probably not the vasopressin-sensitive water channel that is recycled in the non-acidic endosomes described above. However, a partial homolog (referred to as WCH1) with approximately 50% sequence identity to

CHIP28, has been identified in the papilla (Sasaka et al., 1992), and antibodies against this protein localize to collecting duct principal cells. This protein is, therefore, a candidate for the vasopressin-regulated water channel. The availability of full-length cDNAs for these water channels will permit the future analysis of structural elements that may determine non-polarized (CHIP28) versus polarized (WCH1, vasopressin-sensitive channel) targeting of these physiologically relevant proteins.

ROLE OF MICROTUBULES IN VESICLE TRAFFICKING

Many studies have shown that microtubules can support the movement of organelles in vitro, and are probably involved in organelle trafficking in vivo. Drugs that disrupt microtubules interfere with secretory events in many cell types (Busson-Mabillot et al., 1982; Orci et al., 1973; Patzelt et al., 1977; Stetson and Steinmetz, 1983; Taylor, 1977) and they result in a redistribution of intracellular organelles including lysosomes, RER and the Golgi apparatus (Dabora and Sheetz, 1988; Heuser, 1989; Kreis, 1989; Matteoni and Kreis, 1987; Moskalewski et al., 1973). Despite these major cellular alterations induced by microtubule disruption, the role of microtubules in determining cell polarity remains controversial (Achler et al., 1989; Gutmann et al., 1989; Hasegawa et al., 1987; Ojakian and Schwimmer, 1988; Pavelka et al., 1983; Rindler et al., 1987; Salas et al., 1986). In particular, some studies using virally infected cells as well as endogenous proteins have shown that microtubule disruption causes apical proteins to appear on both apical and basolateral plasma membranes. In contrast, other work, including our own studies on an apical membrane glycoprotein, gp330, in the proximal tubule, has shown that membrane proteins are not misdirected to an inappropriate membrane domain after microtubule disruption in these cells. In addition, it is generally believed that microtubules are not involved in the polarized insertion of basolateral membrane proteins.

Microtubules are also implicated in the physiological responses of intercalated cells and principal cells. Studies using both amphibian epithelia and mammalian kidney collecting duct have shown that microtubule depolymerizing agents significantly reduce vasopressin-induced transepithelial water flow (DeSousa et al., 1974; Dratwa et al., 1984; Kachadorian et al., 1979; Valenti et al., 1988), and that H^+ secretion is also markedly inhibited by colchicine in turtle bladder (Stetson and Steinmetz, 1983). In both cases, the effect of microtubule disruption seems to occur by reducing the likelihood that vesicles carrying water channels or proton pumps will move to and fuse with the apical plasma membrane. However, because neither water flow nor H^+ secretion are totally inhibited (maximum inhibition is around 60-70%), it appears that some transporting vesicles are still able to fuse with the appropriate target membrane even in the presumed absence of microtubules. This may occur as a result of random vesicle movement within the cell resulting in some residual 'collisions' of these vesicles with the apical membrane, thus allowing the recognition and fusion event to occur normally.

Microtubules and intercalated cell polarity

One possibility that might explain differential targeting of proton pumps to opposite membrane domains in intercalated cells is that the apical and basolateral forms of the proton ATPase may not be identical in subunit composition; this difference could confer domain specificity on the targeting process. There is increasing evidence that different isoforms of some proton pump subunits are selectively amplified and expressed in different cell types, as well as in different membrane domains within the same cell (Nelson et al., 1992; Puopolo et al., 1992). In particular, isoforms of the 56 kDa subunit show distinct patterns of cellular location in the kidney, and one isoform (the so-called 'kidney' isoform) is amplified in intercalated cells, but is not detectable in proximal tubule epithelial cells (Nelson et al., 1992). So far, however, no isoform that is restricted to either the apical or basolateral membrane in intercalated cells has been identified. Another possibility is that the microtubular network is somehow different in cells with apical or basolateral proton pumps, and that vesicles containing the pumps move selectively to only one pole of the cell. As discussed above, it has been proposed that microtubule tracks are important for the delivery of apical proteins, but that basolateral proteins are routed to the base of the cell by a default pathway. In this way, microtubule depolymerization might be expected to result in basolateral, rather than apical insertion of proton pumps. This prediction assumes that vesicles carrying proton pumps are competent to fuse with either apical or basolateral plasma membranes, and that the specificity of the process lies exclusively in the delivery of the vesicles to the appropriate membrane domain. However, this is clearly not the case with another apical membrane protein, gp330, which is present in vesicles that do not fuse with the wrong (i.e. the basolateral) plasma membrane, even when they are apparently close enough for fusion to occur (Gutmann et al., 1989).

To examine the possible involvement of microtubules in the polarized insertion of proton pumps, studies were performed on colchicine-treated rats (Brown et al., 1991). In these animals, proton pumps were no longer polarized to one pole of the cell, but they were concentrated in numerous vesicles scattered throughout the cytoplasm after 4-6 hours of drug treatment. A similar scattered distribution was seen in A and B intercalated cells, as well as in epithelial cells of the proximal tubule (Fig. 6). One especially important result was that A-type cells in the inner stripe of the outer medulla did not concentrate proton pumps in their basolateral plasma membranes. These results indicate that microtubule depolymerization alone is not sufficient to account for the final differences in the membrane distribution of proton pumps seen in A and B intercalated cells. As is also the case for gp330-containing vesicles in the proximal tubule, an additional level of control must govern the final fusion process between these re-routed vesicles and their target membrane region.

The effects of colchicine on the distribution of basolateral proton pumps in intercalated cells did not, however, extend to all basolateral membrane proteins. When the localization of two other exclusively basolateral proteins, the band 3 anion exchanger and a facilitated glucose trans-

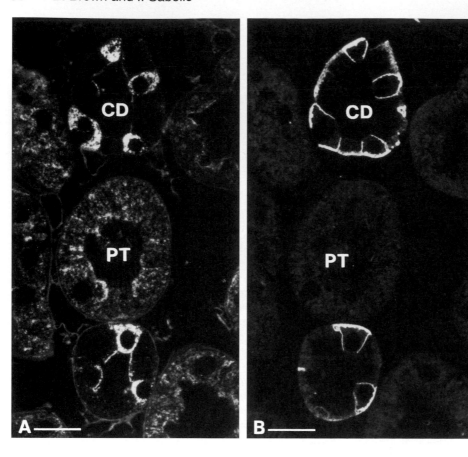

Fig. 6. A 1 μm frozen section of rat kidney cortex from an animal injected with colchicine 8 hours prior to tissue fixation. Section is double-stained to reveal proton pumps (A) and the Glut 1 facilitated glucose transporter (B). Proton pumps are distributed on vesicles scattered throughout the cytoplasm of both proximal tubules (PT) and intercalated cells in the collecting duct (CD); they no longer have a discrete plasma membrane location (compare with control animal in Fig. 2). In contrast, a facilitated glucose transporter, Glut 1, is unaffected by colchicine treatment, and retains a typical basolateral pattern even after prolonged periods of microtubule disruption (B). Intercalated cells show an especially prominent basolateral Glut1 staining. Bar, 20 μm.

porter Glut-1 (Thorens et al., 1990), was examined, no redistribution could be detected. Thus, by double staining the same cell, proton pumps were scattered throughout the cytoplasm as described earlier, but the other basolateral markers were still located in a distinct basolateral pattern (Fig. 6A,B). This result indicates that the effect of microtubule disruption is likely to be protein-specific, rather than membrane domain-specific. It also indicates that proton pumps must be segregated into specific endocytotic vesicles during the recycling process, and that other membrane

proteins, including band 3 and Glut-1, are not internalized in parallel in the same vesicles.

Microtubules and polarity in the proximal tubule

Support for the contention that the microtubule involvement in membrane polarity is protein-specific comes from studies on the proximal tubule. In this nephron segment, the apical membrane is highly active endocytotically, and much of the apical membrane at the base of the microvilli is clathrin-coated (Brown and Orci, 1986; Rodman et al., 1984). Our

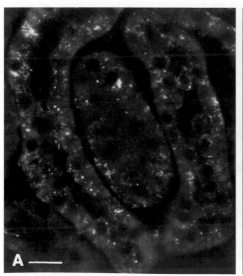
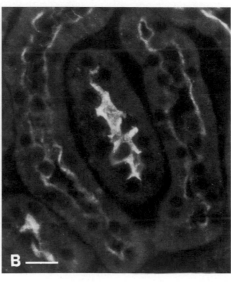

Fig. 7. A 5 μm frozen section of rat kidney cortex from an animal injected with colchicine 8 hours prior to tissue fixation. Section is double-stained to reveal gp330 (A), an apical membrane protein in control animals, and DPP IV (B), which is also an apical protein. Whereas gp330 is redistributed throughout the cytoplasm after colchicine treatment (A), DPP IV retains its original apical location even after microtubule disruption by colchicine. Bar, 15 μm.

previous studies show that proteins (gp330 and H$^+$-ATPase) that are present either in the clathrin-coated membrane domains at the apical membrane, or in the membrane immediately adjacent to these regions at the base of the microvilli, are redistributed in colchicine-treated animals (Fig. 7A). However, some membrane proteins including dipeptidylpeptidase IV (DPP IV) and carbonic anhydrase type IV (CA IV) are restricted to the brush border microvilli (Brown and Waneck, 1992), and are not normally concentrated in the endocytically active zone at the microvillar base. After colchicine treatment, these proteins remain in their original microvillar location, are not redistributed with the other proteins (Fig. 7B). Interestingly, both CA IV and DPP IV are proteins that can be attached to the membrane via a glycosyl phosphatidylinositol anchor (Hooper et al., 1990; Waheed et al., 1992).

Based on results from many groups, the final level of control of vesicle fusion with target membranes could be related to the presence of specific GTP-binding proteins on different populations of vesicles (Balch, 1990; Goud and McCaffrey, 1991), or to the presence of other peripheral and integral membrane proteins that are necessary for specific fusion process to occur (Clary and Rothman, 1990; Clary et al., 1990; Hooper et al., 1990; Weidman et al., 1989). Apical, basolateral and endosomal membranes of many kidney epithelial cells have significant differences with respect to their content of GTP-binding proteins (Stow et al., 1991). The structure of individual membrane proteins may, therefore, contain information ensuring that the protein is packaged into vesicles with the correct address, while other constituents of these vesicles may be responsible for controlling the final series of interactions with target membrane domains. The role of microtubules in this process would be, therefore, to concentrate vesicles containing either newly synthesized or recycling proteins at the appropriate membrane domain, and thereby increase the chances for a subsequent specific fusion event to occur.

REFERENCES

Abramov, M., Beauwens, R. and Cogan, E. (1987). Cellular events in vasopressin action. *Kidney Int.* **32**, Suppl. 21, S56-S66.

Achler, C., Filmer, D., Merte, C. and Drenckhahn, D. (1989). Role of microtubules in polarized delivery of apical membrane proteins to the brush border of the intestinal epithelium. *J. Cell Biol.* **109**, 179-189.

Adams, R. J. and Pollard, T. D. (1986). Propulsion of organelles isolated from Acanthamoeba along actin filaments. *Nature* **322**, 754-756.

Alper, S. L., Natale, J., Gluck, S., Lodish, H. F. and Brown, D. (1989). Subtypes of intercalated cells in rat kidney collecting duct defined by antibodies against erythroid band 3 and renal vacuolar H$^+$-ATPase. *Proc. Nat. Acad. Sci. USA* **86**, 5429-5433.

Alper, S. L., Sabolić, I., Tyszkowski, R. and Brown, D. (1991). Metabolic acidosis and alkalosis modulate anion exchanger (AE1) expression in kidney collecting ducts. *J. Amer. Soc. Nephrol.* **2**, 693a.

Anderson, R. G. W., Falck, J. R., Goldstein, J. L. and Brown, M. S. (1984). Visualization of acidic organelles in intact cells by electron microscopy. *Proc. Nat. Acad. Sci. USA* **81**, 4838-4842.

Balch, W. E. (1990). Small GTP-binding proteins in vesicular transport. *Trends Biochem. Sci.* **15**, 473-477.

Bastani, B., Purcell, H., Hemken, P., Trigg, D. and Gluck, S. (1991). Expression and distribution of renal vacuolar proton-translocating adenosine triphosphatase in response to chronic acid and alkali loads in the rat. *J. Clin. Invest.* **88**, 126-136.

Brown, D. (1989). Membrane recycling and epithelial cell function. *Amer. J. Physiol.* **256**, F1-F12.

Brown, D. (1991a). Cell biology of the cycling of the vasopressin-sensitive water channel. In *Vasopressin* (ed. S. Jard and R. Jamison), pp. 75-83. Paris: John Libbey Eurotext Ltd.

Brown, D. (1991b). Structural-functional features of vasopressin-induced water flow in the kidney collecting duct. *Semin. Nephrol.* **11**, 478-501.

Brown, D., Gluck, S. and Hartwig, J. (1987). Structure of the novel membrane-coating material in proton-secreting epithelial cells and identification as an H$^+$ATPase. *J. Cell Biol.* **105**, 1637-1648.

Brown, D., Hirsch, S. and Gluck, S. (1988a). An H$^+$ATPase is present in opposite plasma membrane domains in subpopulations of kidney epithelial cells. *Nature* **331**, 622-624.

Brown, D., Hirsch, S. and Gluck, S. (1988b). Localization of a proton-pumping ATPase in rat kidney. *J. Clin. Invest* **82**, 2114-2126.

Brown, D. and Orci, L. (1983). Vasopressin stimulates the formation of coated pits in rat kidney collecting ducts. *Nature* **302**, 253-255.

Brown, D. and Orci, L. (1986). The 'coat' of kidney intercalated cell tubulovesicles does not contain clathrin. *Amer. J. Physiol.* **250**, C605-C608.

Brown, D., Sabolić, I. and Gluck, S. (1991). Colchicine-induced redistribution of proton pumps in the proximal tubule. *Kidney Int.* **40** (Suppl. 33), S79-S83.

Brown, D. and Waneck, G. L. (1992). Glycosyl-phosphatidylinositol-anchored membrane proteins. *J. Amer. Soc. Nephrol.* **3**, 895-906.

Brown, D., Weyer, P. and Orci, L. (1988). Vasopressin stimulates endocytosis in kidney collecting duct epithelial cells. *Eur. J. Cell Biol.* **46**, 336-340.

Busson-Mabillot, S., Chambut-Guerin, A.-M., Ovtracht, L., Muller, P. and Rossignol, B. (1982). Microtubules and protein secretion in rat lachrymal glands: localization of short-term effects of colchicine on the secretory process. *J. Cell Biol.* **95**, 105-117.

Clary, D. and Rothman, J. E. (1990). Purification of three related peripheral membrane proteins needed for vesicular transport. *J. Biol. Chem.* **265**, 10109-10117.

Clary, D. O., Griff, I. C. and Rothman, J. E. (1990). SNAPs, a family of NSF attachment proteins involved in intracellular membrane fusion in animals and yeast. *Cell* **61**, 709-721.

Dabora, S. L. and Sheetz, M. P. (1988). The microtubule-dependent formation of a tubulovesicular network with characteristics of the ER from cultured cell extracts. *Cell* **54**, 27-35.

Denker, B. M., Smith, B. L., Kuhajda, F. P. and Agre, P. (1988). Identification, purification and partial characterization of a novel Mr 28,000 integral membrane protein from erythrocytes and renal tubules. *J. Biol. Chem.* **263**, 15634-15642.

DeSousa, R. C., Grosso, A. and Rufener, C. (1974). Blockade of the hydroosmotic effect of vasopressin by cytochalasin B. *Experientia* **30**, 175-177.

Dixon, T. E., Clausen, C., Coachman, D. and Lane, B. (1986). Proton transport and membrane shuttling in turtle bladder. *J. Membr. Biol.* **94**, 233-243.

Dorup, J. (1986). Structural adaptation of intercalated cells in rat renal cortex to acute metabolic acidosis and alkalosis. *J. Ultrastruct. Res.* **92**, 119-131.

Dratwa, M., LeFurgey, A. and Tisher, C. C. (1984). Effects of colchicine and cytochalasin B on hypertonicity-induced changes in toad urinary bladder. *Cell Tiss. Res.* **236**, 585-591.

Drenckhahn, D., Schluter, K., Allen, D. P. and Bennett, V. (1985). Co-localization of Band 3 with ankyrin and spectrin at the basal membrane of intercalated cells in the rat kidney. *Science* **230**, 1287-1289.

Forgac, M., Cantley, L., Wiedenmann, B., Altstiel, L. and Branton, D. (1983). Clathrin-coated vesicles contain an ATP-dependent proton pump. *Proc. Nat. Acad. Sci. USA* **80**, 1300-1303.

Forte, T. M., Machen, T. E. and Forte, J. G. (1977). Ultrastructural changes in oxyntic cells associated with secretory function: a membrane recycling hypothesis. *Gastroenterology* **73**, 941-955.

Fuchs, R., Ellinger, A., Pavelka, M., Peterlik, M. and Mellman, I. (1987). Endocytotic coated vesicles do not exhibit ATP-dependent acidification in vitro. *J. Cell Biol.* **105**, 91a.

Gluck, S., Cannon, C. and Al-Awqati, Q. (1982). Exocytosis regulates urinary acidification in turtle bladder by rapid insertion of H$^+$ pumps into the luminal membrane. *Proc. Nat. Acad. Sci. USA* **79**, 4327-4331.

Goud, B. and McCaffrey, M. (1991). Small GTP binding proteins and their role in transport. *Curr. Opin. Cell Biol.* **3**, 626-633.

Gutmann, E. J., Niles, J. L., McCluskey, R. T. and Brown, D. (1989). Colchicine-induced redistribution of an endogenous apical membrane glycoprotein (gp 330) in kidney proximal tubule epithelium. *Amer. J. Physiol.* **257**, C397-C407.

Handler, J. S. (1988). Antidiuretic hormone moves membranes. *Amer. J. Physiol.* **235**, F375-F382.

Harris, H. W. Jr., Strange, K. and Zeidel, M. L. (1991a). Current understanding of the cellular biology and molecular structure of the antidiuretic hormone-stimulated water transport pathway. *J. Clin. Invest.* **88**, 1-8.

Harris, H. W. Jr., Zeidel, M. L. and Hosselet, C. (1991b). Quantitation and topography of membrane proteins in highly water-permeable vesicles from ADH-stimulated toad bladder. *Amer. J. Physiol.* **261**, C143-C153.

Hasegawa, H., Watanabe, K., Nakamura, T. and Nagura, H. (1987). Immunocytochemical localization of alkaline phosphatase in absorptive cells of rat small intestine after colchicine treatment. *Cell Tiss. Res.* **250**, 521-529.

Hays, R. M. (1983). Alteration of luminal membrane structure by antidiuretic hormone. *Amer. J. Physiol.* **245**, C289-C296.

Hays, R. M., Franki, N. and Ding, G. (1987). Effects of antidiuretic hormone on the collecting duct. *Kidney Int.* **31**, 530-537.

Heuser, J. (1989). Changes in lysosome shape and distribution correlated with changes in cytoplasmic pH. *J. Cell Biol.* **108**, 855-864.

Hooper, N. M., Hryszko, J. and Turner, H. J. (1990). Purification and characterization of pig kidney aminopeptidase P. A glycosyl-phosphatidylinositol-anchored ectoenzyme. *Biochem. J.* **267**, 509-515.

Johnston, G. C., Prendergast, J. A. and Singer, R. A. (1991). The *Saccharomyces cerevisiae* MYO2 gene encodes an essential myosin for vectorial transport of vesicles. *J. Cell Biol.* **113**, 539-551.

Kachadorian, W. A., Ellis, S. J. and Muller, J. (1979). Possible roles for microtubules and microfilaments in ADH action on toad urinary bladder. *Amer. J. Physiol.* **236**, F14-F20.

Koichi, Y., Satlin, L. M. and Schwartz, G. J. (1992). Adaptation of rabbit cortical collecting duct to in vitro acidification. *Amer. J. Physiol.* **263**, F749-F756.

Kreis, T. (1989). Reclustering of scattered Golgi elements occurs along microtubules. *Eur. J. Cell Biol.* **48**, 250-263.

Lai, S., Randall, S. K. and Sze, H. (1988). Peripheral and integral subunits of the tonoplast H⁺-ATPase from oat roots. *J. Biol. Chem.* **263**, 16731-16737.

Lencer, W. I., Brown, D., Ausiello, D. A. and Verkman, A. S. (1990a). Endocytosis of water channels in rat kidney: cell specificity and correlation with in vivo antidiuresis. *Amer. J. Physiol.* **259**, C920-C932.

Lencer, W. I., Verkman, A. S., Arnaout, A., Ausiello, D. A. and Brown, D. (1990b). Endocytic vesicles from renal papilla which retrieve the vasopressin-sensitive water channel do not contain a functional H⁺ATPase. *J. Cell Biol.* **111**, 379-390.

Lewis, S. A. and DeMoura, J. L. C. (1984). Apical membrane area of rabbit urinary bladder increases by fusion of intracellular vesicles: an electrophysiological study. *J. Membr. Biol.* **82**, 123-136.

Madsen, K. M. and Tisher, C. C. (1983). Cellular response to acute respiratory acidosis in rat medullary collecting duct. *Amer. J. Physiol.* **245**, F670-F679.

Madsen, K. M. and Tisher, C. C. (1986). Structure-function relationships along the distal nephron. *Amer. J. Physiol.* **250**, F1-F15.

Madsen, K. M., Verlander, J. W., Kim, J. and Tisher, C. C. (1991). Morphological adaptation of the collecting duct to acid-base disturbances. *Kidney Int.* 40 (Suppl. 33), S57-S63.

Matteoni, R. and Kreis, T. E. (1987). Translocation and clustering of endosomes and lysosomes depends on microtubules. *J. Cell Biol.* **105**, 1253-1265.

Moskalewski, S., Thyberg, J. and Friberg, U. (1973). In vitro influence of colchicine on the Golgi complex in A- and B-cells of guinea pig pancreatic islets. *J. Ultrastruct. Res.* **54**, 304-317.

Nelson, R. D., Guo, X.-L., Masood, K., Brown, D., Kalkbrenner, M. and Gluck, S. (1992). Selectively amplified expression of an isoform of the vacuolar H+ATPase Mr 56,000 subunit in renal intercalated cells. *Proc. Nat. Acad. Sci. USA* **89**, 3541-3545.

Nielsen, S., Smith, B. L., Christensen, E. I., Knepper, M. A. and Agre, P. (1993). CHIP28 water channels are localized in constitutively waterpermeable segments of the nephron. *J. Cell Biol.* **120**, 371-383.

Ojakian, G. K. and Schwimmer, R. (1988). The polarized distribution of an apical cell surface glycoprotein is maintained by interactions with the cytoskeleton of Madin-Darby canine kidney cells. *J. Cell Biol.* **107**, 2377-2387.

Orci, L., Le Marchand, Y., Singh, A., Assimacopoulos-Jeannet, F., Rouiller, C. and Jeanrenaud, B. (1973). Role of microtubules in lipoprotein secretion by the liver. *Nature* **244**, 30-32.

Patzelt, C., Brown, D. and Jeanrenaud, B. (1977). Inhibitory effect of colchicine on amylase secretion by rat parotid glands. Possible localization in the Golgi area. *J. Cell Biol.* **73**, 578-593.

Pavelka, M., Ellinger, A. and Gangl, A. (1983). Effect of colchicine on rat small intestinal adsorptive cells I. Formation of basolateral microvillus borders. *J. Ultrastruct. Res.* **85**, 249-259.

Puopolo, K., Kumamoto, I., Adachi, I., Magner, R. and Forgac, M. (1992). Differential expression of the 'B' subunit of the vacuolar H⁺ ATPase in bovine tissues. *J. Biol. Chem.* **267**, 3696-3706.

Rindler, M. J., Ivanov, I. E. and Sabatini, D. D. (1987). Microtubule-acting drugs lead to the nonpolarized delivery of the influenza hemagglutinin to the cell surface of polarized Madin-Darby canine kidney cells. *J. Cell Biol.* **104**, 231-241.

Rodman, J. S., Kerjaschki, D., Merisko, E. and Farquhar, M. G. (1984). Presence of an extensive clathrin coat on the apical plasmalemma of the rat kidney proximal tubule cell. *J. Cell Biol.* **98**, 1630-1636.

Sabolić, I., Valenti, G., Verbavatz, J.-M., Van Hoek, A. N., Verkman, A. S., Ausiello, D. A. and Brown, D. (1992a). Localization of the CHIP28 water channel in rat kidney. *Amer. J. Physiol.* **263**, C1225-C1233.

Sabolić, I., Wuarin, F., Shi, L.-B., Verkman, A. S., Ausiello, D. A., Gluck, S. and Brown, D. (1992b). Apical endosomes isolated from kidney collecting duct principal cells lack subunits of the proton pumping ATPase. *J. Cell Biol.* **119**, 111-122.

Salas, P., Misek, D., Vega-Salas, D., Gundersen, D., Cereijido, M. and Rodriguez-Boulan, E. (1986). Microtubules are not critically involved in the biogenesis of epithelial cell surface polarity. *J. Cell Biol.* **102**, 1853-1867.

Sasaka, S., Fushimi, K., Uchida, S. and Marumo, F. (1992). Regulation and localization of two types of water channels in the rat kidney. *J. Amer. Soc. Nephrol.* **3**, 798a.

Satlin, L. M. and Schwartz, G. J. (1989). Cellular remodelling of HCO3⁻ secreting cells in rabbit renal collecting duct in response to an acidic environment. *J. Cell Biol.* **109**, 1279-1288.

Schroer, T. A. and Sheetz, M. P. (1991). Functions of microtubule-based motors. *Annu. Rev. Physiol.* **53**, 629-652.

Schuster, V. L. (1988). Cortical collecting duct anion transport. In *Nephrology: Proceedings of the Xth International Congress of Nephrology* (ed A. M. Davison), pp. 283-293. Tokyo: Balliere Tindall.

Schuster, V. L., Bonsib, S. M. and Jennings, M. L. (1986). Two types of collecting duct mitochondria-rich (intercalated) cells: lectin and band 3 cytochemistry. *Amer. J. Physiol.* **251**, C347-C355.

Schwartz, G. J. and Al-Awqati, Q. (1985). Carbon dioxide causes exocytosis of vesicles containing H⁺ pumps in isolated perfused proximal and collecting tubules. *J. Clin. Invest.* **75**, 1638-1644.

Schwartz, G. J., Barasch, J. and Al-Awqati, Q. (1985). Plasticity of functional epithelial polarity. *Nature* **318**, 368-371.

Stetson, D. A. and Steinmetz, P. R. (1985). A and B types of carbonic anhydrase-rich cells in turtle bladder. *Amer. J. Physiol.* **249**, F553-F565.

Stetson, D. L. and Steinmetz, P. R. (1983). Role of membrane fusion in CO₂ stimulation of proton secretion by turtle bladder. *Amer. J. Physiol.* **245**, C113-C120.

Stone, D. (1988). Proton-translocating ATPases: issues in structure and function. *Kidney Int.* **33**, 767-774.

Stow, J. L., Sabolić, I. and Brown, D. (1991). Heterogeneous localization of G protein α-subunits in rat kidney. *Amer. J. Physiol.* **261**, F831-F840.

Strange, K., Willingham, M. C., Handler, J. S. and Harris, H. W. Jr (1988). Apical membrane endocytosis via coated pits is stimulated by removal of antidiuretic hormone from isolated, perfused rabbit cortical collecting tubule. *J. Membr. Biol.* **103**, 17-28.

Suzuki, K. and Kono, T. (1980). Evidence that insulin causes translocation of glucose transport activity to the plasma membrane from an intracellular storage site. *Proc. Nat. Acad. Sci. USA* **77**, 2542-2545.

Taylor, A. (1977). Role of microtubules and microfilaments in the action of vasopressin. In *Disturbances in Body Fluid Osmolality* (ed. T. E. Andreoli, J. J. Grantham and F. C. Rector), pp. 97-124. Bethseda: Amer. Physiol. Soc.

Thorens, B., Lodish, H. F. and Brown, D. (1990). Differential localization of two glucose transporter isoforms in rat kidney. *Amer. J. Physiol.* **259**, C286-C294.

Vale, R. D. (1987). Intracellular transport using microtubule-based motors. *Annu. Rev. Cell Biol.* **3**, 347-378.

Valenti, G., Hugon, J. S. and Bourguet, J. (1988). To what extent is microtubular network involved in antidiuretic response? *Amer. J. Physiol.* **255**, F1098-F1106.

Verkman, A. S. (1989). Mechanisms and regulation of water permeability in renal epithelia. *Amer. J. Physiol.* **257**, C837-C850.

Verlander, J. W., Madsen, K. M. and Tisher, C. C. (1988). Effect of acute respiratory acidosis on two populations of intercalated cells in rat cortical collecting duct. *Amer. J. Physiol.* **253**, F1142-F1156

Waheed, A., Zhu, X. L. and Sly, W. S. (1992). Membrane-associated carbonic anhydrase from rat lung. Purification, characterization, tissue distribution, and comparison with carbonic anhydrase IV's of other mammals. *J. Biol. Chem.* **267**, 3308-3311.

Weidman, P. J., Melancon, P., Block, M. R. and Rothman, J. E. (1989). Binding of and *N*-ethylmaleimide-sensitive fusion protein to Golgi membranes requires both a soluble protein and an integral membrane receptor. *J. Cell Biol.* **108**, 1589-1596.

Xie, X.-S. and Stone, D. K. (1986). Isolation and reconstitution of the clathrin-coated vesicle proton translocating complex. *J. Biol. Chem.* **261**, 2492-2495.

Zhang, R., Skach, W., Hasegawa, H., Van Hoek, A. N. and Verkman, A. S. (1993). Cloning, functional analysis and cell localization of a kidney proximal tubule water transporter homologous to CHIP28. *J. Cell Biol.* **120**, 359-369.

Zot, H. G., Doberstein, S. K. and Pollard, T. D. (1992). Myosin-I moves actin filaments on a phospholipid substrate: implications for membrane targetting. *J. Cell Biol.* **116**, 367-376.

Journal of Cell Science, Supplement 17, 61-64 (1993)
Printed in Great Britain © The Company of Biologists Limited 1993

Phenotypic conversions in renal development

D. Herzlinger[1], R. Abramson[2] and D. Cohen[1]

[1]Department of Physiology and Biophysics, and [2]Division of Urology, Department of Surgery, Cornell University Medical College, New York, NY 10021, USA

SUMMARY

The transporting epithelia of the kidney are derived from an embryonic rudiment containing two distinct cell populations: ureteric bud epithelia and mesenchymal cells of the metanephric blastema. The ureteric bud is a caudal outgrowth of the Wolffian Duct and gives rise to the renal collecting system by branching morphogenesis. The metanephric blastema gives rise to diverse cells of the nephron after receiving an inductive stimulus. It has been proposed that mesenchymal progenitors of the metanephric blastema derive directly from intermediate mesoderm, although this hypothesis has never been tested directly. Utilizing direct lineage analysis techniques we demonstrate, in an organ culture system, that mesenchymal nephron progenitors are immediate descendants of ureteric bud epithelia. Ureteric bud epithelia can give rise to mesenchymal nephron progenitors that populate the metanephric blastema by undergoing an epithelial-to-mesenchymal transition followed by delamination. If this process occurs in vivo, renal morphogenesis can be characterized by two phenotypic conversions: an epithelial-to-mesenchymal transition leading to the generation of mesenchymal-nephron progenitors, followed by a mesenchymal-to-epithelial transition leading to the generation of diverse nephron epithelial cell types. We have immortalized an embryonic renal mesenchymal cell line and demonstrate that the clonal cell line, RSTEM-1, undergoes phenotypic conversions in vitro, providing a suitable model to study the regulation of the epithelial phenotype.

Key words: epithelia, mesenchyme, kidney, development

INTRODUCTION

Epithelial cells can be characterized by several criteria, including a polarized cell surface, the presence of junctional complexes, and the expression of epithelial-specific proteins such as cytokeratin and uvomorulin. Much insight into the cellular and genetic regulation of the epithelial phenotype has been gained by utilizing epithelial and fibroblastic cell culture systems, where the epithelial phenotype can be experimentally manipulated (see review by Rodriguez-Boulan and Nelson, 1989). However, a model system to elucidate the in vivo biological signals that regulate the epithelial phenotype has been lacking.

Epithelial-to-mesenchymal, and the opposite, mesenchymal-to-epithelial conversions occur throughout embryonic development, mediating the formation of diverse organ systems (Gilbert, 1991). The developing kidney can be utilized as a model system to study the biogenesis of epithelial cell surface polarity because the polarized epithelia of the nephron are derived from unpolarized mesenchymal progenitors of the metanephric blastema (Grobstein, 1956; Saxen, 1987; Ekblom, 1981). Utilizing recently developed lineage tracing techniques we have re-examined renal differentiation, and show that mesenchymal progenitors of the metanephric blastema are direct descendants of the ureteric bud.

DEVELOPMENT OF THE URETERIC BUD

Serial sections of rat kidney rudiments at the first identifiable stage of metanephric kidney formation were examined. The rudiment at this stage of development (gestation day 12.5) consists of the epithelial ureteric bud surrounded by the mesenchymal cells of the metanephric blastema. Sections of such rudiments were assayed for the binding of the lectin Dolichos Bifloris (DB), specific for the ureteric bud, and antibodies directed against epithelial-specific intermediate filament proteins (cytokeratin) and vimentin, the only intermediate filament protein expressed by mesenchymal cells (Franke, 1982). Such studies demonstrate that the majority of cells comprising the ureteric bud are DB[+] epithelia (Table 1). However, cells of the ureteric bud at its terminal, branching tips exhibit a mesenchymal phenotype identical to cells of the metanephric blastema (Table 1). In addition, utilizing antibodies directed against collagen type IV, we observed basement membrane discontinuities at the terminal tips of the ureteric bud. These results suggested that ureteric bud epithelia may undergo an epithelial-to-mesenchymal transition and delaminte into the metanephric blastema.

To test this hypothesis, ureteric buds were isolated from gestation day 12.5 kidney rudiments. The purity of such preparations was assessed by electron microscopy. Isolated

Table 1. Immunostaining of ureteric bud cells

	Ureteric bud	Ureteric bud terminal tip	Metanephric blastema
Dolichos Bifloris (DB)	+	−	−
Cytokeratin	+	−	−
Vimentin	+/−	+	+

Gestation day 12.5 rat kidney rudiments were processed for cryosectioning as described by Herzlinger et al. (1982). Serial frozen sections (4 µm) were incubated with FITC-labeled Dolichos Bifloris (DB), an antibody directed against all cytokeratin isoforms, and antibodies directed against vimentin. The binding of such antibodies was visualized by FITC-labeled second antibody incubations. Most cells of the ureteric bud stained with the lectin, Dolichos Bifloris, and expressed the epithelial-specific cytoskeletal protein, cytokeratin. Many of such cells co-expressed vimentin with cytokeratin. Cells at the terminal tips of the ureteric bud but within the confines of its basement membrane were DB-negative and expressed only vimentin, exhibiting an identical phenotype to cells of the metanephric blastema.

Table 2. Immunostaining of developing ureteric bud epithelia

Days of culture (DiI+cells)	Phenotype		
	Ureteric bud	Mesenchyme	Renal epithelia
1	+	−	−
	Around tip of ub +		
3	+	+	−
5	+	+	+

Frozen sections of organ cultures established with DiI-labeled ureteric buds were prepared after 1, 3 and 5 days of culture (Herzlinger et al., 1982). DiI labeling was colocalized with the binding of FITC labeled ureteric-bud-specific lectin, Dolichos Bifloris, to identify ureteric bud. DiI labeling was also co-localized with the binding of antibodies directed against the following terminal differentiation antigens: glomerulus (the clearance atrial naturetic peptide receptor); proximal tubule epithelia (aminopeptidase N and maltase, provided by A. Quaroni), and distal tubule epithelia (Tamms-Horsfall protein). By 1 day of culture, the majority of DiI-labeled cells were defined as ureteric bud. Some DiI-labeled cells exhibited a mesenchymal morphology, and were clearly outside the confines of the ureteric bud basement membane. By 3 days of culture, a large proportion of DiI-labeled cells exhibited a mesenchymal morphology and were clearly intermixing with unlabeled metanephric mesenchyme. By 5 days of culture, DiI labeled-cells could be seen to express terminal differentiation antigens.

buds were labeled with DiI (Honig and Hume, 1989) and the fate of such tagged ureteric bud epithelia and their immediate progeny followed after culture in the presence of unlabeled metanephric blastema to facilitate renal differentiation (Fig. 1). Conversely, control cultures containing labeled metanephric blastema and unlabeled ureteric buds were established to determine the extent of DiI transfer by cell-cell contact. In such control cultures, no DiI-labeled ureteric bud epithelia were observed, demonstrating that the label can only be transferred in a heritable manner. Results from cultures established with DiI-labeled ureteric bud demonstrate that clusters of DiI-labeled cells integrate into the surrounding unlabeled metanephric blastema (Fig. 1). Such cell clusters were clearly separated from the branching portion of the ureteric bud. Thus, the ureteric bud undergoes delamination as well as branching morphogenesis during renal development. The phenotype of DiI-labeled

ureteric bud epithelia and their immediate progeny was followed over five days (Fig. 2, Table 2). Results of such analyses demonstrate that over time DiI-labeled cells formed metanephric blastema and ultimately differentiated into nephron epithelia.

The fate of ureteric bud epithelia was also assessed by retroviral-mediated gene transfer (Jaenisch and Soriano, 1986; Sanes, et al., 1986; Price et al., 1987; Herzlinger et al., 1992). Importantly, retroviral-mediated gene transfer is not dependent on the purity of ureteric bud preparations, since the progenies of a single viral-infected cell are exam-

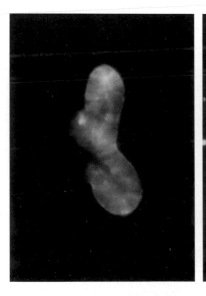
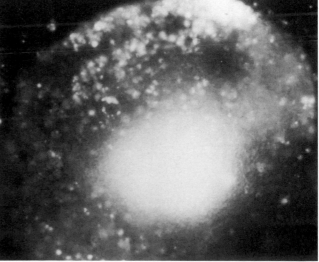

Fig. 1. DiI-labeled ureteric bud. (A) Ureteric buds were isolated from gestation 12.5-13 day rat kidney rudiments and labeled with DiI (Honig and Hume, 1989). Representative example of isolated bud after DiI-labeling before culture with unlabeled metanephric blastema. (B) Localization of DiI-labeled cells from labeled buds after three days of co-culture with unlabeled metanephric blastema. DiI-labeled cells have left the branching portion of the ureteric bud (out of focus, bright center) and have integrated into the unlabeled metanephric blastema.

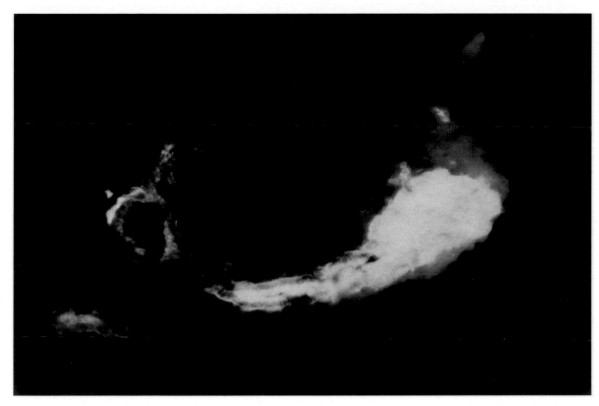

Fig. 2. Frozen section of DiI-labeled ureteric bud after three days of culture with unlabeled metanephric blastema assayed for Dolichos Bifloris binding. Frozen sections were prepared and processed for the binding of FITC-labeled ureteric bud-specific lectin, Dolichos Bifloris, as described. DiI-labeled cells were observed in the ureteric bud (yellow, due to DiI- and FITC-labeling) as well as in the metanephric blastema (red only). By three days of culture, the ureteric bud contains many DiI-negative cells.

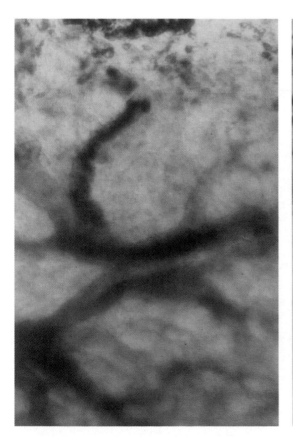

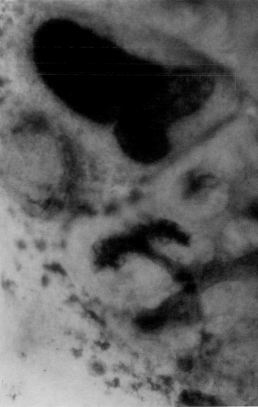

Fig. 3. Clonally derived retroviral tagged colonies present in organ cultures established with BAG-infected ureteric buds. Ureteric buds were isolated from gestation 12.5 day rat kidney rudiments and incubated with a limiting dilution of the BAG retrovirus as described by Herzlinger et al. (1992). Cultures containing single, β-gal-expressing colonies were processed for Dolichos Bifloris histochemistry utilizing peroxidase-labeled DB. (A) Micrograph of a colony containing β-gal-labeled cells restricted to the ureteric bud. (B) Colony exhibiting β-gal-labeled ureteric bud cells as well as β-gal-labeled cells in more proximal nephron segments (β-gal-positive, DB-negative).

Table 3. Differentiation of RSTEM-1 cells into diverse renal epithelial cell types

	Phenotype of RSTEM-1		
Days after trypsinization	Ureteric bud	Mesenchyme	Renal epithelia
3	–	+	–
14	–	–	+

RSTEM-1 cell cultures were trypsinized and new cultures initiated at a density of 3×10^5 cells/cm^2 on polycarbonate filters. Cultures were assayed at the given times and conditions for DB binding, the expression of cytoskeletal proteins vimentin and cytokeratin, and terminal differentiation antigens as described as Table 2. Ureteric bud epithelia were characterized as DB-positive and cytokeratin-positive. Mesenchyme was characterized by the exclusive expression of vimentin and the expression of the p75 nerve growth factor receptor. Renal epithelia were characterized by the expression of cytokeratin and terminal differentiation antigens.

ined. Isolated ureteric buds were infected with decreasing concentrations of the BAG retrovirus and cultured with uninfected metanephric blastema for seven days prior to fixation and visualization of β-galactosidase (β-gal) activity and Dolichos Bifloris binding. The dilution of retrovirus resulting in single β-gal-expressing colonies per sample was determined. Such samples, containing single clonally dervied colonies were serially sectioned and the phenotype of cells contained in clonal colonies determined. Importantly, DB is specific for the ureteric bud in these cultures. All clonal colonies examined exhibited DB$^+$ cells, demonstrating a ureteric bud derivation. Whole-mount analysis of such colonies demostrate that many clonal colonies contained β-gal-labeled cells in tubules classified as ureteric bud (DB$^+$), as well as more proximal segments of the nephron that were DB negative (Fig. 3). Serial sections of the latter colonies demonstrate that β-gal-positive cells were present on segments of forming nephrons, including the primitive glomeruli. These data corroborate the results obtained with DiI-labeling, that is, that the ureteric bud is a multipotent renal stem cell, that forms the metanephric blastema.

To examine a phenotypic conversion mediating nephrogenesis, we established a clonal, immortalized, renal mesenchymal cell line. Gestation 12.5 day rat kidney rudiments were infected with the ts58 retrovirus, which encodes for temperature-sensitive SV40 large T antigen and neomycin resistance (Frederikson et al., 1988). Such immortalized cell populations were selected by growth in the neomycin analogue, G418, and clonal cell lines prepared by three rounds of limiting dilution cloning.

One clonal cell line, designated RSTEM-1, fulfills the criteria expected of a multipotent renal progenitor cell. At the non-permissive temperature, large T antigen expression is turned off in RSTEM-1. RSTEM-1 cells integrate into the metanephric blastema of gestation day 12.5 rat kidney rudiments and form tubules after extended growth in co-culture. Additionally, after extended growth as monolayers without passage, on conventional tissue culture substrates, RSTEM-1 changes from a homogeneous population of mes-

enchymal cells to a population of epithelial cells that ultimately express terminal differentiation antigens characteristic of glomerular, proximal and distal tubule epithelia (Table 3) (Ekblom et al., 1981). These results demonstrate that RSTEM-1 has the potential to undergo mesenchymal to epithelial transitions leading to terminal differentiation in culture.

CONCLUSIONS

In conclusion, we demonstrate that nephrogeneis may be a process that can be divided into two phenotypic conversions. First, the ureteric bud delaminates, forming the mesenchymal nephron progenitors of the metanephric blastema and second, this blastema differentiates into the diverse epithelia of the nephron. The renal stem cell line (RSTEM-1) undergoes this latter transition in culture.

We thank C. Cepko and R. McKay for providing the retroviruses utilized for this study, and A. Quaroni for providing antibodies to the proximal tubule.

REFERENCES

Ekblom, P. (1981). Determination and differentiation of the nephron. *Med. Biol.* **59**, 139-160.

Ekblom, P., Miettinen, A., Virtnaen, I., Wahstrom, Y., Dawnay, A. and Saxen, L. (1981). In vitro segmentation of the metanephric nephron. *Dev. Biol.* **84**, 88-95.

Franke, W. W., Schmid, E., Schiller, P. L., Winter, S., Jarasch, E. C., Denk, H., Jackson, B. W. and Illmensee, K. (1982). Differentiation related patterns of expression of proteins of intermediate size filaments in tissues and in cultured cells. *Cold Spring Harb. Symp. Quant Biol.* **46**, 431-438.

Frederiksen, K., Jat, P. S., Valtx, N., Levy, D. and McKay, R. (1988). Immortalization of precursor cells from the mammalian CNS. *Neuron* **1**, 439-448.

Gilbert, S. F. (1991). *Developmental Biology*, 3rd edn. Sunderland, MA: Sinauer Assoc.

Grobstein, C. (1956). Transfilter induction of tubules in mouse metanephrogenic mesenchyme. *Exp. Cell Res.* **10**, 424-440.

Herzlinger, D., Koseki, C., Mikawa, T. and Al-Awqati, Q. (1992). Metanephric mesenchyme contains multipotent stem cells whose fate is restricted after induction. *Development* **114**, 565-572.

Herzlinger, D., Easton, T. and Ojakian, G. K. (1982). The MDCK epithelial cell line expresses a cell surface antigen of the kidney distal tubule. *J. Cell Biol.* **93**, 269-277.

Honig, M. G. and Hume, R. I. (1989). DiI and DiO: versatile dyes for neuronal labeling and pathway tracing. *Trends Neurosci.* **12**, 333-341.

Jaenisch, R. and Soriano, P. (1986). Retroviruses as tools for mammalian development. *Symp. Fundam. Cancer Res.* **39**, 59-65.

Price, J., Turner, D. and Cepko, C. (1987). Lineage analysis in the vertebrate nervous system by retrovius-mediated gene transfer. *Proc. Nat. Acad. Sci. USA* **84**, 156-160.

Rodriguez-Boulan, E. and Nelson, J. (1989). Morphogenesis of the polarized epithelial phenotype. *Science* **245**, 718-725.

Sanes, J. R., Rubenstein, J. L. R. and Nicolas, J. F. (1986). Use of recombinant retrovirus to study post-implantation cell lineage in mouse embryos. *EMBO J.* **5**, 3133-3142.

Saxen, L. (1987). *Organogenesis of the Kidney.* Cambridge: Cambridge University Press.

Journal of Cell Science, Supplement 17, 65-73 (1993)
Printed in Great Britain © The Company of Biologists Limited 1993

The cytoskeleton in development of epithelial cell polarity

Karl R. Fath, Salim N. Mamajiwalla and David R. Burgess

246 Crawford Hall, Department of Biological Sciences, University of Pittsburgh, Pittsburgh, PA 15260, USA

SUMMARY

The polarization of intestinal epithelial cells and the stereotypic arrangement of their actin-based cytoskeleton have made these epithelia an excellent system to explore the organization and formation of a cortical actin-based cytoskeleton. Through a combined morphological and biochemical analysis, the molecular arrangement of many of the components of the brush border has been elucidated. Study of brush border assembly in the Crypts of Lieberkühn suggests that cytoskeletal mRNA and protein expression, as well as morphological development, occur rapidly following cell differentiation. Protein kinases appear to be important regulators of intestinal cell growth, for differentiating cells in the crypts possess 15-fold higher levels of tyrosine phosphorylated proteins than differentiated cells of the villus. One of these kinases, pp60^{c-src}, has a 4- to 7-fold higher activity in crypts and increased association with the cytoskeleton than it has in villus cells.

The development and maintenance of polarization in epithelial cells require the targeting and transport of specific proteins to the apical and basolateral plasma membrane. It has been proposed that a dynein-like, microtubule-based motor is involved in the transport of apically directed materials from the *trans*-Golgi to the apical plasma membrane. However, microtubules do not reach the plasma membrane, but terminate below the actin-rich network of filaments comprising the terminal web. We propose that vesicles translocate from the Golgi to the apical cytoplasm along microtubules using dynein, and then move through the terminal web to reach the apical plasma membrane using the actin-based motor myosin-I. Our isolation of Golgi-derived vesicles possessing both myosin-I and dynein on their cytoplasmic surface is consistent with this hypothesis.

Key words: brush border, tyrosine kinases, myosin I

INTRODUCTION

In order to understand many cell processes, scientists often exploit model systems that exaggerate or simplify these processes. The simplicity and stereotypic arrangement of the brush border (BB) cytoskeleton have made the enterocyte an excellent model for analyzing the organization and development of an actin-based cytoskeleton (see reviews by Heintzelman and Mooseker, 1992; Mamajiwalla et al., 1992). In addition to an understanding of the architecture of the cortical cytoplasm, this polarized epithelium has been invaluable in dissecting the synthesis and transport of membranous proteins from their origins in the Golgi apparatus to their sites of utilization in the apical or basolateral plasma membrane. In this review we will first briefly describe the intestinal BB and then outline morphological and biochemical changes during its assembly in the adult intestine. We will then discuss the possible role of molecular motors in the transport and/or targeting of apically targeted plasma membrane constituents

INTESTINAL BRUSH BORDER MOLECULAR ARCHITECTURE

The cytoskeletal proteins and their arrangement in the

intestinal brush border (BB) cytoskeleton has been well characterized (Burgess, 1987; Mooseker, 1985). The mature BB is structurally divided into two parts, the microvilli and the terminal web (Fig. 1). Microvilli are approximately 1.5-2 µm long and 100 nm in diameter. A microvillus contains a core bundle of actin filaments extending from the tip of the microvillus to the base of the terminal web. The actin filaments are polarized with their plus or barbed (fast growing) ends at the microvillus tip and are crosslinked by the actin-bundling proteins fimbrin and villin. The other major actin-binding protein of the microvillus core is myosin I, first identified as the 110 kDa protein (Matsudaira and Burgess, 1979). Myosin I, coupled with calmodulin, forms a double spiral of cross bridges linking the actin bundle to the plasma membrane (Matsudaira and Burgess, 1982). A small amount of myosin I has also been localized to the basolateral membranes by immunofluorescence (Coudrier et al., 1981; Heintzelman and Mooseker, 1990). Although myosin I is a mechanochemical motor (see below), no movement of microvilli or their constituents has been observed. The core actin filaments extend out of the microvillus into the terminal web, where they terminate as rootlets. In addition to villin, fimbrin and myosin I, tropomyosin is also bound to the rootlet actin filaments.

Subjacent to the apical plasma membrane, and sur-

Enterocyte Brush Border

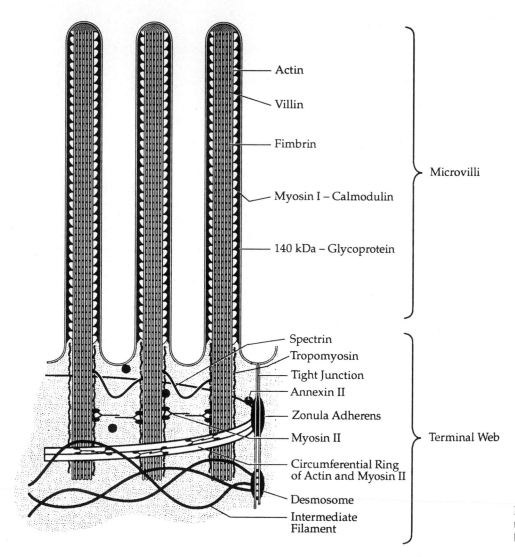

Actin

Villin

Fimbrin

Myosin I – Calmodulin

140 kDa – Glycoprotein

Microvilli

Spectrin
Tropomyosin
Tight Junction
Annexin II
Zonula Adherens
Myosin II
Circumferential Ring
of Actin and Myosin II
Desmosome
Intermediate
Filament

Terminal Web

Fig. 1. Molecular organization of the chicken intestinal brush border.

rounding the microvillar rootlets, is a complex anastomosing meshwork of filaments called the terminal web. The terminal web is a network of actin filaments that are crosslinked with myosin II, nonerythroid spectrins (fodrin and TW 260/240), α-actinin and tropomyosin. Immunolocalization and quick freeze, deep etch analyses localize BB spectrin and TW260/240 to the entire terminal web, and myosin II to the lower portion of the terminal web (Glenney and Glenney, 1983; Hirokawa et al., 1982, 1983; Hirokawa and Heuser, 1981). It is likely that the myosin is in the form of bipolar filaments that connect rootlet bundles and that the spectrin forms similar contacts in addition to attaching the actin to the plasma membrane.

The other major domain of actin cytoskeletal filaments in the BB is the zonula adherens circumferential ring that was first noted by Hull and Staehelin (1979). Subsequent analysis of this ring demonstrated the presence of both actin and myosin II and that this ring was tethered to the lateral

membranes at adherens junctions (Bretscher and Weber, 1978). This circumferential ring can be induced to constrict in vitro, much like a contractile ring (Burgess and Prum, 1982; Keller et al., 1985), probably modulating transepithelial resistance.

BRUSH BORDER ASSEMBLY IN INTESTINAL CRYPTS

Although much is known about the structure of the BB, little is known about its assembly. Early research on BB cytoskeleton formation focused on embryonic chickens, mice and rats (Chambers and Grey, 1979; Ezzell et al., 1989; Maunoury et al., 1988; Rochette and Haffen, 1987; Shibayama et al., 1987; Stidwill and Burgess, 1986; Takemura et al., 1988), with subsequent work utilizing cell lines (Dudouet et al., 1987; Peterson et al., 1992). Recently, attention has turned to understanding the development of the BB in adult tissues. In the adult, there is continual enterocyte differentiation as cells are born in the intestinal crypts and later assemble a BB as they migrate from the crypt onto the villus. This continuum of differentiation has been amenable to ultrastructural and immunocytochemical analysis of BB development (Fath et al., 1990; Heintzelman and Mooseker, 1990). Only a small subpopulation of cells in the basal crypt is structurally undifferentiated. These cells probably correspond to the crypt stem cells which give rise to absorptive columnar, goblet and entero-endocrine cells (Cheng and Leblond, 1974; Gordon, 1989; Potten and Morris, 1988). Initially, cells destined to become enterocytes have domed apical surfaces extending into the gut lumen. These cells express a few microvilli which arise from the center of the lumen, near the top of the dome. The microvilli are approximately 0.5 μm long and run at many angles relative to the cell surface. The microvillar rootlets are longer than the microvilli, and extend as much as 1 μm into the apical cytoplasm (Fath et al., 1990). As the enterocyte further develops, the number and length of the microvilli gradually increase and the rootlets shorten. The microvillus core actin filaments, although bundled in the early microvilli, become more regularly arrayed as the microvilli orient perpendicular to the cell surface. This increased order may reflect a change in the number or identity of the actin-binding and cross-linking elements. Because the total length of the core actin bundle (including the microvillus and rootlet) is approximately the same in the crypt and villus, we have proposed that the microvillus elongates by membrane addition at the microvillus base (Fath et al., 1990). Such addition would in effect lengthen the microvillus and shorten the rootlet. This proposal is consistent with our observations using the electron microscope (Fath et al., 1990).

The ability to isolate pure populations of intestinal crypts containing relatively immature enterocytes and pure intestinal villi containing fully formed enterocytes, made it possible to correlate morphological and biochemical changes during BB assembly (Table 1, and Fath et al., 1990). We wished to determine whether the formation and assembly of the BB cytoskeleton correlated with changes in the levels of mRNAs encoding the constituent cytoskeletal proteins. Using enterocytes isolated from crypts, villus middle or villus tip, we quantified relative RNA levels using northern and dot blot analysis with radiolabeled cDNA clones. Along the crypt-villus axis we detected 2- to 3-fold increases in the steady-state levels of villin, β-tropomyosin and calmodulin mRNAs, no change in the levels of spectrin and actin mRNAs, and a less statistically significant 3-fold decrease in myosin message. This constant level of actin mRNA expression is consistent with in situ hybridization studies in the mouse intestine that report a uniform density of actin mRNA along the crypt-villus axis (Cheng and Bjerknes, 1989). In contrast to the changes in mRNA levels, the corresponding levels of these cytoskeletal proteins did not change, as determined by ELISA analysis. These results are consistent with immunofluorescent images which show that all major actin cytoskeleton proteins are present at their full abundance and are concentrated in the apical enterocyte cytoplasm, even in cells with only a rudi-

Table 1. Changes in cytoskeletal proteins and RNA during brush border assembly

| | Relative abundance | | | | Immunofluorescent distribution | |
| | mRNA | | Protein | | | |
	Crypt	Villus	Crypt	Villus	Crypt	Villus
Actin	1	1	1	1	Luminal	Luminal
α-actinin	ND	ND	1	1	Luminal	Luminal
Myosin I	ND	ND	1	1	Diffuse	Luminal
Myosin II	1	0.3	1	1	Luminal	Luminal
Spectrin	1	1	1	1	Luminal	Luminal
Tropomyosin	1	2	1	1	Luminal	Luminal
Villin	1	3	1	1	Luminal	Luminal

ND, not determined.
From Fath et al. (1990).

mentary BB (Fath et al., 1990; Heintzelman and Mooseker, 1990). Although the cytoskeletal protein levels remain constant, the levels of luminal membrane enzymes such as oligosaccharidases, peptidases and alkaline phosphatase (Weiser et al., 1986) and the level of phosphotyrosine-containing proteins (Burgess et al., 1989) change dramatically as enterocytes migrate to the upper crypt and onto the villus. These changes, among others, have been noted in isolated villus cell fractions and confirm the validity of the cell isolation paradigm for quantitating changes in cytoskeletal protein expression during enterocyte differentiation.

In addition to transcriptional and translational regulation of cytoskeletal protein expression, BB formation may be regulated by the state of assembly of actin, a principal structural element of the BB. To discover whether increases in polymerized actin correlated with assembly of the BB, we measured G- and F-actin levels using the DNase-inhibition assay (Fath et al., 1990). We detected no significant increase in relative levels of total cellular polymerized actin in crypt, mid-villus and villus tip cells. The mean percentage of actin that was polymerized in the crypt, mid-villus and villus tip cells was 69, 68 and 73, respectively. The level in the tip is comparable to that in differentiated adult enterocytes (Stidwill and Burgess, 1986).

Since our results indicated that cytoskeletal proteins and F-actin levels do not change during differentiation, we have proposed that the expression of a minor component may regulate microvillus formation (Fath et al., 1990). This component may be integral to the bundling and stabilization of actin filaments in the microvillus core or it may be a membrane-associated protein which nucleates microvillus assembly. Low levels of this component would generate few microvilli, whereupon increased synthesis would permit the utilization of the abundant pool of cytoskeletal proteins to allow immediate, synchronous and abundant microvillar formation. Alternatively, some secondary message or signaling pathway may trigger assembly of the BB cytoskeleton and polarization of the epithelial cell.

ROLE OF KINASES IN INTESTINAL DEVELOPMENT

Development of the intestinal epithelium cannot be regulated solely by the cytoskeleton. Stem cell division in the crypts must be in steady state to ensure proper self-maintenance, otherwise the tissue will atrophy or hypertrophy. It is becoming increasingly clear that the generation of metaplastic and eventualy neoplastic epithelia most probably results from the loss of control over division of stem cells in the crypts. This control is due in part to extracellular and intracellular factors which exert their effects either from the luminal side and/or from the base of the cells. These factors might include growth factors such as epidermal growth factor (Baliga et al., 1990; Huang et al., 1991; Murthy et al., 1989), amphiregulin (Johnson et al., 1992), gastrin (Chicone et al., 1989; Majumdar, 1990), TGF-β (Kurokowa et al., 1987) and proto-oncogenes such as pp60$^{c\text{-}src}$ (Cartwright et al., 1989, 1990, 1993). Many of the growth factors exert their effects by binding to their respective receptors and subsequently activating the receptor's intrinsic or associated tyrosine kinase activity.

Protein tyrosine kinases appear to be important regulators of intestinal cell growth. Unlike the adult, in the embryonic intestine, mitotic cells are evenly distributed throughout the duodenal epithelium (Levine et al., 1990). During this period of rapid proliferation, the embryonic intestine contains high levels of tyrosine kinase activity (Maher, 1991; Maher and Pasquale, 1988) and the substrates of tyrosine kinases are concentrated at the epithelial cell membranes (Takata and Singer, 1988). In the adult chicken, mitotic cells are restricted to the crypts, and these cells possess 15-fold higher levels of tyrosine phosphorylated proteins than do the differentiated cells of the villus (Maunoury et al., 1988). In addition, most of the tyrosine kinase activity and the tyrosine phosphorylated proteins associate with the Triton-insoluble cytoskeleton. The nature of the tyrosine kinase substrates is currently unknown. It is also significant that high tyrosine kinase activity is found in human colon carcinoma (Sakanoue et al., 1991). These findings confirm that protein tyrosine phosphorylation plays a significant role in the development of the intestinal epithelium.

pp60$^{c\text{-}src}$, and it viral homologue pp60$^{v\text{-}src}$, are cytoplasmic, membrane-associated tyrosine kinases (Cooper, 1990; Bishop, 1991; Hunter, 1991; Cantley et al., 1991). There is a strong correlation between elevated pp60^{src} kinase activity and its association with the cytoskeleton. In transformed fibroblasts, for example, more than 70% of pp60$^{v\text{-}src}$ or mutants of pp60$^{c\text{-}src}$ with elevated tyrosine kinase activity, associate with the cytoskeleton (Loeb et al., 1987; Hamaguchi and Hanafusa, 1987). In contrast, in normal fibroblasts more than 70% of pp60$^{c\text{-}src}$ or kinase inactive mutants of pp60$^{v\text{-}src}$ are soluble. In human colon carcinomas, malignant adenomas or benign adenomas at greatest risk for developing cancer, pp60$^{c\text{-}src}$ has significantly higher protein tyrosine kinase activity than the adjacent normal colonic epithelia (Cartwright et al., 1989, 1990). We have recently found a similar situation in the cells of the crypts of the small intestine (Cartwright et al., 1993). We observed that pp60$^{c\text{-}src}$ activity in crypt cytoskeletons is higher (on average, 4-fold as measured by enolase phosphorylation, or 7-fold as measured by autophosphorylation) than pp60$^{c\text{-}src}$ activity in differentiated villus tip cytoskeletons (Table 2). Moreover, crypt cytoskeletal-associated pp60$^{c\text{-}src}$, unlike that of differentiated enterocytes, appears to have higher specific activity than does soluble pp60$^{c\text{-}src}$ (Table 3). Inter-

Table 2. Relative levels of pp60$^{c\text{-}src}$ protein and in vitro tyrosine kinase activity in cells along the crypt-villus axis of chicken duodena

Cell fraction	Cell type	pp60$^{c\text{-}src}$ protein levels	Enolase phosphorylation	pp60$^{c\text{-}src}$ phosphorylation
Cytoskeleton	villus, tip	1.0	1.0	1.0
	villus, base	1.6±0.2	2.8±0.4	4.2±1.0
	crypt	1.9±0.4	4.2±0.5	6.9±1.3
Whole cell	villus, tip	1.0	1.0	1.0
	villus, base	1.2±0.1	1.2±0.2	1.3±0.4
	crypt	1.0±0.1	0.8±0.2	1.0±0.2

Values for crypt and villus base cells are expressed relative to those for villus tip cells, and each represents the mean ± s.e.m. for 13 independent cytoskeletal preparations (26 chickens) and 7 whole cell preparations (14 chickens).
From Cartwright et al. (1993).

Table 3. Fraction of total cellular pp60$^{c\text{-}src}$ protein and kinase activity that is associated with the cytoskeleton

Cell type	pp60$^{c\text{-}src}$	Enolase phosphorylation	pp60$^{c\text{-}src}$ phosphorylation
Villus, tip	0.21±0.06	0.17±0.03	0.11±0.01
Villus, base	0.24±0.07	0.33±0.05	0.18±0.06
Crypt	0.27±0.10	0.66±0.04	0.53±0.09

Values are expressed as a ratio of cytoskeleton to whole cell ^{32}P incorporation and represent the mean ± s.e.m. for 7 preparations (14 chickens).
From Cartwright et al. (1993).

estingly, the subcellular localization of pp60$^{c\text{-}src}$ in crypts is also similar to that described above for transformed fibroblasts. These results clearly implicate an important role for pp60$^{c\text{-}src}$ in the normal development and differentiation of the intestinal epithelium. Of course it would be naive to suppose that pp60$^{c\text{-}src}$ is the only tyrosine kinase responsible for the high level of tyrosine phosphorylation observed in these cells. Clearly, other tyrosine kinases, both cytoplasmic and growth factor-associated, must also be involved. We are currently attempting to identify novel tyrosine kinases in the cells of the crypt by molecular cloning techniques. pp60$^{c\text{-}src}$ can serve in some cases as an upstream activator of mitogen activated protein (MAP) kinases (Wang and Erikson, 1992; Gupta et al., 1992). MAP kinases have been the focus of recent research involving signal transduction pathways (Thomas, 1992; Sturgill and Wu, 1991; Crews et al., 1992; Pelech and Sanghera, 1992), as they are thought to play important roles in relaying signals from the cell surface to the nucleus. At present, we are investigating the possible role of MAP kinases during differentiation of the intestinal epithelium.

What role pp60$^{c\text{-}src}$ might have, if any, in the assembly of the brush border is not known. Recent experiments have suggested a possible role for pp60$^{c\text{-}src}$ in both endocytosis and exocytosis (Linstedt et al., 1992; Kaplan et al., 1992). It has been suggested (Linstedt et al., 1992) that tyrosine kinase activity, such as by pp60$^{c\text{-}src}$, may trigger disassembly of the cortical cytoskeleton allowing exocytosis

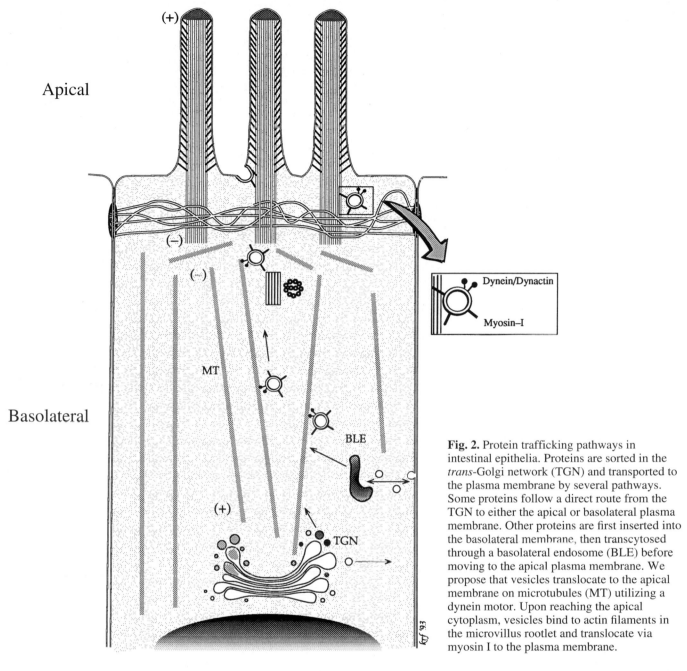

Fig. 2. Protein trafficking pathways in intestinal epithelia. Proteins are sorted in the *trans*-Golgi network (TGN) and transported to the plasma membrane by several pathways. Some proteins follow a direct route from the TGN to either the apical or basolateral plasma membrane. Other proteins are first inserted into the basolateral membrane, then transcytosed through a basolateral endosome (BLE) before moving to the apical plasma membrane. We propose that vesicles translocate to the apical membrane on microtubules (MT) utilizing a dynein motor. Upon reaching the apical cytoplasm, vesicles bind to actin filaments in the microvillus rootlet and translocate via myosin I to the plasma membrane.

and/or endocytosis. Perhaps the dramatic increase in microvillar height during differentiation results from the increased addition of membrane due to the high tyrosine kinase activity in maturing crypt cells (Burgess et al., 1989).

TRANSPORT AND TARGETING OF PLASMA MEMBRANE CONSTITUENTS

Not only is the enterocyte apical cortical actin cytoskeleton different from other regions of the cell, as with other polarized epithelia, but the apical plasma membrane is also specialized. The plasma membrane in polarized epithelia is differentiated into two functionally and structurally distinct domains, the apical or BB and the basolateral membranes (Fig. 2). These domains are separated by a circumferential band of tight junctions and actin filaments near the cell apex. Many of the proteins and phospholipid constituents of these membranes are unique for each domain (for a review, see Hubbard et al., 1989). The mechanisms of sorting and pathways by which constituents reach the apical or basolateral plasma membranes vary between types of polarized epithelial cells; (see *Seminars in Cell Biology*, vol. **2**, 1992, for a collection of papers reviewing epithelial cell protein trafficking). In intestinal epithelia, sorting of many newly synthesized proteins targeted for the apical and basolateral compartments is thought to occur in the *trans*-Golgi (Danielsen and Cowell, 1985; Griffiths and Simons, 1986). Once sorted, proteins destined for each domain apparently translocate to the plasma membrane by different mechanisms. Transport of apically directed materials appears to rely at some stage on microtubules (MTs; see below), while that of materials destined for the basolateral membrane occurs in the apparent absence of MTs (Achler et al., 1989; Rindler et al., 1987).

Pharmacological studies suggest that although not absolutely required, the efficient transport of apically directed membranes in polarized epithelia requires intact MTs (Achler et al., 1989; Bennett et al., 1984; Breitfeld et al., 1990; Hugon et al., 1987; Parczyk et al., 1989). When polarized epithelia are treated with MT-disruptive drugs, there is a decrease in delivery of materials to the apical plasma membrane, although nearly 50% of the materials still reach the apical domain. The remaining materials are missorted to the basolateral domain. The decreased apical transport is probably not simply the result of the disorganization of the Golgi, which has been shown to interact with MTs in cultured astrocytes (Cooper et al., 1990), as the packaging and transport of materials to basolateral membranes continues unabated. Because isolated, Golgi-derived vesicles can bind to MTs in vitro (Coffe and Raymond, 1990; van der Sluijs et al., 1990), and MT binding proteins have been localized to the Golgi apparatus (Bloom and Brashear, 1989), MTs may play some direct role in the translocation of vesicles in vivo. Support for such a role comes from studies showing that the fusion of apically and basolaterally derived endosomes isolated from MDCK (a polarized epithelial cell line; Madin-Darby canine kidney) cells requires MTs, and the motor proteins dynein and kinesin (Bomsel et al., 1990).

The MTs in polarized epithelia are arranged with their minus ends (their slowest growing ends) in the apical cytoplasm (Achler et al., 1989; Drenckhahn and Dermietzel, 1988; Sandoz et al., 1985). The MTs extend in bundles to the basal cytoplasm with their plus ends (or most rapidly growing ends) near the cell base (Fig. 2). There is also a collection of MTs running transversely in the apical cytoplasm, below the cortical actin network in MDCK cells (Bacallao et al., 1989) or the terminal web in enterocytes (Sandoz et al., 1985). Although centrioles in polarized epithelia are located subjacent to the cortical actin cytoskeleton where bundles of MTs terminate, there is no apparent association with the ends of MTs, nor is there pericentriolar material (Bacallao et al., 1989; Drenckhahn and Dermietzel, 1988; Sandoz et al., 1985). Because the plus ends of the MTs are nearest the Golgi complex, a MT-based system for translocating membranes from the Golgi complex to the apical cortex would probably require a minus-end-directed motor, such as dynein.

The decreased, but not eliminated, delivery of membrane to the apical plasma membrane in the presence of microtubule-disruptive drugs suggests that either some stable MTs remain intact, or that MTs are only necessary to provide directionality while an alternative transport system is utilized. Since the average pore size of cytoplasm is smaller than vesicles (Luby-Phelps et al., 1987), passive diffusion alone probably cannot account for movement of vesicles from the trans-Golgi to the apical plasma membrane; some active mechanism is required. Furthermore, enterocyte MTs do not extend to the apical surface, but terminate below, or rarely, within the actin-rich BB terminal web (Sandoz et al., 1985). Because the highly cross-linked actin-rich terminal web appears to exclude organelles from the apical

membrane, it is unlikely that vesicles can simply diffuse from the ends of MTs through the terminal web to reach the plasma membrane (Achler et al., 1989; Sandoz et al., 1985). Another motor, perhaps attached to the same vesicle translocated first along MTs, may be required to move vesicles through the actin-rich terminal web to reach the plasma membrane (Fig. 2). It has been proposed that perhaps an actin-based motor such as myosin I, is required to move vesicles through this meshwork to the membrane (Achler et al., 1989; Fath and Burgess, 1993; Sandoz et al., 1985). Because the disruption of microfilaments by cytochalasin D has no apparent affect on the efficiency of delivery or targeting of vesicles to the apical plasma membrane (Parczyk et al., 1989; Rindler et al., 1987), it has been suggested that actin filaments have no role in apical vesicle trafficking. However, these studies must be interpreted with caution since not all microfilaments are depolymerized by cytochalasin (Burgess and Grey, 1974; Gottlieb et al., 1993; Parczyk et al., 1989).

A good candidate for a motor functioning in the cell cortex is the actin-based motor, myosin I. The myosin Is are a class of actin-activated mechanochemical motors directed toward the barbed, or faster growing ends of actin filaments (Cheney and Mooseker, 1992; Pollard et al., 1991). Myosin I has been identified in many cell types and is probably associated with both intracellular and plasma membranes (Adams and Pollard, 1986; Baines and Korn, 1990; Hayden et al., 1990; Korn and Hammer, 1988; Miyata et al., 1989). The members of the myosin I family all contain a conserved head domain with an ATP-sensitive actin binding site that is similar to myosin II, or conventional myosin. Myosin Is from different species, and different isoforms from the same species, contain a variable tail domain that may contain a positively charged membrane-binding domain and/or another actin binding site (see reviews by Cheney and Mooseker, 1992; Pollard et al., 1991). Because purified myosin I can bind to vesicles comprising isolated membranes (Adams and Pollard, 1986; Doberstein and Pollard, 1992), and can move actin filaments on planar phospholipid substrates (Zot et al., 1992), it is proposed to be a motor for intracellular vesicle movement.

Based largely on conjecture developed from its in vitro properties, it has been proposed that myosin I in the intestinal epithelium moves membranous vesicles transporting proteins and lipids from the Golgi to their sites of incorporation into the apical plasma membrane (Collins et al., 1990; Conzelman and Mooseker, 1987; Fath et al., 1990; Shibayama et al., 1987). Immunolocalization of myosin I on vesicles in the apical cytoplasm of mature chicken and human enterocytes (Drenckhahn and Dermietzel, 1988) is consistent with a membrane translocation role. We decided to test directly whether myosin I was potentially involved in moving carrier vesicles from the Golgi to the apical plasma membrane. We purified Golgi-enriched vesicles from isolated intestinal epithelial cells, and found that a population of vesicles possesses myosin I as a cytoplasmically oriented, peripheral membrane protein (Fath and Burgess, 1993). Myosin I resides on the vesicle cytoplasmic surface, since intact vesicles could be immunolabeled with myosin I antibodies and the myosin I could be proteolyzed by exogenous proteases. Galactosyltransferase, a marker enzyme for the *trans*-Golgi complex, co-partitioned with intact vesicles that had been immunoisolated with myosin I antibodies. Such co-isolation suggests that at least a subpopulation of *trans*-Golgi-derived vesicles express myosin I on their surface. The apically targeted enzyme alkaline phosphatase was also present in these fractions. Because these vesicles could aggregate actin filaments in an ATP-dependent manner, we proposed that these vesicles could represent a population of Golgi-derived vesicles carrying apically directed lipid and protein (Fath and Burgess, 1993).

Although we identified Golgi-derived vesicles with associated myosin I, and previous immunomicroscopy identified vesicles in the enterocyte apical cytoplasm with associated myosin I on their surface (Drenckhahn and Dermietzel, 1988), clearly a myosin-I-mediated motility from the Golgi apparatus to the apical plasma membrane cannot account for the entire pathway, for several reasons. First, there are no large actin filament tracks leading from the Golgi to the cell apex on which myosin-I-coated vesicles could translocate. Second, the general consensus is that MTs are required at some step in the transport of membranes to the apical plasma membrane. To determine whether apically-targeted vesicles utilize both a microtubule- and microfilament-based motility, we have begun looking for vesicles expressing several motors. In preliminary studies from our laboratory, we found that in addition to myosin I, cytoplasmic dynein and its activator dynactin are also associated with the Golgi vesicles isolated from chicken enterocytes, while kinesin was absent. These Golgi vesicles could bind MTs in an ATP-dependent manner in pelleting assays. Because myosin I also pelleted with vesicles bound to MTs, we propose that some vesicles contain both myosin I and dynein on their surfaces (Fig. 2). Our finding of two motors on one vesicle is consistent with immunocytochemical evidence that both kinesin and dynein are found on anterogradely transported vesicles in mouse axons (Hirokawa et al., 1990). In the past several years it has become well accepted that members of the kinesin and dynein families are responsible for the transportation of vesicles along MT substrates in many cells (Bloom, 1992; Schroer and Sheetz, 1991). Other work has suggested that motors using actin filament substrates can also move membranes within cells (Adams and Pollard, 1986; Kachar, 1985). Quite surprisingly, recent studies in *S. cerevisiae* (Johnston et al., 1991; Lillie and Brown, 1992) and squid axoplasm (Kuznetsov et al., 1992) have concluded that there may be a functional redundancy in motor mechanisms such that a single vesicle may translocate by either an actin-based or a MT-based motor (reviewed by Atkinson et al., 1992). Individual organelles may posses both types of motors which may be activated or differentially regulated in different cell regions. Only further work will determine the roles and regulation of multiple cytoskeletal motors in sorting and trafficking of Golgi vesicles.

This work was supported by NIH grant no. DK31643.

REFERENCES

Achler, C., Filmer, D., Merte, C. and Drenckhahn, D. (1989). Role of microtubules in polarized delivery of apical membrane proteins to the brush border of the intestinal epithelium. *J. Cell Biol.* **109**, 179-189.

Adams, R. J. and Pollard, T. D. (1986). Propulsion of organelles isolated from *Acanthamoeba* along actin filaments by myosin I. *Nature* **322**, 754-756.

Atkinson, S. J., Doberstein, S. K. and Pollard, T. D. (1992). Moving off the beaten track. *Curr. Biol.* **2**, 326-328.

Bacallao, R., Antony, C., Dotti, C., Karsenti, E., Stelzer, E. H. K. and Simons, K. (1989). The subcellular organization of Madin-Darby Canine Kidney cells during the formation of a polarized epithelium. *J. Cell Biol.* **109**, 2817-2832.

Baines, I. C. and Korn, E. D. (1990). Localization of myosin IC and myosin II in *Acanthamoeba castellanii* by indirect immunofluorescence and immunogold electron microscopy. *J. Cell Biol.* **111**, 1895-1904.

Baliga, B. S., Borowitz, S. M. and Barnard, J. A. (1990). Modulation of EGF-receptors by phorbol ester in small intestinal crypt cells. *Biochem. Internat.* **20**, 161-168.

Bennett, G., Carlet, E., Wild, G. and Parsons, S. (1984). Influence of colchicine and vinblastine on the intracellular migration of secretory and membrane glycoproteins. III. Inhibition of intracellular migration of membrane glycoproteins in rat intestinal columnar cells and hepatocytes as visualized by light and electron-microscope radioautography after ^{3}H-fucose injection. *Amer. J. Anat.* **170**, 545-566.

Bishop, J. M. (1991). Molecular themes in oncogenesis. *Cell* **64**, 235-248.

Bloom, G. S. (1992). Motor proteins for cytoplasmic microtubules. *Curr. Opin. Cell Biol.* **4**, 66-73.

Bloom, G. S. and Brashear, T. A. (1989). A novel 58 kDa protein associates with the Golgi apparatus and microtubules. *J. Biol. Chem.* **264**, 16083-16092.

Bomsel, M., Parton, R., Kuznetsov, S. A., Schroer, T. A. and Gruenberg, J. (1990). Microtubule- and motor-dependent fusion in vitro between apical and basolateral endocytic vesicles from MDCK cells. *Cell* **62**, 719-731.

Breitfeld, P. P., McKinnon, W. C. and Mostov, K. E. (1990). Effect of nocadazole on vesicular traffic to the apical and basolateral surfaces of polarized MDCK cells. *J. Cell Biol.* **111**, 2365-2373.

Bretscher, A. and Weber, K. (1978). Localization of actin microfilament associated proteins in the microvilli and terminal web of the intestinal brush border by immunofluorescent microscopy. *J. Cell Biol.* **79**, 839-845.

Burgess, D. R. (1987). The brush border: a model for structure, biochemistry, motility, and assembly of the cytoskeleton. In *Advances in Cell Biology*, vol. 1 (ed. K. R. Miller), pp. 31-58. JAI Press Inc., Greenwich, Conn.

Burgess, D. R. and Prum, B. E. (1982). A re-evaluation of brush border motility. Calcium induces core filament solution and microvillar vesiculation. *J. Cell Biol.* **94**, 97-107.

Burgess, D. R., Jiang, W., Mamajiwalla, S. and Kinsey, W. (1989). Intestinal crypt stem cells possess high levels of cytoskeletal-associated phosphotyrosine-containing proteins and tyrosine kinase activity relative to differentiated enterocytes. *J. Cell Biol.* **109**, 2139-2144.

Burgess, D. R. and Grey, R. D. (1974). Alterations in morphology of developing microvilli elicited by cytochalasin B. *J. Cell Biol.* **62**, 566-574.

Cantley, L. C., Auger, K. R., Carpenter, C., Duckworth, B., Graziani, A., Kapeller, R. and Soltoff, S. (1991). Oncogenes and signal transduction. *Cell* **64**, 281-302.

Cartwright, C. A., Meisler, A. I. and Eckhart W. (1990). Activation of the pp60[c-src] protein kinase is an early event in colonic carcinogenesis. *Proc. Nat. Acad. Sci. USA* **87**, 558-562.

Cartwright, C. A., Kamps, M. P., Meisler, A. I., Pipas, J. M. and Eckhart, W. (1989). pp60[c-src] activation in human colon carcinoma. *J. Clin. Invest.* **83**, 2025-2033.

Cartwright, C. A., Mamajiwalla, S., Skolnick, S. A., Eckhart, W. and Burgess, D. R. (1993). Intestinal crypt cells contain higher levels of cytoskeletal-associated pp60[c-src] protein-tyrosine kinase activity than do differentiated enterocytes. *Oncogene* (in press).

Chambers, C. and Grey, R. D. (1979). Development of the structural components of the brush border in the absorptive cells of the chick intestine. *Cell Tiss. Res.* **204**, 387-405.

Cheney, R. E. and Mooseker, M. S. (1992). Unconventional myosins. *Curr. Opin. Cell Biol.* **4**, 27-35.

Cheng, H. and Leblond, C. P. (1974). Origin, differentiation and renewal of the four main epithelial types in the mouse small intestine. *Amer. J. Anat.* **141**, 537-562.

Cheng, H. and Bjerknes, M. (1989). Asymmetric distribution of actin mRNA and cytoskeletal pattern generation in polarized epithelial cells. *J. Mol. Biol.* **210**, 541-549.

Chicone, L., Narayan, S., Townsend, C. J. and Singh, P. (1989). The presence of a 33-40 kDa gastrin binding protein on human and mouse colon cancer. *Biochem. Biophys. Res. Commun.* **164**, 512-519.

Coffe, G. and Raymond, M.-N. (1990). Association between microtubules and Golgi vesicles isolated from rat parotid glands. *Biol. Cell.* **70**, 143-152.

Collins, K., Sellers, J. R. and Matsudaira, P. (1990). Calmodulin dissociation regulates brush border myosin I (110-kDa-calmodulin) mechanochemical activity in vitro. *J. Cell Biol.* **110**, 1137-1147.

Conzelman, K. A. and Mooseker, M. S. (1987). The 110-kDa protein-calmodulin complex of the intestinal microvillus is an actin-activated MgATPase. *J. Cell Biol.* **105**, 313-324.

Cooper, J. A. (1990). Oncogenes and anti-oncogenes. *Curr. Opin. Cell Biol.* **2**, 285-295.

Cooper, M. S., Cornell-Bell, A. H., Chernjavsky, A., Dani, J. W. and Smith, S. J. (1990). Tubulovesicular processes emerge from *trans*-Golgi cisternae, extend along microtubules, and interlink adjacent *trans*-Golgi elements into a reticulum. *Cell* **61**, 135-145.

Coudrier, E., Reggio, H. and Louvard, D. (1981). Immunolocation of the 110, 000 molecular weight cytoskeletal protein of intestinal microvilli. *J. Mol. Biol.* **152**, 49-66.

Crews, C. M., Alessandrini, A. and Erikson, R. L. (1992). Erks: their fifteen minutes have arrived. *Cell Growth Differ.* **3**, 135-142.

Danielsen, M. and Cowell, G. M. (1985). Biosynthesis of intestinal microvillar proteins: evidence for an intracellular sorting taking place in, or shortly after, exit from the Golgi complex. *Eur. J. Biochem.* **152**, 493-499.

Doberstein, S. K. and Pollard, T. D. (1992). Localization and specificity of the phospholipid and actin binding sites on the tail of *Acanthamoeba* myosin IC. *J. Cell Biol.* **117**, 1241-1249.

Drenckhahn, D. and Dermietzel, R. (1988). Organization of the actin filament cytoskeleton in the intestinal brush border: a quantitative and qualitative immunoelectron microscope study. *J. Cell Biol.* **107**, 1037-1048.

Dudouet, B., Robine, S., Huet, C., Sahuquillo, M. C., Blair, L., Coudrier, E. and Louvard, D. (1987). Changes in villin synthesis and subcellular distribution during intestinal differentiation of HT29-19 cells. *J. Cell Biol.* **105**, 359-369.

Ezzell, R. M., Chafel, M. M. and Matsudaira, P. T. (1989). Differential localization of villin and fimbrin during development of the mouse visceral endoderm and intestinal epithelium. *Development* **106**, 407-419.

Fath, K. R. and Burgess, D. R. (1993). Golgi-derived vesicles from developing epithelial cells bind actin filaments and possess myosin I as a cytoplasmically oriented peripheral membrane protein. *J. Cell Biol.* **120**, 117-127.

Fath, K. R., Obenauf, S. D. and Burgess, D. R. (1990). Cytoskeletal protein and mRNA accumulation during brush border formation in adult chicken enterocytes. *Development* **109**, 449-459.

Glenney, J. R. and Glenney, P. (1983). Spectrin, fodrin, and TW 260/240: a family of related proteins lining the plasma membrane. *Cell Motil.* **3**, 671-682.

Gordon, J. I. (1989). Intestinal epithelial differentiation: new insights from chimeric and transgenic mice. *J. Cell Biol.* **108**, 1187-1194.

Gottlieb, T. A., Ivanov, I. E., Adesnik, M. and Sabatini, D. D. (1993). Actin microfilaments play a critical role in endocytosis at the apical but not the basolateral surface of polarized epithelial cells. *J. Cell Biol.* **120**, 695-710.

Griffiths, G. and Simons, K. (1986). The *trans* Golgi network: sorting at the exit site of the Golgi complex. *Science* **234**, 438-443.

Gupta, S. K., Gallego, C., Johnson, G. L. and Heasley, L. E. (1992). MAP kinase is constitutively activated in *gip2* and *src* transformed Rat 1a fibroblasts. *J. Biol. Chem.* **267**, 7987-7990.

Hamaguchi, M. and Hanafusa, H. (1987). Association of p60^{src} with Triton X-100-resistant cellular structure correlates with morphological transformation. *Proc. Nat. Acad. Sci. USA* **84**, 2312-2316.

Hayden, S. M., Wolenski, J. S. and Mooseker, M. S. (1990). Binding of brush border myosin I to phospholipid vesicles. *J. Cell Biol.* **111**, 443-451.

Heintzelman, M. B. and Mooseker, M. S. (1990). Assembly of the brush border cytoskeleton: changes in the distribution of microvillar core proteins during enterocyte differentiation in adult chicken intestine. *Cell Motil. Cytoskel.* **15**, 12-22.

Heintzelman, M. B. and Mooseker, M. S. (1992). Assembly of the intestinal brush border cytoskeleton. *Curr. Topics Dev. Biol.* **26**, 93-122

Hirokawa, N. and Heuser, J. E. (1981). Quick-freeze, deep-etch visualization of the cytoskeleton beneath surface differentiations of intestinal epithelial cells. *J. Cell Biol.* **91**, 399-409.

Hirokawa, N., Tilney, L. G., Fujiwara, K. and Heuser, J. E. (1982). The organization of actin, myosin, and intermediate filaments in the brush border of intestinal epithelial cells. *J. Cell Biol.* **94**, 425-443.

Hirokawa, N., Cheney, R. E. and Willard, M. (1983). Location of a protein of the fodrin-spectrin-TW 260/240 family in the mouse intestinal brush border. *Cell* **32**, 953-965.

Hirokawa, N., Sato-Yoshitake, R., Yoshida, T. and Kawashima, T. (1990). Brain dynein (MAP1C) localizes on both anterogradely and retrogradely transported membranous organelles in vivo. *J. Cell Biol.* **111**, 1027-1037.

Huang, S., Lin, P. F., Fan, D., Price, J. E., Trujillo, J. M. and Chakrabarty, S. (1991). Growth modulation by epidermal growth factor (EGF) in human colonic carcinoma cells: constitutive expression of the human EGF gene. *J. Cell Physiol.* **148**, 220-227.

Hubbard, A. L., Stieger, B. and Bartles, J. R. (1989). Biogenesis of endogenous plasma membrane proteins in epithelial cells. *Annu. Rev. Physiol.* **51**, 755-770.

Hugon, J. S., Bennett, G., Pothier, P. and Ngoma, Z. (1987). Loss of microtubules and alteration of glycoprotein migration in organ cultures of mouse intestine exposed to nocadazole or colchicine. *Cell Tiss. Res.* **248**, 653-662.

Hull, B. E. and Staehelin, L. A. (1979). The terminal web. A re-evaluation of its structure and function. *J. Cell Biol.* **81**, 67-82.

Hunter, T. (1991). Cooperation between oncogenes. *Cell* **64**, 249-270.

Johnson, G. R., Saeki, T., Gordon, A. W., Shoyab, M., Salomon, D. S. and Stromberg, K. (1992). Autocrine action of amphiregulin in a colon carcinoma cell line and immunocytochemical localization of amphiregulin in human colon. *J. Cell Biol.* **118**, 741-751.

Johnston, G. C., Prendergast, J. A. and Singer, R. A. (1991). The *Saccharomyces cerevisiae* MYO2 gene encodes an essential myosin for vectorial transport of vesicles. *J. Cell Biol.* **113**, 539-551.

Kachar, B. (1985). Direct visualization of organelle movement along actin filaments dissociated from Characean algae. *Science* **227**, 1355-1357.

Kaplan, K. B., Swedlow, J. R., Varmus, H. E. and Morgan, D. O. (1992). Association of p60^{c-src} with endosomal membranes in mammalian fibroblasts. *J. Cell Biol.* **118**, 321-333.

Keller, T., Conzelman, K. A., Chasan, R. and Mooseker, M. S. (1985). The role of myosin in terminal web contraction in isolated intestinal epithelial brush borders. *J. Cell Biol.* **100**, 1647-1655.

Korn, E. D. and Hammer, J. A. I. (1988). Myosins of nonmuscle cells. *Annu. Rev. Biophys. Biophys. Chem.* **17**, 23-45.

Kurokowa, M., Lynch, K. and Podolsky, D. K. (1987). Effects of growth factors on an intestinal epithelial cell line: transforming growth factor β inhibits proliferation and stimulates differentiation. *Biochem. Biophys. Res. Commun.* **142**, 775-782.

Kuznetsov, S. A., Langford, G. M. and Weiss, D. G. (1992). Actin-dependent organelle movement in squid axoplasm. *Nature* **356**, 722-725.

Levine, B. A., Moir, A., Patchell, V. B. and Perry, S. V. (1990). The interaction of actin with dystrophin. *FEBS Lett.* **263**, 159-162.

Lillie, S. H. and Brown, S. S. (1992). Suppression of a myosin defect by a kinesin-related gene. *Nature* **356**, 358-361.

Linstedt, A. D., Vetter, M. L., Bishop, J. M. and Kelly, R. B. (1992). Specific association of proto-oncogene product pp60^{c-src} with an intracellular organelle, the PC12 synaptic vesicle. *J. Cell Biol.* **117**, 1077-1084.

Loeb, D. M., Woolford, J. and Beemon, K. (1987). pp60^{c-src} has less affinity for the detergent-insoluble cellular matrix than do pp60^{v-src} and other viral protein-tyrosine kinases. *J. Virol.* **61**, 2420-2427.

Luby-Phelps, K., Castle, P. E., Taylor, L. and Lanni, F. (1987). Hindered diffusion of inert tracer particles in the cytoplasm of mouse 3T3 cells. *Proc. Nat. Acad Sci. USA* **84**, 4910-4913.

Maher, P. A. (1991). Tissue-dependent regulation of protein tyrosine kinase activity during embryonic development. *J. Cell Biol.* **112**, 955-963.

Maher, P. A. and Pasquale, E. B. (1988). Tyrosine phosphorylated proteins in different tissues during chick embryo development. *J. Cell Biol.* **106**, 1747-1755.

Majumdar, A. (1990). Role of tyrosine kinases in gastrin induction of ornithine decarboxylase in colonic mucosa. *Amer. J. Physiol. Gastrointest. Liver Physiol.* **259**, G626-G630.

Mamajiwalla, S. N., Fath, K. R. and Burgess, D. R. (1992). Development of the chicken intestinal epithelium. In *Current Topics in Developmental Biology*, vol. 26 (ed. E. L. Bearer), pp. 123-143. Academic Press, Inc., San Diego, CA.

Matsudaira, P. T. and Burgess, D. R. (1979). Identification and organization of the components in the isolated microvillus cytoskeleton. *J. Cell Biol.* **83**, 667-673.

Matsudaira, P. T. and Burgess, D. R. (1982). Organization of the cross-filaments in intestinal microvilli. *J. Cell Biol.* **92**, 657-664.

Maunoury, R., Robine, S., Pringault, E., Huet, C., Guénet, J. L., Gaillard, J. A. and Louvard, D. (1988). Villin expression in the visceral endoderm and in the gut anlage during early mouse embryogenesis. *EMBO J.* **7**, 3321-3329.

Miyata, H., Bowers, B. and Korn, E. D. (1989). Plasma membrane association of *Acanthamoeba* myosin I. *J. Cell Biol.* **109**, 1519-1528.

Mooseker, M. S. (1985). Organization, chemistry and assembly of the cytoskeletal apparatus of the intestinal brush border. *Annu. Rev. Cell. Biol.* **1**, 209-241.

Murthy, U., Anzano, M. A. and Greig, R. G. (1989). Expression of TGF-α/EGF and TGF-β receptors in human colon carcinoma cell lines. *Internat. J. Cancer* **44**, 110-115.

Overton, J. and Shoup, J. (1964). Fine structure of cell surface specializations in the maturing duodenal mucosa of the chick. *J. Cell Biol.* **21**, 75-85.

Parczyk, K., Haase, W. and Kondor-Koch, C. (1989). Microtubules are involved in the secretion of proteins at the apical cell surface of the polarized epithelial cell, Madin-Darby Kidney. *J. Biol. Chem.* **264**, 16837-16846.

Pelech, S. L. and Sanghera, J. S. (1992). Mitogen-activated protein kinases: versatile transducers for cell signalling. *Trends Biochem. Sci.* **17**, 233-238.

Peterson, M. D. and Mooseker, M. S. (1992). Characterization of the enterocyte-like brush border cytskeleton of the C2_{BBe} clones of the human intestinal cell line, Caco-2. *J. Cell Sci.* **102**, 581-600.

Pollard, T. D., Doberstein, S. K. and Zot, H. G. (1991). Myosin I. *Annu. Rev. Physiol.* **53**, 653-681.

Potten, C. S. and Morris, R. J. (1988). Epithelial stem cells in vitro. *J. Cell Sci. Suppl.* **10**, 45-62.

Quaroni, A., Kirsch, K. and Weiser, M. M. (1979). Synthesis of membrane glycoproteins in rat small-intestinal villus cells. Effect of colchicine on the redistribution of L-[1, 5, 6-^{3}H]fucose-labelled membrane glycoproteins among Golgi, lateral basal and microvillus membranes. *Biochem. J.* **182**,

Rindler, M. J., Ivanov, I. E. and Sabatini, D. D. (1987). Microtubule-acting drugs lead to the nonpolarized delivery of the influenza hemagglutinin to the cell surface of polarized Madin-Darby Canine Kidney cells. *J. Cell Biol.* **104**, 231-241.

Rochette, E. C. and Haffen, K. (1987). Developmental pattern of calmodulin-binding proteins in rat jejunal epithelial cells. *Differentiation* **35**, 219-227.

Sahanouc, Y., Kusunoki, M., Hatada, T., Sakiyama, T., Yamamura, T. and Utsunomiya, J. (1991). Altered protein tyrosine kinase levels in human colon carcinoma. *Cancer* **67**, 590-596.

Sandoz, D., Lainé, M.-C. and Nicolas, G. (1985). Distribution of microtubules within the intestinal terminal web as revealed by quick-freezing and cryosubstitution. *Eur. J. Cell Biol.* **39**, 481-484.

Schroer, T. A. and Sheetz, M. P. (1991). Functions of microtubule-based motors. *Annu. Rev. Physiol.* **53**, 629-652.

Shibayama, T., Carboni, J. M. and Mooseker, M. S. (1987). Assembly of the intestinal brush border: appearance and redistribution of microvillar core proteins in developing chick enterocytes. *J. Cell Biol.* **105**, 335-344.

Stidwill, R. P. and Burgess, D. R. (1986). Regulation of intestinal brush border microvillus length during development by the G- to F-actin ratio. *Dev. Biol.* **114**, 381-388.

Sturgill, T. W. and Wu, J. (1991). Recent progress in characterization of protein kinase cascades for phosphorylation of ribosomal protein S6. *Biochim. Biophys. Acta* **1092**, 350-357.

Takata, K. and Singer, S. J. (1988). Phosphotyrosine-modified proteins are concentrated at the membranes of epithelial and endothelial cells during tissue development in chick embryos. *J. Cell Biol.* **106**, 1757-1764.

Takemura, R., Masaki, T. and Hirokawa, N. (1988). Developmental organization of the intestinal brush-border cytoskeleton. *Cell Motil. Cytoskel.* **9**, 299-311.

Thomas, G. (1992). MAP kinase by any other name smells just as sweet. *Cell* **68**, 3-6.

van der Sluijs, P., Bennett, M. K., Antony, C., Simons, K. and Kreis, T. E. (1990). Binding of exocytic vesicles from MDCK cells to microtubules in vitro. *J. Cell Sci.* **95**, 545-553.

Wang, H. R. and Erikson, R. L. (1992). Activation of protein serine/threonine kinases p42, p63, and p87 in Rous sarcoma virus-transformed cells: signal transduction/transformation-dependent MBP kinases. *Mol. Biol. Cell.* **3**, 1329-1337.

Weiser, M. M., Walters, J. and Wilson, J. R. (1986). Intestinal cell membranes. *Int. Rev. Cytol.* **101**, 1-57.

Zot, H. G., Doberstein, S. K. and Pollard, T. D. (1992). Myosin I moves actin filaments on a phospholipid substrate: implications for membrane targeting. *J. Cell Biol.* **116**, 367-376.

Journal of Cell Science, Supplement 17, 75-79 (1993)
Printed in Great Britain © The Company of Biologists Limited 1993

Synaptic vesicle proteins and regulated exocytosis

Lisa A. Elferink and Richard H. Scheller

Howard Hughes Medical Institute, Department of Molecular and Cellular Physiology, Stanford University Medical Center, Stanford CA 94305, USA

SUMMARY

The recent identification of novel proteins associated with the membranes of synaptic vesicles has ignited the field of molecular neurobiology to probe the function of these molecules. Evidence is mounting that the vesicle proteins vamp (synaptobrevin), rab3A, synaptophysin, synaptotagmin (p65) and SV2 play an important role in regulated exocytosis, by regulating neurotransmitter uptake, vesicle targeting and fusion with the presynaptic plasma membrane.

Key words: regulated exocytosis, synaptic vesicle proteins

INTRODUCTION

The process of exocytosis in eukaryotic cells involves the fusion of secretory vesicles with the plasma membrane. While most secreted proteins are released in a constitutive fashion, some mammalian cells, such as neurons and neuroendocrine cells, contain an additional secretory pathway which functions in response to cell stimulation (Burgess and Kelly, 1987). In neurons, the quantal release of neurotransmitters is a highly regulated process. Synaptic vesicles contain neurotransmitters which, prior to release, accumulate in the nerve terminal. In response to the appropriate signal, an increase in cytosolic Ca^{2+} promotes the fusion of synaptic vesicles with the active zone of the presynaptic plasma resulting in neurotransmitter release. Following exocytosis, the synaptic vesicle proteins are actively retrieved from the presynaptic membrane by endocytosis (Kelly, 1988; Südhof and Jahn, 1991; Trimble et al., 1991). While regulated exocytosis may share some overlapping molecular components with constitutive secretion, specific proteins must also exist to explain the apparent differences. Whereas constitutive vesicles undergo exocytosis without an intermediate storage stage, regulated exocytosis in neurons involves the concentration of neurotransmitters into secretory vesicles, temporary storage of a vesicle pool in close proximity to the release sites and the release of the vesicle contents in response to cell stimulation. In this article, we will focus on the characterization of five synaptic vesicle membrane proteins, all of which exist as members of small gene families. The biochemical and functional studies of these proteins suggest that they play specific roles in regulated exocytosis at the nerve terminal.

MOLECULAR ANALYSIS OF SYNAPTIC VESICLE PROTEINS

Synaptic vesicle proteins may be classified into two broad functional categories. The first category includes those involved in the uptake and storage of neurotransmitters, such as transporters and membrane pumps. Vesicle-specific transporter molecules have been implicated in the uptake of neurotransmitters into synaptic vesicles, in a process driven by a proton gradient (Forgac, 1989). Whereas a vacuolar proton pump localized to several membrane compartments including synaptic vesicles is responsible for establishing the proton gradient, the nature of the vesicle transporters has remained elusive (Yamagata and Parsons, 1989; Floor et al., 1990). A cDNA clone encoding a vesicular amine transporter from PC12 cells was recently identified by its ability to confer MPP^+ resistance when expressed in CHO cells (Liu et al., 1992). The cDNA encodes a protein which is predicted to span the membrane 12 times and shares homology with a class of bacterial drug resistance transporters. Whereas the vesicular uptake of dopamine and serotonin by this transporter is displaced by reserpine, amine uptake by a brain-specific homolog of this transporter is sensitive to tetrabenazine (Liu et al., 1992). The synaptic vesicle protein SV2, previously identified as a component of synaptic vesicle membranes, also displays sequence characteristics reminiscent of transporter molecules (Fig. 1). The amino acid sequences of two highly related SV2 proteins from rat brain are predicted to span the vesicle membrane 12 times, with a large glycosylated intravesicular loop between transmembrane domains 7 and 8 (Bajjalieh et al., 1992, 1993; Feany et al., 1992). Sequence comparison revealed that SV2 homologs do not share significant sequence homology with the mammalian plasma membrane transporters for the neurotransmitters γ-aminobutyric acid, glycine and dopamine, or with the vesicular amine transporter. There is however, significant amino acid identity with arabinose and quinate bacterial transporters, molecules which also require a membrane H^+ gradient for activity. While no functional data is available concerning the nature of the molecules potentially transported across the membrane by SV2 proteins, their sequence

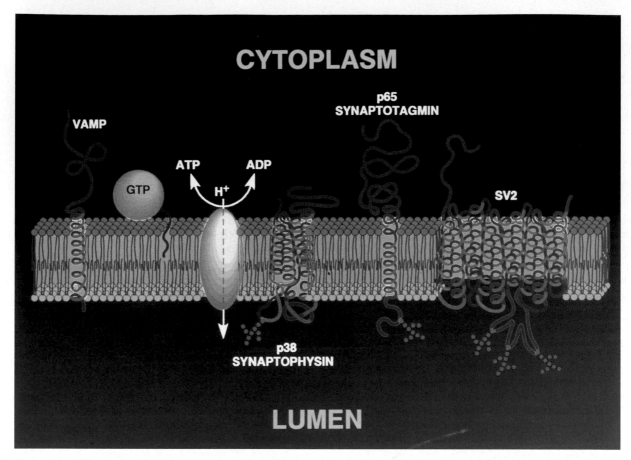

Fig. 1. Synaptic vesicle proteins. Schematic representation of the vacuolar proton pump and five characterized synaptic vesicle proteins showing the predicted membrane topologies. The approximate locations of the glycosylation sites are indicated.

homology, membrane topology and specific localization to secretory vesicles in a number of neural and neuroendocrine cells, strongly suggest that these proteins represent a novel family of vesicle transporters.

A second class of synaptic vesicle proteins includes those responsible for the vectorial transport of synaptic vesicles to the active zone of the presynaptic membrane, the fusion of these membrane compartments and subsequent recovery and reconstitution of synaptic vesicles within the nerve terminal. This class includes vamp, rab3A, synaptophysin and synaptotagmin proteins. Biochemical and genetic studies support the involvement of GTP hydrolysis in mediating a variety of steps in intracellular membrane trafficking and secretion. Using cell free systems, it has been demonstrated that a nonhydrolyzable analog of GTP, GTPγS, inhibits vesicle-mediated transport between the ER and Golgi compartments, within the Golgi, and from endosomes to the *trans*-Golgi network (Balch, 1989). The ability of GTP analogs to stimulate Ca^{2+}-independent exocytosis when introduced into mast cells and the dependence of secretory vesicle budding on GTP hydrolysis in vitro, further implicate a role for GTP in multiple steps of secretion (Aridor et al., 1990; Oberhauser et al., 1992; Tooze and Huttner, 1990). Molecular cloning techniques have identified a family of closely related low molecular weight (LMW) GTP-binding proteins termed rab3, which are specifically expressed in the nervous system (Fig. 1). Members of the

rab3 family all contain four highly conserved domains essential for the binding of GTP. In addition, rab3 proteins contain an effector domain for interaction with GAP proteins which regulate the GTPase activity of these proteins, and a hypervariable carboxy-terminal domain which is important for the correct targeting and attachment of these proteins to membrane compartments (Araki et al., 1991; Johnston et al., 1991; Burnstein and Macara, 1992). Rab3A is highly enriched on secretory vesicles from mammalian brain (Fischer von Mollard et al., 1990; Johnston et al., 1991), chromaffin cells (Darcen et al., 1990) and neuroendocrine cells (Matteoli et al., 1991; Ngsee et al., 1993). Although rab3A is attached to the synaptic vesicle membrane via a carboxy-terminal Cys-X-Cys sequence which is post-translationally polyisoprenylated, it has been proposed that rab3A cycles between a vesicle-bound state and a cytosolic form during exocytosis in vivo (Fischer von Mollard et al., 1991). Although there is still much uncertainty as to the precise function of rab3A in the secretory pathway, initial functional analysis suggests a role in targeting synaptic vesicles to release sites, in a process which involves the binding and hydrolysis of GTP. Using patch clamp techniques to measure exocytosis from mast cells, synthetic peptides corresponding to the effector domain of rab3A cause complete degranulation, in a similar fashion to that observed with GTPγS. The response is selective to rab3A peptides and can be accelerated with the nonhydrolyzable analog GDPβS, suggesting that the rab3A peptides compete with endogenous rab3A for target effector proteins, which in turn catalyze the process of exocytosis (Oberhauser et al., 1992). Mutational analysis of the marine ray homolog o-rab3 revealed that mutations predicted to alter the binding or rate of GTP hydrolysis, blocked the localization of o-rab3 at the tips of processes, when expressed in neuroendocrine AtT20 cells. Since the mutations also disrupted the sequestration of ACTH-containing secretory vesicles to the tips of these cells but not the rate of ACTH release, some members of the rab3 family may have a role in sequestration and storage of secretory vesicles near release sites (Ngsee et al., 1993).

Vamp (a.k.a. synaptobrevin), is a highly conserved 18 kDa protein anchored to the synaptic vesicle membrane via a single membrane domain, with the remainder of the protein oriented towards the cytoplasm (Fig. 1). Although two vamp isoforms, designated vamp 1 and 2, have been identified by cloning techniques from rat and human brain, in situ hybridization studies revealed that vamps 1 and 2 are differentially expressed in rat brain (Elferink et al., 1989; Trimble et al., 1990). Vamp2 is expressed throughout the brain, with highest levels in nuclei associated with autonomic and neuroendocrine function. Vamp1 is found predominantly in motoneurons and a subset of nuclei that innervate them. Although the functional significance of this distribution remains unclear, it suggests that the differential expression of vamps may confer specialized properties to different synapses. Each vamp is composed of three distinct structural motifs, including an NH_2-terminal domain rich in proline and alanine residues, a central hyrophilic core and a carboxy-terminal membrane anchor (Trimble et al., 1988; Elferink et al., 1989). Although the precise role of vamp in the exocytotic process remains unclear, recent studies by Schiavo and coworkers (1992) demonstrated that tetanus and botulinum-B toxins not only block the release of neurotransmitters, but also specifically cleave the cytoplasmic domain of vamp2. The ability of vamp2 peptides containing the toxin cleavage sites to competitively delay the inhibition of neurotransmitter release by tetanus toxin suggests that vamp2 is an essential component of neurotransmission, perhaps by interacting with proteins present in the cytoplasm or on the cytoplasmic face of the plasma membrane. In addition to its presence on neural and neuroendocrine-cell-derived vesicles (Trimble et al., 1988; Baumert et al., 1989), proteins which are structurally and immunologically related to vamp have been detected in peripheral mammalian tissues as well as in yeast. A vamp-like protein has been detected immunologically on the membranes of adiopocyte-derived, Glut 4-containing vesicles, which fuse with the plasma membrane in response to insulin (Corley et al., 1992). Since the cycle of insulin-stimulated exocytosis followed by internalization through vesicular endocytosis is very similar to that proposed for synaptic vesicles, vamp homologs may also have a role in this secretory pathway. Evidence for a more direct role for vamps in secretion has come from genetic manipulations performed in yeast. Two proteins encoded by the *sly2* and *sly12* (*bet1*) loci, have been identified as essential for vesicular transport between the ER and Golgi compartments (Dascher et al., 1991). Although sly2p and sly12p share only 30% amino acid identity with the mammalian vamps, they contain the highly conserved structural motifs characteristic of this family of vesicle proteins. The ability of the sly proteins to suppress a temperature-sensitive mutation in yeast secretion, which encodes the LMW GTP-binding protein ypt1, not only implicates these vamp homologs in yeast secretion, but suggests that these proteins may mediate their effects through a rab-like GTP-binding protein.

Synaptophysin is an abundant, 38 kDa vesicle membrane glycoprotein which spans the membrane four times, with its NH_2 and COOH termini localized to the cytoplasmic surface of the vesicle (Buckley et al., 1987; Leube et al., 1989; Südhoff et al., 1987). Its orientation in the vesicle membrane and the phosphorylation of synaptophysin on tyrosine residues within the carboxy-terminal tail, suggest that this region may serve as a binding site for additional cellular factors (Fig. 1). Sedimentation and crosslinking studies have revealed that synaptophysin forms a large homo-oligomeric structure which displays many of the structural characteristics of gap junction proteins (Thomas et al., 1988). Given the detection of membrane capacitance changes in the membranes of fused Torpedo synaptic vesicle preparations by patch clamp analysis, synaptophysin has been proposed either to form membrane channels or, alternatively, to play a structural role in organizing the synaptic vesicle membrane into a pre-exocytotic pore complex which facilitates the fusion of the vesicle with the plasma membrane (Rahamimoff et al., 1988; Thomas et al., 1988). In keeping with this hypothesis, purified synaptophysin has been reported to form channel-like structures when reconstituted into black lipid membranes (Thomas et al., 1988). Direct evidence for the involvement of synaptophysin in neurotransmitter release has come from reconstitution experiments in Xenopus oocytes (Alder et al., 1992). Ca^{2+}-dependent exocytosis was reconstituted in oocytes by the microinjection of total rat cerebellar RNA. Coinjection of antisense oligonucleotides or antibodies specific to synaptophysin, reduced the expression of synaptophysin in these cells and diminished the release of glutamate by Ca^{2+}-dependent exocytosis.

Synaptotagmin (p65) is an abundant synaptic vesicle protein which has been proposed to play a role in regulating either the translocation of synaptic vesicles to the plasma membrane or the subsequent fusion of these membrane compartments (Perin et al., 1991; Wendland et al., 1991). Two isoforms have been detected in rat brain and in cholinergic vesicles purified from the electric organ of marine rays (Perin et al., 1990, 1991; Wendland et al., 1991). Synaptotagmins are anchored to the vesicle membrane by a single transmembrane domain, have a NH_2-terminal intravesicular domain and a cytoplasmic domain which contains two homologous C2 regulatory domains (Fig. 1). Analogous C2 repeats are found in proteins such as protein kinase C and phospholipase A2, which translocate to the plasma membrane in a Ca^{2+}- and phospholipid-dependent manner. In synaptic vesicles, synaptotagmin exists as a homo-oligomeric complex which binds acidic phospholipids in a Ca^{2+}-dependent fashion (Perin et al., 1990; Brose et al., 1992). Proteolytic cleavage studies revealed that the Ca^{2+}- and lipid-binding activities of synaptotagmin are localized to the cytoplasmic portion of the protein, although the involvement of the two C2 regulatory domains remains to be established (Brose et al., 1992). The cytoplasmic domain of synaptotagmin has been shown to be a substrate for phosphorylation by casein kinase II (Bennett et al., 1993). Although phosphorylation has been proposed to play a role in neurotransmission at the synapse, the physiological consequences of synaptotagmin phosphorylation on neurotransmitter release remains unclear. Two sets of studies endeavored to assess the functional role of synaptotagmin in regulated exocytosis. Neuroendocrine PC12 cells, which express endogenous forms of synaptic vesicle proteins, were depleted of synaptotagmin by successive rounds of immune cytolysis (Shoji-Kasai et al., 1992). When depolarized, catecholamines and ATP were released from the variant cells in a Ca^{2+}-dependent manner, suggesting that synaptotagmin is not an essential component of the secretory machinery. However, the ability of antibodies and recombinant fragments of synaptotagmin to abolish the release of catecholamines when microinjected directly into PC12 cells, suggests that synaptotagmin may have a more modulatory role in Ca^{2+}-regulated exocytosis (Elferink et al., 1993). Following vesicle docking at the plasma membrane, synaptotagmin may interact with components of the secretory machinery to reduce the probability of a fusion event. This inhibitory activity may be relieved by Ca^{2+} binding, suggesting that the subsequent fusion of vesicles with the plasma membrane involves additional Ca^{2+}-dependent components. The ability of synaptotagmin to function as a Ca^{2+} sensor to regulate vesicle fusion is further supported by its interactions with proteins localized to the presynaptic plasma membrane. Synaptotagmin has been shown in vitro to bind syntaxin, a molecule associated with Ca^{2+} channels (Bennett et al., 1992), and to interact with the cytoplasmic domain of the α-latrotoxin receptor (Petrenko et al., 1991). Furthermore, synaptotagmin fragments bind RACKs (receptors for activated C kinase) in a phospholipid- and Ca^{2+}-dependent manner (Mochly-Rosen et al., 1992), potentially through the C2 domains.

The five vesicle proteins described represent only a small collection of the membrane-bound components potentially involved in Ca^{2+}-regulated exocytosis from neurons. Regulated secretory events will most certainly involve cytosolic components such as NSF and SNAPs (Rothman and Orci, 1992), proteins implicated in triggering the bilayer fusion of different membrane compartments, annexins (Curetz, 1992), and p145 (Walent et al., 1992), a novel brain protein which is able to reconstitute Ca^{2+}-dependent secretion from semi-intact PC12 cells. However, the identification of several novel vesicle proteins illustrates the complexity of the secretory process. A current challenge now is to elucidate the individual roles of these proteins in regulated exocytosis. The availability of cDNA clones and antibodies for several synaptic vesicle proteins should enable us to gain further insight into the complex neural circuitry underlying brain function and to determine how changes in synaptic transmission contribute to alterations in synaptic strength in normal and pathological states.

We thank Mark Bennett, Sandy Bajjalieh, Tony Ting and Beverly Wendland for critical reading of this manuscript.

REFERENCES

Alder, J., Lu, B., Valtorta, F., Greengard, P. and Poo, M. (1992). Calcium-dependent transmitter secretion reconstituted in Xenopus oocytes: requirement for synaptophysin. *Nature* **257**, 657-661.

Araki, S., Kaibuchi, K., Sasaki, T., Hata, Y. and Takai, Y. (1991). Role of the C-terminal region of smgp25A in its interaction with membranes and the GDP/GTP exchange protein. *Mol. Cell. Biol.* **11**, 1438-1447.

Aridor, M., Traub, L. M. and Sagi-Eisenberg, R. (1990). Exocytosis in mast cells by basic secretogogues: evidence for direct activation of GTP binding proteins. *J. Cell Biol.* **111**, 909-917.

Bajjalieh, S. M., Peterson, K., Shinghal, R. and Scheller, R. H. (1992). SV2, a brain synaptic vesicle protein homologous to bacterial transporters. *Science* **257**, 1271-1273.

Bajjjalieh, S.M., Peterson, K., Linial, M. and Scheller, R. H. (1993). Brain contains two forms of synaptic vesicle protein 2. *Proc. Nat. Acad. Sci. USA* (in press).

Balch, W. E. (1989). Biochemistry of interorganelle transport. *J. Biol. Chem.* **264**, 16965-16968.

Baumert, M., Maycox, P. R., Navone, F., DeCamilli, P. and Jahn, R. (1989). Synaptobrevin: an integral membrane protein of 18,000 daltons present in small synaptic vesicles of rat brain. *EMBO J.* **8**, 379-384.

Bennett, M. K., Calakos, N. and Scheller, R. H. (1992). Syntaxin: a synaptic protein implicated in docking of synaptic vesicles at presynaptic active zones. *Science* **257**, 255-259.

Bennett, M. K., Miller, K. G. and Scheller, R. H. (1993). Casein kinase II phosphorylates the synaptic vesicle protein p65. *J. Neurosci.* **13**, 1701-1707.

Brose, N., Petrenko, A. G., Südhof, T. C. and Jahn, R. (1992). Synaptotagmin: A calcium sensor on the synaptic vesicle surface. *Science* **256**, 1021-1025.

Buckley, K. M., Floor, E. and Kelly, R. B. (1987). Cloning and sequence analysis of cDNA encoding p38, a major synaptic vesicle protein. *J. Cell Biol.* **105**, 2447-2456.

Burgess, T. L. and Kelly, R. B. (1987). Constitutive and regulated secretion of proteins. *Annu. Rev. Cell Biol.* **3**, 243-293.

Burnstein, E. S. and Macara, I. G. (1992). Characterization of a guanine nucleotide-releasing factor and a GTPase-activating protein that are specific for the ras-related protein p25rab3A. *Proc. Nat. Acad. Sci. USA* **89**, 1154-1158.

Corley, C. C., Trimble, W. S. and Lienhard, G. E. (1992). Members of the VAMP family of synaptic vesicle proteins are components of glucose transporter-containing vesicles from rat adipocytes. *J. Biol. Chem.* **267**, 11681-11684.

Cruetz, C. E. (1992). The annexins and exocytosis. *Science* **258**, 924-931.

Darcen, P., Zahraoui, A., Hammel, F., Monteils, M.-P., Tavitan, A. and Scherman, D. (1990). Association of the GTP-binding protein rab3A with bovine chromaffin granules. *Proc. Nat. Acad. Sci. USA* **87**, 5692-5696.

Dascher, C., Ossig, R., Gallwitz, D. and Schmitt, H. D. (1991). Identification and structure of four yeast genes (SLY) that are able to suppress the functional loss of ypt1, a member of the ras superfamily. *Mol. Cell. Biol.* **11**, 872-885.

Elferink, L. A., Trimble, W. S. and Scheller, R. H. (1989). Two vesicle-associated membrane protein genes are differentially expressed in the rat central nervous system. *J. Biol. Chem.* **264**, 11061-11064.

Elferink, L. A., Peterson, M. R. and Scheller, R. H. (1993). A role for synaptotagmin (p65) in regulated exocytosis. *Cell* **72**, 153-159.

Feany, M. B., Lee, S., Edwards, R. H. and Buckley, K. M. (1992). The synaptic vesicle protein SV2 is a novel type of transmembrane transporter. *Cell* **70**, 861-867.

Fischer von Mollard, G., Mignery, G. A., Baumert, M., Perin, M. S., Hanson, T. J., Burger, P. M., Jahn, R. and Südhof, T. C. (1990). rab3 is a small GTP-binding protein exclusively localized to synaptic vesicles. *Proc. Nat. Acad. Sci. USA* **87**, 1988-1992.

Fischer von Mollard, G., Südhof, T. C. and Jahn R. (1991). A small GTP-binding protein dissociates from synaptic vesicles during exocytosis. *Nature* **349**, 79-81.

Floor, E., Leventhal, P. S. and Schaeffer, S. F. (1990). Partial purification and characterization of the vacuolar H^+-ATPase of mammalian synaptic vesicles. *J. Neurochem.* **55**, 1663-1670.

Forgac, M. (1989). Structure and function of vacuolar class of ATP-driven proton pumps. *Physiol. Rev.* **69**, 765-796.

Johnston, J. P., Archer III, B. T., Robinson, K., Mignery, G. A., Jahn, R.

and Südhoff, T. C. (1991). Rab3A attachment to the synaptic vesicle membrane mediated by a conserved polyisoprenylated carboxy-terminal sequence. *Neuron* **7**, 101-109.

Kelly, R.B. (1988). The cell biology of the nerve terminal. *Neuron* **1**, 431-438.

Leube, R. E., Wiedenmann, B. and Franke, W. W. (1989). Topogenesis and sorting of synaptophysin: synthesis of a synaptic vesicle protein from a gene transfected into non-neuroendocrine cells. *Cell* **59**, 433-446.

Liu, Y., Peter, D., Roghani, A., Schuldiner, S., Privé, G. G., Eisenberg, D., Brecha, N. and Edwards, R. H. (1992). A cDNA that suppresses MPP+ toxicity encodes a vesicular amine transporter. *Cell* **70**, 539-551.

Matteoli, M., Tahei, K., Cameron, R., Hurlbut, P., Johnston, P. A., Südhof, T. C., Jahn, R. and DeCamilli, P. (1991). Association of rab3A with synaptic vesicles at late stages of the secretory pathway. *J. Cell Biol.* **115**, 625-633.

Mochly-Rosen, D., Miller, K. G., Scheller, R. H., Khaner, H., Lopez, J. and Smith, B. L. (1992). p65 fragments, homologous to the C2 region of protein kinase C, bind to the intracellular receptors for protein kinase C. *Biochemistry* **31**, 8120-8124.

Ngsee, J. K., Fleming, A. M. and Scheller, R. H. (1993). A rab protein regulates localization of secretory granules in AtT20 cells. *Mol. Biol. Cell* **4**, 747-756.

Oberhauser, A. F., Monck, J. R., Balch, W. E. and Fernandez, J. M. (1992). Exocytotic fusion is activated by rab3A peptides. *Nature* **360**, 270-273.

Perin, M. S., Fried, V.A., Mignery, G. A., Jahn, R. and Südhof, T. C. (1990). Phospholipid binding by a synaptic vesicle protein homologous to the regulatory region of protein kinase C. *Nature* **345**, 260-263.

Perin, M. S., Brose, N., Jahn, R. and Südhof, T. C. (1991). Domain structure of synaptotagmin (p65). *J. Biol. Chem.* **266**, 623-629.

Petrenko, A. G., Perin, M. S., Davletov, B. A., Ushkaryov, Y., Geppert, M. and Südhof, T. C. (1991). Binding of synaptotagmin to the α-latrotoxin receptor implicates both in synaptic vesicle exocytosis. *Nature* **353**, 65-68.

Rahamimoff, R., DeRiemer, S. A., Sahmann, B., Stadler, H. and Yakir, N. (1988). Ion channels in synaptic vesicles from Torpedo electric organ. *Proc. Nat. Acad. Sci. USA* **85**, 5310-5314.

Rothman, J. E. and Orci, L. (1992). Molecular dissection of the secretory pathway. *Nature* **355**, 409-415.

Schiavo, G., Benfenati, F., Poulain, B., Rossetto, O., Polverino de Laureto, P., DasGupta, B. R., Montecucco, C. (1992). Tetanus and botulinum B neurotoxins block neurotransmitter release by proteolytic cleavage of synaptobrevin. *Nature* **359**, 832-835.

Shoji-Kasai, Y., Yoshida, A., Sato, K., Hoshino, T., Ogura, A., Kondo, S., Fujimoto, Y., Kuwahara, R., Kato, R. and Takahashi, M. (1992). Neurotransmitter release from synaptotagmin-deficient clonal variants of PC12 cells. *Science* **256**, 1020-1823.

Südhof, T. C. and Jahn, R. (1991). Proteins of synaptic vesicles involved in exocytosis and membrane recycling. *Neuron* **6**, 665-677.

Südhof, T. C., Lottspeich, F., Greengard, P., Mehl, E. and Jahn R. (1987). A synaptic vesicle protein with a novel cytoplasmic domain and four transmembrane regions. *Science* **238**, 1142-1144.

Trimble, W. S., Cowan, D. M. and Scheller, R. H. (1988). VAMP-1: a synaptic vesicle-associated integral membrane protein. *Proc. Nat. Acad. Sci. USA* **85**, 4538-4542.

Trimble, W. S., Gray, T. S., Elferink, L. A., Wilson, M. C. and Scheller, R. H. (1990). Distinct patterns of expression of two VAMP genes within the rat brain. *J. Neurosci.* **10**, 1380-1387.

Trimble, W. S., Linial, M. and Scheller, R. H. (1991). Cellular and molecular biology of the presynaptic nerve terminal. *Annu. Rev. Neurosci.* **14**, 93-122.

Thomas, L., Hartung, K., Langosch, D., Rehm, H., Bamberg, E., Franke, W. W. and Betz, H. (1988). Identification of synaptophysin as a hexameric channel protein of the synaptic vesicle membrane. *Science* **242**, 1050-1053.

Tooze, S. A. and Huttner, W. B. (1990). Cell-free protein sorting to the regulated and constitutive secretory pathways. *Cell* **60**, 837-847.

Walent, J. H., Porter, B. W. and Martin, T. F. J. (1992). A novel 145 kD brain cytosolic protein reconstitutes Ca2+-regulated secretion in permeable neuroendocrine cells. *Cell* **70**, 765-775.

Wendland, B., Miller, K. G., Schilling, J. and Scheller, R. H. (1991). Differential expression of the p65 gene family. *Neuron* **6**, 993-1007.

Yamagata, S. K. and Parsons, S. M. (1989). Cholinergic synaptic vesicles contain a V-type and a P-type ATPase. *J. Neurochem.* **53**, 1354-1362.

Journal of Cell Science, Supplement 17, 81-83 (1993)
Printed in Great Britain © The Company of Biologists Limited 1993

Biogenesis of synaptic vesicles

R. B. Kelly, Frank Bonzelius, Ann Cleves, Lois Clift-O'Grady, Eric Grote and Gary Herman

Department of Biochemistry and Biophysics and the Hormone Research Institute, University of California, San Francisco, USA

SUMMARY

The basic endosomal recycling pathway can be modified to generate transcytotic vesicles, storage vesicles and synaptic vesicles. Sorting into synaptic vesicles requires specialized sorting information not present in the transcytotic and storage vesicle proteins. Using mutagenesis we have distinguished the signals for rapid endocytosis and SV targeting in synaptobrevin. Finally, we have evidence that synaptic vesicles can be generated from an endosomal compartment in vitro.

Key words: synaptic vesicles, endosome, synaptobrevin, VAMP, PC12 cells

SPECIALIZATION OF THE ENDOSOMAL PATHWAY

Two factors have helped make the biogenesis of synaptic vesicles an attractive area for study. The first is that synaptic vesicles can be found in cultured endocrine cell lines, particularly the pheochromocytoma cell line, PC12. The second factor is that synaptic vesicle generation in PC12 cells and in neurons is by endocytosis. Endocytosis is probably one of the best understood aspects of cell biology.

Although it is well established that synaptic vesicles arise by endocytosis, it is still not certain whether an endosome is involved. Favoring an endosomal origin are the data that synaptic vesicle membrane proteins co-localize with endosomal markers in neurons, in PC12 cells and in transfected fibroblasts (Cameron et al., 1991; Linstedt and Kelly, 1991). Furthermore, using chimeric proteins, we have been able to show that a synaptic vesicle membrane protein, synaptophysin, has all the sorting information necessary to target it to the LDL receptor-containing endosomes and to recycle back to the cell surface with approximately the same kinetics as the LDL receptor itself (Kaneda, F. Bonzelius, G. Herman and R. B. Kelly, unpublished). It is generally assumed therefore that synaptophysin, the transferrin receptor and the LDL receptor are co-targeted in transfected fibroblasts and PC12 cells to endosomes. In PC12 cells, however, synaptic vesicles arise from the endosome by sorting proteins such as synaptophysin from other endosomal proteins such as the LDL receptor.

The synaptic vesicle, then, is a specialized endocytotic compartment. Other cells have specialized endocytotic compartments that also exclude recycling endosome markers such as the LDL receptor. In epithelial cells, for example, the transferrin and LDL receptors go only to the basolateral endosomes. The apical membrane of epithelial cells gives rise to specialized endocytotic vesicles, for example those that store plasma membrane proteins such as water channels, the chloride channels or the proton pumps in an intracellular pool (Kaplan, this volume; Brown, this volume). A second specialized endocytotic vesicle of epithelial cells is the transcytotic vesicle, which carries, for example, the polyIg receptor from basolateral to apical surfaces. Because of the parallels that it is suggested occur between neurons and epithelial cells (Dotti, this volume), PC12 cells were transfected with DNA encoding the polyIg receptor to discover whether there is any similarity between transcytotic and synaptic vesicles. We found that the polyIg receptor was excluded from synaptic vesicles when we used either the wild-type polyIg receptor, or the Asp664 mutant form, which is targeted to transcytotic vesicles better than wild-type receptor. Even when the PC12 cells were exposed to NGF or the immunoglobulin ligand for the polyIg receptor, synaptic vesicles were free of the polyIg receptor.

Storage endocytotic vesicles are used to provide an intracellular pool of surface proteins in cells other than epithelial cells. In adipose and muscle cells, one form of the glucose transporter (GLUT4) is internalized by endocytosis, but sorted from the endosome into a small vesicle or tubulovesicular structure of approximately the dimensions of the synaptic vesicle. These vesicles accumulate in the cytoplasm in the vicinity of the Golgi complex (Slot et al., 1991). They are believed to contain an analogue of VAMP (Cain et al., 1992) and also a form of the Rab3 protein (Baldini et al., 1992). Like synaptic vesicles, these storage endocytotic vesicles undergo regulated exocytosis. When adipose and muscle cells are exposed to insulin, the rate of fusion of these vesicles with the plasma membrane is markedly increased (Jhun et al., 1992; Yang and Holman, 1993). To test the possible similarities between the two endosomal pathways we transfected GLUT4 into PC12 cells. Once again however we found that GLUT4 was completely excluded from synaptic vesicles. We conclude that the formation of synaptic vesicles involves a unique modification of the endosomal recycling pathway, using sorting signals different from those used in either the generation of transcytotic vesicles or the GLUT4-containing storage endocytotic vesicles.

Although GLUT4 is not in synaptic vesicles in PC12 cells, it is almost exclusively found in a population of vesicles that sediment only slightly faster than synaptic vesicles. The GLU-4-enriched vesicles exclude the polyIg receptor, the synaptic vesicle protein SV2 and the LDL receptor. In PC12 cells, therefore, there may be two independent modifications of the standard endosomal recycling pathway, one which generates the GLUT4 vesicle, and the other which generates the synaptic vesicle.

SORTING INTO SYNAPTIC VESICLES

To be targeted to synaptic vesicles, synaptic vesicle membrane proteins must have sorting information that is absent from other endocytosed proteins such as the LDL receptor, the polyIg receptor or GLUT4. To identify such sorting domains we have begun an analysis of one of the synaptic vesicle proteins, synaptobrevin or VAMP. VAMP is a type II membrane protein which has only two amino acids of its carboxy terminus in its lumenal domain, located inside the synaptic vesicle (Trimble et al., 1991). To follow the targeting of VAMP inside transfected cells, we modified that intralumenal carboxy-terminal region of VAMP by the addition of a T-antigen epitope tag and transfected DNA encoding the construct (VAMP-Tag) into CHO and PC12 cells.

We were concerned that the addition of a large epitope and spacer to the lumenal domain would alter the ability of the T antigen to insert into plasma membranes. Our worry was unfounded. The modified epitope-tagged VAMP reaches the plasma membrane and is endocytosed. The addition of antibodies against the epitope tag to the outside of transfected PC12 cells and transfected fibroblasts has shown us that the endocytosis rates of the VAMP-Tag are comparable to those of other endocytosed markers. Finally, a fraction of the endocytosed VAMP can be recovered inside synaptic vesicles isolated by velocity sedimentation. Since the extension of VAMP-Tag was driven by a cytomegalovirus promoter, we were able to elevate the expression levels of the constructs by adding butyrate to the transfected cells. In this way we could achieve expression levels of the epitope-tagged VAMP that were 5-10 times greater than that of the endogenous VAMP. Despite this overexpression, endogenous VAMP could still be recovered in synaptic vesicles, implying that we had not saturated the sorting system.

To make a preliminary identification of endocytosis and synaptic vesicle sorting domains, constructs were prepared that expressed variants of epitope-tagged VAMP that lacked 30 amino acids from the cytoplasmic amino-terminal domain (del 2-30), that lacked 60 amino acids (del 2-60)

or with the transmembrane domain of VAMP replaced by that of the transferrin receptor (TfR-TM). A fourth construction in which the cytoplasmic domain of VAMP-Tag was replaced with that of the transferrin receptor failed to reach the cell surface. When endocytosis of surface-labeled VAMP-Tag was measured, the extent of endocytosis was higher than wild type for two of the variants (del 2-30 and TfR-TM) and about half that of normal VAMP for the third (del 2-60). We conclude that the amino-terminal domain has no affect on endocytosis, and amino acids between 30 and 60, a small effect.

We examined targeting of the constructs into synaptic vesicles by two techniques, looking at the distribution by western blotting across a velocity gradient and by looking at the targeting of anti-epitope antibodies to the synaptic vesicles from the cell surface. Both techniques gave the same result, namely that a region between amino acids 30 and 60 is necessary to allow targeting to synaptic vesicles. However, while the endocytosis rates were faster in those proteins containing the 30-60 amino acid sequence, targeting to synaptic vesicles was 5-20% of normal.

The endocytosis targeting signal is a robust one and is relatively unaffected by the mutations made in the VAMP molecule. However, in contrast to the endocytosis signal, the signals which target to synaptic vesicles are much more labile. To get the maximum efficiency of targeting to synaptic vesicles, the transmembrane region and the variable amino terminal region are both required.

BIOGENESIS OF SYNAPTIC VESICLES IN VITRO

To identify cytosolic components that might be interacting with sorting domains on synaptic vesicle membrane proteins, we have examined synaptic vesicle biogenesis in vitro. We began our reconstitution with a membrane fraction that contained endosomes that had been washed free of synaptic vesicles. When this fraction was incubated with ATP and cytosol, it generated a population of small vesicles that could be readily identified by velocity sedimentation. Generation of these vesicles was blocked by N-ethylmaleimide.

To determine if the synaptic vesicle-sized vesicles generated in our in vitro system were arising from endosomes, we labeled the endosomal compartment. To do this, PC12 cells were biotinylated on their surface in the cold. The cells were washed and incubated for 20 minutes at 20°C, conditions which do not allow the biotin label to get to synaptic vesicles but which readily labeled endosomal compartments. Surface label was then stripped from the cells. When biotinylated membranes were incubated with ATP in cytosol, small vesicles of the size of synaptic vesicles were generated which contained the biotin label. The biotinylated proteins that were in the budded vesicle compartment were not identical to those in the starting material. One of them appeared to be synaptophysin.

We conclude, therefore, that we can observe the generation in vitro of vesicles that co-migrate with synaptic vesicles and which are derived from endosomes.

REFERENCES

Baldini, G., Hohl, T., Lin, H. Y. and Lodish, H. F. (1992). Cloning of a Rab3 isotype predominately expressed in adipocytes. *Proc. Nat. Acad. Sci. USA* **89**, 5049-5052.

Cain, C. C., Trimble, W. S. and Leinhard, G. E. (1992). Members of the VAMP family of synaptic vesicle proteins are components of glucose transporter containing vesicles from rat adipocytes. *J. Biol. Chem.* **267**, 11681-11684.

Cameron, P. L., Sudhof, T. C., Jahn, R. and De Camilli, P. (1991). Colocalization of synaptophysin with transferrin receptors: implications for synaptic vesicle biogenesis. *J. Cell Biol.* **115**, 151-164.

Jhun, B. H., Rampal, A. L., Liu, H., Lachaal, M. and Jung, C. Y. (1992). Effects of insulin on steady state kinetics of GLUT4 subcellular distribution in rat adipocytes. *J. Biol. Chem.* **267**, 17710-17715.

Linstedt, A. and Kelly, R. B. (1991). Synaptophysin is sorted from endocytotic markers in neuroendocrine PC12 cells but not transfected fibroblasts. *Neuron* **7**, 309-317.

Slot, J. W., Geuze, H. J., Gigengack, S., Lienhard, G. E. and James, D. E (1991). Immuno-localization of the insulin regulatable glucose transporter in brown adipose tissue of the rat. *J. Cell Biol.* **113**, 123-135.

Trimble, W. S., Linial, M. and Scheller, R. H. (1991). Cellular and molecular biology of the presynaptic nerve terminal. *Annu. Rev. Neurosci.* **14**, 93-122.

Yang, J. and Holman, G. D. (1993). Comparison of GLUT4 and GLU1 subcellular trafficking in basal and insulin-stimulated 3T3-L1 cells. *J. Biol. Chem.* **268**, 4600-4603.

Journal of Cell Science, Supplement 17, 85-92 (1993)
Printed in Great Britain © The Company of Biologists Limited 1993

Membrane traffic in polarized neurons in culture

Meltsje J. de Hoop and Carlos G. Dotti

Cell Biology Program, European Molecular Biology Laboratory, D-6900 Heidelberg, Germany

SUMMARY

Fetal hippocampal neurons develop axons and dendrites in culture. To study how neurons form and maintain different plasma membrane domains, hippocampal neurons were infected with RNA viruses and the distribution of the viral glycoproteins was analyzed by light and electron microscopy. Infection of hippocampal cells with vesicular stomatitis virus (VSV) and fowl plague virus (FPV) resulted in the polarized distribution of the newly synthesized viral glycoproteins. The VSV glycoprotein appeared firstly in the Golgi apparatus and then in the dendrites. In contrast, the hemagglutinin of FPV, after accumulation in the Golgi apparatus, moved to the axons. These results suggest that the mechanism of sorting of viral glycoproteins might be similar in neurons and MDCK cells, a cell line of epithelial origin. In these cells the VSV glycoprotein and the hemagglutinin of FPV distribute to the basolateral and apical membranes, respectively. Transport of viral glycoproteins to both neuronal domains was microtubule dependent. Nocodazole treatment of infected neurons inhibited the delivery of axonal and dendritic viral glycoproteins equally.

To investigate if the analogy between epithelial cells and neurons extended to include an endogenous plasma membrane protein, the distribution of Thy-1, a GPI-linked protein, was analyzed. By immunofluorescence and immunoelectron microscopy, Thy-1 was found exclusively along the axonal surface. In epithelial cells GPI-anchored proteins are located apically.

The existence of a barrier on the neuronal plasma membrane that would prevent intermixing of axonal and dendritic proteins was analyzed by a liposome-fusion assay. Fluorescently labeled liposomes containing the $GD_{1\alpha}$ ganglioside were added to FPV-infected neurons. The liposomes bound specifically to the hemagglutinin protein, expressed on the axonal surface. After fusion, fluorescent labelling was observed along the axon but not diffusing into the cell body and dendrites. The barrier that prevented lipid diffusion appeared to be located in the axonal hillock region.

Our work shows that experimental strategies that have proven useful in the understanding of membrane sorting in epithelial cells, can also be used to unveil the mechanism of neuronal sorting.

Key words: polarity, sorting, cytoskeleton

INTRODUCTION

Neurons are highly asymmetric cells equipped with long extensions: axons and dendrites. The dendrites receive and process information and the axons transmit it to the target cell at specialized sites: the synapses. This functional polarity is illustrated by an asymmetric distribution of many cell components. Although there are some exceptions, in most neuronal cells ribosomes (Barlett and Banker, 1984) and RNA are segregated (Davis et al., 1987; Steward and Banker, 1992) into the dendrites and the cell body, whereas synaptic vesicles are in the axon. The cytoskeleton is also organized in a polarized fashion: phosphorylated MAP 1B, tau and neurofilament H are exclusively axonal, while MAP 2 and dystrophin are somatodendritic (Sato-Yoshitake et al., 1989; Kosik and Finch, 1987; Shaw et al., 1985; Caceres et al., 1984; Lidov et al., 1990). Plasma membrane components are segregated as well: the transferrin receptor is localized on the dendrites (Cameron et al., 1991; Parton et al., 1992), neurotransmitter receptors are in the postsynaptic area of the dendrite (Killisch et al., 1991), and acetylcholinesterase (G4 form) and TAG-1 (axonin-1) are present on the axonal plasma membrane (Rotundo and Carbonetto, 1987; Ruegg et al., 1989; Furley et al., 1990). Endocytosis takes place in the dendrites, the cell body and the presynaptic terminals but not from the axon shaft (Parton et al., 1992).

Little is known about how this morphological and functional polarization is accomplished. Studies on neuronal polarity have been hampered by technical limitations. Firstly, in situ studies are difficult because of the complexity of the brain. Secondly, no polarized neuronal cell lines exist. We have analyzed neuronal membrane sorting in hippocampal neurons in culture (an example of such a cell is shown in Fig. 1). Experimentally, we used the same strategies that have been used successfully to understand polarized membrane traffic in epithelial cell.

MEMBRANE TRAFFIC IN EPITHELIAL CELLS

In epithelial cells, the sorting between apical and basolat-

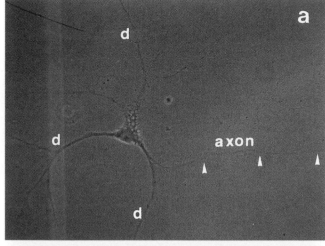

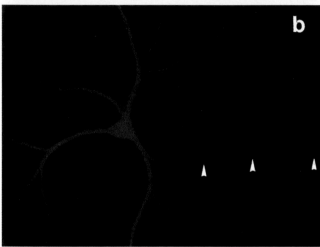

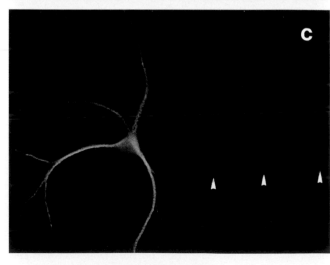

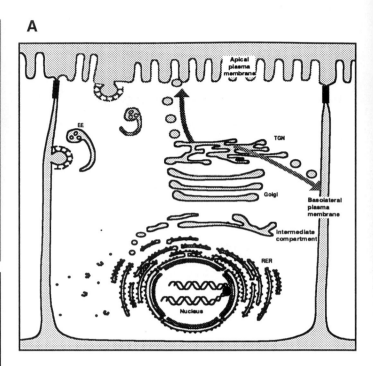

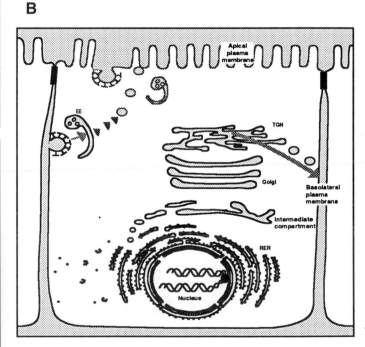

Fig. 1. Morphological and molecular differences between axons and dendrites of hippocampal neurons in culture. Phase-contrast microscopy shows that axon and dendrites can be distinguished by morphological criteria (a). The axon (arrowheads, axon) is thin and of uniform diameter whereas the dendrites (d) are thick at their origin but taper with distance from the cell body. An endogenous cytoskeletal protein, MAP 2 (a microtubule-associated protein), is present in the cell body and dendrites (b). In the same cell, the M protein of VSV is also segregated to the cell body and dendrites (c).

Fig. 2. Schematic representation of the pathways of membrane sorting in epithelial cells. In (A) the direct pathway is shown: *trans*-Golgi network (TGN) to apical and TGN to basolateral surfaces (arrows). In (B) the indirect pathway: from the Golgi complex to the basolateral surface (large arrow) and from there, after endocytosis (small arrow), sorting to the apical surface via transcytotic vesicles (arrowheads). Some epithelial cells use a combination of (A) and (B) to produce distinct apical and basolateral membranes. The viral paradigm in neuronal cells shows that the direct pathway exists. It is possible that the indirect, transcytotic, pathway operates as well.

eral plasma membrane proteins can be executed at two positions: at the *trans*-Golgi network (direct sorting) and at the endosomes/plasma membrane (indirect sorting), (Simons and Wandinger-Ness, 1990; Wessels et al., 1990; Jalal et al., 1991; Schell et al., 1992; Nelson, 1992). Studies with viral glycoproteins show that Madin-Darby canine kidney (MDCK) cells predominantly separate their membrane proteins at the *trans*-Golgi network into vesicles that are destined either for the apical or the basolateral domain (direct sorting). Hepatocytes target most, if not all, proteins to the basolateral domain first. From here, apically destined proteins are rerouted via transcytosis to the apical site of the cell (indirect sorting). The intestinal epithelial cell line Caco-2 uses both the direct and the indirect pathways. The sorting machinery of both the *trans*-Golgi network and the plasma membrane/endosome seems to recognize the same signals, since most polarized membrane proteins have the same distribution in MDCK and hepatocytes. Fig. 2 shows schematically the direct and indirect pathways of epithelial cells.

The analysis of mutated viral-envelope proteins and endogenous plasma membrane proteins led to the concept that specific signals determine vectorial polarized traffic. The first signal was identified in glycoproteins that are anchored to the plasma membrane via a glycosyl-phosphatidylinositol (GPI). In epithelial cells, GPI-linked proteins were found exclusively in the apical membrane (Lisanti et al., 1990). The GPI-anchor is added in the endoplasmic reticulum to those proteins that contain a cleavable hydrophobic signal for GPI attachment at their C terminus (Lisanti and Rodriguez-Boulan, 1990). Adding this signal to basolaterally sorted proteins redirects them to the apical membrane. However, apical targeting signals can also reside in the protein itself. For example, the nerve growth factor (NGF) receptor is a transmembrane protein, so does not contain a GPI anchor, but is apically directed in MDCK cells (Le Bivic et al., 1991). Some GPI-anchored proteins contain an additional apical targeting signal in their ectodomains, which, in the absence of the GPI anchor still directs them apically (Lisanti and Rodriguez-Boulan, 1990).

Basolateral targeting signals have also been discovered. One signal has been identified within a 14 amino acid segment of the poly-immunoglobulin receptor (Casanova et al., 1991). Other signals have been found in the cytoplasmic tail of several basolateral proteins. Upon removal of the signals, the proteins are targeted to the apical site (Townbridge, 1991; and see reviews by Hopkins, 1991, 1992). Very interestingly, in several cases a correlation exists between basolateral sorting signals and signals for clathrin-mediated endocytosis (Mostov et al., 1992; Brewer and Roth, 1991).

Since neurons can be cultured in vitro as polarized cells, it is now possible to test whether the sorting mechanisms discovered in epithelial cells are also utilized by polarized neurons. Such studies, recently performed in our laboratory, are described below.

RECENT STUDIES

Distribution of viral and endogenous plasma membrane proteins in hippocampal neurons in culture

In culture fetal rat hippocampal neurons establish axonal and dendritic arbors and a molecular organization similar to their counterparts in situ (Dotti et al., 1988; Banker and Waxman, 1988).

The same viruses that have been successfully used to study protein sorting in epithelial cells were employed to determine the sorting of newly synthesized membrane glycoproteins (Dotti and Simons, 1990; Dotti et al., 1993). Polarized neurons were infected with the temperature-sensitive mutant VSV ts045. The location of the viral glycoprotein during its biosynthetic route is dependent on the temperature. At the non-permissive temperature of 39°C, viruses can infect the cells. However, the synthesis of the vesicular stomatitis virus (VSV) glycoprotein is arrested in the rough endoplasmic reticulum. At 20°C the glycoproteins can leave the rough endoplasmic reticulum, but are arrested in the *trans*-Golgi network. When the temperature

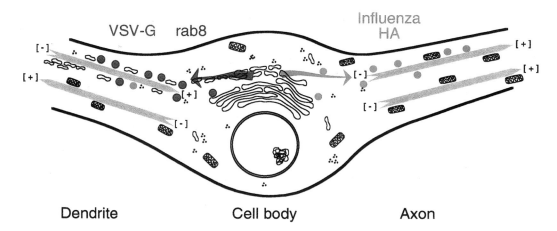

Fig. 3. Schematic representation of the pathways followed by different viral glycoproteins in infected polarized neurons. The VSV glycoprotein is delivered from the Golgi complex to the dendrites. The FPV hemagglutinin follows the route from Golgi to axon. Recent experiments suggest that rab8 is important for the dendritic delivery of VSV glycoprotein but not for the delivery of FPV hemagglutinin (Huber et al., 1993).

is raised to the permissive temperature of 32°C, a synchronous and massive transport from the Golgi apparatus to the plasma membrane takes place. After various times post-infection, neurons were fixed and processed for immunofluorescence. At the end of the 20°C block, the VSV glycoprotein was only observed in the cell body, consistent with a location in the Golgi complex. After one hour of incubation at the permissive temperature (32°C) intense labelling of both the cell body and the dendrites was observed. However, axons were devoid of labelling. Similarly, upon infection with Semliki Forest virus, the viral glycoproteins were only seen in the somatodendritic domain.

When hippocampal cells were infected with the avian fowl plague virus (FPV), the hemagglutinin protein was preferentially inserted into the axonal plasma membrane. Four hours after infection with the wild-type FPV virus, hemagglutinin fluorescence was predominantly observed in the cell body, in accordance with a distribution in the Golgi complex. One hour later, staining was present in all the axons as well. Dendritic labelling was variable; some dendrites were completely devoid of labelling, others showed staining in their proximal parts, which might represent either viral protein processing in the dendritically located Golgi cisternae or mis-sorting of the hemagglutinin. These immunofluorescence experiments were confirmed by quantitative immunoelectron microscopy. The illustration in Fig. 3 summarizes the findings of the neuronal infection approach.

These results show that the viral glycoproteins are transported from the *trans*-Golgi network to the axonal or dendritic plasma membrane via a direct pathway. It was thus suggested that the mechanism used by neurons to deliver newly synthesized viral glycoproteins to the axons and dendrites was similar to that operating in MDCK cells. In these cells the hemagglutinin protein is sorted directly to the apical membrane and the VSV glycoprotein to the basolateral domain.

To analyze whether the correlation in the sorting of viral proteins between epithelial cells and neurons would also hold for the sorting of glypiated proteins, the distribution of Thy-1, a GPI-linked protein, was investigated in hippocampal neurons in culture (Dotti et al., 1991). In polarized epithelial cells GPI-anchored proteins are preferentially targeted to the apical surface. First of all we demonstrated that in the hippocampal neurons Thy-1 was indeed membrane bound via a GPI-anchor. Secondly, immunofluorescence and immunoelectron microscopy revealed the exclusive distribution of Thy-1 on the axonal surface. This result strengthened our early hypothesis that the axonal domain is the analogue of the apical domain of the epithelial MDCK cells and that the dendritic plasma membrane is equivalent to the basolateral membrane. As discussed below, subsequent work has supported, as well as contradicted, this rule.

In support of the axonal/apical and dendritic/basolateral rule are studies concerning the localization of several GPI-linked and integral membrane proteins. GPI-anchored (like 5'-nucleotidase) TAG-1, F3/F11 and acetylcholinesterase are present in the axonal domain (Grondal and Zimmermann, 1987; Dodd et al., 1988; Furley et al., 1990; Faivre-

Sarrailh et al., 1992; Rotundo and Carbonetto, 1987). Moreover, a neuronal GPI-linked protein, an isoform of N-CAM, when expressed in epithelial cells follows the apical route (Powell et al., 1991). The similarities also extend to certain integral membrane proteins. For example, the transferrin receptor, which is present in the basolateral plasma membrane of epithelial cells (Fuller and Simons, 1986) is restricted to the dendritic plasma membrane of neurons (Cameron et al., 1991; Parton et al., 1992). The voltage-dependent sodium channel, preferentially restricted to the axon hillock and the nodes of Ranvier (Srinivasan et al., 1988; Joe and Angelides, 1992), is routed to the apical domain when expressed in MDCK cells (Angelides and Wible, unpublished data).

Contradictions to the rule axonal/apical-dendritic/basolateral have been described as well. The GPI-linked protein F3/F11, which is axonal in neuronal granule cells, is uniformly distributed in neuronal Golgi cells (Faivre-Sarrailh et al., 1992). Thus, one conclusion from these results would be that there is no uniformity on how different neuronal cells sort the same protein. Therefore, and because of this lack of uniformity, epithelial and neuronal cells cannot be compared. However, the absence of unity in the sorting mechanism of a given protein is also true for epithelial cells. In FRT cells, a polarized epithelial cell line derived from thyroid tissue, GPI-anchored proteins are either unsorted or routed to the basolateral domain (Zurzolo et al., 1993). The glycoproteins of certain viruses also follow divergent routes in different epithelial cells. The glycoproteins of Sindbis and Semliki Forest viruses, which are normally sorted to the basolateral domain of MDCK cells, are apically delivered in FRT cells (Zurzolo et al., 1992). The distribution of the human low-density lipoprotein (LDL) receptor constitutes another example of sorting divergence among epithelia. In transgenic mice, the receptor is found in the basolateral surface of hepatocytes and intestinal epithelial cells, but apical in the renal tube epithelium (Pathak et al., 1990).

The distribution of the Na⁺,K⁺-ATPase in neuronal and epithelial cells also contradicts the hypothesis of an axonal/apical-dendritic/basolateral rule (Pietrini et al., 1992). When the neuron-specific Na⁺,K⁺-ATPase was expressed in polarized epithelial cells, it was found on the basolateral surface. The endogenous protein is, however, uniformly distributed on the neuronal surface. The differences in distribution of this protein between epithelia and neurons may be due to specific interactions with the cytoskeleton. In epithelial cells newly synthesized Na⁺,K⁺-ATPase is delivered to both the apical and the basolateral domains. Upon insertion into the apical domain it is selectively removed, while in the basolateral membrane it is stabilized via interactions with the polarized cytoskeletal ankyrin/fodrin complex (Hammerton et al., 1991; Nelson and Veshnock, 1987; Nelson and Hammerton, 1989). The importance of the ankyrin/fodrin complex for the localization of the Na⁺,K⁺ pump is illustrated by the fact that a reversal of the ankyrin/fodrin polarity changes the polarity of Na⁺,K⁺-ATPase as well (Gundersen et al., 1991). The unpolarized distribution of Na⁺,K⁺-ATPase in hippocampal neurons might therefore by related to a lack of polarization of this cytoskeletal complex.

The role of microtubules in polarized protein transport

After leaving the *trans*-Golgi network, different proteins are packed into vesicles destined for either the axonal or the dendritic plasma membrane domain. How are these different vesicles transported to their correct destinations? Newly synthesized membrane proteins are transported by fast-axonal transport, a microtubule dependent event (Hammerschlag and Brady, 1988; Sheetz et al., 1989; Schroer, 1992). Nothing is known on how newly synthesized membrane proteins reach the dendritic plasma membrane. To determine whether or not microtubules are involved in the delivery of both axonal and dendritic exocytic vesicles, the effect of nocodazole on the delivery of viral envelope proteins was studied (C. G. Dotti and K. Simons, unpublished data). The addition of nocodazole inhibited transport of influenza hemagglutinin out of the cell body to the axon, resulting in an intense staining of the cell body. The dendritic delivery of the glycoprotein from VSV was affected similarly; in 71% of the infected cells dendritic transport was abolished and again intense labelling of the cell body was observed in these cells. Although the transport from the Golgi apparatus to the dendrites was inhibited, budding of the VSV virus still occurred in the cell body area. This indicates that the inhibition of viral protein delivery was due to the lack of microtubules and not caused by a functional impairment of the Golgi apparatus. The effects of nocodazole treatment were reversible. Already 1.5 hours after removal of nocodazole the VSV glycoprotein was observed again in the dendrites and the hemagglutinin of FPV in the axon. These results suggest that the delivery of both axonal and dendritic exocytic vesicles is mediated by microtubuli.

Since the peripherally located microtubules of axons and dendrites are of uniform polarity, with their plus ends directed distally (Baas et al., 1988), our results pose a challenge to the newly formed axonal and dendritic plasma membrane proteins: how to choose the right microtubules. The answer to that question appears complicated and several specific molecular interactions have to come into place simultaneously. A simple scenario would be as follows. Axonal and dendritic membrane proteins are packed in different vesicles at the *trans*-Golgi network, each one having specific proteinaceous and lipidic partners, as demonstrated for apical and basolateral vesicles of epithelial cells (Wandinger-Ness et al., 1990; Kurzchalia et al., 1992). After budding from the *trans*-Golgi network, different microtubule-vesicle-binding motors with a plus-end, kinesin-like, directed force will associate with axonal and dendritic vesicles (Hirokawa et al., 1991). This is quite likely considering the number, at least 35, of members in the kinesin family (Goldstein, 1991). Some of them are known to associate specifically with a certain class of vesicles like synaptic vesicles (for the kinesin Unc104) or vesicles containing neurotransmitter channels (Hall and Hedgecock, 1991; Gho et al., 1992). The last condition would then be the recognition of the axonal and dendritic plus-ended microtubules. The different MAPs that associate with axonal or dendritic microtubules (Kosik and Finch, 1987; Sato-Yoshitade et al., 1989; Caceres et al., 1984) can act as such recognition molecules.

Maintenance of polarity

Although the axonal and dendritic plasma membranes have different compositions, the plasma membrane is in principle continuous. The two membrane domains still maintain their unique features, indicating that diffusion obviously does not occur. In epithelial cells, tight junctions, located at the border between the apical and the basolateral domain, prevent mixing of the different membrane components (van Meer and Simons, 1986; Gumbiner, 1987). To determine whether a diffusion barrier is present in neurons, experiments similar to those described by van Meer and Simons (1986) were performed (Kobayashi et al., 1992). Vesicles containing water-insoluble fluorescent lipids were added to influenza virus-infected polarized neurons. Taking advantage of the fusogenic activity of the influenza hemagglutinin protein at low pH, fluorescent vesicles fused exclusively to the axonal domain. Uninfected neurons never showed any labelling, indicating that the fusion process was indeed hemagglutinin dependent. Although the fluorescent lipids were mobile in the axonal domain, as shown by energy transfer and fluorescence recovery after photobleaching, diffusion of labelling to the cell body or dendrites was never observed; the fluorescence terminated abruptly at the axon origin (Fig. 4). Since the hemagglutinin was inserted along the entire axonal surface, from the axon origins to their ends, it is unlikely that the lack of labelling in the cell soma is due to the slow diffusion of the labelled lipids. Even four hours after fusion, labelling of the somatodendritic domain was not observed (T. Kobayashi and C. G. Dotti, unpublished observation). The diffusion barrier was not located in the axonal cytosol; fusion of liposomes containing the fluorescent water-soluble calcein resulted in labelling of the entire cell cytosol, including the somatodenditic part. By fusing both symmetrically and asymmetrically labeled vesicles, which contain the fluorescent lipids in both leaflets or only the inner leaflet of the vesicle, respectively, it became clear that the diffusion barrier was in both leaflets of the plasma membrane. This is in contrast to the barrier of epithelial cells, which is present in the outer leaflet of the plasma membrane only (van Meer and Simons, 1986).

Although the precise molecular composition of this diffusion barrier is unknown, it must block the diffusion of plasma membrane proteins as well because many, including GPI-linked proteins, are highly mobile in the plasma membrane (Zhang et al., 1991; Ishihara et al., 1987), but do not mix with the dendritic domain (Dotti et al., 1991). It is plausible that a submicroscopic organization is responsible for such a fence. However, its true nature is still a mystery.

Onset of neuronal polarity

Morphological polarity of hippocampal neurons in culture is visible early after plating. Between two and three days of culture, the future axon can be distinguished from the other outgrowing neurites (Dotti et al., 1988). We referred to those young polarized neurons as 'stage 3' neurons. This morphological polarization is not yet fixed in this phase of development. Amputating the major neurite, which will develop into the axon, resulted in the outgrowth of one of

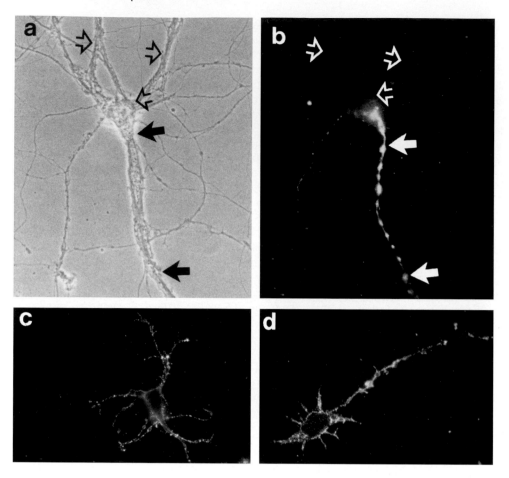

Fig. 4. pH-mediated fusion of fluorescently labeled liposomes containing the ganglioside $GD_{1\alpha}$ to FPV-infected neurons. In stage 5 neurons (a-b) the fluorescent liposomes label the axon (filled arrows), indicating that binding and fusion are hemagglutinin-specific. Labeling is absent from the cell body and dendrites (open arrows), which suggests that a barrier prevents the diffusion of the labeled lipids from the axonal shaft. This cell was photographed 90 minutes after fusion. A similar infection protocol followed by liposome binding (c) and fusion (d) shows uniform labeling on all processes of a stage 2 cell (c) and on the axon and dendrites of a stage 3 (c) neuron.

the remaining smaller neurites (Dotti and Banker, 1987). Lack of sorting of certain molecules accompanies this absence of morphological commitment. Thus, Thy-1, which is axonal in the mature hippocampal neurons, was found in axons and dendrites of stage 3 cells (C. Dotti, R. Parton and K. Simons, unpublished results) and the same was found when the distribution of viral glycoproteins was analyzed (Dotti and Simons, 1990). Other examples of proteins that show a polarized distribution in the mature but not in the young cells are the transferrin receptor, the cytoskeletal proteins MAP 2 and tau and the small GTP-binding protein rab8 (Dotti and Simons 1990; Dotti et al., 1990, 1991; Cameron et al., 1991; Kosik and Finch, 1987; Huber et al., 1993). Even GAP-43, a protein specifically involved in the early stages of axonal growth, has recently been shown to be present in axon and dendrites (van Lookeren Campagne et al., 1992; however, see Goslin et al., 1988). It is therefore obvious to ask when and how molecular sorting first occurs in neuronal cells. Will epithelial cells help to disclose the mechanisms underlying the initial stages of neuronal sorting? In epithelia, the development of polarity seems to be induced by cell-cell and cell-substratum contact (Gumbiner and Simons, 1986). This results in the gradual redistribution of ankyrin and spectrin, which leads to a polarized organization of Na^+,K^+-ATPase and probably triggers other intracellular mechanisms involved in the polarized delivery of newly synthesized proteins (Rodriguez-Boulan and Nelson, 1989; McNeill et al., 1990). During neuronal development, numerous cell contacts take place. However, these are transitory. The fixed neuronal circuitry, in the form of synaptic appositions, occurs at later times. Thus, one may speculate that molecular sorting would take place after the final synaptic contacts have been established. Whether electrical activity or cellular interactions are responsible for the triggering of molecular sorting must be tested experimentally.

PERSPECTIVES

Neurons polarize in a very complicated fashion. Some neurons are unipolar, some are bipolar and some are multipolar. Even among the same type, there are numerous differences: in the type of neurotransmitter, in the length of the axon, in the target cells, in the growing environment and in the number of dendrites. As they are such complex and heterogeneous cells, the mechanisms of sorting will be varied and complex. However, it is still possible that some of the basic mechanisms are conserved. To analyze this, we asked if the mechanisms of sorting of epithelial cells also existed in a neuronal cell type. We found some striking similarities but also divergences. Nevertheless, and independently of resemblances and differences, subordination to epithelial cell biology has been rewarding and we have answered some specific neurobiological questions. More importantly, new questions have been engendered and it may be that neurons, because of their special morphological features, become useful for studying some problems of intracellular sorting that are difficult to approach in epithelial cells; for instance, the direct observation of membrane traffic, as recently shown during endocytosis (Parton et al., 1992).

Special thanks are given to Liane Meyn for her excellent technical assistence and to Kai Simons for his constant encouragement and advice. We also thank Anne Walter (Cell Biology Program, EMBL) for help in the preparation of the manuscript, and Toshihide Kobayashi and Lukas Huber (EMBL), who worked on some of the experiments described here. Meltsje de Hoop is a recipient of a Human Frontier Science Program fellowship (LT 118/92).

REFERENCES

Baas, P. W., Deitch, J. S., Black, M. M. and Banker, G. (1988). Polarity orientation of microtubules in hippocampal neurons: Uniformity in the axon and nonuniformity in the dendrite. *Proc. Nat. Acad. Sci. USA* **85**, 8335-8339.

Banker, G. A. and Waxman, A. B. (1988). Hippocampal neurons generate natural shapes in cell culture. In *Intrinsic Determinants of Neuronal Form and Function* (ed. R. J. Lasek), pp. 61-82. New York: Alan Liss.

Barlett, W. P. and Banker, G. A. (1984). An electron microscopic study of the development of axons and dendrites by hippocampal neurons in culture. *J. Neurosci.* **4**, 1944-1953.

Brewer, C. B. and Roth, M. G. (1991). A single amino acid change in the cytoplasmic domain alters the polarized delivery of influenza virus hemagglutinin. *J. Cell Biol.* **114**, 413-421.

Caceres, A., Banker, G. A., Steward, O., Binder, L. and Payne, M. (1984). MAP2 is localized to the dendrites of hippocampal neurons which develop in culture. *Dev. Brain Res.* **13**, 314-318.

Cameron, P. L., Südhof, T. C., Jahn, R. and De Camilli, P. (1991). Colocalization of synaptophysin with transferrin receptors: Implications for synaptic vesicle biogenesis. *J. Cell Biol.* **116**, 151-164.

Casanova, J. E., Apodaca, G. and Mostov, K. E. (1991). An autonomous signal for basolateral sorting in the cytoplasmic domain of the polymeric immunoglobulin receptor. *Cell* **66**, 65-75.

Davis, L., Banker, G. A. and Steward, O. (1987). Selective dendritic transport of RNA in hippocampal neurons in culture. *Nature* **330**, 477-479.

Dodd, J., Morton, S. B., Karagogeos, D., Yamamoto, M. and Jessell, T. M. (1988). Spatial regulation of axonal glycoprotein expression on subsets of embryonic spinal neurons. *Neuron* **1**, 105-116

Dotti, C. G. and Banker, G. A. (1987). Experimentally induced alteration in the polarity of developing neurons. *Nature* **330**, 255-257.

Dotti, C. G., Kartenbeck, J., Parton, R. and Simons, K. (1993). Polarized distribution of the viral glycoproteins of vesicular stomatitis, fowl plague and semliki forest viruses in hippocampal neurons in culture: a light and electron microscopy study. *Brain Res.* **610**, 141-147.

Dotti, C. G., Parton, R. and Simons, K. (1991). Polarized sorting of glypiated proteins in hippocampal neurons. *Nature* **349**, 158-161.

Dotti, C. G. and Simons, K. (1990). Polarized sorting of viral glycoproteins to the axon and dendrites of hippocampal neurons in culture. *Cell* **62**, 63-72.

Dotti C. G., Sullivan, C. A. and Banker, G. A. (1988). The establishment of polarity by hippocampal neurons in culture. *J. Neurosci.* **8**, 1454-1468.

Faivre-Sairrailh, C., Gennarini, G., Goridis, C. and Rougon, G. (1992). F3/F11 cell surface molecule expression in the developing mouse cerebellum is polarized at synaptic sites and within granule cells. *J. Neurosci.* **12**, 257-267.

Fuller, S. D. and Simons, K. (1986). Transferrin receptor polarity and recycling accuracy in 'tight' and 'leaky' strains of Madin-Darby canine kidney cells. *J. Cell Biol.* **103**, 1767-1779.

Furley, A. J., Morton, S. B., Manalo, D., Karagogoes, D., Dodd, J. and Jesell, T. M. (1990). The axonal glycoprotein TAG-1 is an immunoglobulin superfamily member with neurite outgrowth-promoting activity. *Cell* **61**, 157-170.

Gho, M., Mcdonald, K., Ganetzky, B. and Saxton, W. M. (1992). Effects of kinesin mutations on neuronal functions. *Science* **258**, 313-316.

Goldstein, L. (1991). The kinesin superfamily: tails of functional redundancy. *Trends Cell Biol.* **1**, 93-99.

Goslin, K., Schereyer, D., Skene, J. H. and Banker, G. (1988). Development of neuronal polarity: GAP43 distinguishes axonal from dendritic growth cones. *Nature* **336**, 672-680.

Grondal, E. J. M. and Zimmermann, H. (1987). Purification, characterization and cellular localization of 5'-nucleotidase from *Torpedo* electric organ. *Biochem. J.* **245**, 805-810.

Gumbiner, B. (1987). Structure, biochemistry and assembly of epithelial tight junctions. *Amer. J. Physiol.* **253**, C749-C758.

Gumbiner, B. and Simons, K. (1986). A functional assay for proteins involved in establishing an epithelial occluding barrier: Identification of a uvomorulin-like polypeptide. *J. Cell Biol.* **102**, 457-468.

Gunderson, D., Orlowski, J. and Rodriguez-Boulan, E. (1991). Apical polarity of Na, K-ATPase in retinal pigment epithelium is linked to a reversal of the ankyrin-fodrin submembrane cytoskeleton. *J. Cell Biol.* **112**, 863-873.

Hall, D. H. and Hedgecock, E. M. (1991). Kinesin-related gene unc104 is required for axonal transport of synaptic vesicles in *C. elegans. Cell* **65**, 837-847.

Hammerschlag, R. and Brady, S. (1988). The cytoskeleton and axonal transport. In *Basic Neurochemistry* (ed. G. Siegel, B. Alberts, B. Agranoff and P. Molinof), pp. 457-478. Raven Press, New York.

Hammerton, R. W., Krzeminski, K. A., Mays, R. W., Ryan, T. A., Wollner, D. A. and Nelson, W. J. (1991). Mechanism for regulating cell surface distribution of Na+,K+-ATPase in polarized epithelial cells. *Science* **254**, 847-850.

Hirokawa, N., Sato-Yoshitake, R., Kobayashi, N., Pfister, K., Bloom, G. and Brady, S. (1991). Kinesin associates with anterogradely transported organelles in vivo. *J. Cell Biol.* **114**, 295-302.

Hopkins, C. R. (1991). Polarity signals. *Cell* **66**, 827-829.

Hopkins, C. R. (1992). Selective membrane protein trafficking: vectorial flow and filter. *Trends Biochem. Sci.* **17**, 27-33.

Huber, L., de Hoop, M., Dupree, P., Zerial, M, Simons, K. and Dotti, C. (1993). Protein transport ti the dendritic plasma membrane of cultured neurons is regulated by rab8p. *J. Cell Biol.* **123**, 47-55.

Ishihara, A., Hou, Y. and Jacobson, (1987). The Thy-1 antigen exhibits rapid lateral diffusion in the plasma membrane of rodent lymphoid cells and fibroblasts. *Proc. Nat. Acad. Sci. USA* **84**, 1290-1293.

Jalal, F., Lemay, G., Zollinger, M., Berteloot, A. Boileau, G. and Grine, P. (1991). Neutral endopeptidase, a major brush border protein of the kidney proximal nephron, is directly targeted to the apical domain when expressed in Madin-Darby Canine Kidney cells. *J. Biol. Chem.* **266**, 19826-19832.

Joe, E. and Angelides, K. (1992). Clustering of voltage-dependent sodium channels on axons depends on Schwann cell contact. *Nature* **356**, 333-335

Killisch, I., Dotti, C. G., Laurie, D. J., Luddens, H. and Seeburg, P. H. (1991). Expression patterns of GABA$_A$ receptor subtypes in developing hippocampal neurons. *Neuron* **7**, 927-936.

Kobayashi, T., Storrie, B., Simons, K. and Dotti, C. G. (1992). A functional barrier to movement of lipids in polarized neurons. *Nature* **359**, 647-650.

Kosik, K. S. and Finch, E. A. (1987). MAP2 and tau segragate into dendritic and axonal domains after after the elaboration of morphologically distinct neurites: an immunocytochemical study. *J. Neurosci.* **7**, 3142-3153.

Kurzchalia, T. V., Dupree, P., Parton, R., Kellner, R., Virta, H., Lehnert, M. and Simons, K. (1992). VIP21, a 21-kD membrane protein is an integral component of *trans*-Golgi-network-derived transport vesicle. *J. Cell Biol.* **118**, 1003-1014.

Le Bivic, A., Sambuy, Y., Patzak, A., Patil, N., Chao, M. and Rodriguez-Boulan, E. (1991). An internal deletion in the cytoplasmic tail reverses the apical localization of the human NGF receptor in trasnfected MDCK cells. *J. Cell Biol.* **115**, 607-618.

Lidov, H. G. W., Byers, T. J., Watkins, S. C. and Kunkel, L. M. (1990). Localization of dystrophin to postsynaptic regions of the central nervous system of cortical neurons. *Nature* **348**, 725-727.

Lisanti, M. P., Le Bivic, A., Saltiel, A. R. and Rodriguez-Boulan, E. (1990). Preferred apical distribution of glycosyl-phosphatidylinositol (GPI) anchored proteins: A highly conserved feature of the polarized epithelial cell phenotype. *J. Membr. Biol.* **113**, 155-167.

Lisanti, M. P. and Rodriguez-Boulan, E. (1990). Glycophospholipid membrane anchoring provides clues to the mechanism of protein sorting in polarized epithelial cells. *Trends Biochem. Sci.* **15**, 113-118.

McNeill, H., Ozawa, M., Kemler, R. and Nelson, W. J. (1990). Novel function of the cell adhesion molecule uvomorulin as an inducer of cell surface polarity. *Cell* **62**, 309-315.

Mostov, K., Apodaca, G., Aroeti, B. and Okamoto, C. (1992). Plasma membrane protein sorting in polarized epithelial cells. *J. Cell Biol.* **116**, 577-583.

Nelson, W. J. (1992). Regulation of cell surface polarity from bacteria to mammals. *Science* **258**, 948-955.

Nelson, W. J. and Hammerton, R. W. (1989). A membrane-cytoskeletal complex containing Na+,K+-ATPase, ankyrin and fodrin in Madin-Darby Canine Kidney (MDCK) cells: Implications for the biogenesis of epithelial cell polarity. *J. Cell Biol.* **108**, 893-902.

Nelson, W. J. and Veshnock, P. (1987). Ankyrin binding to Na+,K+-ATPase and implications for the organization of membrane domains in polarized cells. *Nature* **328**, 533-536.

Parton, R. G., Simons, K. and Dotti, C. G. (1992). Axonal and dendritic endocytic pathways in cultured neurons. *J. Cell Biol.* **119**, 123-137.

Pathak, R. K., Yokode, M., Hammer, R. E., Hofmann, S. L., Brown, M. S., Goldstein, J. L. and Anderson, R. G. W. (1990). Tissue-specific sorting of the human LDL receptor in polarized epithelia of transgenic mice. *J. Cell Biol.* **11**, 347-359.

Pietrini, G., Matteoli, M., Banker, G. and Caplan, M. (1992). Isoforms of the Na, K-ATPases are present in both axons and dendrites of hippocampal neurons in culture. *Proc. Nat. Acad. Sci. USA* **89**, 8414-8418.

Powell, S. K., Cunningham, B. A., Edelman, G. M. and Rodriguez-Boulan, E. (1991). Transmembrane and GPI anchored forms of NCAM are targeted to opposite domains of a polarized epithelial cell. *Nature* **353**, 76-77.

Rodriguez-Boulan, E. and Nelson, W. J. (1989). Morphogenesis of the polarized epithelial cell phenotype. *Science* **245**, 718-725.

Rotundo, R. L. and Carbonetto, S. T. (1987) Neurons segregate clusters of membrane-bound acetylcholinesterase along their neurites. *Proc. Nat. Acad. Sci. USA* **84**, 2063-2067.

Ruegg, M. A., Stoeckli, E. T., Kuhn, T. B., Heller, M., Zuellig, R and Sonderegger, P. (1989). Purification of axonin-1, a protein that is secreted from axons during neurogenesis. *EMBO J.* **6**, 55-63.

Sato-Yoshitake, R., Shiomura, Y. Miyasaka, H. and Hirokawa, N. (1989). Microtubule-associated protein 1B: Molecular structure, localization and phosphorylation-dependent expression in developing neurons. *Neuron* **1**, 229-238.

Scheetz, M. P., Steuer, E. R. and Schroer, T. A. (1989). The mechanism and regulation of fast axonal transport. *Trends Neurosci.* **12**, 474-478.

Schell, M. J., Maurice, M., Stieger, B. and Hubbard, A. L. (1992). 5′Nucleotidase is sorted to the apical domain of hepatocytes via an indirect route. *J. Cell Biol.* **119**, 1173-1182.

Schroer, T. A. (1992). Motors for fast axonal transport. *Curr. Opin. Neurobiol.* **2**, 618-621.

Shaw, G., Banker, G. A. and Weber, K. (1985). An immunofluorescence study of neurofilament protein expression by developing hippocampal neurons in tissue culture. *Eur. J. Cell Biol.* **39**, 205-216.

Simons, K. and Wandinger-Ness, A. (1990). Polarized sorting in epithelia. *Cell* **62**, 207-210.

Srinivasan, Y., Elmer, L., Davis, J., Bennett, V and Angelides, K. (1988). Ankyrin and spectrin associate with voltage-dependent sodium channels in brain. *Nature* **333**, 177-180.

Steward, O. and Banker, G. A. (1992). Getting the message from the gene to the synapse: sorting and intracellular transport of RNA in neurons. *Trends Neurosci.* **15**, 180-186.

Townbridge, I. S. (1991). Endocytosis and signals for internalization. *Curr. Opin. Cell Biol.* **3**, 634-641.

van Lookeren Campagne, M., Dotti, C. G., Verkleij, A. J., Gispen, W. H. and Oestereicher, A. B. (1992). Redistribution of B-50/growth cone associated protein 43 during differentiation and maturation of rat hippocampal neurons in vitro. *Neuroscience* **51**, 601-619.

van Meer, G. and Simons, K. (1986). The function of tight junctions in maintaining differences in lipid composition between the apical and the basolateral cell surface domains of MDCK cells. *EMBO J.* **5**, 1455-1464.

Wandinger-Ness, A., Bennett, M. K., Antony, C. and Simons, K. (1990). Distinct transport vesicles mediate the delivery of plasma membrane proteins to the apical and basolateral domain. *J. Cell Biol.* **111**, 9487-1000.

Wessels, H. P., Hansen, G. H., Fuhrer, C., Look, A. T., Sjöström, H., Norén, O. and Spiess, M. (1990). Aminopeptidase N is directly sorted to the apical domain in MDCK cells. *J. Cell Biol.* **111**, 2923-2930.

Zhang, F., Crise, B., Su, B., Hou, Y., Rose, J. K., Bothwell, A. and Jacobson, K. (1991). Lateral diffusion of membrane-spanning and glycosylphosphatidylinositol-linked proteins: towards establishing rules governing the lateral mobility of membrane proteins. *J. Cell Biol.* **115**, 75-84.

Zurzolo, C., Polistina, C., Saini, M., Gentile, R., Aloj, L., Migliaccio, G., Bonatti, S. and Nitsch, L. (1992). Opposite polarity of virus budding and of viral envelope glycoprotein distribution in epithelial cells derived from different tissues. *J. Cell Biol.* **117**, 551-564.

Zurzolo, C., Lisanti, M., Caras, I., Nitsch, L. and Rodriguez-Boulan, E. (1993). Glycosylphosphatidylinositol-anchored proteins are preferentially targeted to the basolateral surface in Fischer rat thyroid epithelial cells. *J. Cell Biol.* **121**, 1031-1039.

Journal of Cell Science, Supplement 17, 93-100 (1993)
Printed in Great Britain © The Company of Biologists Limited 1993

Traffic of synaptic vesicle proteins in polarized and nonpolarized cells

Patricia Cameron, Olaf Mundigl and Pietro De Camilli

Department of Cell Biology, Howard Hughes Medical Institute and Yale University School of Medicine, 333 Cedar Street, New Haven, CT 06510, USA

SUMMARY

Neurons have at least two pathways of regulated secretion, which involve two classes of secretory organelles: typical synaptic vesicles (SVs) and large dense-core vesicles. Large dense-core vesicles store and secrete peptide neurotransmitters and amines, and may be seen as the neuronal counterpart of secretory granules of endocrine cells. SVs are highly specialized secretory organelles, which store and secrete non-peptide hormones and play a dominant role in the fast, point-to-point signalling typical of the nervous system. Microvesicles that share a variety of biochemical and functional similarities with SVs (synaptic-like microvesicles) have recently been described in endocrine cells. SVs and synaptic-like microvesicles are closely related to vesicular carriers of the receptor-mediated recycling pathway. They undergo repeated cycles of exo-endocytosis, which are thought to involve endosomal intermediates.

In mature neurons, SVs are concentrated in axon endings. To gain insight into the mechanisms responsible for SV targeting, we have studied the traffic of SV proteins in both endocrine cells and developing hippocampal neurons in primary culture at different stages of differentiation. Additionally, the distribution of the SV protein synaptophysin, when expressed by transfection in fibroblastic cells or in polarized epithelial cells (MDCK cells), was investigated.

SV proteins are already present in developing neurons at stages preceding the establishment of neuronal polarity. As axons and dendrites form, SV proteins are found in both types of processes, although they become progressively more concentrated in the axon. Throughout these developmental stages SVs undergo active exo-endocytotic recycling. The nonpolarized distribution of SV proteins is observed even at stages when the transferrin receptor, a protein that is present in epithelial cells only at the basolateral surface, is already restricted to dendrites. This indicates that, in immature neurons, SV proteins are not selectively targeted to axons and that the accumulation in axons may at least partially result from a specific retention. In agreement with this finding, synaptophysin, when transfected into MDCK cells, was targeted to both the basolateral and the apical plasma membrane. Brefeldin A, a fungal metabolite that induces a modification of the steady-state localization of endosomal proteins in a variety of cell types, was found to have a different effect on the distribution of SV proteins in dendrites and in axons. Taken together, these observations support the existence of two separate endosomal systems in axons and dendrites, which have differential properties, are enriched in different proteins, and may be related to the basolateral and apical endosomes of epithelial cells.

Key words: synaptophysin, transferrin receptor, endosomes

INTRODUCTION

Neurons are highly polarized cells that are specialized for the reception, integration and emission of signals. The perikaryal-dendritic region is specialized for receptive functions, the axon for the translocation of signals over long distances, and the axon terminal for the regulated secretion of signal molecules. Two main classes of organelles participate in regulated secretion from nerve terminals: large dense-core vesicles and synaptic vesicles (SVs) (Hökfelt et al., 1986). Large dense-core vesicles store and secrete peptide neurotransmitters and may also contain amines. They are the neuronal equivalent of secretory granules of endocrine cells, which secrete amines and peptide hor-

mones. Large dense-core vesicles have a scattered distribution in nerve terminals where their exocytosis is not restricted to the synaptic region and is preferentially triggered by trains of closely spaced action potentials. Secretion via large dense-core vesicles plays primarily a modulatory role at synapses (De Camilli and Jahn, 1990; Thureson-Klein et al., 1988). SVs store and secrete 'fast' non-peptide neurotransmitters and represent a highly specialized class of secretory organelles. They are homogeneous in size and they form large clusters in which SVs are connected to each other by a cytoskeletal matrix. These clusters, in turn, are docked to the region of the plasmalemma that faces the synaptic cleft. Exocytosis of SVs takes place selectively at this region and is stimulated with an extremely short latency (less than 1 millisecond) by nerve terminal depolarization. Secretion via synaptic vesicles is responsible for the fast point-to-point signalling typical of synapses as well as for modulatory signalling (Pappas and Purpura, 1972; De Camilli and Jahn, 1990).

The biogenesis of large dense-core vesicles is well established. Like endocrine secretory granules, large dense-core vesicles are assembled and loaded with their contents in the region of the *trans*-Golgi network (TGN) and are transported to the cell periphery as mature organelles (Tooze, 1991). The site where SVs are first generated remains unclear, but is well known that SVs undergo cycles of exo-endocytosis in nerve terminals and that at each cycle they are re-loaded with neurotransmitter content by transporters and enzymes present in the axon ending (Ceccarelli et al., 1973; Heuser and Reese, 1973; Betz and Bewick, 1992). Thus, these organelles can be continuously re-formed at a site distant from the TGN (Regnier-Vigouroux et al., 1991; Cameron et al., 1991; Lindstedt and Kelly, 1991).

The precise recycling pathway of SVs and the molecular mechanisms underlying this process have become the focus of intense investigation over the last several years (De Camilli and Jahn, 1990; Südhof and Jahn, 1991; Trimble et al., 1991; Greengard et al., 1993; Kelly, 1993). The most widely accepted hypothesis is that SV recycling involves clathrin-coated vesicles and early endosomal intermediates (Heuser, 1989; Maycox et al., 1992), but a direct re-formation of SVs from the plasmalemma cannot be ruled out. If the re-formation of SVs involves fusion of coated vesicle-derived structures with early endosomes and budding from endosomes, the recycling of SVs can be seen as a special case of the receptor-mediated recycling pathway (Mellman et al., 1987). By extension, it would also represent a special case of vesicular recycling, which takes place at all the stations of the secretory and endocytic pathway where

anatomically distinct compartments are functionally interconnected by vesicular traffic. Thus, the study of the mechanisms involved in budding, docking and fusion of SVs and SV-derived structures may shed light on mechanisms of vesicular traffic in general. A unique advantage offered by the study of SVs as a prototypic vesicular carrier is the possibility of isolating them in high yield and purity (Huttner et al., 1983). This facilitates the identification and characterization of the main molecular components of their membranes, an important first step in elucidating molecular mechanisms. Many protein families present in SV membranes have already been identified. In order to establish how this information is relevant to other aspects of membrane traffic it is important to establish the precise relationship between SV recycling and other types of membrane recycling. This short review will address this relationship.

Synaptic vesicles represent one of the best-characterized transport vesicles. A schematic drawing, which illustrates some of the main protein components that have been identified on SVs, is shown in Fig. 1 (for reviews see De Camilli et al., 1990; Trimble et al., 1991; Südhof and Jahn, 1991; Bennett et al., 1992; Jessel and Kandel, 1993; Greengard et al., 1993).

SV RECYCLING AND CONSTITUTIVE PLASMALEMMA-ENDOSOME RECYCLING IN ALL CELLS: CLUES FROM TRANSFECTED FIBROBLASTS

One approach, which has been taken to elucidate the relationships between the trafficking of SV proteins and well-established traffic pathways of all cells, is to transfect SV proteins in cells that do not contain SVs and to monitor

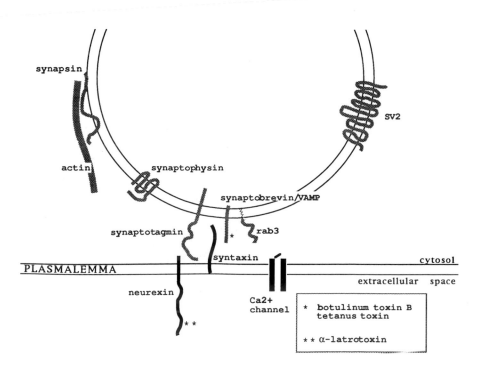

Fig. 1. Schematic drawing illustrating some the major protein families of synaptic vesicles and of the presynaptic plasmalemma. Synaptobrevin is the target for the endopeptidase activity of botulinus toxin B and tetanus toxin; the neurexin family includes the receptor for α-latrotoxin (reviewed by De Camilli et al., 1990; Südhof and Jahn, 1991; Bennett et al., 1992; Jessel and Kandel, 1993; Greengard et al., 1993; see also Scheller et al., this volume).

their targeting in this ectopic environment. The rationale behind this approach is that a SV protein will follow the intracellular trafficking route more closely related to the trafficking route of SVs in neurons. When synaptophysin, one of the most abundant SV membrane proteins (Wiedenmann and Franke, 1985; Jahn et al., 1985), was expressed in fibroblastic CHO cells, its intracellular distribution was virtually identical to that of transferrin and LDL receptors, two proteins that undergo constitutive recycling through the receptor-mediated recycling pathway (Johnston et al., 1989; Cameron et al., 1991; Linstedt and Kelly, 1991). Colocalization was demonstrated by a variety of complementary procedures including immunocytochemistry, immunoisolation, and equilibrium and velocity centrifugation. Additionally, brefeldin A (BFA) induced a redistribution into the same tubular network of both the transferrin receptor and synaptophysin (Fig. 2). BFA is a fungal metabolite that induces a massive fusion of early endosomes with each other and with elements of the TGN, resulting in the formation of an interconnected network of tubules where proteins of early endosomes and the TGN are intermixed (Lippincott-Schwartz et al., 1991).

Similar results were obtained when synaptoporin was expressed in CHO cells (Fykse et al., 1993). These findings indicate that at least two abundant SV proteins have targeting information, which leads to their accumulation in the receptor-mediated recycling pathway. They support the hypothesis that the recycling of SVs is closely related to the vesicular recycling between early endosomes and the plasmalemma.

PARTIAL OVERLAP OF SV RECYCLING AND TRANSFERRIN RECEPTOR RECYCLING IN ENDOCRINE CELLS

The elucidation of the relationship between the SV recycling pathway and the receptor-mediated recycling pathway in neurons is complicated by the presence of distinct cellular compartments specialized for different functions. It would be useful to compare these two pathways in cells that contain SVs but that are not polarized. Cell lines derived from endocrine cells that secrete amines and/or peptide hormones have these properties.

Until recently, SVs were considered neuron-specific organelles. However, it is now clear that organelles closely related to SVs (referred to as synaptic-like microvesicles) are present in endocrine cells (De Camilli, 1991). Synaptic-like microvesicles have a membrane composition very similar to that of SVs and, like SVs, undergo exocytosis, endocytosis and recycling (Navone et al., 1986; Wiedenmann et al., 1988; Baumert et al., 1990; Cameron et al., 1991; Linstedt and Kelly, 1991; Régnier-Vigouroux et al., 1991). In addition, they appear to share with SVs the property of storing and secreting signalling molecules: synaptic-like microvesicles of pancreatic β-cell lines were shown to contain GABA (Thomas-Reetz et al., 1993) and those of the chromaffin cell-derived PC12 cells were shown to contain acetylcholine (Bauerfeind et al., 1993). Thus, synaptic-like microvesicles of endocrine cell lines represent a useful model system with which to study basic aspects of SV traffic in a non-polarized cell.

In endocrine cells SV proteins are present primarily in two pools. One pool is localized in organelles with the same morphology and sedimentation characteristics as SVs, i.e. in bona fide synaptic-like microvesicles. The other pool is colocalized with the transferrin receptor and the LDL receptor in tubulovesicular structures with the morphology and sedimentation characteristics of early endosomes. The two pools of SV proteins present in a low-speed cell supernatants of endocrine cell lines (RIN cells and PC12 cells) are dramatically demonstrated by velocity sedimentation in glycerol gradients (Cameron et al., 1991; Lindstedt and Kelly, 1991). In immunoisolation experiments carried out with PC12 cells, about two-thirds of the transferrin receptor was recovered with synaptophysin-containing membranes (Cameron et al., 1991). Upon BFA treatment, a large fraction of synaptophysin is redistributed in the same tubular network, which is positive for transferrin receptor (our unpublished observations).

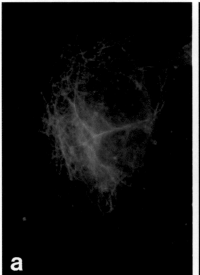

Fig. 2. Colocalization of synaptophysin and internalized rhodaminated transferrin after BFA treatment in transfected CHO cells that stably express synaptophysin. Cells were treated with 10 μg/ml BFA during the last 20 minutes of a 1 hour incubation with rhodamine-transferrin. Subsequently, cells were fixed and stained for synaptophysin. The TGN-endosome tubular network induced by BFA is positive for both synaptophysin (a) and transferrin (b). Bars, 20 μm.

Taken together these data suggest that in endocrine cells the traffic of SV proteins and the constitutive recycling of transferrin receptor are highly interrelated. A cartoon, which summarizes possible relationships of synaptic-like microvesicles to early endosomes in endocrine cells, is shown in Fig. 3. The model predicts that at each exo-endocytotic cycle, membrane proteins of synaptic-like microvesicles are internalized together with recycling receptors via clathrin-coated vesicles and are then delivered to early endosomes. Subsequently, SV proteins are sorted away from recycling receptors in early endosomes and are assembled into membrane microdomains, which bud off as synaptic-like microvesicles. Whether or not SLMVs may also be re-formed directly from the plasmalemma is not known at present.

SEGREGATION OF SYNAPTIC VESICLE RECYCLING FROM TRANSFERRIN RECEPTOR RECYCLING IN POLARIZED NEURONS

In mature neurons, the presynaptic terminal is the cellular compartment specialized for the recycling of SV proteins. However, it is clear that endosome-plasmalemma recycling pathways operate both in axons and in dendrites. Until recently, little information was available regarding recycling traffic in the perikaryal-dendritic region of neurons. Given the complexity of neuronal tissue, an analysis of these traffic pathways cannot be practically performed on neurons in situ using either morphological or biochemical methods. However, central nervous system neurons can be grown in primary culture, and cultured neurons represent a powerful system for studying protein and organelle traffic using morphological techniques. It was shown that cultured hippocampal neurons faithfully express many of the properties of their in situ counterparts. These neurons establish axonal and dendritic polarity even when grown in isolation, thus allowing for the study of those features of cell polarity that are intrinsic to a neuron irrespective of its contact with neighboring cells (Goslin and Banker, 1989).

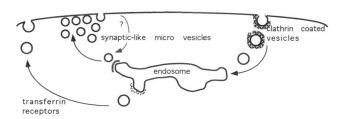

Fig. 3. Hypothetical models concerning the recycling of synaptic-like microvesicle- (SLMVs) proteins in endocrine cells. The model proposes that SLMVs proteins follow the same pathway of internalization as transferrin receptors (clathrin-coated vesicles) and are then sorted away from recycling receptors in early endosomes. The demonstration that a significant fraction of the transferrin receptor is colocalized with SLMVs proteins in endocrine cell lines (Johnston et al., 1989; Cameron et al., 1991; Linstedt and Kelly, 1991) strongly suggests that the recycling of SLMVs proteins involves transit through early endosomes. However, the coexistence of a direct route from the plasmalemma to SLMVs cannot be excluded.

SV proteins are already present in hippocampal neurons in vitro at stages that precede the growth of an axon (stage 2, see Dotti et al., 1988). As soon as the axon begins to differentiate (i.e. one of the cell processes acquires a unique morphology and starts elongating at a faster rate), SV proteins become concentrated in this process. Their concentration in dendrites slowly declines, but never falls to undetectable levels (Matteoli et al., 1991, 1992; Mundigl et al., 1993). When viewed by immunofluorescence microscopy, immunoreactivity for SV proteins in isolated axons appears with a punctate distribution throughout the axonal arbor. When axons form synaptic contacts with other cells, these fine immunoreactive puncta coalesce into much brighter and larger puncta, which correspond to synaptic clustering of SVs (Fletcher et al., 1991; Matteoli et al., 1991).

Do SVs present in the processes of isolated neurons already undergo exocytosis and recycling? Typically, SV exocytosis is monitored by post-synaptic electrical recording, but this assay cannot be applied to isolated neurons. To answer this question, a morphological assay to detect SV exocytosis was developed (Matteoli et al., 1992). This assay, which is independent of the release of neurotransmitter, is based on the detection of lumenal epitopes of the SV protein synaptotagmin I, which are exposed to the cell surface as a result of exocytosis. Only a very small pool of synaptotagmin I is present at the cell surface under control conditions (Matteoli et al., 1992).

Application of this assay demonstrated a very active exo-endocytosis of synaptotagmin-I-containing vesicles in the developing axons of isolated neurons (Fig. 4) (Matteoli et al., 1992). Furthermore, it indicated a very long half-life of SVs in the axon. Binding of antibodies to the lumenal domain of synaptotagmin I did not appear to target the protein for lysosomal degradation and SVs were found to recycle for several days with the antibodies present in their lumen. In contrast, another endocytic marker, wheat-germ agglutinin (WGA), was taken up by the axon, but rapidly targeted to a population of vacuoles distinct from SVs and cleared from the axon by transport to the cell body within less than 24 hours (Matteoli et al., 1992).

In the same neurons, the transferrin receptor was primarily restricted to the perikaryal-dendritic region at all stages of differentiation. This was shown both by immunostaining the receptor in fixed permeabilized cells with monoclonal antibodies, and by steady-state labeling of living neurons with fluorescent transferrin. In both cases the two staining patterns were identical, consistent with a constitutive exo-endocytotic recycling of transferrin receptor in dendrites. As soon as an axon emerges, the transferrin receptor is preferentially excluded from that process. In more mature axons the transferrin receptor is virtually undetectable (Cameron et al., 1991; Mundigl et al., 1993). The distribution of transferrin receptor immunoreactivity in dendrites is similar to the distribution of the dendritic pool of several SV proteins (SV2, protein p29, synaptotagmin, synaptobrevin, rab3A), and almost identical to that of synaptophysin (Cameron et al., 1991; Mundigl et al., 1993).

These observations suggest the existence of at least two distinct pathways of recycling between intracellular vesicles and the plasmalemma in neurons. The two pathways are anatomically separate and operate in different regions

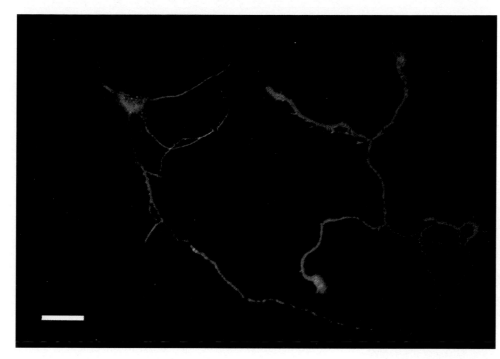

Fig. 4. SV exocytosis in a rat hippocampal neuron developing in isolation in primary culture. The neuron was incubated for 1 hour in the presence of CY3-conjugated antibodies directed against the lumenal domain of synaptotagmin I (red fluorescence). Following the incubation the cell was fixed and counterstained with antibodies directed against the dendritic marker MAP2 (De Camilli et al., 1984) (green fluorescence). The red fluorescence visible throughout the axon demonstrates the occurrence of exo-endocytosis of SVs throughout the axonal arbour at this stage of differentiation. A weaker red fluorescence in dendrites is masked by the MAP2 counterstaining (see study by Matteoli et al., 1992). Bar, 34 μm.

of the cell, the perikaryal-dendritic region and the axon. The transferrin receptor is present only in the perikaryal-dendritic recycling pathway. SVs proteins are enriched in the axonal recycling pathway.

To elucidate further the properties of these two recycling pathways the effects of BFA were investigated. Addition of 5-10 μg/ml BFA for 20 minutes to isolated hippocampal neurons induced a massive tubulation of perikaryal-dendritic early endosomes as indicated by the massive tubulation of transferrin receptor immunoreactivity. In addition, BFA induced a massive co-tubulation of dendritic synaptophysin and transferrin receptor. Unexpectedly, it did not induce an identical co-tubulation of other SV proteins. Furthermore, the distribution of SV proteins in axons was virtually unaffected (Mundigl et al., 1993). These results strengthen the hypothesis that dendritic and axonal recycling pathways differ in some fundamental property. Additionally, they suggest that SV proteins are differentially sorted in the perikaryal dendritic region. While the significance of these findings remains unclear and requires future studies, they clearly indicate that SV proteins are not directly assembled into mature SV membranes when they first exit the Golgi complex as newly synthesized proteins. This is in agreement with recent results obtained in PC12 cells indicating that newly synthesized synaptophysin is transported to the cell surface by the constitutive pathway (Régnier-Vigouroux et al., 1991).

In summary, the perikaryal-dendritic region of isolated hippocampal neurons developing in culture contain early endosomes where the transferrin receptor is colocalized with synaptophysin and with partial pools of other SV proteins. These endosomes may represent the neuronal equivalent of typical early endosomes, which are found in all cells. Recycling of SVs in axons seems to occur via endosomal intermediates with unique properties. The two recycling compartments may be functionally interconnected via

vesicular carriers, since transcytosis in both an anterograde and a retrograde direction has been documented in neurons (Kuypers and Ugolini, 1990). While the transferrin receptor is excluded from axons, SV proteins are greatly concentrated in these processes, where they have a long half-life, but are not excluded from dendrites. The striking concentration of SVs observed in axons may be the result of both selective targeting and selective retention.

TWO DISTINCT RECYCLING COMPARTMENTS: SIMILARITIES BETWEEN NEURONS AND POLARIZED EPITHELIAL CELLS

The existence of functionally distinct early endosomal systems operating at two distinct poles of the cell has been documented in polarized epithelial cells (Parton et al., 1989; Rodriguez-Boulan and Powell, 1992). Several similarities have already emerged between the sorting of membrane components to the apical and basolaterals domains of epithelial cells and the sorting of membrane components to the axonal and dendritic plasmalemmal domains, respectively (Dotti et al., this volume). When hippocampal neurons in culture are infected with the vesicular stomatitis virus (VSV), the VSV glycoprotein, which is sorted to the basolateral domain in MDCK cells, is localized exclusively to cell bodies and dendrites. In contrast the hemaglutinin protein of the avian influenza fowl plague virus (FPV), which is an apically sorted protein in MDCK cells, is directed preferentially, but not exclusively, to the axon in neurons (Dotti and Simons, 1990). In addition, Thy-1, a glycosyl phosphotidylinositol anchored protein that is apically located in MDCK cells, is sorted to the axonal domain of cultured hippocampal neurons (Dotti et al., 1991).

The selective localization of the transferrin receptor in dendrites and perikarya of hippocampal neurons in primary cultures (Cameron et al., 1991; Mundigl et al., 1993) is in agreement with the selective localization of this protein in basolateral endosomes of epithelial cells (Fuller and Simons, 1986). Polarized epithelial cells do not contain SVs. If mechanisms that target proteins to recycling compartments of axons are similar to those that target proteins to the apical region of epithelial cells, SV proteins may be at least partially directed to the apical pole if expressed by transfection in polarized epithelial cells. To test this hypoth-

esis, MDCK cells that stably express synaptophysin were prepared and the localization of synaptophysin in these cells was investigated.

Laser confocal microscopy analysis of confluent monolayers of transfected MDCK cells after synaptophysin immunostaining revealed a punctate fluorescence distribution apically, intracellularly and along the lateral plasma membrane (Fig. 5). Synaptophysin colocalized in part with the 135 kDa glycoprotein (gp135), which is localized only to the apical cell surface (Ojakian and Schwimmer, 1988), and in part with the β-subunit of the Na/K-ATPase (not shown), which is localized at the basolateral plasma membrane (Smith et al., 1987). However, an additional intracellular pool of synaptophysin was also visible (Fig. 5, and our unpublished observations).

To assess further the cell surface domains at which synaptophysin is exposed, transfected cells were surface-labeled using a membrane-impermeant biotin analog (sulfo-NHS-biotin; Graeve et al., 1989). Cells were grown to confluency on polycarbonate filters to allow for the selective biotinylation of either the apical or the basolateral plasma membrane domains. Synaptophysin became labeled when the biotinylation reagent was added to the apical or to the basolateral side of the monolayer at 0°C, demonstrating that synaptophysin is exposed to both plasmalemmal domains (Fig. 6 and our unpublished observations). Additionally, following both apical or basolateral biotynylation, labeled synaptophysin became internalized. This was demonstrated by results obtained with the cleavable biotin analog NHS-SS-biotin (Graeve et al., 1989). The basolateral or the apical plasma membranes were selectively biotinylated with this compound at 0°C, and then incubated at 37°C to allow endocytosis to occur. Biotin remaining at the cell surface was stripped by reduction with glutathione and then alkylated using iodoacetamide. Endocytosis of synaptophysin was measured by the increase in the amount of biotinylated synaptophysin that became resistant to reduction by extra-

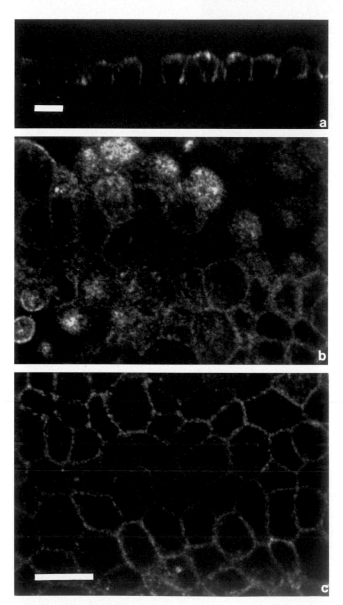

Fig. 5. Localization of synaptophysin in transfected MDCK cells by indirect immunofluorescence. Confluent monolayers of stably transfected cells were grown on polycarbonate filters, fixed, stained for synaptophysin by immunofluorescence and analyzed by laser confocal scanning microscopy. (a) Optical cross-section of the monolayer showing synaptophysin immunoreactivity along both the apical and the basolateral cell surfaces. (b and c) Horizontal sections of the apical surface and of a deeper region of the monolayer, respectively. Synaptophysin immunoreactivity is detected in association with the apical region as well as along the lateral surface. Bars, 14 μm.

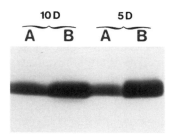

Fig. 6. Detection of synaptophysin at both the apical and basolateral plasma membranes of transfected cells after domain selective biotinylation. Transfected MDCK cells, grown at confluency for 5 (5 D) and 10 days (10 D) on polycarbonate filters, were biotinylated using sulfo-NHS-biotin added to either the apical or the basolateral side of the filter chambers at 0°C in order to selectively label each cell surface. Labeled cell monolayers were detergent solubilized, extracts were prepared and used to precipitate biotinylated proteins with avidin-agarose beads. Precipitates were analyzed by immunoblotting with antibodies directed against synaptophysin. Synaptophysin was labeled when the biotinylation reagent was added to either the apical (A) or the basolateral (B) side of the monolayer.

cellular glutathione over time (Graeve et al., 1989; and our unpublished observations).

Taken together these results suggest that synaptophysin is targeted to both basolateral and apical recycling compartments of the cell. These findings indicate a parallel with the distribution of the protein in isolated hippocampal neurons in primary culture: in these neurons synaptophysin as well as other SV proteins are concentrated in axons, but not excluded from dendrites. MDCK cells may represent an useful experimental system with which to identify the motifs of SV proteins that are required for axonal targeting.

It will be of interest to determine whether synaptophysin is targeted apically in MDCK cells via a direct route or by following transcytosis from the basolateral surface. Such an indirect route for apical delivery has been documented in polarized epithelial cells (Rodriguez-Boulan and Powell, 1992). It will also be of interest to determine whether dendritic synaptophysin can be targeted to axons by an analogous transcytotic route.

CONCLUDING REMARKS

SVs are highly specialized secretory organelles by which neurons secrete non-peptide neurotransmitters at synapses. Their recycling pathway appears to be closely related to the receptor-mediated recycling pathway that functionally interconnects early endosomes and the plasmalemma in all cells. In non-polarized cells that express SV proteins, the recycling of SVs partially overlaps with the recycling of transferrin receptor. In neurons, SV proteins are progressively segregated away from transferrin receptors in parallel with the establishment of dendritic and axonal polarity. This segregation correlates with the organization of two anatomically and functionally distinct recycling pathways, which may be closely related to the two recycling pathway present at the apical and basolateral domains of polarized epithelial cells.

We thank Dr T. Südhof for the gift of the synaptophysin cDNA clone, which was used to prepare stably transfected MDCK cell lines.

REFERENCES

Bauerfeind, R., Régnier-Vigouroux, A., Flatmark, T. and Huttner, W. B. (1993). Selective storage of acetylcholine, but not catecholamines, in neuroendocrine synaptic-like microvesicles of early endosomal origin. *Neuron* **11**, 105-121.

Baumert, M., Takei, K., Hartinger, H., Burger, P. M., Fischer von Mollard, G., Maycox, P. R., De Camilli, P. and Jahn, R. (1990). P29, a novel tyrosine-phosphorylated membrane protein present in small clear vesicles of neurons and endocrine cells. *J. Cell Biol.* **110**, 1285-1294.

Bennett, M. K., Calakos, N. and Scheller, R. H. (1992). Syntaxin: a synaptic protein implicated in docking of synaptic vesicles at presynaptic active zones. *Science* **257**, 255-259.

Betz, W. J. and Bewick, G. S. (1992). Optical analysis of synaptic vesicle recycling at the frog neuromuscular junction. *Science* **255**, 133-256.

Cameron, P. L., Südhof, T. C., Jahn, R. and De Camilli, P. (1991). Colocalization of Synaptophysin with transferrin receptors: implications for synaptic vesicle biogenesis. *J. Cell Biol.* **115**, 151-164.

Ceccarelli, B., Hurlbut, W. P. and Mauro, A. (1973). Turnover of

transmitter and synaptic vesicles at the frog neuromuscular junction. *J. Cell Biol.* **57**, 499-524.

De Camilli, P. (1991). Co-secretion of multiple signal molecules from endocrine cells via distinct exocytic pathways. *Trends Pharmacol. Sci.* **12**, 446-448.

De Camilli, P. and Jahn, R. (1990). Pathways to regulated exocytosis in neurons. *Annu. Rev. Physiol.* **52**, 625-645.

De Camilli, P., Navone, F., Miller, P., Theurkauf, W. E. and Vallee, R. B. (1984). Distribution of microtubule-associated protein 2 (MAP2) in the nervous system of the rat studied by immunofluorescence. *Neuroscience* **11**, 819-846.

DeCamilli, P., Benfenati, F., Valtorta, F. and Greengard, P. (1990). The Synapsins. *Annu. Rev. Physiol.* **6**, 433-460.

de Hoop, M. J. and Dotti, C. G. (1993). Membrane traffic in polarized neurons in culture. *J. Cell Sci., Supplement* **17**, 85-92.

Dotti, C., Parton, and Simons, K. (1991). Polarized sorting of glypiated proteins in hippocampal neurons. *Nature* **349**, 158-161.

Dotti, C. G. and Simons, K. (1990). Polarized sorting of viral glycoproteins to the axon and dendrites of hippocampal neurons in culture. *Cell* **62**, 63-72.

Dotti, C. G., Sullivan, C. A. and Banker, G. A. (1988). The establishment of polarity by hippocampal neurons in culture. *J. Neurosci.* **8**, 1454-1468.

Elferink, L. A. and Scheller, R. H. (1993). Synaptic vesicle proteins and regulated exocytosis. *J. Cell Sci., Supplement* **17**, 75-79.

Fletcher, T. L., Cameron, P. L., De Camilli, P. and Banker, G. (1991). The distribution of Synapsin I and Synaptophysin in hippocampal neurons developing in culture. *J. Neurosci.* **11**, 1617-1626.

Fuller, S. D. and Simons, K. (1986). Transferrin Receptor Polarity and recycling accuracy in 'Tight' and 'Leaky' strains of Madin-Darby canine kidney cells. *J. Cell Biol.* **103**, 1767-1779.

Fykse, M., Takei, K., Walch-Solimena, C., Geppert, M., Jahn, R., DeCamilli, P. and Südhof, T. C. (1993). Relative properties and localizations of synaptic vesicle protein isoforms: The case of the synaptophysins. *J. Neurosci.* (in press).

Goslin, K. and Banker, G. A. (1989). Experimental observations on the development of polarity by hippocampal neurons in culture. *J. Cell Biol.* **108**, 1507-1511.

Graeve, L., Drickamer, K. and Rodriguez-Boulan, E. (1989). Polarized endocytosis by Madin-Darby canine kidney cells transfected with functional chicken liver glycoprotein receptor. *J. Cell Biol.* **109**, 2809-2816.

Greengard, P., Valtorta, F., Czernik, A. J. and Benfenati, F. (1993). Synaptic vesicle phosphoproteins and regulation of synaptic function. *Science* **259**, 780-785.

Heuser, J. (1989). The role of coated vesicles in recycling of synaptic vesicle membrane. *Cell Biol. Int. Rep.* **13**, 1063-1076.

Heuser, J. E. and Reese, T. S. (1973). Evidence for recycling of synaptic vesicle membrane during transmitter release at the frog neuromuscular junction. *J. Cell Biol.* **57**, 315-344.

Hökfelt, T., Fuxe, K. and Pernow, P. (1986). Coexistence of neutronal messengers. *Progress Brain Res.* **68**, 1-411.

Huttner, W. B., Schiebler, W., Greengard, P. and De Camilli, P. (1983). Synapsin I (Protein I), a nerve terminal-specific phosphoprotein. III. Its association with synaptic vesicles studied in a highly purified synaptic vesicle preparation. *J. Cell Biol.* **96**, 1374-1388.

Jahn, R., Schiebler, W., Quimet, C. and Greengard, P. (1985). A 38,000 dalton membrane protein (p38) is present is synaptic vesicles. *Proc. Nat. Acad. Sci. USA* **82**, 4137-4141.

Jessel, T. M. and Kandel, E. R. (1993). Synaptic transmission: a bidirectional and self-modifiable form of cell-cell communication. *Cell* **10**, 1-30.

Johnston, P. A., Cameron, P. L., Stukenbrok, H., Jahn, R. and Südhof, T. C. (1989). Synaptophysin is targeted to similar microvesicles in CHO and PC12 cells. *EMBO J.* **8**, 2863-2872.

Kelly, R. B. (1993). Storage and release of neurotransmitters. *Cell/Neuron* **72/10**, 43-54.

Kuypers, H. G. J. M. and Ugolini, G. (1990). Viruses as transneuronal tracers. *Trends Neurol. Sci.* **13**, 71-75.

Linstedt, A. D. and Kelly, R. B. (1991). Synaptophysin is sorted from endocytic markers in neuroendocrine PC12 cells but not transfected fibroblasts. *Neuron* **7**, 309-317.

Lippincott-Schwartz, J., Yuan, L., Tipper, C., Amherdt, M., Orci, L. and Klausner, R. D. (1991). Brefeldin A's effects on endosomes, lysosomes and the TGN suggest a general mechanism for regulating organelle structure and membrane traffic. *Cell* **67**, 601-616.

Matteoli, M., Takei, K., Cameron, R., Hurlbut, P., Johnston, P. A., Südhof, T. C., Jahn, R. and De Camilli, P. (1991). Association of Rab 3A with synaptic vesicles at late stages of the secretory pathway. *J. Cell Biol.* **115**, 625-633.

Matteoli, M., Takei, K., Perin, M. S., Südhof, T. C. and De Camilli, P. (1992). Exo-endocytotic recycling of synaptic vesicles in developing processes of cultured hippocampal neurons. *J. Cell Biol.* **117**, 849-861.

Maycox, P., Link, E., Reetz, A., Morris, S. A. and Jahn, R. (1992). Clathrin-coated vesicles in nervous tissue are involved primarily in synaptic vesicle recycling. *J. Cell Biol.* **118**, 1379-1388.

Mellman, I., Howe C. and Helenius. A. (1987). The control of membrane traffic on the endocytic pathway. In Current Topics in Membranes and Transport, pp. 255-288. Academic Press, Orlando.

Mundigl, O., Matteoli, M., Daniell, L., Thomas-Reetz, A., Metcalf, A., Jahn, R. and De Camilli, P. (1993). Synaptic vesicle proteins in cultured hippocampal neurons: differential effects of Brefeldin A in axon and dendrites. *J. Cell Biol.* **122**, 1207-1221.

Navone, F., Jahn, R., di Gioia, G., Stukenbrok, H., Greengard, P. and De Camilli, P. (1986). Protein p38: an integral membrane protein specific for small vesicles of neurons and neuroendocrine cells. *J. Cell Biol.* **103**, 2511-2527.

Ojakian, G. K. and Schwimmer, R. (1988). The polarized distribution of an apical cell surface glycoprotein is maintained by interactions with the cytoskeleton of Madin-Darby canine kidney cells. *J. Cell Biol.* **107**, 2377-2387.

Pappas, G. D. and Purpura, D. P. (1972). Structure and Function of Synapses. New York: Raven Press.

Parton, R. G., Prydz, K., Bomsel, M., Simons, K. and Griffith, G. (1989). Meeting of the apical and basolateral endocytic pathways of the Madin-Darby canine kidney cell in late endosomes. *J. Cell Biol.* **109**, 3259-3272.

Rodriguez-Boulan, E. and Powell, S. K. (1992). Polarity of epithelial and neuronal cells. *Annu. Rev. Inc.* **8**, 395-427.

Régnier-Vigouroux, A., Tooze, S. A. and Huttner, H. B. (1991). Newly synthesized synaptophysin is transported to synaptic-like microvesicles via constitutive secretory vesicles and the plasma membrane. *EMBO J.* **10**, 3589-3601.

Smith, Z. D. J., Caplan, M. J., Forbush, III and Jamieson, J. D. (1987). Monoclonal antibody localization of Na^+,K^+-ATPase in the exocrine pancreas and parotid of the dog. *Amer. J. Physiol.* **253**, G99-G109.

Südhof, T. C. and Jahn, R. (1991). Proteins of synaptic vesicles involved in exocytosis and membrane recycling. *Neuron* **6**, 665-677.

Thomas-Reetz, A., Hell, J., During, M. J., Walch-Solimena, C., Jahn, R. and De Camilli, P. (1993). A GABA transporter driven by a proton pump is present in synaptic like microvesicles of pancreatic β-cells. *Proc. Nat. Acad. Sci. USA* **90**, 5317-5321.

Thureson-Klein, A. K., Klein, R. L., Zhu P. C. and Kong. J. Y. (1988). Differential release of transmitters and neuropeptides co-stored in central and peripheral neurons. In *Cellular and Molecular Basis of Synaptic Transmission* (ed. H. Zimmermann), pp. 137-151. Springer Verlag, Berlin.

Tooze, S. A. (1991). Biogenesis of secretory granules. Implications arising from the immature secretory granule in the regulated pathway of secretion. *FEBS Lett.* **285**, 220-224.

Trimble, W. S., Linial, M. and Scheller, R. H. (1991). Cellular and molecular biology of the presynaptic nerve terminal. *Annu. Rev. Neurosci.* **14**, 93-122.

Wiedenmann, B. and Franke, W. W. (1985). Identification and localization of synaptophysin, an integral membrane glycoprotein of M_r 38,000 characteristic of presynaptic vesicles. *Cell* **41**, 1017-1028.

Wiedenmann, B., Rehm, H., Knierim, M. and Becker, C. M. (1988). Fractionation of synaptophysin-containing vesicles from rat brain and cultured PC12 pheochromocytoma cells. *FEBS Lett.* **240**, 71-77.

Journal of Cell Science, Supplement 17, 101-108 (1993)
Printed in Great Britain © The Company of Biologists Limited 1993

Involvement of neurofilaments in motor neuron disease

Zuoshang Xu[1], Linda C. Cork[2], John W. Griffin[3,4] and Don W. Cleveland[1,4]

Departments of [1]Biological Chemistry, [2]Comparative Medicine, [3]Neurology and [4]Neuroscience, 725 North Wolfe Street, The Johns Hopkins University School of Medicine, Baltimore, Maryland 21205, USA

SUMMARY

Motor neuron disease is clinically characterized by progressive muscle wasting leading to total muscle paralysis. A long history of pathological study of patients has firmly established that the primary lesion site is in spinal and cortical motor neurons. In addition to the widespread loss of these neurons, neuronal abnormalities including massive accumulation of neurofilaments in cell bodies and proximal axons have been also widely observed, particularly in the early stages of the disease. To test whether high accumulation of neurofilaments directly contributes to the pathogenic process, transgenic mice that produce high levels of neurofilaments in motor neurons have been generated. These transgenic mice show most of the hallmarks observed in motor neuron disease, including swollen perikarya with eccentrically localized nuclei, proximal axonal swellings, axonal degeneration and severe skeletal muscle atrophy. These data indicate that extensive accumulation of neurofilaments in motor neurons can trigger a neurodegenerative process and may be a key intermediate in the pathway of pathogenesis leading to neuronal loss.

Key words: membrane-cytoskeleton linkage, spectrin, ankyrin, cell adhesion molecule, Ig-super family

INTRODUCTION

Neurofilaments are 10 nm filaments in many types of neurons. Assembled from three polypeptide subunits, NF-L (68 kDa), NF-M (95 kDa) and NF-H (115 kDa), neurofilaments are the most abundant structure in large myelinated axons, such as those elaborated by spinal motor neurons. Mounting evidence has strengthened the view that neurofilaments play a critical role in the development and maintainence of axonal caliber (Friede and Samorajski, 1970; Hoffman et al., 1987; Cleveland et al., 1991; Yamasaki et al., 1992), a crucial determinant for conduction velocity of axons and perhaps also a trigger for myelination (Arbuthnott et al., 1980; Voyvodic, 1989).

In addition to a function in supporting the growth and maintenance of axonal caliber in normal neurons, neurofilaments have been suspected to play a role in the pathogenesis of several types of neurodegenerative diseases, including motor neuron disease, e.g. amyotrophic lateral sclerosis or ALS (Banker, 1986; Carpenter, 1968; Inoue and Hirano, 1979; Hirano et al., 1984a,b; Mulder, 1984, 1986) and infantile spinal muscular atrophy (Byers and Banker, 1961; Wiley et al., 1987). The common clinical symptom of motor neuron diseases is progressive loss of motor neuron function, which in turn leads to wasting of skeletal muscle, paralysis and ultimately death (for reviews, see Mulder, 1984, 1986; Gomez, 1986). For most cases, neither the primary causes nor the mechanism of pathogenesis have been elucidated. A long history of pathological

examination, dating from the middle of the last century, has firmly established that the primary lesion of the disease lies predominantly in the cortical and spinal motor neurons (Betz cells and the anterior horn α-motor neurons). Various degrees of motor neuron loss in either of these two areas (or both) are seen as the major pathological hallmark (Chou, 1992). However, in those cases (e.g. infantile muscular atrophy, the adult diseases which progress relatively rapidly, and the early stage of ALS), significant numbers of surviving motor neurons are observed in post-mortem examination. Most of these remaining motor neurons display various abnormal morphologies (Fig. 1A and B), including swollen cell bodies and dispersal of the rough endoplasmic reticulum (often called Nissl substance). Further, large axonal swellings that sometimes reach the size of the cell body are found (Carpenter, 1968; Chou, 1992). These swollen structures are strongly stained with silver (Fig. 1C) suggesting that they are rich in neurofilaments (Carpenter, 1968; Hughes and Jerrome, 1971; Chou and Fakadej, 1971; Inoue and Hirano, 1979; Hirano et al., 1984a,b). Many electron microscopic studies have unequivocally established that the swollen neurons and axons contain abundant swirls of neurofilaments (Carpenter, 1968; Hughes and Jerrome, 1971; Chou and Fakadej, 1971; Hirano et al., 1984a,b).

Motor neuron disease, with symptoms resembling infantile spinal muscular atrophy, has also been described in a number of animal species. Remarkable neurofilament accumulation in the anterior horn α-motor neurons has been

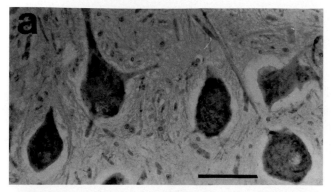

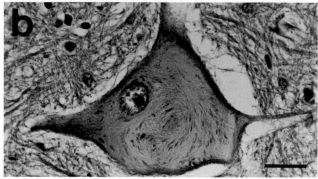

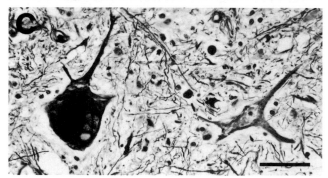

Fig. 1. Swollen neurons in the anterior horn of the spinal cord from human ALS. (a,b) Swollen neurons with neurofilament accumulation from a case of infantile spinal muscular atrophy stained with hematoxylin and eosin. Bars: (a) 150 μm; (b) 25 μm. Reproduced with permission from Wiley et al. (1987). (c) A swollen neuron from a case of familial ALS stained by Bielschowsky's silver impregnation. Bar, 50 μm. Reproduced with permission from Hirano et al. (1984).

found in all such cases (Delahunta and Shively, 1974; Vandevelde et al., 1976; Higgins et al., 1977, 1983; Shields and Vandevelde, 1978; Cork et al., 1982). These studies have collectively fueled the speculation that neurofilament accumulation may represent a common initial pathology of the motor neuron disease process.

Additional experimental support for this view has emerged from various toxin-induced neuropathies. Intoxication with aluminum, β,β′-iminodiproionitrile (IDPN) or 3,4-dimethyl-2,5-hexanedione (DMHD) causes prominent axonal swelling as well as (in the case of aluminum intoxication) swollen neuronal soma. In each case the swellings are accompanied by massive accumulation of neurofilaments in the anterior horn of the spinal cord (Troncoso et

al., 1982; Chou and Hartman, 1965; Anthony et al., 1983). Impairment of slow axonal transport of neurofilaments has been demonstrated in both the IDPN- and aluminum-treated animals (Griffin et al., 1978; Bizzi et al., 1984; Troncoso et al., 1985).

Despite these widely observed examples of neurofilament misaccumulation in α-motor neurons in humans and animals with motor neuron disease, a central unsolved question is whether the aberrant accumulation is merely a harmless by-product of the pathogenic process or a central element in the pathogenic pathway that leads to neuronal dysfunction and ultimately cell death. To distinguish between these these two possibilities, transgenic technology has now been used to demonstrate that forcing neurons to increase expression of neurofilaments is sufficient to yield morphologic features of motor neuron disease, including excessive accumulation of neurofilaments in perikarya and proximal axons and increased axonal degeneration (Xu et al., 1993; Cote et al., 1993). In addition, these neuronal changes result in neuronal dysfunction, as indicated by severe skeletal muscle atrophy. These results demonstrate that misaccumulation of neurofilaments can be a integral part of the pathogenic pathway in motor neuron degeneration.

RESULTS

Doubly transgenic lines accumulate high levels of NF-L in their nervous tissue

To examine the consequence of forcing increased expression of wild-type murine NF-L, several lines of transgenic mice were produced that accumulated amounts up to twice the normal level of wild-type NF-L in peripheral nerves. No overt phenotypic change was observed in any of these transgenic mice (Monteiro et al., 1990). To increase further the number of neurofilaments in the nervous tissue, we mated two independent, highly expressing NF-L lines (MSV-NF-L58 and MSV-NF-L103) and screened for progeny that carried copies of both transgenes. Since transgenes of both transgenic lines are incorporated in a tandem, repeated fashion but have integrated at different chromosomal loci, we could distinguish the presence of each transgene by using genomic DNA blotting to detect the unique sized fragments located at the 5′ junction of the incorporation sites. Using this approach, we readily detected animals that carry transgenes from both founder lines (to be referred to as doubly NF-L transgenic mice).

To determine the levels of accumulated NF-L in doubly transgenic animals, we used protein immunoblotting of extracts of sciatic nerves from 3-week-old control and transgenic animals (Fig. 2). We analyzed known amounts of purified neurofilament proteins in parallel, to provide accurate quantitation standards. The level of NF-L in either parental transgenic line was increased approximately 2-fold (Fig. 2, lanes 2 and 3) more than wild-type controls (Fig. 2, lane 1) and 4-fold in the doubly transgenic animals (Fig. 2, lane 4), reaching about 2% of the total sciatic nerve protein. Immunohistochemistry of spinal cord and sciatic nerves revealed that accumulated NF-L, both endogenous

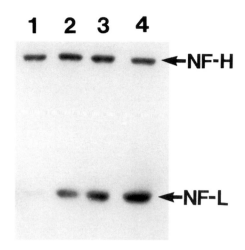

Fig. 2. Accumulation of excess NF-L in sciatic nerves of singly and doubly transgenic mice determined by immunoblot. Total proteins extracted from the sciatic nerve of wild-type (lane 1), line MSV-NF-L103 (lane 2), line MSV-NF-L58 (lane 3) and a doubly transgenic mouse (lane 4) were taken from 20-day-old animals, separated by SDS-PAGE and immunoblotted with a mixture of anti-NF-L and phosphorylation-independent NF-H monoclonal antibodies.

and transgene-encoded, was present only in the neurons, with none detectable in the surrounding Schwann cells or oligodendrocytes (see also Monteiro et al., 1990).

Accumulation of high levels of NF-L results in morphologic characteristics of motor neuron disease

Inspection of litters during the first 21 postnatal days revealed that some mice from matings of the two transgenic lines were significantly smaller in size than their littermates (around 1/3-2/3 of the normal weight) and all displayed progressive reduction in kinetic activity, cultimating in eventual death during the third postnatal week. With careful feeding, two of these doubly transgenic animals survived

past 3 weeks of age. Genomic DNA blotting revealed that 8 of 8 animals showing this slow growth phenotype were doubly transgenic mice, while all other littermates were wild type or singly transgenic.

To determine the consequence of increased NF-L accumulation, four of the doubly transgenic animals were sacrificed by perfusion at day 21 or 22 and their tissues examined morphologically. In all of these animals, striking changes were observed, predominantly in the anterior horn motor neurons of the spinal cord. Compared with non-transgenic littermates, almost all of the motor neurons (at all levels of the spinal cord) displayed features of chromatolysis, including enlarged, ballooned perikarya with depleted rough endoplasmic reticulum and eccentrically positioned nucleus (Fig. 3A). These features are strikingly similar to what has been seen in many reported cases of motor neuron disease (e.g. Fig. 1).

At higher magnification, massive accumulation of filaments in all motor neuron compartments (cytoplasm, dendrites and axons) was confirmed (Fig. 3B; see also Xu et al., 1993). Accompanying this increased accumulation of filaments were two obvious axonal abnormalities. First, as in ALS, on the edge of the anterior horn of a 2-month-old doubly transgenic mouse, numerous axonal swellings were present (Fig. 4A). These swellings were filled with neurofilaments (Fig. 4B). Second, in the ventral roots containing the corresponding motor axons from doubly transgenic animals of various ages, degenerating axons were present (Fig. 4C). While the proportion of degenerating axons was less than 0.2%, this does represent a marked increase in the frequency of degeneration from that seen in control littermates. From the four ventral roots examined from doubly transgenic animals, three degenerating axons were found, whereas an exhaustive search of three ventral roots from control animals revealed no degenerating axons.

The two doubly NF-L transgenic mice that survived past 3 weeks of age gradually recovered, and by 2 months of age were four-fifths of the weight of littermate con-

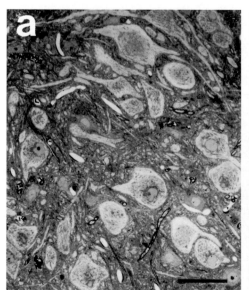

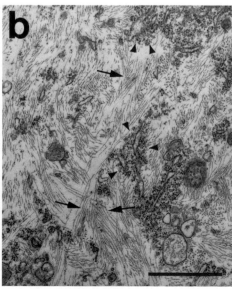

Fig. 3. Morphology of spinal anterior horn motor neurons expressing high levels of NF-L. (a) The anterior horn of a spinal cord from a 21-day-old MSV-NF-L58/MSV-NF-L103 doubly transgenic animal. Sections (1 μm) stained with toliudine blue. Bar, 60 μm. (b) Electron micrograph of the cytoplasm from doubly transgenic anterior horn motor neurons showing massive filament accumulation. Arrows point to bundles of filaments; arrowheads point to clusters of RER. Bar, 1 μm.

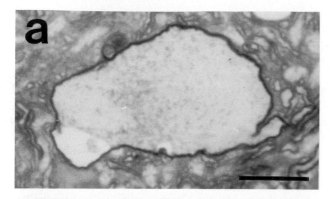

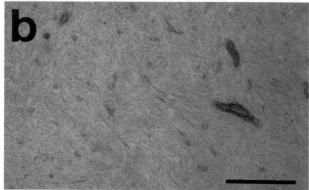

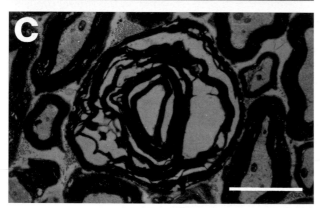

Fig. 4. Axonal abnormalities in the doubly transgenic NF-L mice. (a) Light microscopic view of an axonal swelling in the proximal axon of an anterior horn motor neuron from a doubly transgenic animal. Bar, 10 μm. (b) Higher magnification view of an area inside the axonal swelling. Bar, 1.5 μm. (c) Degenerated axon from a ventral root of a doubly transgenic NF-L mouse. Bar, 3 μm.

trols. The non-progressive course of transgene-mediated pathology in these animals was a surprise, initially. However, quantitation of protein blots of sciatic nerve extracts from both doubly and singly NF-L transgenic mice revealed that although NF-L accumulation initially rises significantly above littermate controls, after 3 weeks of age it gradually falls back to about the same as in wild-type animals (Table I). Concomitant with this decrease in excessive NF-L, morphological examination of one doubly transgenic animal revealed restoration of a nearly wild-type appearance at 9 months of age. Similarly, neurofilament density in axons also declined with age. Since

Table 1. Comparison of NF-L levels in the sciatic nerves of MSVNF-L transgenic and wild-type mice at different ages

Transgenic lines	NF-L in transgenic mice* NF-L in wild-type mice*		
	20-day-old	120-day-old	300-day-old
58	2-3	2	1
103	~2	1	1
58-103	>4	n.d.	1-2

*The quantification was carried out by immunoblotting using the total proteins extracted from sciatic nerve as described in the legend to Fig. 2.

the only difference between the transgene and the wild-type gene lies in their promoters, the most reasonable explanation for the decline in transgene-encoded NF-L is an age-dependent reduction in activity of the MSV promoter used to drive transgene transcription. In any event, loss of both phenotypic and morphological abnormalities in neurons, coincident with the age-dependent reduction in NF-L content, combined with the absence of abnormalities in either singly transgenic mouse line, strongly support the view that only those increases in neurofilament economy above a threshold level result in obvious neurological abnormalities.

Spinal motor neurons with high neurofilament accumulation contain phosphorylated NF-H, a marker of motor neuron pathology

Aberrant accumulation of phosphorylated NF-H in motor neuron soma has been described in a number of motor neuron disease cases, in both human and animal species (Cork et al., 1988; Munoz et al., 1988; Manetto et al., 1988; Sobue et al., 1990). Although this phenomenon is not specific for motor neuron disease, it is an indication that the neuron is undergoing a pathological process. In spite of the fact that more than 20 phosphates are added to NF-H (Julien and Mushynski, 1982; Jones and Williams Jr, 1982; Wong et al., 1984), most of the phosphates are normally added only in the axon so that antibodies specific to the phosphorylated NF-H do not detect reactivity in the cell bodies (Sternberger and Sternberger, 1983). To test whether increased expression of wild-type NF-L and the corresponding accumulation of large numbers of filaments in motor neuron cell bodies was associated with phosphorylation of NF-H, the spinal cords from wild-type and doubly transgenic NF-L mice were embedded in paraffin, sectioned and stained for phosphorylated NF-H. In doubly transgenic animals (Fig. 5A), hematoxylin- and eosin-stained sections revealed strikingly similar neuronal morphologies to motor neurons in human motor neuron disease (compare Fig. 5A to Fig. 1). These include swollen perikarya, depleted Nissl substance and eccentric nuclei in the motor neurons of the anterior horn. Using a well characterized monoclonal antibody that only detects phosphorylated NF-H (Sternberger and Sternberger, 1983), strong staining was found in the transgenic soma (Fig. 5C), while no staining was detectable in a parallel analysis of normal motor neurons (Fig. 5D).

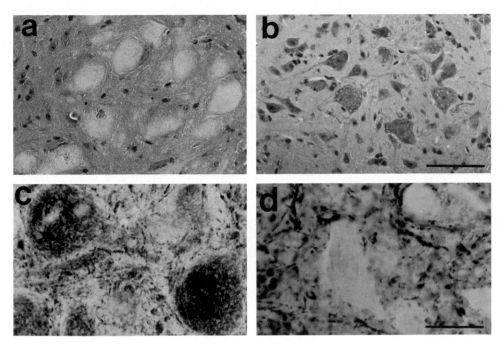

Fig. 5. Abnormal masses of filaments in the neuronal cell bodies of doubly transgenic mice contain phosphorylated NF-H. (a,b) Hematoxylin- and eosin-stained paraffin sections of the anterior horn of the spinal cord from a 21-day-old doubly transgenic (a) and a control mouse (b). Bar, 80 μm. (c,d) Anterior horn motor neurons from a doubly transgenic (c) and a control mouse (d) stained with an anti-phosphorylated NF-H antibody (Ab3-44). Bar, 25 μm.

Abnormal morphological changes in motor neurons are accompanied by severe muscle atrophy

The low body weight phenotype of the doubly transgenic mice was accompanied by a progressive loss in kinetic activity of the doubly transgenic animals. Postmortem examination of 21-day-old animals revealed widespread skeletal muscle atrophy. For example, Fig. 6A,B displays cross sections of the anterior tibial muscle from a doubly transgenic and an age-matched control animal. Individual muscle fibers in the transgenic sample are <20% of the cross sectional area of the wild type, a phenotype consistent with denervation-induced muscle atrophy. However, as noted

previously for the singly transgenic lines (Monteiro et al., 1990), transgene-encoded NF-L is not expressed exclusively in neurons but also accumulates in skeletal muscles. To distinguish whether atrophy was a consequence of nerve dysfunction or a direct effect of NF-L accumulation in muscle, we evaluated the level of NF-L in muscles from animals of different ages (Fig. 7). In contrast to the decline of transgene expression in neurons as the animals age beyond 21 days (Table 1), NF-L accumulation in muscle continues to increase up to 2 months of age (Fig. 7B, lane 2) and remains higher than the level seen in a 2.5-week-old animal for at least 11 months thereafter (compare lanes 3 and 1 in Fig. 7B). Since the muscle was most severely

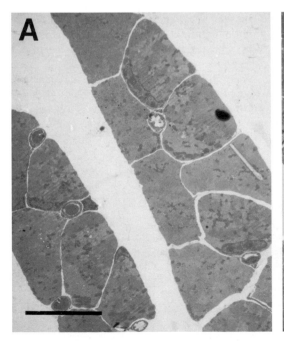

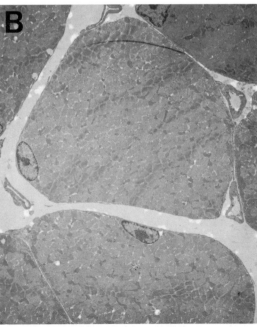

Fig. 6. Severe muscle atrophy in NF-L doubly transgenic mice. (A,B) Electron micrographs of cross sections of muscle fibers from anterior tibial muscle of a 21-day-old doubly transgenic mouse (A) or a non-transgenic littermate (B). Bar, 10 μm. Reproduced with permission from Xu et al. (1993).

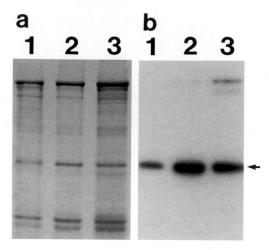

Fig. 7. The level of NF-L accumulation in skeletal muscle does not correlate with the severity of muscle atrophy. (a) Total proteins (10 µg) extracted from skeletal muscle (biceps) from 18-day-old (lane 1), 2.5-month-old (lane 2) and 11-month-old (lane 3) transgenic animals of line MSV-NF-L58 were separated by SDS-PAGE and stained with Coomassie blue. (b) A duplicate gel was immunoblotted with anti-NF-L monoclonal antibodies. An arrow points to the NF-L band.

atrophic between 2 and 3 weeks of age but recovered to nearly normal size by 2 months despite the increasing burden of transgene encoded NF-L, we conclude that there is no correlation between the level of NF-L accumulation in muscle and muscle atrophy. In contrast, the muscle atrophy correlates well with the peak accumulation of NF-L in neurons. These data strongly support the view that the predominant cause of muscle atrophy is the dysfunction of motor neurons resulting from the excessive accumulation of neurofilaments.

DISCUSSION

Neurofilamentous accumulations in perikarya, dendrites and axons occur in a variety of degenerative, toxic and heritable diseases. Particularly striking examples have been reported in different types of motor neuron diseases, including infantile spinal muscular atrophy (Byers and Banker, 1961; Chou and Fakadej, 1971; Wiley et al., 1987), familial ALS (Hughes and Jerrome, 1971; Takahashi et al., 1972; Hirano et al., 1984b) and sporadic ALS (Carpenter, 1968;

Schochet, Jr et al., 1969; Hirano et al., 1984a). In various animal species including dog (Delahunta and Shively, 1974; Cork et al., 1982), zebra (Higgins et al., 1977), rabbit (Shields and Vandevelde, 1978), cat (Vandevelde et al., 1976), pig (Higgins et al., 1983) and cattle (Rousseaux et al., 1985), spontanous motor neuron disease with symptoms resembling those of human infantile spinal muscular atrophy have been reported. Invariably, in each of these cases, severe neurofilament accumulation in the anterior horn α-motor neurons has been found, although in none of these diseases is the pathogenesis fully understood. Even in animal models where similar neurofilament accumulations in the α-motor neurons were induced by administration of neurotoxins (e.g. Chou and Hartman, 1965; Troncoso et al., 1982; Anthony et al., 1983), the precise mechanisms of injury are only partially understood (Griffin et al., 1978; Bizzi et al., 1984; Troncoso et al., 1985), since the agents may have multiple effects on neurons. The present results, in conjunction with similar findings using transgenic technology to force excessive accumulation of NF-H (Cote et al., 1993) provide an unambiguous demonstration that primary alterations in neurofilament economy can (1) lead to structural changes of the type seen in these neurodegenerative disorders and (2) ultimately lead to axonal breakdown and loss.

The morphological effects of over-producing neurofilaments in motor neurons bears most striking resemblance to those observed in rapidly progressing infantile spinal muscular atrophy (Byers and Banker, 1961; Chou and Fakadej, 1971; Wiley et al., 1987) and the early stages of ALS (Inoue and Hirano, 1979; Hirano et al., 1984a,b). This raises an interesting speculation that marked neurofilament accumulation in perikarya and proximal axons may be an early pathological change that preceeds the widespread neuronal loss. Consistent with this is the observation that in virtually all the reported cases of spinal muscular atrophy from various animal species, large numbers of swollen neurons with high neurofilament accumulation are a prominent feature. Further, in dogs with rapidly progressing spinal muscular atrophy, severe neurofilamentous accumulations are accompanied by only a minor motor neuron loss. However, in the cases in which the disease progresses relatively slowly, more prominent motor neuron loss is observed (Cork et al., 1982). In this context, in many human examples a relatively low frequency of swollen perikarya and a higher proportion of degenerating axons may simply reflect the slow progression of disease which allows compromised neurons to initiate subsequent degeneration. From a slightly

Fig. 8. Schematic model for involvement of neurofilaments in motor neuron disease. Reproduced with permssion from Xu et al. (1993).

different perspective, the remarkable extent of neurofilament accumulation in both naturally occurring motor neuron disease and the transgenic mice further indicates a great degree of tolerance of the neuron for the substantial increases in total 'neurofilament burden', suggesting that filament-induced degeneration is a slow process. This is consistent with the gradual progression of many of the disorders with neurofilament accumulation.

Although direct measurements of motor neuron function have not been carried out, the presence of widespread muscle atrophy in the doubly transgenic mice suggests that severe misaccumulation of neurofilaments can cause an impairment of motor neuron function. Consistent with this are the human cases where muscle atrophy becomes prominent before the widespread loss of motor neurons (Inoue and Hirano, 1979; Wiley et al., 1987). In dogs with spinal muscular atrophy, a disproportionately greater muscle weakness relative to neuronal loss has also been reported (Cork et al., 1982).

If it is true, as our data imply, that NF accumulation may be an active participant in the pathogenesis of motor neuron disease, then what mechanisms can lead to the accumulation of neurofilaments in the perikarya and proximal axons? The various possibilities (shown in Fig. 8) include increased synthesis, decreased degradation, and defective transport of neurofilaments. Slowed degradation seems unlikely in the pathogenesis of motor neuron disease because increased neurofilament stability would be expected to lead to more extreme distal accumulations of neurofilaments, which has not been observed. While a concomitant increase in neurofilament synthesis is a possibility, the most plausible mechanism (and one which appears to be consistent with the neuropathological findings) is an alteration in slow axonal transport of neurofilaments. This could be derived from defects either in the machinery that moves the filaments or in the filaments themselves. The former may be a realistic possibility for cases in which not only neurofilaments but also other organelles accumulate in perikarya and proximal axons (Chou and Fakadej, 1971; Cork et al., 1982; Hirano et al., 1984b). However, the latter alternative is also attractive, particularly in cases where abnormal filament structure and organization are found, including paracrystalline arrays, beaded filaments or various types of focal accumulation of neurofilaments (Schochet et al., 1969; Hirano et al., 1984a; Banker, 1986).

If neurofilamentous accumulations are important intermediates in the neurodegenerative process, how can this be reconciled with the recent discovery that half of the familial cases of ALS ($\approx$5% of total ALS cases) result from mutations in the enzyme superoxide dismutase (SOD) (Rosen et al., 1993)? How too can we explain the puzzle that SOD mutations lead to the selective death of motor neurons even though SOD is expressed in most (possibly all) cells? Since SOD acts to block oxidative damage by converting oxygen radicals into peroxide (Fridovich, 1986), and if the sites of primary damage are proteins, we suggest that it is reasonable that the most affected proteins will be those that have long turnover times, since proteins with short half-lives are quickly replaced. In this context, neurofilaments are slowly transported proteins with transit times from synthesis to arrival near a nerve terminus as long as three years (calcu-

lated for a meter-long axon and a rate of transport at 1 mm/day; see Oblinger and Lasek, 1985). It is conceivable, therefore, that damaged proteins of this class of slowly transported proteins gradually accumulate to poison the transport machinary. Such a mechanism can explain the particular vulnerability of motor neurons in motor neuron disease: whatever the cause, if damage to neurofilaments or their transport ultimately results in neuronal degeneration, then cells that normally have the highest neurofilament burden will be the ones first and most severely affected. Consistent with this prediction, both in our mice and in human motor neuron diseases, the neurons that are most severely affected by accumulation of neurofilaments are among the largest neurons with the longest axons that normally contain abundant amounts of neurofilaments.

In any event, our evidence has established one point of pathological significance for human motor neuron disease: primary changes in the cytoskeleton, and specifically in neurofilaments, are sufficient to produce most of the pathological changes encountered in neurodegenerative diseases such as ALS. Our data further promote the suggestion (shown in Fig. 8) of a common pathogenetic sequence that includes neurofilament accumulation as a central pathological intermediary, leading to subsequent axonal swelling and degeneration. Even in disorders where the neurofilamentous abnormalities are secondary to other types of neuronal injury, neurofilaments may contribute to the ultimate loss of the neuron or its axon. Indeed, cytoskeletal abnormalities may increase the susceptibility of the neuron to other insults (e.g. excitotoxicity), so that multiple factors could culminate in production of disease.

We thank Drs Clayton Wiley (University of California, San Diego) and Dr A. Hirano (Montifiore Medical Center, New York) for providing the micrographs of neurons from patients with infantile spinal muscular atrophy and familial ALS. This work has been supported by grants from the NIH to D.W.C. and J.W.G. Z-S.X. has been supported by a postdoctoral fellowship from the Muscular Dystrophy Society.

REFERENCES

Anthony, D. C., Giangaspero, F. and Graham, D. G. (1983). The spatio-temporal pattern of the axonopathy associated wiht the neurotoxicity of 3, 4-dimethyl-2, 5-hexanedione in the rat. *J. Neuropath. Exp. Neurol.* **42**, 548-560.

Arbuthnott, E. R., Boyd, I. A. and Kalu, K. U. (1980). Ultrastructural dimensions of myelinated peripheral nerve fibres in the cat and their relation to conduction velocity. *J. Physiol.* **308**, 125-157.

Banker, B. Q. (1986). The pathology of the motor neuron disorders. In *Myology* (ed. A. G. Engel and B. Q. Banker), pp. 2031-2066. McGraw-Hill, New York.

Bizzi, A., Crane, R. C., Autilio-Cambetti, L. and Gambetti, P. (1984). Aluminum effect on slow axonal transport: a novel impairment of neurofilament transport. *J. Neurosci.* **4**, 722-731.

Byers, R. K. and Banker, B. Q. (1961). Infantile spinal muscular atrophy. *Arch. Neurol.* **5**, 140-164.

Carpenter, S. (1968). Proximal axonal enlargement in motor neuron disease. *Neurology* **18**, 841-851.

Chou, S. M. (1992). Pathology - light microscopy of amyotrophic lateral sclerosis. In *Handbook of Amyotrophic Lateral Sclerosis* (ed. R. A. Smith), pp. 133-181. Marcel Dekker, Inc.

Chou, S. M. and Fakadej, A. V. (1971). Ultrastructure of chromatolytic motor neurons and anterior spinal roots in a case of Werdnig-Hoffmann Disease. *J. Neuropathol. Exp. Neurol.* **30**, 368-379.

Chou, S. M. and Hartmann H. A. (1965). Electron microscopy of focal neuroaxonal lesions produced by β-β'-iminodipropionitrile (IDPN) in rats. *Acta Neuropathol.* **4**, 590-603.

Cleveland, D. W., Monteiro, M. J., Wong, P. C., Gill, S. R., Gearhart, J. D. and Hoffman, P. N. (1991). Involvement of neurofilaments in the radial growth of axons. *J. Cell Sci.* **15**, 85-95.

Cork, L. C., Troncoso, J. C., Klavano, G. G., Johnson, E. S., Sternberger, L. A., Sternberger, N. H. and Price, D. L. (1988). Neurofilamentous abnormalities in motor neurons in spontaneously occurring animal disorders. *J. Neuropathol. Exp. Neurol.* **47**, 420-431.

Cork, L. C., Griffin, J. W., Choy, C., Padula, C. A. and Price, D. L. (1982). Pathology of motor neurons in accelerated hereditary canine spinal muscular atrophy. *Lab. Invest.* **46**, 89-99.

Cote, F., Collard, J.-F. and Julien, J-P. (1993). Progressive neuronopathy in transgenic mice expressing the human neurofilament heavy gene: a mouse model of amyotrophic lateral sclerosis. *Cell* **73**, 35-46.

Delahunta, A. and Shively J. N. (1974). Neurofibrillary accumulation in a puppy. *Cornell Vet.* **65**, 240-247.

Fridovich, I. (1986). Superoxide dismutase. *Advan. Enzymol.* **58**, 61-97.

Friede, R. L. and Samorajski, T. (1970). Axon caliber related to neurofilaments and microtubules in sciatic nerve fibers of rats and mice. *Anat. Rec.* **167**, 379-388.

Gomez, M. R. (1986). Motor neuron diseases in children. In *Myology* (ed. A. G. Engel and B. Q. Banker), pp 1993-2012. McGraw-Hill, New York.

Griffin, J. W., Hoffman, P. N., Clark, A. W., Carroll, P. T. and Price, D. L. (1978). Slow axonal transport of neurofilament proteins: impairment by β, β'-iminodipropionitrile administration. *Science* **202**, 633-636.

Higgins, R. J., Rings, D. M., Fenner, W. R. and Stevenson, S. (1983). Spontaneous lower motor neuron disease with neurofibrillary accumulation in young pigs. *Acta Neuropathol. (Gerl)* **59**, 288-294.

Higgins, R. J., Vandevelde, M., Hoff, E. J., Jagar, J. E., Cork, L. C. and Selbermann M. S. (1977). Neurofibrillary accumulation in the zebra (Equus burchelli). *Acta Neuropathol. (Gerl)* **37**, 1-5.

Hirano, A., Donnenfeld, H., Shoichi, S. and Nakano, I. (1984a). Fine structural observations of neurofilamentous changes in amyotrophic lateral sclerosis. *J. Neuropathol. Exp. Neurol.* **43**, 461-470.

Hirano, A., Nakano, I., Kurland, L. T., Mulder, D. W., Holley, P. W. and Sccomanno, G. (1984b). Fine structural study of neurofibrillary changes in a family with amyotrophic lateral sclerosis. *J. Neuropathol. Exp. Neurol.* **43**, 471-480.

Hoffman, P. N., Cleveland, D. W., Griffin, J. W., Landes, P. W., Cowan, N. J. and Price, D. L. (1987). Neurofilament gene expression: a major determinant of axonal caliber. *Proc. Nat. Acad. Sci. USA* **84**, 3272-3476.

Hughes, J. T. and Jerrome, D. (1971). Ultrastucture of anterior horn motor neurons in the Hirano-Kurland-Sayre type of combined neurological system degeneration. *J. Neurol. Sci.* **13**, 389-399.

Inoue, K. and Hirano, A. (1979). Early pathological changes of amyotrophic lateral sclerosis--autopsy findings of a case of 10 months' duration. *Neurol. Med. (Tokyo)* **11**, 448-455.

Jones, S. M. and Williams, R. C., Jr (1982). Phosphate content of mammalian neurofilaments. *J. Biol. Chem.* **257**, 9902-9905.

Julien, J.-P. and Mushynski, W. E. (1982). Multiple phosphorylation sites in mammalian neurofilament polypeptides. *J. Biol. Chem.* **257**, 10467-10470.

Manetto, V., Sternberger, N. H. and Gambetti, P. (1988). Phosphorylation of neurofilaments is altered in amyotrophic lateral sclerosis. *J. Neurol. Sci.* **47**, 642-653.

Monteiro, M. J., Hoffman, P. N., Gearhart, J. D. and Cleveland, D. W. (1990). Expression of NF-L in both neuronal and nonneuronal cells of transgenic mice: increased neurofilament density in axons without affecting caliber. *J. Cell Biol.* **111**, 1543-1557.

Mulder, D. W. (1984). Motor neuron disease. In *Peripheral Neuropathy* (ed. P. J. Dyck, P. K. Thomas, E. H. Lambert and R. Bunge), pp. 1525-1536. Saunders, Philadelphia.

Mulder, D. W. (1986). Motor neuron disease in adults. In *Myology* (ed. A. G. Engel and B. Q. Banker), pp 2013-2029. McGraw-Hill, New York.

Munoz, D. G., Greene, C., Perl, D. P. and Selkoe, D. J. (1988). Accumulation of phosphorylated neurofilaments in anterior horn motoneuron of amyotrophic lateral sclerosis patients. *J. Neuropath. Exp. Neurol.* **47**, 9-18.

Oblinger, M. M. and Lasek, R. J. (1985). Selective regulation of two axonal cytoskeletal networks in dorsal root ganglion cells. In *Neurobiology: Molecular Biological Approaches to Understanding Neuronal Function and Development* (ed. P. O'Lagre), pp The Shering Corp.: UCLA Symposium on Molecular and Cellular Biology, vol. 24. New York: Liss.

Rosen, D. R., Siddique, T., Patterson, D. et al. (1993). Mutations in Cu/Zn superoxide dismutase gene are associated with familial amyotrophic lateral sclerosis. *Nature* **362**, 59-62.

Rousseaux, C. G., Klavano, G. G., Johnson, E. S., Shnitka, T. K., Harries, W. N. and Snyder, F. F. (1985). 'Shaker' calf syndrome: A newly recognized inherited neurodegenerative disorder of horned Hereford calves. *Vet. Pathol.* **22**, 104-111.

Schochet, S. S. Jr, Hardman, J. M., Ladewig, P. P. and Earle, K. M. (1969). Intraneuronal conglomerates in sporadic motor neuron disease. *Arch. Neurol.* **20**, 548-553.

Shields, R. P. and Vandevelde, M. (1978). Spontaneous lower motor neuron disease in rabbits (Oryctolagus cuniculus). *Acta Neuropathol. (Berl)* **44**, 85-90.

Sobue, G., Hshizume, Y., Yasuda, T., Mukai, E., Kumagai, T., Mitsuma, T. and Trojanowski, J. Q. (1990). Phosphorylated high molecular weight neurofilament protein in lower motor neurons in amyotrophic lateral sclerosis and other neurodegenerative diseases involving ventral horn cells. *Acta Neuropathol.* **79**, 402-408.

Sternberger, L. A. and Sternberger, N. H. (1983). Monoclonal antibodies distinguish phosphorylated and nonphosphorylated forms of neurofilaments *in situ*. *Proc. Nat. Acad. Sci. USA* **80**, 6126-6130.

Takahashi, K., Nakamura, H. and Okada, E. (1972). Hereditary amyotrophic lateral sclerosis. *Arch. Neurol.* **27**, 292-299.

Troncoso, J. C., Hoffman, P. N., Griffin, J. W., Hess-Kozlow, K. M. and Price, D. L. (1985). Aluminum intoxication: a disorder of neurofilament transport in motor neurons. *Brain Res.* **342**, 172-175.

Troncoso, J. C., Price, D. L., Griffin, J. W. and Parhad, I. M. (1982). Neurofibrillary axonal pathology in aluminum intoxication. *Ann. Neurol.* **12**, 278-283.

Vandevelde, M., Greene, C. E. and Hoff, E. J. (1976). Lower motor neuron disease with accumulation of neurofilaments in a cat. *Vet. Pathol.* **13**, 428-435.

Voyvodic, J. T. (1989). Target size regulates caliber and myelination of sympathetic axons. *Nature* **342**, 430-432.

Wiley, C. A., Love, S., Skoglund, R. R. and Lampert, P. W. (1987). Infantile neurodegenerative disease with neuronal accumulation of phosphorylated neurofilaments. *Acta Neuropathol.* **72**, 369-376.

Wong, J., Hutchison, S. B. and Liem, R. K. H. (1984). An isoelectric variant of the 150,000-dalton neurofilament polypeptide. *J. Biol. Chem.* **259**, 4019-4025.

Xu, Z-S., Cork, L. C., Griffin, J. W. and Cleveland, D. W. (1993). Increased expression of neurofilament subunit NF-L produces morphological alterations that resemble the pathology of human motor neuron disease. *Cell* **73**, 23-33.

Yamasaki, H., Bennett, G. S., Itakura, C. and Mizutani, M. (1992). Defective expression of neurofilament protein subunits in hereditary hypotrophic axonopathy of quail. *Lab. Invest.* **66**, 734-743.

Journal of Cell Science, Supplement 17, 109-117 (1993)
Printed in Great Britain © The Company of Biologists Limited 1993

Ankyrin-binding activity of nervous system cell adhesion molecules expressed in adult brain

Jonathan Q. Davis and Vann Bennett

Howard Hughes Medical Institute and Department of Biochemistry, Duke University Medical Center, Durham, NC 27710, USA

SUMMARY

A family of ankyrin-binding glycoproteins have been identified in adult rat brain that include alternatively spliced products of the same pre-mRNA. A composite sequence of ankyrin-binding glycoprotein (ABGP) shares 72% amino acid sequence identity with chicken neurofascin, a membrane-spanning neural cell adhesion molecule in the Ig super-family expressed in embryonic brain. ABGP polypeptides and ankyrin associate as pure proteins in a 1:1 molar stoichiometry at a site located in the predicted cytoplasmic domain. ABGP polypeptides are expressed late in postnatal development to approximately the same levels as ankyrin, and comprise a significant fraction of brain membrane proteins. Immunofluorescence studies have shown that ABGP polypeptides are co-localized with ankyrin$_B$. Major differences in developmental expression have been reported for neurofascin in embryos compared with the late postnatal expression of ABGP, suggesting that ABGP and neurofascin represent products of gene duplication events that have subsequently evolved in parallel with distinct roles. Predicted cytoplasmic domains of rat ABGP and chicken neurofascin are nearly identical to each other and closely related to a group of nervous system cell adhesion molecules with variable extracellular domains, including L1, Nr-CAM and Ng-CAM of vertebrates, and neuroglian of *Drosophila*. A hypothesis to be evaluated is that ankyrin-binding activity is shared by all of these proteins.

Key words: cell adhesion molecule, ankyrin, spectrin, membrane-cytoskeletal interaction

INTRODUCTION

This article will focus on recent biochemical evidence for a direct association between a family of membrane-spanning cell adhesion molecules and ankyrins in the adult nervous system of mammals. Ankyrins are a family of structural proteins strategically located on the cytoplasmic surface of the plasma membrane with recognition sites for both membrane-spanning integral membrane proteins and spectrin (reviewed by Bennett, 1990; 1992). Ankyrins are ancient components of the nervous system that are expressed in *Caenorhabditis elegans* (Otsuka et al., 1991), and comprise 0.5-1% of the membrane protein in adult vertebrate brain (Bennett, 1979; Davis and Bennett, 1984). Multiple isoforms of ankyrin are expressed in brain, with diversity due to distinct genes as well as to alternative splicing of mRNAs: 220 kDa ankyrin$_B$, which is generally distributed in neurons and glial cells of adult brain; 440 kDa ankyrin$_B$, an alternatively spliced form highly expressed in neonatal development and located in neuronal processes; 215 kDa ankyrin$_R$, which is confined to cell bodies and dendrites of a subset of neurons, and ankyrin$_{node}$, localized at axonal initial segments and nodes of Ranvier. A common feature of the ankyrin family is a membrane-binding domain comprising 24 repeats of a 33-residue motif, impli-cated in macromolecular recognition in a variety of proteins (reviewed by Michaely and Bennett, 1992).

Initial characterization of membrane-binding sites for ankyrin in mammalian brain revealed a class of integral membrane proteins capable of high affinity association with the membrane-binding domain of ankyrin$_B$, and these proteins are present in amounts comparable to ankyrin (Davis and Bennett, 1986). The sites detetected in these binding assays are likely to be distinct from membrane proteins currently known to associate with ankyrin, such as the voltage-dependent sodium channel (Srinivasan et al., 1988; Kordeli et al., 1990; Srinivasan et al., 1992) and the Na/K ATPase (Nelson and Veshnock, 1987; Koob et al., 1987; Morrow et al., 1989), based on their abundance and resistance to high pH.

IDENTIFICATION OF ANKYRIN-BINDING GLYCOPROTEINS (ABGPs) IN ADULT BRAIN

A family of membrane glycoproteins was identified in adult brain and found to associate with 33-residue ankyrin repeats, using the following strategy (Davis et al., 1993). The membrane-binding domain of ankyrin$_B$ (residues 190-947, comprising repeats 5-24 plus a portion of the spectrin-

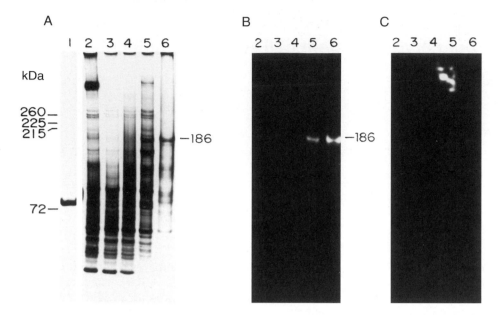

Fig. 1. Identification in adult rat brain of a 186 kDa membrane glycoprotein with ankyrin-binding activity. Triton-X-100-solubilized membrane proteins from 10 g of adult rat brain were applied at 4°C to an ankyrin$_B$ (residues 190-947)-affinity column, and the column washed with ten column volumes of 0.1 M KCl dissolved in column buffer (0.5 % Triton X-100, 0.01 % phosphatidylcholine, 10 mM Hepes, 2 mM dithiothreitol, 1 mM sodium azide, pH 7.4). The adsorbed proteins were eluted with 1 M NaBr in column buffer and applied to a wheat germ agglutinin-agarose affinity column, which was washed with ten volumes of loading buffer, and adsorbed proteins eluted with 0.2 M *N*-acetyl glucosamine. Peak fractions were analyzed by SDS-electrophoresis, and polypeptides detected either by silver stain (A) or by blot-binding with 10 nM ^{125}I-labeled ankyrin$_B$ (residues 190-947) following electrophoretic transfer of polypeptides to nitrocellulose paper (B). A control blot was performed with a 20-fold excess of unlabeled ankyrin (C). Lane 1, Coomassie Blue-stained gel of ankyrin$_B$ (residues 190-947) expressed in *E. coli* (Davis et al., 1991); lane 2, total rat brain membranes; lane 3, Triton X-100 extract of brain membranes; lane 4, Triton X-100 extract following passage over the ankyrin-affinity column; lane 5, polypeptides eluted from the ankyrin-affinity column; lane 6, polypeptides eluted from the wheat germ affinity column. (From Davis et al., 1993.)

binding domain) was expressed in bacteria (Davis et al., 1991) and used to prepare an affinity adsorbent. Proteins from detergent extracts of brain membranes were adsorbed to the ankyrin-affinity column, resulting in selection of at least ten polypeptides (Fig. 1, lane 5). Glycoproteins in this group of ankyrin-binding polypeptides were isolated using a wheat germ agglutinin-affinity column (Fig. 1, lane 6). Finally, a 186 kDa polypeptide capable of direct association with ankyrin was identified in the eluate from the wheat germ agglutinin-affinity column by blot-binding with ^{125}I-labeled ankyrin (Fig. 1, right panels). Direct evidence that the 186 kDa polypeptide is glycosylated was provided by its reduction to a molecular mass of 180 kDa following digestion with endoglycosidase H and to 165 kDa by digestion with endoglycosidase F (Davis et al., 1993).

Affinity-purified antibody against the 186 kDa polypeptide also cross-reacted with two sequence-related polypeptides of molecular masses 155 and 140 kDa (Fig. 2). The 155 and 140 kDa polypeptides were isolated and found to have identical N-terminal sequences to the 186 kDa polypeptide, except for a deletion of six residues (Fig. 2). These polypeptides were alternatively spliced products of the same pre-mRNA based on alternate sequences observed in cDNA clones (see below), and exhibited distinct patterns of expression in regions of the brain. Within the forebrain, 186 kDa and 155 kDa ABGP exhibited a striking segregation between white matter and grey matter, with 186 kDa ABGP present almost exclusively in grey matter and the 155 kDa polypeptide restricted to white matter. The presence of 155 kDa ABGP-1 in white matter, and its location in spinal cord and peripheral nerve, suggested that this polypeptide is a component of myelinated axon tracts.

Association of ankyrin and ABGP polypeptides was measured in quantitative assays using native proteins immobilized through their carbohydrate residues by adsorption to Concanavalin A-coated beads (Fig. 3). The ankyrin domain (residues 190-947) bound to purified ABGP186 with a K_D of 65 nM and with a stoichiometry close to 1:1. Association of ankyrin domain was also measured with isolated ABGP155/140 that as separated from ABGP186 (Fig. 3). A 270 kDa polypeptide identified as the IP3 receptor (data not shown) was also present in this preparation (Fig. 2). However, the 270 kDa polypeptide did not interfere with the assay, since it was not adsorbed to the beads under these experimental conditions. The affinity of ABGP155/140 for ankyrin was reduced 10-fold compared to ABGP186, with a K_D of 600 nM, although the stoichiometry was approximately 1:1. The values for affinity and 1:1 molar stoichiometry are consistent with a selective, site-specific interaction between ankyrin and ABGP186, 155 and 140. The differences in affinity between ABGP186 and 155/140, combined with different regional distributions, suggests that these polypeptides perform related but distinct functions.

PRIMARY STRUCTURE AND DOMAIN ORGANIZATION OF ANKYRIN-BINDING GLYCOPROTEINS

A composite sequence of ABGP encoding 1347 residues was deduced from analysis of multiple overlapping clones, including clones with internal deletions, presumably due to alternative splicing of pre-mRNA (Fig. 4). The predicted sequence of the ankyrin-binding glycoproteins contains five types of domains: (1) six Ig domains of the C2 type (residues 25-611); (2) four fibronectin type 3 domains

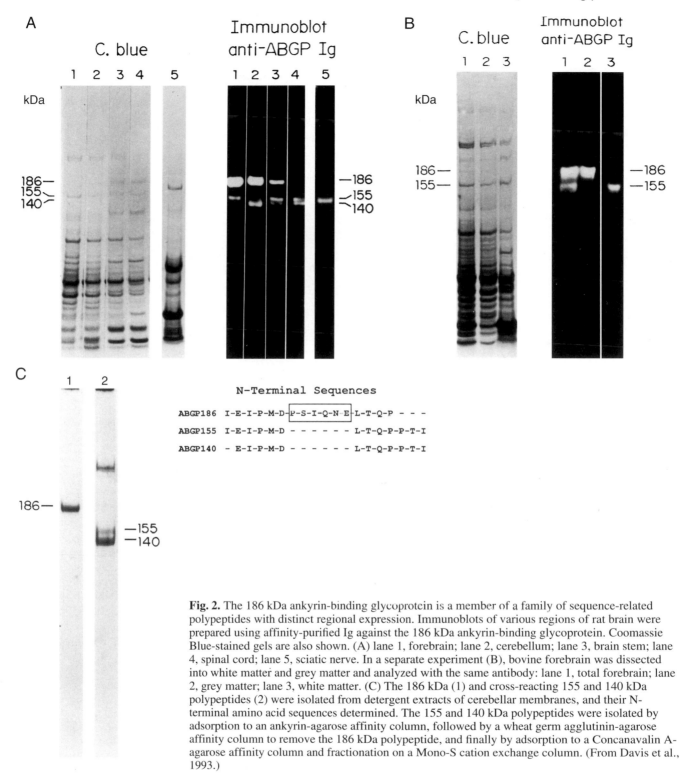

Fig. 2. The 186 kDa ankyrin-binding glycoprotein is a member of a family of sequence-related polypeptides with distinct regional expression. Immunoblots of various regions of rat brain were prepared using affinity-purified Ig against the 186 kDa ankyrin-binding glycoprotein. Coomassie Blue-stained gels are also shown. (A) lane 1, forebrain; lane 2, cerebellum; lane 3, brain stem; lane 4, spinal cord; lane 5, sciatic nerve. In a separate experiment (B), bovine forebrain was dissected into white matter and grey matter and analyzed with the same antibody: lane 1, total forebrain; lane 2, grey matter; lane 3, white matter. (C) The 186 kDa (1) and cross-reacting 155 and 140 kDa polypeptides (2) were isolated from detergent extracts of cerebellar membranes, and their N-terminal amino acid sequences determined. The 155 and 140 kDa polypeptides were isolated by adsorption to an ankyrin-agarose affinity column, followed by a wheat germ agglutinin-agarose affinity column to remove the 186 kDa polypeptide, and finally by adsorption to a Concanavalin A-agarose affinity column and fractionation on a Mono-S cation exchange column. (From Davis et al., 1993.)

(residues 626-1029); (3) a 173-residue domain with a high percentage of proline and threonine (residues 1030-1203); (4) a hydrophobic stretch of 23 amino acids (residues 1216-1238) representing a putative membrane-spanning segment; (5) a putative cytoplasmic domain of 109 amino acids (residues 1239-1347). The Ig domains are in the C2 category, based on spacing of conserved cysteines 48-55 amino acids apart and distinctive residues near the C-terminal cys-

teines (Williams and Barclay, 1988). The fibronectin type 3 repeats have characteristic conserved tryptophans spaced about 50 amino acids from tyrosines (Patthy, 1990), and the third repeat contains a RGD motif. The 173 residues from 1030-1203 have an unusual amino acid composition with a high proportion of proline (9%) and threonine (27%), as well as alanine (9%) and valine (8%). Domains with a similar composition are present in other membrane glyco-

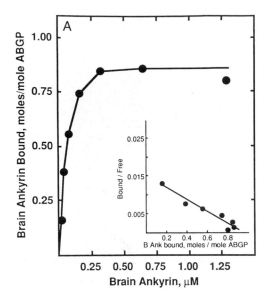

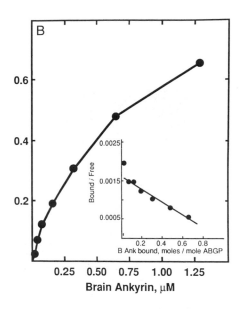

Fig. 3. Measurement of association of ^{125}I-labeled ankyrin$_B$ (brain ankyrin) (residues 190-947) with ankyrin-binding glycoproteins: 186 kDa polypeptide (A) and 155/140 kDa polypeptides (B). Ankyrin-binding glycoproteins adsorbed to the surface of Concanavalin A-coated beads were incubated for 2 hours on ice with increasing concentrations of ^{125}I-labeled ankyrin. Samples were layered onto 200 μl of 10% glycerol dissolved in assay buffer and beads with adsorbed proteins pelleted by centrifugation at 5,000 g for 15 minutes. The tubes were frozen and tips containing the beads cut off and assayed for ^{125}I in a gamma counter. Values for nonspecific binding were determined using a 50-fold excess of unlabeled ankyrin over radiolabeled ankyrin (10 nM), and were subtracted. Data points are the mean of duplicate determinations, and are expressed as moles of ankyrin bound per mole of ankyrin-binding glycoprotein (assuming a monomer), and by the method of Scatchard (insert). (From Davis et al., 1993.)

proteins including the LDL receptor (Yamamoto et al., 1984), platelet glycoprotein 1b (Lopez et al., 1987), and N-CAM (Walsh et al., 1989), and are sites of *O*-glycosylation.

Four candidate sites for alternative splicing of pre-mRNA can be deduced based on alternative sequences among the cDNA clones: one encoding six residues at the N terminus (residues 31-36), one encoding 15 residues between Ig and fibronectin type 3 domains (residues 611-625), and two sites in the proline/threonine domain, residues 1030-1035 and 1036-1203 (Fig. 8). The alternate six residues at the N terminus correspond to the additional amino acids present in the 186 kDa polypeptide and are missing from the 155 and 140 kDa forms (Fig. 4). The 15 residues between Ig and fibronectin domains include two prolines and may be configured as an unstructured loop that provides some flexibility between the domains. The potential for multiple alternative sites raises the question of what combination of deletions/insertions are actually expressed as polypeptides. It also follows that the composite sequence does not necessarily correspond to that of any of the major polypeptides.

Ig and fibronectin type 3 domains are independently folded, and molecules with multiple domains of this would be expected to have the configuration of a relatively rigid rod (Hall and Rutishauser, 1987; Becker et al., 1989; Staunton et al., 1990). The 186 kDa ankyrin-binding glycoprotein, visualized by electron microscopy following rotary shadowing with platinum and carbon, also has an elongated shape, 40-60 nm in length (Fig. 5). Some images were twice this length, and could be due to head-head homophilic interactions. Rosettes of 3-5 molecules were also observed, as has been found for N-CAM, and interpreted as association of these proteins through their hydrophobic domains (Becker et al., 1989). The fact that the ankyrin-binding glycoprotein has the predicted configuration, in addition to correlation of the protein-derived

sequence and deduced sequence provides compelling evidence that the cDNA clones actually encode this protein.

The ankyrin-binding site of 186 kDa ABGP is located in the predicted cytoplasmic domain, based on two observations. Cleavage of the C-terminal 21 kDa, which includes the cytoplasmic domain, results in loss of binding of ankyrin$_B$ (Fig. 6).

ABGPS ARE MEMBERS OF THE Ig SUPERFAMILY OF CELL ADHESION MOLECULES

The amino acid sequence of ABGP is closely related to previously identified nervous system cell adhesion molecules of the Ig super family (Fig. 7). These proteins contain six Ig type C2 domains and four to five fibronectin type 3 domains, and highly conserved cytoplasmic domains. The highest degree of similarity, with 71% sequence identity, is with chicken neurofascin, with lower degrees of identity with mouse L1 (36%), chicken Nr-CAM (47%) and chicken Ng-CAM (30%) (Table 1). *Drosophila* neuroglian, a cell adhesion molecule with similarity to L1 (Bieber et al., 1989), also shares extensive homology with the vertebrate proteins in the cytoplasmic domain.

The predicted cytoplasmic domains are most conserved

Table 1. Comparison of amino acid sequence similarity of ABGP with vertebrate nervous system cell adhesion molecules

| | Percentage identity to ABGP | | | | |
| | | Domains | | | |
Proteins	Overall	Ig	FNIII	PAT	Cytoplasmic
Chicken neurofascin	71	80	71	19	86
Chicken Nr-CAM	47	53	45	--	73
Mouse L1	36	38	38	--	50
Chicken Ng-CAM	30	36	29	--	34

```
MARQQAPPWV HVALILFLLS LGGAIEIPMD PSIONELTQP PTITKQSVKD   50
HIVDPRDNIL IECEAKGNPA PSFHWTRNSR FFNIAKDPRV SMRRRSGTLV  100
IDFRSGGRPE EYEGEYQCFA RNKFGTALSN RIRLQVSKSP LWPKENLDPV  150
VVQEGAPLTL QCNPPPGLPS PVIFWMSSSM EPITQDKRVS QGHNGDLYFS  200
NVMLQDMQTD YSCNARFHFT HTIQQKNPFT LKVLTTRGVA ERTPSFMYPQ  250
GTSSSQMVLR GMDLLLECIA SGVPTPDIAW TKNGQDLPGD KAKFENFNKA  300
LRITNVSEED SGEYFCLASN KMGSIRHTIS VRVKAAPYWL DEPKNLILAP  350
GEDGRLVCRA NGNPKPTVQW LVNGDPLQSA PPNPNREVAG DTIIFRDTQI  400
SSRAVYQCNT SNEHGYLLAN AFVSVLDVPP RMLSPRNQLI RVILYNRTRL  450
DCPFFGSPIP TLRWFKNGQG SNLDGGNYHV YQNGSLEIKM IRKEDQGIYT  500
CVATNILGKA ENQVRLEVKD PTRIYRMPED QVAKRGTTVQ LECRVKHDPS  550
LKLTVSWLKD DEPLYIGNRM KKEDDSLTIF GVAERDQGSY TCMASTELDQ  600
DLAKAYLTVL ADQATPTNRL AALPKGRPDR PRDLELTDLA ERSVRLTWIP  650
GDDNNSPITD YVVQFEEDQF QPGVWHDHSK FPGSVNSAVL HLSPYVNYQF  700
RVIAVNEVGS SHPSLPSERY RTSGAPPESN PSDVKGEGTR KNNMEITWTP  750
MNATSAFGPN LRYIVKWRRR ETRETWNNVT VWGSRYVVGQ TPVYVPYEIR  800
VQAENDFGKG PEPETVIGYS GEDYPRAAPT EVKIRVLNST AISLQWNRVY  850
PDTVQGQLRE YRAYYWRESS LLKNLWVSQK RQQASFPGDR PRGVVGRLFP  900
YSNYKLEMVV VNGRGDGPRS ETKEFTTPEG VPSAPRRFRV RQPNLETINL  950
EWDHPEHPNG ILIGYTLRYV PFNGTKLGKQ MVENFSPNQT KFSVQRADPV 1000
SRYRFSLSAR TQVGSGEAAT EESPTPPNEA TPTAAPPTLP PTTVGTTGLV 1050
SSTDATALAA TSEATTVPII PTVVPTTVAT TIATTTTTTA AATTTTTTES 1100
PPTTTTGTKI HETAPDEQSI WNVTVLPNSK WANITWKHNF RPGTDFVVEY 1150
IDSNHTKKTV PVKAQAQPIQ LTDLFPGMTY TLRVYSRDNE GISSTVITFM 1200
TSTAYTNNQT DIATQGWFIG LMCAIALLVL ILLIVCFIKR SRGGKYPVRE 1250
KKDVPLGPED PKEEDGSFDY SDEDNKPLQG SQTSLDGTIK QQESDDSLVD 1300
YGEGGEGQFN EDGSFIGQYT VRKDKEETEG NESSEATSPV NAIYSLA     1347
```

between ankyrin-binding glycoproteins, neurofascin, L1, Nr-CAM and Ng-CAM, with some regions that are identical among all five of these proteins (Table 1, Fig. 8). In addition to sequence similarity, cytoplasmic domains of chicken neurofascin (Volkmer et al., 1992) rat and human L1 (Miura et al., 1991; Kobayashi et al., 1991; Reid and

Fig. 4. Primary structure of ankyrin-binding glycoproteins deduced from analysis of cDNAs isolated from rat brain. An initial cDNA clone was isolated from a lambda gt11 expression library prepared from rat brain using poly(A) and random hexamers as primers (Clonetech), using affinity-purified polyclonal antibody against the 186 kDa ankyrin-binding glycoprotein. cDNAs encoding the complete polypeptide were isolated using the first clone and subsequent clones as probes. A stop codon was present in three independent clones. Portions of sequence corresponding to nucleotides 1130-1142, 2870-2914, 4131-4145 and 4146-4652 were deleted in some of the clones and represent candidates for alternative splicing of pre-mRNA. Hydrophobic portions of the sequence representing a predicted signal peptide (residues 1-24) and membrane-spanning region (residues 1216-1238) are underlined and in italics. Alternate sequences are boxed: residues 31-36; 611-625 and 1001-1203. Conserved cysteines of the six Ig-like repeats, and tryptophans and tyrosines of the four fibronectin type 3 repeats are enlarged in bold. Potential *N*-glycosylation sites in the predicted extracellular domain and phosphorylation sites in the cytoplasmic domain are bold and underlined, and a RGD motif (residues 914-916) is in bold. Portions of the deduced sequence confirmed by analysis of N-terminal sequences of polypeptides isolated by Mono Q chromatography of V8 proteolytic digests are underlined. (From Davis et al., 1993.)

Hemperly, 1992) and chicken Nr-CAM (Grumet et al., 1991; Kayyem et al., 1992) also share alternative splicing involving a tetrapeptide, RSLE. The cytoplasmic domain of rat ABGP contains the ankyrin-binding site (Fig. 6; Michaely and Bennett, 1993), suggesting the possibility that other members of this group also interact with either the same ankyrin or with a related member of the ankyrin family. A 440 kDa alternatively spliced form of ankyrin$_B$ is expressed prior to birth (Kunimoto et al., 1991), and it also is possible that other forms of ankyrin are present in early development.

Neurofascin was initially characterized as a membrane protein, hypothesized to play a role in extension of neurites and stabilization of bundles of axons during development of the nervous system (Rathjen et al., 1987; Volkmer et al., 1992). A significant discovery from this study is that ABGPs, which are closely related to neurofascin, are most prominent in adult brain, with a 10-20-fold increased expression following the major phases of neuronal migration (see below; Fig. 9). It is not certain at this

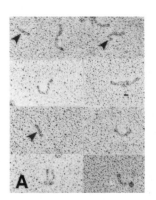
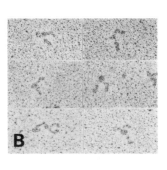
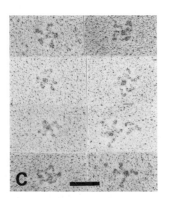

Fig. 5. Visualization of the 186 kDa ankyrin-binding glycoprotein by electron microscopy. The 186 kDa ankyrin-binding glycoprotein (300 µg/ml) in a buffer containing 0.1% Triton X-100, 0.01% phosphatidylcholine, 10 mM Hepes, pH 7.4, was diluted twenty-fold with 30% glycerol, 0.1 M ammonium formate, pH 7.0, and immediately sprayed onto freshly cleaved mica. The samples were then rotary shadowed at an angle of 6 degrees with platinum followed by carbon, and the replicas visualized by electron microscopy. (A) Single molecules (arrowheads); (B) head-head pairs; (C) rosettes of 3-5 molecules. Bar, 100 nm. (From Davis et al., 1993.)

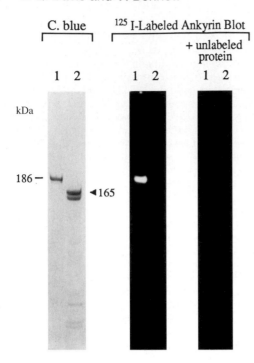

N-Terminal Sequence
ABGP186 I-E-I-P-M-D-P-S-I-Q-N-E-L-T-Q-P-
V8 165 I-E-I-P-M-D-P-S-I-Q-N-E-L-T-Q-P-

Fig. 6. Localization of the ankyrin-binding site to the C-terminal 21 kDa of the ABGP186 polypeptide. ABGP186 (0.1 mg/ml in a buffer containing 50 mM NaCl, 10 mM Hepes, pH 7.4, 0.5 % Triton X-100, 0.01% phosphatidylcholine. 0.5 mM dithiothreitol, 1 mM sodium azide) was digested with Staphylococcal V8 protease (20 μg/ml for 60 minutes at 24°C), and the products resolved by chromatography on a Mono-Q anion exchange column. A 165 kDa polypeptide was resolved, which retained the N terminus based on amino acid sequence, and was missing the C-terminal 21 kDa. Binding of ^{125}I-labeled ankyrin_B (residues 190-947) to 186 kDa and 165 kDa polypeptides was determined following electrophoretic transfer of polypeptides to nitrocellulose paper. (A) Coomassie Blue-stained polypeptides; (B,C) autoradiograms of nitrocellulose paper incubated with 36 nM ^{125}I-labeled ankyrin_B (residues 190-947), either alone or with a 75-fold excess unlabeled ankyrin to displace nonspecific binding. (From Davis et al., 1993.)

time whether the ABGP polypeptides are encoded by the identical gene to chicken neurofascin. The similarity in amino acid sequence and conservation of sites of alterna-

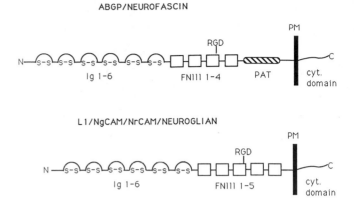

Fig. 7. Schematic model for the domain organization of ankyrin-binding glycoproteins, neurofascin and related nervous system cell adhesion molecules. PM, plasma membrane; Ig, type C2 domains; FNIII, fibronectin type 3 domains (from Davis et al., 1993).

tive splicing strongly support the interpretation that ABGPs and neurofascin genes share a common ancestor. However, the major differences in developmental expression and divergence in some areas of the sequence (Fig. 9) suggest that ABGPs and neurofascin represent products of gene duplication events that have subsequently evolved in parallel with distinct roles in development. Important issues for the future will be to determine whether multiple copies of the ABGP and neurofascin genes indeed exist, or if the same gene plays roles both in fetal development and in adult brain.

ANKYRIN AND ABGPs ARE CO-LOCALIZED AND CO-EXPRESSED DURING DEVELOPMENT

The question of whether the association of ankyrin and ankyrin-binding glycoproteins actually occurs in vivo will require experiments beyond the scope of this initial, biochemically oriented work. However, circumstantial evidence consistent with interaction of these proteins in brain tissue is that ABGP polypeptides are expressed at approximately the same levels as ankyrin, co-expressed with the adult form of ankyrin_B late in postnatal development, and are co-localized with ankyrin_B by immunofluorescence. Ankyrin-binding glycoproteins are expressed in the forebrain at relatively low levels until after birth, when the level

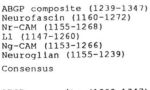
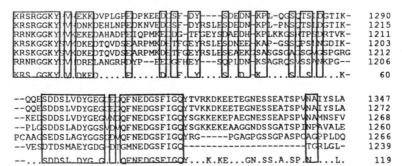

Fig. 8. Aligned sequences of putative cytoplasmic domains of rat ankyrin-binding glycoproteins, and related neural adhesion molecules. (From Davis et al., 1993.)

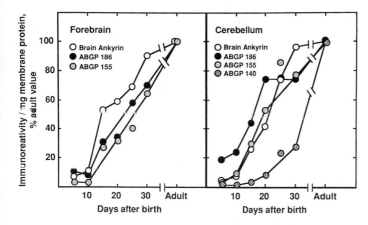

Fig. 9. Ankyrin-binding glycoproteins and the adult form of ankyrin$_B$ are expressed late in post-natal development of rat brain. Samples of forebrain and cerebellum obtained from rats of various ages were analysed by immunoblots using ^{125}I-labeled Protein A and affinity-purified Ig against the 186 kDa ankyrin-binding glycoprotein and ankyrin$_B$, following resolution of polypeptides by SDS-electrophoresis and transfer to nitrocellulose paper. Amounts of immunoreactive 186, 155 and 140 kDa polypeptides were compared by densitometry of autoradiograms, and these values were then normalized with respect to amount of protein applied to the gel. Protein was estimated by elution of dye from Coomassie blue-stained gels with 25% pyridine followed by measurement of absorbance at 550 nm. The ratios of immunoreactivity/ protein are expressed as a percentage of the adult values. (From Davis et al., 1993.)

Fig. 10. (a) Ankyrin-binding glycoproteins are highly concentrated at the node of Ranvier in peripheral nerve. Frozen sections (10 μm) of rat sciatic nerve were examined by immunofluorescence using affinity-purified Ig against the ankyrin-binding glycoproteins. (b) Sciatic nerve with a DIC image showing a node of Ranvier (arrowhead) below the same section viewed by immunofluorescence. Bar, 20 μm. (From Davis et al., 1993.)

of expression increases over 20-fold between day 10 and day 50 (Fig. 9, left panel). The 220 kDa adult form of ankyrin$_B$ exhibited a similar time course, with expression accelerating after day 10 (Fig. 9). Similar profiles were observed for forebrain and cerebellum (Fig. 10, right panel), although 186 kDa ABGP is expressed in the cerebellum (less than 25% of adult values) before day 10. ABGP140 is selectively expressed in the cerebellum, and appears only

after day 20, almost two weeks after ABGP186 and AGBP155. Events known to occur in the cerebellum late in postnatal development following the major phases of neuronal mitosis and migration which coincide with expression of ankyrin-binding glycoproteins include synaptogenesis followed by ensheathing of Purkinje cells by glial cells (Altman, 1972).

Immunofluorescence studies in frozen sections of brain and peripheral nerve indicate that ankyrin and the ankyrin-binding polypeptides are both present in low amounts in central tracts of myelinated axons, highly expressed in unmyelinated axons, and present at this level of resolution in both neurons and glial cells. Ankyrin-binding glycoprotein immunoreactivity is highly concentrated at nodes of Ranvier in myelinated axons of peripheral nerve (Fig. 10), and this is also the site of localization of a form of ankyrin (Kordeli and Bennett, 1991; Kordeli et al., 1990). The staining at nodes of Ranvier is probably due to the 155 kDa polypeptide which is the only form detectable by immunoblots in peripheral nerve (Fig. 2). Punctate staining could also be detected at higher magnification in myelinated regions of the forebrain and cerebellum, which may represent nodes of Ranvier smaller and more difficult to resolve by light microscopy than those in peripheral nerve (not shown). Since the 155 kDa form is the major polypeptide detectable in dissected white matter from forebrain (Fig. 2), the 155 kDa polypeptide is probably a component of nodes of Ranvier in the central nervous system as well as peripheral nerve.

CONCLUSION

Associations of ABGPs with ankyrin, of ankyrin with spectrin (Davis and Bennett, 1984), and of spectrin with actin (Bennett et al., 1982; Glenney et al., 1982) provide an example of a series of protein-protein interactions extending from the extracellular space to the cytoplasm that have been defined in terms of affinity and stoichiometry with pure components. These proteins are abundant in brain, with spectrin representing 3%, ankyrins 1% and ABGPs 0.3-0.5% of the total membrane protein. This system of proteins thus represents a major class of membrane-cytoskeletal linkages in the nervous system. Interactions among these proteins have the potential to be utilized in diverse contexts in cells, since ABGPs and ankyrins are each capable of multiple types of interaction. ABGPs include several polypeptides derived from alternative splicing of pre-mRNA, and these forms exhibit differences in affinity for ankyrin, regional distribution and time of expression during development (Fig. 9). In addition to alternative splicing, another level of diversity is provided by the subgroup of cell adhesion molecules with cytoplasmic domains related to ABGP and neurofascin which are candidates for association with ankyrins (Fig. 9). Interactions, in addition to homophilic associations, have been observed for other cell adhesion molecules containing Ig and fibronectin type 3 repeats and may also be available to ABGPs. Examples include binding to soluble extracellular matrix molecules (Reyes et al., 1990; Kuhn et al., 1991; Rathjen et al., 1991), lateral association with other cell adhesion molecules to form complexes capable of cell-cell interactions (Kadmon et al., 1990) and heterophilic interactions with integral membrane proteins on adjacent cells (Marlin and Springer, 1987). It is clear that a simple interaction between ankyrins and ABGPs and perhaps other cell adhesion molecules with conserved cytoplasmic domains can, in principle, be utilized to establish a variety of membrane-cytoskeletal connections in the nervous system. The node of Ranvier is one example of a specialized membrane domain containing isforms of ankyrin and ABGP polypeptides (Fig. 7) (Kordeli et al., 1990; Kordeli and Bennett, 1991).

The high expression of rat ABGP in postnatal and adult brain strongly suggests that the function(s) of this protein includes roles in addition to activities attributed to cell adhesion molecules during prenatal development. Possibilities include a role in developing and or maintaining specialized membrane domains such as unmyelinated axons and the node of Ranvier discussed above. Another consequence of associations between these proteins may be structural support for the adult brain, which is dependent on cell-cell contacts and lacks a collagen-based basement membrane utilized by cells in most tissues. Coupling between the elongated extracellular domain of ABGP polypeptides and the cytoskeleton would provide a mechanical buffer, allowing distribution of shear stresses and deformations throughout the tissue. Another possible role of ABGPs could be related to cell signaling, and result in stabilizing neurons and glial cells that maintain appropriate cellular contacts.

A prominent role of ABGPs in adult mammalian brain has potential clinical implications, since defects in these proteins may be compatible with survival but with impaired neurological or cognitive development. It is of interest in this regard that abnormal splicing of human L1 premRNA, a related cell adhesion molecule, results in hydrocephalus and mental retardation (Rosenthal et al., 1992). Another potential clinical implication is that ABGPs may play a role as receptors for neurotropic viruses, as occurs for Rhinoviruses in lymphocytes (Staunton et al., 1990).

Brenda Sampson is gratefully acknowledged for help in preparing the manuscript.

REFERENCES

Altman, J. (1972). Postnatal development of the cerebellar cortex in the rat. *J. Comp. Neurol.* **145**, 399-464.

Becker, J., Erickson, H., Hoffman, S., Cunningham, B. and Edelman, G. (1989). Topology of cell adhesion molecules. *Proc. Nat. Acad. Sci. USA* **86**, 1088-1092.

Bennett, V. (1979). Immunoreactive forms of human erythrocyte ankyrin are present in diverse cells and tissues. *Nature* **281**, 597-599.

Bennett, V. (1990). The spectrin-based membrane skeleton: a multipotential adaptor between membrane and cytoplasm. *Physiol. Rev.* **70**, 1029-1066.

Bennett, V. (1992). Ankyrins: adaptors between diverse plasma membrane proteins and cytoplasm. *J. Biol. Chem.* **267**, 8703-8706.

Bennett, V., Davis, J. and Fowler, V. W. (1982). Brain spectrin, a membrane-associated protein related in structure and function to erythrocyte spectrin. *Nature* **299**, 126-131.

Bieber, A. J., Snow, P. M., Hortsch, M., Patel, N. H., Jacobs, J. R., Traquina, Z. R., Schilling, J. and Goodman, C. S. (1989). *Drosophila* neuroglian: a member of the immunoglobulin superfamily with extensive homology to the vertebrate neural cell adhesion molecule L1. *Cell* **59**, 447-460.

Davis, J. and Bennett, V. (1984). Brain ankyrin - a membrane-associated protein with binding sites for spectrin, tubulin and the cytoplasmic domain of the erythrocyte anion channel. *J. Biol. Chem.* **259**, 13550-13559.

Davis, J. and Bennett, V. (1986). Association of brain ankyrin with brain membranes and isolation of active proteolytic fragments of membrane-associated ankyrin-binding proteins. *J. Biol. Chem.* **261**, 16198-16206.

Davis, L. and Bennett, V. (1990). Mapping the binding sites of human erythrocyte ankyrin for the anion exchanger and spectrin. *J. Biol. Chem.* **265**, 10589-10596.

Davis, L., Otto, E. and Bennett, V. (1991). Specific 33-residue repeat(s) of erythrocyte ankyrin associate with the anion exchanger. *J. Biol. Chem.* **266**, 11163-11169.

Davis, J. Q., McLaughlin, T. and Bennett, V. (1993). Ankyrin-binding proteins related to nervous system cell adhesion molecules: Candidates to provide transmembrane and intercellular connections in adult brain. *J. Cell Biol.* (in press).

Glenney, J., Glenney, P., Osborn, M. and Weber, K. (1982). An F-actin- and calmodulin-binding protein from isolated intestinal brush borders has a morphology related to spectrin. *Cell* **28**, 843-854.

Grumet, M., Mauro, V., Burgoon, M. P., Edelman, G. M. and Cunningham, B. A. (1991). Structure of a new nervous system glycoprotein, Nr-CAM and its relationship to subgroups of neural cell adhesion molecules. *J. Cell Biol.* **113**, 1399-1412.

Hall, A. K. and Rutishauser, U. (1987). Visualization of neural cell adhesion molecule by electron microscopy. *J. Cell Biol.* **104**, 1579-1586.

Kadmon, G., Kowitz, A., Alevogt, P. and Schachner, M. (1990). The neural cell adhesion molecule N-CAM enhances L1-dependent cell-cell interactions. *J. Cell Biol.* **110**, 193-208.

Kayyem, J. F., Roman, J. M., de la Rosa, E., Schwarz, U. and Dreyer, W. J. (1992). Bravo/Nr-CAM is closely related to the cell adhesion molecules L1 and Ng-CAM and has a similar heterodimer structure. *J. Cell Biol.* **118**, 1259-1270.

Kobayashi, M., Miura, M., Asou, H. and Uyemura, K. (1991). Molecular cloning of cell adhesion molecule L1 from human nervous tissue: a comparison of the primary sequences of L1 molecules of different origin. *Biochim. Biophys. Acta* **1090**, 238-240.

Koob, R., Zimmermann, M., Schone, W. and Drenckhahn, D. (1987). Colocalization and coprecipitation of ankyrin and Na$^+$,K$^+$-ATPase in kidney epithelial cells. *Eur. J. Cell Biol.* B, 230-237.

Kordeli, E. and Bennett, V. (1991). Distinct ankyrin isoforms at neuron cell bodies and nodes of Ranvier resolved using erythrocyte ankyrin-deficient mice. *J. Cell Biol.* **114**, 1243-1259.

Kordeli, E., Davis, J., Trapp, B. and Bennett, V. (1990). An isoform of ankyrin is localized at nodes of Ranvier in myelinated axons of central and peripheral nerves. *J. Cell Biol.* **110**, 1341-1352.

Kuhn, T. B., Stoeckli, E. T., Condrau, M. A., Rathjen, F. G. and Sonderegger, P. (1991). Neurite outgrowth on immobilized axonin-1 is mediated by heterophilic interaction with L1. *J. Cell Biol.* **115**, 1113-1126.

Kunimoto, M., Otto, E. and Bennett, V. (1991). A new 440-kD isoform is the major ankyrin in neonatal rat brain. *J. Cell Biol.* **115**, 1319-1331.

Lopez, J., Chung, D., Fujikawa, K., Hagen, F. S., Papayannopoulou, T. and Roth, G. (1987). Cloning of the α chain of human platelet glycoprotein 1b: a transmembrane protein with homology to leucine-rich α$_2$ glycoprotein. *Proc. Nat. Acad. Sci. USA* **84**, 5615-5619.

Marlin, S. D. and Springer, T. A. (1987). Purified intercellular adhesion molecule-1 (ICAM-1) is a ligand for lymphocyte function-associated Antigen 1 (LFA-1). *Cell* **51**, 813-819.

Michaely, P. and Bennett, V. (1992). The ANK repeat: a ubiquitous motif involved in macromolecular recognition. *Trends Cell Biol.* **2**, 127-129.

Miura, M., Kobayashi, M., Asou, H. and Uyemura, K. (1991). Molecular cloning of cDNA encoding the rat neural cell adhesion molecule L1. *FEBS Lett.* **289**, 91-95.

Morrow, J. S., Cianci, C. D., Ardito, T., Mann, A. S. and Kashgarian, M. (1989). Ankyrin links fodrin to the alpha subunit of Na,K-ATPase in Madin-Darby canine kidney cells and in intact renal tubule cells. *J. Cell Biol.* **108**, 455-465.

Nelson, W. J. and Veshnock, P. J. (1987). Ankyrin binding to the (Na$^+$ + K$^+$) ATPase and implications for the organization of membrane domains in polarized cells. *Nature* **328**, 533-535.

Otsuka, A. J., Franco, R., Yang, B., Shim, K.-H., Tang, L. Z.,

Jeyaprakash, A. and Boontrakulpoontawee. (1991). The Caenorhabditis elegans unc-44 axonal guidance gene contains an ankyrin-like spectrin-binding domain. *J. Cell Biol.* **115**, 465a.

Patthy, L. (1990). Homology of a domain of the growth hormone/prolactin receptor with type III modules of fibronectin. *Cell* **61**, 13-14.

Rathjen, F. G. and Jessel, T. M. (1991). Glycoproteins that regulate the growth and guidance of vertebrate axons: domains and dynamics of the immunoglobulin/fibronectin type III subfamily. *The Neurosciences* **3**, 297-307.

Rathjen, F. G., Wolff, J. M. and Chiquet-Ehrismann, R. (1991). Restrictin: a chick neural extracelular matrix protein involved in cell attachment co-purifies with the cell recognition molecule F11. *Development* **113**, 151-164.

Rathjen, F. G., Wolff, J. M., Chang, S., Bonhoeffer, F. and Raper, J. (1987). Neurofascin: A novel chick cell-surface glycoprotein involved in neurite-neurite interactions. *Cell* **51**, 841-849.

Reid, R. A. and Hemperly, J. J. (1992). Variants of human L1 cell adhesion-molecule arise through alternate splicing of RNA. *J. Mol. Neurosci.* **3**, 127-135.

Rosenthal, A., M. Jonet and S. Kenwrich (1992). Aberrant splicing of neural cell adhesion molecule L1 mRNA in a family with x-linked hydrocephalus. *Nat. Genet.* **2**, 107-112.

Reyes, A. A., Akeson, R., Brezina, L. and Cole, G. J. (1990). Structural requirements for neural cell adhesion molecule-heparin intraction. *Cell Regul.* **1**, 567-576.

Sadoul, R., Kirchhoff, F. and Schachner, M. (1989). A protein kinase activity is associated with and specifically phosphorylates the neural cell adhesion molecule L1. *J. Neurochemistry* **53**, 1471-1478.

Srinivasan, Y., Elmer, L., Davis, J., Bennett, V. and Angelides, K. (1988). Ankyrin and spectrin associate with voltage-dependent sodium channels in brain. *Nature* **333**, 177-180.

Srinivasan, Y., Lewallen, M. and Angelides, K. J. (1992). Mapping the binding site on ankyrin for the voltage-dependent sodium channel from brain. *J. Biol. Chem.* **267**, 7483-7489.

Staunton, D. E., Dustin, M. L., Erickson, H. P. and Springer, T. A. (1990). The arrangement of the immunolobulin like domains of ICAM-1 and the binding sites for LFA-1 and Rhinovirus. *Cell* **61**, 243-254.

Volkmer, H., Hassel, B., Wolff, J. M., Frank, R. and Rathjen, F. G. (1992). Structure of the axonal surface recognition molecule neurofascin and its relationship to a neural subgroup of the immunoglobulin superfamily. *J. Cell Biol.* **118**, 149-161.

Walsh, F. S., Parekh, R. B., Moore, S. E., Dickson, G., Barton, C. H., Gower, H., Dwek, R. A. and Rodemarcher, T. W. (1989). Tissue-specific O-linked glycosylation of the neural cell adhesion molecule (N-CAM). *Development* **105**, 803-811.

Williams, A. F. and Barclay, A. N. (1988). The immunoglobulin superfamily - Domains for cell surface recognition. *Annu. Rev. Immunol.* **6**, 381-405.

Yamamoto, T., Davis, C. G., Brown, M., Schneider, W., Casey, M., Goldstein, J. and Russell, D. (1984). The human LDL receptor: a cysteine-rich protein with multiple Alu sequences in its mRNA. *Cell* **39**, 27-38.

Journal of Cell Science, Supplement 17, 119-125 (1993)
Printed in Great Britain © The Company of Biologists Limited 1993

Biogenesis of structural intercellular junctions during cleavage in the mouse embryo

Tom P. Fleming, Qamar Javed, Jane Collins and Mark Hay

Department of Biology, Biomedical Sciences Building, University of Southampton, Bassett Crescent East, Southampton SO9 3TU, UK

SUMMARY

The preimplantation embryo differentiates the trophectoderm epithelium which, from the 32-cell stage, generates the blastocoel of the blastocyst and, after implantation, gives rise to most extraembryonic lineages of the conceptus. Trophectoderm differentiation begins at compaction (8-cell stage) when cell-cell adhesion, mediated by uvomorulin, and epithelial cell polarisation first occur. Here, we review our work on the biogenesis of tight junctions and desmosomes during epithelial differentiation. Tight junction construction begins at compaction and appears to be a gradual process, both at morphological and molecular levels. This maturation pattern may be due in part to sequential expression of tight junction constituents from the embryonic genome. Tight junction formation is dependent upon uvomorulin adhesion but can be inhibited by different means without apparently disturbing cell adhesion or polarisation. Cell interactions appear to regulate tight junction tissue specificity, in part by controlling the level of synthesis of constituents. Desmosome formation begins at the 32-cell stage, particularly as the embryo initiates blastocoel accumulation, and, in contrast with tight junction formation, does not appear to be a gradual process. Thus, nascent desmosomes appear mature in terms of their molecular composition. Desmosomal proteins are synthesised well in advance of desmosome formation but the synthesis of the principal glycoprotein components begins at the blastocyst stage and may regulate the timing of junction assembly. Implications of these differing patterns of biogenesis for the embryo are discussed.

Key words: epithelium, cell adhesion, cell polarity, differentiation, mouse embryo, trophectoderm, ICM, blastocyst, uvomorulin, E-cadherin, intercellular junctions, tight junction, zonula occludens, ZO-1, cingulin, desmosome

INTRODUCTION

In our laboratory, we study the process of epithelial differentiation and polarization in the cleaving mouse embryo. The epithelium in question, the trophectoderm, forms the wall of the blastocyst at about 3.5 days post-fertilization and encloses the ICM (inner cell mass; progenitor of foetus) and blastocoelic cavity. The first developmental function of the nascent trophectoderm is to generate the blastocoel by vectorial transport (Wiley, 1987; Manejwala et al., 1989; Wiley et al., 1990) and to regulate metabolic exchange with the ICM. After further expansion of the blastocoel, the trophectoderm contributes to embryo hatching from the zona pellucida by enzymic secretion (Perona and Wassarman, 1986; Sawada et al., 1992). It then engages, at 4.5-5.5 days post-fertilization, in specific adhesive and invasive cellular interactions with maternal tissue to accomplish implantation (Holmes and Lindenberg, 1988; Lindenberg et al., 1990). After implantation, trophectoderm (trophoblast) cell lineages contribute exclusively to extra-embryonic tissues, notably giant cells, extraembryonic ectoderm, ectoplacental cone and chorionic ectoderm (Gardner and Beddington,

1988). Our interest in trophectoderm lies in understanding its derivation from non-epithelial and non-polar blastomeres and how the epithelial phenotype is propagated selectively in this lineage of the blastocyst (Fleming and Johnson, 1988; Fleming, 1992).

There are three main constraints in studying the trophectoderm as a model for epithelial differentiation: preimplantation embryos are expensive to generate, there is only limited material to work with and, because of inherent developmental asynchrony, staging of embryos must be tackled carefully. However, we believe that there are some real advantages. First, the trophectoderm is a native tissue with important consequences for morphogenesis and development, and hence is of clear medical interest. Second, its formation is rather slow (about 24 hours), providing time for analysis of mechanisms. Third, and perhaps most important, the epithelium differentiates de novo after normal cell cycling and 'housekeeping' functions have been reestablished in the embryo following release from oocyte meiotic arrest (Pratt, 1989; Fleming, 1992). Thus, it is possible to study gene and protein expression events required for epithelial differentiation, in addition to changes in cell organisation. Recently, we have studied maturation of cell-cell adhesion during trophectoderm differentiation, in particular the formation of structural intercellular junctions. Here, we provide a brief review of this work.

ADHESION AND POLARISATION

Cell-cell adhesion between blastomeres begins at the 8-cell stage when the embryo compacts and each cell polarises along its apicobasal axis, generating a proto-epithelial phenotype. Adhesion is achieved by uvomorulin (120×10^3 M_r, E-cadherin) intercellular binding (Hyafil et al., 1980; Peyrieras et al., 1983). Uvomorulin is synthesised and is present in the membrane in a non-polar and non-adhesive state from early cleavage; at compaction, it becomes adhesive and progressively basolateral in distribution (i.e. at cell-cell contact sites) (Vestweber et al., 1987). The mechanism causing uvomorulin adhesion at compaction is not known but coincides with the onset of uvomorulin phosphorylation (Sefton et al., 1992). Moreover, treatment of pre-compact embryos with phorbol ester to activate protein kinase C causes premature compaction (Winkel et al., 1990), further suggesting a role for phosphorylation in initiating adhesion.

As adhesion commences, the proto-epithelial organisation generated in 8-cell blastomeres includes changes in the distribution of cytoskeletal elements (actin filaments, microtubules), cytoplasmic organelles (mostly endocytic vesicles) and components of the membrane and underlying cortex (e.g. microvilli, actin-binding proteins) (reviewed by Fleming and Johnson, 1988; Fleming, 1992; Gueth-Hallonet and Maro, 1992). Experimental evidence suggests that certain, as yet undefined, aspects of polarisation in the membrane and cortex (cytocortex) are of fundamental importance in guiding the reorganisation of other cellular structures (Johnson and Maro, 1985, 1986; Fleming et al., 1986; Johnson et al., 1986a; Wiley and Obasaju, 1988). This primary cyto-cortical state appears also to act as a stable 'memory' of the polar axis in subsequent cell cycles, since during mitosis aspects of polarity are transiently run down before being reestablished in the next interphase (Johnson et al., 1988). What is the relationship between cell adhesion and polarisation at compaction? If the onset of adhesion is prevented (by, for example, incubation with uvomorulin antibody), polarisation is delayed, disoriented with respect to cell contact patterns, but is not inhibited (Johnson et al., 1986b). This suggests that adhesion may act normally to induce and orient polarisation but the molecular pathway involved is not known. In the absence of adhesion, however, other non-specific factors may induce polarisation, reflecting the 'programmed' state of blastomeres to begin differentiation. 'Programming' for polarisation at compaction requires RNA, DNA and protein synthesis in the 2-cell embryo, 24 hours earlier, but apparently not subsequently (Kidder and McLachlin, 1985; Smith and Johnson, 1985; Levy et al., 1986).

TIGHT JUNCTION CONSTRUCTION

The first epithelial-type junctions to form in the embryo are gap and tight junctions during the 8-cell stage, although an analysis of adherens junction formation has not yet been conducted systematically (Reima, 1990). The process of tight junction (zonula occludens) formation will be considered here; gap junction formation and function during preimplantation development have been discussed elsewhere recently (Barron et al., 1989; Bevilacqua et al., 1989; Nishi et al., 1991; Fleming, 1992; Fleming et al., 1992).

Ultrastructural analysis of embryos indicates that tight junctions begin to form at compaction; however, this process is not completed until the late morula stage (16- to 32-cell stage), up to 24 hours later (Ducibella and Anderson, 1975; Ducibella et al., 1975; Magnuson et al., 1977; Pratt, 1985). Once completed, vectorial transport and blastocoel accumulation can begin, dependent upon the segregation of Na$^+$,K$^+$-ATPase to basolateral trophectoderm membranes (Watson and Kidder, 1988). During the tight junction construction period, the apicolateral contact region between outside blastomeres displays sites of apparent membrane fusion and lanthanum exclusion, corresponding with a freeze-fracture morphology of anastomosing strands and grooves in complementary faces. These sites first appear as a discontinuous series along the apicolateral border and gradually extend laterally to become continuous (zonular) during the morula stage.

We have examined the molecular maturation of the tight junction in embryos using antibodies to peripheral membrane (cytoplasmic face) tight junction proteins. For a review of tight junction molecular composition, see Anderson and Stevenson (1991). Since embryos develop asynchronously, to improve accuracy in the relative timing of assembly of different components, we have used natural 8-cell couplets (2/8 cells), synchronised from their time of division from single 4-cell blastomeres (1/4 cells). These couplets engage in adhesion and polarisation at compaction in a similar way to blastomeres in intact embryos. The assembly of ZO-1 (225×10^3 M_r; Stevenson et al., 1986; Anderson et al., 1988) at the junction begins 1-2 hours after compaction initiates and precedes the assembly of cingulin (140×10^3 M_r; Citi et al., 1988, 1989) which, on average, assembles about 10 hours later, usually during the 16-cell stage (Fleming et al., 1989, 1993). For both proteins, assembly is at first punctate before gradually becoming zonular. Thus, in double-labelled 2/8 couplets recently compacted, ZO-1 but not cingulin is detectable at the tight junction site (Fig. 1A,B). Our results imply, therefore, that junction formation is progressive, not only in morphological terms but also at the molecular level. Double immunogold analysis of ZO-1 and cingulin localisation at the tight junction in chick and rat epithelia indicate that ZO-1 is positioned closer to the membrane than cingulin (Stevenson et al., 1989). Assuming these proteins occupy similar relative positions in the mouse embryo junction, our results are also consistent with molecular maturation proceeding in the membrane-to-cytoplasm direction (Fleming et al., 1992).

What factors might influence the sequential nature of tight junction protein assembly during cleavage? To investigate this, we have studied the ontogeny of expression of

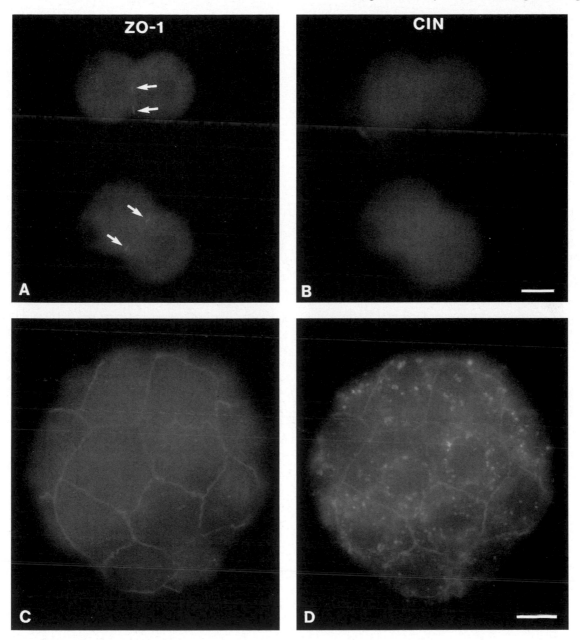

Fig. 1. Double immunofluorescence labelling of whole-mount embryo samples for the tight junction proteins ZO-1 (A,C) and cingulin (B,D). (A,B) Synchronised 2/8 couplets 8 hours post-division from 1/4 cells and 2 hours after blastomere adhesion initiated (compaction). The onset of ZO-1 assembly is detectable (arrows, A) as a weak discontinuous reaction at the periphery (apicolateral region) of the adhesive contact site between blastomeres. At this early stage in tight junction biogenesis, cingulin is not detectable (B). (C,D) Early expanding blastocyst (32- to 64-cell stage) viewed tangentially. Trophectoderm cells are bordered by a continuous (zonular) distribution of ZO-1 (C) and cingulin (D) that appear colocalised. Perinuclear cytoplasmic foci of cingulin, but not ZO-1, are evident, derived from endocytic turnover of cingulin sites in the apical cytocortex. Bar, 20 μm.

junction components at the protein level. Immunoblot analysis indicates detectable expression of ZO-1 from the late 4-cell stage, some 5-6 hours before ZO-1 incorporation into junctions is evident cytochemically (Fleming et al., 1989). The biosynthesis of cingulin is more complex than that of ZO-1 because this protein is expressed from both the maternal and embryonic genomes (Javed et al., 1993). Thus, immunoblot and immunoprecipitation data show synthesis of cingulin, but not ZO-1, during oogenesis. Maternal cingulin has a short metabolic half-life, ceases synthe-

sis during the 2-cell stage when maternal transcripts degrade globally, and localises in the oocyte cortex where it may participate in the oocyte-cumulus cell interaction (Javed et al., 1993; Fleming et al., 1993). Biochemical and embryo manipulation experiments indicate that this maternal pool does not contribute to tight junction formation as trophectoderm differentiates. However, the cortical binding site for maternal cingulin persists during cleavage (on embryo outer surface) long after the maternal expression programme has ceased, and presumably embryonic cingulin replaces maternal cingulin at this binding site. Cortical cingulin is finally degraded by endocytic turnover of the embryo outer surface in late morulae and early blastocysts (Fleming et al., 1993), resulting in cingulin cytoplasmic foci (Fig. 1C,D). Synthesis of cingulin from the embryonic genome is detectable at trace levels during early cleavage (about ten-fold less than in the egg) but a significant increase occurs at compaction, and continues to increase during later cleavage (Javed et al., 1993). The significant enhancement in cingulin synthesis from compaction at the 8-cell stage precedes by approx 5-10 hours the detection of cingulin assembly at the tight junction. This surge in cingulin synthesis is clearly later than the onset of detectable ZO-1 protein expression in the late 4-cell embryo. These differing expression patterns for ZO-1 and embryonic cingulin during cleavage are consistent with, and may control, the sequential membrane assembly pattern at the tight junction. Future work will investigate whether tight junction protein expression is regulated by sequential transcription and/or translation.

What is the relationship between the onset of tight junction formation at compaction and the concurrent differentiation of blastomeres into a proto-epithelial phenotype?

Different experimental situations employing synchronised 2/8 cell couplets cultured during the fourth cell cycle have been used to investigate this question (Fig. 2A; Fleming et al., 1989). If uvomorulin adhesion is inhibited (anti-uvomorulin antibody; calcium removal), ZO-1 membrane assembly is both delayed and distributed randomly (i.e. not at apicolateral contact site), while microvillus polarisation is similarly delayed and oriented randomly, as mentioned earlier (Fig. 2A). Thus, adhesion is necessary both for normal tight junction assembly and for regulating the timing and orientation of cell polarity. If 2/8 couplets are treated with cycloheximide from the time of their division from 1/4 cells, adhesion and microvillus polarisation occur as normal at compaction but ZO-1 membrane assembly is inhibited. Also, if newly formed 1/8 blastomeres are contacted with newly formed 1/4 blastomeres, these heterogeneous couplets will subsequently adhere together with the 1/8 cell polarising apparently normally, but ZO-1 assembly in the 1/8 cell is delayed and randomly distributed (Fig. 2A). These two latter treatments divorce tight junction formation from epithelial polarisation and intercellular adhesion in the embryo (Fleming et al., 1989). Junction formation, but not polarisation or adhesion, requires (i) proximate

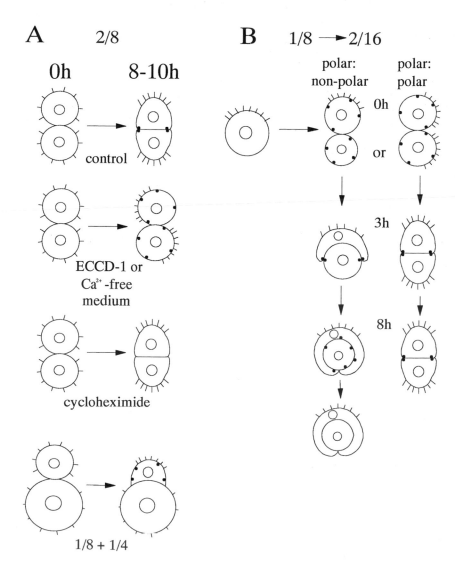

Fig. 2. (A) Schematic representations of ZO-1 distribution (black dots) in 2/8 and heterogeneous couplets in different experimental situations. Control couplets, by 8-10 hours post-division, have adhered together, polarised (here shown by apical microvilli), and assembled ZO-1 at periphery of contact site. Inhibition of uvomorulin function by ECCD-1 uvomorulin antibody or calcium-free medium treatment prevents adhesion and randomises both the orientation of polarity and the membrane distribution of ZO-1. Cycloheximide treatment does not perturb adhesion or polarity but inhibits ZO-1 assembly. 1/8 cells combined with 1/4 cells become adhesive and polarise but ZO-1 membrane assembly is randomly distributed. After Fleming et al. (1989). (B) ZO-1 distribution in 2/16 couplets at different times post-division from 1/8 cell. Differentiative or conservative divisions yield polar:non-polar or polar:polar couplets, depending on whether the apical pole is inherited by one or both cells. Polar:polar couplets assemble ZO-1 at the periphery of their contact site and this pattern is maintained throughout the cell cycle. Polar:non-polar couplets display a similar ZO-1 distribution until the non-polar cell is enveloped, at which time membrane-associated ZO-1 is run down. Equivalent cell interactions regulate maintenance or loss of ZO-1 membrane assembly in trophectoderm and ICM lineages respectively of intact embryos (after Fleming and Hay, 1991).

translation and (ii) adjacent blastomeres to be equally competent to assemble ZO-1 at the correct membrane site. The capacity to inhibit or perturb normal tight junction formation at compaction without apparently affecting epithelial polarisation or cell-cell adhesion argues against the tight junction having a fundamental role in the establishment of a proto-epithelial phenotype in the embryo, data consistent with other systems (e.g. McNeill et al., 1990).

Why does the tight junction develop only in the trophectoderm lineage of the blastocyst? To investigate this question, we have compared cingulin synthesis in trophectoderm and ICM tissues and found that, as blastocyst expansion progresses, the level of cingulin synthesis declines in the ICM and increases in trophectoderm such that the difference between these two tissues reaches fifteen-fold (Javed et al., 1993). Differential translation of tight junction proteins may therefore provide a biosynthetic mechanism to explain tight junction tissue specificity. How might blastomeres perceive their tissue type and modulate their expression pattern accordingly? Trophectoderm and ICM lineages derive from differentiative divisions of certain polarised 8- and 16-cell blastomeres (Johnson and Ziomek, 1981; Pedersen et al., 1986; Fleming, 1987). Daughter cells (at 16- or 32-cell stage) inheriting the apical microvillus domain (plus the cytocortical 'memory' of epithelial polarity, see earlier) remain on the outside of the embryo and continue to differentiate into trophectoderm. Daughter cells not inheriting this domain occupy an internal position in the embryo and differentiate into non-polar ICM cells (Fig. 2B). Polarised 8- and 16-cell blastomeres may also divide conservatively such that both daughters inherit part of the apical domain and continue to differentiate into trophectoderm (Fig. 2B). In newly formed 16- and 32-cell couplets following either differentiative or conservative cleavage, ZO-1 protein is present in both cells and soon associates with the apicolateral region of cell-cell contact between them (Fig. 2B; Fleming and Hay, 1991). Thus, tight junction tissue specificity cannot be explained by differential inheritance of junctional proteins and their membrane binding site (cf. the apical microvillus domain). Following differentiative cleavage, non-polar cells gradually become enveloped by polar cells until all contact-free membrane is lost. Once this has occurred, membrane-associated ZO-1 in non-polar cells is rapidly run down whilst at polar:polar contacts, apicolateral ZO-1 assembly is maintained (Fig. 2B). If contact-free membrane is regained by non-polar cells (e.g. by isolating the ICM), ZO-1 membrane assembly is re-established within a few hours. This assembly process does not require transcription but does require protein synthesis (Fleming and Hay, 1991). These results suggest the following model for tight junction tissue specificity which is currently being tested in our laboratory. Cell position, and hence tissue type, is intepreted by cell-cell contact patterns which regulate tight junction assembly competence. In the absence of membrane assembly (ICM lineage), expression is down-regulated at the protein level but appropriate transcripts are retained. These putative transcripts would allow for rapid formation of a new tight junction network once contact asymmetry is provided. This mechanism, if substantiated, is perhaps required for rapid delamination of primary endoderm by the ICM at the time of implantation, or for replacing damaged trophectoderm cells (Fleming and Hay, 1991).

DESMOSOME FORMATION

Desmosome junctions, characterised by their disc-shaped, membrane-associated plaques and inserted cytokeratin filaments, have been reviewed recently at cellular (Garrod and Collins, 1992) and molecular (Buxton and Magee, 1992; Legan et al., 1992) levels. Desmosomes form relatively late in the process of trophectoderm differentiation, at the 32-cell stage once blastocoel formation has begun (Ducibella et al., 1975; Magnuson et al., 1977; Jackson et al., 1980; Fleming et al., 1991). In contrast to the tight junction, the first desmosomes do not appear to form gradually, but rather display a mature morphology and molecular composition. Thus ultrastructurally, nascent desmosomes, although rather small, contain membrane-associated cytoplasmic plaques with inserted cytokeratin filaments and an intercellular adhesive domain possessing a dense midline (Fleming et al., 1991). These early desmosomes show immunoreactivity for the major desmosomal proteins, desmoplakin (dp1+2) and plakoglobin (dp3), and glycoproteins, desmoglein (dg1) and desmocollins (dg2+3). In time-course assays, all of these components first assemble at basolateral membranes from the 32-cell stage and, with the exception of plakoglobin, only after blastocoel fluid accumulation has initiated. Plakoglobin may assemble slightly earlier in the same cell cycle, before fluid accumulation begins. The close temporal relationship between the assembly of desmosomes and the start of blastocoel formation suggests that desmosomes may have an important role in blastocyst expansion, perhaps to stabilise the trophectoderm layer as the cavity enlarges.

What mechanisms may control the timing of desmosome formation in the embryo? We have monitored the pattern of synthesis of desmosomal constituents and found that plakoglobin and desmoplakin are both synthesised significantly in advance of their time of membrane assembly at the 32-cell stage. However, synthesis of desmoglein and desmocollins is not detectable before the 32-cell stage, suggesting that their synthesis may be regulatory for desmosome formation at cavitation (Fleming et al., 1991). Currently, we are investigating the time at which transcription of desmocollins begins using the reverse transcriptase-PCR technique. Our preliminary data indicate that desmocollin transcripts are first expressed from the embryonic genome in the 16-cell morula (J. Collins and T. Fleming, unpublished), an event that may therefore regulate desmocollins synthesis and the timing of desmosome assembly. Finally, the close link between desmosome formation in trophectoderm and the start of blastocoel accumulation suggests that other non-biosynthetic processes may 'fine-tune' assembly timing. Cavitation, like compaction, is an integrated differentiation event. Tight junction formation is completed, apical and basolateral membrane domains become segregated, Na^+,K^+-ATPase localises on basal membranes and vectorial transport initiates (e.g. DiZio and Tasca, 1977; Kaye et al., 1982; Watson and Kidder, 1988; Watson et al., 1990). Under these circumstances, it is plausible that newly synthesised desmosomal glycoproteins, restricted to baso-lateral membranes by the 'fence' activity of the tight junction, would rapidly accumulate to a threshold level appropriate for desmosome assembly.

CONCLUSIONS

Programmes of expression of junctional constituents in the embryo, in combination with cell-cell interactions, appear to control the timing, characteristics and tissue specificity of assembly of structural intercellular junctions. Biogenesis of the tight junction network is gradual (approximately 24 hours), both in morphological and molecular terms. In contrast, the first desmosomes are constructed, with apparent full molecular complexity, over a relatively short time period. The slower maturation of the tight junction may reflect in part its larger, zonular configuration, requiring a sequential pattern of expression of constituents to achieve efficient assembly. In contrast, the formation of smaller, disc-shaped desmosomes may be controlled by a different mechanism, the later expression of specific constituents (desmosomal glycoproteins) that act as limiting factors for complete assembly. Both of these junction types, however, appear to function for the first time when the embryo accumulates blastocoelic fluid. Their varied patterns of biogenesis may therefore explain why they begin to form at different times during trophectoderm differentiation and perhaps why compaction must occur a day in advance of cavitation.

We are grateful for the financial assistance provided by The Wellcome Trust and the Wessex Medical Trust for research in our laboratory. We are also grateful for essential supplies of antibodies to adhesion and junctional proteins, particularly from Drs B. Stevenson (University of Alberta), S. Citi (Cornell University Medical College), D. Garrod (University of Manchester) and M. Takeichi (Kyoto University).

REFERENCES

Anderson, J. M. and Stevenson, B. R. (1991). The molecular structure of the tight junction. In *Tight Junctions* (ed. M. Cereijido), pp. 77-90. Florida: CRC Press.

Anderson, J. M., Stevenson, B. R., Jesaitis, L. A., Goodenough, D. A. and Mooseker, M. S. (1988). Characterization of ZO-1, a protein component of the tight junction from mouse liver and Madin-Darby canine kidney cells. *J. Cell Biol.* **106**, 1141-1149.

Barron, D. J., Valdimarsson, G., Paul, D. L. and Kidder, G. M. (1989). Connexin32, a gap junction protein, is a persistent oogenetic product through preimplantation development of the mouse. *Dev. Genet.* **10**, 318-323.

Bevilacqua, A., Loch-Caruso, R. and Erickson, R. P. (1989). Abnormal development and dye coupling produced by antisense RNA to gap junction protein in mouse preimplantation embryos. *Proc. Nat. Acad. Sci. USA* **86**, 5444-5448.

Buxton, R. S. and Magee, A. I. (1992). Structure and interactions of desmosomal and other cadherins. *Semin. Cell Biol.* **3**, 157-167.

Citi, S., Sabanay, H., Jakes, R., Geiger, B. and Kendrick-Jones, J. (1988). Cingulin, a new peripheral component of tight junctions. *Nature* **333**, 272-276.

Citi, S., Sabanay, H., Kendrick-Jones, J. and Geiger, B. (1989). Cingulin: characterization and localization. *J. Cell Sci.* **93**, 107-122.

DiZio, S. M. and Tasca, R. J. (1977). Sodium-dependent amino acid transport in preimplantation embryos. III. Na^+,K^+-ATPase linked mechanism in blastocysts. *Dev. Biol.* **59**, 198-205.

Ducibella, T., Albertini, D. F., Anderson, E. and Biggers, J. D. (1975). The preimplantation mammalian embryo: characterization of intercellular junctions and their appearance during development. *Dev. Biol.* **45**, 231-250.

Ducibella, T. and Anderson, E. (1975). Cell shape and membrane changes in the 8-cell mouse embryo: prerequisites for morphogenesis of the blastocyst. *Dev. Biol.* **47**, 45-58.

Fleming, T. P. (1987). A quantitative analysis of cell allocation to trophectoderm and inner cell mass in the mouse blastocyst. *Dev. Biol.* **119**, 520-531.

Fleming, T. P. (1992). Trophectoderm biogenesis in the preimplantation mouse embryo. In *Epithelial Organization and Development* (ed. T. P. Fleming), pp. 111-136. London: Chapman and Hall.

Fleming, T. P., Cannon, P. M. and Pickering, S. J. (1986). The cytoskeleton, endocytosis and cell polarity in the mouse preimplantation embryo. *Dev. Biol.* **113**, 406-419.

Fleming, T. P., Garrod, D. R. and Elsmore, A. J. (1991). Desmosome biogenesis in the mouse preimplantation embryo. *Development* **112**, 527-539.

Fleming, T. P. and Hay, M. J. (1991). Tissue-specific control of expression of the tight junction polypeptide ZO-1 in the mouse early embryo. *Development* **113**, 295-304.

Fleming, T. P., Hay, M. J., Javed, Q. and Citi, S. (1993). Localization of tight junction protein cingulin is temporally and spatially regulated during early mouse development. *Development* **117**, 1135-1144.

Fleming, T. P., Javed, Q. and Hay, M. (1992). Epithelial differentiation and intercellular junction formation in the mouse early embryo. *Development. Suppl.*, 105-113.

Fleming, T. P. and Johnson, M. H. (1988). From egg to epithelium. *Annu. Rev. Cell Biol.* **4**, 459-485.

Fleming, T. P., McConnell, J., Johnson, M. H. and Stevenson, B. R. (1989). Development of tight junctions de novo in the mouse early embryo: control of assembly of the tight junction-specific protein, ZO-1. *J. Cell Biol.* **108**, 1407-1418.

Gardner, R. L. and Beddington, R. S. P. (1988). Multi-lineage 'stem' cells in the mammalian embryo. *J. Cell Sci. Suppl.* **10**, 11-27.

Garrod, D. R. and Collins, J. E. (1992). Intercellular junctions and cell adhesion in epithelial cells. In *Epithelial Organization and Development* (ed. T. P. Fleming), pp. 1-52. London: Chapman and Hall.

Gueth-Hallonet, C. and Maro, B. (1992). Cell polarity and cell diversification during early mouse embryogenesis. *Trends Genet.* **8**, 274-279.

Holmes, P. V. and Lindenberg, S. (1988). Behaviour of mouse and human trophoblast cells during adhesion to and penetration of the endometrial epithelium. In *Eukaryotic Cell Recognition: Concepts and Model Systems* (ed. G. P. Chapman, C. C. Ainsworth and C. J. Chatham), pp. 225-237. Cambridge: Cambridge University Press.

Hyafil, F., Morello, D., Babinet, C. and Jacob, F. (1980). A cell surface glycoprotein involved in the compaction of embryonal carcinoma cells and cleavage stage embryos. *Cell* **21**, 927-934.

Jackson, B. W., Grund, C., Schmid, E., Burki, K. and Franke, W. W. (1980). Formation of cytoskeletal elements during mouse embryogenesis. *Differentiation* **17**, 161-179.

Javed, Q., Fleming, T. P., Hay, M. J. and Citi, S. (1993). Tight junction protein cingulin is expressed by maternal and embryonic genomes during early mouse development. *Development* **117**, 1145-1151.

Johnson, M. H., Chisholm, J. C., Fleming, T. P. and Houliston, E. (1986a). A role for cytoplasmic determinants in the development of the mouse early embryo? *J. Embryol. Exp. Morph. 97 Suppl.*, 97-121.

Johnson, M. H. and Maro, B. (1985). A dissection of the mechanisms generating and stabilising polarity in mouse 8- and 16-cell blastomeres: the role of cytoskeletal elements. *J. Embryol. Exp. Morph.* **90**, 311-334.

Johnson, M. H. and Maro, B. (1986). Time and space in the mouse early embryo: a cell biological approach to cell diversification. In *Experimental Approaches to Mammalian Embryonic Development* (ed. J. Rossant and R. A. Pedersen), pp. 35-66. New York: Cambridge University Press.

Johnson, M. H., Maro, B. and Takeichi, M. (1986b). The role of cell adhesion in the synchronisation and orientation of polarisation in 8-cell mouse blastomeres. *J. Embryol. Exp. Morph.* **93**, 239-255.

Johnson, M. H., Pickering, S. J., Dhiman, A., Radcliffe, G. S. and Maro, B. (1988). Cytocortical organisation during natural and prolonged mitosis in mouse 8-cell blastomeres. *Development* **102**, 143-158.

Johnson, M. H. and Ziomek, C. A. (1981). The foundation of two distinct cell lineages within the mouse morula. *Cell* **24**, 71-80.

Kaye, P. L., Schultz, G. A., Johnson, M. H., Pratt, H. P. and Church, R. B. (1982). Amino acid transport and exchange in preimplantation mouse embryos. *J. Reprod. Fertil.* **65**, 367-380.

Kidder, G. M. and McLachlin, J. R. (1985). Timing of transcription and protein synthesis underlying morphogenesis in preimplantation mouse embryos. *Dev. Biol.* **112**, 265-275.

Legan, P. K., Collins, J. E. and Garrod, D. R. (1992). The molecular biology of desmosomes and hemidesmosomes: 'what's in a name?' *BioEssays* **14**, 385-393.

Levy, J. B., Johnson, M. H., Goodall, H. and Maro, B. (1986). Control of the timing of compaction: a major developmental transition in mouse early development. *J. Embryol. Exp. Morph.* **95**, 213-237.

Lindenberg, S., Kimber, S. and Hamberger, L. (1990). Embryo-endometrium interaction. In *From Ovulation to Implantation* (ed. J. H. L. Evers and M. H. Heineman), pp. 285-295. Elsevier Science Publishers B.V. (Biomedical Division).

Magnuson, T., Demsey, A. and Stackpole, C. W. (1977). Characterization of intercellular junctions in the preimplantation mouse embryo by freeze-fracture and thin-section electron microscopy. *Dev. Biol.* **61**, 252-261.

Manejwala, F. M., Cragoe, E. J. and Schultz, R. M. (1989). Blastocoel expansion in the preimplantation mouse embryo: role of extracellular sodium and chloride and possible apical routes of their entry. *Dev. Biol.* **133**, 210-220.

McNeill, H., Ozawa, M., Kemler, R. and Nelson, W. J. (1990). Novel function of the cell adhesion molecule uvomorulin as an inducer of cell surface polarity. *Cell* **62**, 309-316.

Nishi, M., Kumar, N. M. and Gilula, N. B. (1991). Developmental regulation of gap junction gene expression during mouse embryonic development. *Dev. Biol.* **146**, 117-130.

Pedersen, R. A., Wu, K. and Balakier, H. (1986). Origin of the inner cell mass in mouse embryos: cell lineage analysis by microinjection. *Dev. Biol.* **117**, 581-595.

Perona, R. M. and Wassarman, P. M. (1986). Mouse blastocysts hatch *in vitro* by using a trypsin-like proteinase associated with cells of mural trophectoderm. *Dev. Biol.* **114**, 42-52.

Peyrieras, N., Hyafil, F., Louvard, D., Ploegh, H. L. and Jacob, F. (1983). Uvomorulin: a non-integral membrane protein of early mouse embryo. *Proc. Nat. Acad. Sci. USA* **80**, 6274-6277.

Pratt, H. P. M. (1985). Membrane organization in the preimplantation mouse embryo. *J. Embryol. Exp. Morph.* **90**, 101-121.

Pratt, H. P. M. (1989). Marking time and making space: chronology and topography in the early mouse embryo. *Int. Rev. Cytol.* **117**, 99-130.

Reima, I. (1990). Maintenance of compaction and adherent-type junctions in mouse morula-stage embryos. *Cell Differen. Devel.* **29**, 143-153.

Sawada, H., Hoshi, M., Someno, T., Suzuki, R. and Yamazaki, K. (1992). Inhibition of mouse blastocyst hatching by subsite-specific trypsin inhibitors, peptidyl argininals. *Dev. Growth Differ.* **34**, 357-362.

Sefton, M., Johnson, M. H. and Clayton, L. (1992). Synthesis and phosphorylation of uvomorulin during mouse early development. *Development* **115**, 313-318.

Smith, R. K. W. and Johnson, M. H. (1985). DNA replication and compaction in the cleaving embryo of the mouse. *J. Embryol. Exp. Morph.* **89**, 133-148.

Stevenson, B. R., Heintzelman, M. B., Anderson, J. M., Citi, S. and Mooseker, M. S. (1989). ZO-1 and cingulin: tight junction proteins with distinct identities and localizations. *Amer. J. Physiol.* **257**, C621-C628.

Stevenson, B. R., Siliciano, J. D., Mooseker, M. S. and Goodenough, D. A. (1986). Identification of ZO-1: a high molecular weight polypeptide associated with the tight junction (zonula occludens) in a variety of epithelia. *J. Cell Biol.* **103**, 755-766.

Vestweber, D., Gossler, A., Boller, K. and Kemler, R. (1987). Expression and distribution of cell adhesion molecule uvomorulin in mouse preimplantation embryos. *Dev. Biol.* **124**, 451-456.

Watson, A. J., Damsky, C. H. and Kidder, G. M. (1990). Differentiation of an epithelium: factors affecting the polarized distribution of Na$^+$,K$^+$-ATPase in mouse trophectoderm. *Dev. Biol.* **141**, 104-114.

Watson, A. J. and Kidder, C. M. (1988). Immunofluorescence assessment of the timing of appearance and cellular distribution of Na/K-ATPase during mouse embryogenesis. *Dev. Biol.* **126**, 80-90.

Wiley, L. M. (1987). Trophectoderm: the first epithelium to develop in the mammalian embryo. *Scanning Microsc.* **2**, 417-426.

Wiley, L. M., Kidder, G. M. and Watson, A. J. (1990). Cell polarity and development of the first epithelium. *BioEssays* **12**, 67-73.

Wiley, L. M. and Obasaju, M. F. (1988). Induction of cytoplasmic polarity in heterokaryons of mouse 4-cell-stage blastomeres fused with 8-cell- and 16-cell-stage blastomeres. *Dev. Biol.* **130**, 276-284.

Winkel, G. K., Ferguson, J. E., Takeichi, M. and Nuccitelli, R. (1990). Activation of protein kinase C triggers premature compaction in the four-cell stage mouse embryo. *Dev. Biol.* **138**, 1-15.

Journal of Cell Science, Supplement 17, 127-132 (1993)
Printed in Great Britain © The Company of Biologists Limited 1993

The making of a tight junction

M. Cereijido, L. González-Mariscal, R. G. Contreras, J. M. Gallardo, R. García-Villegas and J. Valdés

Center for Research and Advanced Studies, Apartado Postal 14-740, México, DF, 07000 México

SUMMARY

MDCK (epithelial cells from the dog kidney) plated at confluence, establish tight junctions in 12-15 hours through a process that requires protein synthesis, formation of a ring of actin filaments in close contact with the lateral membrane of the cells, calmodulin, and a Ca^{2+}-dependent exocytic fusion of tight junction (TJ)-associated components. Monolayers incubated in the absence Ca^{2+} make no TJs. Yet, if Ca^{2+} is added under these circumstances, TJs are made with a faster kinetics. Ca^{2+} is needed mainly at a site located on the outer side of the cell membrane, where it activates uvomorulin and triggers the participation of the cellular components mentioned above, via G-proteins associated with phospholipase C and protein kinase C. In principle, the sites of all these molecules and mechanisms involved in junction formation may be where a variety of agents (hormones, drugs, metabolites) act to produce epithelia with a transepithelial electrical resistance (TER) ranging from 10 to 10,000 $\Omega.cm^2$. This range may be also due to a variety of substances found in serum and in urine, that increase the TER in a reversible and dose-dependent manner.

Key words: tight junctions, epithelial cells, Ca^{2+}, G-proteins, uvomorulin, phospholipase C, protein kinase C, calmodulin, urine extracts

INTRODUCTION

For a long while, roughly from the second half of the nineteenth century to the middle of the present one, the observation that epithelia mounted between two chambers with identical saline solutions maintain a spontaneous electrical potential appeared to be in violation of the laws of physics (Cereijido et al., 1989; Cereijido, 1992). However, in 1958 Koefoed-Johnson and Ussing put forward a model for the frog skin that accounted for such asymmetry, and gave rise to a successful period during which physiologists explained the movement of substances across epithelia, ranging from the sheep rumen to the human intestine, and from the cecropia midgut to the choroid plexus. The crucial features of these explanations were (a) tight junctions (TJs) that seal the interspace between epithelial cells, and (b) apical/basolateral polarity that gives rise to vectorial fluxes. By 1970, in spite of such accomplishments, the mechanisms that synthesize, assemble and seal TJs and generate apical/basolateral polarity were still unknown.

A suitable preparation was needed to learn about asymmetry, polarization and the formation of TJs. Oxender and Christensen (1959) devised a system consisting of Ehrlich ascites cells sandwiched between two Millipore filters, and mounted between two chambers, one with pyridoxal phosphate and the other with an excess of K^+ or alanine (Fig. 1). Although the cells were able to transport a net amount of amino acids from the first to the second chamber, the cells lacked an intrinsic asymmetry and junctional complexes, and remained randomly oriented within the multicellular layer.

We attempted another approach. We disassembled the epithelium of the frog skin with proteases and EGTA, made a suspension in which the cells had no junctions or polarity (Zylber et al., 1973, 1975; Rotunno et al., 1973) and replated them at confluence on Millipore filters, hoping that they would repolarize and restore TJs. Although the cells were able to keep their Na^+, K^+, Cl^- or water balance for several hours, they where hard to culture, and did not polarize or establish TJs (Fig. 1).

Although epithelial cell lines are able to grow in vitro, nobody suspected that they could polarize and make TJs, until Leighton and his group (1969, 1970) attributed the blistering activity of monolayers of MDCK cells to transport and accumulation of fluid under the monolayer. Therefore, following this observation the next step was to culture MDCK cells on permeable supports (Misfeld et al., 1976; Cereijido et al., 1978a,b; Rabito et al., 1978). When mounted as a flat sheet between two chambers, these monolayers behave in several respects like natural epithelia. The procedure was soon adapted to form monolayers with cells derived from different epithelia (e.g. see Rabito and Ausiello, 1980; Handler et al., 1984) and endothelia (Shivers et al., 1985).

TJ FORMATION IN THE MONOLAYER OF MDCK CELLS

We use mainly two protocols (Fig. 2). The first one consists of plating the cells at confluence on a permeable support, allowing 20-60 minutes for attachment, and transfer-

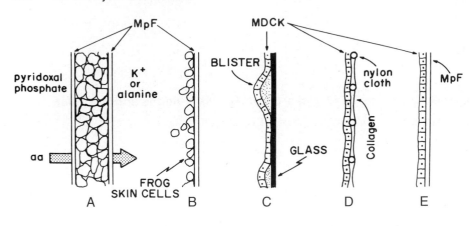

Fig. 1. History of the efforts to develop an asymmetric 'epithelium'.
(A) Ehrlich ascites cells contained between two filters (MpF), and mounted between two asymmetric solutions, one containing pyridoxal phosphate and the other a high concentration of K+ or alanine. Although the preparation did show a net flux of amino acids (aa), cells were not able to develop TJs or asymmetry.
(B) Cells dissociated from frog skin and plated on filter paper were able to maintain their own water and salt balance for a few hours, but they attached too weakly and failed to
develop TJs and polarity. (C) MDCK cells attach, grow for several days, form TJs and polarize on non-permeable supports (glass, plastic). The accumulation of fluid under the monolayer develops blisters. On permeable supports like a nylon cloth coated with collagen (D) or a Millipore filter (E) they form a monolayer that behaves in many respects like a natural epithelium.

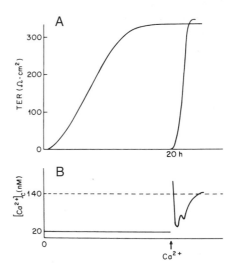

Fig. 2. (A) Development of transepithelial electrical resistance (TER) across monolayers of MDCK cells. The slow curve corresponds to cells plated and cultured in NC medium (1.8 mM Ca^{2+}), and the fast one to cells plated in 1.8 mM Ca^{2+} but transferred 20-40 minutes later to LC medium (1-5 µM), cultured in this medium until the 20th hour, and then switched to NC.
(B) Intracellular concentration of Ca^{2+} as measured with the probe indo-1/AM in cells incubated in CDMEM and in LC medium. After transfer to NC the intracellular concentration of Ca^{2+} shows an initial 'spike', and the concentration rises thereafter with some oscillations towards steady values.

ring this support with the monolayer to fresh medium. Cells form a continuous monolayer, polarize and establish TJs, a process that can be gauged through the development of a TER (transepithelial electrical resistance), and reaches a maximum in 12-15 hours (Fig. 2). The second protocol ('Ca-switch') consists of allowing 20-60 minutes for cell attachment in Ca^{2+}-containing medium (CDMEM or NC, 1.8 mM), and then transferring the monolayers to low-calcium medium (LC, 1-5 µM). Twenty hours later, while monolayers incubated in normal calcium exhibit 200-300 $\Omega.cm^2$, those left in LC have a negligible TER. If at this time these monolayers are transferred to NC, they develop

a TER with a much faster kinetics (Fig. 2) (González-Mariscal et al., 1985). For reviews of the properties of these monolayers see Cereijido (1992) and Schneeberger and Lynch (1992).

Using these approaches, it was found that, in order to make TJs, newly plated cells do not require synthesis of RNA, but do require synthesis of proteins, as the use of cycloheximide or puromycin during the first 4-5 hours after plating blocks the development of TER (Cereijido et al., 1978b, 1981). This synthesis may proceed in the absence of cell-cell contacts and of Ca^{2+} in the bathing media. Accordingly, the development of TER during the Ca-switch is not inhibited by cycloheximide (González-Mariscal et al., 1985).

Although several peptides (ZO-1, ZO-2, cingulin, etc.) were found in close and specific association with the TJs (see Anderson and Stevenson, 1992), no information is available on whether the strands of the TJ that appear as ridges in the P face of freeze-fracture replicas, are themselves made up of proteins. In fact, a model in which these strands consist of inverted cylindrical micelles made of lipids was put forward by Pinto da Silva and Kachar (1982). However, models comprising pure lipidic micelles do not seem to meet some expectations regarding the diffusion of lipid probes along the surface of the membrane (van Meer et al., 1986).

Observations performed with transmission electron microscopy indicate that junctional components are addressed polarizedly to the apical/basolateral limit (Vega-Salas et al., 1988). This possibility is in keeping with the observations made with freeze-fracture replicas, revealing that upon switching to Ca^{2+}, strands start to develop through the formation of isolated segments that occupy from the beginning the place that they will fill in the mature TJ (González-Mariscal et al., 1985).

The observation that cytochalasin B, but not colchicine, prevents junction formation and opens already sealed TJs in a few hours, is taken to indicate that microfilaments but not microtubules are involved in junction formation. In fact, while microfilaments form a continuous ring under the lateral plasma membrane, in close contact with the zonula adherens, microtubules are distributed mainly in the vicin-

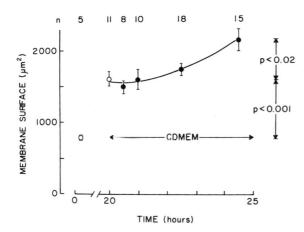

Fig. 3. Membrane area of MDCK cells as measured by the membrane capacitance method during the Ca-switch procedure. Newly plated cells have a small area (first point on the left); 20 hours later the area increases in spite of the low extracellular (1-5 μM) and intracellular (~20 nM) concentration of Ca^{2+}. After the Ca-switch cells increase their surface by 22%, coincident with the process of junction formation. Prevention of this increase with 25 μM chloroquine blocks the development of TJs. (Taken, with kind permission, from González-Mariscal et al. (1990).)

Table 1. Effect of different cations on tight junction formation during a Ca^{2+}-switch

Cations	Concentration (mM)	TER ($\Omega \cdot cm^2$)	n
LC medium			
None		2±10	18
Ca*	1.8	676±48	24
Mg	2.0	6±4	7
Ba*	1.0	3±1	6
Sr*	2.0	37±13	7
Mn*	1.0	3±0	6
Cd*	1.0	1±6	6
La*	1.0	3±1	6
NC buffer			
Ca+Mg		694±131	13
Ca+Ba		603±112	13
Ca+Sr		623±121	13
Ca+La		425±30	6
Ca+Mn		186±57	13
Ca+Cd		2±1	13

Values are means ± s.e.; *n*, no. of observations. Cells were plated on nitrocellulose filters in NC medium for 1 hour and then washed 3 times with phosphate-buffered saline without Ca^{2+} and transferred to low Ca^{2+} (LC) medium. After 20 hours medium was changed to either LC medium or NC buffer containing the indicated multivalent cations. NC buffer composition was (in mM): 140 NaCl, 5 KCl, 10 dextrose, 1.8 $CaCl_2$, and 20 Tris-HCl, pH 7.4, at room temperature. (Taken, with kind permission, from Contreras et al., 1992.)
*Mg was present at 1.0 mM.

ity of the nucleus (Meza et al., 1980, 1982). The possibility exists that actin filaments form a scaffold that helps the cells to adapt their borders to each other so TJs can be established and sealed, and lead the peptide-containing vesicles to the points where junctions are to be assembled, etc. In the absence of Ca^{2+}, vesicles containing TJ-associated peptides are retained in the cytoplasm. Upon switching the monolayers to Ca^{2+} these vesicles fuse to the plasma membrane, along with two other populations of vesicles that are vectorialy addressed and fused to the apical (Vega-Salas et al., 1988) or to the basolateral domain (Contreras et al., 1989a,b), a process that increases the surface area by some 22% (Fig. 3), as measured by the 'whole cell clamp' method (González-Mariscal et al., 1990).

THE ROLE OF CALCIUM

Ca^{2+}, besides of triggering the assembly and sealing of the TJ (Fig. 2), is also needed for maintaining the sealed state, as junctions may be opened and resealed by removal and restoration of this ion (Sedar and Forte, 1964; Meldolesi et al., 1978; Cereijido et al., 1978a; Martínez-Palomo et al., 1980; Gumbiner and Simons, 1986).

We investigated the ability of Ca^{2+} to trigger junction formation in the presence of ions and drugs like La^{3+} and verapamil that inhibit its penetration into the cytoplasm, as indicated by the measurement of ^{45}Ca influx and the use of intracellular Ca^{2+} probes (González-Mariscal et al., 1990; Contreras et al., 1992a,b). As shown in Table 1, only Ca^{2+} among the ions tested is able to promote the development of TER. This was taken as an indication that Ca^{2+} acts on an extracellular site. La^{3+} for instance, is able to block Ca^{2+} penetration but does not substitute for this ion in triggering junction formation. Interestingly, Cd^{2+} is able to block

Ca^{2+} penetration and sealing, but fails to trigger junction formation by itself. These results were interpreted in terms of two sites with different affinities: one used by Ca^{2+} to penetrate into the cytoplasm, where other multivalent ions may compete; and a second one, where this ion triggers junction formation, that has a much higher Ca^{2+} affinity.

In keeping with this interpretation, we found that using 0.1 mM Ca^{2+} to trigger the Ca-switch, elicits junction formation without a detectable increase in intracellular Ca^{2+} (González-Mariscal et al., 1990).

These studies were done with indo-1/AM, measuring the overall Ca^{2+} concentration in the cytoplasm. Niggam et al. (1992) used instead a digital imaging procedure, and found some indications that this ion may accumulate in a sub-membranal intracellular compartment, small enough as to escape detection by the methods that we have used.

THE NEED OF A TRANSDUCTING MECHANISM

As shown by Gumbiner and Simons (1987), junction formation requires cell-cell attachment provided by Ca^{2+}-dependent uvomorulin molecules, located in the lateral membrane of MDCK cells. Therefore, uvomorulin may constitute one of the extracellular sites where Ca^{2+} acts to promote the making of TJs. However, as mentioned above, Ca^{2+} touches off a series of intracellular events that result in the assembly and sealing of TJs, suggesting the existence of a mechanism that would convey the information from the extracellular site(s) to those involved in the rearrangement of actin filaments, exocytic fusion, assembly of the strands, etc.

Looking for this transducting mechanisms, we found that

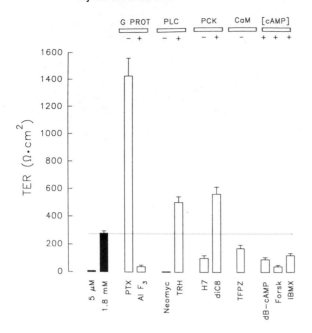

Fig. 4. Filled columns: values of TER during a control Ca-switch from 5 μM to 1.8 mM in 5 hours. The rest of the columns correspond to similar Ca-switches made in the presence of 14 ng ml^{-1} PTX, which inhibits, and 2 mM AlF$_3$, which activates the action of inhibitory G proteins; 110 μM neomycin, which inhibits, and 2 μM TRH, which stimulates PLC; 50 μM H7, which inhibits, and 100 μg ml^{-1} diC8, which stimulates PKC; 25 μM TFPZ, which inhibits calmodulin; 2.5 mM dB-cAMP (a permeable analog of cAMP), 120 μM forskolin (a stimulator of adenylate cyclase) and 120 μM IBMX (a phosphodiesterase inhibitor). See text for abbreviations.

blockers and enhancers of an inhibitory G protein, respectively (Fig. 4). This is further suggested by the fact that GTP$_\gamma$S blocks the development of a cell border pattern of ZO-1 peptides, as observed by immunofluorescence in MDCK cells permeabilized with digitonin. At least two different G proteins may participate in the formation of TJs: (1) an inhibitory G protein modulating phospholipase C (PLC) and protein kinase C (PKC) probably participate in these processes, because activation of PLC by thyrotropin-1-releasing hormone (TRH) increases TER, and its inhibition by neomycin blocks the development of this resistance. Also, 1,2-dioctanoylglycerol (diC8), an activator of PKC,

junction formation may be stimulated by pertussis toxin (PTX) and prevented by AlF$_3$ and carbamil choline, i.e. by

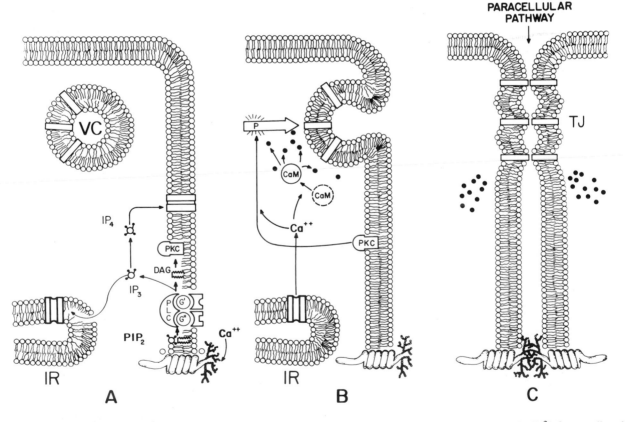

Fig. 5. A highly schematic view of the process of junction formation during the Ca-switch. (A) Cells incubated in Ca^{2+}-free medium have a cytoplasmic vesicular compartment (VC) where junctional components might be stored. Extracellular Ca^{2+} activates a uvomorulin-like molecule and permits attachment to neighboring cells. Cell-cell contact would stimulate PLC that is connected to membrane receptors via two G proteins and convert phosphatidylinositol (PIP$_2$) into inositol trisphosphate (IP$_3$) and diacylglycerol (DAG). IP$_3$ mobilizes Ca^{2+} from an internal reservoir (IR), D-*myo*-inositol 4-monophosphate (IP$_4$) decreases Ca^{2+} permeability, and DAG activates protein kinase C (PKC). (B) This cascade of reactions provokes phosphorylation (P) and incorporation of junctional components through exocytic fusion of the VC and activation of calmodulin (CaM). (C) Activation of CaM causes actin filaments to form into a continuous ring that circles the cells (represented by two groups of filled circles); the paracellular space is sealed, and TER develops.

stimulates TER development, while polymyxin B and 1-(5-isoquinoline sulfonyl)-2-methyl-piperazine dihydrochloride (H7), which inhibits this enzyme, abolish TER (Balda et al., 1991). In turn, freeze-fracture electron microscopy reveals that diC8 triggers the formation of junctional strands. (2) Another G protein that may also participate in junctional events, is the one modulating the reactions involving adenylate cyclase. This stems from the fact that $N^6,O^{2'}$-dibutyryladenosine 3′-5′-cyclic monophosphate (dB-cAMP) a permeable analogue of cAMP, forskolin that stimulates adenylate cyclase, and 3-isobutyl-1-methylxanthine (IBMX), which inhibits phosphodiesterase, produce significant decreases in TER (Fig. 4).

Junction formation may be prevented by the use of trifluoperazine (TFPZ) and calmidazoline, two inhibitors of calmodulin (CaM) (Balda et al., 1991). This is a puzzling observation because, whereas activation of PLC and PKC may be elicited from an extracellular site through G proteins, calmodulin is an intracellular molecule that requires Ca^{2+}, i.e. the mere information that this ion is present on the extracellular side does not suffice. This opens up at least two possibilities: (1) the signal transduced through the G proteins would cause the release of Ca^{2+} from an internal reservoir, presumably by the IP_3 split from PIP_2; or (2), as suggested by the observations of Niggam et al. (1992), there may be a small and localized increase in Ca^{2+} concentration that would escape detection by most methods. Fig. 5 offers a very schematic summary of these results.

TER VARIES IN DIFFERENT EPITHELIA BY OVER THREE ORDERS OF MAGNITUDE

As the nephron progresses from the proximal to the collecting duct, the value of TER across the epithelia forming its walls increases by two orders of magnitude, a feature paralleled by an increase in the number of strands in the tight junctions (Claude and Goodenough, 1973). We investigated whether the increase in TER may be attributed to a substance that, traveling with the filtrate through the lumen, would be finally eliminated in the urine. Accordingly, we prepared a dialyzed and lyophilized extract of urine (DLU) of normal dogs that, when applied to the basolateral (Fig. 6, 2nd column) or to the apical side (Fig. 6, 3rd column) of the MDCK monolayer, enhances TER (Gallardo et al., 1993). This effect is dose-dependent (not shown). When applied simultaneously to both sides of the monolayer the effect is significatively smaller (Fig. 6, 6th column), suggesting that DLU also has a TER-depressing component that acts mainly from the apical side. Only this second component is inactivated by heat, so that when DLU is boiled for 10 minutes before addition to both sides, the TER-enhancing effect prevails and reaches the level achieved with basolateral applications only (Fig. 6, 6th column). The effects of DLU can be completely abolished by incubation with protease type I (Fig. 6, 4th column). Since in its transit from glomerulus to collecting duct the filtrate is concentrated 100- to 200-fold, it is suggested that the TER-enhancing component plays a major role in the making of distal segments with tighter paracellular pathways.

In summary, the study of the TJ over more than a cen-

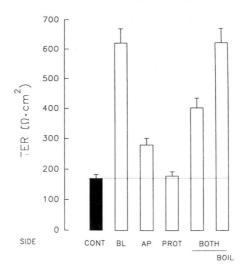

Fig. 6. Effects of a dialyzed and lyophilized extract of dog urine (DLU) on the value of TER in monolayers of MDCK cells. The effect is concentration dependent, but here is only shown at 30% DLU/70% DMEM. Filled column corresponds to control; (2nd) DLU added for 20 hours to the basolateral side; (3rd) to the apical; (4th) to the basolateral side after treatment with protease type I; (5th) to both sides; and (6th) to both sides after boiling the DLU solution for 10 minutes.

tury has shown that this structure is by no means a mere 'terminal bar', a 'tight seal', or a static structure. It may confer a TER of only 10 Ω.cm² , as in the case of the proximal tubule of the kidney, or several thousands, as in the case of the mucosa of the urinary bladder, and can modify the permeability of an epithelium in response to physiological requirements and pharmacological challenges. It is expected that many of the factors involved in the formation of a TJ (Fig. 5) will one day explain the wide range of TERs as well as the TJ's dynamic behaviour.

We thank the National Research Council of México (CONACYT) and the Mexican Health Foundation for their economic support.

REFERENCES

Anderson, J. M. and Stevenson, B. R. (1992). The molecular structure of the tight junction. In *Tight Junctions* (ed. M. Cereijido), pp. 77-90. CRC Press, Boca Raton, Florida.

Balda, M. S., González-Mariscal, L., Contreras, R. G., Macias-Silva, M. Torres-Marquez, M. E., García-Sains, J. A. and Cereijido, M. (1991). Participation of a G protein modulation system in the assembly and sealing of tight junctions. *J. Membr. Biol.* **122**, 193-202.

Cereijido, M. (1992). *Tight Junctions.* CRC Press, Boca Raton, Florida.

Cereijido, M. and Martínez-Palomo, A. (1981). Occluding junctions in cultured epithelial monolayers. *Amer. J. Physiol.* **240**, C96-C102.

Cereijido, M., Ponce, A. and González-Mariscal, L. (1989). Tight junctions and apical/basolateral polarity. *J. Membr. Biol.* **110**, 1-9.

Cereijido, M., Robbins, E. S., Dolan, W. J., Rotunno, C. A. and Sabatini, D. D. (1978a). Polarized monolayers formed by epithelial cells on a permeable and translucent support. *J. Cell Biol.* **77**, 853-880.

Cereijido, M., Rotunno, C. A., Robbins, E. S. and Sabatini, D. D. (1978b). Polarized epithelial membranes produced in vitro. In *Membrane Transport Processes* (ed. J. F. Hoffman), pp. 433-461. Raven Press, New York.

Claude, P. and Goodenough, D. A. (1973). Fracture faces of zonulae occludentes from 'tight' and 'leaky' epithelia. *J. Cell Biol.* **58**, 390-400.

Contreras, R. G., Avila, G., Gutiérrez, C., Bolivar, J. J., González-Mariscal, L., Darzon, A., Beaty, G., Rodríguez-Boulán, E. and Cereijido, M. (1989a). Repolarization of Na-K-Pumps during establishment of epithelial monolayers. *Amer. J. Physiol.* **257**, C896-C905.

Contreras, R. G., González-Mariscal, L., Balda, M. S., García-Villegas, M. R. and Cereijido, M. (1992b). The role of calcium in the making of a transporting epithelium. *News Physiol. Sci.* **7**, 105-108.

Contreras, R. G., Miller, J., Zamora, M., González-Mariscal, L. and Cereijido, M. (1992). The interaction of calcium with the plasma membrane of epithelial (MDCK) cells during junction formation. *Amer. J. Physiol.* **263**, C313-C318.

Gallardo, J. M., Hernández, J. M., García-Villegas, M. R., Contreras, R. G., González-Mariscal, L. and Cereijido, M. (1993). A urine extract that enhances the electrical resistance across monolayers of epithelial cells (MDCK). *Amer. J. Physiol.*

González-Mariscal, L., Chávez de Ramírez, B. and Cereijido, M. (1985). Tight junction formation in cultured epithelial cells (MDCK). *J. Membr. Biol.* **86**, 113-125.

González-Mariscal, L., Contreras, R. G., Bolívar, J. J., Ponce, A., Chávez de Ramírez, B. and Cereijido, M. (1990). The role of calcium in tight junction formation between epithelial cells. *Amer. J. Physiol.* **259**, C978-C986.

Gumbiner, B. and Simons, K. (1986). A functional assay for proteins involved in establishing an epithelial occluding barrier: Identification of an uvomorulin-like peptide. *J. Cell Biol.* **102**, 457-468.

Gumbiner, B. and Simons, K. (1987). The role of uvomorulin in the formation of epithelial occluding junctions. In *Junctional Complexes of Epithelial Cells* (ed. G. Bock and S. Clark), pp. 168-186. J. Wiley, Chichester.

Handler, J. S., Preston, A. S. and Steele, R. E. (1984). Factors affecting the differentiation of epithelial transport and responsiveness to hormones. *Fed. Proc. Fed. Amer. Socs Exp. Biol.* **43**, 2221-2224.

Koefoed-Johnson, V. and Ussing, H. H. (1958). The nature of the frog skin potential. *Acta Physiol. Scand.* **42**, 298-308.

Leighton, J. L., Brada, Z., Estes, L. W. and Justh, G. (1969). Secretory activity and oncogenicity of a cell line (MDCK) derived from canine kidney. *Science* **163**, 472-473.

Leighton, J. L., Estes, L. W., Mansukhani, S. and Brada, Z. (1970). A cell line derived from a normal dog kidney (MDCK) exhibiting qualities of papillary adenocarcinoma and renal tubular epithelium. *Cancer* **26**, 1022-1028.

Martínez-Palomo, A., Meza, I., Beaty, G. and Cereijido, M. (1980). Experimental modulation of occluding junctions in a cultured transporting epithelium. *J. Cell Biol.* **87**, 736-745.

Meldolesi, J., Castiglioni, G., Parma, R., Nassivera, N. and De-Camilli, P. (1978). Ca++-dependent disassembly and reassembly of occluding junctions in guinea pig pancreatic acinar cells. *J. Cell Biol.* **79**, 156-172.

Meza, I., Ibarra, G., Sabanero, M., Martínez-Palomo, A. and Cereijido, M. (1980). Occluding junctions and cytoskeletal components in a cultured transporting epithelium. *J. Cell Biol.* **87**, 746-754.

Meza, I., Sabanero, M., Stefani, E. and Cereijido, M. (1982). Occluding junctions in MDCK cells: Modulation of transepithelial permeability by the cytoskeleton. *J. Cell. Biochem.* **18**, 407-421.

Misfeld, D. S., Hamamoto, S. T. and Pitelka, D. R. (1976). Transepithelial transport in cell culture. *Proc. Nat. Acad. Sci. USA* **73**, 1212-1216.

Niggam, S. K., Rodríguez-Boulán, E. and Silver, R. B. (1992). Changes in intracellular calcium during the development of epithelial polarity and junctions. *Proc. Nat. Acad. Sci. USA* **89**, 6162-6166.

Oxender, D. L. and Christensen, H. N. (1959). Transcellular concentration as a consequence of intracellular accumulation. *J. Biol. Chem.* **234**, 2321-2324.

Pinto da Silva, P. and Kachar, B. (1982). On tight junction structure. *Cell* **28**, 441-450.

Rabito, C. A. and Ausiello, D. A. (1980). Na-dependent sugar transport in a cultured epithelial cell line from pig kidney. *Amer. J. Physiol.* **250**, F734-F743.

Rabito, C. A., Tchao, R. Valentich, J. and Leighton, J. (1978). Distribution and characteristics of the occluding junctions in a monolayer of a cell line (MDCK) derived from a canine kidney. *J. Membr. Biol.* **43**, 351-365.

Rotunno, C. A., Zylber, E. and Cereijido, M. (1973). Ion and water balance in the epithelium of the abdominal skin of the frog Leptodactylus ocellatus. *J. Membr. Biol.* **13**, 217-232.

Schneeberger, E. and Lynch, R. D. (1992). Structure, function, and regulation of cellular tight junctions. *Amer. J. Physiol.* **262**, L647-L661.

Sedar, A. W. and Forte, J. G. (1964). Effects of calcium depletion on the junctional complex between oxyntic cells of gastric glands. *J. Cell Biol.* **22**, 173-188.

Shivers, R., Bowman, P. and Martin, K. (1985). A model for the novo synthesis and assembly of tight intercellular junctions. Ultraestructural correlates and experimental verification of the model revealed by freeze-fracture. *Tissue & Cell* **17**, 417-440.

van Meer, G., Gumbiner, B. and Simons, K. (1986). The tight junction does not allow lipid molecules to diffuse from one epithelial cell to the next. *Nature* **322**, 639-641.

Vega-Salas, D. E., Salas, P. J. I. and Rodríguez-Boulán, E. (1988). Exocytosis of a vacuolar apical comparment (VAC): a cell-cell contact controlled mechanism for the establishment of the apical plasma membrane domain in epithelial cells. *J. Cell Biol.* **107**, 1717-1728.

Zylber, E., Rotunno, C. A. and Cereijido, M. (1973). Ion and water balance in the isolated epithelial cells of abdominal skin of the frog Leptodatylus ocellatus. *J. Membr. Biol.* **13**, 199-216.

Zylber, E., Rotunno, C. A. and Cereijido, M. (1975). Ionic fluxes in isolated epithelial cells of the abdominal skin of the frog *Leptodatylus ocellatus*. *J. Membr. Biol.* **22**, 265-284.

Journal of Cell Science, Supplement 17, 133-138 (1993)
Printed in Great Britain © The Company of Biologists Limited 1993

Gap junctions and tissue business: problems and strategies for developing specific functional reagents

Daniel A. Goodenough and Linda S. Musil

Department of Anatomy and Cellular Biology, Harvard Medical School, 220 Longwood Avenue, Boston, MA 02115, USA

SUMMARY

The complex and overlapping tissue distribution of different members of the gap junctional connexin protein family is reviewed. Intermixing of different connexins in the building of intercellular channels and translational and posttranslational regulation of gap junctional channels add additional challenges to the interpretation of the possible functions played by gap junction-mediated intercellular communication in tissue business.

Key words: gap junctions, intercellular communication, phosphorylation

THE PROBLEMS: GAP-JUNCTIONAL CHANNELS ARE BIOCHEMICALLY AND PHYSIOLOGICALLY COMPLEX

Problem A: many proteins and overlapping expression

Gap junctions are membrane channels that directly join the cytoplasms of adjacent cells, forming the basis for synchronous electrical activity between excitable cells (Bennett and Goodenough, 1978; Bennett et al., 1991). Gap-junctional intercellular channels are almost universal between non-excitable cells as well, although their roles in diverse tissue functions, in cellular and tissue homeostasis and in differentiation, are largely unknown. A current challenge to research is to develop strategies for specifically interfering with junctional communication, such that the functional sequellae of junctional blockade can be directly observed. There are several experimental obstacles that make junctional blockade and interpretation of the data difficult.

The junctional intercellular channels are composed of paired connexons, oligomeric protein assemblies in each cell membrane (Caspar et al., 1977; Makowski et al., 1977; Unwin and Ennis, 1984). The connexins, a family of proteins that form the connexons (Beyer et al., 1988, 1990), have a complex, overlapping distribution in different cell types (Beyer et al., 1987, 1989; Bennett et al., 1991). The family can be divided into two general classes, called α and β (Kumar and Gilula, 1992) or I and II (Bennett et al., 1991), on the basis of sequence homology. Many (perhaps most) tissues express more than one type of connexin. In the lens there are three known connexins: connexin43 (Cx43), joining the epithelial cells (Beyer et al., 1989), and two connexins found in the junctions joining the lens fibers, Cx46 and Cx50 (also known as MP70) (Kistler et al., 1985; Paul et al., 1991; White et al., 1992; Tenbroek et al., 1992). Three connexins have been described in the chick heart

(Veenstra et al., 1992). In some cases, individual cells express more than one connexin type. In stratified squamous epithelium, for example, there is a complex distribution of connexins (Hennemann et al., 1992a,b; Hoh et al., 1991) that varies as a function of the differentiated state of the cells and with the age of the animal (Risek et al., 1992).

In addition to overlap of expression, the levels of expression of connexins may vary as a function of physiological state. The explosive increase in expression of Cx43 in the myometrium immediately prior to parturition is a classic example, when smooth muscle cells acquire powerful synchronous contractility (MacKenzie and Garfield, 1985; Miller et al., 1989; Risek et al., 1990; Tabb et al., 1992). In a more functionally obscure example, Sertoli cells in the testis show a variation in the levels of Cx43 expression as a function of the cycle of the spermatogenic cells (Risley et al., 1992). The cellular location of Cx33, a testis-specific connexin (Haefliger et al., 1992), and its degree of overlap with Cx43 have not yet been studied.

Problem B: many channels, diverse physiological properties

Gap-junctional channels are generally thought of as weakly selective with respect to ions (Brink and Dewey, 1980; Brink, 1983; Brink et al., 1984; Baker et al., 1985; Verselis and Brink, 1986). Intercellular transfer of second messengers and metabolites has been demonstrated in a variety of cellular systems; for example, data are available that demonstrate a key role for gap junctions in the intercellular spread of calcium waves between glial cells, a long-range signaling phenomenon inducible with glutamate and blocked by conditions that activate protein kinase C (Cornell-Bell et al., 1990; Charles et al., 1991; Enkvist and McCarthy, 1992). A similar spread of calcium waves may be essential for ciliary metachronasy (Moss and Tamm, 1987; Sanderson et al., 1988). This intercellular synchronization may result from passage of either Ca^{2+} or IP_3 between cells through gap junctions (Berridge and Irvine, 1989; Saez et al., 1989).

Data are accumulating from studies with transfected cells and other cell lines that show that the different connexin types have different single channel conductances, generally in the range of 50-150 pS (Jaslove and Brink, 1989; Brink and Fan, 1989; Dermietzel et al., 1991; Eghbali et al., 1990; Moreno et al., 1991a,b; Donaldson and Kistler 1992; Fishman et al., 1990; Moore et al., 1991; Salomon et al., 1992; Rup et al., 1993; Bennett and Verselis, 1992). Larger and smaller conductances are also observed (Spray et al., 1991; Perez-Armendiriz et al., 1991), as well as complex intermediate states, which may result from different conductance states of a single channel (Chen and DeHaan, 1992), simultaneous opening of more than one channel, or from channels consisting of more than one connexin type. This exquisite fine tuning of channel conductance between the different connexin types adds another level of complexity to the possible functions, and additional complexity to the interpretation of specific connexin ablation.

Problem C: selectivity and mixing in connexin interactions

Dahl and Werner (Dahl et al., 1987, 1988) have developed a *Xenopus* oöcyte-pair assay, in which individual oöcytes can be directed to synthesize specific connexins by intracellular injection of the appropriate cRNAs. Pairs of injected oöcytes that have had their vitelline envelopes removed can be manipulated into contact such that they form gap junctions. The functional participation of an endogenous *Xenopus* connexin can be substantively controlled by preinjecting oöcytes with antisense oligonucleotides specific for *Xenopus* Cx38 (Barrio et al., 1991; Willecke et al., 1991; White et al., 1992). Using this assay, it has been possible to demonstrate that heterotypic intercellular channels form between oöcytes expressing different connexins (Swenson et al., 1989; Werner et al., 1989; see also Rook et al., 1992). In some cases, the formation of heterotypic intercellular channels by programming each oöcyte with a different cRNA results in a channel with hybrid electrical characteristics. This has been demonstrated by pairing oöcytes injected with rat connexin32 and -26 cRNAs (Barrio et al., 1991). Cx32 and Cx26 are found naturally intermixed in gap junctions joining rat hepatocytes in situ, albeit with functionally obscure individual gradients across the hepatic lobule. Barrio et al. (1991) have shown that connexins26 and -32 are differently affected by applied voltage when assembled in heterotypic 26/32 pairs as compared to when they are assembled in homotypic 32/32 and 26/26 channels. These data suggest a *trans* effect on electrical properties exerted by one connexin on another in an adjacent cell. The observation that Cx43 injected into one oöcyte is able to recruit endogenous *Xenopus* Cx38 in the other oöcyte of the pair demonstrates that individual connexins may also exert complex *trans* effects on gap junction assembly (Swenson et al., 1989; Werner et al., 1989).

While it is possible for heterotypic channels to form using some connexins, it has become equally clear that other connexins are unable to pair with each other in the *Xenopus* oöcyte assay. This selectivity has been studied in detail in the case of rat connexins 43, 40 and 37 (Bruzzone et al., 1993). The 43/37 and 37/40 heterotypic intercellular channels readily assemble, each showing asymmetric voltage profiles characteristic of each connexin. In contrast, 43/40 heterotypic channels do not form, even though the proteins are expressed at high levels. While the meaning of this selectivity is not clear, it may certainly permit the formation of communication compartments within a given organ where adjacent cells are functionally required to maintain separate domains of homeostasis.

Problem D: regulation of gap junctions at multiple levels

There is a substantial amount of literature that has reported studies of the regulation of gap-junctional intercellular communication. It is almost axiomatic that cells that are joined by low resistance channels must have fail-safe systems to close the channels, should either of the cells undergo injury or apoptosis, since a catastrophic loss of membrane potential of one cell would rapidly depolarize an adjacent cell to which it was junctionally joined. Perhaps related to this fail-safe system are the data that demonstrate that gap-junctional channels between cells are sensitive to increases in intracellular calcium and/or decreases in intracellular pH (Rose and Loewenstein, 1975; Turin and Warner, 1980; Obaid et al., 1983). These injury-related responses are of particular interest to the student of myocardial cells, since ischemic injury may trigger these uncoupling mechanisms by Ca^{2+}, pH or lipid metabolites (Burt, 1987, 1989), and their rapid reversal may represent a critical survival mechanism (Burt et al., 1991; Moore et al., 1991). There are documented experimental and developmental situations when groups of cells establish or terminate intercellular communication in the absence of tissue injury (Potter et al., 1966; Dixon and Cronly-Dillon, 1974; Nagajski et al., 1989; Olson et al., 1991; Olson and Moon, 1992; Warner, 1992). Given the relatively short half-life of certain connexins both in vivo and in vitro (Fallon and Goodenough, 1981; Yancey et al., 1981; Musil et al., 1990a), it is possible that these changes in gap-junctional communication levels are regulated at the level of either transcription or translation. The very close temporal correspondence between the metabolic turnover of Cx32 and the loss of morphological and physiological gap-junctional channels in regenerating liver provides a compelling example (Yee and Revel, 1978; Meyer et al., 1981; Dermietzel et al., 1987; Traub et al., 1989). In some systems, the regulation of connexin gene expression has been studied, and this promises to be an interesting area of investigation in the future (reviewed by Musil and Goodenough, 1990).

Gap-junctional channels can also be regulated post-translationally by a variety of effectors (reviewed by Bennett et al., 1991). In many instances, this regulation is thought to involve phosphorylation of connexins, several of which have been shown to be phosphoproteins (e.g. connexins 32, 43, 46 and 50 (MP70) Swenson et al., 1990; Crow et al., 1990; Musil et al., 1990a,b; Musil and Goodenough, 1991; Filson et al., 1990; Saez et al., 1986; Tenbroek et al., 1992). In nontransformed cells, connexin phosphorylation is largely confined to serine residues (Saez et al., 1986, 1990; Swenson et al., 1990; Musil et al., 1990b). Expression of the transforming tyrosine protein kinase pp60[v-src] results in tyrosine phosphorylation of Cx43 (but not Cx32) and selective inhibition of Cx43-mediated gap-junctional conductance between *Xenopus* oöcytes (Swenson et al., 1990). Mutation of tyrosine 265 to phenylalanine prevents both tyrosine phosphorylation of Cx43 and loss of gap-junctional conductance in the presence of pp60^{v-src}, demonstrating that Cx43 is a functional substrate for this transforming tyrosine kinase in the oöcyte-pair system. The tyrosine phosphorylation of Cx43 and concomitant loss of cell-cell communication has also been observed in tissue culture cells infected with Rous sarcoma virus (Crow et al., 1990; Filson et al., 1990).

In contrast to tyrosine phosphorylation, the functions subserved by phosphorylation of Cx43 on serine residues are not yet understood. It has been shown that serine phosphorylation to the mature Cx43-P$_2$ form, which results in a shift in the electrophoretic mobility of Cx43 to a more slowly migrating species, does not occur unless gap junctions are assembled (Musil et al., 1990b). Non-phosphorylated Cx43 can be solubilized with Triton X-100 buffers, leaving Cx43-P$_2$ in the insoluble pellet (Musil and Goodenough, 1991). Using this fractionation method in combination with pulse-chase and cell surface biotinylation studies, it is clear that nonphosphorylated Cx43 can be exported to the cell surface in a Triton-soluble form prior to assembly into Triton-insoluble gap-junctional maculae. Phosphorylation of Cx43 in NRK cells therefore does not serve as an export signal to target transport of Cx43 through intracellular compartments to the cell surface. This conclusion is indirectly supported by the demonstration that a mutant of Cx43, which had much of its cytoplasmic tail truncated, was able to assemble into functional channels in transfected SKHep cells (Fishman et al., 1991).

Evidence supporting a role for Cx43 phosphorylation in gap junction formation and/or function came from studies with the communication-deficient S180 and L929 cell lines, which lack morphologically or physiologically recognizable gap junctions. In these cells, Cx43 is not phosphorylated to the P$_2$ form despite being synthesized and degraded with kinetics equivalent to that seen in NRK cells, which both assemble gap junctions and phosphorylate Cx43. Gap-junctional assembly and communication in S180 cells can be 'rescued' by stable transfection with a cDNA encoding the cell-cell adhesion molecule L-CAM (Mege et al., 1988), which results in the phosphorylation of Cx43 to the P$_2$ form (Musil et al., 1990b). Acute uncoupling of NRK or other communication-competent cells by cytoplasmic acidification or with 1-heptanol does not result in measurable Cx43 dephosphorylation (Musil et al., 1990), suggesting that the experimentally induced fail-safe gating response occurs via mechanisms other than gross changes in Cx43 phosphorylation.

Cx43 cDNA-transfected SKHep cells, which have had intracellular protein kinases stimulated, show differences in single channel conductance and in the kinetics of voltage dependence, suggesting that phosphorylation may alter these electrophysiological parameters (Moreno et al., 1992). Changes in single channel conductance have also been seen in cardiac myocytes expressing endogenous Cx43 in response to stimulation of cyclic GMP protein kinase (Takens-Kwak and Jongsma, 1992). Direct demonstration that a change in gap-junctional single channel conductance is due to Cx43 phosphorylation is experimentally difficult, however, and it is also clear that Cx43 experiences multiple phosphorylations, leaving open the possibility that several functions may be involved. Given the meager knowledge of the function of gap junctions as outlined above, a detailed dissection of the function of connexin phosphorylation is likely to involve students of intercellular communication for some time.

STRATEGIES FOR SPECIFIC ABLATION OF GAP-JUNCTIONAL INTERCELLULAR COMMUNICATION

In addition to changes in intracellular pH and/or calcium levels, gap-junctional intercellular communication is sensitive to exogenous compounds normally not present in a cell's life history, such as alkanols (Johnston et al., 1980) and local anesthetics (Hauswirth, 1968; Burt and Spray, 1989). However, the mechanisms of action of any of these uncoupling agents are largely unknown, and each agent has additional effects on the biology of the cell. It is not possible to use these uncouplers to experimentally determine the roles of gap-junctional communication in tissue biology.

Strategy A: use of specific antisera and peptides
In theory, the intracellular injection of anti-connexin sera would be an effective way to specifically block gap-junctional communication. A few polyclonal antisera directed against one or more connexins have been reported in the literature as being effective in inhibiting gap-junctional communication (Hertzberg et al., 1985; Traub et al., 1989; Yancey et al., 1989), but these have not been used for further functional studies. In one notable exception, Warner et al. (1984) microinjected an active antiserum into embryonic cells in the mouse and the frog and reduced ionic conductance or transfer of the tracer dye Lucifer Yellow (Warner et al., 1984; Lee et al., 1987). When the injected cells included precursors of the anterior central nervous system, abnormalities in the development of the brain, eye and other anterior structures result (Warner et al., 1984). Developmental effects following injection of other lineages have also been reported (Warner, 1985). These results might indicate the involvement of junctional communication in any of a series of tissue interactions, since a block to coupling is present throughout a prolonged and ill-defined period. It is possible, for instance, that gap junctions could play a role in a progression of cell-cell signaling and interactional events that are essential for proper specification of mesoderm, for neural plate induction by the underlying dorsal mesoderm, for neural plate folding, or simply for maintenance of the ectoderm and later neural epithelium. Although Warner and Gurdon (1987) showed in recombination experiments that induction of muscle differentiation in ectoderm is unaffected by inhibiting junctional permeability among cells of the inductively active blastula endoderm, they did not investigate the role of coupling within the responding tissue, nor could they determine whether the pattern of mesodermal induction was perturbed. Preliminary studies have shown the feasibility of using anti-Cx43 antisera directed against putative extracellular domains as a method for blocking gap junction assembly in cultured cells (Meyer et al., 1992). Similarly, channel assembly between *Xenopus*

oöcytes can be blocked using synthetic peptides corresponding to the extracellular loop sequences of Cx32 (Dahl et al., 1992). To date none of these extracellularly targeted reagents have been used for functional studies.

While these studies provide clear information, the methodology of injecting antisera is experimentally difficult with some cell types. In addition, it is difficult to inject whole populations of cells for study. This problem was circumvented by Fraser et al. (1987), who were able to disrupt patterning during regeneration in *Hydra* by loading all the cells with an active anti-gap-junction antiserum using a DMSO procedure.

Strategy B: development of dominant negative inhibitors and transgenic animals

A relatively unexplored possibility for the development of specific inhibitors of gap-junctional function would be a study that focuses on the coöligomerization of different connexins into heteromeric connexons and intercellular channels. *cis* interactions between connexins in the formation of intercellular channels, if they exist, offer the possibility of developing dominant negative constructs that would be of great value in specific knockout of gap junction function. Indeed, it might be feasible to design a dominant negative specific for each connexin, such that the meaning of the overlapping distribution of different connexins could be functionally understood. Design strategies would be to combine sequences between two connexins that are unable to pair in *trans*, such as Cx43 and Cx40, to create a single chimeric molecule capable of physically, but not functionally, interacting with one or both of the parental connexins. An interacting but non-functional connexin might also be designed by selectively deleting or mutating highly conserved regions common to all connexins (Dahl et al., 1992). Once developed, these dominant-negative connexins, under the control of tissue-specific promoters, could be used to construct transgenic animals for functional studies, where a given connexin is ablated in a specific tissue at a defined developmental time. Alternatively, the single-copy connexin genes (Willecke et al., 1990; Hsieh et al., 1991; Haefliger et al., 1992; Hennemann et al., 1992a,b) could be ablated by homologous recombination, denying expressing of a specific connexin in all its developmental and tissue locations.

CONCLUSION

The application of molecular biological methods to the study of intercellular communication via gap junctions has revealed a number of single-copy genes that code for the connexins, a family of oligomeric integral membrane proteins. The cloning of a large number of these genes has opened up the possibility of using genetic strategies to specifically interfere in gap-junctional communication, including development of transgenic animals with individual connexins knocked out by homologous recombination, or of transgenics engineered with connexin-specific dominant negative constructs driven by tissue-specific promoters. The design and interpretation of such experiments will, however, have to take into account several of the complexities of gap junction structure and functional regulation discussed above. First, connexins show a complicated, overlapping tissue and cellular distribution, such that knocking out a specific connexin may well leave cells functionally coupled by other members of the connexin family. Second, knockout of a widely distributed connexin such as Cx43 is both a potentially lethal event and experimentally complex, since this connexin is found not only very early in development (Barron et al., 1989; Nishi et al., 1991; Yancey et al., 1992) but also in a myriad of different tissue locations (Kadle et al., 1991; Ruangvoravat and Lo, 1992), under different regulatory control in different cell types (Risek et al., 1990). As a further complication to the understanding of gap junction function, the degrees to which different connexins assemble into heteromeric connexons, and different connexons into heterotypic intercellular channels, are not yet fully known. Furthermore, genetic approaches do not address the fact that gap junction function can be regulated post-translationally. Despite these complexities, it is anticipated that genetic manipulation of the expression of specific connexins will serve as a powerful tool to elucidate the functions of individual connexins in tissue business.

REFERENCES

Baker, T. S., Sosinsky, G. E., Caspar, D. L. D., Gall, C. and Goodenough, D. A. (1985). Gap junction structures. VII. Analysis of connexon images obtained with cationic and anionic negative stains. *J. Mol. Biol.* **184**, 81-98.

Barrio, L. C., Suchyna, T., Bargiello, T., Xu, L. X., Roginski, R. S., Bennett, M. V. L. and Nicholson, B. J. (1991). Gap junctions formed by connexins 26 and 32 alone and in combination are differently affected by voltage. *Proc. Nat. Acad. Sci. USA* **88**, 8410-8414.

Barron, D. J., Valdimarsson, G., Paul, D. L. and Kidder, G. M. (1989). Connexin32, a gap junction protein, is a persistent oögenetic product through preimplantation development of the mouse. *Dev. Genet.* **10**, 318-323.

Bennett, M. V. L., Barrio, L. C., Bargiello, T. A., Spray, D. C., Hertzberg, E. and Saez, J. C. (1991). Gap junctions: new tools, new answers, new questions. *Neuron* **6**, 305-320.

Bennett, M. V. L. and Goodenough, D. A. (1978). Gap junctions, electrotonic coupling, and intercellular communication. *Neurosci. Res. Prog. Bull.* **16**, 373-486.

Bennett, M. V. L. and Verselis, V. K. (1992). Biophysics of gap junctions. *Semin. Cell Biol.* **3**, 29-47.

Berridge, M. J. and Irvine, R. F. (1989). Inositol phosphates and cell signalling. *Nature* **341**, 197-205.

Beyer, E. C., Goodenough, D. A. and Paul, D. L. (1988). The connexins, a family of related gap junction proteins. In *Gap Junctions* (ed. E. L. Hertzberg and R. G. Johnson), pp. 167-175. New York: Alan R. Liss, Inc.

Beyer, E. C., Kistler, J., Paul, D. L. and Goodenough, D. A. (1989). Antisera directed against connexin43 peptides react with a 43-kD protein localized to gap junctions in myocardium and other tissues. *J. Cell Biol.* **108**, 595-605.

Beyer, E. C., Paul, D. L. and Goodenough, D. A. (1987). Connexin43: a protein from rat heart homologous to a gap junction protein from liver. *J. Cell Biol.* **105**, 2621-2629.

Beyer, E. C., Paul, D. L. and Goodenough, D. A. (1990). Connexin family of gap junction proteins. *J. Membr. Biol.* **116**, 187-194.

Brink, P. R. (1983). Effect of deuterium oxide on junctional membrane channel permeability. *J. Membr. Biol.* **71**, 79-87.

Brink, P. R. and Dewey, M. M. (1980). Evidence for fixed charge in the nexus. *Nature* **285**, 101-102.

Brink, P. R. and Fan, S. (1989). Patch clamp recordings from membranes which contain gap junction channels. *Biophys. J.* **56**, 579-593.

Brink, P. R., Verselis, V. and Barr, L. (1984). Solvent-solute interactions within the nexal membrane. *Biophys. J.* **45**, 121-124.

Bruzzone, R., Haefliger, J.-A., Gimlich, R. L. and Paul, D. L. (1993). Connexin40, a component of gap junctions in vascular endothelium, is restricted in its ability to interact with other connexins. *Mol. Biol. Cell* **4**, 7-20.

Burt, J. M. (1987). Block of intercellular communication: interaction of intracellular H+ and Ca2+. *Amer. J. Physiol.* **253**, C607-C612.

Burt, J. M. (1989). Uncoupling of cardiac cells by doxyl stearic acids: specificity and mechanism of action. *Amer. J. Physiol.* **256**, C913-C924.

Burt, J. M., Massey, K. D. and Minnich, B. N. (1991). Uncoupling of cardiac cells by fatty acids: structure activity relationships. *Amer. J. Physiol.* **260**, C439 C448

Burt, J. M. and Spray, D. C. (1989). Volatile anesthetics block intercellular communication between neonatal rat myocardial cells. *Circ. Res.* **65**, 829-837.

Caspar, D. L. D., Goodenough, D. A., Makowski, L. and Phillips, W. C. (1977). Gap junction structures. I. Correlated electron microscopy and X-ray diffraction. *J. Cell Biol.* **74**, 605-628.

Charles, A. C., Dirksen, E. R. and Sanderson, M. J. (1991). Intercellular signaling in glial cells: calcium waves and oscillations in response to mechanical stimulation and glutamate. *Neuron* **6**, 938-992.

Chen, Y.-H. and DeHaan, R. L. (1992). Multiple-channel conductance states and voltage regulation of embryonic chick cardiac gap junctions. *J. Membr. Biol.* **127**, 95-111.

Cornell-Bell, A. H., Finkbeiner, S. M., Cooper, M. S. and Smith, S. J. (1990). Glutamate induces calcium waves in cultured astrocytes: long-range glial signaling. *Science* **247**, 470-474.

Crow, D. S., Beyer, E. C., Paul, D. L., Kobe, S. S. and Lau, A. F. (1990). Phosphorylation of connexin43 gap junction protein in uninfected and Rous sarcoma virus-transformed mammalian fibroblasts. *Mol. Cell. Biol.* **10**, 1754-1763.

Dahl, G., Miller, T., Paul, D., Voellmy, R. and Werner, R. (1987). Expression of functional cell-cell channels from cloned rat liver gap junction complementary DNA. *Science* **236**, 1290-1293.

Dahl, G., Werner, R. and Levine, E (1988). Paired oöcytes: an expression system for cell-cell channels. In *Gap Junctions* (ed. E. L. Hertzberg and R. G. Johnson), pp. 183-197. New York: Alan R. Liss, Inc.

Dahl, G., Werner, R., Levine, E. and Rabadan-Diehl C. (1992). Mutational analysis of gap junction formation. *Biophys J.* **62**, 187-195.

Dermietzel, R., Hertzberg, E. L., Kessler, J. A. and Spray, D. C. (1991). Gap junctions between cultured astrocytes: immunocytochemical, molecular, and electrophysiological analysis. *J. Neurosci.* **11**, 1421-1432.

Dermietzel, R., Yancey, S. B., Traub, O., Willecke, K. and Revel, J. P. (1987). Major loss of the 28-kD protein of gap junction in proliferating hepatocytes. *J. Cell Biol.* **105**, 1925-1934.

Dixon, J. S. and Cronly-Dillon, N. R. (1974). Intercellular gap junctions in pigment epithelium cells during retinal specification in *Xenopus laevis*. *Nature* **251**, 505.

Donaldson, P. and Kistler, J. (1992). Reconstitution of channels from preparations enriched in lens gap junction protein, MP70. *J. Membr. Biol.* **129**, 155-165.

Eghbali, B., Kessler, J. A. and Spray, D. C. (1990). Expression of gap junction channels in communication-incompetent cells after stable transfection with cDNA encoding connexin 32. *Proc. Nat. Acad. Sci. USA* **87**, 1328-1331.

Enkvist, M. W. and McCarthy, K. D. (1992). Activation of protein kinase C blocks astroglial gap junction communication and inhibits the spread of calcium waves. *J. Neurochem.* **59**, 519-526.

Fallon, R. F. and Goodenough, D. A. (1981). Five hour half-life of mouse liver gap-junction protein. *J. Cell Biol.* **90**, 521-526

Filson, A. J., Azarnia, R., Beyer, E. C., Loewenstein, W. R. and Brugge, J. S. (1990). Tyrosine phosphorylation of a gap junction protein correlates with inhibition of cell-to-cell communication. *Cell Growth Differ.* **1**, 661-668.

Fishman, G., Moreno, A. P., Spray, D. C. and Leinwand, L. A. (1991). Functional analysis of human cardiac gap junction channel mutants. *Proc. Nat. Acad. Sci. USA* **88**, 3525-3529.

Fishman, G. I., Spray, D. C. and Leinwand, L. A. (1990). Molecular characterization and functional expression of the human cardiac gap junction channel. *J. Cell Biol.* **111**, 589-598.

Fraser, S. E., Green, C. R., Bode, H. R. and Gilula, N. B. (1987). Selective disruption of gap-junctional communication interferes with a patterning process in *Hydra*. *Science* **237**, 49-55.

Haefliger, J.-A., Bruzzone, R., Jenkins, N. A., Gilbert, D. J., Copeland, N. G. and Paul, D. L. (1992). Four novel members of the connexin family of gap junction proteins. Molecular cloning, expression, and chromosome mapping. *J. Biol. Chem.* **267**, 2057-2064.

Hauswirth, O. (1968). The influence of halothane on the electrical properties of cardiac Purkinje fibres. *J. Physiol.* **201**, 42P-43P.

Hennemann, H., Dahl, E., White, J. B., Schwarz, H. J., Lalley, P. A., Chang, S., Nicholson, B. J. and Willecke, K. (1992a). Two gap junction genes, connexin31. 1 and 30. 3, are closely linked on mouse chromosome 4 and preferentially expressed in skin. *J. Biol. Chem.* **267**, 17225-17233.

Hennemann, H., Schwarz, H.-J. and Willecke, K. (1992b). Characterization of gap junction genes expressed in F9 embryonic carcinoma cells: molecular cloning of mouse connexin31 and -45 cDNAs. *Eur. J. Cell Biol.* **57**, 51 58.

Hertzberg, E. L., Spray, D. C. and Bennett, M. V. L. (1985). Reduction of gap-junctional conductance by microinjection of antibodies against the 27-kDa liver gap junction polypeptide. *Proc. Nat. Acad. Sci. USA* **82**, 2412-2416.

Hoh, J. H., John, S. A. and Revel, J.-P. (1991). Molecular cloning and characterization of a new member of the gap junction gene family, connexin-31. *J. Biol. Chem.* **266**, 6524-6531.

Hsieh, C.-L., Kumar, N. M., Gilula, N. B. and Francke, U. (1991). Distribution of genes for gap junction membrane channel proteins on human and mouse chromosomes. *Somat. Cell Mol. Genet.* **17**, 191-200.

Jaslove, S. W. and Brink, P. R. (1989). Permeability and conductance of gap junction channels. In *Cell Interactions and Gap Junctions* (ed. N. Sperelakis and W. C. Cole), pp. 203-224. Boca Raton: CRC Press.

Johnston, M. F., Simon, S. A. and Ramon, F. (1980). Interaction of anaesthetics with electrical synapses. *Nature* **286**, 498-500.

Kadle, R., Zhang, J. T. and Nicholson, B. J. (1991). Tissue-specific distribution of differentially phosphorylated forms of Cx43. *Mol. Cell Biol.* **11**, 363-369.

Kistler, J., Kirkland, B. and Bullivant, S. (1985). Identification of a 70,000-D protein in lens membrane junctional domains. *J. Cell Biol.* **101**, 28-35.

Kumar, N. M. and Gilula, N. B. (1992). Molecular biology and genetics of gap junction channels. *Semin. Cell Biol.* **3**, 3-16.

Lee, S., Gilula, N. B. and Warner, A. E. (1987). Gap-junctional communication and compaction during preimplantation stages of mouse development. *Cell* **51**, 851-860.

MacKenzie L. W. and Garfield, R. E. (1985). Hormonal control of gap junctions in the myometrium. *Amer. J. Physiol.* **248**, C296-C308.

Makowski, L., Caspar, D. L. D., Phillips, W. C. and Goodenough, D. A. (1977). Gap junction structures. II. Analysis of the X-ray diffraction data. *J. Cell Biol.* **74**, 629-645.

Mege, R. M., Matsuzaki, F., Gallin, W. J., Goldberg, J. I., Cunningham, B. A. and Edelman, G. M. (1988). Construction of epithelioid sheets by transfection of mouse sarcoma cells with cDNAs for chicken cell adhesion molecules. *Proc. Nat. Acad. Sci. USA* **85**, 7274-7278.

Meyer, R. A., Laird, D. W., Revel, J.-P. and Johnson, R. G. (1992). Inhibition of gap junction and adherens junction assembly by connexin and A-CAM antibodies. *J. Cell Biol.* **119**, 179-189.

Meyer, D. J., Yancey, B., Revel, J. P. and Peskoff, A. (1981). Intercellular communication in normal and regenerating rat liver: a quantitative analysis. *J. Cell Biol.* **91**, 505-523.

Miller, S. M., Garfield, R. E. and Daniel, E. E. (1989). Improved propagation in myometrium associated with gap junctions during parturition. *Amer. J. Physiol.* **256**, C130-C141.

Moore, L. K., Beyer, E. C. and Burt, J. M. (1991). Characterization of gap junction channels in A7r5 vascular smooth muscle cells. *Amer. J. Physiol.* **260**, C975-C981.

Moreno, A. P., Eghbali, B. and Spray, D. C. (1991a). Connexin32 gap junction channels in stably transfected cells: unitary conductance. *Biophys. J.* **60**, 1254-1266

Moreno, A. P., Eghbali, B. and Spray, D. C. (1991b). Connexin32 gap junction channels in stably transfected cells: equilibrium and kinetic properties. *Biophys. J.* **60**, 1267-1277.

Moreno, A. P., Fishman, G. I. and Spray, D. C. (1992). Phosphorylation shifts unitary conductance and modifies voltage dependent kinetics of human connexin43 gap junction channels. *Biophys. J.* **62**, 51-53.

Moss, A. G. and Tamm, S. L. (1987). A calcium regenerative potential controlling ciliary reversal is propagated along the length of ctenophore comb plates. *Proc. Nat. Acad. Sci. USA* **84**, 6476-6480.

Musil, L. S., Beyer, E. C. and Goodenough, D. A. (1990a). Expression of the gap junction protein connexin43 in embryonic chick lens: molecular cloning, ultrastructural localization, and post-translational phosphorylation. *J. Membr. Biol.* **116**, 163-175.

Musil, L. S., Cunningham, B. A., Edelman, G. M. and Goodenough, D.

A. (1990b). Differential phosphorylation of the gap junction protein connexin43 in junctional communication-competent and -deficient cell lines. *J. Cell Biol.* **111**, 2077-2088.

Musil, L. S. and Goodenough, D. A. (1990). Gap-junctional intercellular communication and the regulation of connexin expression and function. *Curr. Opin. Cell Biol.* **2**, 875-880.

Musil, L. S. and Goodenough, D. A. (1991). Biochemical analysis of connexin43 intracellular transport, phosphorylation, and assembly into gap-junctional plaques. *J. Cell Biol.* **115**, 1357-1374.

Nagajski, D. J., Guthrie, S. C., Ford, C. C. and Warner, A. E. (1989). The correlation between patterns of dye transfer through gap junctions and future developmental fate in *Xenopus*: the consequences of u. v. irradiation and lithium treatment. *Development* **105**, 747-752.

Nishi, M., Kumar, N. M. and Gilula, N. B. (1991). Developmental regulation of gap junction gene expression during mouse embryonic development. *Dev. Biol.* **146**, 117-130.

Obaid, A. L., Socolar, S. J. and Rose, B. (1983). Cell-to-cell channels with two independently regulated gates in series: analysis of junctional conductance modulation by membrane potential, calcium, and pH. *J. Membr. Biol.* **73**, 69-79.

Olson, D. J., Christian, J. L. and Moon, R. T. (1991). Effect of wnt-1 and related proteins on gap-junctional communication in *Xenopus* embryos. *Science* **252**, 1173-1176.

Olson, D. J. and Moon, R. T. (1992). Distinct effects of ectopic expression of wnt-1, activin B, and bFGF on gap-junctional permeability in 32-cell *Xenopus* embryos. *Dev. Biol.* **151**, 204-212.

Paul, D. L., Ebihara, L., Takemoto, L. J., Swenson, K. I. and Goodenough, D. A. (1991). Connexin46, a novel lens gap junction protein, induces voltage-gated currents in nonjunctional plasma membrane of *Xenopus* oöcytes. *J. Cell Biol.* **115**, 1077-1089.

Perez-Armendiriz, M., Roy, C., Spray, D. C. and Bennett, M. V. L. (1991). Biophysical properties of gap junctions between freshly dispersed pairs of mouse pancreatic beta cells. *Biophys. J.* **59**, 76-92.

Potter, D. D., Furshpan, E. J. and Lennox, E. X. (1966). Connections between cells of the developing squid as revealed by electrophysiological methods. *Proc. Nat. Acad. Sci. USA* **55**, 328-335.

Risek, B., Guthrie, S. Kumar, N. and Gilula, N. B. (1990). Modulation of gap junction transcript and protein expression during pregnancy in the rat. *J. Cell Biol.* **110**, 269-282.

Risek, B. Klier, R. G. and Gilula, N. B. (1992). Multiple gap junction genes are utilized during rat skin and hair development. *Development* **116**, 639-651

Risley, M. S., Tan, I. P., Roy, C. and Saez, J. C. (1992). Cell-, age- and stage-dependent distribution of connexin43 gap junction in testes. *J. Cell Sci.* **103**, 81-96.

Rook, M. B., Van Ginneken, A. C. G., De Gonge, B., El Auomari, A., Gros, D. and Jongsma, H. J. (1992). Differences in gap junction channels between cardiac myocytes, fibroblasts, and heterologous pairs. *Amer. J. Physiol.* **263**, C959-C977.

Rose, B. and Loewenstein, W. R. (1975). Permeability of cell junction depends on local cytoplasmic calcium activity. *Nature* **254**, 250-252.

Ruangvoravat, C. P. and Lo, C. W. (1992). Connexin43 expression in the mouse embryo: localization to transcripts within developmentally significant domains. *Dev. Dynam.* **194**, 261-281.

Rup, D. M., Veenstra, R. D., Wang, H.-Z., Brink, P. R. and Beyer, E. C. (1993). Chick connexin-56, a novel lens gap junction protein. *J. Biol. Chem.* **268**, 706-712.

Saez, J. C., Connor, J. A., Spray, D. C. and Bennett, M. V. L. (1989). Hepatocyte gap junctions are permeable to the second messenger, inositol 1. 4, 5-trisphosphate, and to calcium ions. *Proc. Nat. Acad. Sci. USA* **86**, 2708-2712.

Saez, J. C., Nairn, A. C., Czernik, A. J., Spray, D. C., Hertzberg, E. L.,Greengard, P. and Bennett, M. V. L. (1990). Phosphorylation of connexin32, the hepatocyte gap-junction protein, by cAMP-dependent protein kinase, protein kinase C and Ca^{2+}/calmodulin-dependent protein kinase II. *Eur. J. Biochem.* **192**, 263-273.

Saez, J. C., Spray, D. C., Nairn, A. C., Hertzberg, E., Greengard, P. and Bennett, M. V. L. (1986). cAMP increases junctional conductance and stimulates phosphorylation of the 27-kDa principal gap junction polypeptide. *Proc. Nat. Acad. Sci. USA* **83**, 2473-2477.

Salomon, D., Chanson, M., Vischer, S., Masgrau, E., Vozzi, C., Saurat, J.-H., Spray D. C. and Meda, P. (1992). Gap-junctional communication of primary human keratinocytes: characterization by dual voltage clamp and dye transfer. *Exp. Cell Res.* **201**, 452-461.

Sanderson, M. J., Chow, I. and Dirksen, E. R. (1988). Intercellular communication between ciliated cells in culture. *Amer. J. Physiol.* **254**, C63-74.

Spray, D. C., Chanson, M., Moreno, A. P., Dermietzel, R. and Meda, P. (1991). Distinctive gap junction channel types connect WB cells, a clonal cell line dreived from rat liver. *Amer. J. Physiol.* **260**, C513-C527.

Swenson, K. I., Jordan, J. R., Beyer, E. C. and Paul, D. L. (1989). Formation of gap junctions by expression of connexins in *Xenopus* oöcyte pairs. *Cell* **57**, 145-155.

Swenson, K. I., Piwnica-Worms, H., McNamee, H. and Paul, D. L. (1990). Tyrosine phosphorylation of the gap junction protein connexin43 is required for the pp60$^{v\text{-}src}$-induced inhibition of communication. *Cell Regul.* **1**, 989-1002.

Tabb, T., Thilander, G., Grover, A., Hertzberg, E. and Garfield, R. (1992). An immunochemical and immunocytologic study of the increase in myometrial gap junctions (and connexin 43) in rats and humans during pregnancy. *Amer. J. Obstet. Gynecol.* **167**, 559-567.

Takens-Kwak, B. R. and Jongsma, H. J. (1992). Cardiac gap junctions: three distinct single channel conductances and their modulation by phosphorylating treatments. *Pflugers Arch.* **422**, 198-200.

Tenbroek, E., Arneson, M., Jarvis, L. and Louis, C. (1992). The distribution of the fiber cell intrinsic membrane proteins MP20 and connexin46 in the bovine lens. *J. Cell Sci.* **103**, 245-257.

Traub, O., Look, J., Dermietzel, R., Brummer, F., Hulser, D. and Willecke, K. (1989). Comparative characterization of the 21-kD and 26-kD gap junction proteins in murine liver and cultured hepatocytes. *J. Cell Biol.* **108**, 1039-1051.

Turin, L. and Warner, A. (1980). Intracellular pH in early *Xenopus* embryos: its effects on current flow between blastomeres. *J. Physiol.* **300**, 489-504.

Unwin, P. N. T. and Ennis, P. D. (1984). Two configurations of a channel-forming membrane protein. *Nature* **307**, 609-613.

Veenstra, R. D., Wang, H.-Z., Westphale, E. M. and Beyer, E. C. (1992). Multiple connexins confer distinct regulatory and conductance properties of gap junctions in developing heart. *Circ. Res.* **71**, 1277-1283.

Verselis, V. and Brink, P. R. (1986). The gap junction channel: its hydrophilic nature, as indicated by deuterium oxide effects. *Biophys. J.* **50**, 1003-1007.

Warner, A. E. (1985). The role of gap junctions in amphibian development. *J. Embryol. Exp. Morphol.* **89** *Suppl.* 365-380.

Warner, A. E. (1992). Gap junctions in development--a perspective. *Semin. Cell Biol.* **3**, 81-91.

Warner, A. E. and Gurdon, J. B. (1987). Functional gap junctions are not required for muscle gene activation by induction in *Xenopus* embryos. *J. Cell Biol.* **104**, 557-564.

Warner, A. E., Guthrie, S. C. and Gilula, N. B. (1984). Antibodies to gap-junctional protein selectively disrupt junctional communication in the early amphibian embryo. *Nature* **311**, 127-131.

Werner, R., Levine, E., Rabadan-Diehl, C. and Dahl, G. (1989). Formation of hybrid cell-cell channels. *Proc. Nat. Acad. Sci. USA* **86**, 5380-5384.

White, T. W., Bruzzone, R., Goodenough, D. A. and Paul, D. L. (1992). Mouse Cx50, a functional member of the connexin family of gap junction proteins, is the lens fiber protein MP70. *Mol. Biol. Cell* **3**, 711-720.

Willecke, K., Heynkes, R., Dahl, E., Stutenkemper, R., Hennemann, H., Jungbluth, S., Suchyna, T. and Nicholson, B. J. (1991). Mouse connexin37: cloning and functional expression of a gap junction gene highly expressed in lung. *J. Cell Biol.* **114**, 1049-1057.

Willecke, K., Jungbluth, S., Dahl, E., Hennemann, H., Heynkes, R. and Grzeschik, K.-H. (1990). Six genes of the human connexin gene family coding for gap-junctional proteins are assigned to four different human chromosomes. *Eur. J. Cell Biol.* **53**, 275-280.

Yancey, S. B., Biswal, S. and Revel, J.-P. (1992). Spatial and temporal patterns of distribution of the gap junction protein connexin43 during mouse gastrulation and organogenesis. *Development* **114**, 203-212.

Yancey, S. B., John, S. A., Ratneshwar, L., Austin, B. J. and Revel, J.-P. (1989). The 43-kD polypeptide of heart gap junctions: immunolocalization, topology, and functional domains. *J. Cell Biol.* **108**, 2241-2254.

Yancey, S. B., Nicholson, B. J. and Revel, J.-P. (1981). The dynamic state of liver gap junctions. *J. Supramol. Struct. Cell Biochem.* **16**, 221-232.

Yee, A. G. and Revel, J.-P. (1978). Loss and reappearance of gap junctions in regenerating liver. *J. Cell Biol.* **78**, 554-564.

Journal of Cell Science, Supplement 17, 139-145 (1993)
Printed in Great Britain © The Company of Biologists Limited 1993

Epithelial cell adhesion and development of cell surface polarity: possible mechanisms for modulation of cadherin function, organization and distribution

Inke S. Näthke[1], Lindsay E. Hinck[1,2] and W. James Nelson[1,2]

Department of Molecular and Cellular Physiology[1] and The Cancer Biology Program[2], Stanford University School of Medicine, Stanford, CA 94305-5426, USA

SUMMARY

Epithelial cell adhesion is principally regulated by calcium-dependent cell adhesion proteins, termed cadherins. Recent studies indicate that cadherin function is modulated by a class of proteins, termed catenins, that bind to the cytoplasmic domain of cadherin. Here we review the evidence that catenins regulate cadherin function in cell-cell adhesion, and discuss their role in inititiating cell surface polarity in epithelial cells.

Key words: epithelia, adhesion, cadherin, cytoskeleton, polarity

INTRODUCTION

Multicellular organisms are composed of heterogeneous cell types that are organized during development into distinct patterns to form tissues and organs. One of the important, primary processes involved in regulating the establishment and maintenance of these patterns is cell-cell adhesion. Pioneering studies by Holtfreter and colleagues, and Steinberg and Moscona and colleagues established the central principle that the interaction between cells within a heterogeneous cell population is based upon the specificity and extent of adhesion between those cells; cells of the same type tended to aggregate and, therefore, be sorted out from the other cells (for discussion, see Trinkaus, 1984). The molecular basis for cell adhesion has since been shown to be due to the cell surface expression of a family of glycoproteins that bind with high specificity to each other on adjacent cells (Kemler, 1992a). These proteins are expressed in distinct patterns during tissue and organ morphogenesis, suggesting that they play an important and direct role in the temporal and spatial regulation of cell interactions and cell sorting during tissue formation. Furthermore, loss of expression of these proteins correlates with loss of intercellular adhesion, which is an early event in the induction of metastatic disease (Vieminckx et al., 1991).

Two functionally distinct mechanisms of cell adhesion have been described: Ca^{2+}-dependent, and Ca^{2+}-independent adhesion (Takeichi, 1977). Both processes are mediated by cell surface glycoproteins that have been classified into three major families of cell adhesion molecules (CAMs): the immunoglobulin (Ig) superfamily, integrins and cadherins (Kemler, 1992b). N-CAM is a well characterized member of the Ig superfamily of CAMs; its interactions on adjacent cells are homotypic and Ca^{2+}-independent (Goridis and Brunet, 1992). Early studies on the function of N-CAM in proteoliposomes provided direct biochemical evidence of modulation of CAM avidity by CAM concentration; a 2-fold increase in the amount of N-CAM produced a 30-fold increase in its binding (Goridis and Brunet, 1992; Rutishauser et al., 1982). The integrin family of CAMs is primarily involved in cell interactions with the substratum (Sanchez-Madrid and Corbí, 1992). However, LFA-1, a member of the integrin family expressed on lymphocytes, interacts with I-CAM, a ligand on the surface of endothelial cells (Sanchez-Madrid and Corbí, 1992). The cadherin family of CAMs mediates Ca^{2+}-dependent cell-cell adhesion in a wide variety of cell types (Kemler, 1992a). Here we discuss possible mechanisms for modulating cadherin function.

CADHERIN FAMILY MEMBERS

Three basic classes of cadherins have been characterized, E-, P- and N-cadherin (Kemler, 1992a; Takeichi, 1977). Initial evidence that cadherins play a role in modulating cell interactions was obtained using antibodies raised against the extracellular domain of a given cadherin, which was released from cells by trypsin in the presence of Ca^{2+} (Gumbiner and Simons, 1986). These antibodies inhibit cell-cell adhesion and cause clusters of cells to disaggregate in tissue culture. Addition of specific cadherin antibodies to preimplantation embryos blocks compaction, and their addition to develop-

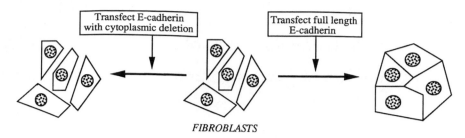

Fig. 1. Fibroblast expression system for analyzing cadherin functions. Fibroblasts do not express cadherins. However, transfection of cadherin full-length cDNA results in expression of the protein at the cell surface, interaction with endogenous catenins, and induction of Ca^{2+}-dependent cell-cell adhesion. Truncation of part of the C-terminal cytoplasmic domain of cadherins results in loss of catenin binding and cell-cell adhesion (for details, see text).

ing tissues in the embryo inhibits further development; similar results have been obtained with antibodies to other CAMs (reviewed by Kemler, 1992a).

Molecular analysis of cadherin structure has provided important insights into the function of different protein domains in homotypic binding between cadherins, and interactions between cadherins and cytoplasmic proteins (Fig. 1). Cadherins span the membrane once with their N termini located in the extracellular space and their C termini in the cytoplasm (Kemler, 1992a); one exception is T-cadherin, which lacks the transmembrane domain and the cytoplasmic tail and appears to be anchored to the membrane via a glycophosphotidylinositol moiety (Vestal and Ranscht, 1992). Different cadherins exhibit an overall sequence identity of 43-58% (Kemler, 1992a). The extracellular domain of different cadherins exhibits the least homology, while the cytoplasmic domain has the highest homology. The extracellular domain comprises three repeat domains (Fig. 1), each of which contains two putative Ca^{2+} binding sites (Ringwald et al., 1987). Mutagenesis of an amino acid in one of the Ca^{2+}-binding sites in the N-terminal repeat domain abolishes cell adhesion (Ozawa et al., 1990a). Recent evidence suggests that the N-terminal repeat contains a cell adhesion recognition motif (Nose et al., 1990). The N-terminal 113 amino acid domain contains a tripeptide, *HAV*, that is highly conserved between cadherin classes (Fig. 1). Antibodies raised against this domain inhibit cadherin function and block cell adhesion (Nose et al., 1990). Additionally, synthetic peptides containing the sequence *HAV* inhibit compaction of mouse preimplantation embryos, which normally occurs through E-cadherin-induced cell adhesion (Blaschuk et al., 1990). These results indicate that the N-terminal repeat domain of cadherins may be important for homotypic binding function. However, little is known about the affinity of these interactions, or whether the cytoplasmic domain plays a role in modulating the avidity of homotypic E-cadherin binding.

Definitive evidence that cadherins are involved in homotypic binding in cell-cell adhesion was obtained when cadherin cDNAs were expressed in fibroblasts (Nagafuchi et al., 1987). Fibroblasts do not exhibit significant Ca^{2+}-dependent cell adhesion properties. However, expression of cadherins in these cells results in Ca^{2+}-dependent cell-cell recognition and the formation of compact cell aggregates (colonies) similar to those formed by epithelial cells (Nagafuchi et al., 1987; see Fig. 1). Mixtures of cells expressing

different classes of cadherins sort out from one another such that cells expressing the same cadherin class, or similar cell surface levels of cadherin, form separate aggregates (Nose et al., 1988). Through studies of cadherin function in this fibroblast expression system, evidence has also been obtained that the cytoplasmic domain of cadherins plays an important role in cell adhesion (Fig. 2). Deletions of the C-terminal half of the cytoplasmic domain result in the expression of a truncated protein at the cell surface with an intact extracellular domain (Ozawa et al., 1989). These cells do not form stable cell-cell contacts, or localize cadherin to cell-cell contacts, even when the cells are grown at high density (McNeill et al., 1990; Ozawa et al., 1989). The loss of cadherin function as a result of these cytoplasmic deletions appears to be due, at least in part, to loss of interactions with cytoplasmic proteins.

CADHERIN-ASSOCIATED CYTOPLASMIC PROTEINS

Indirect evidence that cadherins associate with cytoplasmic proteins has come from the observation that cadherins co-localize to sites of cell contact with actin-associated junctions (Hirano et al., 1987). In addition, a limited number of cytoplasmic proteins have been found to co-immunoprecipitate with cadherins solubilized from whole cells (Fig. 3). The most prominent of these cytoplasmic proteins have apparent molecular masses of 102,000, 92,000 and 84,000 Da and have been termed α-, β- and γ-catenin, respectively (Ozawa et al., 1989). Insight into the possible function of two of the catenins has been recently obtained.

α-Catenin

α-Catenin is approximately 30% identical to vinculin within three conserved domains (Herrenknecht et al., 1991; Nagafuchi et al., 1991). These domains include a region of vinculin that is known to bind talin as well as a region that is thought to be involved in the binding of vinculin molecules to one another (Jones et al., 1989; Molony and Burridge, 1985; Molony-Milam, 1985). Vinculin is found in cell-cell and cell-substratum adhesions and appears to be involved in linking membrane proteins to the cortical cytoskeleton. Similarly, α-catenin may link cadherins to the actin cytoskeleton that co-localizes with cadherin in adherens junctions. It has been demonstrated that the interaction of

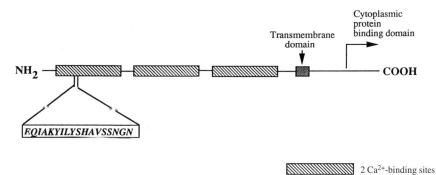

Fig. 2. E-cadherin functional domains (for details, see text).

2 Ca²⁺-binding sites

cadherin complexes with DNAse I (presumably via actin) is dependent on the ability of the cadherin to interact with catenins (Ozawa et al., 1990b).

Cells lacking α-catenin are unable to form stable contacts despite high expression levels of E-cadherin and β-catenin. The ability of these cells to adhere to one another is increased dramatically by the introduction of a neuronal isoform of α-catenin which has been identified as an N-cadherin-associated protein and shows 82% similarity to α-catenin (Hirano et al., 1992). Similarly, cells expressing α-catenin and β-catenin, but lacking cadherins, can be induced to form an epithelioid phenotype by the introduction of N-cadherin or E-cadherin (Hirano et al., 1992). This shows that different cadherin subtypes can interact with different isoforms of α-catenin and vice versa.

β-Catenin/plakoglobin/armadillo family of proteins

The sequence of β-catenin shows ~65% similarity to armadillo, a segment polarity gene in *Drosophila* (McCrea et al., 1991). Additionally, β-catenin shows ~60% similarity to plakoglobin, a major component of desmosomes also found associated with cadherin complexes in adherens junctions. Since plakoglobin and armadillo also share 63% similarity, plakoglobin and β-catenin are considered to be the vertebrate homologues of armadillo (McCrea et al., 1991;

Peifer et al., 1992). All three proteins contain internal repeats in the central part of the protein that may be involved in the formation of homo- or hetero-oligomers (Peifer et al., 1992). All members of this protein family are localized to the plasma membrane and the lateral regions of polarized cells, where they co-localize with the actin cytoskeleton and are associated with intercellular junctions (Peifer and Wiechaus, 1990). All three proteins have been detected in both cytoskeletal-associated and cytoplasmic pools, as judged by Triton X-100 extractability (Peifer et al., 1992; Peifer and Wieschaus, 1990; Riggleman et al., 1990).

γ-Catenin

The amino acid sequence for γ-catenin has not been identified. Its apparent molecular mass is identical to that of plakoglobin and the suggestion that these two proteins are identical has been made (Knudsen and Wheelock, 1992; Peifer et al., 1992). Two pieces of evidence seem to contradict this suggestion: in two-dimensional gels of E-cadherin immunoprecipitates, a protein with a much more acidic pI than plakoglobin can be resolved from plakoglobin; also, E-cadherin immunoprecipitates from which all plakoglobin has been removed still contain a protein that migrates with the same size as γ-catenin (Piepenhagen and Nelson, 1993). However, further study of this putative γ-catenin has

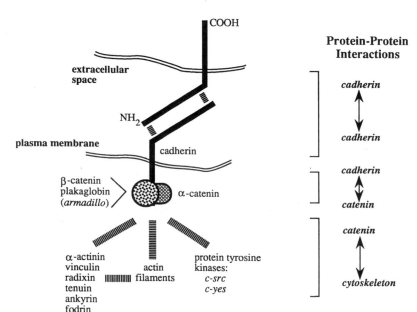

Fig. 3. Protein-protein interactions between the cytoplasmic domain of cadherins, and cytoplasmic proteins - evidence for a linkage between cadherins and the cytoskeleton (for details, see text).

revealed that it may be a proteolytic fragment of cadherin, thereby supporting the idea that plakoglobin is indeed γ-catenin (A. Barth and W. J. Nelson, unpublished observation).

The binding site(s) for catenins on the cytoplasmic domain of cadherins is poorly understood. However, none of the catenins, or membrane-cytoskeleton proteins, are associated with truncated cadherin containing a 72 amino acid deletion of the C-terminal cytoplasmic domain, called LΔC4-17, indicating that these cytoplasmic proteins bind to this region (Ozawa et al., 1989). Since cells expressing cadherin mutant LΔC4-17, lacking the binding site(s) for these cytoplasmic proteins, do not form cell-cell contacts, it is possible that this linkage may play a role in modulating cell adhesion, perhaps by clustering cadherins at the cell surface and increasing the avidity of binding. However, nothing is known about the mechanisms of interaction between cadherins and these cytoplasmic proteins, or their specific roles in modulating cell adhesion.

FROM CELL ADHESION TO CELLULAR REORGANIZATION: REGULATION OF CADHERIN FUNCTION

The results discussed above indicate that cadherins mediate cell-cell recognition and adhesion, and that a direct linkage between cadherins and cytoplasmic (cytoskeletal) proteins is important in cell adhesion and cellular morphogenesis. However, the mechanism(s) involving transduction of cell-cell adhesion, through cadherins, into the reorganization of cell structure and function is unknown. Several levels of complexity are possible. The mechanism could involve increased local concentrations of cadherins at sites of cell-cell contact that cause multivalent stabilization of weak interactions with cytoplasmic proteins through the cytoskeleton. Several examples of this type of mechanism have been cited, including the activation of complement by the binding of Clq to cell surface antigen-IgG complexes, and cellular degranulation triggered by extracellular cross-linking of IgE-receptor complexes (Labrecque et al., 1989; Peerschke and Ghebrehiwet, 1990).

Signal transduction could (also) be involved in mediating cell adhesion by cadherins. Occupancy of cadherin (homotypic binding) could result in the activation of a classical signal transduction response through second messengers (Ca^{2+}, inositol phosphates, protein kinase C). Evidence that second messengers may be involved in N-CAM-mediated adhesion has been reported by Schuch et al. (1989) (see also Doherty et al., 1991), who demonstrated that addition of antibodies to the extracellular domain of the cell adhesion proteins N-CAM or L1 to PC12 cells induced an increase in intracellular Ca^{2+} levels, and a reduction in inositol phosphates and intracellular pH.

EARLY EVENTS IN CELL-CELL INTERACTIONS: FORMATION OF TRANSIENT AND STABLE CELL-CELL CONTACTS

Recent studies have begun to analyze in detail the interaction between epithelial cells and the consequences of cell adhesion on the formation of structurally and functionally distinct membrane domains. These studies indicate that the interaction of cadherin molecules on the surface of neighboring cells is the initial event in a cascade of events that eventually lead to major morphological and biochemical changes within the cells participating in making contacts.

During the initial phases of cell contacts, cells extend a number of filopodia towards one another, transiently form cell contacts which are then retracted, and then establish a stable cell contact. After a variable period of time, the stable contact begins to spread along the apposed membranes by a zippering activity, rather than through the coalescence of multiple individual contacts along the apposed membranes (McNeill et al., 1993). This suggests that a nucleating event may be needed in order to form a stable contact. The direction of zippering does not appear to be biased towards previous sites of transient contacts.

Analysis of the Triton X-100 insolublity of E-cadherin, a preliminary assay for association with the cytoskeleton, revealed no detectable protein at the contact at the time of initiation of a stable cell contact or during the following 10 minutes. However, after ~10 minutes of stable cell contact, rapid acquisition of Triton X-100 insolubility was detected specifically at the contact site (McNeill et al., 1993). It is possible that the increase in the Triton X-100 insoluble pool of E-cadherin was due to accumulation of protein at the contact site. However, the total amount of E-cadherin at the contact remains unchanged during this time (McNeill et al., 1993).

One possible interpretation of the acquisition of Triton X-100 insolubility is that E-cadherin becomes associated with the cytoskeleton after 10 minutes of stable cell-cell contact. However, it is also possible that this is a reflection of another form of molecular reorganization of E-cadherin, like the lateral aggregation of many E-cadherin molecules. The increase in the Triton X-100 insoluble pool of E-cadherin did not correlate with changes in the distribution of actin or fodrin, suggesting that the acquisition of the Triton X-100 insolublity is due to changes in E-cadherin itself, or other closely associated proteins such as the catenins.

MODULATION OF CADHERIN FUNCTION AND DISTRIBUTION DURING THE FORMATION OF CELL-CELL CONTACTS

At present, we have little information on the mechanisms involved in the formation of transient or stable cell-cell contacts. The transient contacts may be mediated by low affinity interactions between randomly distributed cadherin molecules on the surface. This interaction may generate intracellular signals that cause the recruitment of cadherin molecules to the region of the initial contact to increase the local concentration of cadherins leading to the stabilization of cell contacts and the formation of stable adherens junctions.

Signal transduction and second messengers

The signals that could mediate the recruitment of cadherin to sites of cell contact include the activation of second messenger pathways involving G-proteins and the activation of kinases and/or phosphatases. G-proteins have been described to play a role in the morphoregulatory activities of N-cadherin as well as the calcium-independent adhesion molecule N-CAM (Doherty et al., 1991; Schuch et al., 1989). These studies revealed that morphogenic changes mediated by N-cadherin and N-CAM could be inhibited by pertussis toxin, a known inhibitor of G-proteins. The G proteins appeared (at least in part) to mediate their effect by opening calcium channels which in turn could lead to the activation of other intracellular factors that act on the proteins involved in adhesion.

Preliminary results also indicate that extracellular activation of E-cadherin may initiate signal transduction events. It is not clear, however, how, in the cases of these single membrane-spanning proteins, homotypic extracellular binding is transduced across the membrane. Classical studies of signal transduction by the EGF receptor show that binding of EGF induces dimerization of the receptor (Hurwitz et al., 1991) which results in activation of the receptor tyrosine kinase (Kashles et al., 1991). The dimerization is mediated by a region of the protein near the transmembrane domain. E-cadherin and the EGF receptor share amino acid homology in this region, suggesting that E-cadherin may also dimerize.

A change in the phosphorylation state of cadherins and associated proteins may cause a change in the ability of the complex to interact with cytoskeletal components or with other complexes. The cytoskeletal proteins adducin and ankyrin are modulated by phosphorylation, and their ability to crosslink spectrin networks depends on their phosphorylation (Bennett, 1990). E-cadherin and the catenins are phosphorylated in vivo but a correlation between their assembly into complexes with the cytoskeleton or their adhesive function and their phosphorylation state has not been established. However, the observation that tyrosine phosphorylation by v-src interferes with cadherin-mediated cell adhesion suggests a role for phosphorylation in this process (Matsuyoshi et al., 1992). It is possible that the phosphorylation of catenins and/or cadherins modulates the binding of cadherin-catenin complexes to the cytoskeleton or to each other. If each component of the complex regulated different interactions, the activation of kinases or phosphatases specific for each component would regulate different functions of the adhesion complex. This could provide a complex regulatory mechanism that can be finely tuned by the action of several different, possibly independently regulated components.

Regulation of complex formation with catenins

Adhesive function and distribution of cadherin at the cell surface may be modulated by regulation of the binding of cadherin with catenins. Both β-catenin and plakoglobin associate with cadherins immediately following synthesis (Ozawa and Kemler, 1992), indicating that binding is a constitutive process and does not occur in response to cell contact. Newly synthesized α-catenin, on the other hand, is not found in association with newly made cadherin until 30-60 minutes after synthesis (Ozawa and Kemler, 1992) (L. Hinck, J. Papkoff, W. J. Nelson and I. S. Näthke, in preparation); this is similar to the time required for newly syn-

thesized cadherin to be transported to the cell surface (Siemers et al., in preparation). Similarly, β-catenin appears in sites of cell contact with the same kinetics as cadherin after cell contact is initiated, whereas α-catenin is not found at these sites until later times (Hinck et al., in preparation). A large portion of α-catenin is not associated with cadherin and α-catenin is more easily removed from cadherin than β-catenin (McCrea and Gumbiner, 1991; Ozawa and Kemler, 1992). These observations suggest that α-catenin may be able to exchange from one cadherin molecule at the cell surface to another, thus modulating cadherin function at the cell surface. The presence of a large non-cadherin associated pool of α-catenin further reveals that α-catenin may have functions unrelated to cadherin-mediated adhesion.

Based on its similarity to vinculin, it has been proposed that α-catenin links cadherins to the cytoskeleton (Nagafuchi et al., 1991). If indeed it only associates with cadherin on the cell surface it may modulate the association of cadherin-catenin complexes with the cytoskeleton in response to cadherin-mediated adhesion. The titration of α-catenin from a Triton X-100-soluble to a Triton X-100-insoluble pool within 2-6 hours after cell contact is consistent with the idea that its association with the cytoskeleton increases after cadherin-mediated cell contact (Hinck et al., in preparation). Cadherins also increase their association with the cytoskeleton after cell contact, but it has not been established that Triton X-100-insoluble cadherin molecules are always associated with α-catenin molecules.

We have recently shown a mutually exclusive association of E-cadherin with the armadillo family members, resulting in the formation of different pools of E-cadherin containing either β-catenin or plakoglobin (Hinck et al., in preparation). Based on the significant sequence similarity between β-catenin and plakoglobin, it is possible that they compete with one another for the same binding site on cadherins. The central domain containing the internal repeats, thought to be responsible for interaction with other proteins, is the most conserved part between these two proteins (and armadillo) and this region may be involved in their interactions with cadherin (Peifer et al., 1992; Peifer and Wiechaus, 1990). We believe the different complexes may have properties that allow them to perform separate functions including the propagation of different signals. A plakoglobin-containing complex may be able to interact with a different set of second messengers from a β-catenin-containing complex, so that stimulation of a cell surface cadherin bound to plakoglobin would initiate a different cascade of events to that initiated by a cadherin bound to β-catenin. The N- and C-terminal regions of plakoglobin and β-catenin display significant sequence disparity (McCrea et al., 1991) and these regions could be responsible for the interaction with different sets of second messenger proteins. Additionally, plakoglobin and β-catenin may be responsible for the ability of the cadherin complex to interact with different cytoskeletal components. It is also possible that interactions between cadherin and either β-catenin or plakoglobin are modulated differently by phosphorylation.

The fact that many vertebrate cells express both, plakoglobin and β-catenin, and that both proteins are associated with cadherin as soon as they are synthesized, raises the question of how the formation of the complex between cadherin and these proteins is regulated. One possibility is that the relative amounts of plakoglobin and β-catenin in the cell determine how many complexes of each type are formed. Alternatively, post-translational modification of either cadherin or plakoglobin and β-catenin may favor one association over the other. Another question that arises from these observations is whether a cadherin - β-catenin complex on one cell can interact only with a cadherin - β-catenin complex on the contacting cell. This would imply that a conformational difference between the two types of complexes is detectable in the extracellular domain of cadherin.

RECRUITMENT OF CADHERIN TO THE CONTACT SITE

Approximately 1 hour after the establishment of a stable contact there is an increase in the amount of E-cadherin at the contact site (McNeill et al., 1993). Recruitment of E-cadherin to the contact site could be due to diffusion of protein from adjacent non-contacting regions of the membrane to the site of cell contact, similar to ligand-induced capping of cell surface receptors. Most ligand receptors are multivalent, but it is possible that cadherin molecules dimerize to form multivalent receptors for each other. E-cadherin dimerization could potentially be mediated by a short amino acid sequence containing four conserved cysteine residues in the extracellular domain of cadherins, near the transmembrane region.

Another source for recruitment of cadherin to the contact site could be intracellular stores that release cadherins specifically at the site of cell contact. Intracellular compartments containing cadherin are observed by immunofluorescence and intracellular cadherin is rapidly recruited to the plasma membrane after removal of surface cadherin with trypsin (Shore et al., in preparation). The compartment that contains the intracellular cadherin stores does not appear to be an early endosome, as cadherin internalized into early endosomes from the surface is rapidly degraded with a half life of less than 3 hours, whereas the intracellular pool has half life of at least 5 hours.

LATE EVENTS IN CELL-CELL INTERACTIONS: REMODELLING OF THE CELL SURFACE

The long-term effects of cadherin-mediated cell adhesion include extensive reorganization of the membrane and cytoskeletal protein composition of the membrane (Rodriguez-Boulan and Nelson, 1989). This is especially important in polarized, transporting epithelial cells in which distinct cell surface domains are established at the contact site (part of the basal-lateral membrane domain), and at the non-contacting membrane (apical membrane domain).

Interactions between E-cadherin and cytoplasmic (cytoskeleton) proteins may be directly involved in generating structurally and functionally distinct membrane domains. E-cadherin-mediated cell-cell contacts in MDCK cells result in the accumulation of E-cadherin, Na+,K+-ATPase and the membrane-cytoskeleton at sites of cell-cell contact; furthermore, protein complexes containing membrane-cytoskeletal proteins and Na+,K+-ATPase and E-cadherin have been isolated from extracts of MDCK cells (Nelson and Hammerton, 1989). We have proposed that the reorganization of Na+,K+-ATPase is driven by assembly of the membrane-cytoskeleton that is induced by E-cadherin-mediated cell-cell adhesion. This hypothesis was tested by analyzing the distribution of these proteins in fibroblasts transfected with E-cadherin constructs (McNeill et al., 1990). Fibroblasts do not normally express E-cadherin, but constitutively express Na+,K+-ATPase and components of the membrane-cytoskeleton which are uniformly distributed at the surface of cells. Expression of E-cadherin in fibroblasts results in the redistribution of these proteins to sites of cell-cell contacts, in a distribution similar to that in polarized MDCK cells (McNeill et al., 1990). This result provides strong evidence that expression of E-cadherin induces a remodelling of the cell surface distribution of an unrelated membrane protein. That this process requires linkage of these two membrane proteins to cytoplasmic (cytoskeleton) proteins was shown by expressing E-cadherin with the deletion comprising the C-terminal 72 amino acids of the cytoplasmic domain (LΔC4-17). Under those conditions, Na+,K+-ATPase and the membrane-cytoskeleton did not localize to cell-cell contacts, presumably due to loss of the linkage between E-cadherin and Na+,K+-ATPase through the membrane-cytoskeleton as a result of the deletion of the cytoplasmic domain of E-cadherin.

At present we do not know the mechanism(s) involved in inducing assembly of the membrane-cytoskeleton at cell-cell contacts. The membrane-cytoskeleton comprises several well-characterized proteins including: ankyrin, fodrin (spectrin), adducin, protein 4.1 and actin (Bennett, 1990). Adducin, protein 4.1 and actin associate with cell-cell contacts in MDCK cells and are thought to function in the interaction of spectrin and actin filaments (Bennett, 1990). The interaction between these proteins and catenins (see above) is not known. It is noteworthy that protein interactions in the membrane-cytoskeleton are regulated by Ca^{2+} and phosphorylation; phosphorylation of protein 4.1 decreases its affinity for spectrin and its ability to mediate spectrin-actin interactions; adducin bundles actin filaments and is a substrate for phosphorylation by protein kinase C. These post-translational modifications may play an important role in modulating membrane-cytoskeleton assembly in response to E-cadherin-mediated cell-cell adhesion.

This work was supported by grants from the NIH (GM35527) and American Cancer Society to W. J. Nelson. Inke S. Näthke is the recipient of a postdoctoral fellowship from the Damon Runyan-Walter Winchell Cancer Resarch Fund, and Lindsay Hinck is the recipient of a Cancer Biology Predoctoral Fellowship. W. J. Nelson is an Established Investigator of the American Heart Association.

REFERENCES

Bennett, V. (1990). Spectrin-based membrane skeleton: A multipotential adaptor between plasma membrane and cytoplasm. *Physiol. Rev.* **70**, 1029-1065.

Blaschuk, O. W., Pouliot, Y. and Holland, P. C. (1990). Identification of a conserved region common to cadherins and influenza strain A hemagglutinin. *Dev. Biol.* **211**, 679-682.

Doherty, P., Ashton, S. V., Moore, S. E. and Walsh, F. S. (1991). Morphoregulatory activities of NCAM and N-cadherin can be accounted for by G-protein dependent activation of L- and N-type neuronal Ca^{2+} channels. *Cell* **67**, 21-33.

Goridis, C. and Brunet, J. (1992). NCAM: structural diversity, function and regulation of expression. *Semin. Cell Biol.* **3**, 189-197

Gumbiner, B. and Simons, K. (1986). A functional assay for proteins involved in establishing an epithelial occluding barrier: identification of a uvomorulin-like polypeptide. *J. Cell Biol.* **102**, 457-68.

Herrenknecht, K., Ozawa, M., Eckerskorn, C., Lottspeich, F., Lenter, M. and Kemler, R. (1991). The uvomorulin-anchorage protein alpha catenin is a vinculin homologue. *Proc. Nat. Acad. Sci. USA* **88**, 9156-9160.

Hirano, S., Kimoto, N., Shimoyama, Y., Hirohashi, S. and Takeichi, M. (1992). Identification of a neural α-catenin as a key regulator of cadherin function and multicellular organization. *Cell* **70**, 293-301.

Hirano, S., Nose, A., Hatta, K., Kawakami, A. and Takeichi, M. (1987). Calcium-dependent cell-cell adhesion molecules (cadherins): subclass specificities and possible involvement of actin bundles. *J. Cell Biol.* **105**, 2501-2510.

Hurwitz, D. R., Emanuel, S. L., Nathan, M. H., Sarver, N., Ullrich, A., Felder, S., Lax, I. and Schlessinger, J. (1991). EGF induces increased ligand binding affinity and dimerization of soluble epidermal growth factor (EGF) receptor extracellular domain. *J. Biol. Chem.* **266**, 22035-22043.

Jones, P., Jackson, P., Price, G. J., Patel, B., Ohanion, V., Lear, A. L. and Critchley, D. R. (1989). Identification of a talin binding site in the cytoskeletal protein vinculin. *J. Cell Biol.* **109**, 2917-2927.

Kashles, O., Yarden, Y., Fischer, R., Ullrich, A. and Schlessinger, J. (1991). A dominant negative mutation suppresses the function of normal epidermal growth factor receptors by heterodimerization. *Mol. Cell. Biol.* **11**, 1454-1463.

Kemler, R. (1992a). Classical cadherins. *Semin. Cell Biol.* **3**, 149-155.

Kemler, R. (1992b). Introduction: Cell adhesion. *Semin. Cell Biol.* **3**, 147-148.

Knudsen, K. A. and Wheelock, M. J. (1992). Plakoglobin, or an 83-kD homologue distinct from beta-catenin, interacts with E-cadherin and N-cadherin. *J. Cell Biol.* **118**, 671-679.

Labrecque, G. F., Holowka, D. and Baird, B. (1989). Anitgen triggered membrane potential changes in IgE sensitized rat basophilic leukemia cells: Evidence for a repolarizing response that is important in the stimulation of cellular degranulation. *J. Immunol.* **142**, 236-243.

Matsuyoshi, N., Hamaguchi, M., Taniguchi, S., Nagafuchi, A., Tsukita, S. and Takeichi, M. (1992). Cadherin-mediated cell-cell adhesion is perturbed by v-*src* tyrosine phosphorylation in metastatic fibroblasts. *J. Cell Biol.* **118**, 703-714.

McCrea, P. D. and Gumbiner, B. (1991). Purification of a 92 kDa cytoplasmic protein tightly associated with the cell-cell adhesion molecule E-cadherin (uvomorulin). *J. Biol. Chem.* **266**, 4514-4520.

McCrea, P. D., Turck, C. W. and Gumbiner, B. (1991). A homolog of the *armadillo* protein in *Drosophila* (plakoglobin) associated with E-cadherin. *Science* **254**, 1359-1361.

McNeill, H., Ozawa, M., Kemler, R. and Nelson, W. J. (1990). Novel function of the cell adhesion molecule uvomorulin as an inducer of cell surface polarity. *Cell* **62**, 309-16.

McNeill, H., Ryan, T., Smith, S. J. and Nelson, W. J. (1993). Spatial and temporal dissection of immediate and early events following cadherin-mediated epithelial cell adhesion. *J. Cell Biol.* **120**, 1217-1227.

Molony, L. and Burridge, K. (1985). Molecular shape and self-association of vinculin and metavinculin. *J. Cell. Biochem.* **29**, 31-36.

Molony-Milam, L. (1985). Electron microscopy of rotary shadowed vinculin and vinculin complexes. *J. Mol. Biol.* **184**, 543-545.

Nagafuchi, A., Shirayoshi, Y., Okazaki, K., Yasuda, K. and Takeichi, M. (1987). Transformation of cell adhesion properties by exogenously introduced E-cadherin cDNA. *Nature* **329**, 340-343.

Nagafuchi, A., Takeichi, M. and Tsukita, S. (1991). The 102 kd cadherin-associated protein: similarity to vinculin and post-transcriptional regulation of expression. *Cell* **65**, 849-57.

Nelson, W. J. and Hammerton, R. W. (1989). A membrane-cytoskeletal complex containing Na^+,K^+-ATPase, ankyrin and fodrin in Madin-Darby canine kidney (MDCK) cells: implications for the biogenesis of epithelial cell polarity. *J. Cell Biol.* **108**, 893-902.

Nose, A., Nagafuchi, A. and Takeichi, M (1988). Expressed recombinant cadherins mediate cell sorting in model systems. *Cell* **54**, 993-1001.

Nose, A., Tsuji, K. and Takeichi, M. (1990). Localization of specificity determining sites in cadherin cell adhesion molecules. *Cell* **61**, 147-155.

Ozawa, M., Baribault, H. and Kemler, R. (1989). The cytoplasmic domain of the cell adhesion molecule uvomorulin associates with three independent proteins structurally related in different species. *EMBO J.* **8**, 1711-7.

Ozawa, M., Engel, J. and Kemler, R. (1990a). Single amino acid substitutions in one Ca2+ binding site of uvomorulin abolish the adhesive function. *Cell* **63**, 1033-1038.

Ozawa, M. and Kemler, R. (1992). Molecular organization of the uvomorulin-catenin complex. *J. Cell Biol.* **116**, 989-996.

Ozawa, M., Ringwald, M. and Kemler, R. (1990b). Uvomorulin-catenin complex formation is regulated by a specific domain in the cytoplasmic region of the cell adhesion molecule. *Proc. Nat. Acad. Sci. USA* **87**, 4246-50.

Peerschke, E. I. and Ghebrehiwet, B. (1990). Modulation of platelet responses to collagen by C1Q receptors. *J. Immunol.* **144**, 221-225.

Peifer, M., McCrea, P. D., Green, K. J., Wieschaus, E. and Gumbiner, B. M. (1992). The vertebrate adhesive junction proteins beta-catenin and plakoglobin and the *Drosophila* segment polarity gene *armadillo* form a multigene family with similar properties. *J. Cell Biol.* **118**, 681-691.

Peifer, M. and Wieschaus, E. (1990). The segment polarity gene *armadillo* encodes a functionally modular protein that is the *Drosophila* homolog of human plakoglobin. *Cell* **63**, 1167-1178.

Piepenhagen, P. A. and Nelson, W. J. (1993). Defining E-cadherin-associated protein complexes in epithelial cells: plakoglobin, β- and γ-catenin are distinct components. *J. Cell Sci.* **104**, 751-762.

Riggleman, B., Schedl, P. and Wieschaus, E. (1990). Spatial expression of the *Drosophila* segment polarity gene *armadillo* is post-transcriptionally regulated by *wingless*. *Cell* **63**, 549-560.

Ringwald, M., Schuh, R., Vestweber, D., Eistetter, H., Lottspeich, F., Engel, J., Dolz, R., Jähnig, F., Epplen, J., Mayer, S., Müller, C. and Kemler, R. (1987). The structure of the cell adhesion molecule uvomorulin. Insights into the molecular mechanisms of Ca^{2+}-dependent cell adhesion. *EMBO J.* **6**, 3647-3653.

Rodriguez-Boulan, E. and Nelson, W. J. (1989). Morphogenesis of the polarized epithelial cell phenotype. *Science* **245**, 718-725.

Rutishauser, U., Hoffman, S. and Edelman, G. M. (1982). Binding properties of a cell adhesion molecule from neuronal tissue. *Proc. Nat. Acad. Sci. USA* **79**, 685-689.

Sanchez-Madrid, F. and Corbí, A. L. (1992). Leukocyte integrins: structure, function and regulation of their activity. *Semin. Cell Biol.* **3**, 199-210.

Schuch, U., Lohse, M. J. and Schachner, M. (1989). Neural cell adhesion molecules influence second messenger systems. *Neuron* **3**, 13-20.

Takeichi, M. (1977). Functional correlation between cell adhesive properties and some cell surface proteins. *J. Cell Biol.* **75**, 464-474.

Trinkaus, J. P. (1984). *Cells into Organs*. Prentice Hall.

Vestal, D. J. and Ranscht, B. (1992). Glycosyl phosphatidylinositol-anchored T-cadherin mediates calcium-dependent, homophilic cell adhesion. *J. Cell Biol.* **119**, 451-461.

Vieminckx, K., Vakaet, J. L., Mareel, M., Fiers, W. and Van Roy, F. (1991). Genetic manipulation of E-cadherin expression by epithelial tumor cells reveals an invasion suppressor role. *Cell* **66**, 107-119.

Journal of Cell Science, Supplement 17, 147-154 (1993)
Printed in Great Britain © The Company of Biologists Limited 1993

Characterization of recombinant E-cadherin (uvomorulin) expressed in insect cells

Kurt Herrenknecht* and Rolf Kemler

Max-Planck-Institut für Immunbiologie, Stübeweg 51, D-79108 Freiburg, Germany

*Present address: Eisai London Research Laboratories Ltd, Bernard Katz Building, University College London, Gower Street, London WC1E 6BT, UK

SUMMARY

Cadherins are Ca^{2+}-dependent cell adhesion molecules that mediate cell adhesion by homophilic binding. Structural and functional analysis of the extracellular part of cadherins that mediates this binding has often been hampered by the availability of sufficient amount of protein. Therefore, we have expressed the extracellular region of E-cadherin (uvomorulin) using the baculovirus expression vector system (BEVS). A recombinant baculovirus was generated that encodes the signal peptide, the precursor region and the extracellular part of the mature protein, under the control of the promotor for polyhedrin. Infection of insect cells with recombinant virus led to the expression of about 40 mg of the E-cadherin fragment per 2×10^9 infected cells. About half of the protein synthesized was secreted, either as mature protein or in its unprocessed form. The precursor pep-tide was removed by trypsin treatment in the presence of Ca^{2+} and recombinant protein was purified to homogeneity. Biochemical characterization of the recombinant protein revealed a high degree of similarity with the mouse wild-type protein. Recombinant protein exhibited the known resistance to trypsin in the presence of Ca^{2+} and was recognized by two different conformation-sensitive monoclonal anti-E-cadherin antibodies. Rabbit antibodies made against the recombinant protein recognized E-cadherin from different species. In spite of the high degree of structural resemblance recombinant E-cadherin was not able to inhibit E-cadherin mediated cell-cell adhesion.

Key words: cell adhesion molecule, recombinant E-cadherin

INTRODUCTION

Cell-cell interaction during development and in adult tissue is largely mediated by four major protein families of cell adhesion molecules (CAMs), i.e. integrins, the Ig-super-family, selectins and cadherins (for review see Hynes and Lander, 1992). Cadherins comprise the group of Ca^{2+}-dependent CAMs that exhibit their adhesive function only in the presence of Ca^{2+} and that show a remarkable Ca^{2+}-dependent resistance against proteolytic degradation.

The classical cadherins E- (uvomorulin), N-, P-cadherin and L-CAM have been identified in a functional cell adhesion assay in different cell types (Takeichi, 1988; Kemler et al., 1989). Subsequent molecular cloning and comparison of the primary structure revealed that these proteins are highly homologous. Many new members of the cadherin gene family have recently been identified by structural homology (Kemler, 1992). Although involvement in cell-cell interaction has not been demonstrated in all cases, some of these new cadherins are likely to exhibit important biological functions.

Cadherins are cell surface glycoproteins with a single transmembrane domain. Trypsin digestion in the presence of Ca^{2+} releases the extracellular portion of cadherins as a soluble, stable fragment (gp84). The extracellular part of the proteins is largely composed of three repeating domains with internal homology of about 25-30% at the amino acid level (Ringwald et al., 1987). Remarkably, these individual domains are much more strongly conserved between different cadherins, with the most amino-terminal domain exhibiting the highest degree of homology (about 70%). Each of the cadherin domains contains two characteristic motifs for Ca^{2+}-binding, which are located at similar positions in all domains. Secondary structure analysis predicts a loop structure for these motifs. Site-directed mutagenesis in one Ca^{2+}-binding motif demonstrated that the motifs represent structural requirements for the adhesive function of cadherins (Ozawa et al., 1990). It is generally accepted that cad-herins interact in a homophilic manner although the molecular mechanism of this interaction is not completely understood. In order to study the homophilic interaction of cadherins and the role of Ca^{2+} for cadherin structure and function we have expressed the extracellular region of E-cadherin in insect cells using the baculovirus expression vector system.

MATERIALS AND METHODS

Baculovirus expression system

Sf158 cells derived from the fall armyworm *Spodoptera frugiperda* (Vaughn et al., 1977), wild-type baculovirus *Autographa californica* nuclear polyhedrosis virus (AcNPV) and the transfer vector pAc373 were all kindly provided by Dr N. Mueller-Lantzsch (University Hospital Homburg/Saar, Germany) and were used, with permission from Dr M. Summers (Texas A. and M. University, USA).

Antibodies

Rat monoclonal antibodies DE-1 (Hyafil et al., 1981) and DECMA-1 (Vestweber and Kemler, 1985) were raised against the tryptic fragment of mouse E-cadherin (gp84), as was the polyclonal rabbit antiserum anti-gp84 (Vestweber and Kemler, 1984a). Anti-UM/P are polyclonal rabbit antibodies directed against the precursor portion of mouse E-cadherin (Ozawa and Kemler, 1990). Anti-r-gp84 was produced in rabbits by s.c. and i.m. injections of recombinant E-cadherin (30 µg mixed with complete Freund's adjuvant for the first and incomplete adjuvant for all subsequent immunizations).

Cell culture and virus infection

Sf158 cells were cultured at 27°C as monolayers or in suspension in TC-100 medium (Gibco) with 10% heat-inactivated fetal calf serum (FCS) (Summers and Smith, 1987). Viral infections were done using a multiplicity of infection (m.o.i.) of 1 for propagation of virus and a m.o.i. of 10 for production of recombinant protein (Summers and Smith, 1987). Mouse teratocarcinoma cells PCC4a-za1 (Nicholas et al., 1975) were grown in Dulbecco's modified Eagle's medium (DMEM) (Gibco), 15% FCS, in a 10% CO_2 atmosphere at 37°C.

Construction of a baculovirus transfer vector and generation of a recombinant baculovirus

Standard recombinant DNA techniques were used (Sambrook et al., 1989). A *Bgl*II-*Hin*dIII cDNA clone encoding full-length mouse E-cadherin in pBluescript (Ozawa et al., 1989) was cleaved with *Bst*EII and *Hin*dIII to remove the coding sequences for the cytoplasmic domain, the transmembrane domain and 30 amino acid residues of the membrane proximal part of the extracellular region (numbering is according to Ringwald et al., 1987). The plasmid was ligated with a double-stranded synthetic oligonucleotide encoding the extracellular amino acids 3' of the *Bst*EII site, which terminates with codon 543, coding for lysine, and was followed by a stop codon and an artificial *Bgl*II and *Hin*dIII site. This plasmid encoded the entire extracellular part of E-cadherin (including signal and propeptide) and was cloned as a *Bgl*II fragment into the *Bam*HI site of the baculovirus transfer vector pAc373. The final transfer plasmid pAcUm84 contained the E-cadherin start signal for translation and had a 5' nontranslated leader sequence of 27 nucleotides, which is not present in the original polyhedrin gene.

For the generation of recombinant baculovirus, Sf158 cells were cotransfected with circular plasmid pAcUm84 and wild-type AcNPV DNA using the calcium phosphate precipitation technique (Summers and Smith, 1987; Method I). Culture medium containing wild-type and recombinant extracellular virions as collected after 7 days and 6000 p.f.u. were screened for recombinants by dot blot hybridization according to Pen et al. (1989) using the *Bgl*II fragment of pBsUm84 as a probe. Since recombinant viruses turned out to be contaminated by wild-type viruses E-cadherin-positive isolates were additionally subjected to plaque-purification (Summers and Smith, 1987). Briefly, Sf158 cells were infected with dilutions of isolates containing recombinants and after 7 days cells were transferred to nitrocellulose filters and lysed by placing filters on Whatman 3MM paper soaked in 5% SDS for 10 minutes. Filters were baked (1 hour at 50°C) and SDS was removed electrophoretically (buffer: 25 mM Tris-HCl, pH 8.8, 192 mM glycine, 20% (v/v) methanol). Plaques were screened by an immunoblotting procedure with anti-gp84 antibodies. After three rounds of plaque purification recombinant virus strain AcNPV/Um84-1 was isolated and propagated (Summers and Smith, 1987).

Characterization of recombinant protein

Recombinant E-cadherin was characterized from cell extracts or culture medium of infected Sf158 cells grown in 25 cm² flasks. Cells were infected with AcNPV wild-type virus or AcNPV/Um84-1 at MOI of 10. After 1 hour the inoculum was removed and the cells were cultured in TC-100 with or without FCS. For glycosylation studies medium was supplemented with 2 µg/ml tunicamycin (Sigma). For metabolic labeling experiments infected cells (24 hours p.i.) were cultured for 1-2 hours in methionine- and cysteine-free TC-100 and were labeled with L-[^{35}S]methionine and L-[^{35}S]cysteine (each 50 µCi/ml, >1000 Ci/mmol) for 12-16 hours. Unless otherwise stated, 70- to 72-hour p.i. cells and medium were separately subjected to SDS-PAGE and immunochemical analysis. Standard procedures were used for immunoblot and immunoprecipitation analyses (Ozawa et al., 1989). To analyze trypsinized material PCC4aza1 cells and culture medium of AcNPV/Um84-1-infected cells were incubated with 0.1% (w/v) trypsin (Sigma, Type XI) in the presence of 2 mM $CaCl_2$ for 30 minutes at 37°C and subsequently adjusted to 0.2% (w/v) soybean trypsin inhibitor.

Production and purification of r-gp84

For large-scale production of recombinant E-cadherin 2×10^{10} Sf158 cells were infected with AcNPV/Um84-1 (m.o.i.=10) and the culture medium (10 l) of cells grown in serum-free medium was harvested at 72 hours p.i. Extracellular virions were removed by ultrafiltration using the Minitan Acrylglas-Ultrafiltration-System (Millipore), with filters of an exclusion size of 300 kDa (PTMK 300,000 NMGG). The filtrate was concentrated to 100 ml using the same system, with filters of an exclusion size of 30 kDa (PTTK 30,000 NMGG). The concentrate was adjusted to 2 mM $CaCl_2$ and incubated for 2 hours at 37°C with 0.1% (w/v) trypsin (Sigma, Type XI). After extensive ultrafiltration as described above (30 kDa membranes) in 20 mM Tris-HCl, pH 7.5, containing 2 mM $CaCl_2$ (TC-buffer) to remove large amount of trypsin, the material was extensively dialyzed against TC-buffer. The material was applied to a 20 ml TC-equilibrated TSK DEAE-650(S) column (Merck, FPLC, flow rate: 3 ml/min 120 ml, linear gradient of 0 to 0.5 M NaCl in TC). Peak fractions containing r-gp84 were identified by immunoblotting with anti-E-cadherin antibodies and peak fractions were concentrated in Amicon microconcentrators (30 kDa) to a final volume of 1 ml. Concentrated r-gp84 was subjected to gel filtration on a HiLoad 26/60 Superdex 200 prep grade column (Pharmacia) by FPLC (TC-buffer containing 200 mM NaCl, flow rate: 1 ml/min). The r-gp84-containing fractions (although homogeneously purified) still exhibited residual trypsin activity. Therefore, the material was treated twice with 1 ml of carrier-fixed α_2-macroglobulin (Boehringer) equilibrated with 20 mM Tris-HCl, pH 8.2, containing 2 mM $CaCl_2$ plus 200 mM NaCl. Purification steps were quantified using the BCA Protein Assay (Pierce) and analyzed qualitatively by SDS-PAGE analysis and silver staining according to Blum et al. (1987).

Cell adhesion assays

Ca^{2+}-dependent cell aggregation assays (Ozawa et al., 1990) and cell decompaction assays (Vestweber and Kemler, 1984a) were performed using the embryonal carcinoma cell line, PCC4aza1. Mouse preimplantation embryos at the early 8-cell stage were collected from superovulated NMRI females, freed of their zona pellucida and cultured in M6 medium as described (Hogan et al., 1986).

RESULTS

Generation of recombinant baculovirus

The extracellular part of mature E-cadherin contains 42 possible trypsin cleavage sites (trypsin cleaves carboxy-terminal of lysine and arginine). The exact trypsin cleavage site that generates the gp84 fragment from wild-type E-cadherin is not known. Therefore a cDNA was constructed that ended 3′ of position 545 (Lys), encoding a protein that includes the last possible trypsin cleavage site close to the predicted transmembrane domain. The cDNA construct encoding the signal peptide, the precursor region and the extracellular part of the mature protein was cloned in the baculovirus transfer vector pAc373 and subsequently introduced into the genome of the *Autographa californica* nuclear polyhedrosis virus (AcNPV) to generate the recombinant virus AcNPV/Um84-1 by homologous recombination. Site-directed insertion was confirmed by Southern blot analysis (not shown).

Expression of recombinant protein

It was expected that recombinant baculovirus AcNPV/Um84-1 generates a protein that is secreted into the culture medium of infected cells. Culture medium of metabolically labeled Sf158 cells that were either mock infected or infected with wild-type AcNPV or AcNPV/Um84-1 virus were subjected to SDS-PAGE and radio-fluorography. AcNPV/Um84-1-infected cells specifically expressed two proteins with apparent molecular masses of 100 and 80 kDa (Fig. 1, Medium). These proteins were recognized by anti-E-cadherin antibodies in immunoprecipitation (Fig. 1, IP) and immunoblot experiments (Fig. 1, IB). Culture medium of uninfected Sf158 cells and cells infected with wild-type baculovirus were negative in these experiments (not shown). As shown below (see Fig. 4), the 100 kDa protein corresponds to the precursor of E-cadherin and the 80 kDa protein to the processed recombinant form. These results indicate that a substantial amount of recombinant protein is secreted in its unprocessed form.

Synthesis of both proteins started around 24 hours p.i. and reached the highest level at about 48 hours p.i. (Fig. 2). Maximum yields of protein were observed around 72 hours p.i. The relative amounts of secreted versus intracel-

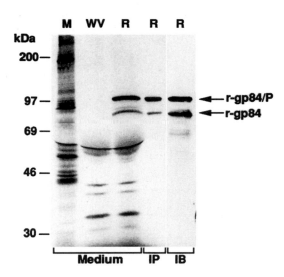

Fig. 1. Expression of recombinant E-cadherin in Sf158 cells. Sf158 cells (3×10^6) were either mock infected (M), or infected with AcNPV wild-type virus (WV) or AcNPV/Um84-1 (R), metabolically labeled and the culture supernatant was analyzed. Medium, culture supernatants, each 50,000 counts (TCA-precipitable) IP, immunoprecipitation with anti-E-cadherin antibodies from culture supernatant of 3.75×10^5 labeled cells infected with AcNPV/Um84-1. IB, immunoblot analysis with supernatant of 1.5×10^5 AcNPV/Um84-1-infected cells with anti-E-cadherin antibodies.

lular protein were compared by quantitative immunoprecipitations from culture medium versus immunoblot analysis from whole cell lysates of AcNPV/Um84-1-infected Sf158 cells at 70 hours p.i. As shown in Fig. 3B, about 50% of the recombinant protein was found to be secreted. Estimating from Coomassie Blue-stained gels this amount corresponds to 40 mg protein per 2×10^9 infected cells grown in the presence of FCS (Fig. 3A).

Immunochemical characterization of recombinant proteins

The secreted recombinant proteins were tested in immunoprecipitation experiments with different anti-E-cadherin antibodies, i.e. rat monoclonal antibody DE-1 and DECMA-1, rabbit anti-precursor peptide (anti-Um/P) and rabbit anti-wild-type gp84 (anti-gp84). DE-1 and DECMA-1 reacted with both the 100 kDa and the 80 kDa protein, as did antigp84 (Fig. 4, left panel). However, antibodies against

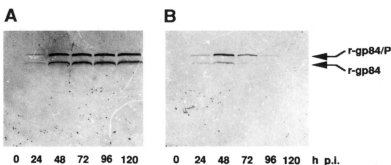

Fig. 2. Kinetics of E-cadherin expression. Sf158 cells were infected with AcNPV/Um84-1 and cultured for 120 hours. In (A) 12 µl samples of culture medium were collected every 24 hours without changing the medium. (B) as in (A) but culture medium was renewed every 24 hours. Immunoblot analysis was carried out with anti-E-cadherin antibodies.

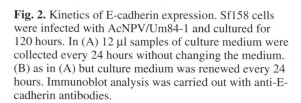

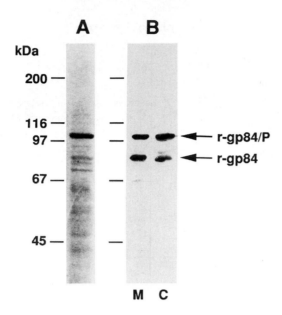

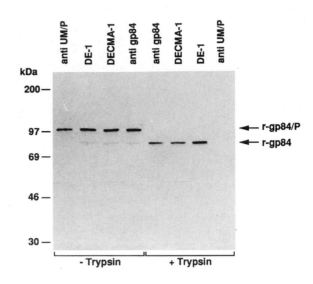

Fig. 3. Synthesis of recombinant E-cadherin. (A) Sf158 cells were infected with AcNPV/Um84-1 and grown in suspension at a cell density of 2×10⁶ cells/ml in the absence of FCS; 75 µl of culture medium (72 hours p.i.) was subjected to SDS-PAGE analysis and stained with Coomassie Brillant Blue. The amount of E-cadherin as calculated by comparison with BSA was 0.75 µg protein for 1.5×10⁵ infected cells. (B) Culture medium (M) from 2.25×10⁵ AcNPV/Um84-1-infected cells was subjected to quantitative immunoprecipitation with anti-E-cadherin antibodies 70 hours p.i. The precipitated recombinant protein was compared with r-gp84 in cell extracts of the respective cells by immunoblot analysis (C). About 50% of the recombinant protein is secreted.

Fig. 4. Precursor and processed recombinant E-cadherin. Culture supernatant of metabolically labeled Sf158 cells infected with AcNPV/Um84-1 with or without trypsin treatment was immunoprecipitated with different antibodies against E-cadherin as indicated (for details see text).

the precursor peptide recognized only the 100 kDa protein. When culture medium was treated with trypsin in the presence of Ca²⁺ and subjected to immunoprecipitations with the same panel of antibodies (Fig. 4, right panel), DE-1, DECMA-1 and anti-gp84 antibodies immunoprecipitated only the 80 kDa protein that has accumulated at the expense of the 100 kDa protein. This protein was no longer recognized by antibodies against the precursor peptide. These results demonstrate that the 100 kDa protein contains the precursor polypeptide of E-cadherin and that the 80 kDa protein represents the processed form. They also demonstrate that the precursor is converted to mature protein by trypsin and that recombinant protein is resistant to further trypsin cleavage in the presence of Ca²⁺. The 100 kDa protein was designated r-gp84/P and the 80 kDa protein r-gp84 (r, recombinant).

To ascertain whether trypsin correctly removes the precursor peptide, which is a prerequisite for E-cadherin function (Ozawa et al., 1990), amino-terminal microsequencing was performed. An amino acid sequence was obtained that was identical to that reported for the mouse protein (DWVIPP, Ringwald et al., 1987). Since the electrophoretic mobilities of trypsinized protein and untreated r-gp84 were indistinguishable, an additional trypsin cleavage in the carboxy-terminal part of the recombinant protein seems unlikely (the next possible cleavage site, 22 amino acid

residues away, if used, would result in a different electrophoretic mobility).

Glycosylation of recombinant E-cadherin

Most post-translational modifications of proteins in insect and mammalian cells are similar, but this is not the case for asparagine-dependent glycosylation. In both cell types the same target amino acids are glycosylated via dolicol pyrophosphate with an oligosaccharide of the high-mannose type, Glc3Man3GlcNAc2. However, only in mammalian cells does this structure become completely processed (Kornfeld and Kornfeld, 1985). Processing in insect cells occurs only to the trimannosyl core oligosaccharide, Man3GlcNAc2 (Hsieh and Robbins, 1984). Terminal glycosylation by the addition of galactose, fucose and sialic acids is absent (Butters and Hughes, 1981; Butters et al., 1981).

Since wild-type E-cadherin harbors four consensus sequences for asparagine-dependent glycosylation (Ringwald et al., 1987), wild-type and recombinant E-cadherin were compared from cells grown in the presence or absence of tunicamycin (Fig. 5). Recombinant E-cadherin appears not to be glycosylated to the same extent as mouse E-cadherin, since the two fragments migrated with different electrophoretic mobilities. However, after trypsin treatment of cells, the resultant native and recombinant gp84 migrated with the same electrophoretic mobility, indicating that the protein backbones of recombinant E-cadherin and the tryptic fragment generated from wild-type E-cadherin are identical (Fig. 5).

Antibodies against r-gp84

Rabbits were immunized with purified recombinant protein. When tested in immunoprecipitation experiments, anti-r-gp84 serum precipitated the known E-cadherin-catenin complex and specifically stained E-cadherin in complexes

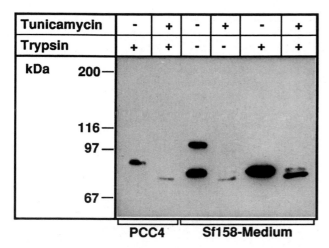

Fig. 5. Glycosylation of recombinant E-cadherin. Sf158 cells were infected with AcNPV/Um84-1 and cultured for 44 hours with or without 2 µg/ml tunicamycin. For comparison, mouse PCC4 cells were cultured for 12 hours with or without 1 µg/ml tunicamycin. PCC4 cells were trypsinized to generate the soluble form of the native protein. Recombinant and native protein were collected by immunoprecipitation and stained in immunoblots with anti-E-cadherin antibodies. The protein backbones of gp84 and r-gp84 exhibit identical electrophoretic mobilities, but r-gp84 appears not to be glycosylated to the same degree as gp84.

collected with anti-gp84 antibodies (Fig. 6). Also, anti-r-gp84 reacted with E-cadherin from different species in immunoblot experiments (not shown).

Large-scale production and purification of recombinant protein

To facilitate the purification of recombinant protein, infected cells were grown in FCS-free medium, which reduced protein synthesis by about 50%. Culture medium from 2×10^{10} Sf158 cells infected with AcNPV/Um84-1 (72 hours p.i.) was cleared of extracellular virus particles, concentrated and treated with trypsin in the presence of Ca^{2+} (see Materials and Methods). Trypsin treatment resulted in the cleavage of the precursor peptide, while digesting protein contaminants not protected by Ca^{2+}. The material was fractionated by a combination of anion exchange chromatography on a DEAE-matrix column and gel filtration on a Superdex™200 column using FPLC. The respective chromatograms and the analysis of protein fractions by SDS-PAGE are given in Figs 7 and 8. In Fig. 9 a summary of the different steps of the purification procedure is presented. With these purification procedures about 20 mg of purified r-gp84 was recovered.

Cell adhesion assays

The embryonal carcinoma cell line PCC4aza1 grows as aggregates in tissue culture and has frequently been used to study E-cadherin-mediated cell adhesion. Purified r-gp84 (25 pM to 2.5 mM) was added to cells to test whether recombinant protein can interfere with E-cadherin-mediated cell adhesion. Monoclonal antibody DECMA-1 was included as a positive control. Recombinant protein had no decompacting activity on preformed cell aggregates and did not inhibit cell aggregation in cell adhesion assays (not

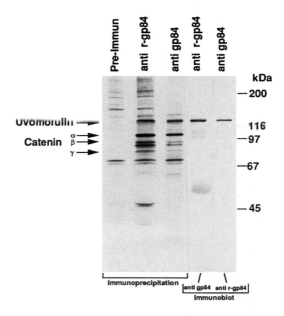

Fig. 6. Characterization of anti-r-gp84 antibodies. Immunoprecipitation: metabolically labeled PCC4 cells were immunoprecipitated with preimmune serum, antiserum against recombinant E-cadherin or affinity-purified anti-mouse gp84 antibodies. Immunoblot: immunocomplexes collected with anti-r-gp84 and anti-gp84 were blotted and reciprocally cross-stained with the same antibodies in immunoblots.

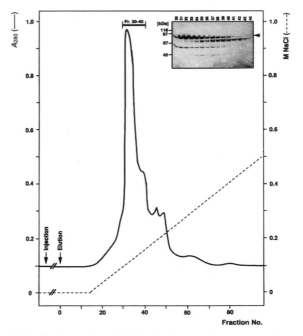

Fig. 7. Purification of r-gp84. Ion exchange chromatography. Culture medium (10 l) from 2×10^{10} AcNPV/Um84-1-infected Sf158 cells were ultrafiltrated, trypsin treated and concentrated to 100 ml as described in Materials and Methods. The concentrate was applied to a 20 ml Fractogel DEAE TSK-650(S) column at a flow rate of 3 ml/min and eluted with a linear 120 ml gradient of 0 to 0.5 M NaCl in TC-buffer. Fractions containing r-gp84 were identified by immunoblot analysis with antibodies against E-cadherin (inset, arrowhead, r-gp84). r-gp84 elutes between 100 mM and 165 mM NaCl. Fractions 31-34 were pooled (6 ml) and concentrated to 1 ml.

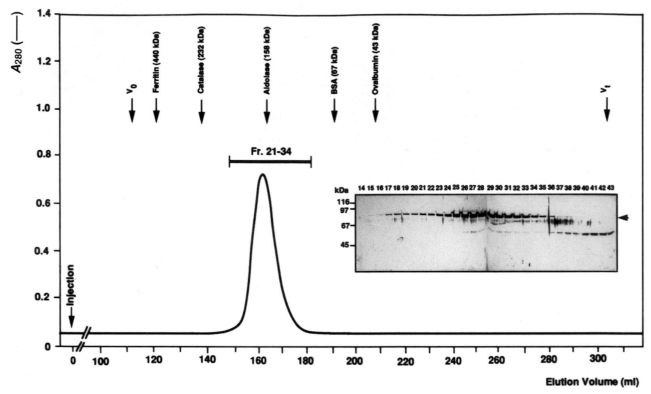

Fig. 8. Purification of r-gp84. Gel filtration. The pooled r-gp84 fractions from Fig. 7 were applied to a HiLoad Superdex 200 prep grade column (flow rate, 1 ml/min; fraction size, 2.3 ml). The fractionation of r-gp84 was monitored by immunoblots as described for Fig. 7. r-gp84 eluted as a broad peak with an apparent molecular mass of 165 kDa. The column was standardized with globular standard proteins (Pharmacia); standards and their elution peaks are indicated.

shown). In another series of experiments the possible inhibitory effect of r-gp84 was tested during the compaction process of mouse preimplantation embryos. Again, r-gp84 exhibited no effect on the compaction of the morula and embryos grown in the presence of r-gp84 developed to blastocysts (not shown).

DISCUSSION

The baculovirus expression system has successfully been used to express large amounts of mammalian proteins (e.g. see Miller, 1993). We report here the expression and characterization of the E-cadherin extracellular region in insect cells. Immunological analysis established that the recombinant protein is very similar, if not identical, to the native form of E-cadherin. Recombinant protein harbors the epitope of a monoclonal antibody that interferes with cell adhesion and is also recognized by other antibodies raised against the wild-type protein. Concordantly, antibodies against recombinant protein react with E-cadherin from mouse and other species. The amino-terminal amino acid sequences of recombinant and native protein are identical, as direct protein sequencing analysis revealed. Although a similar amino acid comparison was not performed at the carboxy terminus, the biochemical analysis supports the view that it is identical for the two proteins. As is well known for cadherins, recombinant protein is resistant to proteolytic degradation in the presence of Ca^{2+}, indicating

overall similarity of the protein conformation (Takeichi, 1988). Recombinant protein appears not to be glycosylated to the same degree as the native form. Since glycosylation seems not to alter the adhesive properties of cadherins

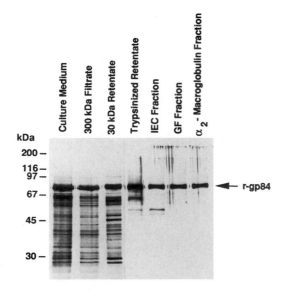

Fig. 9. Summary of r-gp84 purification. Samples from different steps of the r-gp84 purification procedure were subjected to SDS-PAGE and visualized by silver staining. IEC, ion exchange chromatography; GF, gel filtration.

(Vestweber and Kemler, 1984b; Shirayoshi et al., 1986), this difference is not likely to account for the lack of biological activity of recombinant protein discussed below. Of interest is the detection of the recombinant precursor polypeptide secreted into the culture medium, as this has not been observed in mammalian cells. The most likely explanation for this discrepancy is that the processing machinery of insect cells cannot efficiently handle the over-expressed recombinant protein. Trypsin treatment removes the precursor portion and the cleaved protein is indistinguishable from the endogenously generated mature protein, as far as size and amino-terminal amino acid sequences are concerned. As already mentioned, cadherins interact in a homophilic manner, best demonstrated by heterotypic expression studies, which lead to the induction of cadherin-mediated adhesion (Nagafuchi et al., 1987; Hatta et al., 1988; Ozawa et al., 1989). Studies on the homophilic binding have provided some initial insights into the molecular mechanism of this interaction. The expression of chimeric cadherins and cell mixing experiments have clearly pointed to the importance of the amino-terminal region of cadherins for the selectivity of binding (Nose et al., 1990). This view is also supported by studies on the processing of the precursor polypeptide. It was found that exact proteolytic cleavage of E-cadherin is required to initiate its adhesive function (Ozawa and Kemler, 1990). The result that a peptide centering on HAV mediates the homophilic interaction (Blaschuk et al., 1990) is of interest but requires additional experimental support. The possible involvement of the membrane proximal region of E-cadherin has been suggested, since structural alterations in this region affect the adhesive function; additionally, this region harbors the epitopes of two functionally active monoclonal antibodies (Ozawa et al., 1991). These results are consistent with ideas that the entire extracellular region and the particular protein conformation are important for the intermolecular interactions of cadherins. One of the major goals in expressing large amounts of recombinant protein was to test its inhibitory effect in cell adhesion. It has been reported that the extracellular region of human E-cadherin spontaneously produced by MCF-7 cells is able to inhibit adhesion of mouse mammary tumor cells (Wheelock et al., 1987). In contrast, Hyafil et al. (1981) found no inhibitory function of mouse gp84 on the compaction process of mouse preimplantation embryos. Similarly, recombinant protein, even at high protein concentration, did not inhibit the aggregation of embryonal carcinoma cells, nor did it influence the compaction process at the mouse morula stage. Thus, in spite of the high degree of structural similarity between native and recombinant protein, the latter exhibits no functional activity. It may well be that minor structural alterations arising during biosynthesis or in the purification procedure of recombinant protein are responsible for the lack of biological activity. Other possible explanations are even more attractive. It has been discussed that lateral clustering of cadherins on the cell surface is a prerequisite to initiating efficient cell-cell adhesion (Kemler et al., 1989). If so, soluble protein might exhibit only low biological activity since molecules are not arranged properly. Experiments are under way to compare the biological activity of soluble and matrix-bound r-gp84.

The microsequencing analysis was carried out by Paul Jenö (Biozentrum, Basel) and is greatly acknowledged. We thank Andreas Rolke for technical assistence, Rosemary Schneider for typing and Randy Cassada for critically reading the manuscript.

REFERENCES

Blaschuk, W., Sullivan, R., David, S. and Pouliot, Y. (1990). Identification of a cadherin cell adhesion recognition sequence. *Dev. Biol.* **139**, 227-229.

Blum, H., Beier, H. and Gross, H. J. (1987). Improved silver staining of plant proteins, RNA and DNA in polyacrylamide gels. *Electrophoresis* **8**, 93-99.

Butters, T. D. and Hughes, R. C. (1981). Isolation and characterization of mosquito cell membrane glycoproteins. *Biochim. Biophys. Acta* **640**, 655-671.

Butters, T. D., Hughes, R. C. and Visher, P. (1981). Steps in the biosynthesis of mosquito cell membrane glycoproteins and the effects of tunicamycin. *Biochim. Biophys. Acta* **640**, 672-686.

Hatta, K., Nose, A., Nagafuchi, A. and Takeichi, M. (1988). Cloning and expression of cDNA encoding a neural calcium-de-pendent cell adhesion molecule: Its identity in the cadherin gene family. *J. Cell Biol.* **106**, 873-881.

Hogan, B., Constantini, F., Ana Lacy, E. (1986). *Manipulating the Mouse Embryo. A Laboratory Manual.* Cold Spring Harbor Laboratory Press, New York.

Hsieh, P. and Robbins, P. W. (1984). Regulation of apsaragine-linked oligosaccharide processing. *J. Biol. Chem.* **259**, 2375-2382.

Hyafil, F., Babinet, C. and Jacob, F. (1981). Cell-cell interactions in early embryogenesis: a molecular approach to the role of calcium. *Cell* **26**, 447-454.

Hynes, R. O. and Lander, A. D. (1992). Contact and adhesive specifities in the associations, migrations and targeting of cells and axons. *Cell* **68**, 303-322.

Kemler, R., Ozawa, M. and Ringwald, M. (1989). Calcium-dependent cell adhesion molecules. *Curr. Opin. Cell Biol.* **1**, 892-897.

Kemler, R. (1992). Classical cadherins. *Semin. Cell Biol.* **3**, 149-155.

Kornfeld, R. and Kornfeld, S. (1985). Assembly of asparagine-linked oligosaccharides. *Annu. Rev. Biochem.* **54**, 631-664.

Miller, L. K. (1993). Baculoviruses: high level expression in insect cells. *Curr. Opin. Gen. Dev.* **3**, 97-101.

Nagafuchi, A., Shirayoshi, Y., Okazaki, K., Yasuda, K. and Takeichi, M. (1987). Transformation of cell adhesion properties by exogenously introduced E-cadherin cDNA. *Nature* **329**, 341-343.

Nicholas, J. F., Dubois, P., Jakob, B., Gaillard, J. and Jacob, F. (1975). Teratocareinome de la souris: Differentiation en culture d'un lignee de cellules primitives a potentialites multiple. *Ann. Microbiol. (Inst. Pasteur)* **126 A**, 3-22.

Nose, A., Tsuji, K. and Takeichi, M. (1990). Localization of specifity determining sites in cadherin cell adhesion molecules. *Cell* **61**, 147-155.

Ozawa, M., Baribault, H. and Kemler, R. (1989). The cytoplasmic domain of the cell adhesion molecule uvomorulin associates with three independent proteins structurally related in different species. *EMBO J.* **8**, 1711-1717.

Ozawa, M., Engel, I. and Kemler, R. (1990). Single amino acid substitutions in one Ca2+ binding site of uvomorulin abolish the adhesive function. *Cell* **63**, 1033-1038.

Ozawa, M. and Kemler, R. (1990). Correct proteolytic cleavage is required for the cell adhesive function of uvomorulin. *J. Cell Biol.* **111**, 1645-1650.

Ozawa, M., Hoschützky, H., Herrenknecht, K. and Kemler, R. (1991). A possible new adhesive site in the cell-adhesion molecule uvomorulin. *Mech. Dev.* **33**, 49-56.

Pen, J., Welling, G. W. and Welling-Wester, S. (1989). An efficient procedure for the isolation of recombinant baculovirus. *Nucl. Acids Res.* **17**, 451.

Ringwald, M., Schuh, R., Vestweber, D., Eistetter, H., Lottspeich, F., Engel, J., Dölz, R., Jöhnig, F., Eppler, J., Mayer, S., Müller, C. and Kemler, R. (1987). The structure of cell adhesion molecule uvomorulin. Insights into the molecular mechanism of Ca2+-dependent cell adhesion. *EMBO J.* **6**, 3647-3653.

Sambrook, J., Fritsch, E. F., Maniatis, T. (1989). *Molecular Cloning - A Laboratory Manual*, 2nd edn. Cold Spring Harbor Laboratory Press, Cold Spring Harbor, New York.

Shirayoshi, Y., Nose, A., Iwasaki, K. and Takeichi, M. (1986). N-linked oligosaccharides are not involved in the function of a cell-cell binding glycoprotein E-cadherin. *Cell Struct. Funct.* **11**, 245-252.

Summers, M. D. and Smith, G. E. (1987). *A Manual Of Methods For Baculovirus Vectors And Insect Cell Culture Procedures:* Bulletin no. 1555, Texas Agricultural Experimental Station, College Station, TX 77843.

Takeichi, M. (1988). The cadherins: cell-cell adhesion molecules controlling animal morphogenesis. *Development* **102**, 639-655.

Vaughn, J. L., Goodwin, R. H., Tomkins, G. L. and Mccawley, P. (1977). The establishment of two cell lines from the insect Spodoptera frugiperda (lepidoptera: noctuidae). *In Vitro* **13**, 213-217.

Vestweber, D. and Kemler, R. (1984a). Rabbit antiserum against a purified surface glycoprotein decompacts mouse preimplantation embryos and reacts with specific adult tissues. *Exp. Cell Res.* **152**, 169-178.

Vestweber, D. and Kemler, R. (1984b). Some structural and functional aspects of the cell adhesion molecule uvomorulin. *Cell Differ.* **15**, 269-273.

Vestweber, D. and Kemler, R. (1985). Identification of a putative cell adhesion domain of uvomorulin. *EMBO J.* **4**, 3393-3398.

Wheelock, M. J., Buck, C. A., Bechtol, K. B. and Damsky, C. H. (1987). Soluble 80-kd fragment of cell-CAM 120/80 disrupts cell-cell adhesion. *J. Cell Biochem.* **34**, 187-202.

Journal of Cell Science, Supplement 17, 155-158 (1993)
Printed in Great Britain © The Company of Biologists Limited 1993

Catenins as mediators of the cytoplasmic functions of cadherins

Barry M. Gumbiner and Pierre D. McCrea

Cellular Biochemistry and Biophysics Program, Sloan-Kettering Institute, Memorial Sloan-Kettering Cancer Center, Box 564, 1275 York Avenue, New York, NY 10021, USA

SUMMARY

The catenins are polypeptides that bind to the conserved cytoplasmic tail of cadherins and are required for cadherin function. α-Catenin is related to vinculin and seems to be required for the interaction of cadherins with the actin cytoskeleton. β-Catenin is homologous to *armadillo*, a segment polarity gene in *Drosophila* that participates in developmental signaling. Recent findings indicate that β-catenin also participates in developmental signaling and embryonic patterning in *Xenopus*

laevis. At least a portion of the electrophoretic band migrating at the position of γ-catenin consists of plakoglobin, a desmosomal and *zonula adherens* protein that has high sequence similarity to β-catenin and *armadillo*. The catenins may be involved in the regulation of cadherin function during tissue morphogenesis and tumorigenesis.

Key words: catenin, cadherin, adhesion

Cadherins mediate Ca^{2+}-dependent cell-cell adhesion in virtually all solid tissues (Takeichi, 1991). They are homophilic adhesion molecules, and are thought to be responsible for specific cell recognition events during tissue morphogenesis. In epithelia, E-cadherin facilitates the formation of other cell junctions and plays a role in the organization of a polarized cytoskeleton and organelles (Fig. 1). Inhibition of E-cadherin function at the cell surface with antibodies slows the formation of cell junctions (Gumbiner et al., 1988). Furthermore, expression of exogenous cadherins by cDNA transfection can induce the formation of gap junctions between cells and create a communication-competent collective of cells (Matsuzaki et al., 1990; Musil et al., 1990). Therefore, cadherins seem to regulate the state and/or extent of other cell-cell interactions.

The mechanism of cadherin function involves both specific binding of extracellular domains at the cell surface and interactions with components of the cytoplasm. The cadherins seem to interact in some way with actin filaments (Hirano et al., 1987), presumably to fulfill a requirement to generate tension at adhesion sites. The roles of the cytoskeleton and tension generation in cadherin-mediated cell adhesion is probably best exemplified by the process of compaction in mouse embryos and in some cultured cells, whereby the adherent cells flatten extensively against one another (Fleming and Johnson, 1988). Compaction of cells is probably analogous to the spreading of single cells on an extracellular substratum, a process which is mediated primarily by the integrins.

The cytoplasmic tail of the cadherins is a very highly conserved region of the molecules and carries out important functions. Mutant cadherin molecules with deletions in the cytoplasmic domain fail to bring about normal cell adhesion (Nagafuchi and Takeichi, 1989; Ozawa et al.,

1989), despite the fact that the extracellular domain by itself seems to be able to fold properly and to retain some ligand binding activity (Bixby and Zhang, 1990; Wheelock et al., 1987). Furthermore, overexpression of a cadherin molecule lacking virtually all of the extracellular domain in the early *Xenopus* embryo disrupts cell-cell adhesion globally (Kintner, 1992). This mutant cadherin seems to act as a dominant negative inhibitor of endogenous cadherin function, presumably as a result of binding to some limiting intracellular component(s).

The catenins are proteins that interact with the conserved cadherin cytoplasmic domain (Fig. 2) (Magee and Buxton, 1991; Ozawa et al., 1989). They were first identified as a set of three polypeptides (α-, β- and γ-catenins) that co-immunoprecipitate with E-cadherin extracted from cells with nonionic detergents. The catenins bind to the region of the cadherin cytoplasmic tail required for normal cadherin function, as identified by the deletion mutant analysis described above (Ozawa et al., 1990). β-Catenin is known to bind directly to the cadherin cytoplasmic tail even in the absence of the other catenins (McCrea and Gumbiner, 1991). α-Catenin may bind to β-catenin or directly to E-cadherin (Ozawa and Kemler, 1992). γ-Catenin seems to interact less stably with the cadherin-catenin complex, since its recovery in cadherin immunoprecipitates is more variable.

The best candidate for mediating the interaction of cadherins with actin is α-catenin. Its primary amino acid sequence and overall sequence organization is very similar to that of vinculin, a cytoskeletal protein known to be associated with actin filaments at their sites of attachment to the plasma membrane in focal contacts (Herrenknecht et al., 1991; Nagafuchi et al., 1991). There is also some suggestive evidence that α-catenin binds to actin (Ozawa et al.,

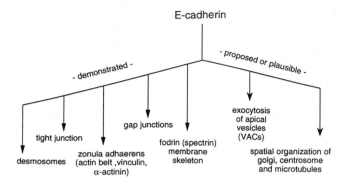

Fig. 1. Structures 'dependent' on the formation of E-cadherin-mediated cell contacts.

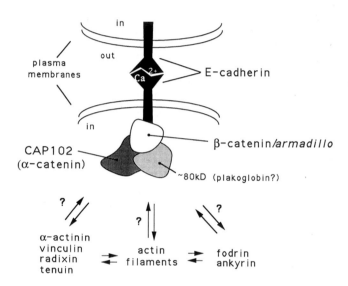

Fig. 2. Cadherin-catenin protein complexes in cells.

1990). A fraction of the E-cadherin-catenin complex binds to a DNase column (DNase is known to bind tightly to actin). By contrast, when the α-catenin is first stripped from the complex by treatment with the detergent octylglucoside, the complex no longer binds to DNase. However, this evidence for an α-catenin/actin interaction is indirect and can account for only a small fraction of the cadherin-catenin complex; there is not yet any evidence that the complex contains significant amounts of actin.

Perhaps the most interesting findings about the function of α-catenin come from studies of α-catenin-deficient car-

cinoma cells (Hirano et al., 1992). These cells express E-cadherin and the other catenins, but are only loosely adherent. When α-catenin is expressed in this cell line by cDNA transfection, the cells undergo a compaction-like process and form epithelial structures. Since actin filaments are involved in compaction, this finding indicates that α-catenin is required in some way for the interaction of E-cadherin with the actin cytoskeleton.

There is intriguing evidence that β-catenin is involved in signal transduction or in the regulation of cadherin function by developmental signals. β-Catenin is highly homologous to a segment polarity gene in *Drosophila* called *armadillo (arm)* (Fig. 3) (McCrea et al., 1991). In *arm* mutants, the posterior compartment of each embryonic segment fails to develop, and is instead replaced by a mirror image of the anterior compartment (Riggleman et al., 1989). *arm* seems to participate in the same developmental signaling pathway as *wingless,* which is a homolog of the vertebrate *wnt* family of growth factors (Peifer et al., 1991; Riggleman et al., 1990). The homology between β-catenin and *armadillo* raises the possibility that β-catenin has a similar developmental signaling role in vertebrates.

We have recently obtained evidence that β-catenin participates in embryonic pattern formation in *Xenopus* (McCrea et al., 1993). Microinjection of anti-β-catenin antibodies into cleaving embryos causes the development of a secondary body axis, as evidenced by the formation of two notochords and two neural tubes, and sometimes even the formation of two complete head structures. This phenotype is remarkably similar to the one caused by the injection of *wnt* mRNA. The anti-β-catenin Fabs, like *wnt* mRNA, are also capable of rescuing a primary dorso-anterior axis in embryos that had been ventralized by treatment with UV light. These findings suggest that a known component of the cell-cell adhesion machinery (β-catenin) participates in developmental signaling. They are also consistent with the notion that β-catenin is part of the same or a related signaling pathway as that utilized by *wnt*, similar to signaling mediated by *arm* and *wingless* in *Drosophila.*

How β-catenin might participate in a developmental signaling event is not yet known. We do not even know whether the microinjected antibody acts in an inhibitory or a stimulatory fashion. Despite the lack of information about biochemical mechanisms, two general kinds of models can be considered (Fig. 4). β-Catenin could act directly in an intracellular signal transduction pathway in response to homotypic binding of cadherins or to occupancy of a *wnt* receptor (model 1). Alternatively, β-catenin could regulate cadherin adhesion activity, perhaps in response to the recep-

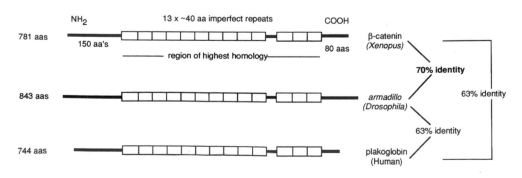

Fig. 3. β-Catenin is homologous to the product of the segment polarity gene *armadillo* in *Drosophila* and to human plakoglobin.

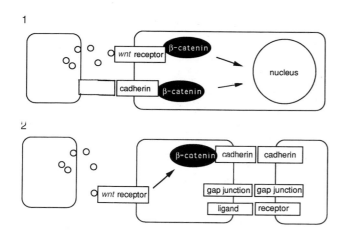

Fig. 4. Proposed models for the *wnt* → β-catenin signaling 'pathway'. (1) β-Catenin is directly involved in signal transduction. (2) *wnt* modulates cadherin-mediated cell recognition via β-catenin, which facilitates signaling through other cell surface molecules.

tion of a *wnt* signal (model 2). Regulating specific cell recognition in this way could determine which cells in a tissue are capable of communicating with each other by other short-range signaling systems. For example, there is already very good evidence that gap junction communication is controlled by specific cadherin-mediated cell recognition (Matsuzaki et al., 1990; Musil et al., 1990). In this regard, it is very intriguing that the *wnts* that induce the formation of a duplicate axis in *Xenopus* also stimulate the extent of gap junction communication between embryonic blastomeres (Olson et al., 1991). Theoretically, this type of regulation could be generalized to any pair of cell surface-bound ligands and receptors (like *sevenless* and *bride of sevenless* in *Drosophila* eye development; Cagan et al., 1992), which have been discovered with increasing frequency. Further experimentation will be required to determine the mechanism by which cadherin-mediated cell-cell adhesion participates in embryonic patterning.

Phosphorylation of β-catenin may be one mechanism for regulating cadherin function at the cell surface. In v-*src*-transformed cells, cadherins are expressed at the cell surface, but are functionally inactive (Matsuyoshi et al., 1992; Volberg et al., 1991). β-Catenin is phosphorylated on tyrosine residues in these cells, but not in normal cells (Behrens et al., 1993; Hamaguchi et al., 1993; Matsuyoshi et al., 1992). However, because v-src is a very promiscuous tyrosine kinase, it is difficult to know whether tyrosine phosphorylation of β-catenin is relevent to the alterations in cell adhesion. Cellular src-like kinases are present at adhesive junctions in normal cells (Tsukita et al., 1991), and could be involved in regulating cadherin-mediated adhesion. There is not yet evidence that tyrosine phosphorylation of β-catenin in nontransformed cells is associated with any developmental or physiological event.

The molecular nature and cellular function of γ-catenin is less well defined. At least one component of the γ-catenin band seems to be plakoglobin, a polypeptide first described as a component of the desmosomal plaque, but also found to be present in *zonula adhaerens* junctions (Cowin et al.,

1986). Plakoglobin shares very high sequence homology with *armadillo* (Peifer and Wieschaus, 1990) and β-catenin (McCrea et al., 1991). Plakoglobin has been found to co-immunoprecipitate with desmoglein-I (Korman et al., 1989), a desmosomal component that is a member of the cadherin superfamily (Goodwin et al., 1990; Koch et al., 1990). It is also present, although apparently with some variability (Butz et al., 1992), in E-cadherin immunoprecipitates, and it co-migrates with the γ-catenin band on 1 dimensional SDS-gels (Knudsen and Wheelock, 1992; Peifer et al., 1992). Preliminary unpublished data indicate that β-catenin and plakoglobin form mutually exclusive cadherin-catenin complexes, and therefor they may interact with the same binding site on E-cadherin. The γ-catenin band may also contain additional polypeptides that have yet to be defined.

Progress has been made in the molecular characterization of the catenins, polypeptides which mediate the cytoplasmic functions of the cadherins. Much remains to be learned about how the catenins themselves interact with the actin cytoskeleton, mediate cadherin-dependent intracellular signaling events, and regulate the functional activity of the cadherins. Understanding these functions of the catenins will reveal much about the mechanisms of cadherins in tissue morphogenesis. With the appropriate molecular tools now available, these questions are subject to rigorous experimental analysis.

REFERENCES

Behrens, J., Vakaet, L., Friis, R., Winterhager, E., Van Roy, F., Mareel, M. M. and Birchmeier, W. (1993). Loss of epithelial differentiation and gain of invasiveness correlates with tyrosine phosphorylation of the E-cadherin/β-catenin complex in cells transformed with a temperature-sensitive v-src gene. *J. Cell Biol.* **120**, 757-766.

Bixby, J. L. and Zhang, R. (1990). Purified N-Cadherin is a potent substrate for the rapid induction of neurite outgrowth. *J. Cell Biol.* **110**, 1253-1260.

Butz, S., Stappert, J., Wessig, H. and Kemler, R. (1992). Plakoglobin and β-catenin: Distinct but closely related. *Science* **257**, 1142-1144.

Cagan, R. L., Kramer, H., Hart, A. C. and Zipursky, S. L. (1992). The bride of sevenless and sevenless interaction: internalization of a transmembrane ligand. *Cell* **69**, 393-399.

Cowin, P., Kapprell, H.-P., Franke, W. W., Tamkun, J. and Hynes, R. O. (1986). Plakoglobin: a protein common to different kinds of intercellular adhering junctions. *Cell* **46**, 1063-1073.

Fleming, T. P. and Johnson, M. H. (1988). From egg to epithelium. *Annu. Rev. Cell Biol.* **4**, 459-485.

Goodwin, L., Hill, J. E., Raynor, K., Raszi, L., Manabe, M. and Cowin, P. (1990). Desmoglein shows extensive homology to the cadherin family of cell adhesion molecules. *Biochem. Biophys. Res. Commun.* **173**, 1224-1230.

Gumbiner, B., Stevenson, B. and Grimaldi, A. (1988). The role of the cell adhesion molecule uvomorulin in the formation and maintenance of the epithelial junctional complex. *J. Cell Biol.* **107**, 1575-1587.

Hamaguchi, M., Matsuyoshi, N., Ohnishi, Y., Gotoh, B., Takeichi, M. and Nagai, Y. (1993). p60*v-src* causes tyrosine phosphorylation and inactivation of the N-cadherin-catenin cell adhesion system. *EMBO J.* **12**, 307-314.

Herrenknecht, K., Ozawa, M., Eckerskorn, C., Lottspeich, F., Lentner, M. and Kemler, R. (1991). The uvomorulin-anchorage protein α catenin is a vinculin homologue. *Proc. Nat. Acad. Sci. USA* **88**, 9156-9160.

Hirano, S., Kimoto, N., Shimoyama, Y., Hirohashi, S. and Takeichi, M. (1992). Identification of a neural α-catenin as a key regulator of cadherin function and multicellular organization. *Cell* **70**, 293-301.

Hirano, S., Nose, A., Hatta, K., Kawakami, A. and Takeichi, M. (1987). Calcium-dependent cell-cell adhesion moelcules (Cadherins): Subclass specificities and possible involvement of actin bundles. *J. Cell Biol.* **105**(6, Pt. 1), 2501-2510.

Kintner, C. (1992). Regulation of embryonic cell adhesion by the cadherin cytoplasmic domain. *Cell* **69**, 225-236.

Knudsen, K. A. and Wheelock, M. (1992). Plakoglobin, or an 83-kD homologue distinct from β-catenin, interacts with E-cadherin and N-cadherin. *J. Cell Biol.* **118**, 671-679.

Koch, P. J., Walsh, M. J., Schmelz, M., Goldschmidt, M. D., Zimbelmann, R. and Franke, W. W. (1990). Identification of desmoglein, a constitutive desmosomal glycoprotein, as a member of the cadherin family of cell adhesion molecules. **53**, 1-12.

Korman, N. J., Eyre, R. W., Klaus-Kovtun, V. and Stanley, J. R. (1989). Demonstration of an adhering-junction molecule (plakoglobin) in the autoantigens of pemphigus foliaceus and pemphigus vulgaris. *N. Engl. J. Med.* **321**, 631-635.

Magee, A. I. and Buxton, R. S. (1991). Transmembrane molecular assemblies regulated by the greater cadherin family. *Curr. Opin. Cell Biol.* **3**, 854-861.

Matsuyoshi, N., Hamaguchi, M., Taniguchi, S., Nagafuchi, A., Tsukita, S. and Takeichi, M. (1992). Cadherin-mediated cell-cell adhsion is perturbed by v-src tyrosine phosphorylation in metastatic fibroblasts. *J. Cell Biol.* **118**, 703-714.

Matsuzaki, F., Mege, R.-M., Jaffe, S. H., Friedlander, D. R., Gallin, W. J., Goldberg, J. I., Cunningham, B. A. and Edelman, G. M. (1990). cDNAs of cell adhesion molecules of different specificity induce changes in cell shape and border formation in cultured S180 cells. *J. Cell Biol.* **110**, 1239-1252.

McCrea, P. and Gumbiner, B. (1991). Purification of a 92-kDa cytoplasmic protein tightly associated with the cell-cell adhesion molecule E-cadherin (uvomorulin): Characterization and extractability of the protein complex from the cell cytostructure. *J. Biol. Chem.* **266**(7), 4514-4520.

McCrea, P. D., Turck, C. W. and Gumbiner, B. (1991). A homolog of the *armadillo* protein Drosophila (Plakoglobin) associated with E-cadherin. *Science* **254**, 1359-61.

McCrea, P. D., Brieher, W. M. and Gumbiner, B. M. (1993). Induction of a secondary body axis in Xenopus by antibodies by β-catenin. *J. Cell Biol.* **123**, 477-484.

Musil, L. S., Cunningham, B. A., Edelman, G. M. and Goodenough, D. A. (1990). Differential phosphorylation of the gap junction protein connexin43 in junctional communication-competent and -deficient cell lines. *J. Cell Biol.* **111**, 2077-2088.

Nagafuchi, A. and Takeichi, M. (1989). Transmembrane control of cadherin-mediated cell adhesion: a 94 kDa protein functionally associated with a specific region of the cytoplasmic domain of E-cadherin. *Cell Regul.* **1**, 37-44.

Nagafuchi, A., Takeichi, M. and Tsukita, S. (1991). The 102 kd cadherin-associated protein: Similarity to vinculin and posttranscriptional regulation of expression. *Cell* **65**, 849-857.

Olson, D. J., Christian, J. L. and Moon, R. T. (1991). Effect of Wnt-1 and Related proteins in gap junctional communication in *Xenopus* embryos. *Science* **252**, 1173-1176.

Ozawa, M., Baribault, H. and Kemler, R. (1989). The cytoplasmic domain of the cell adhesion molecule uvomorulin associates with three independent proteins structurally related in different species. *EMBO J.* **8**, 1711-1717.

Ozawa, M. and Kemler, R. (1992). Molecular organization of the uvomorulin-catenin complex. *J. Cell Biol.* **116**, 989-996.

Ozawa, M., Ringwald, M. and Kemler, R. (1990). Uvomorulin-catenin complex formation is regulated by a specific domain in the cytoplasmic region of the cell adhesion molecule. *Proc. Nat. Acad. Sci. USA* **87**, 4246-4250.

Peifer, M., McCrea, P. D., Green, K. J., Wieschaus, E. and Gumbiner, B. M. (1992). The vertebrate adhesive junction proteins β-catenin and plakoglobin and the *Drosophila* segment polarity gene *armadillo* form a multigene family with similar properties. *J. Cell Biol.* **118**, 681-691.

Peifer, M., Rauskolb, C., Williams, M., Riggleman, B. and Wieschaus, E. (1991). The segment polarity gene *armadillo* interacts with the *wingless* signaling pathway in both embryonic and adult pattern formation. *Development* **111**, 1029-1043.

Peifer, M. and Wieschaus, E. (1990). The segment polarity gene *armadillo* encodes a functionally modular protein that is the Drosophila homolog of human plakoglobin. *Cell* **63**, 1167-1178.

Riggleman, B., Schedl, P. and Wieschaus, E. (1990). Spatial expression of the Drosophila segment polarity gene *armadillo* is posttranscriptionally regulated by *wingless. Cell* **63**, 549-560.

Riggleman, B., Wieschaus, E. and Schedl, P. (1989). Molecular analysis of the *armadillo* locus: uniformly distributed transcripts and a protein with novel internal repeats are associated with a *Drosophila* segment polarity gene. *Genes Dev.* **3**, 96-113.

Takeichi, M. (1991). Cadherin cell adhesion receptors as a morphogenetic regulator. *Science* **251**, 1451-1455.

Tsukita, S., Oishi, K., Akiyama, T., Yamanashi, Y., Tamamoto, T. and Tsukita, S. (1991). Specific proto-oncogenic tyrosine kinases of src family are enriched in cell-to-cell adherens junctions where the level of tyrosine phosphorylation is elevated. *J. Cell Biol.* **113**, 867-879.

Volberg, T., Geiger, B., Dror, R. and Zick, Y. (1991). Modulation of intercellular adherens-type junctions and tyrosine phosphorylation of their components in RSV-transformed cultured chick lens cells. *Cell Regul.* **2**, 105-120.

Wheelock, M. J., Buck, C. A., Bechtol, K. B. and Damsky, C. H. (1987). Soluble 80-kd fragment of cell-CAM 120/80 disrupts cell-cell adhesion. *J. Cell. Biochem.* **34**, 187-202.

Journal of Cell Science, Supplement 17, 159-164 (1993)
Printed in Great Britain © The Company of Biologists Limited 1993

Molecular mechanisms leading to loss of differentiation and gain of invasiveness in epithelial cells

Walter Birchmeier, K. Michael Weidner and Jürgen Behrens

Institute of Cell Biology (Tumor Research), University of Essen Medical School, Virchowstr. 173, 4300 Essen 1, Germany

Present address: Max-Delbrück-Centrum for Molecular Medicine, Robert-Rössle-Str. 10, 13122 Berlin-Buch, Germany

SUMMARY

It has been realized for some time that the loss of epithelial differentiation in carcinomas, which is accompanied by higher mobility and invasiveness of the tumor cells, is a consequence of reduced intercellular adhesion. A variety of recent reports have indicated that the primary cause for the 'scattering' of the cells in invasive carcinomas is a loss of the integrity of intercellular junctions. Thus, defects in expression or structure of several components of the epithelial adherens junctions (e.g. E-cadherin, α-catenin) can occur, and our increased knowledge about the molecules of the junctions allows an explanation of these defects in molecular terms in some of the cases. Furthermore, tyrosine phosphorylation of junctional components (e.g. β-catenin) appears to play a role in the assembly and disassembly of cell-cell contacts. Some of the effectors of epithelial junction formation are tyrosine protein kinases, e.g. the scatter factor/hepatocyte growth factor receptor c-Met, the FGF receptors and the $pp60^{src}$ kinase. The importance of tyrosine phosphorylation in junctions during tumor development is becoming increasingly evident.

Key words: tumor differentiation, adherens junctions, catenins, E-cadherin promoter, scatter factor, hepatocyte growth factor

INVASIVE CARCINOMA CELLS EXHIBIT REDUCED INTERCELLULAR ADHESION

Pathologists have observed for some decades that invasive carcinomas generally show reduced epithelial differentiation, and that this is particularly prominent at invasion fronts where carcinoma cells break into surrounding mesenchymal tissue (Weinstein et al., 1976; Gabbert et al., 1985). The invading cells lose their epithelial appearance (they become amorphic, spindle-shaped, fibroblastoid, more mobile) and in the electron microscope a reduced number of intercellular junctions are observed. Desmosomes (spot desmosomes) represent the intercellular junctions which are most easily detected by electron microscopy in intact tissue. Together with adherens junctions (belt desmosomes), they constitute the main adhering junctions of epithelial cells. Other known junctions (tight, gap) do not primarily function in intercellular adhesion; the hemidesmosomes (and the focal contacts) play a specific role in cell-basement membrane contacts.

In recent years, our laboratory and others have set out to examine molecular components responsible for the generation of invasive, dedifferentiated epithelial (carcinoma) cells (Imhof et al., 1983; Behrens et al., 1985, 1989, 1993; Frixen et al., 1991; Weidner et al., 1991). We were not simply interested in markers which would be differentially expressed in differentiated and dedifferentiated epithelial cells. Instead we concentrated on the identification of molecular components which are directly responsible for the loss or maintenance of epithelial differentiation and junction formation.

THE ROLE OF THE CELL ADHESION MOLECULE E-CADHERIN

It became apparent by the work of our and other laboratories that the epithelial cell adhesion molecule E-cadherin is one potent regulator of the epithelial phenotype and of junction formation. For instance, forced expression of E-cadherin in nonepithelial cells by cDNA transfection induces junction formation, and disturbance of E-cadherin function in epithelial cells by specific antibodies leads to loss of junctions and to a fibroblast-like morphology (Behrens et al., 1985; Gumbiner and Simons, 1986; Nagafuchi et al., 1987; Matsuzaki et al., 1990; McNeill et al., 1990). E-cadherin, a 120 kDa transmembrane glycoprotein, is enriched in the adherens junctions of epithelial cells and interacts with the cytoskeleton via associated cytoplasmic molecules, the catenins (Boller et al., 1985; Behrens et al., 1985; Nagafuchi and Takeichi, 1988; Ozawa et al., 1989, 1990b; Ozawa and Kemler 1992). The cDNAs for α- and β-catenin have recently been characterized; they show sequence similarities to the cDNAs of other well known junction-associated proteins, i.e. vinculin and plakoglobin, respectively (Nagafuchi et al., 1991; Herrenknecht et al., 1991; McCrea and Gumbiner, 1991; McCrea et al., 1991). β-catenin is homologous to the armadillo gene product of Drosophila (McCrea et al., 1991). E-cadherin expression is frequently downregulated in highly invasive, poorly differentiated carcinomas (Behrens et al., 1989; Schipper et al., 1991; Frixen et al., 1991; Shiozaki et al., 1991; Shimoyama and Hirohashi, 1991a,b; Mayer et al., 1993; Moll et al., 1993), and re-expression of E-cadherin by cDNA transfection in poorly differentiated carcinoma cell lines inhibits invasiveness (Frixen et al., 1991; Vleminckx et al., 1991; Chen and Öbrink 1991; Navarro et al., 1991). Thus, E-cadherin seems to act as a kind of master molecule for maintaining the differentiation of normal epithelial cells, and loss of expression or function of E-cadherin in transformed epithelial cells appears to be a key step in the progression of the cells to a malignant phenotype (see Behrens et al., 1992, for a review).

EXCEPTIONS TO THE RULE

It has recently become clear, however, that loss of differentiation of epithelial (carcinoma) cells in vitro and in vivo can also occur while E-cadherin expression is maintained. Scatter factor/hepatocyte growth factor is a motility and growth factor for various cell types and has multiple effects on MDCK epithelial cells. It leads to the dissociation of the cells, to increased cell motility, to a change from an epithelial to a fibroblastoid shape, to invasiveness into collagen gels, but not to a loss of E-cadherin expression (Weidner et al., 1990, 1991; see also below). Similar results were observed in dissociation experiments of rat bladder carcinoma cells with acidic fibroblast growth factor (Jouanneau et al., 1991). Transformation of MDCK epithelial cells with a temperature-sensitive v-src gene leads to morphology changes and invasiveness at the permissive temperature, but not to a loss of E-cadherin expression (Behrens et al., 1993; see also below). Similarly, expression of an estrogen receptor-fos hybrid gene in breast epithelial cells results in a hormone-inducible, rapid loss of differentiation of the cells, but E-cadherin expression is only affected after prolonged hormone exposure (Reichmann et al., 1992). Furthermore, in a number of 'scattered' gastric carcinomas, E-cadherin was found to be present (Shimoyama and Hirohashi, 1991a). In one case of a poorly differentiated lung carcinoma cell line (PC 9), E-cadherin expression was unchanged, but the E-cadherin-associated protein α-catenin was not expressed, probably due to homozygous mutation in the α-catenin gene (Hirano et al., 1992; Shimoyama et al., 1992). Other cases in which E-cadherin expression is observed in poorly differentiated carcinomas have been reported by Eidelman et al. (1989) and Moll et al. (1993). However, in all of these studies E-cadherin was analyzed by immunological techniques only. Whether the molecule is functionally intact in all of these examples is unkown.

Abberations that result in direct junction defects have been studied recently in molecular terms. For instance, expression of E-cadherin without a cytoplasmic domain resulted in defective cell-cell adhesion. Apparently, the truncated E-cadherin is unable to interact with the catenins and, therefore, proper junctions cannot be formed (Nagafuchi and Takeichi, 1988; Ozawa et al., 1990b). E-cadherin without the entire extracellular domain acted in a dominant-negative fashion. It is likely that these truncated molecules collect catenins which are thus not available to form proper complexes with intact E-cadherin (Kintner, 1992). Furthermore, a point mutation generated in the Ca^{2+}-binding region of the first extracellular repeat of E-cadherin also resulted in non-functional cell adhesion molecules (Ozawa et al., 1990a). Similar mutations in the extracellular portions of E-cadherin have recently been found in two non-adhesive cell lines from gastric carcinomas (S. Hirohashi, Tokyo, personal communication). The adhesive properties of PC 9 lung cancer cells, which harbor a null mutation in the α-catenin gene, could be restored by transfection with α-catenin cDNA (Hirano et al., 1992; Shimoyama et al., 1992).

In our lab, we have recently found that the v-src oncogene is a potent effector of epithelial differentiation and invasiveness without affecting E-cadherin expression. MDCK epithelial cells transformed with a temperature-sensitive mutant of v-src exhibit a strictly epithelial phenotype at the nonpermissive temeprature for $pp60^{v\text{-}src}$ activity (40.5°C), but rapidly lose cell-to-cell contacts and acquire a fibroblast-like morphology after culture at the permissive temperature (35°C). Furthermore, the invasiveness of the cells into collagen gels or into chick heart fragments was increased at the permissive temperature (Behrens et al., 1993). The profound effects of v-src on intercellular adhesion were not linked to changes in the levels of expression of E-cadherin. Rather, we observed an increase in tyrosine phosphorylation of β-catenin. Similar data were reported by Matsuyoshi et al. (1992). These results suggest a mechanism by which v-src counteracts junctional assembly and thereby promotes invasiveness and dedifferentiation of epithelial cells through phosphorylation of the E-cadherin/catenin complex.

CONTROL OF EXPRESSION OF JUNCTIONAL COMPONENTS: THE E-CADHERIN PROMOTER

In addition to mutation and post-translational modification, adherens junction integrity could also be affected by changes in the regulation of gene expression of particular junctional constituents. Thus, any variation in the battery of the many transcription factors which regulate the promoters of the adherens junction proteins might lead to changes in the invasiveness of carcinoma cells. These studies are still at the beginning stage since the promoters of most of the involved genes have not been characterized.

We have recently identified the E-cadherin promoter in order to study the mechanisms that regulate epithelial-specific expression of E-cadherin and possible downregulation of expression during dedifferentiation of carcinomas (Behrens et al., 1991). We found that a −178 to +92 bp upstream fragment of the E-cadherin gene induced specific expression of a CAT reporter gene in epithelial cells, whereas in nonepithelial cells this fragment was inactive, indicating the presence of cell type-specific regulatory elements in this region. A further deletion fragment (from −58 bp to +92 bp) resulted in fivefold-reduced activity that was still epithelium-specific. Importantly, both the −178 bp and the −58 bp fragments were highly active in differentiated breast carcinoma cells, but were inactive in a line of dedifferentiated carcinoma cells. In these dedifferentiated breast carcinoma cells we detected a change in the activity of transcription factors responsible for the epithelial specificity of E-cadherin expression. By DNase footprinting and gel retardation analysis we could identify binding of nuclear factors to three regions within the −178 to +92 bp E-cadherin promoter fragment: first, to a GC-rich region at −58 to −25, second, to a palindromic sequence centered at −86 (named E-pal) which harbors two copies of the CANNTG consensus sequence for binding of helix-loop-helix transcription factors, and third, to the CAAT box. Identification of factors binding to and regulating the E-cadherin promoter is currently being pursued.

EPITHELIAL MOTILITY FACTORS: THE ROLE OF SCATTER FACTOR/HEPATOCYTE GROWTH FACTOR

Cell motility factors have been described previously as a group of proteins that selectively stimulate cell motility with little or no effect on cell proliferation. This group of proteins includes scatter factor (SF), which is secreted by mesenchymal cells and increases the motility of epithelial and endothelial cells in a paracrine fashion (Stoker et al., 1987; Rosen et al., 1990; Weidner et al., 1990, 1991), autocrine motility factor, which is derived from melanoma and breast carcinoma cells (Liotta et al., 1986), and migration-stimulating factor, which affects fibroblasts in an autocrine way (Grey et al., 1989). However, in the course of more thorough investigations of the phenomena of cell motility and growth, it became clear that motility factors often also act as growth factors, and vice versa. For instance, SF was shown to be identical to hepatocyte growth factor (HGF; Weidner et al., 1991) and vascular permeability factor (VPF) was identified as vascular endothelial growth factor (VEGF; Leung et al., 1989). Furthermore, many well known growth factors such as PDGF, FGF, EGF, Il-6, NGF or IGF-1 were also found to affect cell motility (see Stoker and Gherardi, 1991, for a review). We have examined the effect of SF/HGF on the invasiveness of various epithelial cell lines into extracellular matrices. SF/HGF induces the invasion of MDCK epithelial cells into collagen in a dose-dependent manner. Some human carcinoma cell lines respond to SF/HGF by movement whereas others are insensitive to the factor (Weidner et al., 1990).

The SF/HGF cDNA, recently isolated from several sources such as placenta, liver, leukocytes or fibroblasts (Miyazawa et al., 1989; Nakamura et al., 1989; Seki et al., 1990; Rubin et al., 1991; Weidner et al., 1991), encodes a 83 kDa protein with sequence and overall structure similar to plasminogen and other enzymes involved in blood clotting, fibrinolysis and complement activation. The primary translation product is an inactive precursor (Hartmann et al., 1992; Lokker et al., 1992) which is proteolytically processed into the active, disulfide-linked heterodimer. The

heavy (H) chain is composed of a short N-terminal region followed by four kringle modules, and the light (L) chain exhibits sequence similarity to serine proteases, but SF/HGF has no detectable proteolytic activity, possibly due to alterations of two of three amino acid residues forming the catalytic site (serine and histidine residues are replaced by tyrosine and glutamine, respectively). The light chain is produced by proteolytic processing of the precursor at a dibasic cleavage site.

The receptor for SF/HGF has recently been identified as the c-Met protooncogene product (Bottaro et al., 1991; Naldini et al., 1991), which is a transmembrane protein with tyrosine kinase activity. The MET gene is expressed in a variety of epithelial cells as well as in a number of tumors of epithelial origin (Di Renzo et al., 1991). The Met receptor is a 190 kDa heterodimer made up of a 50 kDa α-subunit disulphide-linked to a 145 kDa β-subunit which is synthesized as a single-chain precursor and then proteolyzed to yield the mature two-chain protein (Giordano et al., 1989). The α chain and the N-terminal portion of the β chain are located in the cytoplasm and contain the tyrosine kinase domain as well as phosphorylation sites involved in the regulation of the activity of the protein and in signal transduction. Binding of SF/HGF to the Met receptor was demonstrated by coprecipitation in immunocomplexes, by chemical crosslinking to the β-subunit of the Met protein and by ligand-induced tyrosine phosphorylation of the receptor (Naldini et al., 1991). In addition to the specific, high affinity receptor Met, low affinity/high capacity binding sites of SF/HGF have been detected in binding experiments (Naldini et al., 1991). Since it is known that SF/HGF binds to heparin, it is likely that heparan sulfate proteoglycans of the extracellular matrix and the cell surface provide these additional binding sites.

Expression of naturally occurring splice variants and in vitro-mutagenized cDNAs of SF/HGF allowed us to define the biological activities of different SF/HGF isoforms. The recombinant molecules also enabled us to delineate the protein domains of SF/HGF necessary for Met receptor interaction and activation (Hartmann et al., 1992). The results were as follows. (1) A single-chain SF/HGF resulting from the destruction of the protease cleavage site between heavy and light chain (Arg-494 + Gln) was largely inactive, indicating that proteolytic cleavage is essential for acquisition of the biologically active conformation. (2) A SF/HGF splice variant encoding a protein with a 5-amino acid deletion in the first kringle domain was as highly active as the wild-type molecule. (3) The separately expressed light chain (with serine protease homology) was inactive in all assays tested. (4) The separate heavy chain as well as a naturally occurring splice variant consisting of the N terminus and the first two kringle domains bound the c-Met receptor, stimulated tyrosine autophosphorylation, and induced scattering of epithelial cells but not mitogenesis. These data indicate that a functional domain in the N terminus/first two kringle regions of SF/HGF is sufficient for binding to the Met receptor and that this leads to the activation of the downstream signal cascade involved in the motility response. However, the complete SF/HGF protein seems to be required for mitogenic activity.

We have also addressed the question of whether all biological signals of SF/HGF are actually transmitted into the cell by the Met receptor. For this purpose, we have introduced into epithelial cells a cDNA expression vector encoding a hybrid tyrosine kinase receptor, which consists of the membrane-spanning and cytoplasmic domains of Met fused to the extracellular domain of the NGF receptor (trk) (Weidner et al., 1993). It has previously been shown that the extracellular domains of such hybrid receptors provide the ligand specificity, whereas the tyrosine kinase domain is responsible for the signalling specificity (Riedel et al., 1989; Bernhanu et al., 1990). We then asked which of the biological activities normally induced by SF/HGF could now be observed in response to NGF. We could demonstrate that all biological effects of SF/HGF upon epithelial cells such as the induction of cell motility, proliferation, invasiveness and tubular morphogenesis (Montesano et al., 1991) are now triggered by the addition of NGF. Thus, it is likely that all known biological signals of SF/HGF are transduced through the receptor tyrosine kinase encoded by the c-Met protooncogene (Weidner et al., 1993).

Coordinated movement, growth and differentiation of cells are essential prerequisites for embryonal development and tissue regeneration in vivo. A recurring picture in development is that certain groups of cells influence motility, growth and differentiation of other cells in their vicinity. In particular, exchange of signals between epithelial and mesenchymal cell compartments are major driving forces in development (cf. Ekblom 1989; Gumbiner 1992, for reviews). Recently, several receptor tyrosine kinases expressed in epithelia and their mesenchymally derived ligands have been implicated in these mesenchymal-epithelial interactions (see Stern et al., 1990; Montesano et al., 1991; Sonnenberg et al., 1991, 1992; Wen et al., 1992; Holmes et al., 1992; cf. Birchmeier and Birchmeier, 1993, for a review). The best characterized of these receptor/ligand systems involved in mesenchymal-epithelial interactions is SF/HGF/c-Met. Studies of SF/HGF and Met expression in cell culture show that the ligand is generally not produced by the same cells which respond to it and which express the receptor (Stoker et al., 1987; Weidner et al., 1991; Naldini et al., 1991). Furthermore, during mouse embryogenesis the cells expressing SF/HGF are also different but often in close vicinity to cells which transcribe the c-Met gene, suggesting a paracrine mode of action in vivo as well. For example, during kidney development c-Met is expressed in the epithelia of the ureter buds and of the proximal and distal tubules; transcripts for SF/HGF are found in the surrounding nephrogenic mesenchyme (Sonnenberg et al., 1992). Our present data suggest that the paracrine effects of SF/HGF in vivo leading to changes in cell motility, migration, differentiation and proliferation, are also mediated through the protooncogene product c-Met.

How could signal transduction through the Met receptor result in disturbance of intercellular junctions? The Met tyrosine kinase could directly phosphorylate junctional components, as seen in the case of the v-src gene product. Alternatively, the Met kinase could activate downstream targets such as c-src and thus indirectly induce phosphorylation of junctional complexes. No such reactions have so far been discovered. However, c-src seems to be involved in downstream signalling of other receptor tyrosine kinases.

Lastly, activation of Met could lead to changes in gene expression, which might indirectly affect junctional complexes.

We thank B. Lelekakis for excellent secretarial work and the Deutsche Forschungsgemeinschaft and the Deutsche Krebshilfe for financial support.

REFERENCES

Behrens, J., Birchmeier, W., Goodman, S. L. and Imhof, B. A. (1985). Dissociation of Madin-Darby canine kidney epithelial cells by the monoclonal antibody anti-Arc 1: Mechanistic aspects and identification of the antigens as a component related to uvomorulin. *J. Cell Biol.* **101**, 1307-1315

Behrens, J., Frixen, U., Schipper, J., Weidner, M. and Birchmeier, W. (1992). Cell adhesion in invasion and metastasis. *Semin. Cell Biol.* **3**, 169-178.

Behrens, J., Löwrick, O., Klein-Hitpass, L. and Birchmeier, W. (1991). The E-cadherin promoter: Functional analysis of a GC-rich region and an epithelial cell-specific palindromic regulatory element. *Proc. Nat. Acad. Sci. USA* **88**, 11495-11499.

Behrens, J., Mareel, M. M., Van Roy, F. M. and Birchmeier, W. (1989). Dissecting tumor cell invasion: Epithelial cells acquire invasive properties after the loss of uvomorulin-mediated cell-cell adhesion. *J. Cell Biol.* **108**, 2435-3447.

Behrens, J., Vakaet, L., Friis, R., Winterhager, E., Van Roy, F., Mareel, M. M. and Birchmeier, W. (1993). Loss of epithelial differentiation and gain of invasiveness correlates with tyrosine phosphorylation of the E-cadherin/β catenin complex in cells transformed with a temperature-sensitive v-src gene. *J. Cell Biol.* **120**, 757-766.

Berhanu, P., Rohilla, A. M. K. and Rutter, W. J. (1990). Replacement of the human insulin receptor transmembrane and cytoplasmic domains by corresponding domains of the oncogene product v-ros leads to accelerated internalization, degradation, and down-regulation. *J. Biol. Chem.* **265**, 9505-9511.

Birchmeier, C. and Birchmeier, W. (1993). Molecular aspects of mesenchymal-epithelial interactions. *Annu. Rev. Cell Biol.* (in press).

Boller, K., Vestweber, D. and Kemler, R. (1985). Cell adhesion molecule uvomorulin is localized in the intermediate junctions of adult intestinal epithelial cells. *J. Cell Biol.* **100**, 327-332.

Bottaro, D. P., Rubin, J. S., Faletto, D. L., Chan, A. M.-L., Kmiecik, T. E., Vande Woude, G. F. and Aaronson, S. A. (1991). Identification of the hepatocyte growth factor receptor as the c-met proto-oncogene product. *Science* **251**, 802-804.

Chen, W. and Öbrink, B. (1991). Cell contacts mediated by E-cadherin (uvomorulin) restrict invasive behavior of L-cells. *J. Cell Biol.* **114**, 319-327.

Di Renzo, M. F., Narsimhan, R. P., Olivero, M., Bretti, S., Giordano, S., Medico, E., Gaglia, P., Zara, P. and Comoglio, P. M. (1991). Expression of the Met/HGF receptor in normal and neoplastic human tissues. *Oncogene* **6**, 1997-2003.

Eidelman, S., Damsky, C. H., Wheelock, M. J. and Damianov, I. (1989). Expression of the cell-cell adhesion glycoprotein cell-CAM 120/80 in normal human tissues. *Amer. J. Pathol.* **135**, 101-110.

Ekblom, P. (1989). Developmentally regulated conversion of mesenchyme to epithelium. *Fedn. Proc. Fedn. Amer. Socs. Exp. Biol.* **3**, 2141-2150.

Frixen, U., Behrens, J., Sachs, M., Eberle, G., Voss, B., Warda, A., Löchner, D. and Birchmeier, W. (1991). E-cadherin mediated cell-cell adhesion prevents invasiveness of human carcinoma cell lines. *J. Cell Biol.* **111**, 173-185.

Gabbert, H., Wagner, R., Moll, R. and Gerharz, C.-D. (1985). Tumor dedifferentiation: An important step in tumor invasion. *Exp. Metastasis* **3**, 257-279.

Giordano, S., Ponzetto, C., Di Renzo, M. F., Cooper, C. S. and Comoglio, P. M. (1989). Tyrosine kinase receptor indistinguishable from the c-met protein. *Nature* **339**, 155-156.

Grey, A.-M., Schor, A. M., Rushton, G., Ellis, I. and Schor, S. L. (1989). Purification of the migration stimulating factor produced by fetal and breast cancer patient fibroblasts. *Proc. Nat. Acad. Sci. USA* **86**, 2438-2442.

Gumbiner, B. and Simons, K. (1986). A functional assay for proteins involved in establishing an epithelial occluding barrier: identification of a uvomorulin-like polypeptide. *J. Cell Biol.* **102**, 457-468.

Gumbiner, B. M. (1992). Epithelial morphogenesis. *Cell* **69**, 385-387.

Hartmann, G., Naldini, L., Weidner, K. M., Sachs, M., Vigna, E., Comoglio, P. M. and Birchmeier, W. (1992). A functional domain in the heavy chain of scatter factor/hepatocyte growth factor binds the c-Met receptor, induces cell dissociation but not mitogenesis. *Proc. Nat. Acad. Sci. USA* (in press).

Herrenknecht, K., Ozawa, M., Eckerskorn, C., Lottspeich, F., Lenter, M. and Kemler, R. (1991). The uvomorulin-anchorage protein α catenin is a vinculin homologue. *Proc. Nat. Acad. Sci. USA* **88**, 9156-0160.

Hirano, S., Kimoto, N., Shimoyama, Y., Hirohashi, S. and Takeichi, M. (1992). Identification of a neural α-catenin as a key regulation of cadherin function and multicellular organization. *Cell* **70**, 293-301.

Holmes, W. E., Sliwkowski, M. X., Akita, R. W., Henzel, W. J., Lee, J., Park, J. W., Yansura, D., Abadi, N., Raab, H., Lewis, G. D., Shepard, H. M., Kuang, W.-J., Wood, W. I., Goeddel, D. V. and Vandlen, R. L. (1992). Identification of heregulin, a specific activator of p185/erbB2. *Science* **256**, 1205-1210.

Imhof, B. A., Vollmers, H. P., Goodman, S. L. and Birchmeier, W. (1983). Cell-cell interaction and polarity of epithelial cells: Specific perturbation using a monoclonal antibody. *Cell* **35**, 667-675.

Jouanneau, J., Gavrilowic, J., Caruelle, D., Jaye, M., Moens, G., Caruelle, J.-P. and Thiery, J. P. (1991). Secreted or non-secreted forms of acid fibroblast growth factor produced by transfected epithelial cells influence cell morphology, motility, and invasive potential. *Proc. Nat. Acad. Sci. USA* **88**, 2893-2997.

Kintner, C. (1992). Regulation of embryonic cell adhesion by the cadherin cytoplasmic domain. *Cell* **69**, 225-236.

Leung, D. W., Cachlanes, G., Kuang, W.-J., Goeddel, D. V. and Ferrara, N. (1989). Vascular endothelial growth factor is a secreted angiogenic mitogen. *Science* **246**, 1306-1309.

Liotta, L. A., Mandler, R., Murano, G., Katz, D. A., Gordon, R. K., Ching, P. K. and Schiffmann, E. (1986). Tumor cell autocrine motility factor. *Proc. Nat. Acad. Sci. USA* **83**, 3302-3306.

Lokker, N. A., Mark, M. R., Luis, E. A., Bennett, G. L., Robbins, K. A., Baker, J. B. and Godowsky, P. J. (1992). Structure-function analysis of hepatocyte growth factor: Identification of variants that lack mitogenic activity yet retain high affinity receptor binding. *EMBO J.* **11**, 2503-2510.

Matsuyoshi, N., Hamaguchi, M., Taniguchi, S., Nagafuchi, A., Tsuchita, S. and Takeichi, M. (1992). Cadherin mediated cell-cell adhesion is perturbed by v-src tyrosine phosphorylation in metastatic fibroblasts. *J. Cell Biol.* **118**, 703-714.

Matsuzaki, F., Mege, R.-M., Jaffe, S. H., Friedlander, D. R., Gallin, W., Goldberg, J. I., Cunningham, B. A. and Edelman, G. M. (1990). cDNAs of cell adhesion molecules of different specificity induce changes in cell shape and border formation in cultured S180 cells. *J. Cell Biol.* **110**, 1239-1252.

Mayer, B., Johnson, J. P., Leitl, F., Jauch, K. W., Heiss, M. M., Schildberg, F. W., Birchmeier, W. and Funke, I. (1993). E-cadherin expression in primary and metastatic gastric cancer: Downregulation correlates with cellular dedifferentiation and glandular disintegration. *Cancer Res.* (in press).

McCrea, P. D. and Gumbiner, B. M. (1991). Purification of a 92-kDa cytoplasmic protein tightly associated with the cell-cell adhesion molecule E-cadherin (uvomorulin). *J. Biol. Chem.* **266**, 4514-4520.

McCrea, P. D., Turck, C. W. and Gumbiner, B. (1991). A homolog of the armadillo protein in Drosophila (plakoglobin) associated with E-cadherin. *Science* **254**, 1359-1361.

McNeill, H., Ozawa, M., Kemler, R. and Nelson, W. J. (1990). Novel function of the cell adhesion molecule uvomorulin as an inducer of cell surface polarity. *Cell* **62**, 309-316.

Miyazawa, K., Tsubouchi, H., Naka, D., Takahashi, K., Okigaki, M., Arakaki, N., Nakayama, H., Hirono, S., Sakiyama, O., Takahashi, K., Gohda, E., Daikuhara, Y. and Kitamura, N. (1989). Molecular cloning and sequence analysis of cDNA for human hepatocyte growth factor. *Biochem. Biophys. Res. Commun.* **163**, 967-973.

Moll, R., Mitze, M., Frixen, H. and Birchmeier, W. (1993). Differentiated loss of E-cadherin expression on infiltrating ductal and lobular breast carcinomas. *Amer. J. Pathol.* (in press).

Montesano, R., Matsumoto, K., Nakamura, T. and Orci, L. (1991). Identification of a fibroblast-derived epithelial morphogen as hepatocyte growth fator. *Cell* **67**, 901-908.

Nagafuchi, A. and Takeichi, M. (1988). Cell binding function of E-cadherin is regulated by the cytoplasmic domain. *EMBO J.* **7**, 3679-3684.

Nagafuchi, A., Shirayoshi, Y., Okazaki, K., Yasuda, K. and Takeichi, M. (1987). Transformation of cell adhesion properties by exogenously introduced E-cadherin cDNA. *Nature* **329**, 340-343.

Nagafuchi, A., Takeichi, M. and Tsukita, S. (1991). The 102 kd cadherin-associated protein: similarity to vinculin and posttranscriptional regulation of expression. *Cell* **65**, 849-857.

Nakamura, T., Nishizawa, T., Hagiya, M., Seki, T., Shimouishi, M., Sugimura, A., Tashiro, K. and Shimizu, S. (1989). Molecular cloning and expression of human hepatocyte growth factor. *Nature* **342**, 440-443.

Naldini, L., Weidner, K. M., Vigna, E., Gaudino, G., Bardelli, A., Ponzetto, C., Narsimhan, R. P., Hartmann, G., Zarnegar, R., Michalopoulos, G. K., Birchmeier, W. and Comoglio, P. M. (1991). Scatter factor and hepatocyte growth factor are indistinguishable ligands for the MET receptor. *EMBO J.* **10**, 2867-2878.

Navarro, P., Gomez, M., Pizarro, A., Gamallo, C., Guintanilla, M. and Cano, A. (1991). A role for the E-cadherin cell adhesion molecule during tumor progression of mouse epidermal carcinogenesis. *J. Cell Biol.* **115**, 517-533.

Ozawa, M. and Kemler, R. (1992). Molecular organization of the uvomorulin-catenin complex. *J. Cell Biol.* **116**, 989-996.

Ozawa, M., Baribault, H. and Kemler, R. (1989). The cytoplasmic domain of the cell adhesion molecule uvomorulin associates with three independent proteins structurally related in different species. *EMBO J.* **8**, 1711-1717.

Ozawa, M., Engel, J. and Kemler, R. (1990a). Single amino acid substitutions in one Ca^{2+} binding site of uvomorulin abolish the adhesive function. *Cell* **63**, 1033-1038.

Ozawa, M., Ringwald, M. and Kemler, R. (1990b). Uvomorulin-catenin complex formation is regulated by a specific domain in the cytoplasmic region of the cell adhesion molecule. *Proc. Nat. Acad. Sci. USA* **87**, 4246-4250.

Reichmann, E., Schwarz, H., Deiner, E. M., Leitner, I., Eilers, M., Berger, J., Busslinger, M. and Beug, H. (1992). Activation of an inducible c-fos-ER fusion protein causes loss of epithelial polarity and triggers epithelial-fibroblastoid cell conversion. *Cell* **71**, 1103-116.

Riedel, H., Dull, T. J., Honegger, A. M., Schlessinger, J. and Ullrich, A. (1989). Cytoplasmic domains determine signal specificity, cellular routing characteristics and influence ligand binding of epidermal growth factor and insulin receptors. *EMBO J.* **8**, 2943-2954.

Rosen, E. M., Meromsky, L., Setter, E., Vinter, D. W. and Goldberg, I. D. (1990). Purified scatter factor stimulates epithelial and vascular endothelial cell migration. *Proc. Soc. Exp. Biol. Med.* **195**, 34-43.

Rubin, J. S., Chan, A. M.-L., Bottaro, D. P., Burgess, W. H., Taylor, W. G., Cech, A. C., Hirschfield, D. W., Wong, J., Miki, T., Finch, P. W. and Aaronson, S. A. (1991). A broad-spectrum human lung fibroblast-derived mitogen is a variant of hepatocyte growth factor. *Proc. Nat. Acad. Sci. USA* **88**, 415-419.

Schipper, J. H., Frixen, U. H., Behrens, J., Unger, A., Jahnke, K. and Birchmeier, W. (1991). E-cadherin expression in squamous cell carcinomas of head and neck: inverse correlation with tumor dedifferentiation and lymph node metastasis. *Cancer Res.* **51**, 6328-6337.

Seki, T., Ihara, I., Sugimura, A., Shimonishi, M., Nishizawa, T., Asami, O., Hagiya, M., Nakamura, T. and Shimizu, S. (1990). Isolation and expression of cDNA for different forms of hepatocyte growth factor from human leukocyte. *Biochem. Biophys. Res. Commun.* **172**, 321-327.

Shimoyama, Y. and Hirohashi, S. (1991a). Expression of E- and P-cadherin in gastric carcinomas. *Cancer Res.* **51**, 2185-2192.

Shimoyama, Y. and Hirohashi, S. (1991b). Cadherin intercellular adhesion molecule in hepatocellular carcinomas: loss of E-cadherin expression in an undifferentiated carcinoma. *Cancer Lett.* **57**, 131-135.

Shimoyama, Y., Nagafuchi, A., Fujita, S., Gotoh, M., Takeichi; M., Tsukita, S. and Hirohashi, S. (1992). Cadherin dysfunction in a human cancer cell line: Possible involvement of loss of α-catenin expression in reduced cell-cell adhesiveness. *Cancer Res.* **52**, 1-5.

Shiozaki, H., Tahara, H., Oka, H., Miyata, M., Kobayashi, K., Tamura, S., Iihara, K., Doki, Y., Hiran, S., Takeichi, M. and Mori, T. (1991). Expression of E-cadherin adhesion molecules in human cancers. *Amer. J. Pathol.* **139**, 17-23.

Sonnenberg, E., Gödecke, A., Walter, B., Bladt, F. and Birchmeier, C. (1991). Transient and locally restricted expression of the ros 1 protooncogene during mouse development. *EMBO J.* **10**, 3693-3702.

Sonnenberg, E., Weidner, K. M. and Birchmeier, C. (1992). Expression of the met-receptor and its ligand, scatter factor/hepatocyte growth factor, during mouse development. In *Hepatocyte Growth Factor/Scatter Factor and the c-met Receptor* (ed. I. D. Goldberg). Birkäuser Verlag, Basel (in press).

Stern, C. D., Ireland, G. W., Herrick, S. E., Gherardi, E., Gray, J., Perryman, M. and Stoker, M. (1990). Epithelial scatter factor and development of the chick embryonic axis. *Development* **110**, 1271-1284.

Stoker, M. and Gherardi, E. (1991). Regulation of cell movement: The mitogenic cytokines. *Biochim. Biophys. Acta* **1072**, 81-102.

Stoker, M., Gherardi, E., Perryman, M. and Gray, J. (1987). Scatter factor is a fibroblast-derived modulator of epithelial cell motility. *Nature* **327**, 239-242.

Vleminckx, K., Vakaet, L., Mareel, M., Fiers, W. and Van Roy, F. (1991). Genetic manipulation of E-cadherin expression by epithelial tumor cells reveals an invasion suppressor role. *Cell* **66**, 107-119.

Weidner, K. M., Arakaki, N., Hartmann, G., Vandekerckhove, J., Weingart, S., Rieder, H., Fonatsch, C., Tsubouchi, H., Hishida, T., **Daikuhara, Y. and Birchmeier, W.** (1991). Evidence for the identity of human scatter factor and hepatocyte growth factor. *Proc. Nat. Acad. Sci. USA* **88**, 7001-7005.

Weidner, K. M., Behrens, J., Vandekerckhove, J. and Birchmeier, W. (1990). Scatter factor: Molecular characteristics and effect on the invasiveness of epithelial cells. *J. Cell Biol.* **111**, 2097-2108.

Weidner, K. M., Sachs, M. and Birchmeier, W. (1993). The *Met* receptor tyrosine kinase transduces motility, proliferation, and morphogenic signals of scatter factor/hepatocyte growth factor in epithelial cells. *J. Cell Biol.* **121**, 145-154.

Weinstein, R. S., Merk, F. B. and Alroy, J. (1976). The structure and function of intercellular junctions in cancer. *Advan. Cancer Res.* **23**, 23-89.

Wen, D., Peles, E., Cupples, R., Suggs, S. V., Bacus, S. S., Luo, Y., Trail, G., Hu, S., Silbiger, S. M., Levy, R. B., Koski, R. A., Lu, H. S. and Yarden, Y. (1992). Neu differentiation factor: A transmembrane glycoprotein containing an EGF domain and an immunoglobulin homology unit. *Cell* **69**, 559-572.

Journal of Cell Science, Supplement 17, 165-169 (1993)
Printed in Great Britain © The Company of Biologists Limited 1993

Patches and fences: probing for plasma membrane domains

Michael Edidin

Biology Department, The Johns Hopkins University, Baltimore, MD 21218, USA

SUMMARY

Cell plasma membranes appear to be composed of domains, patches whose composition and function differ from the average for an entire membrane surface. Proteins and lipids may be segregated into domains by different mechanisms. Some of these mechanisms are discussed, followed by a summary of the evidence for membrane domains obtained in my laboratory. This evidence is largely based on measurements of the lateral diffusion of membrane proteins and lipids. Recent new approaches to the interpretation of lateral diffusion measurements, consideration of so-called fractal or long time-tails promise to give new insights into the stability and lifetime of membrane domains.

Key words: plasma membrane, lateral diffusion, fluorescence, FPR, domains

INTRODUCTION

For many years my laboratory's work has focused on problems concerning the lateral diffusion of plasma membrane proteins and lipids. These studies began with Larry Frye's demonstration that some integral membrane proteins, class I MHC molecules, were indeed mobile in the plane of the bilayer (Frye and Edidin, 1970). The demonstration that lateral mobility was due to Brownian motion, diffusion, and not to convection or other ATP-driven processes (Edidin and Wei, 1977) was the starting point for a series of studies quantitating lateral diffusion and investigating the molecular constraints to diffusion. The studies began with an important assumption: the fluid bilayer is a random mixture of lipids and proteins. However, as our measurements progressed, particularly as we began to compare the diffusion of different but related lipid probes (Wolf et al., 1981a), we found that our assumption was not correct. Lateral diffusion of both lipids and proteins appears to reflect a membrane that is patchy, one whose component molecules interact with one another. Diffusion measurements then become a way of describing the lateral organization of membranes (Edidin, 1990, 1992). In this paper I will first briefly summarize the ways in which inhomogeneous, patchy membranes might form and raise some unresolved problems with the nature of these membranes. Then, I will illustrate the problem with some of the evidence for inhomogeneities obtained in my laboratory. Finally, I will mention an alternative approach to thinking about membrane organization.

LIPIDS AND PROTEINS IN MEMBRANE DOMAINS

Inhomogeneities in plasma membranes in the size range of tens to thousands of nm, that persist on a time scale of tens to thousands of seconds, are commonly termed membrane domains. Broadly speaking there are two bases for the formation of these domains, namely segregation and self-association of membrane lipids, to form patches whose composition differs from that of the average lipid composition of the bilayer, and corraling of membrane proteins by proteins of the cytoskeleton. Lipid segregation is generally thought of in terms of the separation of immiscible species - at the extreme the separation of gel and liquid-crystalline lipid phases (Vaz, 1992). Corrals may enhance the aggregation of membrane proteins, and proteins may be anchored to their component fences, but they are primarily barriers to lateral diffusion (Edidin, 1992).

Though the two forms of domain seem to be antithetical, they in fact overlap a good deal. There is evidence that the formation of lipid domains in erythrocyte membranes is promoted by membrane proteins (see Glaser, 1992; Gawrisch et al., 1993). These effects could be due to the selective binding of lipids by membrane proteins. For example, the boundary lipids associated with the transmembrane domains of membrane proteins (Marsh, 1983) could serve to nucleate the formation of lipid domains. Or, lipid domains could be created by the lateral pressure of transmembrane and cytoskeleton proteins on the bilayer (McGregor and Hunt, 1990). On the other hand, proteins may form domains by aggregation. Protein/protein associations in turn are enhanced if a population of proteins is confined to a small area of the membrane by barriers (Peters, 1988).

The physical basis for domain formation is related to another critical issue, the lifetime and stability of domains. We know that lipid domains are not likely to be immiscible phases in equilibrium with the rest of a membrane; such an equilibrium system is dead. However, if they are not phases, then what are they? It has been suggested that they reflect non-ideal mixing of lipids (Wolf, 1992). In that case most of the features detected as lipid domains are relatively short-lived, perhaps with lifetimes not much longer than the few minutes required to make a lateral diffusion measurement. However, the suggestion also implies that membrane lipids are delivered to the surface in patches. This simply moves the problem of selective association of lipids back to the sites of their synthesis in endomembranes. A mechanism for lipid patching in the Golgi membranes has been proposed to explain the polarized sorting of glycolipids and glycolipid-anchored proteins in morphologically polarized cells (Simons and van Meer, 1988; Lisanti and Rodriguez-Boulan, 1990). With only a few exceptions (Thompson and Tillack, 1985; Hannan et al., 1993), the evidence for glycolipid and GPI-protein clusters is the isolation of detergent-resistant complexes enriched in these components from polarized epithelial cells (Brown and Rose, 1992) and from lymphoblasts (Stefanova et al., 1991, 1992). These complexes can only be isolated at 4°C, raising the question of their physiological relevance.

Similar arguments apply to protein-enriched domains. Some of these, for example proteins localized to basal surfaces of epithelial cells, form aggregates associated with the cytoskeleton (Nelson et al., 1990). Clusters of acetylcholine receptors also form in this way (Wang and Axelrod, 1993). Though there may be exchange of molecules between the clusters and the rest of the membrane, the clusters themselves persist for days. On the other hand, as we will see below, some domains defined in fibroblasts and hepatoma cells reflect the average state of a membrane cytoskeleton that itself is constantly remodeled.

USING FLUORESCENCE PHOTOBLEACHING AND RECOVERY (FPR) TO DETECT MEMBRANE DOMAINS

FPR, a microscope-based technique, evolved to quantitate lateral diffusion of membrane components (Axelrod et al., 1976; Jacobson et al., 1976; Edidin et al., 1976). Diffusion of a population of fluorescent membrane molecules, lipid analogs or integral proteins labeled with fluorescent antibody fragments, is monitored by partly bleaching a spot (usually a few μm^2) in the membrane and then following the recovery of fluorescence after the bleach. The shape of the recovery curve may be used to distinguish diffusion from flow. The extent of recovery of fluorescence gives an indication of the fraction of fluorescent molecules that is free to move in the time of observation, and the time required to reach half-maximum recovery, together with area bleached (measured independently), reflects the diffusion coefficient of the fluorescent label. The technical approaches and problems in making FPR measurements are well discussed in a recent article (Wolf, 1989).

FPR, LIPID PROBES AND LIPID DOMAINS

FPR measurements of a series of fluorescent lipid probes, carbocyanine dyes, DiI Cn (Sims et al., 1974), gave us our

first indications of heterogeneity of membrane lipids. The probes all have the same fluorophore headgroup, indocarbocyanin iodide, DiI. Two saturated hydrocarbon chains are attached to each fluorophore and members of the DiI Cn series differ from one another in the length of these chains (n). Lipid-soluble forms of the probe have chain lengths ranging from 10 to 22 carbons, DiI C10 to DiI C22. Klausner and Wolf (1980) showed that in liposomes, DiI Cn partition between fluid and solid phases, depending on their hydrocarbon chain length. Short-chain molecules are concentrated in fluid phospholipid phases, while long-chain molecules, up to C20, concentrate in gel phases. C22 and longer chains extend more than the average thickness of a half bilayer, curl back on themselves and perturb the bilayer, so these show a preference for fluid lipids.

If a cell plasma membrane is a fluid mixture of randomly dispersed lipids and proteins, then we expect that the observed diffusion coefficient, D, and the mobile fraction, R, will be the same for all DiI, independent of the hydrocarbon chain length (n). If the membrane contains patches of different compositions and viscosities, then we expect to see a dependence of D and R on the length of the DiI hydrocarbon chains (Fig. 1). Indeed, we found this dependence when comparing diffusion of DiI probes in sea urchin and mouse egg plasma membranes (Wolf et al., 1981a,b).

In recent experiments on membranes of human lymphoblasts, we found that DiI C18 probed different regions of the cell membrane when cells were labeled at 20°C from when they were labeled at 37°C. R, the mobile fraction of

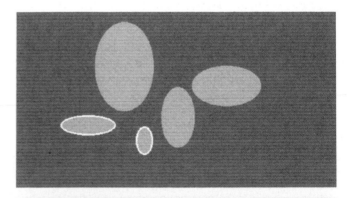

Fig. 1. Partition of indocarbocyanin iodide, DiI, fluorescent lipid probes into gel and fluid phases. Dark shading, short-chain DiI, light shading, long-chain DiI. Top, a bilayer membrane that consists of gel phase lipid domains in a fluid continuum. Bottom, a membrane that consists of fluid lipid domains in a gel phase continuum. After Klausner and Wolf, 1980.

DiI C18, did not change with temperature when cells were labeled at 20°C and diffusion of the probe at 20°C was compared with its diffusion at 35°C. In contrast, when cells were labeled at 37°C the mobile fraction of the probe was very sensitive to temperature, increasing about twofold when the temperature was increased by 15°C. It appears that at 37°C, DiI C18 can partition into regions of the cell membrane that are inaccessible to the probe at 20°C.

The results just quoted suggest that some membrane lipids are segregated from the bulk of the membrane when cells are cooled from growth temperature, 37°C. The chemical and physical composition of these domains will differ from those of the rest of the membrane and they are also likely to contain a sample of membrane proteins that differs from the average. The experiments still do not show if lipid patches of different compositions and physical properties exist at 37°C. A different way of using FPR, applicable to lipids and proteins, may allow us to detect patches that occur in mammalian cells at physiological temperatures.

FPR AS A GENERAL METHOD FOR DETECTING MEMBRANE DOMAINS

In a model FPR experiment, the time for recovery of fluorescence depends upon the size of the area bleached, a, but the extent of recovery is independent of a until $a \to a$ significant fraction of the total labeled surface, A (Wey et al., 1981). The experiments summarized in the last section kept a constant and varied the chain length of the fluorescent probes. The experiments summarized in this section depend upon using a single probe and varying a. If the probe labels a membrane continuum then the recovery of fluorescence ought to be independent of a for $a \ll A$. On the other hand, if the probe labels patches of membrane with area P, itself $\ll A$, then the recovery of fluorescence will fall as $a \to A$ and will be even lower for $a > A$.

Based on the preceding argument, we expect to detect domains by observing a systematic fall in fluorescence recovery when FPR measurements are made on a single population of cells, labeled with only one fluorescent label, but using a series of different-sized measuring spots. Unlike the experiments with lipid analogs, this FPR experiment is

perfectly general. No matter what the fluorescent label, any time we find the relationship:

$$R = k \, 1/a, \qquad (1)$$

(where k is some constant of proportionality), we are detecting membrane domains.

Membrane domains, defined by the kinds of FPR experiments just described, are detectable in several different kinds of cells: normal and transformed human fibroblasts, human T-lymphoblasts, and mouse hepatoma cells (Yechiel and Edidin, 1987; Edidin and Stroynowski, 1991; Edidin, unpublished). The diI probes and GPI-anchored proteins do not seem to be included in these domains, but several kinds of transmembrane proteins, as well as the lipid analog NBD-PC, are found there. The diffusion behavior of the NBD-PC analog suggests that as we use it, adding it to membranes from a stock solution in ethanol, it binds to proteins and so reports patches of proteins that need not be lipid domains as well (Yechiel and Edidin, 1987).

We can estimate the size of the domains from a simple geometric argument. As long as $a < P$, then in equation 1:

$$k = a/P, \qquad (2)$$

but if $a > P$ then:

$$k = \sqrt{a}/\sqrt{P}, \qquad (3)$$

(Fig. 2). Beginning with the smallest a, we find that the regression of R on a is fit well by 2 until $a \sim 3 \ \mu m^2$, that is until the radius of the bleached spot is about 1 μm. Beginning with the largest a, we find that the regression of R on a is fit well by 3, again until $a \sim 3 \ \mu m^2$. Both forms of k (2 and 3) assume $a \neq P$. The value at which both fits deviate from the experimental data then is close to $a = P$. Hence the radii of domains defined by this experiments is around 1 μm.

BEYOND FPR AND BEYOND STATIC DOMAINS

The definition of domains by either of our FPR experiments is a static definition. Domains seem to have a lifetime of at least a few minutes since this is the time required for a FPR measurement, but we cannot learn anything more about them from FPR.

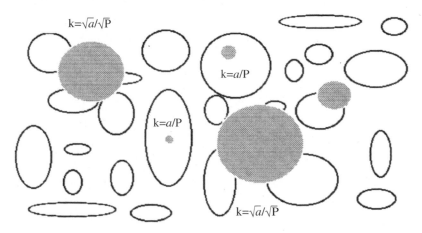

Fig. 2. FPR geometry and membrane domains. The cell membrane is drawn as a collection of closed domains (unshaded ovals) in a phopholipid continuum. Domains may be enriched in particular proteins or may represent lipids that are immiscible in the phospholipid continuum. Projections of the laser beam used in FPR for bleaching and measuring fluorescence are shown as shaded circles. If these spots are small relative to the domains, then the recovery depends upon the ratio of the area of the laser beam to the area of a domain, noted on the diagram as k=a/P (see equations (2) and (3) in the text). For large spots, recovery depends upon the ratio of the perimeters of the beam and the domains, noted on the diagram as k=$\sqrt{a}$/$\sqrt{P}$.

We obtained a different view of membrane domains in experiments with Michael Sheetz in which membrane proteins were labeled by 40 nm gold beads coated with small numbers of specific antibodies. The beads were then gripped in a laser optical trap (Kuo and Sheetz, 1992) and moved through the cell membrane by translating the microscope stage with a piezoelectric controller. Some beads could not be moved at all, but most moved a significant distance before meeting an obstacle and being torn out of the laser trap. At 23°C the average barrier-free path of beads attached to molecules of a transmembrane protein, the class I MHC molecule H-2D^b, was about 0.6 μm, a good approximation to the value of 1 μm estimated from FPR experiments. The average barrier-free path of a GPI-anchored form of class I MHC molecule, Qa2, was 3× larger (Edidin et al., 1991), consistent with the apparent ability of this molecule to cross domain boundaries. When the measurements were repeated at 34°C we found that gold/H-2D^b traveled an average of 3.5 μm before meeting an obstacle and gold/Qa2 traveled an average of 8.5 μm. Thus, the barriers to lateral movement defined as static domains by FPR experiments prove to be dynamic, and what were previous seen as the radii of membrane domains should be considered as averages of distributions of the probability of a molecule meeting an obstacle in a given distance of lateral travel. Patches are not static.

THE STATISTICS OF DIFFUSION

The dynamic picture of membrane domains obtained from optical trap experiments contrasts with the view from FPR. Membrane domains are not static; they constantly change in extent and in composition. We need another way to describe the constraints to lateral dynamics of membrane proteins.

A general approach to the lateral dynamics of interacting systems is offered by a consideration not of R, the recovery of fluorescence in an FPR experiment, but of D. Just as R is not expected to scale with a, so, if a is known, D, the observed diffusion coefficient, is not expected to scale with a; only the observed half-time for recovery should change. Again, this is not the case; D for membrane proteins increases with increasing a, reaching a limit set by membrane lipid viscosity (Edidin and Stroynowski, 1991). This paradox is rationalized when we consider the FPR recovery curve as the sum of the recoveries of many smaller populations of molecules whose members are in different membrane environments. Labeled molecules that do not interact with their neighbors, or that do not meet barriers in their diffusion, contribute to a rapid recovery of fluorescence, while labeled molecules that do meet barriers, or that interact with membrane or cytoskeleton, will arrive more slowly at the bleach site and contribute to a prolonged, slow fluorescence recovery. If one waits long enough both sorts of recoveries will be detected. In practice FPR measurements using small spots miss unhindered diffusion and underestimate D. FPR measurements using large spots miss hindered diffusion and so underestimate recovery, while yielding higher D. Another way of stating the problem is to say that D varies with the time of measurement. Long time tails, time-dependent D and R indicate interactions between diffusing molecules and other components of the membrane (Nagle, 1992; Brust-Mascher et al., 1993).

The approach just taken is very general and makes no assumptions about the nature of the molecular interactions that give rise to long or fractal time tails. It would be worth applying not only to problems in protein/protein interactions in membranes, but to a reconsideration of the experiments on the detergent solubility of GPI-proteins and glycolipids (Brown and Rose, 1992; Stefanova and Horejsi, 1991; Stefanova et al., 1992). The detergent-insoluble molecular complexes isolated at 4°C may represent dynamic, but real, associations of membrane components, stabilized at low temperature. Their components certainly seem to interact strongly enough to allow signaling through GPI-molecules (Hahn and Soloski, 1988; Davis et al., 1988; Thompson et al., 1988). To understand these and other membrane events we will need to think more about the statistics, rather than the statics of molecular interactions in membranes.

REFERENCES

Axelrod, D., Koppel, D. E., Schlessinger, J., Elson, E. and Webb, W. W. (1976). Mobility measurement by analysis of fluorescence photobleaching recovery kinetics. *Biophys. J.* **16**, 1055-1069.

Brown, D. A. and Rose, J. K. (1992). Sorting of GPI-anchored proteins to glycolipid enriched membrane subdomains during transport to apical cell surface. *Cell* **67**, 533-544.

Brust-Mascher, I., Feder, T. J., Slattery, J. P., Baird, B. and Webb, W. W. (1993). FPR data on mobility of cell surface proteins reevaluated in terms of temporarily constrained molecular motions. *Biophys J.* **64**, A354.

Davis, L. S., Patel, S. S., Atkinson, J. P. and Lipsky, P. E. (1988). Decay-accelerating factor functions as a signal transducing molecule for human T-cells. *J. Immunol.* **141**, 2246-2252.

Edidin, M. (1990). Molecular associations and membrane domains. *Curr. Topics Memb. Trans.* **36**, 81-96.

Edidin, M. (1992). Patches, posts and fences: proteins and plasma membrane domains. *Trends Cell Biol.* **2**, 376-380.

Edidin, M. and Wei, T. (1977). Diffusion rates of cell surface antigens of mouse-human heterokaryons. I. Analysis of the population. *J. Cell Biol.* **75**, 475-482.

Edidin, M. and Stroynowski, I. (1991). Differences between the lateral organization of conventional and inositol phospholipid-anchored membrane proteins. A further definition of micrometer scale membrane domains. *J. Cell Biol.* **112**, 1143-1150.

Edidin, M., Zagyansky, Y. and Lardner, T. J. (1976). Measurement of membrane protein lateral diffusion in single cells. *Science* **191**, 466-468.

Edidin, M., Kuo, S. C. and Sheetz, M. P. (1991). Lateral movements of membrane glycoproteins are restricted by dynamic cytoplasmic barriers. *Science* **254**, 1379-1382.

Frye, L. D. and Edidin, M. (1970). The rapid intermixing of cell surface antigens after formation of mouse-human heterokaryons. *J. Cell Sci.* **7**, 319-335.

Gawrisch, K., Han, K-H, Yang, J-S, Bergelson, L. D. and Ferretti, J. A. (1993). Energetics of binding of a highly amphipathic peptide to membranes: Lipid domain formation and peptide structure. *Biophys J.* **64**, A60.

Glaser, M. (1992). Characterization and formation of lipid domains in vesicles and erythrocyte membranes. *Commun. Molec. Cell. Biophys.* **8**, 37-51.

Hahn, A. and Soloski, M. J. (1988). Anti-Qa2-induced cell activation. *J. Immunol.* **143**, 407-413.

Hannan, L. A., Lisanti, M. P., Rodriguez-Boulan, E. and Edidin, M. (1993). Correctly sorted molecules of a GPI-anchored protein are clustered and immobile when they arrive at the apical surface of MDCK cells. *J. Cell Biol.* **120**, 353-358.

Jacobson, K., Wu, E.-S. and Poste, G. (1976). Measurement of the translational mobility of concanavalin A in glycerol-saline solutions and on the cell surface by fluorescence recovery after photobleaching. *Biochim. Biophys. Acta* **433**, 215-222.

Klausner, R. D. and Wolf, D. E. (1980). Selectivity of fluorescent lipid analogues for lipid domains. *Biochemistry* **19**, 6199-6203.

Kuo, S. C. and Sheetz, M. P. (1992). Optical tweezers in cell biology. *Trends Cell Biol.* **2**, 116-117.

Lisanti, M. P. and Rodriguez-Boulan, E. (1990). Glycosphingolipid membrane anchoring provides clues to the mechanism of protein sorting in polarized epithelial cells. *Trends Biochem. Sci.* **15**, 113-118.

Marsh, D. (1983). Spin-label answers to lipid-protein interactions. *Trends Biochem. Sci.* **8**, 330.

McGregor, R. D. and Hunt, C. A. (1990). Artificial red cells. A link between the membrane skeleton and RES detectability? *Biomater. Artif. Cells Artif. Organs* **18**, 329-343.

Nagle, J. F. (1992). Long tail kinetics in biophysics? *Biophys. J.* **63**, 366-370.

Nelson, W. J., Shore, E. M., Wang, A. Z. and Hammerton, R. W. (1990). Identification of a membrane-cytoskeletal complex containing the cell adhesion molecule uvomorulin (E-cadherin), ankyrin and fodrin in Madin-Darby canine kidney epithelial cells. *J. Cell Biol.* **110**, 349-357.

Peters, R. (1988). Lateral mobility of proteins and lipids in the red cell membrane and the activation of adenylate cyclase by Beta-adrenergic receptors. *FEBS Lett.* **234**, 1-19.

Simons, K. and van Meer G. (1988). Lipid sorting in epithelial cells. *Biochemistry* **27**, 6197-6202.

Sims, P. J., Waggoner, A. S., Wang, C.-H. and Hoffman, J. F. (1974). Studies on the mechanism by which carbocyanine dyes measure membrane potential in red blood cells and phosphatidylcholine vesicles. *Biochemistry* **13**, 3315-3330.

Stefanova, I. and Horejsi, V. (1991). Association of the CD59 and CD55

cell surface glycoproteins with other membrane molecules. *J. Immunol.* **147**, 1587-1592.

Stefanova, I., Horejsi, V., Ansotegui, I. J., Knapp, W. and Stockinger, H. (1992). GPI-anchored cell-surface molecules complexed to protein tyrosine kinases. *Science* **254**, 1016-1019.

Thompson, T. E. and Tillack, T. W. (1985). Organization of glycosphingolipids in bilayers and plasma membranes of mammalian cells. *Annu. Rev. Biophys. Biophys. Chem.* **14**, 361-386.

Thompson, L. I., Ruedel, J. M., Glass, A., Low, M. F. and Lucas, A. H. (1988). Antibodies to 5′-nucleotidase (CD73), a glycosylphosphatidylinositol-anchored protein, cause human peripheral blood T-cells to proliferate. *J. Immunol.* **143**, 1815-1821.

Vaz, W. L. C. (1992). Translational diffusion in phase-separated lipid bilayer membranes. *Commun. Molec. Cell. Biophys.* **8**, 17-36.

Wang, D. and Axelrod, D. (1993). Time-lapse movies of acetylcholine receptor cluster formation on cultured rat myotubes. *Biophys. J.* **64**, A84.

Wey, C-L., Edidin, M. A. and Cone, R. A. (1981). Lateral diffusion of rhodopsin in photoreceptor cells measured by fluorescence photobleaching and recovery (FPR). *Biophys. J.* **33**, 225-232.

Wolf, D. E. (1989). Designing, building and using a fluorescence recovery after photobleaching instrument. In *Methods in Cell Biology,* vol. 39 (ed. D. L. Taylor and Y.-L. Wang), pp. 271-332. New York: Academic Press.

Wolf, D. E. (1992). Lipid domains: The parable of the blind men and the elephant. *Commun. Molec. and Cell. Biophys.* **8**, 83-95.

Wolf, D. E., Kinsey, W., Lenarz, W. and Edidin, M. (1981a). Changes in the organization of the sea urchin egg plasma membrane upon fertilization: Indications from lateral difusion rates of lipid-soluble fluorescent dyes. *Dev. Biol.* **81**, 133-138.

Wolf, D. E., Edidin, M. E. and Handyside, A. H. (1981b). Changes in the organization of the mouse egg plasma membrane upon fertilization and first cleavage: Indications from the lateral diffusion rates of fluorescent lipid analogs. *Dev. Biol.* **85**, 195-198.

Yechiel, E. and Edidin, M. (1987). Micrometer scale domains in fibroblast plasma membranes. *J. Cell Biol.* **105**, 755-760.

Journal of Cell Science, Supplement 17, 171-181 (1993)
Printed in Great Britain © The Company of Biologists Limited 1993

Apical junctions and cell signalling in epithelia

Daniel F. Woods and Peter J. Bryant

Developmental Biology Center, University of California, Irvine, CA 92717, USA

SUMMARY

Genetic analysis in *Drosophila* has led to the identification of several proteins that mediate cell-cell interactions controlling the fate and proliferation of epithelial cells. These proteins are localized or enriched in the adherens and septate junctions at the apical end of the lateral membranes between cells. The proteins localized or enriched at adherens junctions include Notch, which is important for the cell interactions controlling neuroblast and bristle patterning; Boss and sevenless, which are required for the cell interaction that establishes the R7 photoreceptor cell; and Armadillo, required for the wingless-dependent cell interactions that control segment polarity and imaginal disc patterning. Proteins localized at septate junctions include the product of the tumor suppressor gene *dlg*, which is required for septate junction formation, apical basal cell polarity, and the cell interactions that control proliferation. The results suggest that the cell signalling events important for cell fate determination and for cell proliferation control in epithelia occur at the apical junctions. The migration of the nucleus to the apical surface of the epithelium for mitosis may enable it to interact directly with the junction-associated signalling mechanisms.

Key words: adherens junction, septate junction, epithelial cell, mitosis, pattern formation, imaginal disc, ommatidia, *Drosophila*

INTRODUCTION

Epithelial cell layers protect the organism from its environment, separate different compartments of the organism, transport materials from one compartment to another, and produce both liquid- and solid-phase extracellular components of the body. These functions depend upon the physical integrity and impermeability of the epithelial sheet, and on the apical-basal polarity of its constituent cells. The specialized junctions that are formed between adjacent epithelial cells are critical to epithelial properties: they provide a strong physical attachment between cells, they provide a tight barrier to transepithelial movement of molecules and ions, and they restrict mobile membrane proteins to either the apical or the basal-lateral membrane domain, thus contributing to apical-basal cell polarity (Rodriguez-Boulan and Nelson, 1989). These functions of specialized junctions have been revealed by molecular, physiological and cell biological studies. However, evidence from genetic analysis is now suggesting an additional and critically important role of apical cell junctions in the development of epithelial cell populations. These structures appear to mediate the interactions between cells and their neighbors that control both cell proliferation and the formation of spatial patterns of differentiation.

Intercellular junctions of vertebrate epithelial cells include, in apical-basal order (Fig. 1): tight junctions (also called occluding junctions or zonulae occludens), adherens junctions (also called belt desmosomes or zonulae adherens), both of which form belts around the apical end

of the cell, as well as gap junctions and desmosomes scattered along the lateral membrane basal to the adherens junctions (Rodriguez-Boulan and Nelson, 1989). In arthropods the tight junction is missing, but an additional junction, the septate junction, is found basal to the adherens junction (Figs 1 and 2).

Interactions between epithelial cells and their neighbors control cell proliferation, differentiation and morphogenesis, and these interactions must take place via the unspecialized lateral membrane or via the specialized junctions listed above. At the present state of knowledge any or all of the specialized junctions connecting epithelial cells could be involved in these cell interactions. Most investigations of cell communication have been focused on gap junctions, at least in part because simple physiological tests for their function are available. However, an increasing volume of evidence points to the apical junctions as the sites of developmentally significant cell interactions. Much of this evidence comes from immunolocalization of proteins identified by genetic analysis in *Drosophila,* and a summary of the locations of these proteins is presented in Table 1.

MOLECULAR NATURE AND POSSIBLE FUNCTIONS OF APICAL JUNCTIONS

Adherens junctions

The adherens junction is a thick density that forms a continuous belt around the apical end of each epithelial cell

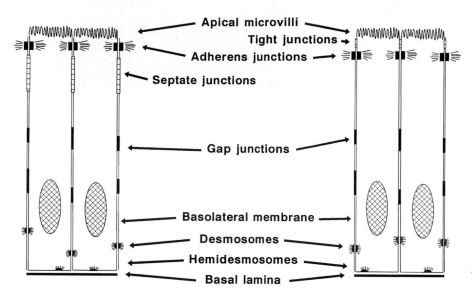

Fig. 1. The distribution of cellular junctions in arthropod and vertebrate epithelia.

Table 1. Surface domains of imaginal disc cells

Domain		Structures present	Molecular markers	
			Localized	Enriched
Apical		Microvilli	*boss* (Krämer et al., 1991; Cagan and Ready, 1989b) *sevenless* (Banerjee et al., 1987; Tomlinson et al., 1987) *crumbs* (Tepass et al., 1990)	
Lateral:	Apical	Adherens junctions	Phosphotyrosine (J.-W. Wu, D. F. Woods and P. J. Bryant, unpublished) *boss* (Krämer et al., 1991; Cagan et al., 1992) *sevenless* (Banerjee et al., 1987; Tomlinson et al., 1987) *Notch* (Artavanis-Tsakonas et al., 1991; Fehon et al., 1991)	*armadillo* (Peifer and Wieschaus, 1990) *wingless* (González et al., 1991) Actin Neuroglian (Bieber et al., 1989) D*abl* (Bennett and Hoffmann, 1992)
	Subapical	Septate junctions	*dlg* (Woods and Bryant, 1991) Fasciclin III (Snow et al., 1989) DA.1B6 antigen (Brower et al., 1980) Band 4.1 (R. Fehon, personal communication)	α-Spectrin (Dubreuil et al., 1987)
	Basal	Gap junctions (scattered)	PS2 antigen (Brower et al., 1985) (enriched basally) F7D6 (Bedian and Jungklaus, 1987) (enriched basally)	Neuroglian (Bieber et al., 1989)
		Desmosomes (scattered)		
Basal		Hemi-desmosomes (scattered) Basal lamina		

and is associated with actin microfilaments (Poodry and Schneiderman, 1970; Rodriguez-Boulan and Nelson, 1989). One of the main functions of adherens junctions appears to be in cell adhesion (Geiger et al., 1987) and at least one group of cell adhesion molecules, the cadherins, and their associated anchoring molecules, the catenins, have been localized at adherens junctions (Geiger and Ayalon, 1992).

Recent studies of human tumor cells show that loss of expression of cadherins and related molecules is associated with loss of cell proliferation control as well as adhesion (Schipper et al., 1991; Shimoyama and Hirohashi, 1991; Field, 1992). In fact, the E-cadherin locus at chromosome band 16q22.1 (Natt et al., 1989) may correspond to a candidate tumor suppressor gene identified by loss of heterozygosity in hepatocellular, breast and prostate carcinomas (Carter et al., 1990; Sato et al., 1990; Tsuda et al., 1990; Zhang et al., 1990). Furthermore, treatment with anti-E-cadherin antibodies can lead to invasive behavior of otherwise non-invasive epithelial and carcinoma cell lines (Behrens et al., 1989; Frixen et al., 1991) and transfection with E-cadherin cDNA can reverse the invasiveness of invasive carcinoma cell lines (Frixen et al., 1991). On the other hand some transformed cells show loss of adhesiveness while maintaining cadherin expression. For example, the lung cancer cell line PC-9 shows reduced adhesiveness

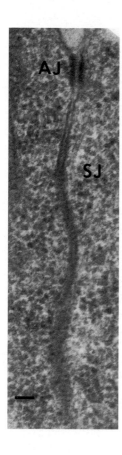

Fig. 2. Electron micrograph showing the adherens (AJ) and septate (SJ) junctions between epithelial cells of a *Drosophila* wing imaginal disc. The apical surface of the epithelium is at the top of the figure. Bar, 0.1 μm.

oncogenic pp60[v-src] in epithelial cells causes abnormally high levels of tyrosine phosphorylation, breakdown of adherens junctions and loss of cell-cell adhesion (Warren and Nelson, 1987; Volberg et al., 1991). Inhibiting the activity of phosphatases with vanadate and thereby increasing the level of tyrosine phosphorylation at adherens junctions can also cause breakdown of these junctions and changes in cell properties that suggest loss of adhesiveness (Matsuyoshi et al., 1992; Volberg et al., 1992).

An important substrate of pp60[v-src] at adherens junctions appears to be the cadherin/catenin complex. Thus in fibroblasts or epithelial cells transformed with v-src, cadherins are expressed and localized at the cell surface but are apparently unable to function properly in cell adhesion or metastasis suppression. These transformed cells show a high level of pp60[v-src]-mediated tyrosine phosphorylation on catenins, and a lower level on cadherins (Matsuyoshi et al., 1992; Behrens et al., 1993; Hamaguchi et al., 1993). This raises the intriguing possibility that the adhesive functions of cadherins depend critically on their association with catenins, and that this association is (or can be) functionally modulated by tyrosine phosphorylation mediated by PTKs.

Adherens junctions are clearly important for cell adhesion, but genetic studies show that they are also sites of developmentally significant signalling between epithelial cells. Studies of the *Drosophila* embryo have provided highly suggestive evidence for a role of adherens junctions in cell-cell interactions controlling the spatial pattern of cell differentiation. Prior to cellularization, the spatial patterns of gene expression that lead to anterior-posterior patterning of the embryo are controlled by the distribution of maternal products and interactions between nuclei in the syncytium. Soon after cellularization, however, the patterns of gene expression come to depend on interactions between the newly formed cells (for review see Woods and Bryant, 1992). This is seen most clearly in genes in the segment polarity class, such as *wingless* (*wg*) and *engrailed* (*en*). Lethal mutations in these genes cause loss of structures normally found in the posterior parts of body segments and their replacement by anterior structures. The expression of *en* in the posterior part of each embryonic segment depends on the expression of the *wingless* gene in anteriorly adjacent cells (DiNardo et al., 1988) as shown by the premature loss of *en* expression in *wg* embryos (Heemskerk et al., 1991) and by the expanded domain of *en* expression produced by ectopic expression of *wg* (Noordermeer et al., 1992). The sequence of the *wg* gene shows that it encodes a protein with a signal sequence but no transmembrane domain, indicating that it is secreted (Cabrera et al., 1987; Rijsewijk et al., 1987). This prediction is confirmed by immunocytochemical studies, which show that the Wg protein is actually transfered from the expressing cell into the responding cell across the boundary separating the anterior from the posterior compartment of the body segment. The transfer occurs in the apical part of the cell just basal to the adherens junctions (González et al., 1991).

A segment polarity phenotype similar to that of *wg* is also produced by mutations in the *armadillo* (*arm*) gene, which encodes an adherens junction protein (Peifer, 1993; Peifer et al., 1993) showing highly significant homology with the vertebrate adherens junction protein β-catenin

in spite of apparently normal cadherin expression. This is apparently because α-catenin is not expressed in these cells, and lack of this molecule prevents cadherin function (Shimoyama et al., 1992).

Lethal mutations at the *fat* locus in *Drosophila*, which encodes an enormous cadherin-like transmembrane protein, cause hyperplastic overgrowth of the imaginal discs (Mahoney et al., 1991). In the mutant imaginal discs, some of the excess cells are shed as small closed vesicles, which are lost from the epithelium, suggesting a failure of cell adhesion (Bryant et al., 1988). The phenotypes of these mutants suggest an important role for this cadherin-related molecule in the control of *Drosophila* cell growth. However, it is not yet known whether the protein is localized in cell junctions.

Adherens junctions appear to participate in cell-cell interactions not only through the cadherin/catenin complex but also through their association with a protein tyrosine kinase (PTK)-mediated signalling pathway. Tyrosine phosphorylation is very rare in normal vertebrate cells, accounting for only 0.02-0.05% of all protein phosphorylation events (Sefton et al., 1980). However, in epithelial cells of both vertebrates (Maher et al., 1985; Takata and Singer, 1988; Tsukita et al., 1991; Volberg et al., 1991) and *Drosophila* (J.-W. Wu, D. F. Woods and P. J. Bryant, unpublished data) most of the small amount of phosphotyrosine is highly localized at adherens junctions.

Tyrosine phosphorylation at adherens junctions is at least partly a function of non-receptor PTKs. Two of these enzymes, pp62[c-yes] and pp60[c-src], are highly enriched in the adherens junctions of hepatocytes, kidney epithelial cells and keratinocytes (Tsukita et al., 1991). Expression of the

(Peifer et al., 1992). β-Catenin is known to interact with α-catenin and the cytoplasmic domain of cadherins in a multi-molecular complex at the adherens junction (Magee and Buxton, 1991). In a similar way, the Arm protein interacts with the *Drosophila* α-catenin homolog and a glycoprotein similar in size to vertebrate cadherins (Peifer, 1993). In the female germ line, although well-defined adherens junctions are not present, the Arm protein appears to be required for cell adhesion and cytoskeletal integrity (Peifer et al., 1993). It is therefore possible that *arm* mutations produce a *wg*-like phenotype in developing embryos and imaginal discs (Peifer et al., 1991) because they disrupt adherens junctions, which are required for the normal functioning of the *wg* signal.

Somewhat later in *Drosophila* development, cell-cell interactions are important for regulating the spatial distribution of neuroblasts in the developing central nervous system (Artavanis-Tsakonas et al., 1991). After many small groups of cells (proneural clusters) become neuroblast-competent, lateral inhibition between the cells of each cluster results in one cell acquiring the neuroblast fate, and the remainder becoming epidermis (for review see Woods and Bryant, 1992). The *Notch* gene product, a transmembrane protein with 36 sequences homologous to epidermal growth factor (EGF) in its extracellular domain, is required for these cell interactions as well as others controlling neurogenesis in the peripheral nervous system (Artavanis-Tsakonas et al., 1991), and for several different cell interactions controlling the fate of cells in the developing retina (Cagan and Ready, 1989b). Embryos lacking *Notch* function give rise to neoplastic tissue when transplanted into adult female hosts (Gateff and Schneiderman, 1974) suggesting an additional role for the gene product in the cell interactions controlling proliferation. The product of the *Delta* gene, which like the *Notch* gene product is required for the cell interactions leading to neuroblast specification, is also a transmembrane protein containing multiple EGF repeats in its extracellular domain (Vässin et al., 1987). Delta and Notch proteins expressed on different cells can mediate adhesion between them (Fehon et al., 1990), and genetic studies provide evidence for direct interactions between these two proteins in vivo (Xu et al., 1990). Notch protein is localized at apical junctions in various epithelia (Fehon et al., 1991), and the same seems to be true of Delta in the follicular epithelium of the ovary (Bender et al., 1993) although its localization in other cell types has not been reported. Nevertheless, many lines of evidence at the molecular and genetic levels are consistent with the hypothesis that these two proteins act as a signal-receptor pair for cell-cell interactions operating at apical junctions to determine cell fates. Studies of genetic mosaics in imaginal discs indicate that cells mutant for *Notch* autonomously adopt the mutant phenotype of excess bristle production, whereas cells mutant for *Delta* mutations can non-autonomously show the wild-type phenotype if they are adjacent to wild-type cells (Heitzler and Simpson, 1991). These results argue in favor of a model in which the *Delta* product is the signal and the *Notch* product is the receptor for the signalling event that specifies bristle sites.

During the development of the pattern of ommatidia in the forming eye imaginal disc, a series of fate-determining interactions occurs between the individual cells of each developing ommatidium. The best understood of these interactions is the induction of the R7 photoreceptor cell by the R8 cell (for review see Woods and Bryant, 1992). Analysis of genetic mosaics indicates that the *bride-of-sevenless* (*boss*) product is required in the R8 precursor (Reinke and Zipursky, 1988) and the *sevenless* (*sev*) product is required in the R7 precursor (Tomlinson and Ready, 1987) for a successful inductive event. The predicted *boss* product has seven transmembrane segments as well as extracellular and cytoplasmic domains (Hart et al., 1990). The predicted *sev* product is a transmembrane protein with a functional protein tyrosine kinase catalytic domain in the cytoplasmic tail (Hafen et al., 1987; Basler and Hafen, 1988; Bowtell et al., 1988; Simon et al., 1989). Both Sev and Boss proteins are predicted transmembrane proteins, leading to the idea that the *boss* protein expressed on the surface of the R8 cell directly induces the adjacent cell to develop into R7, by interacting with the Sev protein expressed on the surface of the responding cell. Immunocytochemistry using epitope-specific antibodies shows that the entire Boss protein is transferred into the R7 precursor cell during the interaction, and is contained in a prominent multivesicular body similar to a late endosome (Cagan et al., 1992). Both Sev (Cagan et al., 1992) and Boss (Tomlinson et al., 1987) proteins are localized at apical microvilli and adherens junctions, and the internalization of Boss protein occurs in the apical part of the cell. Furthermore, the Drk protein, which functions immediately downstream of *sev* in the signalling pathway, is also localized to the apical plasma membrane of epithelial cells in the eye imaginal disc (Olivier et al., 1993).

Other *Drosophila* PTKs and growth factor homologs may be associated with adherens junctions. The non-receptor PTK Dabl is enriched at adherens junctions (Bennett and Hoffmann, 1992) and the 66 kDa src-related protein encoded by the Dsrc28C locus is localized to the cell periphery (Vincent et al., 1989), possibly at adherens junctions. DER, the *Drosophila* homolog of the epidermal growth factor receptor, has been described as being present at the apical microvillar surface of imaginal discs cells (Zak and Shilo, 1992), but the data are also consistent with localization at the adherens junction. Finally, the product of the *crumbs* gene, a transmembrane protein with EGF-like repeats in its extracellular domain (Tepass et al., 1990) that is required to maintain epithelial integrity in the early embryo, is localized apically (Tepass and Knust, 1990), possibly at adherens junctions, in embryonic epithelia.

Tight junctions

In the epithelia of vertebrates, tight junctions form a belt around the end of the cell, apical to the adherens junctions. They provide a transepithelial diffusion barrier to movements of ions and small molecules, and restrict mobile membrane proteins to either the apical or the basal-lateral membrane domains, thus maintaining apical-basal cell polarity (Rodriguez-Boulan and Nelson, 1989). Breakdown of tight junctions by treatment of cells with proteases or chelating agents leads to loss of apical-basal polarity and intermixing of apical and basal-lateral membrane proteins (Pisam and Ripoche, 1976; Ziomek et al., 1980; Herzlinger and Ojakian, 1984). Some protein components of tight junctions have been identified, including ZO-1 (Anderson et al., 1989), ZO-2 (Gumbiner et al., 1991), cingulin (Citi et al., 1991), and the protein identified by antibody 7H6 (Zhong et al., 1993). However, critical tests of the developmental functions of tight junctions have not yet been reported.

Septate junctions

The most obvious difference between arthropod and vertebrate epithelia is that, in general, arthropods have septate junctions but no tight junctions, whereas vertebrates have tight junctions but no septate junctions. Septate junctions (Fig. 2) are characterized by electron-dense septa between cells and are associated with both actin filaments and microtubules (Lane, 1991). Although claims have been made for the existence of tight junctions at the blood/brain barrier in insects (Lane, 1992), other studies of this region show the presence of typical septate junctions (Juang and Carlson, 1992). Because they replace each other and show some structural and functional similarities (Green and Bergquist, 1982; Wood, 1990), it has been suggested that tight and septate junctions have similar roles (Noirot-Timothee and Noirot, 1980), even though the septate junctions are basal to the adherens junctions whereas tight junctions are apical (Figs 1 and 2). Our results support the idea that the septate junctions also maintain apical-basal polarity, and they further suggest that these junctions play an important role in the cell-cell interactions controlling proliferation.

The first protein to be identified at septate junctions was the product of the *discs-large* (*dlg*) tumor suppressor gene in *Drosophila* (Woods and Bryant, 1991). Mutations in this gene cause the imaginal discs, which are normally single-layered, to overgrow and become disorganized masses in which the cells have almost completely lost apical-basal polarity (Fig. 3). The discs also lose the abil-

ity to develop into adult parts after transplantation into normal hosts. As shown using antibodies against recombinant Dlg protein, the gene product is expressed in most epithelial tissues throughout development, and it also shows expression in other tissues including the nervous system (Woods and Bryant, 1991). In the carboxy-terminal 179 amino acids, the predicted Dlg protein shows 35.5% identity to yeast guanylate kinase (Stehle and Schulz, 1992), an enzyme that catalyzes the conversion of GMP to GDP, using ATP as the phosphate donor. However, although the GMP-binding features of yeast GUK are highly conserved in Dlg, the putative ATP-binding site has a three-amino acid deficiency (Koonin et al., 1992), suggesting that the protein may have lost its kinase function during evolution and may now have a different function dependent on GMP binding.

The predicted Dlg protein, as well as its two mammalian homologs (Bryant and Woods, 1992; Cho et al., 1992), also includes a copy of the 71-amino acid SH3 domain (Musacchio et al., 1992a,b), which is found in many membrane-associated signal transduction proteins and is thought to mediate binding to other proteins. Recently a protein that binds with high affinity to the SH3 domain of the c-abl protein was identified and found to show homology to the GTPase activating protein associated with the ras-related protein rho (Cicchetti et al., 1992). The rho protein is involved in actin bundling and regulates the assembly of focal adhesions (Ridley and Hall, 1992). Other binding targets for SH3 include the GTP-hydrolyzing motor protein dynamin (Booker et al., 1993), and guanine nucleotide exchange factors (Olivier et al., 1993; Rozakis-Adcock et al., 1993). The Dlg protein also contains an OPA repeat (Wharton et al., 1985) and a PEST motif (Rogers et al., 1986), both of which are thought to control protein synthesis and turnover rates. The N-terminal half of the mol-

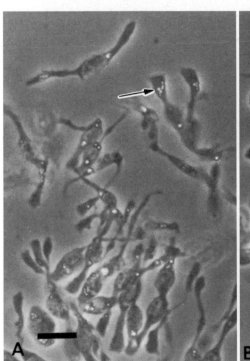
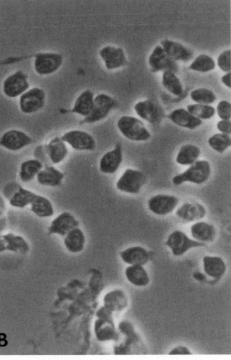

Fig. 3. Micrograph of normal (A) and *dlg⁻* (B) wing imaginal disc epithelial cells after citric acid fixation and dissociation. Note the highly polarized normal cells containing lipid droplets (arrow). The *dlg⁻* cells appear cuboidal with no obvious apical-basal polarity. Bar, 10 μm.

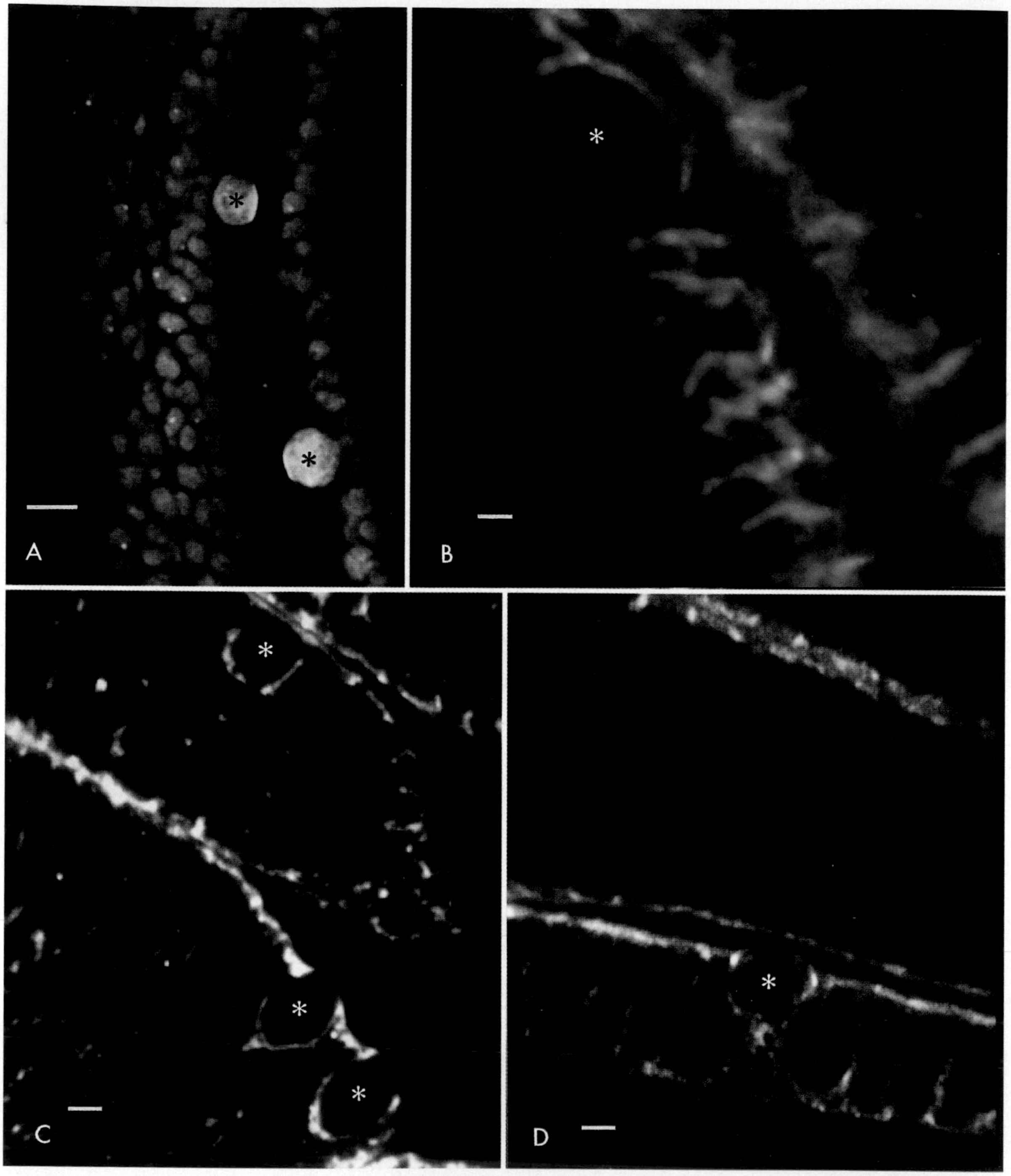

Fig. 4. Immunolocalization of various proteins in *Drosophila* wing imaginal disc cells using confocal microscopy. (A) Cells stained with the antibody MPM-2, a marker for cells in mitosis (Millar et al., 1987). Two apical layers are facing each other across a luminal space. The brightly staining mitotic nuclei (∗) have migrated to the apical surface of the epithelium. Bar, 4 μm. (B) Two epithelial layers stained with antibodies against phosphotyrosine (red) and the *dlg* protein (green). The phosphotyrosine is found mainly at the most apical end of the lateral membrane, at the position of the adherens junctions (J.-W. Wu, D. F. Woods and P. J. Bryant, unpublished data). The *dlg* protein is restricted to a slightly more basal location on the lateral membrane, at the level of the septate junctions (Woods and Bryant, 1991). Note the change in protein distribution in the mitotic cell (∗). Bar, 1 μm. (C) Cells stained with phalloidin to visualize filamentous actin, showing enrichment in the adherens junction. Actin forms a cup under the nucleus during mitosis (∗). Bar, 2 μm. (D) Cells stained with antibodies against the *armadillo* (*arm*) protein (Peifer and Wieschaus, 1990), showing enrichment in the adherens junction and staining most of the rest of the membrane at reduced levels. The adherens junction staining persists during mitosis (∗). Bar, 2 μm.

ecule contains three copies of a ~91-amino-acid motif called GLGF (Cho et al., 1992) or DHR (Bryant et al., 1993), the function of which is unknown. The results obtained with the *dlg* gene suggest that cell interactions important for growth control occur at septate junctions, that the Dlg protein is important in morphogenesis of the septate junction,

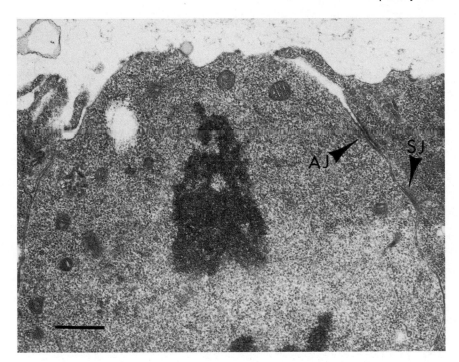

Fig. 5. Electron micrograph showing the nucleus of a wing imaginal disc cell during mitosis. The nucleus has migrated to the apical surface of the epithelium. AJ, adherens junction; SJ, septate junction. Bar, 0.5 μm.

and that it may also regulate the production, at these junctions, of guanine nucleotides that act as messenger molecules within the cell.

In epithelial cells the Dlg protein is localized at the apical end of the lateral cell membrane, just basal to the adherens junctions (Fig. 4B). This is exactly the location of the septate junction (Fristrom, 1982). Furthermore, our genetic studies (unpublished) show that the *dlg* product is required for the formation of septate junctions. The effects of *dlg* mutations on cell polarity, adhesion and proliferation may therefore be a result of disruption of the septate junction. A cell adhesion molecule, fasciclin III, is localized at septate junctions (Table 1), so some of the effects of *dlg* mutations, including the loss of cell adhesion, could be mediated by their effects on the localization or function of this molecule.

ELEVATOR MOVEMENTS OF THE NUCLEUS IN EPITHELIAL CELLS

If cell communication occurs at apical junctions, the signals generated must be transmitted to the nucleus where they can be translated into effects on patterns of gene expression and/or replication. This might suggest the need for a signal transduction mechanism to relay the signal through the cytoplasm to the nucleus, and many molecules that may participate in this signal transduction have recently been identified (Pelech and Sanghera, 1992). However, a special aspect of the biology of epithelial cells provides a natural mechanism for direct interaction between the nucleus and apical cell junctions.

Epithelial cells undergo a characteristic set of morphological changes during the course of a cell cycle (Figs 4, 5 and 6; Fujita, 1962). The nucleus is basal during S phase, but it migrates apically during G_2, and goes through mito-

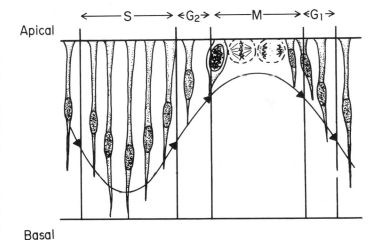

Fig. 6. Nuclear migration in epithelial cells during the cell cycle. The nucleus oscillates between a basal position during S phase and an apical position during M phase. Redrawn after Fujita (1962). S, G_2, M, G_1: the different phases of the cell cycle. The extent to which the cell retains a connection to the basal lamina during mitosis is not known.

sis at the extreme apical end of the cell. At this time the cell itself rounds up (Figs 4 and 5), but at least in *Drosophila* imaginal epithelium the cell retains a thin connection to the basal lamina (Mathi and Larsen, 1988). Following mitosis the cell regains its columnar shape, and the nucleus migrates basally to begin the next S phase. This apical-basal 'elevator movement' (Jinguji and Ishikawa, 1992) accounts for the original erroneous interpretation of simple epithelia as stratified, with a layer of 'germinal cells' at the apical surface. Thymidine incorporation studies (Fujita, 1962) clearly reveal that cells seen at different apical-basal levels are simply cells at different stages of the

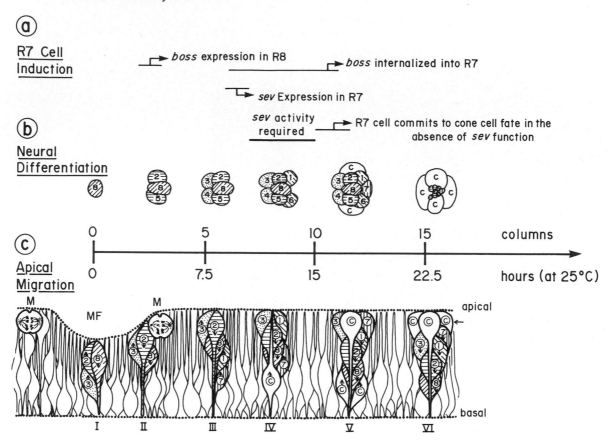

Fig. 7. Cell interactions and nuclear migrations involved in ommatidial patterning. (a) Expression patterns and requirements for *boss* and *sev* in R7 photoreceptor cell induction; (b) the time course of neural differentiation as seen by the production of neuronal markers at the apical surface of the epithelium; (c) apical-basal movements of nuclei in the epithelium (only one of each pair of cells showing similar behavior is shown). The nucleus of each cell of the cluster (shown as a bulge in the outline) migrates to the apical side of the epithelium just before differentiation begins in that cell, then returns to a more basal position. The time scale is shown in hours as well as in photoreceptor cluster columns, measured from the position of the morphogenetic furrow at 0 columns and 0 hours. From Woods and Bryant (1992), redrawn from Rubin (1991) and Tomlinson (1988).

cell cycle (Fig. 6). In vertebrate cells the tight junctions remain intact during the entire cell cycle, preserving the integrity of the epithelium as a barrier to trans-epithelial diffusion (Jinguji and Ishikawa, 1992). In *Drosophila* the adherens and septate junctions are also maintained in cells through mitosis (Figs 4 and 5).

When an epithelial cell rounds up and its nucleus enters M phase there is very little, if any, cytoplasm surrounding the nucleus (Fujita, 1962). Thus, when the nuclear envelope breaks down, the nuclear contents are apparently in direct contact with the cell membrane including the apical junctions (Fig. 5). We therefore suggest that signals generated by interactions with adjacent cells at cell junctions are translated directly into effects on transcription and replication factors in the nucleus, without the need for an elaborate cytoplasmic signal transduction mechanism or transport of signals through the cytoplasm. The signals could be mediated by phosphorylation events controlled by junction-associated protein kinases. This hypothesis implies that such signals have their effect on nuclear factors only during M phase, and that the nucleus implements the signals autonomously during the subsequent interphase.

The cell fate decisions that occur during the develop-

ment of photoreceptor clusters in the *Drosophila* eye disc provide strong circumstantial evidence for cell-fate decisions associated with nuclear elevator movements (Fig. 7). The elevator movements in this system occur in a precisely defined sequence that is not associated with mitosis but is correlated with specifically defined cell interactions establishing cell fates, some of which can be recognized at the molecular level. The sequence of events is best understood in the determination of the R7 cell (for review see Woods and Bryant, 1992), which requires the expression of the *boss* gene in the R8 precursor cell at about 3 hours after the furrow passes. *boss* protein is internalized into the adjacent R7 cell at 6-11 hours, and the expression of the *sev* protein in R7 is required at 6-7 hours. In the absence of this inductive signal from R8, the R7 cell becomes committed to develop into a cone cell instead of a photoreceptor cell. Committment to the R7 fate occurs after the R7 cell is exposed to the *sev* signal for about six hours (Mullins and Rubin, 1991), and the nucleus of R7 is apical at exactly this time (Tomlinson and Ready, 1987). Nuclei of the other photoreceptor cells also migrate apically in a sequence that corresponds to the sequence of their subsequent differentiation, and the same is true later of the cone cells. Thus the detailed information available from this system is strikingly consistent with the idea that cell interactions controlling cell fate occur via the apical junctions, where both Boss and Sev protein are localized and where Boss is transferred and internalized, and that this interaction directly programs the nucleus at the time when it is apically positioned.

CONCLUSIONS

Molecular genetic studies are providing strong evidence for the idea that apical cell junctions, both adherens and septate, are the main sites of the interactions between epithelial cells that control their developmental fates and proliferative behavior. The well-known elevator movements of epithelial cell nuclei may reflect a mechanism providing for the presentation of signals generated at the apical junctions to the mechanisms that control gene expression and replication in the nucleus. Most of the evidence for this model comes from genes that function in the undifferentiated imaginal disc epithelium or the undifferentiated ectoderm of the *Drosophila* embryo. In both systems there is a dynamic pattern of spatially organized gene expression that ultimately leads to the intricate spatial pattern of differentiation seen in the cuticle and other derivatives (Akam, 1987; Bryant, 1993). Cell signalling mechanisms operating at the apical junctions appear to be intimately involved in setting up these spatially ordered patterns of gene expression.

We thank Dr Mark Peifer for a gift of antibody against the *armadillo* protein, and Dr Francis Davis for a gift of the anti-MPM-2 antibody. Our research is supported by grants from the National Institutes of Health and the National Science Foundation.

REFERENCES

Akam, M. (1987). The molecular basis for metameric pattern in the *Drosophila* embryo. *Development* **101**, 1-22.
Anderson, J. M., Van Itallie, C. M., Peterson, M. D., Stevenson, B. R., Carew, E. A. and Mooseker, M. S. (1989). ZO-1 mRNA and protein expression during tight junction assembly in Caco-2 cells. *J. Cell Biol.* **109**, 1047-1056.
Artavanis-Tsakonas, S., Delidakis, C. and Fehon, R. G. (1991). The *Notch* locus and the cell biology of neuroblast segregation. *Annu. Rev. Cell Biol.* **7**, 427-452.
Banerjee, U., Renfranz, P. J., Hinton, D. R., Rabin, B. A. and Benzer, S. (1987). The *sevenless*+ protein is expressed apically in cell membranes of developing *Drosophila* retina; it is not restricted to cell R7. *Cell* **51**, 151-158.
Basler, K. and Hafen, E. (1988). Control of photoreceptor cell fate by the *sevenless* protein requires a functional tyrosine kinase domain. *Cell* **54**, 299-311.
Bedian, V. and Jungklaus, C. E. (1987). Expression of the differentiation antigen F7D6 in tumorous tissues of *Drosophila*. *Dev. Genet.* **8**, 165-177.
Behrens, J., Mareel, M. M., Van Roy, F. M. and Birchmeier, W. (1989). Dissecting tumor cell invasion: epithelial cells acquire invasive properties after the loss of uvomorulin-mediated cell-cell adhesion. *J. Cell Biol.* **108**, 2435-2447.
Behrens, J., Vakaet, L., Friis, R., Winterhager, E., Van Roy, F., Mareel, M. M. and Birchmeier, W. (1993). Loss of epithelial differentiation and gain of invasiveness correlates with tyrosine phosphorylation of the E-cadherin/β-catenin complex in cells transformed with a temperature-sensitive v-*src* gene. *J. Cell Biol.* **120**, 757-766.
Bender, L. B., Kooh, P. J. and Muskavitch, M. A. T. (1993). Complex function and expression of *Delta* during *Drosophila* oogenesis. *Genetics* **133**, 967-978.
Bennett, R. L. and Hoffmann, F. M. (1992). Increased levels of the *Drosophila* Abelson tyrosine kinase in nerves and muscles: Subcellular localization and mutant phenotypes imply a role in cell-cell interactions. *Development* **116**, 953-966.
Bieber, A. J., Snow, P. M., Hortsch, M., Patel, N. H., Jacobs, J. R., Traquina, Z. R., Schilling, J. and Goodman, C. S. (1989). *Drosophila* neuroglian: a member of the immunoglobulin superfamily with extensive homology to the vertebrate neural adhesion molecule L1. *Cell* **59**, 447-460.
Booker, G. W., Gout, I., Downing, A. K., Driscoll, P. C., Boyd, J., Waterfield, M. D. and Campbell, I. D. (1993). Solution structure and ligand-binding site of the SH3 domain of the p85α subunit of phosphatidylinositol 3-kinase. *Cell* **73**, 813-822.
Bowtell, D. D., Simon, M. A. and Rubin, G. M. (1988). Nucleotide sequence and structure of the *sevenless* gene of *Drosophila melanogaster*. *Genes Dev.* **2**, 620-634.
Brower, D. L., Smith, R. J. and Wilcox, M. (1980). A monoclonal antibody specific for diploid epithelial cells in *Drosophila*. *Nature* **285**, 403-405.
Brower, D. L., Piovant, M. and Reger, L. A. (1985). Development analysis of *Drosophila* position-specific antigens. *Dev. Biol.* **108**, 120-130.
Bryant, P. J. (1993). The polar coordinate model goes molecular. *Science* **259**, 1741-1742.
Bryant, P. J., Huettner, B., Held, L. I., Jr., Ryerse, J. and Szidonya, J. (1988). Mutations at the *fat* locus interfere with cell proliferation control and epithelial morphogenesis in *Drosophila*. *Dev. Biol.* **129**, 541-554.
Bryant, P. J., Watson, K. L., Justice, R. W. and Woods, D. F. (1993). Tumor suppressor genes encoding proteins required for cell interactions and signal transduction in *Drosophila*. *Development* (in press).
Bryant, P. J. and Woods, D. F. (1992). A major palmitoylated membrane protein of human erythrocytes shows homology to yeast guanylate kinase and to the product of a *Drosophila* tumor suppressor gene. *Cell* **68**, 621-622.
Cabrera, C. V., Alonso, M. C., Johnston, P., Phillips, R. G. and Lawrence, P. A. (1987). Phenocopies induced with antisense RNA identify the *wingless* gene. *Cell* **50**, 659-663.
Cagan, R. L., Krämer, H., Hart, A. C. and Zipursky, S. L. (1992). The *bride of sevenless* and *sevenless* interaction: internalization of a transmembrane ligand. *Cell* **69**, 393-399.
Cagan, R. L. and Ready, D. F. (1989b). *Notch* is required for successive cell decisions in the developing *Drosophila* retina. *Genes Dev.* **3**, 1099-1112.
Carter, B. S., Ewing, C. M., Ward, W. S., Treiger, B. F., Aalders, T. W., Schalken, J. A., Epstein, J. I. and Isaacs, W. B. (1990). Allelic loss of chromosomes 16q and 10q in human prostate cancer. *Proc. Nat. Acad. Sci. USA* **87**, 8751-8755.
Cho, K.-O., Hunt, C. A. and Kennedy, M. B. (1992). The rat brain postsynaptic density fraction contains a homolog of the *Drosophila discs-large* tumor suppressor protein. *Neuron* **9**, 929-942.
Cicchetti, P., Mayer, B. J., Thiel, G. and Baltimore, D. (1992). Identification of a protein that binds to the SH3 region of Abl and is similar to Bcr and GAP-rho. *Science* **257**, 803-806.
Citi, S., Amorosi, A., Franconi, F., Giotti, A. and Zampi, G. (1991). Cingulin, a specific protein component of tight junctions, is expressed in normal and neoplastic human epithelial tissues. *Amer. J. Pathol.* **138**, 781-789.
DiNardo, S., Sher, E., Heemskerk-Jongens, J., Kassis, J. A. and O'Farrell, P. H. (1988). Two-tiered regulation of spatially patterned *engrailed* gene expression during *Drosophila* embryogenesis. *Nature* **332**, 604-609.
Dubreuil, R., Byers, T. J., Branton, D., Goldstein, L. S. and Kiehart, D. P. (1987). *Drosophila* spectrin. I. Characterization of the purified protein. *J. Cell Biol.* **105**, 2095-2102.
Fehon, R. G., Johansen, K., Rebay, I. and Artavanis-Tsakonas, S. (1991). Complex cellular and subcellular regulation of *Notch* expression during embryonic and imaginal development of *Drosophila*: Implications for *Notch* function. *J. Cell Biol.* **113**, 657-669.

Fehon, R. G., Kooh, P. J., Rebay, I., Regan, C. L., Xu, T., Muskavitch, M. A. T. and Artavanis-Tsakonas, S. (1990). Molecular interactions between the protein products of the neurogenic loci *Notch* and *Delta*, two EGF-homologous genes in *Drosophila*. *Cell* **61**, 523-534.

Field, J. K. (1992). Oncogenes and tumour-suppressor genes in squamous cell carcinoma of the head and neck. *Eur. J. Cancer [B]* **28B**, 67-76.

Fristrom, D. K. (1982). Septate junctions in imaginal disks of *Drosophila*: a model for the redistribution of septa during cell rearrangement. *J. Cell Biol.* **94**, 77-87.

Frixen, U. H., Behrens, J., Sachs, M., Eberle, G., Voss, B., Warda, A., Lochner, D. and Birchmeier, W. (1991). E-cadherin-mediated cell-cell adhesion prevents invasiveness of human carcinoma cells. *J. Cell Biol.* **113**, 173-185.

Fujita, S. (1962). Kinetics of cellular proliferation. *Exp. Cell Res.* **28**, 52-60.

Gateff, E. A. and Schneiderman, H. A. (1974). Developmental capacities of benign and malignant neoplasms of *Drosophila*. *Roux's Arch. Develop. Biol.* **176**, 23-65.

Geiger, B. and Ayalon, O. (1992). Cadherins. *Annu. Rev. Cell Biol.* **8**, 307-332.

Geiger, B., Volk, T., Volberg, T. and Bendori, R. (1987). Molecular interactions in adherens-type contacts. *J. Cell Sci. Suppl.* **8**, 251-272.

González, F., Swales, L., Bejsovec, A., Skaer, H. and Martínez-Arias, A. (1991). Secretion and movement of *wingless* protein in the epidermis of the *Drosophila* embryo. *Mech. Dev.* **35**, 43-54.

Green, C. R. and Bergquist, P. R. (1982). Phylogenetic relationships within the Invertebrata in relation to the structure of septate junctions and the development of 'occluding' junctional types. *J. Cell Sci.* **53**, 279-305.

Gumbiner, B., Lowenkopf, T. and Apatira, D. (1991). Identification of a 160-kDa polypeptide that binds to the tight junction protein ZO-1. *Proc. Nat. Acad. Sci. USA* **88**, 3460-3464.

Hafen, E., Basler, K., Edstroem, J. E. and Rubin, G. M. (1987). *Sevenless*, a cell-specific homeotic gene of *Drosophila*, encodes a putative transmembrane receptor with a tyrosine kinase domain. *Science* **236**, 55-63.

Hamaguchi, M., Matsuyoshi, N., Ohnishi, Y., Gotoh, B., Takeichi, M. and Nagai, Y. (1993). p60^{v-src} causes tyrosine phosphorylation and inactivation of the N-cadherin-catenin cell adhesion system. *EMBO J.* **12**, 307-314.

Hart, A. C., Krämer, H., Van Vactor, D. L., Jr., Paidhungat, M. and Zipursky, S. L. (1990). Induction of cell fate in the *Drosophila* retina: The *bride of sevenless* protein is predicted to contain a large extracellular domain and seven transmembrane segments. *Genes Dev.* **4**, 1835-1847.

Heemskerk, J., DiNardo, S., Kostriken, R. and O'Farrell, P. H. (1991). Multiple modes of *engrailed* regulation in the progression towards cell fate determination. *Nature* **352**, 404-410.

Heitzler, P. and Simpson, P. (1991). The choice of cell fate in the epidermis of *Drosophila*. *Cell* **64**, 1083-1092.

Herzlinger, D. A. and Ojakian, G. K. (1984). Studies on the development and maintenance of epithelial cell surface polarity with monoclonal antibodies. *J. Cell Biol.* **98**, 1777-1787.

Jinguji, Y. and Ishikawa, H. (1992). Electron microscopic observations on the maintenance of the tight junction during cell division in the epithelium of the mouse small intestine. *Cell Struct. Funct.* **17**, 27-37.

Juang, J.-L. and Carlson, S. D. (1992). Fine structure and blood-brain barrier properties of the central nervous system of a dipteran larva. *J. Comp. Neurol.* **324**, 343-352.

Koonin, E. V., Woods, D. F. and Bryant, P. J. (1992). dlg-R proteins: modified guanylate kinases. *Nature Genet.* **2**, 256-257.

Krämer, H., Cagan, R. L. and Zipursky, S. L. (1991). Interaction of *bride of sevenless* membrane-bound ligand and the *sevenless* tyrosine-kinase receptor. *Nature* **352**, 207-212.

Lane, N. J. (1991). Cytoskeletal associations with intercellular junctions in arthropods. In *Form and Function in Zoology*, Selected Symposia and Monographs UZI vol. 5 (ed. G. Lanzavecchia and R. Valvassori), pp. 87-102. Mucchi, Modera.

Lane, N. J. (1992). Anatomy of the tight junction: invertebrates. In: Tight junctions (Cereijido, M., Ed.), pp. 23-48. CRC Press, Boca Raton.

Magee, A. I. and Buxton, R. S. (1991). Transmembrane molecular assemblies regulated by the greater cadherin family. *Curr. Opin. Cell Biol.* **3**, 854-861.

Maher, P. A., Pasquale, E. B., Wang, J. Y. J. and Singer, S. J. (1985). Phosphotyrosine-containing proteins are concentrated in focal adhesions and intercellular junctions in normal cells. *Proc. Nat. Acad. Sci. USA* **82**, 6576-6580.

Mahoney, P. A., Weber, U., Onofrechuk, P., Biessmann, H., Bryant, P. J. and Goodman, C. S. (1991). The *fat* tumor suppressor gene in *Drosophila* encodes a novel member of the cadherin gene superfamily. *Cell* **67**, 853-868.

Mathi, S. K. and Larsen, E. (1988). Patterns of cell division in imaginal discs of *Drosophila*. *Tissue & Cell* **20**, 461-472.

Matsuyoshi, N., Hamaguchi, M., Taniguchi, S., Nagafuchi, A., Tsukita, S. and Takeichi, M. (1992). Cadherin-mediated cell-cell adhesion is perturbed by v-*src* tyrosine phosphorylation in metastatic fibroblasts. *J. Cell Biol.* **118**, 703-714.

Millar, S. E., Freeman, M. and Glover, D. M. (1987). The distribution of a 'mitosis-specific' antigen during *Drosophila* development. *J. Cell Sci.* **87**, 95-104.

Mullins, M. C. and Rubin, G. M. (1991). Isolation of temperature-sensitive mutations of the tyrosine kinase receptor *sevenless* (*sev*) in *Drosophila* and their use in determining its time of action. *Proc. Nat. Acad. Sci. USA* **88**, 9387-9391.

Musacchio, A., Gibson, T., Lehto, V.-P. and Saraste, M. (1992a). SH3--An abundant protein domain in search of a function. *FEBS Lett.* **307**, 55-61.

Musacchio, A., Noble, M., Pauptit, R., Wierenga, R. and Saraste, M. (1992b). Crystal structure of a Src-homology 3 (SH3) domain. *Nature* **359**, 851-855.

Natt, E., Magenis, R. E., Zimmer, J., Mansouri, A. and Scherer, G. (1989). Regional assignment of the human loci for uvomorulin (UVO) and chymotrypsinogen B (CTRB) with the help of two overlapping deletions on the long arm of chromosome 16. *Cytogenet. Cell Genet.* **50**, 145-148.

Noirot-Timothee, C. and Noirot, C. (1980). Septate and scalariform junctions in arthropods. *Int Rev. Cytol.* **63**, 97-140.

Noordermeer, J., Johnston, P., Rijsewijk, F., Nusse, R. and Lawrence, P. A. (1992). The consequences of ubiquitous expression of the *wingless* gene in the *Drosophila* embryo. *Development* **116**, 711-719.

Olivier, J. P., Raabe, T., Henkemeyer, M., Dickson, B., Mbamalu, G., Margolis, B., Schlessinger, J., Hafen, E. and Pawson, T. (1993). A *Drosophila* SH2-SH3 adaptor protein implicated in coupling the *sevenless* tyrosine kinase to an activator of *Ras* guanine nucleotide exchange. *Sos. Cell* **73**, 179-191.

Peifer, M., McCrea, P. D., Green, K. J., Wieschaus, E. and Gumbiner, B. M. (1992). The vertebrate adhesive junction proteins β-catenin and plakoglobin and the *Drosophila* segment polarity gene *armadillo* form a multigene family with similar properties. *J. Cell Biol.* **118**, 681-691.

Peifer, M. (1993). The product of the *Drosophila* segment polarity gene *armadillo* is part of a multi-protein complex resembling the vertebrate adherens junction. *J. Cell Sci.* **105**, 993-1000.

Peifer, M., Orsulic, S., Sweeton, D. and Wieschaus, E. (1993). A role for the *Drosophila* segment polarity gene *armadillo* in cell adhesion and cytoskeletal integrity during oogenesis. *Development* **118**, 1191-1207.

Peifer, M., Rauskolb, C., Williams, M., Riggleman, B. and Wieschaus, E. (1991). The segment polarity gene *armadillo* interacts with the *wingless* signaling pathway in both embryonic and adult pattern formation. *Development* **111**, 1029-1043.

Peifer, M. and Wieschaus, E. (1990). The segment polarity gene *armadillo* encodes a functionally modular protein that is the *Drosophila* homolog of human plakoglobin. *Cell* **63**, 1167-1178.

Pelech, S. L. and Sanghera, J. S. (1992). MAP kinases: charting the regulatory pathways [comment]. *Science* **257**, 1355-1356.

Pisam, M. and Ripoche, P. (1976). Redistribution of surface macromolecules in dissociated epithelial cells. *J. Cell Biol.* **71**, 907-920.

Poodry, C. A. and Schneiderman, H. A. (1970). The ultrastructure of the developing leg of *Drosophila melanogaster*. *Roux's Arch. Develop. Biol.* **166**, 1-44.

Reinke, R. and Zipursky, S. L. (1988). Cell-cell interaction in the *Drosophila* retina: the *bride of sevenless* gene is required in photoreceptor cell R8 for R7 development. *Cell* **55**, 321-330.

Ridley, A. J. and Hall, A. (1992). The small GTP-binding protein rho regulates the assembly of focal adhesions and actin stress fibers in response to growth factors. *Cell* **70**, 389-400.

Rijsewijk, F., Schuermann, M., Wagenaar, E., Parren, P., Weigel, D. and Nusse, R. (1987). The *Drosophila* homolog of the mouse mammary oncogene *int-1* is identical to the segment polarity gene *wingless*. *Cell* **50**, 649-657.

Rodriguez-Boulan, E. and Nelson, W. J. (1989). Morphogenesis of the polarized epithelial cell phenotype. *Science* **245**, 718-724.

Rogers, S., Wells, R. and Rechsteiner, M. (1986). Amino acid sequences common to rapidly degraded proteins: the PEST hypothesis. *Science* **234**, 364-368.

Rozakis-Adcock, M., Fernley, R., Wade, J., Pawson, T. and Bowtell, D. (1993). The SH2 and SH3 domains of mammalian Grb2 couple the EGF receptor to the Ras activator mSos1. *Nature* **363**, 83-85.

Rubin, G. M. (1991). Signal transduction and the fate of the R7 photoreceptor in *Drosophila*. *Trends Genet.* **7**, 372 377.

Sato, T., Tanigami, A., Yamakawa, K., Akiyama, F., Kasumi, F., Sakamoto, G. and Nakamura, Y. (1990). Allelotype of breast cancer: cumulative allele losses promote tumor progression in primary breast cancer. *Cancer Res.* **50**, 7184-7189.

Schipper, J. H., Frixen, U. H., Behrens, J., Unger, A., Jahnke, K. and Birchmeier, W. (1991). E-cadherin expression in squamous cell carcinomas of head and neck: Inverse correlation with tumor dedifferentiation and lymph node metastasis. *Cancer Res.* **51**, 6328-6337.

Sefton, B. M., Hunter, T., Beemon, K. and Eckhart, W. (1980). Evidence that the phosphorylation of tyrosine is essential for cellular transformation by Rous sarcoma virus. *Cell* **20**, 807-816.

Shimoyama, Y. and Hirohashi, S. (1991). Cadherin intercellular adhesion molecule in hepatocellular carcinomas: Loss of E-cadherin expression in an undifferentiated carcinoma. *Cancer Lett.* **57**, 131-135.

Shimoyama, Y., Nagafuchi, A., Fujita, S., Gotoh, M., Takeichi, M., Tsukita, S. and Hirohashi, S. (1992). Cadherin dysfunction in a human cancer cell line: Possible involvement of loss of α-catenin expression in reduced cell-cell adhesiveness. *Cancer Res.* **52**, 5770-5774.

Simon, M. A., Bowtell, D. D. and Rubin, G. M. (1989). Structure and activity of the *sevenless* protein: a protein tyrosine kinase receptor required for photoreceptor development in *Drosophila*. *Proc. Nat. Acad. Sci. USA* **86**, 8333-8337.

Snow, P. M., Bieber, A. J. and Goodman, C. S. (1989). Fasciclin III: a novel homophilic adhesion molecule in *Drosophila*. *Cell* **59**, 313-323.

Stehle, T. and Schulz, G. E. (1992). Refined structure of the complex between guanylate kinase and its substrate GMP at 2.0 Å resolution. *J. Mol. Biol.* **224**, 1127-1141.

Takata, K. and Singer, S. J. (1988). Phosphotyrosine-modified proteins are concentrated at the membranes of epithelial and endothelial cells during tissue development in chick embryos. *J. Cell Biol.* **106**, 1757-1764.

Tepass, U. and Knust, E. (1990). Phenotypic and developmental analysis of mutations at the *crumbs* locus, a gene required for the development of epithelia in *Drosophila melanogaster*. *Roux's Arch. Dev. Biol.* **199**, 189-206.

Tepass, U., Theres, C. and Knust, E. (1990). *crumbs* encodes an EGF-like protein expressed on apical membranes of *Drosophila* epithelial cells and required for organization of epithelia. *Cell* **61**, 787-799.

Tomlinson, A. (1988). Cellular interactions in the developing *Drosophila* eye. *Development* **104**, 183-193.

Tomlinson, A., Bowtell, D. D., Hafen, E. and Rubin, G. M. (1987). Localization of the *sevenless* protein, a putative receptor for positional information, in the eye imaginal disc of *Drosophila*. *Cell* **51**, 143-150.

Tomlinson, A. and Ready, D. F. (1987). Cell fate in the *Drosophila* ommatidium. *Dev. Biol.* **123**, 264-275.

Tsuda, H., Zhang, W. D., Shimosato, Y., Yokota, J., Terada, M., Sugimura, T., Miyamura, T. and Hirohashi, S. (1990). Allele loss on chromosome 16 associated with progression of human hepatocellular carcinoma. *Proc. Nat. Acad. Sci. USA* **87**, 6791-6794.

Tsukita, S., Oishi, K., Akiyama, T., Yamanashi, Y. and Yamamoto, T. (1991). Specific proto-oncogenic tyrosine kinases of src family are enriched in cell-to-cell adherens junctions where the level of tyrosine phosphorylation is elevated. *J. Cell Biol.* **113**, 867-879.

Vässin, H., Bremer, K. A., Knust, E. and Campos-Ortega, J. A. (1987). The neurogenic gene *Delta* of *Drosophila melanogaster* is expressed in neurogenic territories and encodes a putative transmembrane protein with EGF-like repeats. *EMBO J.* **6**, 3431-3440.

Vincent, W. S.,3d., Gregory, R. J. and Wadsworth, S. C. (1989). Embryonic expression of a *Drosophila src* gene: alternate forms of the protein are expressed in segmental stripes and in the nervous system. *Genes Dev.* **3**, 334 347.

Volberg, T., Geiger, B., Dror, R. and Zick, Y. (1991). Modulation of intercellular adherens-type junctions and tyrosine phosphorylation of their components in RSV-transformed cultured chick lens cells. *Cell Regul.* **2**, 105-120.

Volberg, T., Zick, Y., Dror, R., Sabanay, I., Gilon, C., Levitzki, A. and Geiger, B. (1992). The effect of tyrosine-specific protein phosphorylation on the assembly of adherens-type junctions. *EMBO J.* **11**, 1733-1742.

Warren, S. L. and Nelson, W. J. (1987). Nonmitogenic morphoregulatory action of pp60^{v-src} on multicellular epithelial structures. *Mol. Cell. Biol.* **7**, 1326-1337.

Wharton, K. A., Yedvobnick, B., Finnerty, V. and Artavanis-Tsakonas, S. (1985). *opa*: A novel family of transcribed repeats shared by the *Notch* locus and other developmentally regulated loci in *D. melanogaster*. *Cell* **40**, 55-62.

Wood, R. L. (1990). The septate junction limits mobility of lipophilic markers in plasma membranes of *Hydra vulgaris (attenuata)*. *Cell Tiss. Res.* **259**, 61-66.

Woods, D. F. and Bryant, P. J. (1991). The *discs-large* tumor suppressor gene of *Drosophila* encodes a guanylate kinase homolog localized at septate junctions. *Cell* **66**, 451-464.

Woods, D. F. and Bryant, P. J. (1992). Genetic control of cell interactions in developing *Drosophila* epithelia. *Annu. Rev. Genet.* **26**, 305-350.

Xu, T., Rebay, I., Fleming, R. J., Scottgale, T. N. and Artavanis-Tsakonas, S. (1990). The *Notch* locus and the genetic circuitry involved in early *Drosophila* neurogenesis. *Genes Dev.* **4**, 464-475.

Zak, N. B. and Shilo, B. Z. (1992). Localization of DER and the pattern of cell divisions in wild-type and *Ellipse* eye imaginal discs. *Dev. Biol.* **149**, 448-456.

Zhang, W. D., Hirohashi, S., Tsuda, H., Shimosato, Y., Yokota, J., Terada, M. and Sugimura, T. (1990). Frequent loss of heterozygosity on chromosomes 16 and 4 in human hepatocellular carcinoma. *Jpn J. Cancer Res.* **81**, 108-111.

Zhong, Y., Saitoh, T., Minase, T., Sawada, N., Enomoto, K. and Mori, M. (1993). Monoclonal antibody 7H6 reacts with a novel tight junction-associated protein distinct from ZO-1, cingulin and ZO-2. *J. Cell Biol.* **120**, 477-483.

Ziomek, C. A., Schulman, S. and Edidin, M. (1980). Redistribution of membrane proteins in isolated mouse intestinal epithelial cells. *J. Cell Biol.* **86**, 849-857.

Note added in proof

The hypothesis that tight and septate junctions may represent analogous structures has been strengthened by the recent finding that a major protein component of tight junctions, ZO-1, is homologous to the Dlg protein (M. Itoh, A. Nagafuchi, S. Yonemura, T. Kitani-Yasuda and S. Tsukita (1993). *J. Cell Biol.* **121**, 491-502; E. Willot, M. S. Balda, A. S. Fanning, B. Jameson, C. Van Itallie and J. M. Anderson (1993). *Proc. Nat. Acad. Sci. USA* **90**, 7834-7838; D. F. Woods and P. J. Bryant (1994). *Mech. Dev.* (in press).

Journal of Cell Science, Supplement 17, 183-188 (1993)
Printed in Great Britain © The Company of Biologists Limited 1993

Responses to *Wnt* signals in vertebrate embryos may involve changes in cell adhesion and cell movement

Randall T. Moon, Alyce DeMarais and Daniel J. Olson*

Department of Pharmacology, University of Washington School of Medicine, Seattle, WA 98195, USA

*Present address: Division of Plastic Surgery, Penn State University, Hershey, PA 17033, USA

SUMMARY

Wnt genes encode secreted glycoproteins, and, because of their homology with the *Drosophila* segment polarity gene *wingless*, are likely to play important roles as modulators of local intercellular signalling during embryonic development. Although little is known of the mechanisms by which *Wnts* signal in an autocrine or paracrine manner, it is increasingly clear that cells can respond rapidly to *Wnt* signals in the absence of transcription, and that these responses may include changes in cell adhesion and cell movement. We review recent evidence from studies on *Xenopus laevis* and other systems, which demonstrate that (1) a subset of *Wnts* modulate gap junctional permeability, which may be a reflection of changes in cadherin-mediated cell adhesion, (2) embryos express β-catenin and plakoglobin, which are homologs of the *armadillo* gene products, known to be involved in the *wingless* signalling pathway, and known to be found at cell junctions, and (3) overexpression of specific *Wnts* in *Xenopus* embryos leads to clear changes in cell behavior and movement.

Key words: Xenopus, *Wnt*, cell adhesion, cadherin, development

INTRODUCTION

Wnts encode a class of secreted signalling proteins, which are likely to be involved in modulating diverse processes in developing embryos, and in a subset of adult tissues. Interest in *Wnts* stems largely from the discovery that *Wnt-1*, a proto-oncogene expressed in the embryonic central nervous system, is the vertebrate homolog of a segment polarity gene, *wingless*, in *Drosophila*. This suggests that *Wnts* in general may be involved in pattern formation. As recent reviews of these factors (Nusse and Varmus, 1992; McMahon, 1992; Moon, 1993) are still up to date, the dual emphasis of the present review is to build a framework for presenting the specific argument that changes in cell adhesion and cell movement are likely to be among the early responses of cells to *Wnt* signals, and to highlight areas needing further study.

BIOCHEMISTRY AND SUBCELLULAR LOCALIZATION OF Wnts

Although only Wnt-1 has been extensively studied in terms of its biosynthesis, secretion, and subcellular localization (reviewed by Nusse and Varmus, 1992), it is generally presumed that distinct Wnt polypeptides have similar biochemical properties. Most Wnts contain 350-380 amino acids, though in-frame insertions in some Wnts are likely to yield larger polypeptides (Nusse and Varmus, 1992). Wnts are readily recognized from their predicted amino acid sequences by the presence and position of highly conserved cysteine residues, primarily in the carboxy-terminal region. Suggesting that some of these cysteines are indispensible, directed mutagenesis of the penultimate amino acid of Wnt-1, one of these conserved cysteines, abolishes the activity of Wnt-1 in two unrelated bioassays (McMahon and Moon, 1989; reviewed by Nusse and Varmus, 1992). However, it is also important to note that other alterations in the sequences of Wnts diminish their activity, such as insertion of epitope tags for following the polypeptides (McMahon and Moon, 1989), suggesting that Wnt activity is highly dependent upon proper folding and conformation. All reported Wnts have putative leader sequences and N-linked glycosylation sites. Deletion of the leader sequence of Wnt-1 abolishes its activity upon ectopic expression in *Xenopus* embryos (McMahon and Moon, 1989), while mutagenesis of all putative glycosylation sites does not affect its transforming ability in a cultured cell assay (reviewed by Nusse and Varmus, 1992). Little is known about the regulation of Wnt polypeptide stability, though it is interesting to note that Xwnt-8 has a PEST sequence (Christian et al., 1992) and related sequences, found in rapidly degraded proteins (reviewed by Rechsteiner, 1990).

Direct evidence that Wnt-1 is secreted has been obtained from analysis of Wnt-1 in transfected C57 mammary epithelial cells (reviewed by Nusse and Varmus, 1992). Importantly, following secretion, Wnt-1 remains tightly adherent to the plasma membrane of the secreting cell and may interact with the extracellular matrix. Studies of the *wingless* signalling pathway in *Drosophila* also suggest that the distance of action of the *wingless* product is restricted to a few cell diameters from the site of synthesis (reviewed by Nusse and Varmus, 1992; Vincent and O'Farrell, 1992). Combined with the observations that *wingless* in *Drosophila*, and *Wnts* in vertebrates, are highly localized in their sites of synthesis (reviewed by Nusse and Varmus, 1992) it is apparent that the distance of action of *Wnts* is restricted to highly specific regions of embryos.

There are a number of unanswered questions concerning the secretion of Wnts. Pertinent to the topic of this symposium, are Wnts secreted solely to apical domains of epithelial cells, or less specifically to the general cell surface? Following secretion of Wnts, with what do they interact on the cell surface, and what is the stability of Wnts on the cell surface? Although Wnts appear to adhere to the surface of any cell type following transfection, their ability to transform is restricted to C57 mammary epithelial cells (reviewed by Nusse and Varmus, 1992). This raises the possibility that Wnts interact with cell surface or extracellular matrix components present on many cell types, but may activate Wnt receptors in only a few cell types. To date, isolation of Wnt receptors through biochemical approaches has been hindered by the fact that no Wnts have been obtained in a soluble, biologically active form. Is there any evidence that Wnts operate through known second messenger systems? We have previously noted the similarities between the effects of Xwnt-8 and LiCl on *Xenopus* embryos, which support the hypothesis that at least some Xwnts affect IP_3 levels, and hence calcium levels (Christian and Moon, 1993a,b). Direct testing of this hypothesis is underway.

SYSTEMS FOR ANALYZING THE EXPRESSION AND FUNCTIONS OF Wnts DURING VERTEBRATE DEVELOPMENT

As reviewed elsewhere (McMahon, 1992; Nusse and Varmus, 1992; Moon, 1993), most *Wnts* are expressed in the nervous system of developing embryos. That the expression of *Wnts* in the nervous system is likely to be important is clear from disruption of *Wnt-1* expression in mouse, resulting in cerebellar and midbrain defects. Comparing the expression of two of the better studied *Wnts*, *Wnt-1* and *-3A* are expressed in overlapping yet distinct regions (Fig. 1). The overlap in expression of *Wnt-1* and *-3A* has been discussed as a possible basis for the observation that disruption of *Wnt-1* in mice does not appear to perturb formation of the neural tube (McMahon, 1992). Thus, if *Wnt-1* and *-3A* displayed some overlapping and redundant activities in the *Wnt-1*-deficient mouse embryos, one might expect *Wnt-3A* to mask any consequence of the *Wnt-1* deletion. While rigorous testing of this hypothesis requires analysis of embryos deficient in both *Wnt-1* and *-3A*, the observation that ectopic expression of *Wnt-1* and *-3A* in *Xenopus* embryos produces identical defects does suggest that these *Wnts* can activate a common pathway (Wolda et al., 1993). *Wnt-4* is the only *Wnt* reported to be expressed in the floor plate of the neural tube (McGrew et al., 1992), but in the brain it also has areas of overlapping expression with other *Wnts* (reviewed by Moon, 1993).

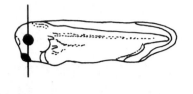

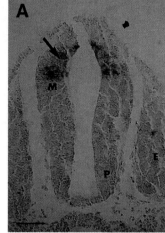 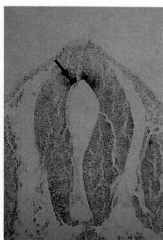

Xwnt-3   *Xwnt-1*

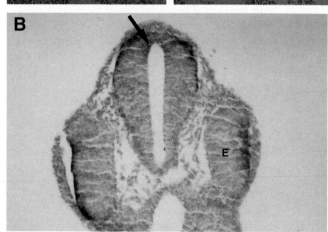

Fig. 1. Overlapping expression of *Xwnt*-3A, *Xwnt*-1 and β-catenin transcripts in the *Xenopus* tadpole. Whole mount in situ hybridization was conducted for *Xwnt*-3A (left panel in (A)), *Xwnt*-1 (right panel in (A); Wolda et al., 1993) or β-catenin (B) (DeMarais and Moon, 1992) transcripts, and tadpole embryos were then sectioned transversely at the level shown in the cartoon. The arrows denote the area of overlapping expression of these transcripts in the mesencephalon (M)/prosencephalon (P) boundary, with dorsal upwards in all panels. The eye (E) is evident in the left panel in (A), and in (B). Bar in (A) is 50 μm.

Outside the nervous system, *Xwnt*-8 is highly restricted in expression to the future ventral and lateral mesoderm of *Xenopus* embryos. This gene is likely to be induced in this limited region of the marginal zone in response to mesoderm-inducing growth factors, which are locally acting in this region of the embryo. Another *Xenopus* Wnt, *Xwnt*-5A, is expressed maternally, and becomes enriched in the head and tail of embryos, in both ectoderm and mesoderm (Moon

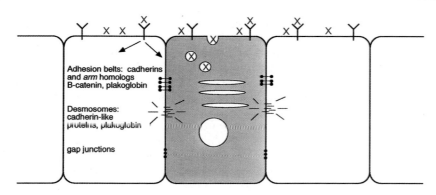

- *Armadillo* is in the *wingless* signalling pathway and is homologous to plakoglobin and B-catenin
- Gap junctional permeability is modulated positively by cadherin-mediated increased adhesion and by *Xwnt*-8
- *Xwnts* directly lead to altered cell spreading, movement *in vivo* and *in vitro*

Fig. 2. Speculative model of *Wnt* signalling and responses at cell junctions. Upon secretion of Wnt from the colored cell, the Wnt may act in an autocrine or paracrine manner via a receptor-mediated signal transduction pathway, though at present there is no direct evidence for a plasma membrane-associated *Wnt* receptor. However, as described in the text, there is now evidence indicating that cells can respond to Wnt signals by modulation of gap junctional permeability, and that this effect may be an indirect consequence of changes in cell adhesion. In addition, *armadillo* is downstream of the *Wnt*-1 signal in *Drosophila*, and the *armadillo* homologs β catenin and plakoglobin are associated with adherens junctions in vertebrate cells, which contain cadherins. Plakoglobin is also found at desmosomes. Finally, as described in the text, there is direct evidence that cells in *Xenopus* embryos undergo changes in cell adhesion and migration in response to *Wnt* signals.

et al., 1993). The only other reported maternal *Wnt, Xwnt*-11, has an enrichment of transcripts in the vegetal hemisphere of the cleavage stage embryo (Ku and Melton, 1993).

Given the observations that vertebrate embryos express multiple *Wnts,* with overlapping patterns of expression and overlapping activities, how can one begin to determine the specific functions, and mechanisms of action, of individual *Wnt* products? Different vertebrate embryos have their own distinct advantages for investigating specific aspects of *Wnt* activity. Since the sequences of specific *Wnt* members are highly conserved between species, and their patterns of expression are strikingly similar (reviewed by Nusse and Varmus, 1992; Moon, 1993), it is likely that the integration of information on *Wnt* functions from different species will indeed be pertinent, and contribute to a much more thorough understanding of *Wnts* than could be obtained from the analysis of any specific species. The use of homologous recombination in mouse to generate the null phenotype for specific *Wnts* will clearly be pivotal in testing whether *Wnts* are required for the formation of specific structures, and in testing whether some *Wnts* have redundant activities. However, in analyzing a mutant phenotype, it is not trivial to distinguish between primary effects of disruption of the gene, and indirect consequences of gene inactivation. Embryos of *Xenopus laevis*, owing to their size, abundance and ease of microinjection, are much better suited for dissecting *Wnt* signalling pathways. This is accomplished through microinjection of synthetic *Wnt* RNAs, and in monitoring rapid cell physiological responses to *Wnt* signals, such as alterations in gap junctional permeability (Olson et al., 1991) and in growth factor responsiveness (Christian et al., 1992). *Xenopus* embryos are also suitable for tissue-tissue recombination studies, allowing one to test whether induction of expression of a given *Wnt* requires specific intercellular contacts (McGrew et al., 1992; Wolda et al., 1993). However, *Xenopus* does not allow targeted gene disruption. Researchers have only recently begun investigating *Wnts* in zebrafish embryos (reviewed by Kelly et al., 1993), though one can anticipate

that the optical clarity of this embryo will allow real-time monitoring of the effects of *Wnt* expression upon cell migration and cell fate. Moreover, the continuing isolation of embryonic lethal mutations may unearth mutations affecting *Wnt* expression, or provide interesting phenotypic backgrounds for overexpression of specific *Wnts,* to ask whether specific aspects of normal development can be rescued by these *Wnts*.

DISTINCT RESPONSES OF *XENOPUS* EMBRYOS TO OVEREXPRESSION OF DIFFERENT *Xwnts*

Although the specific mechanisms of actions of *Wnts* are largely unknown, data to date support the involvement of *Xwnts* in diverse embryological processes extending from the cleavage stages through organogenesis. A few examples of the potential functions of *Xwnts* in *Xenopus* development are described below.

Recent experiments support the hypothesis that a maternal *Wnt*-like activity is operative during mesoderm induction in embryos of *Xenopus*, which commences during early cleavage stages prior to the onset of zygotic transcription. This conclusion was reached by overexpression of *Xwnt*-8, -1 and -3A in embryos, which leads to a duplication of the embryonic axis, and to a rescue of normal axial development in embryos ventralized by UV-irradiation. These results are consistent with these *Xwnts* mimicking, or comprising, the blastula organizer (Nieuwkoop center) activity (reviewed by Christian and Moon, 1993a). However, none of these *Xwnts* appear to be expressed in the proper time and place to have a normal role to play in this blastula organizer, which has been interpreted to suggest that they activate a pathway normally utilized by a maternal *Xwnt*. The search for this hypothesized maternal *Xwnt* continues.

It is now clear that not all *Xwnts* cause the same phenotypic defect when misexpressed in *Xenopus* embryos, supporting the hypothesis that multiple *Wnt* signalling pathways exist, and are functional during early development. A second type of response is obtained by overexpression of *Xwnt*-5A in *Xenopus* embryos. This maternal *Xwnt* does not rescue dorsal structures in UV-irradiated embryos, and overexpression perturbs the movements of gastrulation, resulting in overt defects in the head and elsewhere, which are distinct from any caused by overexpression of *Xwnt*-1, -8, or -3A (Moon et al., 1993). A third response is obtained by *Xwnt*-11, which partially rescues UV-irradiated embryos, but does not rescue formation of a notochord (Ku and Melton, 1993).

Have these studies provided insights into the likely functions of any specific *Xwnt*? Synthesis of several observations suggests that *Xwnt*-8 is normally active in a pathway leading to formation of ventral mesoderm in *Xenopus* (reviewed by Christian and Moon, 1993a). First, the expression of *Xwnt*-8 normally begins with the onset of zygotic transcription and, by the onset of gastrulation, *Xwnt*-8 transcripts are highly localized in future ventral and lateral mesoderm. Second, *Xwnt*-8 can be induced by the mesoderm-inducing growth factors basic fibroblast growth factor (bFGF) and activin, suggesting that it is downstream from the activity of these factors. Third, and consistent with *Xwnt*-8 being downstream from the activities of activin or bFGF, in the absence of these mesoderm-inducing growth factors, *Xwnt*-8 can direct prospective ectoderm into a pathway of differentiation as ventral mesoderm (Christian and Moon, 1993b). Confirmation of this likely role for *Xwnt*-8 awaits experiments blocking the activity of this *Xwnt*.

EVIDENCE THAT *Wnts* MAY ALTER CELL ADHESION AND CELL MOVEMENT

For the past few years there have been suggestive, albeit indirect, observations raising the possibility that cellular responses to *Wnt* signals include changes in cell adhesive properties. These initial indications, as well as some recent direct evidence, are summarized below and in Fig. 2.

Both *Wnt* and cadherin-mediated cell adhesion can modulate gap junctional permeability

In 32-cell embryos of *Xenopus laevis* there is an inherent dorsal-ventral polarity in gap junctional permeability, as monitored by transfer of the fluorescent dye lucifer yellow. Blastomeres on the future dorsal side of the embryo are largely coupled by gap junctions, whereas blastomeres on the future ventral side of the embryo are generally less permeable to dye transfer. Interestingly, injection of *Xwnt*-8 RNA enhances gap junctional permeability on the ventral side of the embryo, so that it now resembles the dorsal side in terms of dye transfer (Olson et al., 1991). In contrast, ectopic expression of *Xwnt*-5A has no measureable effect on gap junctional permeability. As zygotic gene transcription does not commence until the mid-blastula stage, these data demonstrate that cells can respond rapidly to *Wnt* signals in the absence of transcription. Furthermore, these findings indicate that *Xwnts* with different effects upon the embryonic phenotype also have different effects on gap junctional permeability. This suggests that these *Xwnts* activate distinct processes in responsive cells.

At the time of the observations that *Xwnt*-8 enhanced gap junctional permeability in *Xenopus* embryos, it was clear that gap junctional permeability could be modulated by a variety of mechanisms, including phosphorylation of connexins, post-translational recruitment of existing connexins to form gap juctions, and increased cell adhesion (reviewed in Olson and Moon, 1992). Direct evidence that cadherin-mediated increases in cell adhesion can promote increased gap junctional permeability has now been provided by Matsuzaki et al. (1990), showing that transfection of N-cadherin in mouse sarcoma cells increases gap junctions. Similarly, Jongen et al. (1991), have shown that mouse epidermal cells transfected with E-cadherin display enhanced gap junctional coupling. Thus, as previously proposed (Olson et al., 1992), the observation that *Xwnt*-8 enhances gap junctional permeability in the early *Xenopus* embryo might reflect enhanced cell adhesion in response to the *Xwnt* signal. To date, the similar effects on gap junctional permeability of *Xwnt*-8 and enhanced E-cadherin-mediated cell adhesion is only a suggestive correlation requiring further study.

At this point, it is prudent to conclude that although ectopic expression of *Xwnt*-8 enhances gap junctional permeability in 32-cell *Xenopus* embryos, the mechanisms leading to this response remain unknown. Thus far, there have been no data correlating the spatial patterns of expression of endogenous *Wnts* and gap junctional permeability in any embryo. Despite these uncertainties, the data clearly demonstrate the *potential* for *Wnts* to trigger this response; however, whether or not gap junctions are ultimately affected depends on other variables controlling gap junctional permeability.

The *armadillo* gene, involved in the *Wnt-1* signalling pathway in *Drosophila*, has vertebrate homologs found at cell junctions

Lack of function of the *armadillo* gene product in *Drosophila* yields an embryonic phenotype resembling the *wingless* (*Drosophila Wnt*-1) phenotype (reviewed by Riggleman et al., 1990; Peifer and Wieschaus, 1990). In addition, *wingless* expression is thought to modulate the subcellular distribution of *armadillo* (Riggleman et al., 1990). Cloning of the *armadillo* gene revealed that its product is related to the vertebrate protein plakoglobin (Peifer and Wieschaus, 1990), which is a cytoplasmic structural protein found at adherens junctions and desmosomes. Moreover, partial peptide sequencing and cloning of the *Xenopus* E-cadherin-associated protein β-catenin revealed that it was also related to the *armadillo* product (reviewed by Gumbiner, this issue). Thus, there is compelling evidence that a protein involved in the *Wnt*-1 signalling pathway in *Drosophila* is also a protein involved in cadherin-mediated cell adhesion.

Interestingly, as reviewed by Cowin and Brown in this issue, the subcellular distribution of plakoglobin, and its responses to *Wnt* signals, more closely resemble *armadillo* than does β-catenin. Specifically, both *armadillo* in *Drosophila*, and plakoglobin in cultured vertebrate cells, appear to be recruited to the inner surface of the plasma membrane from cytoplasmic pools in response to *Wnt* signals, whereas β-catenin at steady-state is largely restricted to the plasma membrane. While these observations do not prove that vertebrate *Wnts* modulate cell adhesion, the localization of *armadillo* homologs to cell junctions strongly reinforces this hypothesis.

If the cellular responses to *Wnt* signals in vertebrates were to involve either plakoglobin or β-catenin, then these proteins should be coexpressed in embryos and at least overlap with *Xwnts* in their spatial patterns of expression. Evidence that *Xenopus* embryos, which express at least twelve *Wnts* in spatially and temporally specific patterns (reviewed by Moon, 1993) also express both plakoglobin and β-catenin RNAs and polypeptides, has recently been reported (DeMarais and Moon, 1992). Whole mount in situ hybridization reveals that transcripts for both polypeptides are often expressed in regions of the embryo expressing *Wnts*. As shown in Fig. 1, transcripts for β-catenin, *Xwnt*-1, and *Xwnt*-3A are expressed in an overlapping pattern in the dorsal midline of the mesencephalon/prosencephalon boundary of the tadpole. At least one other *Xwnt* overlaps in expression in this region, *Xwnt*-4 (McGrew et al., 1992). Therefore, it is plausible that at least some *Wnt* signals activate pathways which ultimately involve the β-catenin polypeptide. Finally, it is very interesting to note that a substrate of protein tyrosine kinase receptors and of p60^{v-src}, p120, contains four copies of a 42-amino acid repeat also found in plakoglobin, β-catenin, and *armadillo* (Reynolds et al., 1992). Thus, proteins related to *armadillo* may also be phosphorylated in response to intercellular signalling events, potentially modulating their activity. It is tempting to speculate that *Wnts* could also be involved in initiating such phosphorylation events, though this has not been reported.

It is crucial to bear in mind that there is little indication as to how *Wnt* signals are received by responding cells, or how cellular responses are manifested. The data from studies of *wingless* and *armadillo* in *Drosophila*, and data from studies on cultured cells (reviewed by Cowin et al. and Gumbiner, in this issue) suggest the intriguing possibility that some *Wnts* may affect *armadillo* or its homologs in embryos, ultimately resulting in the modulation of cell adhesion. These provocative correlations are currently being investigated.

Direct evidence that *Xwnts* can affect cell movements and migration in vivo and in vitro

Recently we have obtained direct evidence supporting the hypothesis that *Wnts* lead to changes in cell adhesion, which result in altered cell and tissue movements. These experiments employ independent approaches, which yield similar conclusions. First, blastula caps normally respond to treatment with activin by undergoing mesoderm induction, and display the morphogenetic movements associated with this process, resulting in elongated explants. Ectopic expression of *Xwnt*-5A in these blastula caps blocks morphogenetic movements in response to activin, without affecting the cell types induced by activin (Moon et al., 1993). Although this may or may not be due to altered cell adhesive properties, it does display a profound effect of *Xwnt*-5A upon morphogenetic movements. Second, overexpression of *Xwnt*-5A in the dorsal marginal zone of gastrula *Xenopus* embryos profoundly interferes with the movements of gas-

trulation, as observed in explants of the dorsal marginal zone (J. Shih and R. T. Moon, unpublished). Third, *Xenopus* embryos normally display considerable cell mixing by the late gastrula stage. This can be monitored by injection of β-galactosidase RNA into one animal pole blastomere at the 8-cell stage, followed by observation of the localization of β-galactosidase-expressing cells at the late gastrula stage. The results reveal that many progeny of the injected blastomere have migrated throughout the embryo. Co-injection of *Xwnt*-5A RNA with this β-galactosidase RNA substantially reduces the migration of the injected cells, supporting the hypothesis that they display enhanced cell adhesion. Interestingly, the effects of *Xwnt*-5A are the same in this assay (A. A. DeMarais and R. T. Moon, unpublished) as previously reported for overexpression of N-cadherin (Detrick et al., 1990). Fourth, blastula cap cells dissociated and plated on fibronectin substrates normally respond to activin by flattening and spreading on this substrate (Smith et al., 1990; DeSimone and Johnson, 1991). This flattening and spreading is reduced to a statistically significant extent by both *Xwnt*-5A and *Xwnt*-8 (A. A. DeMarais and R. T. Moon, unpublished). The similarities in the response of cells to these two *Xwnts* may in part be due to the artifical substrate employed, but it does demonstrate that both *Xwnts* can affect the behavior of individual cells. In conclusion, we have much to learn regarding how cells receive and transduce *Wnt* signals. However, it is becoming increasingly evident that the cellular responses to *Wnt* signals are likely to include rapid effects upon cell adhesion and cell movement.

REFERENCES

Christian, J. L., Olson, D. J. and Moon, R. T. (1992). *Xwnt*-8 modifies the character of mesoderm induced by bFGF in isolated *Xenopus* ectoderm. *EMBO J.* **11**, 33-41.

Christian, J. L. and Moon, R. T. (1993a). When cells take fate into their own hands: Differential competence to respond to inducing signals generates diversity in the embryonic mesoderm. *BioEssays* **15**, 135-140.

Christian, J. L. and Moon, R. T. (1993b). Interactions between *Xwnt*-8 and Spemann organizer signalling pathways generate dorsoventral pattern in the embryonic mesoderm of *Xenopus*. *Genes Dev.* **7**, 13-28.

DeMarais, A. A. and Moon, R. T. (1992). The *armadillo* homologs β-catenin and plakoglobin are differentially expressed during early development of *Xenopus laevis*. *Dev. Biol.* **153**, 337-346.

DeSimone, D. W. and Johnson, K. E. (1991). The *Xenopus* embryo as a model system for the study of cell-extracellular matrix interactions. *Meth. Cell Biol.* **136**, 527-539.

Detrick, R. J., Dickey, D. and Kintner, C. R. (1990). The effects of N-cadherin misexpression on morphogenesis in *Xenopus* embryos. *Neuron* **4**, 493-506.

Jongen, W. M. F., Fitzgerald, D. J., Asamoto, M., Piccoli, C., Slaga, T. J., Gros, D., Takeichi, M. and Yamasaki, H. (1991). Regulation of connexin 43-mediated gap junctional intercellular communication by Ca^{2+} in mouse epidermal cells is controlled by E-cadherin. *J. Cell Biol.* **114**, 545-555.

Kelly, G. M., Lai, C.-J. and Moon, R. T. (1993). Expression of *Wnt*10a in the central nervous system of the developing zebrafish. *Dev. Biol.* **158**, 113-121.

Ku, M. and Melton, D. A. (1993). *Xwnt*-11: A novel maternally expressed *Xenopus Wnt* gene *Development* (in press).

Matsuzaki, F., Mege, R.-M., Jaffe, S. H., Friedlander, D. R., Gallin, W. J., Goldberg, J. I., Cunningham, B. A. and Edelman, G. M. (1990). cDNAs of cell adhesion molecules of different specificity induce changes in cell shape and border formation in cultured S180 cells. *J. Cell Biol.* **110**, 1239-1252.

McGrew, L. L., Otte, A. P. and Moon, R. T. (1992). Analysis of *Xwnt*-4 in embryos of *Xenopus laevis:* A *Wnt* family member expressed in the brain and floor plate. *Development* **115,** 463-473.

McMahon, A. P. and Moon, R. T. (1989). Ectopic expression of the proto-oncogene *int*-1 in *Xenopus* embryos leads to duplication of the embryonic axis. *Cell* **58,** 1075-1084.

McMahon, A. P. (1992). The *Wnt* family of developmental regulators. *Trends Genet.* **8,** 1-5.

Moon, R. T. (1993). In pursuit of the functions of the *Wnt* family of developmental regulators: Insights from *Xenopus laevis. BioEssays* **15,** 91-97.

Moon, R. T., Campbell, R., Christian, J. L., McGrew, L. L., Shih, J. and Fraser, S. (1993). *Xwnt*-5A: A maternal *Wnt* which affects morphogenetic movements after overexpression in embryos of *Xenopus laevis. Development* **119,** 97-111.

Nusse, R. and Varmus, H. E. (1992). *Wnt* genes. *Cell* **69,** 1073-1087.

Olson, D. J., Christian, J. L. and Moon, R. T. (1991). Effect of *Wnt*-1 and related proteins on gap junctional communication in *Xenopus* embryos. *Science* **252,** 1173-1176.

Olson, D. J. and Moon, R. T. (1992). Distinct effects of ectopic expression of *Wnt*-1, activin B, and bFGF on gap junctional permeability in 32-cell *Xenopus* embryos. *Dev. Biol.* **151,** 204-212.

Peifer, M. and Wieschaus, E. (1990). The segment polarity gene *armadillo* encodes a functionally modular protein that is the *Drosophila* homolog of human plakoglobin. *Cell* **63,** 1167-1178.

Rechsteiner, M. (1990). PEST sequences are signals for rapid intracellular proteolysis. *Semin. Cell Biol.* **1,** 433-440.

Reynolds, A. B., Herbert, L., Cleveland, J. L., Berg, S. T. and Gaut, J. R. (1992). p120, a novel substrate of protein tyrosine kinase receptors and of p60v-src is related to cadherin-binding factors β-catenin, plakoglobin, and *armadillo. Oncogene* **7,** 2439-2445.

Riggleman, B., Schedl, P. and Wieschaus, E. (1990). Spatial expression of the *Drosophila* segment polarity gene *armadillo* is posttranscriptionally regulated by *wingless. Cell* **63,** 549-560.

Smith, J. C., Symes, K., Hynes, R. O. and DeSimone, D. (1990). Mesoderm induction and the control of gastrulation in *Xenopus laevis:* the roles of fibronectin and integrins. *Development* **109,** 229-238.

Vincent, J.-P. and O'Farrell, P. (1992). The state of *engrailed* expression is not clonally transmitted during early *Drosophila* development. *Cell* **68,** 923-931.

Wolda, S. L., Moody, C. J. and Moon, R. T. (1993). Overlapping expression of *Xwnt*-3A and *Xwnt*-1 in neural tissue of *Xenopus laevis* embryos. *Dev. Biol.* **155,** 46-57.

Journal of Cell Science, Supplement 17, 189-195 (1993)
Printed in Great Britain © The Company of Biologists Limited 1993

The retinal pigment epithelium: a versatile partner in vision

Dean Bok

Department of Anatomy and Cell Biology, the Brain Research Institute and the Jules Stein Eye Institute, School of Medicine, University of California, Los Angeles, CA 90024, USA

SUMMARY

The retinal pigment epithelium (RPE) is a monolayer of cuboidal cells that lies in close association with the rod and cone photoreceptors. This epithelium has diverse features, three of which are discussed in some detail in this review, namely the daily phagocytosis of rod and cone outer segment fragments that are shed from their distal ends; the uptake, processing, transport and release of vitamin A (retinol) and some of its visual cycle intermediates (retinoids); and some of the aspects of its apical and basolateral membrane polarity that are the reverse of most other epithelia.

Phagocytosis takes place at the apical surface via membrane receptor-mediated processes that are not yet well defined. Retinol uptake occurs at both the basolateral and apical surfaces by what appear to be separate receptor-mediated processes. The release of a crucial retinoid, 11-*cis* retinaldehyde (11-*cis* retinal), occurs solely across the apical membrane. Delivery of retinol across the basolateral membrane is mediated by a retinol binding protein (RBP) that is secreted by the liver as a complex with retinol (vitamin A). Within the cell, retinol and its derivatives are solubilized by intracellular retinoid binding proteins that are selective for retinol (cellular retinol binding protein, CRBP) and 11-*cis* retinoids (cellular retinal binding protein, CRALBP). Release of 11-*cis* retinal across the apical membrane and re-uptake of retinol from the photoreceptors during the visual cycle is promoted by an intercellular retinoid binding protein (IRBP).

Na,K-ATPase, the membrane-integrated enzyme required to set up the ion gradients that drive other ion transporters, is largely localized to the apical membrane. This is the reverse of most epithelia. The RPE expresses the enveloped viral G protein and hemagglutinin on its basolateral and apical surface, respectively and does not appear to possess a general scheme for reversal of membrane protein polarity. Therefore possible alternative mechanisms for this reversal in Na,K-ATPase polarity are discussed. They include unique domains in the primary amino acid sequence of Na,K-ATPase subunits, cytoskeletal elements and components of the extracellular matrix. The precise mechanism remains unresolved.

Key words: retinal pigment epithelium, vitamin A, retinoids, phagocytosis, Na,K-ATPase

INTRODUCTION

The retinal pigment epithelium (RPE) is a multifunctional and indispensable component of the vertebrate retina. It is strategically placed between the large-bore capillary bed of the choroidal layer of the eye and the photoreceptors of the neurosensory retina. By virtue of this location, it forms part of the blood retinal barrier via its tight junctions (Peyman and Bok, 1972), the other barrier being at the level of retinal blood vessels. Additionally, the RPE is responsible for the net movement of ions and water in an apical to basal direction (retinal to choroidal), thereby maintaining the neurosensory retina in a proper state of dehydration and optical clarity. It absorbs stray light that would otherwise degrade the visual image and plays an adhesive role that aids in the attachment of the retina to the choroidal layer. Among the more fascinating aspects of RPE function are the uptake, processing and transport of retinoids that subserve vision, and the intermittent phagocytosis of detached distal portions of the rod and cone light-sensitive organelles (outer segments), thereby subserving the renewal of each of these organelles by new membrane assembly at their proximal ends.

Early in the life of the individual the activities of the RPE begin. It continues to carry out these functions until it is lost through disease or death of the host. Under normal circumstances the RPE, once differentiated, does not renew itself by cell division. Thus it must remain viable and perform its array of functions throughout the lifetime of the individual, a period that can exceed 100 years in humans.

The RPE is remarkable not only in its versatility but also because it has a feature that makes it virtually unique among epithelia, at least in the view of those investigators who have an interest in epithelial cell polarity. Most of the surface Na,K-ATPase in the RPE is expressed on the apical membrane domain (Steinberg and Miller, 1973; Bok, 1982), a feature that is shared only by the epithelium of the choroid plexus (Quinton et al. 1973), a tissue with which it has some developmental kinship. What follows is a brief review of several of the RPE functions that have held the attention of our laboratory.

PHAGOCYTIC PROPERTIES OF THE RETINAL PIGMENT EPITHELIUM

The outer segments of rods and cones are closely associated with the RPE via villous and pseudopodial attachments. These three cell types (rods, cones and RPE) interact in several ways, one of the most interesting of which involves a limb of the photoreceptor outer segment renewal process, namely RPE phagocytosis of distal portions of rod and cone outer segments (for a review, see Bok, 1985). The definitive evidence for this process relative to rod photoreceptors was gathered by tissue autoradiography following the injection of radioactive amino acids into animals. Radioactive membranous discs of the labeled rod outer segments were intermittently shed and then phagocytosed by the RPE following their displacement from the proximal to distal end of the outer segment by membrane assembly (Young and Bok, 1969). In some animals, such as the rat, this process exhibits a strong circadian rhythm (LaVail, 1976). Although the details of this interaction remain to be worked out, recent evidence from *Xenopus* suggests that the circadian clock for this process resides in the photoreceptor cell itself (Cahill and Besharse, 1992). However the photoreceptor is not solely in control of disc shedding, since it has been observed that close approximation of photoreceptors and RPE is required before the process can take place (Williams and Fisher, 1987). Furthermore, the rat RPE also shows a circadian rhythm with respect to the processing of this phagocytic load. Lysosomal fusion can be triggered by both light and circadian mechanisms (Bosch et al., 1993). Following ingestion of an outer segment fragment (the fragment thereby becoming a phagosome), the lysosomal response occurs in two steps (Fig. 1A and B). First, small lysosomes fuse with the outer segment fragment to form phagolysosomes. Then larger lysosomes, formed by the fusion of smaller precursors, interact with the phagolysosomes through what appear to be bridge-like structures. This process was recently followed in detail by rapid freezing of rat RPE at various times before and after light onset, and monitoring of the fusion of lysosomes with cathepsin D antibodies (Bosch et al., 1993).

Recognition signals that subserve outer segment shedding and phagocytosis also remain unresolved (for a review, see Bok, 1988). It is believed that this process involves receptor-ligand interactions, but these membrane components have not been isolated.

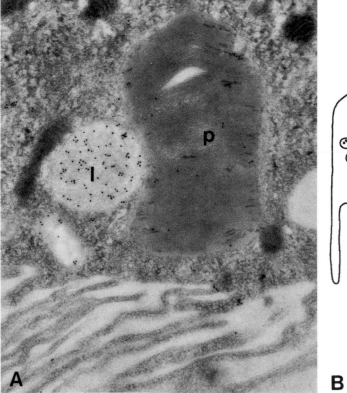 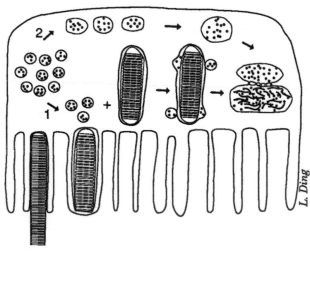

Fig. 1. (A) Rat RPE rapidly frozen and freeze dried prior to analysis by immunogold electron microscopy. The tissue was fixed 30 minutes after light onset. A large lysosome (l), stained for cathepsin D, lies adjacent to a phagolysosome (p), which was produced as a result of rod outer segment shedding. The apical microvilli of the RPE are observed at the bottom of the field. ×27,500. (B) Diagram illustrating a summary of phagolysosome digestion. Digestion occurs in two steps, as observed from fixation and immunostaining of tissue from light-entrained animals at various times during the light-dark cycle. Initially, small lysosomes (1) fuse with ingested outer segment fragments. Additionally, small lysosomes fuse with one another to form larger lysosomes (2). In turn the larger lysosomes interact with phagolysosomes, possibly by exchanging material through bridge-like structures. (From Bosch et al., 1993, with permission.)

Years of daily phagocytosis by the RPE are thought eventually to take their toll in some individuals. Over time, lipofuscin accumulates in the aging RPE until, in some cases, the cells are virtually engorged with this material and function is almost certainly compromised (for a review, see Young, 1987). Some investigators believe that this aging process is a causative factor in age-related macular degeneration, a leading cause of retinal blindness in countries with large senior populations. The macular photoreceptors, which include both rods and cones, then die as a secondary response to an aged and incompetent RPE. Currently, there is considerable interest in developing methods for the transplantation of healthy RPE into these individuals (for a review, see Bok et al., 1993). Transplantation of the RPE is feasible because it is capable of leaving its postmitotic state when placed in culture or the appropriate microenvironment. Indeed, healthy RPE has been transplanted successfully into the retinas of rats that carry a mutation that impairs the phagocytic function of the RPE and leads to photoreceptor death (Bok and Hall, 1971; Mullen and LaVail, 1976). RPE transplantation rescues the adjacent photoreceptors from this fate (Li and Turner, 1988).

UPTAKE PROCESSING, TRANSPORT AND RELEASE OF RETINOIDS BY THE RPE

One of the highly-specialized functions of the RPE is its role in the visual or retinoid cycle (Fig. 2). This involves the repeated movement of vitamin A (retinol) and some of its derivatives (retinoids) back and forth between the rods and cones (photoreceptors) and the RPE (Dowling, 1960). The purpose of this cycle is to regenerate 11-*cis* retinaldehyde, the retinoid that serves as the chromophore for the visual pigments in rod and cone outer segments and whose photon triggered isomerization to the all-*trans* form is the first step in phototransduction. The RPE is the cellular site in which regeneration of 11-*cis*-retinaldehyde (11-*cis*-retinal) takes place (Bernstein et al., 1987). Therefore, all-*trans* retinol, the product of photoisomerization and reduction in the photoreceptor outer segment, must leave the photoreceptors, traverse the extracellular space between the photoreceptors and RPE and undergo reisomerization to 11-*cis* retinal and oxidation prior to returning to the photoreceptors across the extracellular space. This, in summary, is the visual cycle.

During the visual cycle, the retina is conservative with respect to the reutilization of its endogenous retinoids, as indicated by the fact that they are so tightly sequestered there once they are taken up for the circulation (Dowling, 1964). The delivery of retinol from the blood to the retina and its recycling within the retina involve a cohort of binding proteins that solubilize and protect retinol and its derivatives from damage (Fig. 2). Retinol is a lipid-soluble molecule and its solubility in water is in the nanomolar range. Its concentration in the blood, however, is micromolar. This increase in solubility is achieved by plasma retinol binding protein (RBP), with which it is secreted by the liver (Kanai et al., 1968). RBP circulates as a complex with transthyretin, a thyroxin-binding protein, and delivers its cargo of retinol to the RPE by a receptor-mediated process, the precise molecular mechanisms of which remain unresolved (Heller,

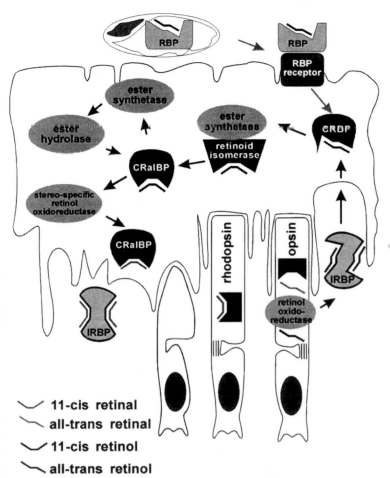

11-cis retinal
all-trans retinal
11-cis retinol
all-trans retinol

Fig. 2. Diagram of the visual cycle. This complicated process involves a group of extracellular and intracellular retinoid binding proteins that solubilize and protect the retinoids and serve as substrate carriers for enzymes. The cycle also involves rod and cone photopigments that initiate phototransduction, plus enzymes that convert retinol into its various visual cycle intermediates, the final product being the photopigment chromophore, 11-*cis* retinaldehyde (11-*cis* retinal). Basolateral uptake and apical uptake and release of retinol are mediated by separate binding proteins. See text for further details.

1975; Heller and Bok, 1976). Putative receptors for RBP exist on the basolateral membrane of the RPE (Bok and Heller, 1976). Autoradiographic studies involving ^{125}I-labeling of RBP strongly suggest that the protein does not enter the RPE cells during retinol delivery. Following the entry of retinol into the cell, its solubilization continues and its processing commences. Studies from a variety of laboratories combine to suggest the following series of events (Fig. 2) that ultimately lead to the release of the finished product, 11-*cis* retinaldehyde, from the apical membrane of the RPE, across the extracellular matrix and into the photoreceptors (for a review, see Saari, 1990).

Within the RPE, retinol is bound to cellular retinol-binding protein (CRBP, Bok et al., 1984), a protein that has no amino acid sequence homology with RBP but belongs instead to a family of fatty acid binding proteins (Sundelin et al. 1985). The bound retinol is esterified primarily to palmitic acid and the resulting retinyl ester serves as both the storage form of retinol in the RPE and the substrate for retinoid isomerase (Barry et al., 1989), a membrane-bound enzyme that converts the ester to 11-*cis*-retinol (Bernstein et al., 1987). This retinoid isomer is bound by yet another intracellular binding protein named cellular retinal binding protein (CRALBP, Futterman et al., 1977). It presents the retinoid to an oxidoreductase (Saari and Bredberg, 1982), which converts it to the final product, 11-*cis* retinaldehyde. The cellular release of 11-*cis*-retinal then takes place across the apical membrane of the RPE. The release process is promoted by a large extracellular retinoid binding glyco-protein (Adler and Klusznik, 1982) called interphotorecep-tor retinoid binding protein (IRBP, Lai et al., 1982; Liou et al., 1982). The mechanism for this release appears to involve a receptor-mediated process by virtue of its speci-ficity for IRBP. In tissue culture (Carlson and Bok, 1992) and in amphibian eyecups (Okajima et al., 1989) that have had the neurosensory retina removed, release of 11-*cis*-reti-nal is up to 5-fold higher in the presence of IRBP than it is when other proteins are substituted for it, including CRALBP, which has a much higher affinity for 11-*cis*-reti-nal than IRBP. IRBP is thought to mediate the delivery of 11-*cis*-retinal to the photoreceptors and the return of all-*trans*-retinol back to the RPE following photobleaching. Again, the mechanisms for this have not been resolved (Saari, 1990). Nonetheless, the efficiency of delivery of all-*trans*-retinol across the apical membrane appears to be at its highest under experimental conditions when the deliv-ery is via IRBP as opposed to non-specific carrier proteins such as bovine serum albumin (Okajima et al., 1989).

Individuals who suffer from a rare autosomal recessive syndrome called Refsum's disease have a deficiency in phy-tanic acid alpha hydroxylase, which leads to the accumu-lation of a branched fatty acid called phytanic acid (Klenk

and Kahlke, 1963; Eldjarn et al., 1966). In addition to neu-rologic disorders, these patients suffer from night blindness and retinitis pigmentosa due to the loss of their RPE and photoreceptors. There are two hypotheses that suggest a molecular mechanism for this cell degeneration. One hypothesis favors a metabolic basis and suggests that phy-tanic acid competes with palmitic acid for the esterification of retinol, thereby competing with retinyl palmitate in the visual cycle (Levy, 1970). The molecular distortion hypoth-esis speculates that phytanic acid, due to its side chains, perturbs the integrity of lipid bilayers and leads to a gen-eral decline in cell function, particularly in regions of high membrane density such as myelin and photoreceptor outer segments (Steinberg, 1978) or perhaps by causing lysoso-mal membranes to become leaky.

Recently, we were able to model Refsum's disease in RPE cell cultures grown on porous supports and to test the antimetabolite hypothesis (Bernstein et al., 1992). Human and bovine RPE cells were exposed to levels of phytanic acid (200 μM) comparable to those measured in human patients. The cells were then analyzed morphologically and by high performance liquid chromatography in order to assess their ability to process retinoids. We were able to show that their ability to esterify retinol and to isomerize all-*trans* retinoids to 11-*cis* retinoids remained intact, in spite of the synthesis of a large amount of retinyl phytanate. This provides evidence against the hypothesis that phytanic acid inhibits retinol processing by the RPE and favors the distortion hypothesis.

RPE POLARITY: THE ISSUE OF Na,K-ATPASE TRAFFICKING AND POLARITY OF VIRAL BUDDING

As mentioned earlier, the RPE shares a unique feature with

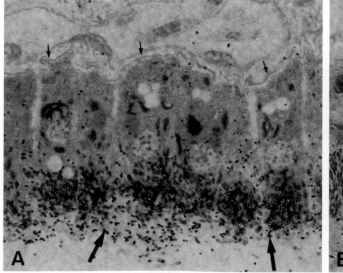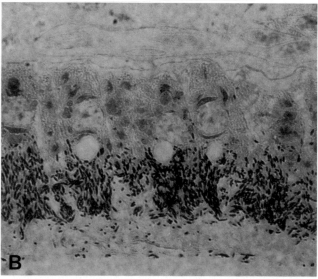

Fig. 3. Light microscopic autoradiograms of apical binding of ³H-ouabain by frog RPE. The tissue was freeze dried and fixed with osmium tetroxide vapors after incubation in this specific marker for Na,K-ATPase. (A) ³H-ouabain binding, as indicated by the location of silver grains, is confined primarily to the apical microvilli (large arrows) with no detectable binding on the basolateral surface (small arrows). (B) Apical binding of ³H-ouabain was significantly reduced when a 3-fold excess of non-radioactive ouabain was present in the incubation medium. ×940. (From Bok, 1982, with permission.)

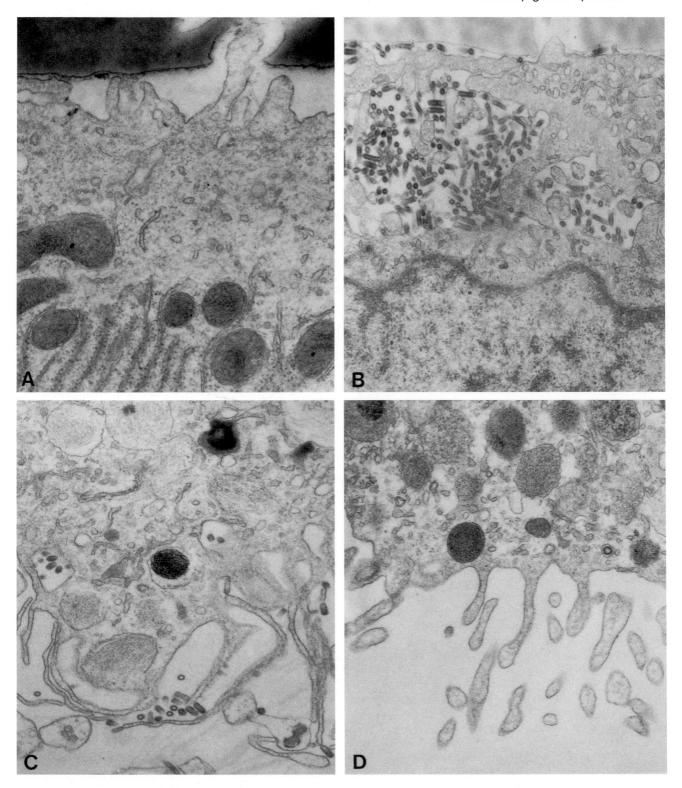

Fig. 4. Polarized budding of vesicular stomatitis virus (VSV) and influenza virus from human RPE cultured from a 2-year-old donor. (A and C) Basolateral and apical surfaces following influenza virus infection. (B and D) basolateral and apical surfaces following VSV infection. The orientation of the micrographs is with the base of the RPE up, in order to be consistent with Figs 1-3. (A-C), ×19,500; (D), ×26,000.

the epithelium of the choroid plexus, namely predominant expression of its Na,K-ATPase on the apical membrane (Fig. 3) rather than the basolateral expression observed in most other epithelia (Steinberg and Miller 1973; Bok, 1982). Due to this reversal in polarity for Na,K-ATPase, we wondered whether the RPE might possess general membrane protein trafficking mechanisms that are the reverse of that in the kidney. To explore this possibility, we infected cultured human and bovine RPE with enveloped viruses whose progeny bud from specific membrane domains (Rodriguez-Boulan and Sabatini, 1978), as dictated by the sorting of their envelope glycoproteins (Rodriguez-Boulan and Pendergast, 1980). Influenza hemagglutinin (HA) is sorted to the apical membrane in kidney (MDCK) and other polarized epithelial cells, whereas vesicular stomatitis (VSV) glycoprotein (G-protein) is targeted to the basolateral membrane. Cultured human (Fig. 4) and bovine RPE cells exhibited the same pattern of viral budding as has been observed in other polarized epithelia (Bok et al., 1992). Therefore, as far as viral envelope glycoproteins are concerned, the RPE does not appear to have a generalized sorting mechanism that is unique.

We must therefore search for alternative mechanisms in order to gain an understanding of Na,K-ATPase trafficking in the RPE. Hammerton et al. (1991) have shown that MDCK cells insert their Na,K-ATPase into both the basolateral and apical membranes, and then achieve polarity by inactivating and then removing the apical proteins. The RPE may do the reverse by inactivation and removal of Na,K-ATPase from the basolateral membrane.

There is a growing impression, based on experimental evidence, that Na,K-ATPase polarity might be dictated by cytoskeletal elements. Fodrin and ankyrin also show a reversal of polarity in the RPE. Gunderson et al. (1991) have shown that these proteins are polarized to the apical domain. Furthermore, Rizzolo and Heiges (1991) have found that apical polarization of the RPE does not occur until day 11 in the chick embryo, a time when the developing photoreceptors begin to elaborate their extracellular matrix. The RPE is peculiar in the sense that both its basolateral and apical membranes are in contact with highly organized extracellular matrices, the basal lamina on the basal side and an intricate system of proteoglycan sheaths surrounding individual photoreceptor outer segments on the apical side (Johnson et al., 1986; Sameshima et al. 1987). Thus interactions between cytoskeletal elements, Na,K-ATPase and extracellular matrix components could be involved in dictating the polarity of this enzyme.

Finally, we should not dismiss the possibility that information for trafficking could reside in the amino acid sequence of the Na,K-ATPase α or β subunits. Protein (McGrail and Sweadner, 1986) and mRNA analysis (Gundersen et al., 1991) suggest that the α isoform is the same in the kidney and RPE, namely α_1. As in the kidney, the β_1 isoform has also been detected with antibodies and by mRNA analysis (Gundersen et al., 1991; Rizzolo and Heiges, 1991), although the abundance of β_1 does not appear to be 1:1 with α_1. Thus it is conceivable that the RPE contains a unique β isoform that dictates polarity.

The mRNA isoform classification of RPE ATPase subunits that has been performed to date has been limited to northern blot analysis. This is a relatively low resolution method, which cannot detect subtle differences in size or nucleotide sequence. Thus we must remain receptive to the possibility that, in spite of apparent isoform identity among α and β subunits in RPE and kidney, minor sequence differences that result in small changes at the protein level

could determine polarity. Brewer and Roth (1991) have shown that a single amino acid change from cysteine to tyrosine in the cytoplasmic domain of influenza HA changes its expression from the apical to the basolateral membrane.

A FEW PARTING POINTS

The RPE presents an interesting target for investigations into its diverse functions in the healthy state as well as for issues involving the process of aging and genetic disorders. Whereas the RPE has not been included in the mainstream investigations of the majority of those interested in epithelial polarity, I hope that this short review has made a case for the versatility of this epithelium and some of the unique features of its polarity. Recent advances in cell culture, particularly in the case of human, bovine and chicken RPE, have made it possible to explore more readily this interesting tissue under a variety of controlled conditions.

Supported by National Eye Institute Grants EY00444, EY00331 and The National Retinitis Pigmentosa Foundation Fighting Blindness, Inc. D.B. is the Dolly Green Professor of Ophthalmology at UCLA. I thank Cherie Hubbell for preparing Fig. 2.

REFERENCES

Adler, A. J. and Klusznik, K. M. (1982). Proteins and glycoproteins of the bovine interphotoreceptor matrix: composition and fractionation. *Exp. Eye Res.* **34**, 423-434.

Barry, R. J., Canada, F. J. and Rando, R. R. (1989). Solubilization and partial purification of retinyl ester synthetase and retinoid isomerase from bovine ocular pigment epithelium. *J. Biol. Chem.* **264**, 9231-9238.

Bernstein, P. S., Law, W. C. and Rando, R. (1987). Isomerization of all-*trans* retinoids to 11-*cis* retinoids in vitro. *Proc. Nat. Acad. Sci. USA* **84**, 1849-1853.

Bernstein, P. S., Lloyd, M. B., O'Day, W. T. and Bok, D. (1992). Effect of phytanic acid on cultured retinal pigment epithelium: an in vitro model for Refsum's disease. *Exp. Eye Res.* **55**, 869-878.

Bok, D. and Heller, J. (1976). Transport of retinol from the blood to the retina: an autoradiographic study of the pigment epithelial cell surface receptor for plasma retinol-binding protein. *Exp. Eye Res.* **22**, 395-402.

Bok, D. (1982). Autoradiographic studies on the polarity of plasma membrane receptors in retinal pigment epithelial cells. In *The Structure of the Eye* (ed. J. G. Hollyfield), pp. 247-256. New York: Elsevier North Holland.

Bok, D. (1985). Retinal photoreceptor-pigment epithelium interactions. *Invest. Ophthalmol. Vis. Sci.* **26**, 1659-1694.

Bok, D. (1988). Retinal photoreceptor disc shedding and pigment epithelium phagocytosis. In *Retinal Diseases: Medical and Surgical Management, Vol I* (ed. S. J. Ryan, T. E. Ogden and A. P. Schachat), pp. 69-81. St. Louis: C. V. Mosby Co.

Bok, D. and Hall, M. O. (1971). The role of the pigment epithelium in the etiology of inherited retinal dystrophy in the rat. *J. Cell Biol.* **49**, 664-682.

Bok, D., Hageman, G. S. and Steinberg, R. H. (1993). Repair and replacement to restore sight. Report from panel on photoreceptor/retinal pigment epithelium. *Arch. Ophthalmol.* **111**, 463-471.

Bok, D., O'Day, W. and Rodriguez-Boulan, E. (1992). Polarized budding of vesicular stomatitis and influenza virus from cultured human and bovine retinal pigment epithelium. *Exp. Eye Res.* **55**, 853-860.

Bok, D., Ong, D. E. and Chytil, F. (1984). Immunocytochemical localization of cellular retinol binding protein in the rat retina. *Invest. Ophthalmol. Vis. Sci.* **25**, 1-7.

Bosch, E., Horwitz, J. and Bok, D. (1993). Phagocytosis of outer segments by retinal pigment epithelium: phagosome-lysosome interaction. *J. Histochem. Cytochem.* **41**, 253-263.

Brewer, C. and Roth, M. G. (1991). A single amino acid change in the cytoplasmic domain alters the polarized delivery of influenza virus hemagglutinin. *J. Cell Biol.* **114**, 413-21.

Cahill, G. M. and Besharse, J. C. (1992). Light-sensitive melatonin synthesis by Xenopus photoreceptors after destruction of the inner retina. *Vis Neurosci.* (in press).

Carlson, A. and Bok, D. (1992). Promotion of the release of 11-*cis* retinal from cultured retinal pigment epithelium by interphotoreceptor retinoid-binding protein. *Biochemistry* **31**, 9056-9062.

Dowling, J. E. (1960). Chemistry of visual adaptation in the rat. *Nature* **188**, 114-118.

Dowling, J. F. (1964). Nutritional and inherited blindness in the rat. *Exp. Eye Res.* **3**, 348-356.

Eldjarn, L., Stokke, O. and Try, K. (1966). α-oxidation of branched chain fatty acids in man and its failure in patients with Refsum's disease showing phytanic acid accumulation. *Scand. J. Clin. Lab. Invest.* **18**, 694-695.

Futterman, S., Saari, J. C. and Blair, S. (1977). Occurrence of a binding protein for 11-*cis* retinol in retina. *J. Biol. Chem.* **252**, 3267-3271.

Gundersen, D., Orlowski, J. and Rodriguez-Boulan, E. (1991). Apical polarity of Na,K-ATPase in retinal pigment epithelium is linked to a reversal of the ankyrin-fodrin submembrane cytoskeleton. *J. Cell Biol.* **112**, 863-872.

Hammerton, R. W., Krzeminski, K. A., Mays, R. W., Ryan, T. A., Wollner, D. A. and Nelson, J. A. (1991). Mechanism for regulating cell surface distribution of Na,K-ATPase in polarized epithelial cells. *Science* **254**, 847-850.

Heller, J. (1975). Interactions of plasma retinol binding protein with its receptor. Specific binding of bovine and human retinol binding protein to pigment epithelium cells from bovine eyes. *J. Biol. Chem.* **250**, 3613-3619.

Heller, J. and Bok, D. (1976). A specific receptor for retinol binding protein as detected by the binding of human and bovine retinol binding protein to pigment epithelial cells. *Amer. J. Ophthalmol.* **81**, 93-97.

Johnson, L. V., Hageman, G. S. and Blanks, J. C. (1986). Interphotoreceptor matrix domains ensheath vertebrate cone photoreceptor cells. *Invest. Ophthalmol. Vis. Sci.* **27**, 129-135.

Kanai, M., Raz, A. and Goodman, D. S. (1968). Retinol binding protein: the transport protein for vitamin A in human plasma. *J. Clin. Invest.* **47**, 2025-2044.

Klenk, E. and Kahlke, W. (1963). Uber das Vorkommen der 3,7,11,15-tetramethyl-hexadecansaure (phytansaure) in den cholesterinestern und anderen Lipoidfractionen der Organe bei einem Krankheitsfall unbekannter Genese (Verdacht auf Heredopathia atactica polyneuritiformis (Refsum Syndrome). *Hoppe Seyler's Z. Physiol. Chem.* **333**, 133-139.

Lai, Y-L., Wiggert, B., Liu, Y-P. and Chader, G. J. (1982). Interphotoreceptor retinol-binding proteins: possible transport vehicles between compartments of the retina. *Nature* **298**, 848-849.

LaVail, M. M. (1976). Rod outer segment disk shedding in the rat retina. Relationship to cyclic lighting. *Science* **194**, 1071-1074.

Levy, I. S. (1970). Refsum's syndrome. *Trans Ophthalmol. Soc. UK* **90**, 181-186.

Li, L. and Turner, J. E. (1988). Inherited retinal dystrophy in the RCS rat: prevention of photoreceptor degeneration by pigment epithelial cell transplantation. *Exp. Eye Res.* **47**, 911-916.

Liou, G. I., Bridges, C. D. B. and Fong, S.-L. (1982). Vitamin A transport between retina and pigment epithelium - an interstitial protein carrying endogenous retinol (interstitial retinol binding protein). *Vision Res.* **22**, 1457-1468.

McGrail, K. and Sweadner, K. (1986). Immunofluorescent localization of two different Na,-ATPase in the rat retina and in identified dissociated retinal cells. *J. Neurosci.* **6**, 1272-1283.

Mullen, R. J. and LaVail, M. M. (1976). Inherited retinal dystrophy: primary defect in pigment epithelium determined with experimental rat chimeras. *Science* **192**, 799-801.

Okajima, T.-I. L., Pepperberg, D. R., Ripps, H., Wiggert, B. and Chader, G. J. (1989). Interphotoreceptor retinoid binding protein: role in delivery of retinol to the pigment epithelium. *Exp. Eye Res.* **49**, 629-644.

Peyman, G. A. and Bok, D. (1972). Peroxidase diffusion in the normal and laser-coagulated primate retina. *Invest. Ophthalmol.* **11**, 35-45.

Quinton, P. M., Wright, E. M. and Tormey, J. McD. (1973). Localization of sodium pumps in the choroid plexus epithelium. *J. Cell Biol.* **58**, 724-730.

Rizzolo, L. J. and Heiges, M. (1991). The polarity of the retinal pigment epithelium is developmentally regulated. *Exp. Eye Res.* **53**, 549-553.

Rodriguez-Boulan, E. and Pendergast, M. (1980). Polarized distribution of viral envelope proteins in plasma membrane of infected epithelial cells. *Cell* **20**, 45-54.

Rodriguez-Boulan, E. and Sabatini, D. (1978). Asymmetric budding of viruses in epithelial monolayers; a model system for study of epithelial polarity. *Proc. Nat. Acad. Sci. USA* **75**, 5071-5075.

Saari, J. C. (1990). Enzymes and proteins of the mammalian visual cycle. In *Progress in Retinal Research* (ed. N. Osborne and G. Chader), pp. 363-382. Oxford: Pergamon Press.

Saari, J. D. and Bredberg, L. (1982). Enzymatic reduction of 11-*cis* retinol bound to cellular retinal-binding protein. *Biochem. Biophys. Acta.* **715**, 266-272.

Sameshima, M., Uehara, E. and Ohba, N. (1987). Specialization of the interphotoreceptor matrices around cone and rod photoreceptor cells in the monkey retina as revealed by lectin cytochemistry. *Exp. Eye Res.* **45**, 751-762.

Steinberg, D. (1978). Phytanic acid storage disease: Refsum's syndrome. In *The Metabolic Basis of Inherited Disease, 4th edn.* (ed. J. B. Stanbury, J. B. Wyngarden and D. S. Fredickson), pp. 688-706. New York; McGraw-Hill.

Steinberg, R. H. and Miller, S. (1973). Aspects of electrolyte transport in frog pigment epithelium. *Exp. Eye Res.* **16**, 36-52.

Sundelin, J., Anundi, H., Tragardh, L., Ericksson, U., Lind, P., Ronne, H., Peterson, P. A. and Rask, L. (1985). The primary structure of rat liver cellular retinol-binding-protein. *J. Biol. Chem.* **260**, 6488-6493.

Williams, D. S. and Fisher, S. K. (1987). Prevention of rod disk shedding by detachment from the retinal pigment epithelium. *Invest. Ophthalmol. Vis. Sci.* **28**, 184-187.

Young, R. W. (1987). Pathophysiology of age-related macular degeneration. *Surv. Ophthalmol.* **31**, 291-306.

Young, R. W. and Bok, D. (1969). Participation of the retinal pigment epithelium in the rod outer segment renewal process. *J. Cell Biol.* **42**, 392-402.

Journal of Cell Science, Supplement 17, 197-208 (1993)
Printed in Great Britain © The Company of Biologists Limited 1993

Epidermal differentiation and keratin gene expression

Elaine Fuchs

Howard Hughes Medical Institute, Department of Molecular Genetics and Cell Biology, The University of Chicago, Chicago, IL 60637, USA

SUMMARY

The epidermis of the skin is a stratified squamous epithelium, which plays an important protective role. It manifests this role by building an extensive cytoskeletal architecture, the unique feature of which is the presence of keratin filaments. There are two major pairs of keratins in the epidermis: one pair is expressed in dividing cells and the other expressed in terminally differentiating cells. As such, keratins provide useful biochemical markers to explore the molecular mechanisms underlying the balance between growth and differentiation in the epidermis. Here, I review what is currently known about epidermal growth and differentiation, and how an understanding of keratin gene expression has been useful in elucidating regulatory pathways in the skin.

Key words: epidermis, differentiation, gene expression, growth control

THE PROGRAM OF TERMINAL DIFFERENTIATION

The epidermis is a stratified squamous epithelium, which forms the protective covering of skin. Only the innermost, basal layer of the epidermis has the capacity for DNA synthesis and mitosis. Under an as yet unidentified trigger of terminal differentiation, a basal cell will begin its journey to the skin surface. In transit, it undergoes a series of morphological and biochemical changes culminating in the production of dead, flattened, enucleated squames, which are sloughed from the surface, and continually replaced by inner cells differentiating outward. The epidermis manifests its protective role by building a three-dimensional network of interconnected keratinocytes, each containing an extensive cytoskeleton of specialized 10 nm keratin filaments, encased by a membranous envelope of highly cross-linked proteins. Mitotically active basal cells adhere to the basement membrane and underlying dermis via specialized, calcium-activated adhesion plaques, called hemidesmosomes (Jones and Green, 1991). Hemidesmosomes contain unique anchoring proteins, including the $\alpha_6\beta_4$ integrin heterodimer and several proteins identified by autoimmune antibodies from sera of patients with bullous pemphigoid. Basal cells interact laterally and suprabasally with their neighbors through calcium-activated membranous plaques, called desmosomes (Jones and Green, 1991). Despite their ultrastructural similarity to hemidesmosomes, desmosomes are composed of distinct proteins, including desmoplakins, desmogleins and desmocollins.

Intracellularly, hemidesmosomes and desmosomes connect with the cytoskeletal network of keratin filaments. The pattern of keratins in the skin is complex. As in basal cells of all stratified squamous epithelia, basal epidermal cells display a keratin network composed of the type II keratin K5 (58 kDa) and the type I keratin K14 (50 kDa) (Fuchs and Green, 1980; Moll et al., 1982; Nelson and Sun, 1983; Roop et al., 1987). These keratins constitute ~15-25% of basal cell protein. As basal epidermal cells differentiate, they downregulate expression of K5/K14 and induce expression of a new set of differentiation-specific keratins (Fuchs and Green, 1980; Moll et al., 1982; Roop et al., 1987). For most body regions, the type II keratin, K1 (67 kDa) and the type I keratin, K10 (56.5 kDa), is expressed (Fuchs and Green, 1980; Roop et al., 1987). As epidermal cells proceed through differentiation, they switch on the expression of an additional type II keratin, K2 (65 kDa) and type I keratin (56 kDa) (Collin et al., 1992). In palmar and plantar skin, an additional type I keratin, K9 (63 kDa) is expressed suprabasally (Fuchs and Green, 1980; Knapp et al., 1986). During wound-healing, the type II keratin, K6 (56 kDa) and type I keratin K16 (48 kDa) are induced suprabasally (Mansbridge and Knapp, 1987). These keratins are also typically expressed in the outer root sheath (ORS) of the hair follicles (Stark et al., 1987; Kopan and Fuchs, 1989a) and in the posterior segments of tongue epithelium (Moll et al., 1982). Other suprabasal keratin pairs, such as K4 and K13, are not expressed in the skin, but have been found in other stratified squamous epithelia (for a review, see Sun et al., 1984).

Even though terminally differentiating cells in the epidermis are post-mitotic, they nevertheless are metabolically active, and the differentiation-associated changes in keratin expression are regulated transcriptionally (Stellmach et al., 1991). In the inner spinous layers, keratins are a mixture of residual K5/K14 and newly synthesized differentiation-specific keratins. As spinous cells continue their path to the skin surface, they devote most of their protein synthesizing machinery to manufacturing differentiation-specific keratins. Given that keratins are also highly stable in filament form, suprabasal keratins eventually constitute >85% of the total protein of a differentiated squame. Although the functional significance of the keratin switch has not yet been unequivocally resolved, K1/K10 filaments aggregate to form tonofibrillar bundles, which are thicker than tonofilament bundles in basal cells (for a review, see Montagna and Lobitz, 1964). This process also takes place in vitro, and appears to be dependent upon the pair(s) of keratins (Eichner et al., 1986). The increase in filament bundling may enhance the ability of keratins to be among the sole survivors of the terminal differentiation process.

As spinous cells reach the granular layer, they undergo a final tailoring in protein synthesis, producing filaggrin, a histidine-rich, basic protein, which may be involved in bundling tonofibrils into large macrofibrillar cables (Dale et al., 1978). This process may impart to keratin filaments their final protection against the destructive phase, which soon ensues. Several other changes occur in the later stages of differentiation. Membrane-coating granules, made earlier, fuse with the plasma membrane and release lipids into intercellular spaces of granular and stratum corneum cells (for a review, see Schurer et al., 1991). In addition, glutamine- and lysine-rich proteins are deposited on the inner surface of the plasma membrane (Rice and Green, 1979). Some of these proteins, such as involucrin, are made early during differentiation (Simon and Green, 1985 and references therein). Others, such as loricrin, are synthesized later (Mehrel et al., 1990). As each differentiating cell becomes permeable during the destructive phase, a calcium influx activates epidermal transglutaminase, which then catalyzes formation of ε-(γ-glutamyl) lysine isopeptide bonds. The envelope proteins are thereby cross-linked into a cage to contain the keratin macrofibrils (for a review, see Greenberg et al., 1991). As lytic enzymes are released, all vestiges of metabolic activity terminate, and the resulting flattened squames are merely cellular skeletons, chock full of keratin macrofibrils. The stratum corneum, composed of squames sealed together by lipids, is an impermeable fortress, keeping microorganisms out and essential bodily fluids in.

In development, progenitor cells for the epidermis are embryonic basal cells (for a review, see Montagna and Lobitz, 1964). They are the first cells to express epidermal markers, synthesizing very low levels of K14 and K5 (Dale et al., 1985; Kopan and Fuchs, 1989a and references therein). If embryonic basal cells come into contact with specialized mesenchymal cells, called dermal papilla cells, they downregulate K5/K14 expression, and begin to grow downward, forming what will ultimately become a hair follicle. In the absence of stimulus from dermal papilla cells, an embryonic basal cell upregulates K5/K14 expression, concomitant with a commitment to an epidermal cell fate. Shortly thereafter, concomitant with stratification, K1 and K10 are made in the suprabasal layers of the developing epidermis. In contrast, six different programs of differentiation take place in the hair follicle, giving rise to terminally differentiated hairs. The program of differentiation in the epidermis is much simpler than that of its appendages, although based on body location, regional differences can give rise to differences in the pattern of gene expression associated with the epidermal program of differentiation (for a review, see Fuchs, 1990).

Terminal differentiation in the epidermis continues throughout life. It takes approximately 2-4 weeks for an epidermal cell to leave the basal layer and reach and be sloughed from the skin surface. Thus, the adult epidermis is rejuvenated every few weeks.

EPIDERMAL CELL CULTURE

Among the most significant contributions to epidermal cell growth in culture are the pioneering studies of Rheinwald and Green (for a review, see Rheinwald, 1980), who realized that epidermal cells are not only dependent upon epidermal growth factor (EGF), but also certain fibroblast factors, one of which is likely to be keratinocyte growth factor (KGF). Thus, when seeded on a lawn of X-irradiated or mitomycin C-treated fibroblasts, and in medium containing the appropriate serum lot, cAMP-inducing agent, growth factors and various additional nutrients, epidermal cells grow for several hundred generations in culture. This system is optimal for generating rapidly growing keratinocytes, although many of the biochemical changes characteristic of terminal differentiation, such K1, K10 and filaggrin expression, do not occur appreciably (Fuchs and Green, 1980; Asselineau et al., 1986).

A number of laboratories have contributed to methods aimed at optimizing terminal differentiation in vitro, and from these studies, clues to extracellular controls of keratinization have been obtained. One of these factors is calcium, a necessary prerequisite for a variety of differentiative processes, including stratification, assembly of desmosomes and activation of epidermal transglutaminase (Rice and Green, 1979; Hennings et al., 1980; Watt et al., 1984; Duden and Franke, 1988). Another important class of regulators are retinoids, which diminish features of terminal differentiation in stratified squamous epithelia, both in vivo (Fell and Mellanby, 1953) and in vitro (Yuspa and Harris, 1974; Fuchs and Green, 1981). When retinol is removed from serum, cultured epidermal cells display many of the morphological and biochemical characteristics of terminal differentiation (Fuchs and Green, 1981). These features include stratification, cell adhesiveness, reduced cell motility, and expression of K1 and K10.

While calcium and retinoids are clearly important, cultures grown on feeder layers in the presence of low concentrations of retinol and high concentrations of calcium produce basal keratinocytes and 1-2 layers of squames, but generate very few spinous and granular cells. However, when epidermal cells are cultured on floating lattices of collagen and fibroblasts at the air-liquid interface, their differentiation is significantly enhanced (see Asselineau et al., 1986 and references therein). Subsequent studies showed that, when coupled with consideration of optimal serum lots, calcium, retinoids and other nutrients, this culture method results in a near optimal balance between growth and differentiation, which is both morphologically and biochemically a faithful representation of epidermis in vivo (Kopan et al., 1987; Choi and Fuchs, 1990). Fig. 1 illustrates the four major programs of differentiation that take

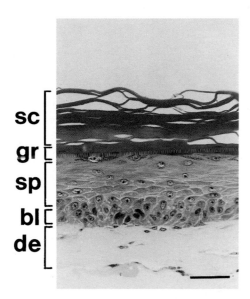

Fig. 1. Morphology of differentiation by cultured human epidermal cells. Human epidermal cells from newborn foreskins were isolated and cultured according to the method of Rheinwald (1980). Cells were transferred to a dish containing a lattice of collagen and fibroblasts, and at confluence, the lattice was raised to the air-liquid interface, and cultured for an additional three weeks (Asselineau et al., 1986; Kopan et al., 1987). The 'tissue' was then fixed in Carnoy's solution, embedded in paraffin, and sectioned (5 μm). A section stained with hematoxylin and eosin (Choi and Fuchs, 1990) is shown. sc, stratum corneum; gr, granular layer; sp, spinous layers; ba, basal layer; de, dermis. Bar, 41 μm.

place in the epidermal raft cultures grown under optimal conditions.

MOLECULAR CONTROLS OF EPIDERMAL GROWTH AND DIFFERENTIATION

Epidermal growth factors and their tyrosine kinase receptors

The search for an optimal culture system uncovered a number of extracellular regulators controlling the balance between growth and terminal differentiation. Stimulators of keratinocyte growth include EGF (Rheinwald, 1980), TGF-α (Coffey et al., 1987; Barrandon and Green, 1987), 10^{-6} to 10^{-10} M retinoic acid (Fuchs and Green, 1981; Kopan and Fuchs, 1989b), KGF (Finch et al., 1989), and the cytokines, IL-6, IL-1_α and IL-8 (for a review, see Luger and Schwarz, 1990). Of these, EGF and TGF-α have been the most extensively studied. EGF and TGF-α are both ligands for the tyrosine kinase-activatable EGF receptors, located primarily on the surface of basal cells (Green et al., 1987). However, these factors do not act simply as mitogens (Barrandon and Green, 1987; Vassar and Fuchs, 1991). In fact, when keratinocyte colonies are small, cell growth is exponential and usually not markedly influenced by additional growth supplements. It is only when colonies become larger that supplemental factors play a significant role in colony expansion. This acquired factor dependency appears to arise from the fact that colony growth occurs predomi-

nantly at the periphery, and hence larger colonies are dependent upon factors that increase cell migration. TGF-α (Barrandon and Green, 1987) and retinoids (Fuchs and Green, 1981) are especially potent in enhancing migration of keratinocytes, and it may be that the growth stimulatory effects of these factors are at least in part related to this ability.

TGF-α differs from EGF in that it is synthesized by keratinocytes both in vitro and in vivo (see Elder et al., 1989). Since epidermal cells autoregulate their own growth via TGF-α production, it is perhaps not surprising to find that such control can go awry, leading to uncontrolled growth. Several reports have implicated an increase in EGF receptors and/or TGF-α levels with epidermal tumorigenesis (Yamamoto et al., 1986; Ozanne et al., 1986). Psoriatic epidermis also contains higher levels of TGF-α than normal skin (Elder et al., 1989). Interestingly, when transgenic mice were engineered to overexpress TGF-α in their basal epidermal cells, newborn mice exhibited some, but not all, of the features typical of psoriatic skin (Vassar and Fuchs, 1991). This included a physical appearance of scaliness at the skin surface. Histologically, the scaliness was accompanied by an increase in epidermal proliferation, leading to a proportional increase in spinous, granular and stratum corneum layers (Fig. 2A, K14-TGF-α mouse skin, 9 days; Fig. 2B, normal mouse skin). While these mice did not develop squamous cell carcinomas, they did produce benign skin papillomas upon wound healing (Fig. 2C-D; Vassar and Fuchs, 1991; Vassar et al., 1992). Unlike chemically induced papillomas, these papillomas did not have mutations in the *Ha-ras* gene (Vassar et al., 1992). Thus, while there are additional steps such as *Ha-ras* in the keratinocyte growth cycle that can be altered, thereby leading to epidermal hyperproliferation and malignant transformation (for examples, see Bailleul et al., 1990 and Greenhalgh et al., 1990), TGF-α seems to be centrally involved in controlling the proper balance between growth and differentiation. Finally, TGF-α overexpression in mice elicited some effects, such as epidermal hypertrophy, which were seemingly unrelated to hyperproliferation (Vassar and Fuchs, 1991).

Keratinocyte growth factor: epithelial-mesenchymal interactions

Keratinocyte growth factor (KGF) is made by stromal fibroblasts and belongs to the seven-member fibroblast growth factor family (for a review see Aaronson et al., 1991). It differs from other FGFs in that its mitogenic activity appears to be specific for keratinocytes, and not fibroblasts or endothelial cells. Similar to those of TGF-α and EGF, the KGF pathway for keratinocyte growth stimulation is activated by a tyrosine kinase surface receptor (Rubin et al., 1989). In vitro studies have shown that the stimulating effects of KGF on DNA synthesis in keratinocytes is 2-10-fold stronger than that of autocrine keratinocyte growth factors such as aFGF, TGF-α and EGF (Rubin et al., 1989). Taken together with the finding that KGF mRNA expression is dramatically elevated after skin injury (Werner et al. 1992), KGF appears to be a major factor in promoting skin cell proliferation.

Given its paracrine effects on the epidermis, KGF has also been implicated as a major player orchestrating the

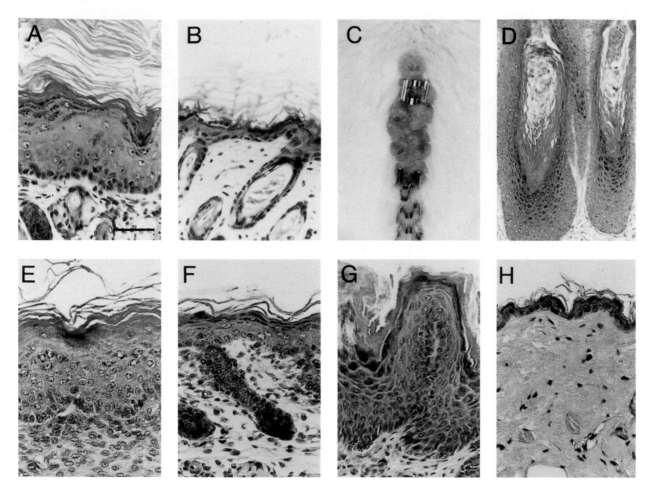

Fig. 2. Histopathology of skin from k14-tgfα and k14-kgf transgenic mice. Human keratin 14 promoter and enhancer were used to drive expression of rat-TGF-α and human KGF in the basal layer of stratified squamous epithelia of transgenic mice (Vassar and Fuchs, 1991; Guo et al., 1993). Tissues processed for histology were fixed in Bouin's fixative, sectioned (5 μm) and stained with hematoxylin and eosin. (A-B) Skins from a 9-day-old F1 transgenic K14-TGF-α mouse (A) and control littermate (B) (Vassar and Fuchs, 1991). (C) Adult K14-TGF-α mouse after wound-healing. Note presence of benign papillomas along the site of the wound (Vassar and Fuchs, 1991). (D) Section from K14-TGF-α transgenic skin of wound-generated papilloma. (E-F) Sections from skins of K14-KGF transgenic newborn exhibiting a severe phenotype (E), and from control littermate (F). (G-H) Sections from eyelid skin of K14-KGF transgenic adult(s) and control littermate (H). Sections (E-H) are reproduced from Guo et al. (1993) by permission of Oxford University Press. Bar, 57 μm (A-B, E-H); 110 μm (D).

epithelial-mesenchymal interactions that are necessary for epidermal cells to grow, develop and differentiate (for a review, see Aronson et al., 1991 and references therein). Other mesenchymal factors that are likely to play a role in this process include extracellular matrix components (Bissell et al., 1982) and cell surface-associated proteins (Sariola et al., 1988; Hirai et al., 1992).

Given that the basal layer of the epidermis has tyrosine kinase receptors for both autocrine (TGF-α) and paracrine (KGF) factors, the question arises as to whether the effects elicited by activation of these receptors are similar. To answer this question, we recently used the same keratin promoter to drive expression of KGF that we used previously to drive expression of TGF-α (Guo et al., 1993). K14-KGF expression consistently exhibited a more potent effect than K14-TGF-α on generating an increase in the number of cells within the basal layer of the epidermis (Fig. 2E, K14-KGF mouse skin, newborn; Fig 2F, control mouse skin,

newborn). In part, this overcrowding may be due to a more potent effect of KGF than TGF-α on epidermal proliferation in vivo. However, a number of major differences existed between the KGF animals and the TGF-α animals that were difficult to explain on the basis of relative degree of potency of these two factors.

One difference was that KGF-expressing epidermal cells were far more crowded and compact than the more loosely interconnected TGF-α-overexpressing epidermal cells. Another difference was in terminal differentiation. While TGF-α-overexpression led to a proportional increase in the number of spinous, granular and stratum corneum layers, KGF expression led to epidermal cells, which prematurely reached the skin surface before completing their program of terminal differentiation (Vassar and Fuchs, 1991; Guo et al., 1993). In addition, while TGF-α overexpression caused epidermal hypertrophy and a larger cytoplasm-to-nuclear ratio (Vassar and Fuchs, 1991), KGF expression produced keratinocytes with a smaller cytoplasm-to-nuclear ratio (Guo et al., 1993). Finally, while TGF-α overexpression in mice was not sufficient to elicit epithelial transformation without TPA treatment or wounding (Vassar and Fuchs, 1991), KGF overexpression led to gross transformations of tongue and skin in adult mice (Fig. 2G and H; Guo et al., 1993). Collectively, these studies suggest that the second messenger signalling that takes place after activation of the KGF receptor may be different from that elicited by activation of the EGF receptor.

One of the most striking phenotypic aberrancies of newborn, high-expressing KGF transgenic mice was the near complete suppression of hair follicle formation concomitant with thickened and grossly wrinkled skin. While other explanations are possible, it seems most likely that a critical, threshold level of K14-KGF expression at a critical time during embryonic development may have prevented some stem cells from choosing a hair follicle cell fate and funneled them into an epidermal cell fate instead. This notion is especially intriguing given that (1) hair follicles and epidermis are derived from the same embryonic stem cells, and (2) K14 expression occurs at a low level in embryonic basal cells at a time when the choice between the hair follicle and epidermal pathways of development is made (Kopan and Fuchs, 1989a).

It is well-established that the developmental choice to hair follicle morphogenesis is based upon the interaction between an embryonic basal cell and a specialized mesenchymal component, the dermal papilla cell (Wessels and Roessner, 1965). In the natural situation, hair follicle morphogenesis seems to be favored, rather than inhibited, when this mesenchymal-epidermal interaction takes place (Kollar, 1970; Dhouailly et al., 1978; Hirai et al., 1992). The inverse correlation between keratinocyte-derived KGF expression and hair follicle number suggests the possibility that KGF expression by an embryonic basal cell may be able to interfere with signals normally transmitted by dermal papilla cells. Further studies will be necessary to assess the extent to which this intriguing possibility may be correct, and if so, precisely how epidermal KGF is able to interfere with this commitment decision.

TERMINAL DIFFERENTIATION IN THE EPIDERMIS: ACTIVE OR PASSIVE?

A major question in epidermal biology is when does an epidermal cell undergo a commitment to terminally differentiate? If commitment takes place in the basal layer, then the population of basal keratinocytes should be heterogeneous. Certainly, as judged by their cell-cycling properties, this appears to be the case (Barrandon and Green, 1987; Potten and Morris, 1988). By this criterion, there seem to be at least two populations of basal cells. One population, stem cells, have a long lifespan, a long cycling phase and short S period (for a review, see Potten and Morris, 1988). The second population, transit amplifying cells or paraclones, undergo only a limited number of divisions prior to terminally differentiating (Barrandon and Green, 1987). Moreover, paraclones seem to arise from stem cells, suggesting further that a sequence of events leading to terminal differ-

entiation may take place prior to movement of a cell out of the basal layer (Barrandon and Green, 1987).

A priori, it might seem attractive to visualize terminal differentiation as a passive event, where an occupied basal layer provides the force to push a cell to the first suprabasal layer, and thereafter, its absence of contact with the basement membrane might trigger cell cycle withdrawal and the cascade of events leading to keratinization. One component of the basement membrane, fibronectin, seems to play a pivotal role in inhibiting the differentiation process, although it does not appear to interfere with cell cycle withdrawal (Adams and Watt, 1990). During suspension-induced differentiation of human keratinocytes, transcription is inhibited for the genes encoding the fibronectin receptor, α5β1 integrin, and concomitantly, the receptors lose their ability to bind fibronectin, and subsequently are lost from the cell surface (Hotchin and Watt, 1992). While loss of fibronectin binding seems to enhance the differentiative process, it is not likely to be the initial trigger of differentiation, since integrin distribution in the basal layer seems to be uniform, whereas cell cycle withdrawal and other features of epidermal differentiation can occur within the basal layer (Watt, 1984; Potten and Morris, 1988; Choi and Fuchs, 1990; Adams and Watt, 1990).

Cell cycle withdrawal: role of TGF-βs

Withdrawal from the cell cycle seems to be a prerequisite for irreversible commitment of a keratinocyte to terminally differentiate. The most extensively studied negative regulators of epidermal cell growth are the TGF-βs, which act at picomolar concentrations to inhibit DNA synthesis and cell division (Shipley et al., 1986; Kopan et al., 1987; Bascom et al., 1989a). The effect of TGF-βs on growth is reversible, at least within a 48 hour frame, and is not accompanied by gross changes in protein or RNA synthesis (Bascom et al., 1989a). While TGF-βs inhibit growth of basal cells, their natural expression in epidermis seems to be predominantly in suprabasal, differentiating layers. Indeed during mammalian development, expression of TGF-β2 mRNA (Pelton et al., 1989) and a related Vgr-1 mRNA (Lyons et al., 1989) coincide with epidermal stratification and keratinization. An interesting parallel occurs in Drosophila, where a TGF-β-like gene called *decapentaplegic* (*dpp*) is expressed dorsally in early embryos, and mutations in the *dpp* gene cause a homeotic transformation of dorsal into ventral epidermis in the fly (Padgett et al., 1987; Arora and Nusslein-Volhard, 1992). In adult mammalian epidermis both in vivo and in vitro, TGF-β1 and TGF-β2 mRNAs are low, but detectable in the differentiating layers (Glick et al., 1989; Bascom et al., 1989b; Pelton et al., 1989, and references therein). In adult epidermis, TGF-β mRNAs can be upregulated (1) in an autoregulatory fashion (Bascom et al., 1989b), and (2) when mouse skin is treated with tumor promoting agent (TPA) (Fowlis et al., 1992), retinoic acid (Glick et al., 1990, 1991; see below) or calcium (Glick et al., 1990), agents known to influence epidermal keratinization. Curiously, TPA also induces TGF-α expression, presumably in basal epidermal cells (Pittlekow et al., 1989), a phenomenon which may explain the seemingly antagonistic effects of TPA, enhancing growth and inducing differentiation in epidermis. Collectively, the timing and location of TGF-β mRNA expression suggests that members of the TGF-β family may be involved in maintaining the cessation of growth in the differentiating cells of epidermis.

Elucidating the functional significance of TGF-β expression has been hampered by the fact that TGF-βs are produced and secreted by cells in a latent form, which must then be activated prior to interaction with TGF-β receptors on the cell surface (Lyons et al., 1988; Pandiella and Massague, 1991). Mere elevation of TGF-β mRNA expression is therefore not automatically an indication that active TGF-βs are being produced. An example of this is the production of latent TGF-β1 by human keratinocytes cultured under serum-free conditions at neutral pH (Bascom et al., 1989a). Thus, even though the correlation between suprabasal TGF-β mRNA expression and cessation of growth in keratinizing cells is compelling, a causal relationship has not yet been unequivocally demonstrated, nor is it clear to what extent the expression of TGF-β mRNAs in vivo is an accurate reflection of active TGF-β secretion.

Because the effects of TGF-βs on basal cell growth appear to be largely reversible, it has been assumed that TGF-βs alone are not sufficient to induce terminal differentiation, a process thought to be irreversible. In support of this notion were early in vitro studies, showing that the biochemical indicators of terminal differentiation were not induced upon treatment of keratinocytes cultured on plastic with TGF-βs (Kopan et al., 1987; Bascom et al., 1989a). More recent studies with differentiating culture systems have revealed that at greatly elevated levels, TGF-βs can influence biochemical markers of keratinization, but at these high levels, they inhibit rather than promote, K1, K10 and filaggrin expression (Mansbridge and Hanawalt, 1988; Choi and Fuchs, 1990). At high concentration, TGF-βs also enhance expression of K6 (56 kDa) and K16 (48 kDa), keratins more commonly associated with suprabasal layers of epidermis undergoing (1) wound-healing (Mansbridge and Knapp, 1987) and (2) hyperproliferation (Weiss et al., 1984; Stoler et al., 1988). Studies using floating epidermal cultures have shown that induction of K6 and K16 is accompanied by morphological changes typical of squamous cell carcinomas, including increased stratification, vacuolization and coilocyte formation (Choi and Fuchs, 1990). Interestingly, TGF-βs seem to elicit these changes in keratinizing epidermal cells at least in part independently of their action on basal cells. Collectively, these studies have led to the notion that the epidermal phenotype associated with wound-healing and many hyperproliferative diseases may not relate to hyperproliferation, per se, but rather is a reflection of environmental changes, which in some circumstances, may include active TGF-βs (Mansbridge and Hanawalt, 1988; Kopan and Fuchs, 1989b; Schermer et al., 1989; Choi and Fuchs, 1990).

A priori, the apparent reversibility of TGF-β-mediated growth inhibition may seem ironic in light of more recent findings that (1) TGF-β mRNA expression is largely confined to suprabasal, terminally differentiating cells, and (2) TGF-βs can upregulate their own expression (Bascom et al., 1989b and references therein). However, the effects of TGF-βs at various stages of epidermal differentiation seem to be quite different (Choi and Fuchs, 1990), and hence it

may be relevant that the reversibility studies were conducted on dividing cells of the population, while TGF-β mRNA synthesis and autoregulation seem to take place in non-dividing cells. In addition, it seems increasingly apparent that while cessation of cell growth by TGF-βs may be necessary, it is not sufficient for commitment to terminal differentiation. In a model where a cascade of biochemical changes is necessary to enter and maintain the differentiation state, TGF-β expression may be among the early steps in the pathway.

Recently, the TGF-β receptors have been cloned (Lopez-Casillas et al., 1991; Wang et al., 1991; Lin et al., 1992; Ebner et al., 1993). While the type III receptor is a surface proteoglycan and may regulate the ligand-binding ability of cells, the type I and II receptor encode a transmembrane serine-threonine kinase, indicating an important role for intracellular signalling. While the sequence of events that follow TGF-β activation of its receptors remains to be elucidated, the retinoblastoma gene product, pRb, seems to be involved. Paradoxically, however, it is the underphosphorylated, rather than the phosphorylated, form of pRb that has a growth-suppressive effect, and TGF-β1 seems to maintain pRb in the underphosphorylated state (Laiho et al., 1990). In turn, pRb inhibits transcription of genes involved in growth control, such as c-myc, and curiously activates transcription of several growth inhibitory genes, including those encoding TGF-βs (Pietenpol et al., 1990; Kim et al., 1992 and references therein). As further studies are conducted, the molecular mechanisms underlying the TGF-β-mediated influence on epidermal growth and differentiation should become more apparent.

Retinoids

While TGF-βs seem to accentuate abnormal and inhibit normal differentiation, retinoids at high concentrations have long been known to have inhibitory effects on both forms of epidermal differentiation. Thus, for example, in organ culture of chick epidermis, vitamin A can induce its transition from a keratinizing to a secretory epithelium (mucous metaplasia) (Fell and Mellanby, 1953). Retinoic acid at 10^{-6} M in mammalian epidermal cultures can suppress differentiative features, including K1/K10 expression (Fuchs and Green, 1981), K6/K16 expression (Kopan and Fuchs, 1989b), cornified envelope production (Yuspa and Harris, 1974) and filaggrin expression (Fleckman et al., 1985). Many of these effects are at the level of mRNA expression (Fuchs and Green, 1981; Kopan et al., 1987; Kopan and Fuchs, 1989b) and transcription (Tomic et al., 1990; Stellmach et al., 1991).

10^{-6} M retinoic acid inhibits proliferation and concomitantly induces secretion of active TGF-β2 in mouse keratinocyte cultures and in mouse skin (Glick et al., 1989; 1990). Conversely, when exposed to 10^{-7} to 10^{-6} M retinoic acid, human keratinocytes show an increase in proliferation and cell migration, with no detectable TGF-β2 induction (Choi and Fuchs, 1990). Whether these differences are a reflection of species-specific variations in dose-response to retinoids or variations in culture conditions awaits further investigation. Nevertheless, the discovery of an autocrine regulatory loop between retinoids and TGF-βs in some keratinocytes under some conditions is exciting, and suggests that both factors may be involved in some common regulatory pathways.

Determining the mechanism of action of retinoids on epidermal differentiation has been hampered by the fact that there are a number of intracellular regulators of retinoids. Among the first to be identified were cellular retinol binding protein (CRBP) and cellular retinoic acid binding protein (CRABP), fatty acid binding-like proteins initially thought to mediate the steroid hormone-like effects of retinoids on epidermal gene expression (Chytil and Ong, 1983), but now thought to play a role in the storage or transport of retinoids. More recently, a family of retinoid receptors has been identified with sequence homologies to classical steroid receptors (see Mangelsdorf et al., 1992 and references therein). Retinoic acid receptors (RAR) are transcription factors activated upon binding of RA, whereas RXR receptors become activated upon binding of 9-*cis* RA, (Zhang et al., 1992b). No analogous retinol receptors have been detected, and it therefore seems likely that the effects of retinol are mediated via intracellular conversion to RA or 9-*cis* RA and subsequent interaction with RARs or RXRs, respectively.

The control of gene transcription by RARs and RXRs is extraordinarily complex, involving a multitude of both indirect and direct mechanisms. RARs can heterodimerize with each other, with thyroid hormone receptors, and with RXRs (Forman et al., 1989; Kliewer et al., 1992; Yu et al., 1991; Zhang et al., 1992a). At least some of these interactions appear to change the DNA affinity and activity of RARs (Husmann et al., 1991; Zhang et al., 1992a). RARs can bind to thyroid response elements, retinoic acid response elements (RAREs) and retinoid X response elements (RXREs) (Mangelsdorf et al., 1991 and references therein). The repertoire of complex DNA interactions exhibited by RARs and RXRs is further expanded by their capacity to interact with AP1 proteins, thereby conferring indirect transcriptional control of genes (Nicholson et al., 1990).

RAR-α, RAR-γ and RXRα are expressed in human epidermis (Elder et al., 1992 and references therein). RAR-γ and RXRα are expressed in skin and only a few other organs, whereas RARα is more broadly expressed (Krust et al., 1989; Mangelsdorf et al., 1992). Although in situ hybridization studies have not yet localized RXR mRNAs in skin, they have shown that RAR mRNAs are most abundant in the keratinizing layers of epidermis (Noji et al., 1989). Although the direct binding of RA-activated, suprabasal RARs to epidermal genes remains to be unequivocally demonstrated, RA-mediated biochemical changes in epidermal differentiation do appear to be mediated by retinoid response elements (Tomic-Canic et al., 1992). The suprabasal location of retinoid receptors might explain why RA inhibits suprabasal functions, and why culturing cells at an air-liquid interface enables suprabasal cells to differentiate via movement away from the retinol-containing serum.

While it is generally accepted that retinoids inhibit terminal differentiation in the epidermis, it has only recently been suggested that retinoids also act to enhance certain features of the differentiated process (Asselineau et al., 1989). This notion has been supported by examining the behavior of keratinocyte lines expressing a truncated RARγ

capable of suppressing action at retinoid response elements (Aneskievich and Fuchs, 1992). In contrast to control lines, the tRARγ lines are basal-like and fail to differentiate. The mechanism by which this tRARγ functions is complex, and it does not seem to act merely as a dominant negative inhibitor of RARs. This said, if RARs/RXRs are able to regulate terminal differentiation in positive as well as negative fashions, this could explain the wide-reaching and often disparate effects of retinoids on epidermal cells in vivo and in vitro. As future studies are conducted, the pathways by which specific RARs or RXRs operate to control the expression of critical genes involved in the differentiative process should become more apparent.

Calcium

When cultured in medium containing 0.05 mM calcium, murine keratinocytes grow as a monolayer, because desmosome assembly is inhibited (Hennings et al., 1980). Upon a switch to high (1.2 mM) calcium, desmosomes form and cells stratify. After 3-7 additional days in culture, epidermal transglutaminase is induced and squames containing cornified envelopes appear in the medium. These data indicate that many features of terminal differentiation can be induced by calcium in vitro. Calcium also seems to play a role in mediating keratinization in vivo: certain calcium ionophores have been shown to enhance action of TPA in promoting epidermal differentiation (Jaken and Yuspa, 1988).

Recent studies have indicated that calcium can act to control the transcription of terminal differentiation-specific genes, including keratins 1 and 10 (Yuspa et al., 1989; Rosenthal et al., 1991) and loricrin (Hohl et al., 1991). In addition, Glick et al. (1990) showed that calcium induces a marked increase in TGF-β2 mRNA expression in murine keratinocytes, thereby implicating calcium in both early and late stages of terminal differentiation.

In some cases, calcium can have a more pronounced effect on regulating differentiation-specific changes in cellular architecture than it has on transcription. Thus, for example, when human cells are cultured in low calcium medium, withdrawal from the cell cycle and involucrin synthesis still occur (Watt, 1984). Similarly, while desmosomes cannot assemble in low calcium, desmosomal proteins are nevertheless synthesized in both low and high calcium medium (Watt et al., 1984; Duden and Franke, 1988). Finally, while changes in calcium concentrations do not seem to have a major effect on filaggrin expression in human keratinocytes (Fleckman et al., 1985), the leader peptide of profilaggrin has a calcium binding domain, suggesting that calcium plays an important role in the formation of keratohyalin and/or the subsequent processing of profilaggrin to filaggrin (Presland et al., 1992). Hence, like other known regulators of epidermal differentiation, calcium seems to have pleiotropic effects.

In summary, we are left with a picture whereby a keratinocyte becomes a terminally differentiating cell as a consequence of a series of biochemical checks and balances. There seem to be several early changes necessary for entry into the differentiation pathway, and among these are likely to be TGF-βs and other agents that slow or inhibit DNA synthesis and cell division. In normal epidermis, movement of a cell from its basement membrane may contribute to, but does not seem sufficient for, instigating a cascade of biochemical changes that culminate in irreversibly sealing the differentiative fate of a keratinocyte. Once a basal cell has left the innermost layer and its biochemical program has begun to change, it seems to be further influenced by retinoids, TGF-βs and calcium primarily in a fashion that appears to allow retailoring of the architecture of the keratinizing layers above. Further investigation will be necessary to determine whether this capacity to redesign the suprabasal program of differentiation affects basal as well as suprabasal cells.

MOLECULAR CONTROLS OF EPIDERMAL GENE EXPRESSION

A knowledge of the major transcription factors controlling keratinocyte-specific gene expression will be of central importance in the quest to elucidate the molecular mechanisms underlying epidermal differentiation. A number of keratinocyte genes have been isolated and characterized, and these serve as a foundation for pursuing factors controlling keratinocyte specificity. They include genes encoding (a) basal keratins K5 (Lersch et al., 1989) and K14 (Marchuk et al., 1984), (b) suprabasal keratins K1 (Johnson et al., 1985), K10 (Rieger and Franke, 1988), K6 (Tyner et al., 1985) and K16 (Rosenberg et al., 1988), (c) a cornified envelope protein, involucrin (Eckert and Green, 1986) and (d) filaggrin (Rothnagel and Steinert, 1990; Presland et al., 1992). Sequence comparisons provide some clues to possible common regulatory elements. One is a putative retinoid response element, found upstream of a number of epidermal genes, and recently suggested to be functional for the human keratin 14 gene (Tomic-Canic et al., 1992). Another is the CK 8-mer sequence 5′ A A N C C A A A 3′, found upstream from a number of epidermal genes (Blessing et al., 1987; Cripe et al., 1987). Blessing et al. (1989) showed that a ~90 bp fragment containing a TATA box and a CK 8-mer sequence provided a 4-fold enhancement of expression of a CAT reporter gene, but Chin and Chow (1989) was unable to demonstrate function for the CK 8-mer sequence in the E6/E7 promoter of a human papillomavirus genome. Hence, if a CK 8-mer-like sequence is involved in keratinocyte gene expression, it may act in concert either in multiple copies or with other regulatory elements in addition to a TATA box.

Several years ago, we identified a different sequence, 5′ G C C T G C A G G C 3′, located 5′ from the TATA box of the human K14 gene, that appears to act in conjunction with a distal element to control its transcription in keratinocytes (Leask et al., 1990). This site also bound a transcription factor, AP2, which was significantly more abundant in epidermal keratinocytes than in other cell types in culture (Leask et al., 1990, 1991). The cDNA for AP2 has been cloned, and in situ hybridization studies have revealed that in vivo, AP2 is expressed in a highly restricted tissue-specific fashion, with cells of neural and epidermal lineage being the predominant AP2 expressers (Mitchell et al., 1991). In addition, the Xenopus equivalent of AP2 has been shown to play a role in embryonic development of the frog

epidermis (Snape et al., 1990, 1991). AP2 has been implicated broadly in the regulation of other endogenous and viral genes that are typically expressed in keratinocytes (see also Royer et al., 1991), and AP2 sites seem to play some role in restricting keratinocyte-specific expression in vivo (Byrne and Fuchs, 1993). This said, AP2 does not appear to be sufficient for keratinocyte specificity on its own (Leask et al., 1990).

Recently, we found that 90 bp of K5 promoter, missing RARE, AP2 and CK8-mer binding sites, was sufficient to direct expression of a reporter β-galactosidase gene predominantly to the epidermis and tongue of transgenic mice, albeit in the suprabasal, rather than basal, compartment, and with some promiscuous expression in a few non-keratinocyte-containing tissues (Fig. 3A, K5βgal90 transgenic foot skin; compare with Fig. 3B, illustrating foot skin from transgenic mouse expressing K5βgal6000, containing 6000 bp of 5′ K5 sequence; see also Byrne and Fuchs, 1993). Replacement of the AP2 site did not restore

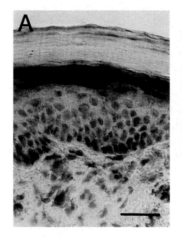

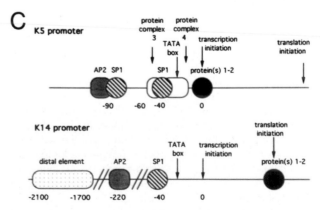

Fig. 3. Expression of K5βgal6000 and K5βgal90 in transgenic mice, and transcription factors involved in keratinocyte specificity in vitro and in vivo. 6000 and 90 bp of 5′ upstream sequence from the human keratin 5 gene were used to drive expression of the β-galactosidase gene in vivo (Byrne and Fuchs, 1993). Tissue sections of transgenic skin were assayed for β-galactosidase activity, yielding a blue-green reaction product. (A) Foot pad of K5βgal90; (B) foot pad of K5βgal6000. Bar, 25 μm. (C) Summary of protein factors that bind to the promoter regions of the human keratin 14 and 5 genes (Byrne and Fuchs, 1993). O, transcription initiation site.

basal expression although it may have restricted some promiscuity in expression (Byrne and Fuchs, 1993). The severely truncated K5 promoter segment also exhibited cell type specificity in culture (Byrne and Fuchs, 1993). These findings enabled us to focus on a relatively small segment of DNA, which we showed bound a number of proteins, some of which are common to both the K5 and K14 promoters (Fig. 3C). These include Sp1, which has a ubiquitous but not necessarily homogenous distribution in vitro (Robidoux et al., 1992), and a protein complex, which we have tentatively termed 1-2, which binds in the vicinity of the transcription and translation initiation regions of these two promoters. The protein complexes that bind to the 90 bp promoter segment are present in a variety of cultured cell types, and thus, at least in vitro, the restricted expression conferred by the truncated K5 promoter does not appear to be achieved by an epidermal-specific, DNA-binding transcription factor. Whether this is also the case in vivo remains to be shown. In this regard, it is notable that in vivo, Sp1 seems to be expressed in a tissue-specific fashion, while in vitro, it is not (Saffer et al., 1991; Robidoux et al., 1992).

Our in vitro studies suggest that the specificity of the truncated K5 promoter may be governed by cell-type specific variations, either in the modifications of the factors that bind to the truncated K5 promoter, or in the non-DNA binding proteins that might associate with these DNA-binding proteins. Whatever the mechanism, protein complex 1-2 seems to be involved since mutations that interfere with protein 1-2 binding also obliterate cell-type specific expression of the K5 promoter in vitro (Byrne and Fuchs, 1993). The protein 1-2 binding sequence (GTTC-CTGGGTAAC) is similar to the consensus binding sequence (GTTAATNATTAAC) for the POU-homeodomain transcription factors HNF-1α and HNF-1β, involved in liver-specific gene expression (reviewed by Johnson, 1990). While proteins 1-2 neither share the cell-type specificity nor the precise binding specificity of HNF-1β and HNF-1β, further studies will be necessary to ascertain whether they might nevertheless be related members of the same family.

This said, it is also possible that this complex may be involved in initiating transcription (Smale and Baltimore, 1989). Such transcription initiating factors have been variously termed δ (Hariharan et al., 1991), YY1 (Shi et al., 1991), TFII-I (Roy et al., 1991), NF-E1 (Park and Atchison, 1991), UCRBP (Flanagan et al., 1991), and are either identical binding factors or belong to a similar classes of factors (Roy et al., 1991; Seto et al., 1991). These factors interact with TFIID, and they can bind DNA and initiate transcription even in the absence of a TATA box. These putative roles for protein 1-2 are intriguing, especially since these types of elements are not necessarily fixed and may be found distal to the initiation site (Nakatani et al., 1990). Additional studies will be needed to fully elucidate the role of proteins 1-2 in keratinocyte specificity.

While some headway has been made in the quest to uncover the factors and sequences that orchestrate tissue-specific gene expression in the epidermis and other stratified squamous epithelia, underlying questions remain concerning how transcriptional factors act at a molecular level to control the balance between gene expression in the basal and suprabasal layers. In this regard, it is clear that epithelial-specific and basal-specific gene expression can be uncoupled, since (a) 90 bp of the basal K5 promoter can target expression in transgenic mice to the suprabasal epidermal layers (Byrne and Fuchs, 1993) and (b) 1500 bp of the suprabasal K1 promoter can target expression in transgenic mice to both the suprabasal and the basal layers (Rosenthal et al., 1991).

Finally, while calcium and retinoids are likely to play a role in the molecular switch of basal and suprabasal epidermal genes, there are probably additional environmental cues, based on our recent studies with the truncated 90 bp K5 promoter. The expression pattern of this gene was unusual in epidermis and tongue in that it was not analogous to any known keratin gene, but rather appeared to be a regional-dependent subset of the combined activities of a number of suprabasal genes, including those encoding K1/K10, K6/K16, K4/K13 and K9 (Byrne and Fuchs, 1993). Thus, the truncated promoter appeared capable of responding to regional variations, and displayed an environmental sensitivity that is absent in the intact promoter from which it was derived. The peculiar behavior of the transgene in skin suggests that the regulatory elements controlling expression of a keratin in one location of the body can differ from those governing expression even in the same tissue, but in a different region of the body. If true, the regulation of keratin gene expression is significantly more complex than previously realized. In the coming years, a major focus in the field of epidermal differentiation will be on keratinocyte-specific and differentiation-specific transcription factors as possible mediators of extracellular regulators and keratinocyte fate.

I am grateful to all of the past and present members of my laboratory for their numerous contributions to the research efforts that were described in this review. In particular, I would like to thank the following scientists for their substantial contributions to the research reviewed here: Dr Robert Vassar, Dr Carolyn Byrne, Dr Brian Aneskievich, Dr Andrew Leask, Dr Raphael Kopan and Lifei Guo. I would also like to thank Lifei Guo, Dr Carolyn Byrne and Dr Brian Aneskievich for providing the photographs used in the Figures in this paper. Work in the author's laboratory is funded by a grant from the National Institutes of Health and from the Howard Hughes Medical Institute.

REFERENCES

Aaronson, S. A., Bottaro, D. P. Miki, T. Ron, D., Finch, P. W., Fleming, T. P., Ahn, J., Taylor, W. G. and Rubin, J. S. (1991). Keratinocyte growth factor: a fibroblast growth factor family member with unusual target cell specificity. *Ann. NY Acad. Sci.* **638**, 62-77.

Adams, J. C. and Watt, F. M. (1990). Changes in keratinocyte adhesion during terminal differentiation: reduction in fibronectin binding precedes alpha5 -beta1 integrin loss from the cell surface. *Cell* **63**, 425-435.

Aneskievich, B. J. and Fuchs, E. (1992). Terminal differentiation in keratinocytes involves positive as well as negative regulation by retinoic acid receptors and retinoid X receptors at retinoid response elements. *Mol. Cell. Biol.* **12**, 4862-4871.

Arora, K. and Nusslein-Volhard, C. (1992). Altered mitotic domains reveal fate map changes in Drosophila embryos mutant for zygotic dorsoventral patterning genes. *Development* **114**, 1003-1024.

Asselineau, D., Bernard, B. A., Bailly, C., Darmon, M. and Prunieras, M. (1986). Human epidermis reconstructed by culture: is it 'normal?' *J. Invest. Dermatol.* **86**, 181-185.

Asselineau, D., Bernard, B. A., Bailly, C. and Darmon, M. (1989). Retinoic acid improves epidermal morphogenesis. *Dev. Biol.* **133**, 322-335.

Bailleul, B., Surani, M. A., White, S., Barton, S. C., Brown, K., Blessing, M., Jorcano, J. and Balmain, A. (1990). Skin hyperkeratosis and papilloma formation in transgenic mice expressing a ras oncogene from a suprabasal keratin promoter. *Cell* **62**, 697-708.

Barrandon, Y. and Green, H. (1987). Cell migration is essential for sustained growth of keratinocyte colonies: The roles of transforming growth factor-alpha and epidermal growth factor. *Cell* **50**, 1131-1137.

Bascom, C. C., Sipes, N. J., Coffey, R. J. and Moses, H. L. (1989a). Regulation of epithelial cell proliferation by transforming growth factors. *J. Cell Biochem.* **39**, 25-32.

Bascom, C. C., Wolfshohl, J. R., Coffey, R. J. J., Madisen, L., Webb, N. R., Purchio, A. R., Derynck, R. and Moses, H. L. (1989b). Complex regulation of transforming growth factor beta1, beta2, and beta3 mRNA expression in mouse fibroblasts and keratinocytes by transforming growth factors beta1 and beta2. *Mol. Cell. Biol.* **9**, 5508-5515.

Bissell, M. J., Hall, H. G. and Parry, G. (1982). How does the extracellular matrix direct gene expression? *J. Theor. Biol.* **99**, 31-68.

Blessing, M., Zentgraf, H. and Jorcano, J. L. (1987). Differentially expressed bovine cytokeratin genes. Analysis of gene linkage and evolutionary conservations of 5′-upstream sequences. *EMBO J.* **6**, 567-575.

Blessing, M., Jorcano, J. L. and Franke, W. W. (1989). Enhancer elements directing cell-type-specific expression of cytokeratin genes and changes of the epithelial cytoskeleton by transfections of hybrid cytokeratin gene. *EMBO J.* **8**, 117-126.

Byrne, C. and Fuchs, E. (1993). Probing keratinocyte and differentiation specificity of the K5 promoter in vitro and in transgenic mice. *Mol. Cell. Biol.* **13**, 3176-3190.

Chin, M. T. and Chow, T. R. B. (1989). Identification of a novel constitutive enhancer element and an associated binding protein: Implications for human papillomavirus type II enhancer regulation. *J. Virol.* **63**, 2967-2976.

Choi, Y. and Fuchs, E. (1990). TGF-beta and retinoic acid: regulators of growth and modifiers of differentiation in human epidermal cells. *Cell Regul.* **1**, 791-809.

Chytil, F. and Ong, D. E. (1983). Cellular retinol- and retinoic acid-binding proteins. *Adv. Nutr. Res.* **5**, 13-29.

Coffey, R. J., Derynck, R., Wilcox, J. N., Bringman, T. S., Goustin, A. S., Moses, H. L. and Pittelkow, M. R. (1987). Production and auto-induction of transforming growth factor-alpha in human keratinocytes. *Nature* **328**, 817-820.

Collin, C., Moll, R., Kubicka, S., Ouhayoun, J-P. and Franke, W.W. (1992). Characterization of human cytokeratin 2, an epidermal cytoskeletal protein synthesized late during differentiation. *Exp. Cell Res.* **202**, 132-141.

Cripe, T. P., Haugen, T. H., Turk, J. P., Tabatabai, F., Schmid, P. G. II, Durst, M., Gissmann, L., Roman, A. and Terek, L. P. (1987). Transcriptional regulation of the human papillomavirus-16 E6-E7 promoter by a keratinocyte-dependent enhancer, and by viral E2 trans-activator and repressor gene products: Implications for cervical carcinogenesis. *EMBO J.* **6**, 3745-3753.

Dale, B. A., Holbrook, K. A. and Steinert, P M. (1978). Assembly of stratum corneum basic protein and keratin filaments in macrofibrils. *Nature* **276**, 729-731.

Dale, B. A., Holbrook, K. A., Kimball, J. R., Hoff, M. and Sun, T.-T. (1985). Expression of epidermal keratins and filaggrin during human fetal skin development. *J. Cell Biol.* **101**, 1257-1269.

Dhouailly, D., Rogers, G. E. and Sengel, P. (1978). The specification of feather and scale protein synthesis in epidermal-dermal recombinations. *Dev. Biol.* **65**, 58-68.

Duden, R. and Franke, W. W. (1988). Organization of desmosomal plaque proteins in cells growing at low calcium concentrations. *J. Cell Biol.* **107**, 1049-1063.

Ebner, R., Chen, R. H., Shum, L., Lawler, S., Zioncheck, T. F., Lee, A., Lopez, A. R. and Derynck, R. (1993). Cloning of a type I TGF-beta receptor and its effect on TGF-beta binding to the type II receptor. *Science* **260**, 1344-1348.

Eckert, R. L. and Green, H. (1986). Structure and evolution of the human involucrin gene. *Cell* **46**, 583-589.

Eichner, R., Sun, T.-T. and Aebi, U. (1986). The role of keratin subfamilies and keratin pairs in the formation of human epidermal intermediate filaments. *J. Cell Biol.* **102**, 1767-1777.

Elder, J. T., Fisher, G. J., Lindquist, P. B., Bennett, G. L., Pittelkow, M. R., Coffey, R. J., Ellingsworth, L., Derynck, R. and Voorhees, J. J. (1989). Overexpression of transforming growth factor alpha in psoriatic epidermis. *Science* **243**, 811-814.

Elder, J. T., Astrom, A., Pettersson, U., Tavakkol, A., Krust, A., Kastner, P., Chambon, P. and Voorhees, J. J. (1992). Retinoic acid receptors and binding proteins in human skin. *J. Invest. Dermatol.* **98**, 36S-41S.

Fell, H. B. and Mellanby, E. (1953). Metaplasia produced in cultures of chick ectoderm by high vitamin A. *J. Physiol* **119**, 470-488.

Finch, P. W., Rubin, J. S., Miki, T., Ron, D. and Aaronson, S. A. (1989). Human KGF is FGF-related with properties of a paracrine effector of epithelial cell growth. *Science* **245**, 752-755.

Flanagan, J. R., Murata, M., Burke, P. A., Shirayoshi, Y., Appella, E., Sharp, P. A. and Ozato, K. (1991). Negative regulation of the major histocompatibility complex class I promoter in embryonal carcinoma cells. *Proc. Nat. Acad. Sci. USA* **88**, 3145-3149.

Fleckman, P., Dale, B. A. and Holbrook, K. A. (1985). Profilaggrin, a high-molecular-weight precursor of filaggrin in human epidermis and cultured keratinocytes. *J. Invest. Dermatol.* **85**, 507-512.

Forman, B. M., Yang, C.-R., Au, M., Casanova, J., Ghysdael, J. and Samuels, H. H. (1989). A domain containing leucine-zipper-like motifs mediate novel in vivo interactions between the thyroid hormone and retinoic acid receptors. *Mol. Endocrinol.* **3**, 1610-1626.

Fowlis, D. J., Flanders, K. C., Duffie, E., Balmain, A. and Akhurst, R. J. (1992). Discordant transforming growth factor beta 1 RNA and protein localization during chemical carcinogenesis of the skin. *Cell Growth Diff.* **3**, 81-91.

Fuchs, E. (1990). Epidermal differentiation: the bare essentials. *J. Cell Biol.* **111**, 2807-2814.

Fuchs, E. and Green, H. (1980). Changes in keratin gene expression during terminal differentiation of the keratinocyte. *Cell* **19**, 1033-1042.

Fuchs, E. and Green, H. (1981). Regulation of terminal differentiation of cultured human keratinocytes by vitamin A. *Cell* **25**, 617-625.

Glick, A. B., Flanders, K. C., Danielpour, D., Yuspa, S. H. and Sporn, M. B. (1989). Retinoic acid induces transforming growth factor-beta2 in cultured keratinocytes and mouse epidermis. *Cell Regul.* **1**, 87-97.

Glick, A. B., Danielpour, D., Morgan, D., Sporn, M. B. and Yuspa, S. H. (1990). Induction and autocrine receptor binding of transforming growth factor-beta2 during terminal differentiation of primary mouse keratinocytes. *Mol. Endocrinol.* **4**, 46-52.

Glick, A. B., McCune, B. K., Abdulkarem, N., Flanders, K. C., Lumadue, J. A., Smith, J. M. and Sporn, M. B. (1991). Complex regulation of TGF beta expression by retinoic acid in the vitamin A-deficient rat. *Development* **111**, 1081-1086.

Green, M. R., Mycock, C., Smith, C. G. and Couchman, J. R. (1987). Biochemical and ultrastructural processing of (125l)epidermal growth factor in rat epidermis and hair follicles: Accumulation of nuclear label. *J. Invest. Dermatol.* **88**, 259-265.

Greenberg, C. S., Birckbichler, P. J. and Rice, R. H. (1991). Transglutaminases: multifunctional cross-linking enzymes that stabilize tissues. *FASEB J.* **5**, 3071-3077.

Greenhalgh, D. A., Welty, D. J., Player, A. and Yuspa, S. H. (1990). Two oncogenes, v-fos and v-ras, cooperate to convert normal keratinocytes to squamous cell carcinoma. *Proc. Nat. Acad. Sci. USA* **87**, 643-647.

Guo, L., Yu, Q.-C. and Fuchs, E. (1993). Epidermal expression of KGF causes remarkable changes in the skin of transgenic mice. *EMBO J.* **12**, 973-986.

Hariharan, N., Kelley, D. E. and Perry, R. P. (1991). Sigma, a transcription factor that binds to downstream elements in several polymerase II promoters, is a functionally versatile zinc finger protein. *Proc. Nat. Acad. Sci. USA* **88**, 9799-9803.

Hennings, H., Michael, D., Cheng, C., Steinert, P. M., Holbrook, K. and Yuspa, S. H. (1980). Calcium regulation of growth and differentiation of mouse epidermal cells in culture. *Cell* **29**, 245-254.

Hirai, Y., Takebe, K., Takashina, M., Kobayashi, S. and Takeichi, M. (1992). Epimorphin: a mesenchymal protein essential for epithelial morphogenesis. *Cell* **69**, 471-481.

Hohl, D., Lichti, U., Breitkreutz, D., Steinert, P. M. and Roop, D. R. (1991). Transcription of the human locrin gene in vitro is induced by calcium and cell density and suppressed by retinoic acid. *J. Invest. Dermatol.* **96**, 414-418.

Hotchin, N. A. and Watt, F. M. (1992). Transcriptional and post-translational regulation of beta 1 integrin expression during keratinocyte terminal differentiation. *J. Biol. Chem.* **267**, 14852-14858.

Husmann, M., Lehmann, J., Hoffmann, B., Hermann, T., Tzukerman, M. and Pfahl, M. (1991). Antagonism between retinoic acid receptors. *Mol. Cell. Biol.* **11**, 4097-4103.

Jaken, S. and Yuspa, S. H. (1988). Early signals for keratinocyte differentiation: role of Ca^{2+}-mediated inositol lipid metabolism in normal and neoplastic epidermal cells. *Carcinogenesis (London)* **9**, 1033-1038.

Johnson, P. F. (1990). Transcriptional activators in hepatocytes. *Cell Growth Differ.* **1**, 47-52.

Johnson, L., Idler, W., Zhou, X.-M., Roop, D. and Steinert, P. (1985). Structure of a gene for the human epidermal 67-kda keratin *Proc. Nat. Acad. Sci. USA* **82**, 1896-1900.

Jones, J. C. and Green, K. J. (1991). Intermediate filament-plasma membrane interactions. *Curr. Opin. Cell Biol.* **3**, 127-132.

Kim, S.-J., Wagner, S., Liu, F., O'Reilly, M. A., Robbins, P. D. and Green, M. R. (1992). Retinoblastoma gene product activates expression of the human TGF-beta2 gene through transcription factor ATF-2. *Nature* **358**, 331-334.

Kliewer, S. A., Umesono, K., Mangelsdorf, D. J. and Evans, R. M. (1992). Retinoid X receptor interacts with nuclear receptors in retinoic acid, thyroid hormone and vitamin D3 signalling. *Nature* **355**, 446-449.

Knapp, A. C., Franke, W. W., Heid, H., Hatzfeld, M., Jorcano, J. L. and Moll, R. (1986). Cytokeratin No. 9, an epidermal type I keratin characteristic of a special program of keratinocyte differentiation displaying body site specificity. *J. Cell Biol.* **103**, 657-667.

Kollar, E. J. (1970). The induction of hair follicles by embryonic dermal papillae. *J. Invest. Derm.* **55**, 374-378.

Kopan, R. and Fuchs, E. (1989a). A new look into an old problem: keratins as tools to investigate determination, morphogenesis, and differentiation in skin. *Genes Dev.* **3**, 1-15.

Kopan, R. and Fuchs, E. (1989b). The use of retinoic acid to probe the relation between hyperproliferation-associated keratins and cell proliferation in normal and malignant epidermal cells. *J. Cell Biol.* **109**, 295-307.

Kopan, R., Traska, G. and Fuchs, E. (1987). Retinoids as important regulators of terminal differentiation: examining keratin expression in individual epidermal cells at various stages of keratinization. *J. Cell Biol.* **105**, 427-440.

Krust, A., Kastner, P., Petkovich, M., Zelent, A. and Chambon, P. (1989). A third human retinoic acid receptor, hRAR-lamba. *Proc. Nat. Acad. Sci. USA* **86**, 5310-5314.

Laiho, M., Decaprio, J. A., Ludlow, J. W., Livingston, D. M. and Massague, J. (1990). Growth inhibition by TGF-beta linked to suppression of retinoblastoma protein phosphorylation. *Cell* **62**, 175-185.

Leask, A., Rosenberg, M., Vassar, R. and Fuchs, E. (1990). Regulation of a human epidermal keratin gene: sequences and nuclear factors involved in keratinocyte-specific transcription. *Genes Dev.* **4**, 1985-1998.

Leask, A., Byrne, C. and Fuchs, E. (1991). Transcription factor AP2 and its role in epidermal-specific gene expression. *Proc. Nat. Acad. Sci. USA* **88**, 7948-7952.

Lersch, R., Stellmach, V., Stocks, C., Giudice, G. and Fuchs, E. (1989). Isolation, sequence, and expression of a human keratin K5 gene: transcriptional regulation of keratins and insights into pairwise control. *Mol. Cell. Biol.* **9**, 3685-3697.

Lin, H. Y., Wang, X. F., Ng-Eaton, E., Weinberg, R. A. and Lodish, H. F. (1992). Expression cloning of the TGF-beta type II receptor, a functional transmembrane serine/threonine kinase. *Cell* **68**, 775-785.

Lopez-Casillas, F., Cheifetz, S., Doody, J., Andres, J. L., Lane, W. S. and Massague, J. (1991). Structure and expression of the membrane proteoglycan betaglycan, a component of the TGF-beta receptor system. *Cell* **67**, 785-795.

Lugar, T. A. and Schwartz, T. (1990). Evidence for an epidermal cytokine network. *J. Invest. Dermatol.* **95**, 1005-1045.

Lyons, K. M., Pelton, R. W. and Hogan, B. L. M. (1989). Patterns of expression of murine Vgr-1 and BMP-2a RNA suggest that transforming growth factor-beta-like genes coordinately regulate aspects of embryonic development. *Genes Dev.* **3**, 1657-1668.

Lyons, R. M., Keski-Oja, J. and Moses, H. L. (1988). Proteolytic activation of latent transforming growth factor-beta from fibroblast-conditioned medium. *J. Cell Biol.* **106**, 1659-1665.

Mangelsdorf, D. J., Borgmeyer, U., Heyman, R. A., Zhou, J. Y., Ong, E. S., Oro, A. E., Kakizuka, A. and Evans, R. M. (1992). Characterization of three RXR genes that mediate the action of 9-cis retinoic acid. *Genes Dev.* **6**, 329-344.

Mangelsdorf, D. J., Umesono, K., Kliewer, S. A., Borgmeyer, U., Ong, E.

S. and Evans, R. M. (1991). A direct repeat in the cellular retinol-binding protein type II gene confers differential regulation by RXR and RAR. *Cell* **66**, 555-561.

Mansbridge, J. N. and Hanawalt, P. C. (1988). Role of transforming growth factor beta in the maturation of human epidermal keratinocytes. *J. Invest. Dermatol.* **90**, 336-341.

Mansbridge, J. N. and Knapp, A. M. (1987). Changes in keratinocyte maturation during wound healing. *J. Invest. Dermatol.* **89**, 253-262.

Marchuk, D., McCrohon, S. and Fuchs, E. (1984). Remarkable conservation of structure among intermediate filament genes *Cell* **39**, 491-498.

Mehrel, T., Hohl, D., Rothnagel, J. A., Longley, M. A., Bundman, D., Cheng, C., Lichti, U., Bisher, M. E., Steven, A. C. and Steinert, P. M. (1990). Identification of a major keratinocyte cell envelope protein, loricrin. *Cell* **61**, 1103-1112.

Mitchell, P. J., Timmons, P. M., Hebert, J. M., Rigby, P. W. J. and Tjian, R. (1991). Transcription factor AP-2 is expressed in neural crest cell lineages during mouse embryogenesis. *Genes Dev.* **5**, 105-119.

Moll, R., Franke, W., Schiller, D., Geiger, B. and Krepler, R. (1982). The catalog of human cytokeratins: patterns of expression in normal epithelia, tumors and cultured cells. *Cell* **31**, 11-24.

Montagna, W. and Lobitz, W. C. (1964). *The Epidermis.* New York: Academic Press.

Murphy, C. S., Pietenpol, J. A., Munger, K., Howley, P. M. and Moses, H. L. (1991). c-*myc* and pRB: role in TGF beta 1 inhibition of keratinocyte proliferation. *CSH Symp. Quant. Biol.* **56**, 129-135.

Nakatani, Y., Horikoshi, M., Brenner, M., Yamamoto, T., Besnard, F., Roeder, R. G. and Freese, E. (1990). A downstream initiation element required for efficient TATA box binding and in vitro function of TFIID. *Nature* **348**, 86-88.

Nelson, W. and Sun, T.-T. (1983). The 50- and 58-kdalton keratin classes as molecular markers for stratified squamous epithelia: cell culture studies. *J. Cell Biol.* **97**, 244-251.

Nicholson, R. C., Mader, S., Nagpal, S., Leid, M., Rochette-Egly, C. and Chambon, P. (1990). Negative regulation of the rat stromelysin gene promoter by retinoic acid is mediated by an AP1 binding site. *EMBO J.* **9**, 4443-4454.

Noji, S., Yamaai, T., Koyama, E., Nohno, T., Fujimoto, W., Arata, J. and Taniguchi, S. (1989). Expression of retinoic acid receptor genes in keratinizing front of skin. *FEBS Lett.* **259**, 86-90.

Ozanne, B., Richards, C. S., Hendler, F., Burns, D. and Gusterson, B. (1986). Over-expression of the EGF receptor is a hallmark of squamous cell carcinomas. *J. Pathol.* **149**, 9-14.

Padgett, R. W., St. Johnston, R. D. and Gelbart, W. M. (1987). A transcript from a Drosophila pattern gene predicts a protein homologous to the transforming growth factor-beta family. *Nature* **325**, 81-84.

Pandiella, A. and Massague, J. (1991). Cleavage of the membrane precursor for transforming growth factor alpha is a regulated process. *Proc. Nat. Acad. Sci. USA* **88**, 1726-1730.

Park, K. and Atchison, M. L. (1991). Isolation of a candidate repressor/activator, NF-E1 (YY-1, sigma) that binds to the immunoglobulin k 3′ enhancer and the immunoglobulin heavy-chain uEi site. *Proc. Nat. Acad. Sci. USA* **88**, 9804-9808.

Pelton, R. W., Nomura, S., Moses, H. L. and Hogan, B. L. M. (1989). Expression of transforming growth factor beta2 during murine embryogenesis. *Development* **106**, 759-767.

Pietenpol, J. A., Stein, R. W., Moran, E., Yaciuk, P., Schlegel, R., Lyons, R. M., Pittelkow, M. R., Munger, K., Howley, P. M. and Moses, H. L. (1990). TGF-beta1 inhibition of c-*myc* transcription and growth in keratinocytes is abrogated by viral transforming proteins with pRB binding domains. *Cell* **61**, 777-785.

Pittelkow, M. R., Lindquist, P. B., Abraham, R. T., Graves-Deal, R., Derynck, R. and Coffey, R. J. J. (1989). Induction of transforming growth factor-alpha expression in human keratinocytes by phorbol esters. *J. Biol. Chem.* **264**, 5164-5171.

Potten, C. S. and Morris, R. J. (1988). Epithelial stem cells in vivo. *J. Cell Sci. Suppl.* **10**, 45-62.

Presland, R. B., Haydock, P. V., Fleckman, P., Nirunsuksiri, W. and Dale, B. A. (1992). Characterization of the human epidermal profilaggrin gene. Genomic organization and identification of an S-100-like calcium binding domain in the amino terminus. *J. Biol. Chem.* **267**, 23772-23781.

Rheinwald, J. G. (1980). Serial cultivation of normal human epidermal keratinocytes. *Meth. Cell Biol.* **21A**, 229-254.

Rice, R. H. and Green, H. (1979). Presence in human epidermal cells of a soluble protein precursor of the cross-linked envelope: activation of the cross-linking by calcium ions. *Cell* **18**, 681-694.

Rieger, M. and Franke, W. W. (1988). Identification of an orthologous mammalian cytokeratin gene. High degree of intron sequence conservation during evolution of human cytokeratin 10. *J. Mol. Biol.* **204**, 841-856.

Robidoux, S., Gosselin, P., Harvey, M., Leclerc, S. and Guerin, S. L. (1992). Transcription of the mouse secretory protease inhibitor p12 gene is activated by the developmentally regulated positive transcription factor Sp1. *Mol. Cell. Biol.* **12**, 3796-3806.

Roop, D. R., Huitfeldt, H., Kilkenny, A. and Yuspa, S. H. (1987). Regulated expression of differentiation-associated keratins in cultured epidermal cells detected by monospecific antibodies to unique peptides of mouse epidermal keratins. *Differentiation* **35**, 143-150.

Rosenberg, M., Raychaudhury, A., Shows, T. B., Le Beau, M. M. and Fuchs, E. (1988). A group of type I keratin genes on human chromosome 17: characterization and expression. *Mol. Cell. Biol.* **8**, 722-736.

Rosenthal, D. S., Steinert, P. M., Chung, S., Huff, C. A., Johnson, J., Yuspa, S. H. and Roop, D. R. (1991). A human epidermal differentiation-specific keratin gene is regulated by calcium but not negative modulators of differentiation in transgenic mouse keratinocytes. *Cell Growth Differ.* **2**, 107-113.

Rothnagel, J. A. and Steinert, P. M. (1990). The structure of the gene for mouse filaggrin and a comparison of the repeating units. *J. Biol. Chem.* **265**, 1862-1865.

Roy, A. L., Meisterernst, M., Pognonec, P. and Roeder, R. G. (1991). Cooperative interaction of an initiator-binding transcription factor and the helix-hoop-helix activator USF. *Nature* **354**, 245-248.

Royer, H.-D., Freyaldenhoven, M. P., Napierski, I., Spitkovsky, D. D., Bauknecht, T. and Dathan, N. (1991). Delineation of human papillomavirus type 18 enhancer binding proteins: the intracellular distribution of a novel octamer binding protein p92 is cell cycle regulated. *Nucl. Acids Res.* **19**, 2363-2371.

Rubin, A. L., Parenteau, N. L. and Rice, R. H. (1989). Coordination of keratinocyte programming in human SCC-13 squamous cell carcinoma and normal epidermal cells. *J. Cell Physiol.* **138**, 208-214.

Saffer, J. D., Jackson, S. P. and Annarella, M. B. (1991). Developmental expression of Sp1 in the mouse. *Mol. Cell. Biol.* **11**, 2189-2199.

Sariola, H., Aufderheide, E., Bernhard, H., Henke-Fahle, S., Dippold, W. and Ekblom, P. (1988). Antibodies to cell surface ganglioside GD3 perturb inductive epithelial-mesenchymal interactions. *Cell* **54**, 235-245.

Schermer, A., Jester, J. V., Hardy, C., Milano, D. and Sun, T.-T. (1989). Transient synthesis of K6 and K16 keratins in regenerating rabbit corneal epithelium: Keratin markers for an alternative pathway of keratinocyte differentiation. *Differentiation* **42**, 103-110.

Schurer, N. Y., Plewig, G. and Elias, P. M. (1991). Stratum corneum lipid function. *Dermatologica* **183**, 77-94.

Schweizer, J. and Winter, H. (1982). Changes in regional keratin polypeptide patterns during phorbol ester-mediated reversible and permanently sustained hyperplasia of mouse epidermis. *Cancer Res* **42**, 1517-1529.

Seto, E., Shi, Y. and Shenk, T. (1991). YY1 is an initiator sequence-binding protein that directs and activates transcription in vitro. *Nature* **352**, 241-245.

Shi, Y., Seto, E., Chang, L.-S. and Shenk, T. (1991). Transcriptional repression by YY1, a human GLI-Kruppel-related protein, and relief of repression by adenovirus E1A protein. *Cell* **67**, 377-388.

Shipley, G. D., Pittelkow, M. R., Willie, J. J., Scott, R. E. and Moses, H. L. (1986). Reversible inhibition of normal human prokeratinocyte proliferation by type beta transforming growth factor-growth inhibitor in serum-free medium. *Cancer Res.* **46**, 2068-2071.

Simon, M. and Green, H. (1985). Enzymatic cross-linking of involucrin and other proteins by keratinocyte particulates in vitro. *Cell* **40**, 677-683.

Smale, S. and Baltimore, D. (1989). The 'initiator' as a transcription control element. *Cell* **57**, 103-113.

Snape, A. M., Jonas, E. A. and Sargent, T. C. (1990). KTF-1, a transcriptional activator of Xenopus embryonic keratin expression. *Development* **109**, 157-165.

Snape, A. M., Winning, R. S. and Sargent, T. D. (1991). Transcription factor AP-2 is tissue-specific in Xenopus in closely related or identical to keratin transcription factor 1 (KTF-1). *Development* **113**, 283-293.

Stark, H.-J., Breitkreutz, D., Limat, A., Bowden, P. and Fusenig, N. E. (1987). Keratins of the human hair follicle: 'hyperproliferative' keratins

consistently expressed in outer root sheath cells in vivo and in vitro. *Differentiation* **35**, 236-248.

Stellmach, V., Leask, A. and Fuchs, E. (1991). Retinoid-mediated transcriptional regulation of keratin genes in human epidermal and squamous cell carcinoma cells. *Proc. Nat. Acad. Sci. USA* **88**, 4582-4586.

Stoler, A., Kopan, R., Duvic, M. and Fuchs, E. (1988). The use of monospecific antibodies and crna probes reveals abnormal pathways of terminal differentiation in human epidermal diseases. *J. Cell Biol.* **107**, 427-446.

Sun, T.-T., Eichner, R., Schermer, A., Cooper, D., Nelson, W. G. and Weiss, R. A. (1984). *The Transformed Phenotype. 1. The Cancer Cell.* pp. 169-176. Cold Spring Harbor, N.Y.

Tomic, M., Jiang, C.-K., Epstein, H. S., Freedberg, I. M., Samuels, H. H. and Blumenberg, M. (1990). Nuclear receptors for retinoic acid and thyroid hormone regulate transcription of keratin genes. *Cell Regul.* **1**, 965-973.

Tomic-Canic, M., Sunjevaric, I., Freedberg, I. M. and Blumenberg, M. (1992). Identification of the retinoic acid and thyroid hormone receptor-responsive element in the human K14 keratin gene. *J. Invest. Dermatol.* **99**, 842-847.

Tyner, A. L., Eichman, M. J. and Fuchs, E. (1985). The sequence of a type II keratin gene expressed in human skin: conservation of structure among all intermediate filament genes. *Proc. Nat. Acad. Sci. USA* **82**, 4683-4687.

Vassar, R. and Fuchs, E. (1991). Transgenic mice provide new insights into the role of TGF-alpha during epidermal development and differentiation. *Genes Dev.* **5**, 714-727.

Vassar, R., Hutton, M. E. and Fuchs, E. (1992). Transgenic overexpression of transforming growth factor alpha bypasses the need for c-Ha-ras mutations in mouse skin tumorigenesis. *Mol. Cell. Biol.* **12**, 4643-4653.

Wang, X. F., Lin, H. Y., Ng-Eaton, E., Downward, J., Lodish, H. F. and Weinberg, R. A. (1991). Expression cloning and characterization of the TGF-beta type III receptor. *Cell* **67**, 797-805.

Watt, F. M. (1984). Selective migration of terminally differentiating cells from the basal layer of cultured human epidermis. *J. Cell Biol.* **98**, 16-21.

Watt, F. M., Mattey, D. L. and Garrod, D. R. (1984). Calcium-induced reorganization of desmosomal components in cultured human keratinocytes. *J. Cell Biol.* **99**, 2211-2215.

Weiss, R. A., Eichner, R. and Sun, T.-T. (1984). Monoclonal antibody analysis of keratin expression in epidermal diseases: a 48- and 56-dalton keratin as molecular markers for hyperproliferative keratinocytes. *J. Cell Biol.* **98**, 1397-1406.

Werner, S., Peters, K. G., Longaker, M. T., Fuller-Pace, F., Banda, M. J. and Williams, L. T. (1992). Large induction of keratinocyte growth factor expression in the dermis during wound healing. *Proc. Nat. Acad. Sci. USA* **89**, 6896-6900.

Wessels, N. K. and Roessner, K. D. (1965). Nonproliferation in dermal condensations of mouse vibrissae and pelage hairs. *Dev. Biol.* **12**, 419-433.

Yamamoto, T., Kamata, N., Kawano, H., Shimizu, S., Kuroki, T., Toyoshima, K., Rikimaru, K., Nomura, N., Ishizaki, R., Pastan, I., Gamou, S. and Shimizu, N. (1986). High incidence of amplification of the epidermal growth factor receptor gene in human squamous carcinoma cell lines. *Cancer Res.* **46**, 414-416.

Yu, V. C., Delsert, C., Andersen, B., Holloway, J. M., Devary, O. V., Naar, A. M., Kim, S. Y., Boutin, J. M., Glass, C. K. and Rosenfeld, M. G. (1991). RXRbeta: A co-regulator that enhances binding of retinoic acid, thyroid hormone, and vitamin D receptors to their cognate response elements. *Cell* **67**, 1251-1266.

Yuspa, S. H. and Harris, C. C. (1974). Altered differentiation of mouse epidermal cells treated with retinyl acetate in vitro. *Exp. Cell Res.* **86**, 95-105.

Yuspa, S. H., Kilkenny, A. E., Steinert, P. M. and Roop, D. R. (1989). Expression of murine epidermal differentiation markers is tightly regulated by restricted extracellular calcium concentrations in vitro. *J. Cell Biol.* **109**, 1207-1217.

Zhang, X.-K., Hoffmann, B., Tran, P. B.-V., Graupner, G. and Pfahl, M. (1992a). Retinoid X receptor is an auxiliary protein for thyroid hormone and retinoic acid receptors. *Nature* **355**, 441-446.

Zhang, X.-K., Lehmann, J., Hoffmann, B., Dawson, M. I., Cameron, J., Graupner, G., Hermann, T., Tran, P. and Pfahl, M. (1992b). Homodimer formation of retinoid X receptor induced by 9-cis retinoic acid. *Nature* **358**, 587-591.

Journal of Cell Science, Supplement 17, 209-215 (1993)
Printed in Great Britain © The Company of Biologists Limited 1993

The role of transepithelial transport by M cells in microbial invasion and host defense

Marian R. Neutra[1] and Jean-Pierre Kraehenbuhl[2]

[1]Department of Pediatrics, Harvard Medical School and GI Cell Biology Laboratory, Children's Hospital, 300 Longwood Avenue, Boston, MA 02115 USA
[2]Swiss Institute for Experimental Cancer Research and Institute of Biochemistry, University of Lausanne, CH-1066 Epalinges, Switzerland

SUMMARY

Transepithelial transport of antigens by M cells in the epithelium associated with lymphoid follicles in the intestine delivers immunogens directly to organized mucosal lymphoid tissues, the inductive sites for mucosal immune responses. We have exploited M cell transport to generate and characterize specific monoclonal IgA antibodies that can prevent interaction of pathogens with epithelial surfaces. The relative protective capacities of specific monoclonal IgA antibodies have been tested in vivo by generation of hybridoma tumors that result in secretion of monoclonal IgA into the intestine. Using this method, we have established that secretion of IgA antibodies recognizing a single surface epitope on enteric pathogens can provide protection against colonization or invasion of the intestinal mucosa.

Key words: mucosal immunity, intestinal epithelium, oral vaccines

INTRODUCTION

The lining of the intestine is a vast monolayer of highly polarized epithelial cells that provides an effective barrier to most of the macromolecules, microorganisms and toxins present in the intestinal lumen. One component of this barrier is the thick and complex coat of glycoproteins and glycolipids on the apical brush borders of intestinal absorptive cells. The epithelium is nevertheless vulnerable to enteric pathogens that express surface adhesins, enzymes, and other specialized mechanisms for colonization of epithelial surfaces and invasion of the mucosa. It is thus not surprising that the intestinal mucosa is heavily populated with cells of the immune system. Indeed, the intestinal lining contains more lymphoid cells and produces more antibodies than any other organ in the body (Mestecky and McGhee, 1987; Seilles et al., 1985). The vast majority of antibodies produced at this site are of the IgA isotype, and are exported into secretions.

Transepithelial transport plays two crucial roles in the mucosal immune response (Fig. 1). First, samples of antigens and microorganisms must be transported from the intestinal lumen across the epithelium in order to be processed in lymphoid tissues and elicit a mucosal immune response (Neutra and Kraehenbuhl, 1992; Kraehenbuhl and Neutra, 1992). This appears to be the special role of M cells, a unique epithelial cell type located exclusively in the lymphoid follicle-associated epithelia over sites containing organized mucosal lymphoid tissue (Bockman and Cooper, 1973; Neutra et al., 1987; Owen 1977). Antigen processing and presentation at these sites results in IgA-committed, antigen-specific B lymphocytes that proliferate locally, then leave the mucosa, migrate via the bloodstream, and finally 'home' to mucosal or glandular sites throughout the intestine as well as other mucosal and secretory tissues (Cebra et al., 1976; McDermott and Bienenstock, 1979). These disseminated cells terminally differentiate to become subepithelial plasma cells that produce polymeric IgA antibodies (Mestecky and McGhee, 1987; Kraehenbuhl and Neutra, 1992). Transepithelial transport in the basal to apical direction is then required for transport of IgA into glandular and mucosal secretions, and this is mediated by polymeric immunoglobulin (poly-Ig) receptors in a variety of epithelial and glandular cells (Mostov et al., 1980; Kuhn and Kraehenbuhl 1982; Apodaca et al., 1991).

Organized mucosal lymphoid tissues, recognized by the presense of lymphoid follicles, are present in the oral cavity, the bronchi, and throughout the small and large intestines (Owen and Ermak, 1990; Owen and Nemanic, 1978). Single follicles or small clusters are located along the length of the gastrointestinal (GI) tract, with increasing frequency in the colon and rectum (O'Leary and Sweeney, 1986; Fujimura et al., 1992) and aggregated follicles are found in the lingual and palatine tonsils, adenoids, appendix and Peyer's patches in the small intestine. Whether single or aggregated, mucosal lymphoid follicles are separated from

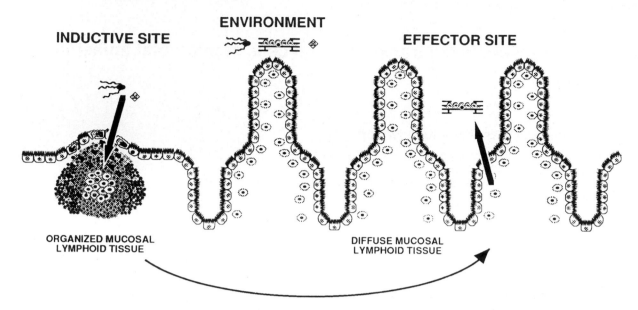

Fig. 1. The role of transepithelial transport in induction and secretion of IgA antibodies. Luminal antigens are separated from cells of the mucosal immune system by the intestinal epithelial barrier. Antigens are transported into the organized mucosa-associated lymphoid tissue of the intestine by M cells in follicle-associated epithelia. Antigen-sensitized, IgA-committed B cells leave the mucosa and migrate to distant glandular and mucosal sites where they terminally differentiate into polymeric IgA-producing plasma cells. Epithelial and glandular cells transport polymeric IgA by receptor-mediated transcytosis, releasing sIgA into secretions where it can interact with antigens and pathogens.

the lumen by a highly specialized epithelium containing antigen-transporting M cells (Fig. 2).

TRANSPORT OF ANTIGENS BY M CELLS

Since transepithelial transport by M cells seems to be required for initiation of a secretory immune response, increasing the efficiency of this transport is an important component of mucosal immunization strategies (Neutra and Kraehenbuhl, 1992). The M cell apical surface lacks the closely packed microvilli and thick enzyme-rich coat of absorptive enterocytes, and displays many broad microdomains from which endocytosis occurs (Neutra et al., 1987). M cell apical membranes nevertheless contain abundant glycoconjugates that can serve as binding sites for cationic macromolecules and possibly for lectin-like microbial surface molecules (Neutra et al., 1987; Bye et al., 1984; Owen and Bhalla, 1983). Microorganisms, particles and lectins that adhere either selectively or nonselectively to M cell apical membranes are endocytosed and transcytosed with high efficiency (Neutra et al., 1987; Pappo and Ermak 1989). This is consistent with the observation that materials that can adhere to mucosal surfaces tend to evoke strong secretory immune responses (DeAizpurua and Russell-Jones, 1988; Mayrhofer, 1984). Certain pathogenic viruses and bacteria adhere selectively to M cells and are efficiently transported, but niether the microbial surface molecules that mediate adherence nor the M cell surface molecules that serve as receptors have been identified. It is probable that microorganisms, which may be considered multivalent particulate ligands, could find their receptors particularly accessible on M cells. It was recently demonstrated that

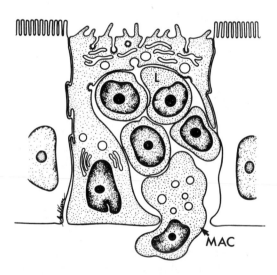

Fig. 2. Diagram of an M cell. The M cell basolateral surface is modified to form an intra-epithelial pocket into which lymphocytes (L) and macrophages (MAC) migrate. Antigens, microorganisms and particles that adhere to the M cell apical membrane are efficiently endocytosed and transported into the pocket, and hence to the underlying mucosal lymphoid tissue.

immunoglobulins in the lumen adhere selectively to the apical membranes of M cells, and IgA-antigen complexes were found to adhere to M cells much more efficiently than antigen alone (Weltzin et al., 1989). This raises the possibility that sIgA could in some cases promote re-uptake of antigens and microorganisms by M cells, perhaps to boost the secretory immune response to pathogens that have not been effectively cleared from the lumen. Studies of this transport system are hampered by the fact that M cells are relatively rare occupants of the intestinal lining, however, and the M cell phenotype has not been replicated in culture.

M cells take up macromolecules, particles and microorganisms by adsorptive endocytosis via clathrin-coated pits and vesicles (Neutra et al., 1987), fluid-phase endocytosis in either coated (Neutra et al., 1987) or uncoated vesicles (Bockman and Cooper, 1973; Owen, 1977), and phagocytosis involving extension of cellular processes and reorganization of submembrane actin assemblies (Winner et al., 1991). Bacteria that adhere to M cells can form broad areas of close interaction: during uptake of *Vibrio cholerae*, for example, the bacterial outer membrane and the M cell apical membrane are separated by a uniform 10-20 nm space. Endocytosed material is delivered into apical endosomal tubules and vesicles (Neutra et al., 1987) some of which contain the late endosome or lysosome membrane marker lgp120 and (in some species) MHC class II antigen (Allan et al., 1993). M cell endosomes are acidified (Allan et al., 1993), but it is not known whether they contain proteases and whether endocytosed materials are partially degraded during transepithelial transport.

The transcytotic pathway of M cells is dramatically shortened by invagination of the basolateral membrane to form a large intra-epithelial 'pocket'. Apical endosomes of M cells deliver their content not to lysosomes but rather directly to the membrane domain lining the pocket, and endocytosed materials are released by exocytosis into the pocket as early as 10 minutes after apical endocytosis (Neutra et al., 1987). Since bacteria and particles are readily released from the membrane into the intra-epithelial space, it is likely that that initial binding involves multiple, low-affinity interaction sites and that the milieu of the transport vesicle or intra-epithelial pocket allows rapid dissociation. Whether apical membrane molecules are replaced by de novo synthesis or by recycling of membrane microdomains from the pocket is not known. Antigens that are transported by M cells may interact first with the antigen-presenting cells and lymphocytes present in the intra-epithelial pocket formed by M cells (Ermak et al., 1990) but it is not known whether an immune response is generated in this sequestered site. In any case, the subepithelial tissue immediately below the follicle-associated epithelium contains IgM+ B cells, CD4+ T cells, dendritic cells and macrophages, and in this cellular network antigens and microorganisms are likely to be efficiently processed and presented (Ermak and Owen, 1986).

INTERACTION OF MICRO-ORGANISMS WITH M CELLS

A common mechanism such as lectin-carbohydrate recognition may allow the M cell to 'sample' pathogenic luminal organisms, either by binding of lectin-like bacterial adhesins to M cell surface glycoconjugates or, conversely, binding of bacterial surface oligosaccharides to M cell surface lectins. M cell binding of noninvasive bacteria such as *Vibrio cholerae* (Winner et al., 1991; Owen et al., 1986) results in efficient sampling by the mucosal immune system, and a strong secretory immune response. In the case

of cholera, secretion of anti-microbial sIgA appears to play a major role in limiting the duration of mucosal disease and preventing re-infection (Svennerholm et al., 1984; Jertborn et al., 1986). A variety of pathogenic bacteria and viruses that bind to M cells, however, exploit the transport mechanism that was intended for mucosal protection by using this transepithelial pathway as an invasion route. For example, transport of *Salmonella typhi* into Peyer's patch mucosa (Kohbata et al., 1986) results in a vigorous anti *Salmonella* mucosal immune response, but this occurs too late to prevent spread of bacteria to the liver and spleen and disseminated systemic disease (Chau et al., 1981; Hohmann et al., 1978). Similarly, M cell binding and transport of *Shigella flexneri* (Wassef et al., 1989) and *Yersinia enterocoliitica* (Grutzkau et al., 1990) allows these organisms to gain access to the lamina propria, where they cause mucosal disease by basolateral invasion of epithelial cells and infection of mucosal macrophages (Isberg, 1990; Sansonetti, 1991).

Viral pathogens also exploit the M cell transport system. This has been amply demonstrated in studies of reovirus pathogenesis in mice (Wolf et al., 1981). Poliovirus adhered to human M cells in organ culture (Sicinski et al., 1990), and the retrovirus HIV-1 adhered to M cells of rabbit and mouse follicle-associated epithelia in mucosal explants (Amerongen et al., 1991). Selective adherence to M cell apical membranes effectively targets these pathogens for efficient transport into the intestinal mucosa. In the case of reovirus type 3 and possibly poliovirus, entry into Peyer's patch mucosa is followed by invasion of neuronal target cells and spread to the central nervous system (Nibert et al., 1991). If HIV is transported by human M cells, the virus would be delivered directly to target T cells within and under the follicle-associated epithelium. Although viral particles are sampled by the mucosal immune system and immune responses may be generated, entry of virus into target cells puts them beyond the reach of anti-viral antibodies. Identification of viral surface components that mediate M cell adherence, and the corresponding M cell receptors, remains an important research priority.

MECHANISM OF IgA PROTECTION

There is considerable indirect evidence that specific secretory IgA in the fluids bathing mucosal surfaces can prevent contact of antigens and pathogens with epithelial cells, a phenomenon called 'immune exclusion' (Tomasi, 1983; Killian et al., 1988). The molecular mechanisms that underlie this protection, however, are not completely understood and it is likely that this unique effector molecule can play multiple roles in the changing mucosal environment of the intestinal lumen. Secretory IgA is an effector molecule, which functions outside the body in environments usually devoid of complement and phagocytic cells. Most IgA antibodies studied to date are not 'neutralizing' in the classic sense as they generally do not opsonize in vitro, do not bind complement or cause release of complement fragment C5a, and do not directly cause bacterial lysis (Tomasi, 1983; Killian et al., 1988; Childers et al., 1989). It has been shown that specific IgA antibodies injected systemically may be ineffective against systemic microbial challenge even when the same antibodies can protect against mucosal challenge when they are present in mucosal secretions (Subbarao and Murphy, 1992; Michetti et al., 1992). IgA antibodies secreted in response to mucosal bacteria and viruses are directed primarily against surface antigens or secreted toxins. Since sIgA is a dimer with 4 antigen binding sites, it can efficiently crosslink target macromolecules and micro-organisms in the intestinal lumen, thus inhibiting motility and facilitating entrapment in mucus and clearance by peristalsis. In the context of the mucosa, sIgA can also collaborate with bacteriostatic proteins and lytic cells to enhance microbial killing in novel ways (Killian et al., 1988; Childers et al., 1989).

Oral or mucosal vaccination has been clearly shown to be the optimal method for induction of secretory IgA and effective immune protection against many enteric pathogens. Thus there is rapidly growing interest in testing and use of novel oral vaccines in experimental animals and humans (Subbarao and Murphy, 1992; Levine and Edelman, 1990; Mekalanos, 1992). The immune responses generated by enteric viral and bacterial infections and by mucosal vaccines usually include other components in addition to secretory IgA, however, such as production of systemic IgG antibodies and cell-mediated immunity (Cancellieri and Fara, 1985). Thus it has been difficult to judge the relative importance of sIgA in protection, or to determine whether 'immune exclusion' by sIgA alone can be sufficient to prevent mucosal infection. It is technically difficult to collect, purify and analyse polyclonal sIgA from secretions and even more difficult to determine which antigenic determinants and antibody specificities contributed to protection. For these reasons, several laboratories including our own have produced monoclonal IgA antibodies and have used them to address these issues in vivo and in vitro.

PRODUCTION AND USE OF MONOCLONAL IgA ANTIBODIES

Mucosal (but not systemic) immunization favors the formation of antigen-sensitized lymphoblasts of the IgA isotype in organized mucosal lymphoid tissues such as Peyer's patches. In our laboratories, we have found that fusion of cells isolated directly from Peyer's patches after a series of mucosal immunizations with viruses, bacteria and protein antigens is an effective method for obtaining IgA hybridomas (Weltzin et al., 1989; Winner et al., 1991; Michetti et al., 1992; Apter et al., 1991). The antigen specificities of the IgA antibodies thus obtained serve to identify the microbial surface molecules that are most immunogenic in the mucosal system. Most of the monoclonal IgAs that we have produced and analysed have been directed against microbial surface components. and this is consistent with the proposed function of sIgA in immune exclusion. Mucosally derived IgA hybridomas produce IgA primarily in dimeric form and these antibodies are recognized by polymeric immunoglobulin receptors on epithelial cells (Weltzin et al., 1989). Thus they can be delivered into secretions of mice in vivo or across epithelial monolayers in vitro via the normal transepithelial transport system with addition of

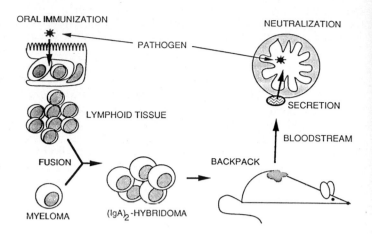

Fig. 3. Protocol for production of IgA hybridomas and secretion of monoclonal sIgA in vivo. After oral immunization of adult mice, Peyer's patch lymphocytes are recovered and fused with myeloma cells. The resulting hybridomas are screened for production of IgA antibodies of the desired specificities. Selected clones of hybridoma cells are injected subcutaneously on the backs of syngeneic mice, where they form hybridoma 'backpack' tumors that produce circulating dimeric IgA. The monoclonal IgA is recognized by epithelial polymeric immunoglobulin receptors in the liver and intestine, and is delivered into bile and intestinal secretions via receptor-mediated transcytosis. This in vivo model allows identification of monoclonal IgA antibodies that can protect against challenge with the corresponding pathogen.

secretory component (Winner et al., 1991; Subbarao and Murphy, 1992) and can bind recombinant secretory component in solution (Michetti et al., 1991). These methods provide an unlimited source of protease-protected IgA antibodies of known epitope specificities that can be separately tested in protection assays.

To obtain continuous secretion of monoclonal IgA antibodies into intestinal secretions and bile of mice via the normal receptor-mediated epithelial transport system, hybridoma cells are injected subcutaneously on the upper backs of Balb/c mice, resulting in hybridoma 'backpack' tumors that release IgA into the circulation (Winner et al., 1991). In tissues such as liver and intestine where capillaries are permeable, dimeric IgA binds to basolateral epithelial poly-Ig receptors and is delivered into secretions as monoclonal sIgA (Fig. 3). We have used the backpack tumor method to analyse the specificity and the mechanisms of IgA protection against micro-organisms in the intestine, using as models two enteric bacterial pathogens: *Vibrio cholerae*, a non-invasive organism that colonizes the mucosal surface and secretes cholera toxin, and *Salmonella typhimurium*, an invasive pathogen.

IgA PROTECTION AGAINST EPITHELIAL COLONIZATION

Vibrio cholerae causes severe diarrheal disease by colonizing the mucosal surface of the small intestine. When vibrios enter the luminal microenvironment the *toxR* regulatory gene is activated resulting in expression of several virulence factors including the pilus protein that promotes mucosal colonization, and cholera toxin (CT) (Miller et al., 1989). Binding of CT to its glycolipid receptor GM1 on epithelial cells initiates a series of intracellular events that result in massive chloride secretion (Holmgren, 1981; Lencer et al., 1992). *V. cholerae* evokes polyclonal secretory IgA antibodies (sIgA) directed against both CT and bacterial surface components including the outer membrane lipopolysaccharide (LPS) (Svennerholm et al., 1984) and these are thought to be involved in limiting the primary infection and providing protection against subsequent reinfection (Svennerholm et al., 1984; Jertborn et al., 1986). Using the hybridoma backpack tumor method, we have shown that secretion of monoclonal sIgA directed against a strain-specific carbohydrate epitope of the surface LPS is sufficient to prevent diarrhea and death in mice after a lethal oral dose of *V. cholerae* (Winner et al., 1991). Furthermore, a single oral dose of 5 mg of the same anti-LPS IgA protected suckling mice against subsequent oral challenge for up to 3 hours, although protection was lost as the IgA was cleared from the upper small intestine by peristalsis (Apter et al., 1991).

To test the ability of IgA to block the effects of CT and prevent diarrheal disease, hybridomas were generated that produce monoclonal IgA antibodies directed against CT; all of the IgAs recognized the B subunit and none was directed against the binding site for GM1, the intestinal cell membrane toxin receptor (Apter et al., 1991). These antibodies were applied to a well-defined intestinal epithelial cell monolayer culture system (Lencer et al., 1992; Dharmsathaphorn and Madara, 1990) to directly measure protection against toxin action in vitro, and were tested in vivo by passive oral administration or the backpack tumor method. When applied to human T84 colon carcinoma cells grown on permeable supports, the IgAs blocked CT-induced Cl$^-$ secretion in a dose-dependent manner and completely inhibited binding of rhodamine-labelled CT to apical cell membranes (Apter et al., 1991). Oral feeding of the monoclonal IgAs protected against oral CT administration in vivo. Both in vitro and in vivo, however, high doses of IgA were required for CT neutralization. In contrast, anti-CTB IgA failed to protect suckling mice against a lethal oral dose of live *V. cholerae* organisms, whether the antibodies were delivered perorally or secreted intraintestinally in mice bearing backpack tumors (Apter et al., 1991). These results corroborate previous human studies in which volunteers orally immunized with multiple large doses of purified CT were not protected against oral challenge with *V. cholerae*, whereas volunteers immunized orally with live *V. cholerae* organisms were completely protected (Levine et al., 1979, 1983). Since CT is not a component of the bacterial surface, anti-CT IgA alone is not likely to prevent *V. cholerae* colonization, and secretion of toxin from adherent organisms on the mucosal surface could deliver high levels of CT directly into the enterocyte glycocalyx and onto apical membranes. Our results show that IgAs directed against the bacterial surface provide most efficient mucosal protection.

IgA PROTECTION AGAINST EPITHELIAL INVASION

The disease caused by *Salmonella typhimurium* infection in mice is similar to typhoid fever caused by *S. typhi* in humans (Edelman and Levine, 1986). In both cases, organisms are ingested orally, rapidly invade the intestinal epithelium, proliferate in the mucosa, and then spread to the liver and spleen resulting in a potentially lethal systemic disease (Hohmann et al., 1978; Edelman and Levine, 1986). Entry into the mucosa occurs first via transepithelial transport by M cells (Kohbata et al., 1986) and then by adherence, invasion and damage of absorptive enterocytes (Takeuchi, 1975). Immunization strategies designed to protect against this disease are aimed at preventing the initial interaction of bacteria with epithelial cells. Indeed, the presense of anti-*Salmonella* IgA in intestinal secretions is known to be closely correlated with protection in experimental animals and humans (Chau et al., 1981; Edelman and Levine, 1986). Using monoclonal IgA antibodies, we have recently demonstrated that secretory IgA antibodies alone can provide this protection.

A series of anti-*Salmonella* IgA hybridomas were generated from Peyer's patch cells and a monoclonal polymeric IgA (Sal4) was characterized that recognizes a surface-exposed carbohydrate epitope on wild type *S. typhimurium* (Michetti et al., 1992). Mice bearing subcutaneous Sal4 hybridoma tumors secreted monoclonal sIgA into their gastrointestinal tracts and were protected against a lethal oral challenge with this bacterium. This protection was directly dependent on specific recognition by Sal4 IgA, since mice secreting Sal4 IgA from hybridoma tumors were not protected against an equally virulent *S. typhimurium* mutant that lacks the epitope recognized by Sal4. In these in vivo studies, secretion of monoclonal IgA was shown to prevent the initial event in pathogenesis, uptake of *Salmonella* by M cells into the Peyer's patch mucosa. We also used monolayer cultures of epithelial cell lines (MDCK and HT29) to test IgA protection against invasion of epithelial cells by *Salmonella*. It had been previously shown that invasion of MDCK cells in vitro correlates closely with invasion of CaCo2 cells and with infection of the small intestinal mucosa in vivo (Finley and Falkow, 1990; Finlay et al., 1988). Using these in vitro models, we have demonstrated that specific IgA antibodies can protect absorptive epithelia against invasive *Salmonella* in the absence of mucus, peristalsis and other protection mechanisms (Michetti et al., unpublished data). Thus, IgA alone can prevent epithelial contact and mucosal invasion.

CONCLUSION

In summary, our studies using monoclonal IgA antibodies have confirmed that the principal role of sIgA in the intestine is to prevent contact of antigens and pathogens with epithelial surfaces. We have established that sIgA of appropriate specificity, if present in sufficiently large amounts, can provide protection of the intestinal mucosa in the absence of other immune protection mechanisms. Identification of protective secretory IgA antibodies provides a means to identify the microbial antigens that should be included in effective oral vaccines. Elucidation of the mechanisms that govern adherence and transepithelial transport by M cells will allow us to target such vaccines to the inductive sites of the mucosal immune system.

We thank the former members of our laboratories who conducted much of the work summarized in this review: Pierre Michetti, Richard Weltzin, Helen Amerongen, Julie Mack, Scott Winner and Felice Apter. We are indebted to our collaborators John Mekalanos, Michael Mahon and James Slauch from the Department of Microbiology and Molecular Genetics at Harvard Medical School. The authors are supported by NIH Research grants HD17557, DK21505 and AI29378 and NIH Center grant DK34854 to the Harvard Digestive Diseases Center (M.R.N.); Swiss National Science Foundation grant 31.246404.89 and Swiss League against Cancer grant 373.89.2 (J.P.K.).

REFERENCES

Allan, C. H., Mendrick, D. L., Trier, J. S. (1993). Rat intestinal M cells contain acidic endosomal-lysosomal compartments and express Class II major histocompatibility complex determinants. *Gastroenterology* **104**, 698-708.

Amerongen, H. M., Weltzin, R. A., Farnet, C. M., Michetti, P., Haseltine, W. A. and Neutra, M. R. (1991). Transepithelial transport of HIV-1 by intestinal M cells: a mechanism for transmission of AIDS. *J. Acquir. Immune Defic. Syndr.* **4**, 760-765.

Apodaca, G., Bomsel, M. Arden, J., Breifteld, P. P., Tang, K. C., Mostov, K. E. (1991). The polymeric immunoglobulin receptor. A model protein to study transcytosis. *J. Clin. Invest.* **87**, 1877-1882.

Apter, F.M., Lencer, W.I., Mekalanos, J.J. and Neutra, M.R. (1991). Analysis of epithelial protection by monoclonal IgA antibodies directed against cholera toxin B subunits in vivo and in vitro. *J. Cell Biol.* **115**, 399a.

Bockman, D. E. and Cooper, M.D. (1973). Pinocytosis by epithelium associated with lymphoid follicles in the bursa of Fabricius, appendix, and Peyer's patches. An electron microscopic study. *Amer. J. Anat.* **136**, 455-478.

Bye W. A., Allan, C. H. and Trier, J. S. (1984). Structure, distribution and origin of M cells in Peyer's patches of mouse ileum. *Gastroenterology* **86**, 789-801.

Cancellieri, V. and Fara, G. M. (1985). Demonstration of specific IgA in human feces after immunization with live Ty21a *Salmonella typhi* vaccine. *J. Infect. Dis.* **151**, 482-484.

Cebra, J. J., Gearheart, P. J., Kamat, R., Robertson, S. M. and Tseng, J. (1976). Origin and differentiation of lymphocytes involved in the secretory IgA response. *Cold Spring Harbor Symp. Quant. Biol.* **41**, 201-215.

Chau, P. Y., Tsang, R. S. W., Lam, S. K., Labrooy, J. T. and Rowley, D. (1981). Antibody response to the lipopolysaccharide and protein antigens of *Salmonella typhi* during typhoid infection. *Clin. Exp. Immunol.* **46**, 515-520.

Childers, N. K., Bruce, M. G. and Mcghee, J. R. (1989). Molecular mechanisms of immunoglobulin A defense. *Annu. Rev. Microbiol.* **43**, 503-536.

DeAizpurua, H. J. and Russell-Jones, G. J. (1988). Oral vaccination: Identification of classes of proteins that provoke an immune response upon oral feeding. *J. Exp. Med.* **167**, 440-451.

Dharmsathaphorn, K. and Madara, J. L. (1990). Established cell lines as model systems for electrolyte transport studies. *Meth. Enzymol.* **192**, 354-359.

Edelman, R. and Levine, M. M. (1986). Summary of an International Workshop on Typhoid Fever. *Rev. Infect. Dis.* **8**, 329-349.

Ermak, T. H. and Owen, R. L. (1986). Differential distribution of lymphocytes and accessory cells in mouse Peyer's patches. *Anat. Rec.* **215**, 144-152.

Ermak, T. H., Steger, H. J. and Pappo, J. (1990). Phenotypically distinct subpopulations of T cells in domes and M-cell pockets of rabbit gut-associated lymphoid tissues. *Immunology* **71**, 530-537.

Finlay, B. B. and Falkow, S. (1990). *Salmonella* interaction with polarized human intestinal Caco-2 epithelial cells. *J. Infect. Dis.* **162**, 1096-1106.

Finlay, B. B., Starnbach, M. N., Francis, C. L. (1988). Identification and characterization of Tn*phoA* mutants of *Salmonella* that are unable to pass through a polarized MDCK epithelial cell monolayer. *Mol. Microbiol.* **2**, 725-766.

Fujimura, Y., Hosobe, M. and Kihara, T. (1992). Ultrastructural study of M cells from colonic lymphoid nodules obtained by colonoscopic biopsy. *Digest. Dis. Sci.* **37**, 1089-1098.

Grutzkau, A., Hanski, C., Hahn, H. and Riecken, E. O. (1990). Involvement of M cells in the bacterial invasion of Peyer's patches: a common mechanism shared by *Yersinia enterocolitica* and other enteroinvasive bacteria. *Gut* **31**, 1011-1015.

Hohmann, A. W., Schmidt, G. and Rowley, D. (1978). Intestinal colonization and virulence of *Salmonella* in mice. *Infect. Immunol.* **22**, 763-770.

Holmgren, J. (1981). Actions of cholera toxin and the prevention and treatment of cholera. *Nature* **292**, 413-417.

Isberg R. R. (1990). Pathways for the penetration of enteropathogenic *Yersinia* into mammalian cells. *Mol. Biol. Med.* **7**, 73-82.

Jertborn, M., Svennerholm, A. M. and Holmgren, J. (1986). Saliva, breast milk, and serum antibody responses as indirect measures of intestinal immunity after oral cholera vaccination or natural disease. *J. Clin. Microbiol.* **24**, 203-209.

Killian, M., Mestecky, J. and Russel, M. W. (1988). Defense mechanisms involving Fc-dependent functions of immunoglobulin A and their subversion by bacterial immunoglobulin A proteases. *Microbiol. Rev.* **52**, 296-303.

Kohbata, S., Yokobata, H. and Yabuuchi, E. (1986). Cytopathogenic effect of *Salmonella typhi* GIFU 10007 on M cells of murine ileal Peyer's patches in ligated ileal loops: An ultrastructural study. *Microbiol. Immunol.* **30**, 1225-1237.

Kraehenbuhl, J. P. and Neutra, M. N. (1992). Molecular and cellular basis of immune protection of mucosal surfaces. *Physiol. Rev.* **72**, 853-879.

Kuhn, L. C. and Kraehenbuhl, J. P. (1982). The sacrificial receptor - translocation of polymeric IgA across epithelia. *Trends Biochem Sci.* **7**, 299-302.

Lencer, W. I., Delp, C., Neutra, M. R. and Madara, J. L. (1992). mechanism of cholera toxin action on a polarized human intestinal epithelial cell line: role of vesicular traffic. *J. Cell Biol.* **6**, 1197-1209.

Levine, M. M. and Edelman, R. (1990). Future vaccines against enteric pathogens. *Infect. Dis. Clin. N. Amer.* **4**, 105-121.

Levine, M. M., Kaper, J. B., Black, R. E. and Clements, M. L. (1983). New knowledge on pathogenesis of bacterial enteric infections as applied to vaccine development. *Microbiol. Rev.* **47**, 510-550.

Levine, M. M., Nalin, D. R., Craig, J. P., Hoover, D., Bergquist, E. J., Waterman, D., Preston-Holley, H., Hornick, R. B. Pierce, N. P. and Libonati, J. P. (1979). Immunity to cholera in man: Relative role of antibacterial verus antitoxic immunity. *Trans. Royal Soc. Trop. Med. Hyg.* **73**, 3-9.

Mayrhofer, G. (1984). Physiology of the intestinal immune system. In *Local Immune Responses of the Gut* (ed. T. J. Newby and C. R. Stokes), pp. 1-96. Boca Raton: CRC Press.

McDermott, M. R. and Bienenstock, J. (1979). Evidence for a common mucosal immunologic system I. Migration of B immunoblasts into intestinal, respiratory, and genital tissues. *J. Immunol.* **122**, 1892-1898.

Mekalanos, J. J. (1992). Bacterial mucosal vaccines. In *Genetically Engineered Vaccines. Advan. Exp. Med. Biol.*, vol. 327 (ed. J. E. Ciardi, J. R. McGhee and J. M. Kieth), pp. 43-50. New York: Plenum Press.

Mestecky, J. and Mcghee, J. R. (1987). Immunoglobulin A (IgA): molecular and cellular interactions involved in IgA biosynthesis and immune response. *Adv. Immunol.* **40**, 153-245.

Michetti, P., Hirt, R., Weltzin, R., Fasel, N., Schaerer, E., Neutra, M. R. and Kraehenbuhl, J. P. (1991). Production and use of monoclonal IgA antibodies complexed with recombinant secretory component for passive immune protection. In *Immunology of Milk and the Neonate. Advan. Exp. Med. Biol.* (ed. J. Mestecky, P. Ogra), pp. 183-187. New York: Plenum Press.

Michetti, P., Mahan, M. J., Slauch J. M., Mekalanos, J. J. and Neutra, M. R. (1992). Monoclonal secretory IgA protects against oral challenge with the invasive pathogen *Salmonella typhimurium*. *Infect. Immunology* **60**, 1786-1792.

Miller, J. F., Mekalanos, J. J. and Falkow, S. (1989). Coordinate regulation and sensory transduction in the control of bacterial virulence. *Science* **243**, 916-922.

Mostov, K. E., Kraehenbuhl, J. P. and Blobel, G. (1980). Receptor mediated transcellular transport of immunoglobulins: synthesis of secretory component as multiple and larger transmembrane forms. *Proc. Nat. Acad. Sci. USA* **77**, 7257-7261.

Neutra, M. N. and Kraehenbuhl, J. P. (1992). Transepithelial transport and mucosal defence I: the role of M cells. *Trends Cell Biol.* **2**, 134-138.

Neutra, M. R., Phillips, T. L., Mayer, E. L. and Fishkind, D. J. (1987). Transport of membrane-bound macromolecules by M cells in follicle-associated epithelium of rabbit Peyer's patch. *Cell. Tiss. Res.* **247**, 537-546.

Nibert, M. L., Furlong, D. B. and Fields, B. N. (1991). Mechanisms of viral pathogenesis. *J. Clin. Invest.* **88**, 727-734.

O'Leary, A. D. and Sweeney, E. C. (1986). Lymphoglandular complexes of the colon: structure and distribution. *Histopathology* **10**, 267-283.

Owen, R. L. (1977). Sequential uptake of horseradish peroxidase by lymphoid follicle epithelium of Peyer's patches in the normal unobstructed mouse intestine: an ultrastructural study. *Gastroenterology* **72**, 440-451.

Owen, R. L. and Bhalla, D. K. (1983). Cytochemical analysis of alkaline phosphatase and esterase activities and of lectin-binding and anionic sites in rat and mouse Peyer's patch M cells. *Amer. J. Anat.* **168**, 199-212.

Owen, R. L. and Ermak, T. H. (1990). Structural specialization for antigen uptake and processing in the digestive tract. *Springer Semin. Immunopathol* **2**, 139-152.

Owen, R. L. and Nemanic P. (1978). Antigen processing structures of the mammalian intestinal tract: an SEM study of lymphoepithelial organs. *Scan. Electron Microsc.* **2**, 367-378.

Owen, R. L., Pierce, N. F., Apple, R. T. and Cray, W. C. J. (1986). M cell transport of *Vibrio cholerae* from the intestinal lumen into Peyer's patches: a mechanism for antigen sampling and for microbial transepithelial migration. *J. Infect. Dis.* **153**, 1108-1118.

Pappo, J. and Ermak, T. H. (1989). Uptake and translocation of fluorescent latex particles by rabbit Peyer's patch follicle epithelium: a quantitative model for M cell uptake. *Clin. Exp. Immunol.* **76**, 144-148.

Sansonetti, P. J. (1991). Genetic and molecular basis of epithelial cell invasion by *Shigella* species. *Rev. Infect. Dis.* **13**, 285-292.

Seilles, E., Vuitton, D., Sava, P., Claude, P., Panouse Perrin, J., Roche, A. and Delacroix, D. L. (1985). IgA and its different molecular forms in the mesenteric, portal and peripheral venous blood in man. *Gastroenterol. Clin. Biol.* **9**, 607-613.

Sicinski, P., Rowinski, J., Warchol, J. B., Jarzcabek, Z., Gut, W., Szczygiel, B., Bielecki, K. and Koch, G. (1990). Poliovirus type 1 enters the human host through intestinal M cells. *Gastroenterology* **98**, 56-58.

Subbarao, E. K. and Murphy, B. R. (1992). A general overview of viral vaccine development. In *Genetically Engineered Vaccines. Advan Exp. Med. Biol.*, vol. 327 (ed. J. E. Ciardi, J. R. McGhee and J. M. Kieth), pp. 51-58. New York: Plenum Press.

Svennerholm, A.-M., Jertborn, M. Gothefors, L., Karim, A. M. M. M., Sack, D. A. and Holmgren, J. (1984). Mucosal antitoxic and antibacterial immunity after cholera disease and after immunization with a combined B subunit-whole cell vaccine. *J. Infect. Dis.* **149**, 884-893.

Takeuchi, A. (1967). Electron microscope studies of experimental *Salmonella* infection into the intestinal epithelium by *Salmonella typhimurium*. *Amer. J. Pathol.* **50**, 109-136.

Tomasi, T. B. (1983). Mechanisms of immune regulation at mucosal surfaces. *Rev. Infect. Dis.* **5**, S784-S792.

Wasseff, J. S., Keren, D. F. and Mailloux, J. L. (1989). Role of M cells in initial antigen uptake and in ulcer formation in the rabbit intestinal loop model of *Shigellosis*. *Infect. Immunol.* **57**, 858-863.

Weltzin, R. A., Lucia-Jandris, P., Michetti, P., Fields, B. N., Kraehenbuhl, J. P. and Neutra, M. R. (1989). Binding and transepithelial transport of immunoglobulins by intestinal M cells: demonstration using monoclonal IgA antibodies against enteric viral proteins. *J. Cell Biol.* **108**, 1673-1685.

Winner, L. S. Iii, Mack, J., Weltzin, R. A., Mekalanos, J. J., Kraehenbuhl, J. P. and Neutra, M. R. (1991). New model for analysis of mucosal immunity: Intestinal secretion of specific monoclonal immunoglobulin A from hybridoma tumors protects against *Vibrio cholerae* infection. *Infect. Immunol.* **59**, 977-982.

Wolf, J. L., Rubin, D. H., Finberg, R. S., Kauffman, R. S., Sharpe, A. H., Trier, J. S. and Fields, B. N. (1981). Intestinal M cells: a pathway for entry of reovirus into the host. *Science* **212**, 471-472.

Journal of Cell Science, Supplement 17, 217-222 (1993)
Printed in Great Britain © The Company of Biologists Limited 1993

Epithelial polarity and differentiation in polycystic kidney disease

Ellis D. Avner

Department of Pediatrics, University of Washington and Division of Nephrology, Children's Hospital and Medical Center, Seattle, Washington, USA

SUMMARY

Renal cysts are central pathological features in a number of human congenital and acquired diseases, and produce significant morbidity and mortality. This review describes our laboratory's efforts to identify specific alterations in epithelial cell polarity and differentiation associated with renal tubular cyst formation and progressive enlargement. Studies in a murine model of human autosomal recessive polycystic kidney disease, the C57BL/6J cpk/cpk (CPK) mouse have demonstrated quantitative (increased activity) and qualitative (apical membrane distribution) alterations in Na⁺,K⁺-adenosine triphosphatase activity that mediate tubular cyst formation. Proximal tubular cyst formation in CPK kidneys is characterized by increased activity of a basolat-

eral Na⁺,K⁺-ATPase, which drives organic anion secretion and consequent tubular fluid secretion. In contrast, collecting tubule cyst formation is characterized by increased apical membrane Na⁺,K⁺-ATPase expression, which may be a marker of the relatively undifferentiated phenotype of cyst lining cells. If such apically expressed enzyme is active, it may have pathogenic import in collecting tubule cyst formation and enlargement by mediating net basal to apical vectorial solute and fluid transport.

Key words: polycystic kidney disease, sodium potassium adenosine triphosphatase, epithelial polarity

INTRODUCTION

Renal cysts are the central pathological feature of a number of human congenital and acquired diseases. The two most common forms of genetically determined renal cystic disease, autosomal dominant polycystic kidney disease (ADPKD) and autosomal recessive polycystic kidney disease (ARPKD) affect over 500,000 individuals in the United States (Welling and Grantham, 1991). Thus, polycystic kidney disease is more common than the combination of trisomy 21, sickle cell anemia, cystic fibrosis, hemophilia and Duchenne's Muscular Dystrophy, and is responsible for 8 to 10% of all patients receiving dialysis or transplantation for end stage renal disease. The cost of these therapies alone, apart from the significant morbidity and mortality caused by renal cystic diseases, was approximately $300,000,000 in 1992. In both ADPKD and ARPKD progressive accumulation of fluid in a subpopulation of renal tubules leads to distortion and destruction of normal adjacent renal tissue and, ultimately, to renal failure. Despite intensive investigation, the genes responsible for ADPKD and ARPKD have not been identified (Germino and Somlo, 1992). Our efforts have predominantly focused on the pathophysiology of renal cyst formation and progressive enlargement (Avner, 1988, 1993; Avner et al., 1990). Data generated from such studies may focus molecular genetic approaches in identifying candidate genes, and, even in the absence of gene identification, may lead to specific therapeutic strategies directed at reducing the

formation and enlargement of cystic lesions. This review will focus on our studies in the C57 BL/6J cpk/cpk (CPK) mouse, a murine model of ARPKD (Avner et al., 1987a,b, 1988), and specifically address the role of altered epithelial polarity and differentiation in PKD.

PATHOGENESIS OF RENAL CYST FORMATION AND PROGRESSIVE ENLARGEMENT

A murine model of PKD: the CPK mouse

In 1977, a spontaneous mutation in the C57 BL/6J murine strain produced animals with autosomal recessive polycystic kidney disease (CPK) (Russell and McFarland, 1977). The cystic CPK strain has subsequently been maintained through controlled breeding of obligatory heterozygotes. CPK animals that appeared normal at birth developed progressive lethargy, abdominal protuberance and wasting, and died in renal failure at 3-4 weeks of postnatal age with massively enlarged kidneys (Preminger et al., 1982). We have studied the morphology and ontogeny of tubular cyst formation in the CPK mouse by light and transmission electron microscopy, and intact nephron microdissection (Avner et al., 1987a). The earliest morphological alterations consisted of tubular dilatation and cyst formation in proximal tubular segments of 17-day affected fetuses. Cysts occurred as outpouchings of proximal tubular segments and remained in continuity with other nephron segments. Transmission electron microscopy revealed widening of the tubular inter-

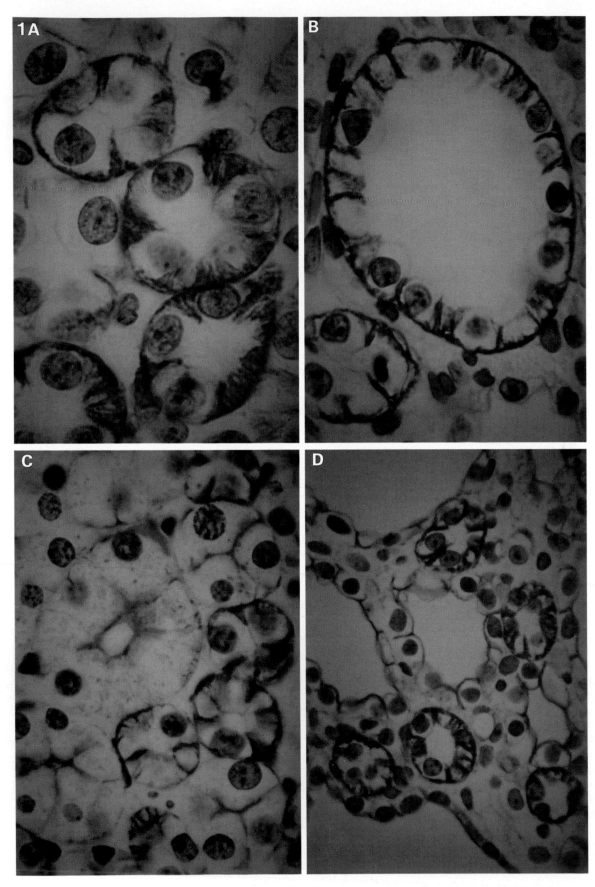

cellular spaces without evidence of cell injury. Nephron microdissection revealed a shift in site of nephron involvement from proximal tubules to cortical and outer medullary collecting tubules as the disease progressed. The distinct shift in the site of nephron involvement at specific stages of renal organogenesis suggests stage-specific alterations in cystic gene expression or a developmentally regulated pattern of tubular responsiveness to cyst-promoting processes.

Increased Na⁺,K⁺-ATPase in PKD

Studies in a variety of in vivo and in vitro experimental models as well as mathematical analysis of cyst growth kinetics demonstrate that two basic criteria necessary for cyst formation are increased epithelial cell proliferation and altered transtubular fluid transport (Avner et al., 1990; Welling, 1990; Wilson and Sherwood, 1991). Altered fluid transport in renal cystic tubular epithelium leading to net tubular secretion and intratubular fluid accumulation could result from alterations in ion pump activity or more global abnormalities of polarized cell structure and function. In normal renal tubular epithelial cells, sodium-potassium adenosine triphosphatase (Na⁺,K⁺-ATPase) is restricted to the basal-lateral membrane. Through coupled sodium-potassium countertransport, Na⁺,K⁺-ATPase is the major driving force for renal tubular sodium reabsorption and the secondary active transport of a number of other solutes (Skou and Esmann, 1992). We, therefore, sought to determine whether alterations in Na⁺,K⁺-ATPase activity or polarized distribution were correlated with tubular cyst formation and enlargement. In CPK kidneys, the earliest phases of proximal tubular cyst formation were paralleled by increases in whole kidney Na⁺,K⁺-ATPase activity (Avner et al., 1988). Increased renal Na⁺,K⁺-ATPase activity occurred before significant epithelial hyperplasia and was not associated with abnormalities in tubular basal laminae glycoprotein expression. This suggested that increased Na⁺,K⁺-ATPase activity with consequent tubular epithelial hyperplasia were early markers of CPK gene expression and cyst formation. Subsequent studies suggested that proximal tubular cyst formation in this murine model, like cyst formation in organ culture models of developing renal tissue, might involve increased organic anion secretion driven by a normally localized basolateral Na⁺,K⁺-ATPase (Avner et al., 1985, 1987b,

1988, 1989, 1990). The intratubular sequestration of osmotically active organic anions would then obligate net intratubular fluid accumulation, resulting in cyst formation and progressive enlargement (Avner, 1988; Avner et al., 1990).

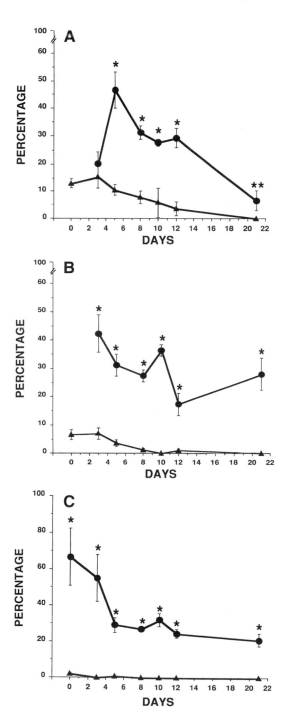

Fig. 2. Localization of Na⁺,K⁺-ATPase α1 subunit to apical, as well as lateral, cell surfaces in cystic CPK (●) and control (▲) collecting tubules. Data are expressed as percentages (mean ± s.d.) of total control or cystic DBA⁺ collecting tubules in outer cortex (A), inner cortex (B), and medulla (C). *$P<0.001$, cystic versus controls; **$P<0.02$, cystic versus controls. (Reprinted from Avner et al. (1992) with the author's permission.)

Fig. 1. Expression of Na⁺,K⁺-ATPase subunits during control and cystic CPK renal tubular development. Immunoperoxidase stain (brown), counterstained with hematoxylin. (A and C) ×165; (B and D) ×130. (A) Control day 3 proximal tubules demonstrate basal-lateral expression of Na⁺,K⁺-ATPase α1 subunit. β1 subunit expression was identical. (B) CPK day 3 cystic proximal tubules, as well as unaffected proximal tubules in the field, demonstrate basal-lateral Na⁺,K⁺-ATPase α1 subunit expression. β1 subunit expression was identical. (C) Control day 8 outer cortical collecting tubule demonstrates apical, as well as lateral, β1 subunit expression. Note the purely basal-lateral staining of other collecting tubules in the field. α1 subunit expression was identical. (D) CPK day 8 cystic outer cortical collecting tubule demonstrates apical, as well as lateral, β1 subunit expression. Note the purely basal-lateral staining of noncystic tubules in the field. α1 subunit expression was identical. (Reprinted from Avner et al. (1992) with the author's permission.)

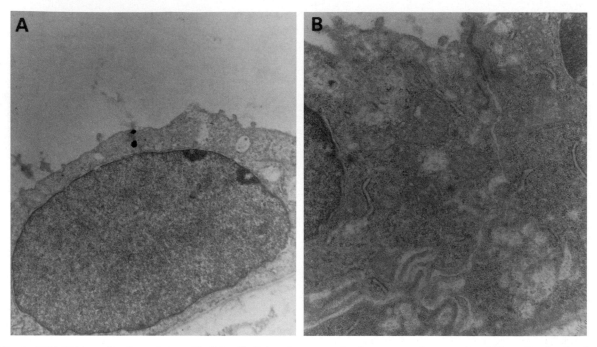

Fig. 3. Cystic CPK DBA+ collecting tubule epithelial cells lining the cyst cavity demonstrate features of undifferentiated collecting tubule principal cells. These include (A) a large nuclear to cytoplasmic ratio, and (B) a paucity of lysozymes and other intracellular organelles, with simple basal-lateral interdigitations. Also noted are apical tight junctions and a normal basal laminae. (A) ×4811; (B) ×9547.

Na+,K+-ATPase polarity and epithelial differentiation in PKD

Altered Na+,K+-ATPase activity might also mediate intratubular fluid accumulation and cyst formation if the ion pump was mislocated to apical membranes of cystic tubular cells. In this location, it could stimulate net basal to apical vectorial transport of sodium and fluid, resulting in tubular fluid secretion and cyst formation. Such mislocation has recently been reported in cultured ADPKD epithelium (Wilson and Sherwood, 1991; Wilson et al. 1991). In collaboration with Dr W. J. Nelson, we, therefore, sought to determine whether abnormal Na pump distribution was associated with cystic tubular maldevelopment in the CPK model (Avner et al., 1992). Such studies were of particular interest given the developmental stage specific formation of cysts in distinct nephron populations in this model, and the fact that Na+,K+-ATPase was reported to be transiently expressed in the apical membrane of collecting tubule epithelium during normal renal development (Holthofer, 1987; Minuth et al., 1987). In addition, the Na+,K+-ATPase is sorted to both apical and basal-lateral domains during establishment of polarity in MDCK cells, a canine renal epithelial cell line (Hammerton et al., 1991).

In these studies, kidney tissue was obtained from control C57BL/6J and cystic CPK mice at 7 postnatal stages: days 0 (newborn), 3, 5, 8, 10, 12 and 21. In CPK mice, day 0 through 5 reflect a proximal and early collecting tubule stage of cystic development, days 8-12 represent predominant cystic collecting tubule development, and day 21 represents the terminal phase of cystic disease (Avner et al., 1987a). Sequential serial sections cut parallel to the long axis of the kidney were stained with antibodies specific for either the a or b subunit of the Na+,K+-ATPase, biotiny-

lated lectins and a series of antibodies to apical and basal lateral membrane marker proteins. Apical membrane markers included γ-glutamyltranspeptidase, GP-135, and the lectins *Lotus tetragonologbus* agglutinin (LTA) and *Dolichos biflorus* agglutinin (DBA). Basolateral domain markers included ZO1, type 4 collagen, laminin, entactin, band 3 anion exchanger, and carbonic anhydrase II. Staining patterns were evaluated separately in outer cortical, inner cortical and medullary zones, which permitted direct comparison of nephron segments in control and cystic tissue at similar developmental stages. Distributions of Na+,K+-ATPase subunits were compared in proximal tubules, proximal tubular cysts, collecting tubules and collecting tubule cysts through systematic evaluation of lectin profiled serial sections. By this method, lectin staining patterns allow clear discrimination of proximal tubules and proximal tubule cysts (LTA positive, DBA negative) from collecting tubule and collecting tubule cysts (LTA negative, DBA positive) in developing murine renal tissue (Avner and Sweeney, 1990; Sweeney and Avner, 1991).

Analysis of control proximal tubules demonstrated restriction of both the α1 and β1 subunits of Na+,K+-ATPase to the basal-lateral membrane domain at all developmental stages (Fig. 1A). Similarly, in cystic CPK proximal tubules, Na+,K+-ATPase subunits were expressed exclusively in basal-lateral membranes (Fig. 1B). Apical membrane expression of Na+,K+-ATPase subunits was not detected in control proximal tubules or unaffected or cystic CPK proximal tubules at any developmental stage. Analysis of other marker proteins of the apical or basal-lateral membrane domain revealed normal distributions in proximal tubule cells.

In the majority of control collecting tubules both α1 and

β1 subunits of Na$^+$,K$^+$-ATPase were localized to the basal-lateral membrane of cells in all nephrogenic zones. However, a subpopulation of control collecting tubules in the outer and inner cortical zones of active tubulogenesis demonstrated apical-lateral as well as low intensity basal membrane staining of both Na$^+$,K$^+$-ATPase subunits (Figs 1C and 2A,B). Apical Na$^+$,K$^+$-ATPase expression was observed in a maximum of 16% of outer cortical, 6% of inner cortical and 2% of medullary collecting tubules at days 0 through 5 (Fig. 2). In all zones, apical membrane Na$^+$,K$^+$-ATPase staining declined progressively at subsequent developmental stages as the normal basal-lateral membrane staining pattern became prominent. These data demonstrate that Na$^+$,K$^+$-ATPase is transiently localized to both apical and lateral membranes of epithelial cells as a normal feature of renal collecting tubule, but not proximal tubule, development. Apical membrane Na$^+$,K$^+$-ATPase expression is a normal, transient phenotypic feature of early collecting tubule differentiation that is lost with subsequent cell maturation.

In cystic CPK collecting tubules, apical and lateral membrane staining of Na$^+$,K$^+$-ATPase α1 and β1 subunits was significantly increased when compared with control tubules (Figs 1D and 2). A maximum of 63% of medullary cystic tubules, 46% of inner cortical, and 47% of outer cortical collecting tubule cysts expressed apical membrane Na$^+$,K$^+$-ATPase. Significant differences were present between Na$^+$,K$^+$-ATPase distributions in cystic and control collecting tubules at progressive developmental stages (Fig. 2). In all nephrogenic zones, the percentage of cystic collecting tubules with apical membrane Na$^+$,K$^+$-ATPase distribution decreased over time paralleling the normal developmental pattern seen in control collecting tubules. No abnormalities in immunolocalization of other apical or basal lateral cell surface marker proteins were detected at any stage of development in control or cystic collecting tubules. Like immature control collecting tubules, cystic collecting tubules demonstrated apical and lateral membrane Na$^+$,K$^+$-ATPase expression. In parallel with control collecting tubules, the percentage of cystic collecting tubules with apical and lateral membrane Na$^+$,K$^+$-ATPase expression decreased in relation to the total cystic nephron population at progressive developmental stages. Thus, a large proportion of cystic collecting tubules exhibit a relatively undifferentiated phenotype in terms of the membrane distribution of Na$^+$,K$^+$-ATPase. This conclusion is consistent with recent reports that cystic CPK collecting tubule epithelium exhibits elevated steady state mRNA levels of the SGP2 gene and a variety of protooncogenes that are normally expressed during an early stage of collecting tubule differentiation (Cowley et al., 1991; Harding et al., 1991). Further, ultrastructural analysis of cystic CPK collecting tubules reveals characteristic anatomical features of a relatively undifferentiated epithelium (Fig. 3).

Distributions of other apical or basolateral membrane marker proteins were unaffected in immature control and cystic collecting tubule epithelial cells. Apical membrane distribution is, thus, not a result of general deregulation of mechanisms involved in establishing and maintaining cell surface polarity. Further, the fact that Na$^+$,K$^+$-ATPase distribution is restricted to the basal lateral membrane of both normal and cystic proximal tubular epithelium indicates that CPK cells are capable of normal Na$^+$,K$^+$-ATPase sorting. On the basis of these data we have speculated that the sorting pathway of Na$^+$,K$^+$-ATPase is the same in normal and cystic epithelial cells, but that Na$^+$,K$^+$-ATPase retention in the apical membrane is transient in normal development, but persists in cystic epithelium. At present, it is not clear whether retention of Na$^+$,K$^+$-ATPase on the apical membrane during normal collecting tubule development or in cystic tubule epithelial cells is due to alterations the assembly of the membrane cytoskeleton at that membrane. Similarly, it is not known whether the distribution of glycosphingolipids is altered in the apical membrane of immature control or cystic tubule cells, or whether retained apical membrane Na$^+$,K$^+$-ATPase functions as an active Na pump. Studies are currently underway to characterize the distribution of membrane cytoskeletal proteins and glycosphingolipids in control and cystic epithelial cells, and determine whether Na$^+$,K$^+$-ATPase activity is affected by its apical membrane microenvironment.

CONCLUSION

On the basis of our studies to date, we conclude that increased basal-lateral membrane Na$^+$,K$^+$-ATPase activity in cystic kidney proximal tubule epithelia may drive organic anion secretion with consequent intratubular fluid accumulation. Further, increased apical membrane Na$^+$,K$^+$-ATPase expression in cystic kidney collecting tubule epithelia may be a marker of the relatively undifferentiated phenotype of cyst lining cells. If such apically expressed enzyme is active, it may have pathogenic import in collecting tubule cyst formation and progressive enlargement by stimulating net basal to apical vectorial solute and fluid transport.

The work described in this review was supported by National Institutes of Health grants DK34891 and DK 44875. The author acknowledges the excellent secretarial assistance of Ms Debbie McNamara in manuscript preparation.

REFERENCES

Avner, E. D. (1988). Renal cystic disease: insights from recent experimental investigations. *Nephron* **48**, 89-93.

Avner, E. D. (1993). Renal developmental diseases. *Semin. Nephrol.* **13**, (in press).

Avner, E. D., McAteer, J. A. and Evan, A. P. (1990). Models of cysts and cystic kidneys. In *The Cystic Kidney* (ed. K. D. Gardner and J. Bernstein), pp. 55-98. Dordrecht, The Netherlands: Kluwer.

Avner, E. D., Studinicki, F. M., Young, M. C., Sweeney, W. E., Piesco, N. P., Ellis, D and Fetterman, G. H. (1987a). Congenital murine polycystic kidney disease: I. The ontogeny of tubular cyst formation. *Pediatr. Nephrol.* **1**, 587-596.

Avner, E. D. and Sweeney, W. E. (1990). Polypeptide growth factors in metanephric growth and segmental nephron differentiation. *Pediatr. Nephrol.* **4**, 372-377.

Avner, E. D., Sweeney, W. E., Jr and Ellis, D. (1989). In vitro modulation of tubular cyst regression in murine polycystic kidney disease. *Kidney Int.* **36**, 960-968

Avner, E. D., Sweeney, W. E., Finegold, D. N., Piesco, N. P. and Ellis, D. (1985). Sodium-potassium ATPase activity mediates cyst formation in metanephric organ culture. *Kidney Int.* **28**, 447-455.

Avner, E. D., Sweeney, W. E. and Nelson, W. J. (1992). Abnormal sodium pump distribution during renal tubulogenesis in congenital murine polycystic disease. *Proc. Nat. Acad. Sci. USA* **89**, 7447-7451.

Avner, E. D., Sweeney, W. E., Piesco, N. P. and Ellis, D. (1987b). Triiodothyronine-induced cyst formation in metanephric organ culture: the role of increased Na$^+$,K$^+$-ATPase activity. *J. Lab. Clin. Med.* **109**, 441-454.

Avner, E. D., Sweeney, W. E. Jr, Young, M. D. and Ellis, D. (1988). Congenital murine polycystic kidney disease. II. Pathogenesis of tubular cyst formation. *Pediatr. Nephrol.* **2**, 210-218.

Cowley, B. D., Chadwich, L. J. and Calvet, J. P. (1991). Elevated protooncogene expression in polycystic kidneys of the C57BL/6J (cpk) mouse. *J. Amer. Soc. Nephrol.* **1**, 1048-1053.

Germino, G. G. and Somlo, S. (1992). A positional cloning approach to inherited renal disease. *Semin. Nephrol.* **12**, 541-553.

Hammerton, R. W., Krzeminski, K. A., Mays, R. W. and Nelson, W. J. (1991). A mechanism for regulating cell surface distribution of Na-K-ATPase in polarized epithelial cells. *Science* **254**, 847-850.

Harding, M. A., Chadwick, L. J., Gattone, V. H. and Calvet, J. P. (1991). The SGP-2 gene is developmentally regulated in the mouse kidney and abnormally expressed in collecting duct cysts in polycystic kidney disease. *Dev. Biol.* **146**, 483-490.

Holthofer, H. (1987). Ontogeny of cell type-specific enzyme reactivities in kidney collecting ducts. *Pediatr. Res.* **22**, 504-508.

Minuth, W. W., Gross, P., Gilbert, P. and Kashgarian, M. (1987).

Expression of the α-subunit of Na/K-ATPase in renal collecting duct epithelium during development. *Kidney Int.* **31**, 1104-1112.

Preminger, G. M., Koch, W. E., Fried, F. A., McFarland, E., Murphy, E. D. and Mandell, J. (1982). Murine congenital polycystic kidney disease: a model for studying development of cystic disease. *J. Urol.* **127**, 556-560.

Russell, E. S. and McFarland, E. C. (1977). Cystic kidneys. *Mouse Newsletter* **56**, 40-43.

Skou, J. C. and Esmann, M. (1992). The Na,K-ATPase. *J. Bioenerg. Biomembr.* **24**, 249-261.

Sweeney, W. E. and Avner, E. D. (1991). Intact organ culture of murine metanephros. *J. Tiss. Cult. Meth.* **13**, 163-168.

Welling, L. W. (1990). Pathogenesis of cysts and cystic kidneys. In *The Cystic Kidney* (ed. K. D. Gardner and J Bernstein), pp. 99-116. Dordrecht, The Netherlands: Kluwer.

Welling, L. W. and Grantham, J. J. (1991). Cystic and developmental diseases of the kidney. In *The Kidney*, 4th edn (ed. B. M. Brenner and F. J. Rector), pp. 1657-1694. Philadelphia: W. B. Saunders.

Wilson, P. D. and Sherwood, A. C. (1991). Tubulocystic epithelium. *Kidney Int.* **39**, 450-463.

Wilson, P. D., Sherwood, A. C., Palla, K., Du, J., Watson, R. and Norman, J. T. (1991). Reversed polarity of Na$^+$,K$^+$-ATPase: mislocation to apical plasma membranes in human polycystic kidney disease epithelia. *Amer. J. Physiol.* **260**, F1-F11.

Journal of Cell Science, Supplement 17, 223-228 (1993)
Printed in Great Britain © The Company of Biologists Limited 1993

Analysis of the *trk* NGF receptor tyrosine kinase using recombinant fusion proteins

Curt M. Horvath, Amy Wolven, Debbie Machadeo, Julie Huber, Lana Boter, Marta Benedetti, Barbara Hempstead and Moses V. Chao

Department of Cell Biology and Anatomy, Hematology/Oncology Division, Cornell University Medical College, 1300 York Avenue, New York 10021, USA

SUMMARY

Nerve growth factor (NGF) represents a family of structurally related trophic factors, including brain-derived neurotrophin factor (BDNF), neurotrophin-3 (NT-3), NT-4, and NT-5. These neurotrophin factors interact with two classes of receptors, the *trk* receptor tyrosine kinase family, and the low affinity p75 neurotrophin receptor. To study potential ligand-receptor interactions, recombinant *trk* fusion proteins have been constructed, and pan-*trk* polyclonal antisera directed against the cytoplasmic tyrosine kinase domain have been generated. The recombinant proteins were assessed for in vitro kinase activity and for the ability of K-252a to inhibit phosphorylation. Antibodies made against the fusion protein recognize all *trk* family members, and are effective in immunoprecipitation of affinity-crosslinked receptors. Comparative crosslinking indicates that NGF can recognize all *trk* receptor members, illustrating the large number of potential ligand-receptor interactions between neurotrophins and their receptors.

Key words: *trk* receptor, NGF, tyrosine kinase, recombinant fusion protein

INTRODUCTION

The classic studies on nerve growth factor (NGF) defined the essential roles of survival and differentiation factors during development of the nervous system (Levi-Montalcini, 1987; Thoenen et al., 1987). The biological actions of NGF include survival of embryonic and adult neurons and induction of neurite outgrowth and neurotransmitter enzymes. The primary target populations in the peripheral nervous system include neural crest-derived sensory neurons and sympathetic neurons. In the central nervous system, NGF is capable of influencing cholinergic neurons in the basal forebrain by the induction of choline acetyltransferase (ChAT) activity (Mobley et al., 1985; Martinez et al., 1987). Accumulating evidence indicates that NGF also displays effects upon selective cell populations in the immune and endocrine systems (Levi-Montalcini et al., 1990).

An essential prerequisite for the actions of NGF is the presence of functional receptors on responsive cells. Two NGF receptors exist that are represented by transmembrane glycoproteins of M_r 75,000 (p75[NGFR]) and 140,000 (p140[trk]; a receptor tyrosine kinase encoded by a proto-oncogene). Both receptor proteins bind NGF, and are co-expressed in vivo in cells responsive to NGF, such as sympathetic ganglia (Schechterson and Bothwell, 1992), sensory ganglia (Buck et al., 1988; Verge et al., 1992; Martin-Zanca et al., 1990), and basal forebrain neurons (Holtzman et al., 1992). PC12 cells also express both p75[NGFR] and p140[trk] (Kaplan

et al., 1991a,b; Klein et al., 1991a). Examples where *trk* is expressed in the absence of p75[NGFR] have been reported (Birren et al., 1992), indicating that p140[trk] can function with or without the low affinity p75 NGF receptor.

The *trk* proto-oncogene product is the NGF receptor. The p75[NGFR] serves as a receptor for all neurotrophins (Rodriguez-Tebar et al., 1990). Both receptors bind NGF individually with low affinity, $K_d \approx 10^{-9}\text{-}10^{-10}$ M (Kaplan et al., 1991b; Hempstead et al., 1991), but the p140[trk] receptor is capable of high affinity site formation, either in the absence (Klein et al., 1991a) or in the presence of p75 receptors (Hempstead et al., 1991). Binding of NGF to p140[trk] results in the autophosphorylation of tyrosine residues on *trk* and cellular protein substrates.

Related molecules to *trk*, such as *trk*B and *trk*C, serve as receptors to other related neurotrophin factors, BDNF, NT-3, NT-4, and NT-5 but not NGF (Soppet et al., 1991; Squinto et al., 1991; Klein et al., 1991b; Cordon-Cardo et al., 1991; Lamballe et al., 1991; Ip et al., 1993), and these *trk* family members bear considerable resemblance to p140[trk] molecule, not only in the consensus tyrosine kinase domain, but also the extracellular ligand-binding domain. Consistent with the identity of BDNF and NT-3 as ligands for these receptors is the highly specific expression of *trk*B (Klein et al., 1989) and *trk*C (Lamballe et al., 1991) in the central nervous system. BDNF (Leibrock et al., 1989) and other closely related neurotrophins such as NT-3, NT-4, and NT-5 display similar biological effects upon distinct but overlapping populations of neuronal cells (Barde, 1989).

Since the neurotrophins and their receptor tyrosine kinases are so closely related in sequence and structure, it is not surprising that a considerable amount of crossreactivity has been detected (Chao, 1992a). For example, *trk*B is the receptor for BNDF (Soppet et al., 1991; Klein et al., 1991b; Squinto et al., 1991), however, NT-3, NT-4 and NT-5 have the capability of binding to *trk*B and initiating biological responses in fibroblast cells (Ip et al., 1993). It is unlikely that all interactions occur in vivo in neuronal cell populations. NT-3 is the most diverse in its ability to bind and stimulate all *trk* family members in heterologous cells.

To study the structural relatedness of the *trk* family of receptors, recombinant fusion proteins have been generated. These fusion proteins utilized the bacterial glutathione S-transferase protein (Smith and Johnson, 1988) as a means to overexpressing defined domains of human p140^{trk}. Here we report that the catalytic domain alone of p140^{trk} serves as the target for a specific inhibitor of NGF action, K-252a (Koizumi et al., 1988; Berg et al., 1992). Antisera against the tyrosine kinase domain of p140^{trk} can effectively recognize other *trk* tyrosine kinase receptors in this subfamily. Moreover, affinity crosslinking experiments indicate that NGF has the potential for interacting with all *trk* family members in heterologous cell types.

MATERIALS AND METHODS

Construction of fusion proteins

Restriction fragments from a full length human *trk* cDNA in the vector pDM69 (Martin-Zanca et al., 1989) were introduced into pGEX3X or pGEX2T to generate fusion proteins. To express the extracellular domain of p140^{trk}, a 1 kb *Ava*I restriction fragment (from amino acids 12 to 387) was introduced in-frame in the *Sma*I site of pGEX2T. The resulting fusion protein was of predicted M_r of 61,960. The entire cytoplasmic portion of p140^{trk} was represented by a GST/*Ear*I construct (367 amino acids of *trk*), made by digestion of pDM69 with *Ear*I and removal of the 5'-overhang by S$_1$ nuclease treatment, and released by *Eco*RI digestion. This fragment was introduced into pGEX3X, digested with *Bam*HI, S$_1$ nuclease, followed by *Eco*RI digestion. The junction sequence was verified by DNA sequencing to be 5'-CGTGGTACG-3'. This fusion protein has a predicted M_r of 66,370.

Additional fragments representing C-terminal sequences of p140^{trk} were employed after digestion at unique sites - *Nco*I (1911 bp), *Eco*RV (2122 bp), *Bgl*II (2158 bp), and *Kpn*I (2285 bp). The *Nco*I fragment was prepared after digestion of pDM69 with *Nco*I, incubation with the Klenow fragment of DNA Polymerase I, and *Eco*RI digestion. The *Nco*I-*Eco*RI gel purified insert was ligated into *Sma*I and *Eco*I digested pGEX3X. The junction sequence was in frame and was found to be 5'-CCCCATGGA-3'. The resulting fusion protein (M_r 47,890) contained 199 amino acids of *trk*. The *Eco*RV fragment was obtained after digestion with *Eco*RV and *Eco*RI, and subcloned into pGEX3X, digested with *Sma* and *Eco*RI. The junction sequence was 5'-CCCATC-3', and the fusion protein resulted in a protein with a predicted M_r of 40,080, with 128 amino acids of *trk*. The GST/*Bgl*II construct contained a *Bgl*II-*Eco*RI fragment from pDM69 subcloned into *Bam*HI/*Eco*RI-digested pGEX3X. The fusion protein product contains 81 amino acids of *trk* and has a predicted M_r of 34,910. The GST/*Kpn*I fusion construct was generated after *Kpn*I digestion and S$_1$ nuclease treatment, and *Eco*RI digestion of pDM69. The fragment was gel purified and introduced into pGEX3X, which had been digested with *Sma*I and *Eco*RI. The fusion protein product con-

tained the last 73 amino acids of *trk*, and has a predicted M_r of 34,030.

Production of antibodies

Bacterial cultures expressing pGEX fusion proteins were grown in 50 µg/ml ampicillin and induced with 100 µM IPTG. Induced bacteria were lysed and centrifuged for 10 minutes. The fusion proteins were separated by preparative polyacrylamide/SDS gels, and electroeluted. Immunizations of rabbits were carried out by subcutaneous injections of emulsified fusion protein (Pocono Rabbit Farm), with boosts every 2-3 weeks. Antisera was collected six weeks after the initial injection.

In vitro phosphorylation

Bacterial cultures were grown for 3-5 hours and treated with IPTG for an additional hour, before harvest and lysis. The pGEX-encoded fusion proteins were isolated using glutathione-coupled beads, and washed in 1× kinase buffer containing 20 mM Hepes, pH 7.4, 25 mM NaCl, 0.05% Triton X-100, 1% glycerol, 10 mM MgCl$_2$, 10 mM MnCl$_2$. Phosphorylation was initiated with the addition of [γ-^{32}P]ATP and allowed to incubate for 15 minutes at 37°C. The effect of K-252a (Kamiya Biochemicals, Thousand Oaks, CA) on protein kinase activity was assayed by resuspending the beads in kinase buffer containing K-252a at a final concentration of 1 µM.

Affinity crosslinking

Crosslinking was carried out on fibroblast cells expressing different *trk* receptor family members with ^{125}I-labelled NGF prepared by lactoperoxidase treatment. Transfected cells were incubated with 1 nM ^{125}I-labelled NGF for 30 minutes at room temperature in the presence of EDAC (1-ethyl-3-(3-dimethylaminopropyl)-carbodimide hydrochloride (Pierce) or DSS, disuccinimidyl suberate, or both reagents simultaneously). The crosslinking reactions were stopped by quenching with PBS + 50 mM lysine at 4°C, and the cells were then pelleted and washed three times in PBS-lysine. The final pellet of cells was resuspended in lysis buffer (10 mM, pH 7.6, 1% NP-40, 0.4% deoxycholate, 66 mM EDTA, 1 mM PMSF, 1 mM leupeptin, and 1 mM aprotinin), and was allowed to sit on ice for 20 minutes. After a high speed final centrifugation for 15 minutes, supernatants were incubated with anti-NGF polyclonal antibodies (Collaborative Research), or anti-*trk* antibodies, as described in the text, and the immune complexes precipitated with Protein A-Sepharose beads (Sigma). The samples were subjected to gel electrophoresis on 7% acrylamide/SDS gels, and crosslinked products visualized after exposure on X-ray film.

RESULTS

The *trk* NGF receptor is a heavily glycosylated transmembrane protein (Martin-Zanca et al., 1989) that exhibits a signal peptide and an extracellular domain distinguished by two short cysteine-rich clusters in the amino terminus, which are separated by three 24 amino acid leucine-rich repeats. Thirteen potential *N*-linked glycosylation sites exist, as well as two consensus IgG domains (Schneider and Schweiger, 1991), and a single transmembrane domain. Cysteine residues in the extracellular domain are conserved among *trk* (or *trk*A), *trk*B, and *trk*C; there is more than 50% conservation in the ligand-binding domains in this subfamily. The catalytic tyrosine kinase domains contain a consensus ATP-binding site and are characterized by dual tyro-

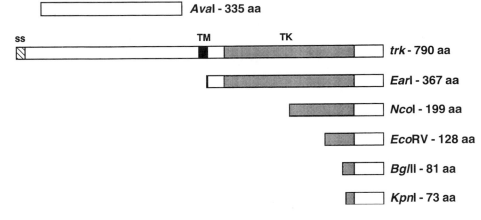

*Ava*I - 335 aa

ss   TM   TK

trk - 790 aa

*Ear*I - 367 aa

*Nco*I - 199 aa

*Eco*RV - 128 aa

*Bgl*II - 81 aa

*Kpn*I - 73 aa

Fig. 1. Trk fusion proteins were produced using the glutathione S-transferase protein. An extracellular, as well as intracellular portions of the human p140^{trk} were constructed and overexpressed after IPTG induction. TM, transmembrane domain; ss, signal peptide; TK, tyrosine kinase.

sine residues at the putative autophosphorylation site, and a short C-terminal tail (Martin-Zanca et al., 1989).

To express discrete domains of the extracellular and intracellular regions of p140^{trk}, a series of fusion proteins was constructed. The extracellular domain of p140^{trk} was represented by an *Ava*I fragment that was introduced into pGEX2X (Fig. 1). This domain extended from amino acid 51, after the first cysteine cluster, to amino acid 387, twenty amino acids above the membrane spanning domain. A series of intracellular fusion proteins was made using selected restriction sites in the human *trk* cDNA. The *Ear*I construct begins at the transmembrane sequence and extends to the C-terminal sequence, and includes the entire tyrosine kinase domain. Other fusion proteins represented smaller C-terminal regions of the kinase domain. All proteins were readily expressed with varying degrees of solubility.

The cytoplasmic fusion proteins were tested for in vitro phosphorylation ability after partial purification on glutathione-coupled beads. Only the full length *Ear*I fusion protein demonstated detectable phosphorylation after incubation with [γ-^{32}P]ATP (Fig. 2A). Although the level of phosphorylation was low, it was readily detectable above background levels. In keeping with the lack of key kinase sequences, the smaller fusion proteins did not display any detectable phosphorylation (Fig. 2B) by this in vitro assay.

Effect of K252-a

The alkaloid K252-a has been shown to inhibit NGF-induced neurite outgrowth and signaling in PC12 cells (Koizumi et al., 1988), and also p140^{trk} autophosphorylation (Berg et al., 1992; Tapley et al., 1992; Nye et al., 1992). The effects of K-252a appear to be specific for the *trk* family of receptor tyrosine kinases, as K-252a does not affect EGF- and FGF-induced phosphorylation in PC12 cells. In addition, K-252a has a direct effect upon the p140^{trk} receptor tyrosine kinase, since it inhibits kinase activity in in vitro phosphorylation reactions (Berg et al., 1992).

These results raise the possibility that K-252a acts directly upon the catalytic activity of p140^{trk}. To test this possibility, the GST/*Ear*I construct was incubated with [γ-^{32}P]ATP in the presence of 1 nM K-252a. The amount of phosphorylated fusion protein was significantly decreased with K-252a (Fig. 2A), suggesting that the inhibition may

A

K252a   −   +

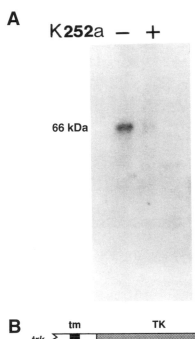

66 kDa

B

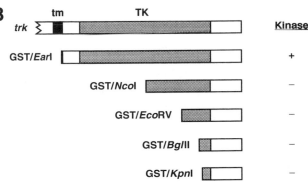

trk

GST/*Ear*I   +

GST/*Nco*I   −

GST/*Eco*RV   −

GST/*Bgl*II   −

GST/*Kpn*I   −

Kinase

Fig. 2. In vitro phosphorylation of recombinant *trk* fusion proteins. (A) The 66 kDa GST/*Ear*I fusion protein was assessed for phosphorylation in in vitro kinase assays (see Berg et al., 1992). The effect of K-252a on phosphorylation was also assayed after gel electrophoresis of the recombinant fusion protein. (B) A summary of the in vitro kinase assay with the *trk* fusion proteins.

have interfered with the cytoplasmic domain and the in vitro kinase activity of *trk*. This result agrees with experiments in PC12 cells, in which immunoprecipitated p140^{trk} kinase activity could be blocked by K-252a treatment (Berg et al., 1992). Other fusion proteins did not give rise to detectable

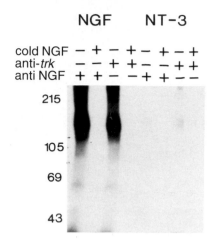

Fig. 3. Affinity crosslinking of iodinated NGF and NT-3. Equal numbers of fibroblast cells (3T3*trk* (2×10⁶) cells were incubated with ¹²⁵I-labelled NGF or ¹²⁵I-labelled NT-3 for 30 minutes and treated to DSS crosslinking. The crosslinked species were subjected to immunoprecipitation with anti-NGF (Collaborative) or anti-*trk* antibodies and analyzed by polyacrylamide gel electrophoresis.

levels of phosphorylation (Fig. 2B) and were unaffected by similar K-252a treatment.

A plausible mechanism by which K-252a may interfere with *trk* autophosphorylation, and not affect other tyrosine kinases encoded by receptors for FGF and EGF, may lie in the sequence of the *trk* tyrosine kinase. In addition to the consensus ATP-binding site, GEGAFGKV at amino acid 511, a second potential site, GSGLQGHI, has been observed at residue 477 (Martin-Zanca et al., 1989). This second site is not observed in other receptor tyrosine kinases, and may provide a means for K-252a to interfere with normal ATP binding.

Affinity crosslinking

Several affinity crosslinking reagents have historically been used to characterize NGF receptors. The most reactive and widely used reagents have compounds, such as ethyl-3-dimethylaminopropyl-carbodiimide (EDAC) and disuccimidyl suberate (DSS). Using affinity crosslinking of ¹²⁵I-labelled NGF with EDAC, the major radioiodinated complex isolated from neurons and tumor cell lines has an apparent molecular mass of 100 kDa (Grob et al., 1983; Taniuchi et al., 1986; Green and Greene, 1986). Treatment with DSS selectively crosslinks ¹²⁵I-labelled NGF with p140^{trk} to produce a species of 160 kDa (Meakin and Shooter, 1991).

Antisera generated against the human *trk* cytoplasmic protein were tested for its ability to immunoprecipitate p140^{trk} after affinity crosslinking. Fibroblast 3T3 cells expressing p140^{trk} were incubated with ¹²⁵I-labelled NGF and DSS, and subjected to immunoprecipitation with anti-*trk* polyclonal antibodies and compared with anti-NGF antibodies. Fig. 3 demonstrates that both antibodies are equally effective in immmunoprecipitation of the crosslinked NGF-*trk* complex of 160 kDa. These complexes were specific, since an excess of unlabelled NGF eliminated the crosslinked species.

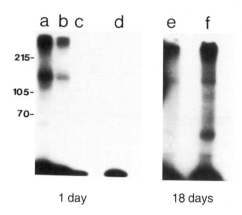

Fig. 4. Binding of NGF to *trk* family members. ¹²⁵I-labelled NGF (3500 cpm/fmole) at a concentration of 1 nM was incubated with fibroblast cells expressing either *trk*, *trk*B, or *trk*C, crosslinked with DSS and EDAC, and immunoprecipitated with antisera against NGF or GST/*trk*. (a) *trk* crosslinked with NGF, immunoprecipitated with anti-NGF antibodies. (b) *trk* immunoprecipitated with anti-*trk*. (c) Cells expressing *trk*B were crosslinked with NGF, immunoprecipitated with anti-NGF. (d) Cells expressing *trk*C were crosslinked with NGF, and the crosslinked species were immunoprecipiated with anti-NGF antibodies. (e,f) Same as (c) and (d), except the X-ray exposure was 18 days at −70°C, instead of 1 day.

NT-3 is known to interact with p140^{trk}, in addition to its principal receptor, *trk*C (Lamballe et al., 1991). We compared the crosslinking of ¹²⁵I-labelled NT-3 to p140^{trk} to NGF, and found that although the relative levels of crosslinked *trk* were diminished, binding of ¹²⁵I-labelled NT-3 to *trk* could also be detected (Fig. 3). This result is consistent with previous observations of increased *trk* autophosphorylation by NT-3 (Cordon-Cardo et al., 1991). Antibodies to NGF were equally effective in immunoprecipitating this complex, and unlabelled NGF was able to compete for the binding of NT-3 and *trk*. The ability of anti-NGF antibodies to recognize NT-3 is consistent with many observations that NGF antisera are not specific to NGF, but recognize other neurotrophins (Acheson et al., 1991).

Antisera against the *trk* cytoplasmic domain was equally effective in recognizing *trk*, as well as *trk*B and *trk*C. Fibroblast cells expressing each of the *trk* receptors were crosslinked with either iodinated NGF or NT-3, and the crosslinked *trk* species was immunoprecipitated with polyclonal antibodies made against the *trk* NGF receptor. In all cases, the antibody specifically recognized each *trk* receptor (data not shown). These experiments demonstrate the crossreactivity of these antibodies against a highly conserved domain.

The close structural relatedness of the *trk* receptors is further mirrored by the ability of each neurotrophin to bind to other family members. NGF and BDNF have traditionally been found to be very exclusive in interacting and stimulating p140^{trk} and p140^{trkB} receptor activities. However, NGF, which does not ordinarily give biological responses through *trk*B and *trk*C (Squinto et al., 1991; Klein et al., 1991b; Soppet et al., 1991; Lamballe et al., 1991), nevertheless, has the capability of weakly binding to *trk*B and *trk*C. When ^{125}I-labelled NGF is crosslinked in the presence of both DSS and EDAC to fibroblast cells expressing each of the three *trk* receptors, the strongest signal was observed with p140^{trk}. However, a long autoradiographic exposure indicates that both *trk*B and *trk*C are crosslinked with [^{125}I]NGF (Fig. 4). Each crosslinked species was immunoprecipitated with anti-GST/*Ear*I *trk* antibodies, demonstrating the ability of these antibodies to recognize similar family members. These experiments also illustrate that a large number of potential interactions between the neurotrophins and *trk* family members may occur in heterologous cells. In the nervous system, it is expected that much more specificity exists to ensure more exclusivity between each neurotrophin and its *trk* receptor.

DISCUSSION

Neurotrophin factors are known to interact specifically with *trk* tyrosine kinase family members, leading to neuronal differentiation and increased cell survival. Autophosphorylation of p140^{trk} in fibroblast cells is induced by not only NGF, but also NT-3 and NT-5 (Berkemeier et al., 1991). The results of this study indicate that antisera to NGF and to the consensus tyrosine kinase domain frequently will recognize related molecules and family members. A considerable amount of caution must be taken to clarify all the potential interactions and crossreactivities using antibody reagents, as well as molecular probes.

The existence of two different classes of neurotrophin receptors implies separate functions for the *trk* family of receptors and the low affinity p75 receptor (Meakin and Shooter, 1992; Chao 1992a). The role of the *trk* tyrosine kinase is to act as the signaling transducing receptor for NGF, and it has been shown to be necessary for NGF function. Initiation of NGF action depends upon increased tyrosine phosphorylation by p140^{trk}. Lack of expression of this receptor leads to NGF unresponsiveness, indicating that p140^{trk} function is essential for NGF signal transduction (Loeb et al., 1991). In contrast, the p75 receptor does not appear to signal independently (Hempstead et al., 1988), but can bind to all neurotrophin family members (Rodriguez et al., 1990, 1992). The p75^{NGFR} should be more appropriately considered as a neurotrophin receptor. Its function is to participate in formation of high affinity binding sites for NGF, and to assist in the discrimination between related neurotrophins. The low affinity p75 receptor may also participate in retrograde transport, and modulation of the tyrosine kinase activities of *trk*. The p75 receptors are expressed throughout development in a variety of diverse cell types (Bothwell, 1990), suggesting that this receptor must acting in a wider manner as a receptor for the family of neurotrophins.

A major unanswered question is how specificity of neurotrophin factors is dictated. The effect of K-252a upon *trk* autophosphorylation is unique among receptor tyrosine kinases, and implies that the initial signaling events carried out my neurotrophins are distinctive. How the signaling pathways differ from other growth factor-mediated events have yet to be determined (Chao, 1992b). The promiscuity of neurotrophin action exhibited in fibroblasts expressing *trk* or *trk*B suggest that neurotrophin action must be examined more closely in neuronal cell environments. The cellular context in which each *trk* tyrosine kinase is expressed will be an extremely important parameter in determining the biological functions of the neurotrophin factor family. It is anticipated that this question will be ultimately answered by examining the pattern of differential expression of *trk* family members, and the p75 neurotrophin receptor during development and maturity, and by determining how each neurotrophin-receptor interaction gives rise to distinctive signaling pathways to promote cell survival and differentiation.

We thank Drs Luis Parada and David Kaplan for reagents and cell lines expressing *trk* family members, and Dr Dionisio Martin-Zanca for the pDM69 expression plasmid. We are grateful to Chiron and Genentech for generously providing human recombinant NT-3. This work was supported by a Zenith Award from the Alzheimers Association, and grants from NIH and the Dorothy Rodbell Cohen Foundation.

REFERENCES

Acheson, A., Barker, P. A., Alderson, R. F., Miller, F. D. and Murphy, R. A. (1991). Detection of brain-derived neurotrophic factor-like activity in fibroblasts and Schwann cells: Inhibition by antibodies to NGF. *Neuron* **7**, 265-275.

Barde, Y.-A. (1989). Trophic factors and neuronal survival. *Neuron* **2**, 1525-1534.

Berg, M. M., Sternberg, D. W., Parada, L. F. and Chao, M. V. (1992). K-252a inhibits nerve growth factor-induced *trk* proto-oncogene tyrosine phosphorylation and kinase activity. *J. Biol. Chem.* **267**, 13-16.

Berkemeier, L. R., Winslow, J. W., Kaplan, D. R., Nikolics, K., Goedell, D. V. and Rosenthal, A. (1991). Neurotrophin-5: a novel neurotrophic factor that activates *trk* and *trk*B. *Neuron* **7**, 857-866.

Birren, S. J., Verdi, J. M. and Anderson, D. J. (1992). Membrane depolarization induces p140^{trk} and NGF responsiveness, but not p75^{NGFR}, in MAH cells. *Science* **257**, 395-397.

Bothwell, M. (1990). Tissue localization of nerve growth factor and nerve growth factor receptors. *Curr. Top. Microbiol. Immunol.* **165**, 55-70.

Buck, C. R., Martinez, H., Chao, M. V. and Black, I. B. (1988). Differential expression of the nerve growth factor receptor gene in the periphery and brain. *Proc. Nat. Acad. Sci. USA* **84**, 3060-3063.

Chao, M. V. (1992a). Neurotrophin receptors: A window into neuronal differentiation. *Neuron* **9**, 583-593.

Chao, M. V. (1992b). Growth factor signaling: where is the specificity? *Cell* **68**, 995-997.

Cordon-Cardo, C., Tapley, P., Jing, S., Nanduri, V., O'Rourke, E., Lamballe, F., Kovary, K., Klein, K., Jones, K. R., Reichardt, L. F. and Barbacid, M. (1991). The *trk* tyrosine protein kinase mediates the mitogenic properties of nerve growth factor and neurotrophin-3. *Cell* **66**, 173-183.

Green, S. H. and Greene, L. A. (1986). A single M_r=103, 000 ^{125}I-β-nerve growth factor-affinity-labeled species represents both the low and high affinity forms of the nerve growth factor receptor. *J. Biol. Chem.* **261**, 15316-15326.

Grob, P. M., Berlot, C. H. and Bothwell, M. A. (1983). Affinity labeling and partial purification of nerve growth factor receptors from rat pheochromocytoma and human melanoma cells. *Proc. Nat. Acad. Sci. USA* **80**, 6819-6823.

Hempstead, B. L., Patil, N., Olson, K. and Chao, M. V. (1988). Molecular analysis of the nerve growth factor receptor. *Cold Spring Harbor Symp. Quant. Biol.* **53**, 477-485.

Hempstead, B. L., Martin-Zanca, D., Kaplan, D., Parada, L. F. and Chao, M. V. (1991). High affinity NGF binding requires co-expression of the *trk* proto-oncogene and the low affinity NGF receptor. *Nature* **350**, 678-683.

Holtzman, D. M., Li. Y., Parada, L. F., Kinsman, S., Chen, C. K., Valletta, J. S., Zhou, J., Long, J. B. and Mobley, W. C. (1992). p140^{trk}

mRNA marks NGF-responsive forebrain neurons: evidence that *trk* gene expression is induced by NGF. *Neuron* **9**, 465-478.

Ip, N. Y., Stitt, T. N., Tapley, P., Klein, R., Glass, D. J., Fandl, J., Greene, L. A., Barbacid, M. and Yancopoulos, G. D. (1993). Similarities and differences in the way neurotrophins interact with the trk receptors in neuronal and nonneuronal cells. *Neuron* **10**, 137-149.

Kaplan, D. R., Martin-Zanca, D. and Parada, L. F. (1991a). Tyrosine phosporylation and tyrosine kinase activity of the *trk* proto-oncogene product induced by NGF. *Nature* **350**, 158-160.

Kaplan, D. R., Hempstead, B. L., Martin-Zanca, D., Chao, M. V. and Parada, L. F. (1991b). The *trk* proto-oncogene product: a signal transducing receptor for nerve growth factor. *Science* **252**, 554-558.

Klein, R., Parada, L. F., Coulier, F. and Barbacid, M. (1989). trkB, a novel tyrosine protein kinase receptor expressed during mouse neural development. *EMBO J.* **8**, 3701-3709.

Klein, R., Jing, S., Nanduri, V., O'Rourke, E. and Barbacid, M. (1991a). The *trk* proto-oncogene encodes a receptor for nerve growth factor. *Cell* **65**, 189-197.

Klein, R., Nanduri, V., Jing, S., Lamballe, F., Tapley, P., Bryant, S., Cordon-Cardo, C., Jones, K. R., Reichardt, L. F. and Barbacid, M. (1991b). The *trk*B tyrosine protein kinase is a receptor for brain-derived neurotrophic factor and neurotrophin-3. *Cell* **66**, 395-403.

Koizumi, S., Contreras, M. L., Matsuda, Y., Hama, T., Lazarovici, P. and Guroff, G. (1988). K-252a: a specific inhibitor of the action of nerve growth factor on PC12 cells. *J. Neurosci.* **8**, 715-721.

Lamballe, F., Klein, R. and Barbacid, M. (1991). trkC, a new member of the *trk* family of tyrosine protein kinases, is a receptor for neurotrophin-3. *Cell* **66**, 967-979.

Leibrock, J., Lottspeich, F., Hohn, A., Hofer, M., Hengerer, B., Masiakowski, P., Thoenen, H. and Barde, Y.-A. (1989). Molecular cloning and expression of brain-derived neurotrophic factor. *Nature* **341**, 149-152.

Levi-Montalcini, R. (1987). The nerve growth factor: Thirty-five years later. *Science* **237**, 1154-1164.

Levi-Montalcini, R., Aloe, L. and Alleva, E. (1990). A role for nerve growth factor in nervous, endocrine, and immune systems. *Prog. Neurol. Endo. Immunol.* **3**, 1-10.

Loeb, D., Martin-Zanca, D., Chao, M. V., Parada, L. F. and Greene, L. A. (1991). The *trk* proto-oncogene rescues NGF responsiveness in mutant NGF-nonresponsive PC12 cell lines. *Cell* **66**, 961-966.

Martinez, H. J., Dreyfus, C. F., Jonakait, G. M. and Black, I. B. (1987). Nerve growth factor selectively increases cholinergic markers but not neuropeptides in rat basal forebrain in culture. *Brain Res.* **412**, 295-301.

Martin-Zanca, D., Hughes, S. H. and Barbacid, M. (1986). A human oncogene formed by the fusion of truncated tropomyosin and protein tyrosine kinase sequences. *Nature* **319**, 743-77.

Martin-Zanca, D., Oskam, R., Mitra, G., Copeland, T. and Barbacid, M. (1989). Molecular and biochemical characterization of the human *trk* proto-oncogene. *Mol. Cell. Biol.* **9** 24-33.

Martin-Zanca, D., Barbacid, M. and Parada, L. F. (1990). Expression of the *trk* proto-onco gene is restricted to the sensory cranial and spinal ganglia of neural crest origin in mouse development. *Genes Dev.* **4**, 683-688.

Meakin, S. O. and Shooter, E. M. (1991). Molecular investigations on the high affinity nerve growth factor receptor. *Neuron* **6**, 153-163.

Meakin, S. O. and Shooter, E. M. (1992). The nerve growth factor family of receptors. *Trends Neurosci.*

Mobley, W. C., Rutkowski, J. L., Tennekoon, G. I., Buchanan, K. and Johnston, M. V. (1985). Choline acetyltransferase activity in striatum of neonatal rats increased by nerve growth factor. *Science* **229**, 284-287.

Nye, S. H., Squinto, S. P., Glass, D. J., Stitt, T. N., Hantzopoulos, P., Macchi, M. J., Lindsay, N. S., Ip, N. Y. and Yancopoulos, G. D. (1992). K-252a and staurosporine selectively block autophosphorylation of neurotrophin receptors and neurotrophin-mediated responses. *Mol. Biol. Cell* **3**, 677-686.

Rodriguez-Tebar, A., Dechant, G. and Barde, Y.-A. (1990). Binding of brain-derived neurotrophic factor to the nerve growth factor receptor. *Neuron* **4**, 187-192.

Rodriguez-Tebar, A., Dechant, G., Gotz, R. and Barde, Y.-A. (1992). Binding of neurotrophin-3 to its neuronal receptors and interactions with nerve growth factor and brain-derived neurotrophin factor. *EMBO J.* **11**, 917-922.

Schechterson, L. C. and Bothwell, M. A. (1992). Novel roles for neurotrophins are suggested by BDNF and NT-3 mRNA expression in developing neurons. *Neuron* **9**, 449-463.

Schneider, R. and Schweiger, M. (1991). A novel modular mosiac of cell adhesion motifs in the extracellular domains of the neurogenic *trk* and *trk*B tyrosine kinase receptors. *Oncogene* **6**, 1807-1811.

Smith, D. B. and Johnson, K. S. (1988). Single-step purification of polypeptides expressed in Escherichia coli as fusions with glutathione S-transferase. *Gene* **67**, 41-40.

Soppet, D., Escandon, E., Maragos, J., Middlemas, D. S., Reid, S. W., Blair, J., Burton, L. E., Stanton, B. R., Kaplan, D. R., Hunter, T., Nikolics, K. and Parada, L. F. (1991). The neurotrophin factors brain-derived neurotrophin factor and neurotrophin-3 are ligands for the *trk*B tyrosine kinase receptor. *Cell* **65**, 895-903.

Squinto, S. P., Stitt, T. N., Aldrich, T. H., Davis, S., Bianco, S. M., Radziejewski, C., Glass, D. J., Masiakowski, P., Furth, M. E., Valenzuela, D. M., DiStefano, P. S. and Yancopoulos, G. D. (1991). trkB encodes functional receptor for brain-derived neurotrophic factor and neurotrophin-3 but not nerve growth factor. *Cell* **65**, 885-893.

Tapley, P., Lamballe, F. and Barbacid, M. (1992). *Oncogene* **7**, 371-381.

Thoenen, H., Bandtlow, C. and Heumann, R. (1987). The physiological function of nerve growth factor in the central nervous system: comparison with the periphery. *Rev. Physiol. Biochem. Pharmacol.* **109**, 145-178.

Verge, V. M. K., Merlio, J. P., Grondin, J., Ernfors, P., Persson, H., Riopelle, R. J., Hokfelt, T. and Richardson, P. M. (1992). Co-localization of nerve growth factor binding sites, *trk* mRNA, and low affinity nerve growth factor receptor mRNA in primary sensory neurons: responses to injury, and infusion by nerve growth factor. *J. Neurosci.* **12**, 4011-4022.

Journal of Cell Science, Supplement 17, 229-233 (1993)
Printed in Great Britain © The Company of Biologists Limited 1993

Defective acidification of the biosynthetic pathway in cystic fibrosis

Jonathan Barasch* and Qais Al-Awqati

Departments of Medicine and Physiology, College of Physicians and Surgeons of Columbia University, 630 W 168th St, New York, NY 10032, USA

*Author for correspondence

SUMMARY

Cystic fibrosis is associated with defective epithelial sodium chloride and fluid secretion in epithelia. In addition, there is widespread reductions in sialylation of secreted proteins and increases in the sulfation and fucosylation of mucus glycoproteins. The major morbidity in the disease is due to the colonization of respiratory epithelia by Pseudomonas. The cystic fibrosis gene (CFTR) is a cyclic AMP activated Cl channel, which when mutated is retained in the endoplasmic reticulum. We postulate that this Cl channel is responsible for effective acidification of the Golgi. In CF cells, we demonstrate the Golgi pH is higher than in normal cells and suggest that the abnormalities in glycoprotein biosynthesis is due to changes in the kinetics of sialyl transferase, a pH sensitive enzyme. Defects in sialylation also result in decreased sialylation of glycolipids and asialogangliosides are potential Pseudomonas receptors.

Key words: chloride channel, Golgi acidification, cystic fibrosis, sialyl transferase

INTRODUCTION

All eukaryotic cells tested have one or more type of chloride channel. In some cells they are present in the plasma membrane where they participate in the control of cell volume (probably in most cells), membrane potential (in muscle and nerve) or the secretion of NaCl and water (in epithelia). In addition, chloride channels have been found in intracellular organelles such as endosomes, lysosomes and Golgi where they are present in parallel to an electrogenic proton translocating ATPase and hence can control the pH gradient and membrane potential of these organelles. Based on single channel behavior, chloride channels exhibit marked diversity in conductance, current-voltage relation and regulation by modulators. Using these functional criteria, it was found that a single cell might contain as many as three types of plasma membrane Cl⁻ channels, in addition to the one or more types of intracellular channels.

Recent studies have identified a number of molecules that code for Cl⁻ channels that do not belong to a single family. The GABA and glycine receptors resembles the nicotinic receptor, a cation channel (Olsen and Tobin, 1990). The cystic fibrosis gene product (CFTR) and the multidrug resistance gene bear similarities to ATP-dependent solute transporters (Riordan, 1992; Welsh et al., 1992). A family of voltage-sensitive chloride channels found in *Torpedo* electric organ, mammalian muscle and epithelial cells do not resemble any known sequences (Steinmayer et al., 1991). Porins in outer membranes of bacteria and mitochondria do not even contain 'canonical' transmembrane hydrophobic helices (Weiss and Schulz, 1992). Neither does a channel

recently cloned from MDCK epithelia (Paulmichl et al., 1992). This diversity suggests that there may be even more types of chloride channels to be discovered. Indeed, using the biochemical approach of solubilization and reconstitution, we (Landry et al., 1989, 1993) and others (Ran and Benos, 1991) have found two additional Cl⁻ channels in epithelial cells.

Most of the studies referred to above were directed towards the identification of plasma membrane Cl⁻ channels. We had discovered that Golgi, endosomes and secretory granules contain chloride channels, which are intimately involved in the control of the pH gradient generated by the H⁺-ATPase (Glickman et al., 1983). That this Cl⁻ channel can control vacuolar pH in vivo was shown when we found that secretagogues induce acidification of secretory granules by opening Cl⁻ channels (Barasch et al., 1988). Since we had demonstrated that Golgi vesicles also contain Cl⁻ channels and they were not maximally acidified, we speculated that control of Golgi pH might profoundly affect the function of Golgi enzymes, many of which are pH-sensitive (Al-Awqati, 1986).

To provide molecular reagents for further analyses of these processes we decided to purify the Cl⁻ channel of intracellular organelles, which we term here a vacuolar chloride channel. We do not know whether there is a single molecular species that codes for vacuolar Cl⁻ channels or whether there are many. Given the level of molecular diversity in Cl⁻ channels already identified, it is probable that there are several kinds of intracellular Cl⁻ channels. We used an inhibitor derived from ethacrynic acid, IAA-94, to purify the drug binding proteins from bovine kidney cortex intracellular vesicles and showed by reconstitution that the affinity-purified proteins contain the Cl^- channel (Landry et al., 1989, 1987). Two proteins were eliminated as drug-binding proteins and one of the remaining, a 64 kDa protein (p64), generated a specific antibody. This antibody was able to deplete all Cl^- channel activity from bovine kidney cortex, suggesting that it is a necessary component of the vacuolar channel (Redhead et al., 1992). We cloned and sequenced the cDNA for p64 and obtained a novel sequence of a membrane protein. Using antibodies we found that p64 is located in the perinuclear region (probably Golgi) and in the apical membrane of some epithelial cells (Landry et al., 1993).

CYSTIC FIBROSIS

The discovery that the phenotypic defect in cystic fibrosis is an abnormality of activation of an epithelial Cl^- channel has galvanized the field of study of Cl^- channels and awarded it a high visibility (Schoumacher et al., 1987; Welsh and Liedtke, 1986). The gene, CFTR, was rapidly identified (Welsh et al., 1986) and its function was analyzed in detail by transfection into heterologous cells where it causes the appearance of a new cyclic AMP- and ATP-activated small Cl^- channel with a linear I-V relationship (Riordan, 1992; Welsh et al., 1992). The major mutation, $\Delta F508$ appears to be a temperature-sensitive mutation that causes an abnormality in proper folding of the protein (Chen et al., 1990; Denning et al., 1992). Such proteins get rapidly identified by a 'quality control' mechanism that leads to their degradation from the endoplasmic reticulum, preventing their progress through the Golgi and on to the apical plasma membrane (Hurtley and Helenius, 1989). Reduction of temperature results in the appearance of cyclic AMP-regulated chloride channels in the plasma membrane that have the same conductance and I-V relationship as the wild-type protein but with a lower open probability.

One puzzling finding is that cystic fibrosis (CF) cells demonstrate abnormalities in two other channels. The amiloride-sensitive Na channel is tonically open (Willumsen and Boucher, 1991). An outwardly rectifying Cl^- channel (ORCC) is present in CF cells but it cannot be regulated by protein kinase A (PKA) (Schoumacher et al., 1987; Welsh et al., 1986); transfection with the wild-type CFTR corrects this defect (Egan et al., 1992). Because the mutant and wild-type CFTR have essentially the same elctrophysiological characterstics (except for open probability), it is likely that the ORCC is a different protein. Since the outward rectifier exhibits defective regulation in CF cells, we can conclude that when CFTR does not leave the endoplasmic reticulum abnormalities in other proteins can result.

As far as we know, p64 is not directly involved in CF. The protein exists in CF epithelial cells and does not seem to have either an abnormal location or an abnormal molecular mass, in that none of these parameters are changed when the cells are transfected with the wild-type CFTR. However, it remains possible that p64 is the outward rectifier channel and we are now attempting to reconstitute the over-expressed protein in order to test this question.

DEFECTIVE ACIDIFICATION OF VACUOLES IN CYSTIC FIBROSIS

The clinical syndrome of cystic fibrosis is characterized by thick mucus in the gastrointestinal and respiratory tracts, and colonization and infection by *Pseudomonas* bacteria (Boat et al., 1989). Chemical analysis of the mucus has demonstrated that the structure of its glycoproteins is different from those of normal mucus, it is undersialyated, oversulfated and overfucosylated (Boat and Cheng, 1980; Cheng et al., 1989). While an abnormality in cyclic AMP-mediated NaCl secretion will lead to thick 'dehydrated' mucus it cannot by itself explain the other findings listed above. We recently provided evidence for a new hypothesis that can explain these manifestations of CF (Barasch et al., 1991). This is based on the fact that the Golgi H^+-ATPase is electrogenic; hence transport of protons results in hyperpolarization of the membrane potential such that continued H^+ transport becomes energetically unfavorable (Glickman et al., 1983). The pH of the Golgi will therefore depend on the number of such channels or on their open probability.

Evidence for acidification in the *trans*-Golgi network

A number of lines of evidence shows that some compartments of the Golgi are acidified. Isolation of vesicles from the *trans*-Golgi, i.e. vesicles enriched for galactosyl transferase, showed that these vesicles acidified their interiors by an electrogenic H^+-ATPase in parallel to a chloride channel (Glickman et al., 1983). Similar results were obtained by others and the ATPase has been purified from this source by two groups (Young et al., 1988; Moriyama and Nelson, 1990). That the enzyme was functional in generating pH gradients across the Golgi membranes was demonstrated by electron microscopy using the weak base DAMP (Anderson et al., 1984; Orci et al., 1987). It is interesting that the pH was not low in the medial and *cis* compartments.

Where estimates of Golgi pH exist, it is about one pH unit lower than the cytoplasm; i.e. around pH 6.4. It is interesting that the enzymes responsible for terminal sialylation of glycoproteins and glycolipids have their optimum function at pH 5.9. Further, mutants selected for a defect in acidification exhibit defective sialylation in the Golgi (Roff et al., 1987). These results demonstrate that the pH of the *trans*-Golgi network is acid and that the low pH plays a functional role in sialylation.

Evidence that opening of Cl^- channels acidifies granules

Parafollicular cells of the thyroid contain large granules, which store serotonin and calcitonin. These granules were isolated and found to contain an electrogenic H^+-ATPase. However, the pH of the granules could not be acidified in vitro unless the membrane potential generated by the ATPase was completely collapsed by the K ionophore valinomycin. These studies suggested that the conductance of the membrane to ions was very low. The pH of these granules was examined in vivo using the permeant weak base DAMP (Anderson et al., 1984; Orci et al., 1987). There was no acidification in resting cells. However, stimulation of the cells by thyroid stimulating hormone (TSH) caused the appearance of acidification. Granules isolated from stimulated cells showed that they could now acidify in vitro and that their acidification was not dependent on valinomycin, suggesting that stimulation by TSH opened a conductance in the membrane. When the Cl⁻ permeability of the stimulated granules was examined it was found to be high while unstimulated granules had no Cl⁻ permeability. These studies demonstrated for the first time that a physiologically relevant change in the Cl⁻ conductance of an intracellular organelle could affect the vacuolar pH. Similar studies were later performed by Bae and Verkman (1990) using kidney cortex endosomes. They found that protein kinase A opened Cl⁻ channels and enhanced the acidification of these organelles.

Evidence for defective acidification of the Golgi in cystic fibrosis

We estimated the pH of the *trans*-Golgi network using the permeant weak base, DAMP. Organelles were identified by morphological and immunocytochemical criteria using the antibody to the mannose 6-phosphate receptor (M6PR). Compartments enriched in the M6PR were taken to represent the prelysosome (late endosome), (Griffiths et al., 1988). The *trans*-Golgi vesicles and the prelysosomes were found to have a higher pH in CF than in matched controls. However, lysosomes had the same pH. Hence, the defect was not simply an artifact of the accumulation or permeability of the cells to DAMP. We isolated light vesicles and heavy vesicles from immortalized respiratory epithelial cells and studied their acidification in vitro. We found that CF light vesicles (Golgi and endosomes) showed defective acidification, which was corrected if the membrane potential generated by the ATPase was nullified by a K ionophore, valinomycin. Light vesicles of normal cells did not require the addition of the ionophore to acidify maximally. Heavy vesicles (lysosomes) isolated from normal and CF cells acidified maximally regardless of the presence of valinomycin. These results confirm the acidification defect identified using the electron microscopic method.

The acidification defect was found in two sets of cells: primary cultures from nasal polyps of CF and normal children and a pair of immortalized respiratory epithelial cell lines, one from a patient with CF and the other from a normal person. Perhaps the most difficult question in these experiments is that of comparing CF cells with normal cells; the natural variation in the function of cells in culture could easily confound the results. To provide more convincing evidence for this hypothesis we have recently extended these observations to two sets of CF-PAC cells that have been 'rescued' by transfection with the wild-type CFTR gene. CF-PAC is a pancreatic adenocarcinoma cell line. In all four sets examined we have found the same defect in the acidification of Golgi and M6PR vesicles. These studies with DAMP are shown in Table 1. Hence, this defect has been observed in four pairs of cells.

Consequences of the acidification defect on sialylation of proteins and lipids

Terminal glycosylation of secreted and membrane-spanning glycoproteins occurs in the *trans*-Golgi, the only region of

Table 1. Accumulation of DAMP in identified compartments

Cell type	Mannose 6-P receptor	n	α-2,6-Sialyl transferase	n
CF-PAC	20.5±4.6	59	17.6±2.8	77
CF-PAC + CFTR	114.5±18	77	71.8±13	60

Values are number of gold dots/μm².

this organelle that is acid. Some of the Golgi enzymes have steep pH optima; 2,6-sialyl transferase has a pH optimum of 5.9 while sulfotransferase has a pH optimum centered around pH 7.0. A large number of investigators have found that cystic fibrosis mucus is poor in terminal 2,6-sialic acid residues but enriched in sulfate. Since sialylation occurs on the same residue as sulfate and since it had been previously shown that the two processes are competitive with each other, reduced sialylation would be expected to cause increased sulfation.

We recently examined the sialylation of secreted proteins in a pair of airway epithelial cell lines. We found that there was a widespread reduction in the addition of sialic acid to these proteins (Barasch et al., 1991). We have repeated these studies now in the CF-PAC cell line and compared the sialylation with that occurring in the same cell line after transfection with the wild-type CFTR gene. We found that the sialylation is higher in the rescued cell compared to the CF cell. Hence, it seems that the defect in sialylation is not restricted to airway epithelial cells but is present in a pancreatic cells as well. It is likely therefore, that the sialylation defect is present in most or all cells that express CFTR. It had previously been demonstrated that gastric mucus isolated from patients with CF is undersialyated.

Expression of a potential *Pseudomonas* receptor

We have also provided evidence that gangliosides such as GM1 are undersialyated in CF cells. It is well known that the respiratory tract of young children with CF get colonized by *Pseudomonas* in the first few months of life, suggesting that a receptor has been exposed. Indeed, most of the morbidity and mortality of CF can be attributed to the consequences of respiratory infection by *Pseudomonas*. Krivan et al. (1988) demonstrated that *Pseudomonas* binds to asialo GM1 but not to (sialo) GM1, suggesting that asialo GM1 is a receptor for *Pseudomonas*. Since glycosphingolipids are targeted to the apical membranes in epithelia (van Meer and Simons, 1988), our hypothesis provides a potential explanation for the infection with *Pseudomonas* that occurs in CF. Recent studies by our colleague at Columbia have shown that CF epithelia bind more *Pseudomonas* organisms than normal respiratory epithelia in culture. Binding of the bacteria to the epithelium is reduced almost to the normal level if the organism is coated with excess asialo GM1 before binding (Saiman and Prince, 1993).

Sulfation in the Golgi and the role of the Cl⁻ channel

Proteins are sulfated on terminal galactose residues by reaction with the sulfate donor, phosphoadenosine monophosphate sulfate (PAPS) where the transfer of the sulfate leads to the formation of 3'AMP and the sulfated protein. We found that the secreted mucus glycoproteins of CF-PAC are oversulfated when compared with the secretion from the same cells transfected with the wild-type CFTR gene.

The sulfate nucleotide is transported into the Golgi by a carrier that exchanges PAPS for 3'AMP. We had previously predicted that PAPS transport might be electrogenic, since PAPS has 4 negative charges while 3'AMP has 2.5. To test this hypothesis we loaded kidney Golgi vesicles with Cl⁻ and passed them down an anion exchange resin to generate a positive membrane potential inside only vesicles that have a Cl⁻ channel. When the vesicles were loaded with 3'AMP there was a large inhibition of the uptake of [³⁵S]PAPS by valinomycin or extravesicular Cl⁻. When vesicles were loaded with PAPS, there was little effect of valinomycin. These results suggest that Golgi vesicles will accumulate larger amount of PAPS if their membrane potential is positive inside. Our hypothesis for CF is that the absent or closed Cl⁻ channel would result in a higher .membrane potential in the Golgi. Hence, the increased sulfation is not only produced by the fact that the activity of sulfotransferase is independent of acidification, but also due to the possibility that there is a greater delivery of PAPS to the enzyme because of a possible hyperpolarization of the membrane. To test this directly, we are developing potential-sensitive probes that could measure the membrane potential in identified intracellular organelles.

The acidification defect is restricted to the biosynthetic pathway

We studied the sialylation of anonymous and known proteins in CF cells. Cells were labelled with [³⁵S]methionine to label amino acids and with the sialic acid precursor, N-[³H]acetyl mannosamine. Secreted proteins were collected and analyzed by SDS-PAGE and bands were cut and counted to obtain ³H/³⁵S ratios, which are measures of the specific activity of sialic acid addition. We found that all secreted proteins from the immortalized CF respiratory epithelial cell lines had reduced sialylation when compared with controls. In addition to these reported studies, we have now examined two pairs of CF-PAC cell lines, one member of each pair was rescued by the transfection of the wild-type CFTR gene. In these cell lines the defect in sialylation was corrected by transfection of the normal gene.

To gain more direct evidence we prepared antibodies to α-2,6-sialyl transferase and measured the pH in the environment of the enzyme using the DAMP method mentioned above. As seen in Table 1 the vesicles containing the transferase had a lower apparent pH (i.e. higher DAMP accumulation) in the rescued cells compared to the mutant cell line. As Table 1 shows, it appears that the pH defect is restricted to the biosynthetic pathway, since it was seen in sialyl transferase vesicles (trans-Golgi and beyond), and in M6PR vesicles, which are prelysosomes. The acidification of CF lysosomes was normal. These results are important, especially in reference to the studies of others who have studied the intravesicular pH of other cell lines. Lukacs et al. (1992) transfected CHO cell lines with CFTR and found that FITC-dextran was internalized into acid compartments that did not seem to be sensitive to cyclic AMP. Since the

endocytosis of dextran and of transferin occurs into early endosomes, which do not intersect with the mannose 6-phosphate receptor compartment (Stoorvogel et al., 1989), it appears that the defective acidification is restricted to the biosynthetic compartment.

We recently started to examine the function of sialyl transferase in CF using our specific antibody to the α-2,6-sialyl transferase. We were startled to find that the trafficking of this enzyme was defective in CF. There was a decrease in the total amount of sialyl transferase in the cell, which was a consequence of increased degradation. Incubation of normal cells with NH₄Cl, an alkalinizing agent, reproduced this increased degradation. Further, addition of bafilomycin, a 'specific' inhibitor of the vacuolar ATPase, led to rapid degradation of sialyl transferase within five minutes of addition. These studies suggest that the acid pH of the Golgi is not only needed for the activity of this enzyme but is also required for correct trafficking. Defective acidification, hence, can cause 'secondary' changes in sialyl transferase, which can amplify the functional defect, thereby accentuating the sialylation defect.

Studies by others on the role of CFTR in vacuolar acidification

Lukacs et al. (1992) transfected CHO cells with wild-type and mutant CFTR and allowed them to internalize FITC-dextran. They found the acidification of the organelles labelled by this ligand to be the same regardless of the type of CFTR transfected. Dextran is internalized into early endosomes and then it is transferred to lysosomes. These compartments do not intersect the mannose 6-phosphate receptor compartment to any great extent. In addition, dextran labels a large number of vesicles, none of which was identified. Finally, it is not clear that transfection of wild-type or mutant CFTR into non-epithelial cells will shed any light on the sialylation and sulfation abnormalities in epithelial cells.

The complexity of vesicle trafficking in the cells and the number of independent pathways have to be taken into consideration when discussing the question of the role of CFTR in the acidifcation of intracellular organelles.

Is CFTR the only Golgi Cl⁻ channel?

Our results show that the absence of CFTR in the trans-Golgi of epithelial cells leads to abnormal acidification with consequent abnormalities in sialylation and sulfation. The question then arises of what is responsible for normal Golgi acidification in cells that do not express CFTR. There are at least two Cl⁻ channel proteins, which are expressed in all cells tested (Jensch et al., 1991; Landry et al., 1993).

The rate of transport of the H⁺-ATPase is low, something of the order of 100 ions/second. The rate of transport of a Cl⁻ channel with a reasonable single channel conductance is at least 1,000,000 ions/second. Hence, to collapse the membrane potential generated by the few H⁺-ATPases likely to be present in a single vesicle would require no more than a single Cl⁻ channel per vesicle, which needs to be open no more than 1% of the time. This calculation assumes that the conductance of the membrane to other ions is extremely low. We have no information regarding the state of membrane conductance of the trans-Golgi. While the electrical conductance of artifical lipid bilayers is extremely low, it does vary with the lipid composition. Hence, it is possible that some cells would acidifiy their Golgi without requiring any Cl⁻ channel. The presence of Cl⁻ channels would accelerate the acidification.

Since the effect of acidification is expected to alter the sialylation and sulfation of some proteins and lipids, and since this process is known to be variable in different cells, it is possible that cells that do not express Golgi Cl⁻ channels could fail to maximally sialyate their proteins.

REFERENCES

Al-Awqati, Q. (1986). Proton translocating ATPases. *Annu. Rev. Cell Biol.* **2**, 179-199.

Anderson, R. G. W., Falk, J. R., Goldstein, J. L. and Brown, M. S. (1984). Visualization of acidic organelles in intact cells by electron microscopy. *Proc. Nat. Acad. Sci. USA* **81**, 4838-4842.

Bae, H.-R. and Verkman, A. S. (1990). Protein kinase A regulates chloride conductance in endocytic vesicles from proximal tubules. *Nature* **348**, 637-639.

Barasch, J., Gershon, M. D., Nunez, E. A., Tamir, H. and Al-Awqati, Q. (1988). Thyrotropin induces the acidification of the secretory granules of parafollicular cells by increasing the chloride conductance of the granular membrane. *J. Cell Biol.* **107**, 2137-2147.

Barasch, J., Kiss, B., Prince, A., Salman, L., Gruenert, D. and Al-Awqati, Q. (1991). Defective acidification of intracellular organelles in cystic fibrosis. *Nature* **352**, 70-73.

Boat, T. J. and Cheng, P. W. (1980). Biochemistry of airway mucus secretions. *Fed. Proc. Fed. Amer. Socs Exp. Biol.* **39**, 3067-3074.

Boat, T. J., Welsh, M. J. and Beaudet, A. L. (1989). Cystic Fibrosis. In *The Metabolic Basis of Inherited Disease*, vol. 2 (ed. C. R. Scriver, A. L. Beaudet, W. S. Sly and D. Valle), pp. 2649-2682. McGraw Hill, New York.

Chen, S. H., Gregory, R. J., Marshall, J., Paul, S., Souza, D. W. White, G. A. O'Riordan, C. R. and Smith, A. E. (1990). Defective intracellular transport and processing of CFTR is the molecular basis of most cystic fibrosis. *Cell* **63**, 827-834.

Cheng, P. W., Boat, T. F., Cranfill, K., Yankaskas, J. R. and Boucher, R. C. (1989). Increased sulfation of glycoconjugates by cultures nasal epithelial cells from patients with cystic fibrosis. *J. Clin. Invest.* **84**, 68-72.

Denning, G. M., Anderson, M. P., Amara, J. F., Marshall, J., Smith A. E. and Welsh, M. J. (1992). Processing of mutant CFTR is temperature sensitive. *Nature* **358**, 761-764.

Egan, F., Flotte, T., Afione, S., Solow, B., Zeitlin, P. L., Carter, B. J. and Guggino, W. B. (1992). Defective regulation of an outwardly rectifying Cl⁻ channels by protein kinase A corrected by insertion of CFTR. *Nature* **358**, 581-584.

Fuller, S. D. and Simons, K. (1986). Transferrin receptor polarity and recycling accuracy in leaky and tight strains of MDCK cells. *J. Cell Biol.* **103**, 1767-1779.

Glickman, J., Croen, K., Kelly, S. and Al-Awqati, Q. (1983). Golgi membranes contain an electrogenic H⁺ pump in parallel to a chloride conductance. *J. Cell Biol.* **97**, 1303-1308.

Griffiths, G., Hoflack, B., Simons, K. and Mellman, I. (1988). The mannose 6-phosphate receptor and the biogenesis of lysosomes. *Cell* **52**, 329-341.

Hurtley, S. M. and Helenius, A. (1989). Protein oligomerization in the endoplasmic reticulum. *Annu. Rev. Cell Biol.* **5**, 277-307.

Krivan, H. C., Roberts, D. D. and Ginsburg, V. (1988b). Many pulmonary pathogenic bacteria bind specifically to the carbohydrate sequence GalNAcβ1-4Gal found in some glycolipids. *Proc. Nat. Acad. Sci. USA* **85**, 6157-6161.

Landry, D. W., Reitman, M., Cragoe, E. J. Jr and Al-Awqati, Q. (1987).

Epithelial chloride channel. Development of inhibitory ligands. *J. Gen. Physiol.* **90**, 779-798.

Landry, D. W., Akabas, M. H., Redhead, C., Edelman, A., Cragoe, E. J. and Al-Awqati, Q. (1989). Purification and reconstitution of chloride channels from kidney and trachea. *Science* **244**, 1469-1472.

Landry, D. W., Sullivan, S., Nicolaides, M., Redhead, C., Edelman, A., Field, M., Al-Awqati, Q. and Edwards, J. (1993). Molecular cloning of p64, a chloride channel protein. *J. Biol. Chem.* **268**, 14948-14955.

Lukacs, G. L., Chang, X. B., Kartner, N., Rotstein, O. D., Riordan, J. R. and Grinstein, S. (1992). The cystic fibrosis transmembrane regulator is present and functional in endosomes. Role as a determinant of endosomal pH. *J. Biol. Chem.* **267**, 14568-1457.

Moriyama, Y., and Nelson, N. (1989). H⁺ translocating ATPase in Golgi apparatus: characterization as vacuolar H⁺-ATPase and its subunit structure. *J. Biol. Chem.* **264**, 18445-18450.

Olsen, R. W. and Tobin, A. J. (1990). Molecular biology of GABAₐ receptors. *FASEB J.* **4**, 469-480.

Orci, L., Ravazzola, M., Amherdr, M., Madsen, O., Perrelet, A., Vassalli, J. D. and Anderson, R. G. W. (1987). Conversion of pro-insulin to insulin occurs coordinately with acidification of maturing secretory granules. *J. Cell Biol.* **103**, 2273-2281.

Paulmichl, M., Li, Y., Wickman, K., Ackerman, M., Peralta, E. and Clapham, D. (1992). New mammalian chloride channel identified by expression cloning. *Nature* **356**, 238-241.

Ran, S. and Benos, D. J. (1991). Purification and reconstitution of a chloride channel from tracheal membranes. *J. Biol. Chem.* **266**, 4782-4788.

Redhead, C. R., Edelman, A., Brown, D., Landry, D. W. and Al-Awqat,. Q. (1992). A ubiquitous 64 kDa protein is a component of a chloride channel of plasma and intracellular membranes. *Proc. Nat. Acad. Sci. USA* **89**, 3716-3720.

Riordan, J. R. (1992). The molecular biology of chloride channels. *Curr. Opin. Nephrol. Hypert.* **1**, 35-42.

Roff, C. F., Fuchs, R., Mellman, I. and Robbins, A. R. (1987). Chinese hamster ovary cell mutants with temperature-sensitive defects in endocytosis. I. Loss of function on shifting to the non-permissive temperature. *J. Cell Biol.* **103**, 2283-2297.

Saiman, L. and Prince, A. (1993). Pseudomonas aeruginosa pili bind to asialo GM, which is increased on the surface of cystic fibrosis epithelial cells. *J. Clin. Invest.* **92**, 1875-1880.

Schmid, S., Fuchs, R., Male, P. and Mellman, I. (1988). Two distinct subpopulations of endosomes involved in membrane recycling and and transport to lysosomes. *Cell* **52**, 73-83.

Schoumacher, R. A., Shoemaker, R. L., Halm, D. R., Tallant, E. A., Wallace, R. W. and Frizzell, R. A. (1987). Phosphorylation fails to activate chloride channels from cystic fibrosis airway cells. *Nature* **330**, 752-754

Steinmayer, K., Ortland, C. and Jentsch, T. J. (1991). Primary structure and functional expression of a developmentally regulated skeletal muscle chloride channel. *Nature* **354**, 301-304.

Stoorvogel, W., Geuze, H. J., Grifith, J. M., Schwartz, A. L. and Strous, G. J. (1989). Relations between the intracellular pathways of the receptors for transferrin, asialoglycoprotein, and mannose 6-phosphate in human hepatoma cells. *J. Cell Biol.* **108**, 2137-2148.

van Meer, G. and Simons, K. (1988). Lipid polarity and sorting in epithelial cells. *J. Cell. Biochem.* **36**, 51-58.

Weiss, M. S. and Schulz, G. E. (1992). Structure of porin refined at 1.8 A resolution. *J. Mol. Biol.* **227**, 493-509.

Welsh, M. J., Anderson, M. P., Rich, D. P., Berger, H. A., Denning, G. M., OStergaard, L. S., Sheppard, D. N., Cheng, S. H., Gregory, R. J. and Smith, A. E. (1992). CFTR: a chloride channel with novel regulation. *Neuron* **8**, 821-829.

Welsh, M. J. and Liedtke, C. M. (1986). Chloride and potassium channels in cystic fibrosis airway epithelia. *Nature* **322**, 467-470.

Willumsen, N. J. and Boucher, R. C. (1991). Na transport and intracellular Na activity in cultured human nasal epithelium. *Amer. J. Physiol.* **261**, C319-C331.

Young, G. P. H., Qiao, J. Z. and Al-Awqati, Q. (1988). Purification and reconstitution of the proton translocating ATPase of Golgi-enriched membranes. *Proc. Nat. Acad. Sci. USA* **85**, 9590-9594.

Journal of Cell Science, Supplement 17, 235-239 (1993)
Printed in Great Britain © The Company of Biologists Limited 1993

Dysfunction of CFTR bearing the ΔF508 mutation

Michael J. Welsh, Gerene M. Denning, Lynda S. Ostedgaard and Matthew P. Anderson

Howard Hughes Medical Institute, Departments of Internal Medicine and Physiology and Biophysics, University of Iowa College of Medicine, Iowa City, Iowa 52242, USA

SUMMARY

The cystic fibrosis transmembrane conductance regulator (CFTR) is mutated in patients with cystic fibrosis (CF). The most common CF-associated mutation is deletion of phenylanine at residue 508, CFTRΔF508. When expressed in heterologous cells, CFTR bearing the ΔF508 mutation fails to progress through the normal biosynthetic pathway and fails to traffic to the plasma membrane. As a result, CFTRΔF508 is mislocalized and is not present in the apical membrane of primary cultures of airway epithelia. Consequently, the apical membrane of CF airway epithelia is Cl⁻-impermeable, a defect that probably contributes to the pathogenesis of the disease.

Key words: cystic fibrosis, chloride channel, processing, trafficking, apical membrane

INTRODUCTION

Cystic fibrosis transmembrane conductance regulator (CFTR) (Riordan et al., 1989) is a regulated Cl⁻ channel located in the apical membrane of several Cl⁻-secretory epithelia (for a review, see Welsh et al., 1992). Mutations in the gene encoding CFTR cause cystic fibrosis (CF) (Kerem et al., 1989; Tsui, 1992). These two observations begin to explain the best characterized physiological defect in CF, namely affected epithelia lack a cAMP-regulated apical membrane Cl⁻ conductance (Quinton, 1990). The loss of cAMP-regulated Cl⁻ permeability is manifest in a number of CF epithelia including the pancreas, the intestine, the sweat gland secretory coil, the sweat gland absorptive duct and the pulmonary airways. In each organ, abnormal transepithelial electrolyte transport is thought to contribute to the pathogenesis of the disease. However, it is lung disease that is the major cause of morbidity and mortality in CF (Boat et al., 1989). In the lung, defective electrolyte transport is thought to alter the quantity and composition of the respiratory tract fluid, thereby contributing to the impaired mucociliary clearance observed in patients with CF.

In order to understand the pathogenesis of CF it is important to understand how mutations cause a loss of CFTR Cl⁻ channel function. The most common CF-associated mutation is deletion of a phenylalanine at residue 508 (ΔF508) (Kerem et al., 1989; Tsui, 1992). This mutation accounts for approximately 70% of CF chromosomes. Here I discuss some of the mechanisms that cause dysfunction of CFTR bearing the ΔF508 mutation.

PREDICTED STRUCTURE OF CFTR

Amino acid sequence analysis and comparison of the sequence with that of other proteins suggested that CFTR consists of five domains (Riordan et al., 1989) (Fig. 1). Beginning at the amino terminus there is a putative membrane-spanning domain (MSD1), composed of six possible membrane-spanning α-helices. MSD1 is followed by a nucleotide-binding domain (NBD1) in which there is sequence similarity with nucleotide-binding sequences from a number of other proteins. Then comes the R (regulatory) domain, which contains multiple phosphorylation sites for cAMP-dependent protein kinase (PKA) and protein kinase C. After the R domain, the protein re-enters the membrane with a second membrane-spanning domain (MSD2) followed by a second nucleotide-binding domain (NBD2).

Sequence similarity between the NBDs and the topology of CFTR (with the exception of the R domain) suggest that CFTR belongs to a family of proteins called the traffic ATPases (Ames et al., 1990), or ATP-Binding Cassette (ABC) transporters (Hyde et al., 1990). Most members of this family are ATP-dependent transporters; they include periplasmic permeases in prokaryotes and P-glycoprotein responsible for multiple drug resistance (MDR) in eukaryotes. However, recent studies indicate that CFTR is a regulated Cl⁻ channel. Studies of CFTR containing site-directed mutations have begun to provide some information about the function of the individual domains (Welsh et al., 1992). The MSDs are thought to contribute to the formation of the channel pore. Mutation of specific basic residues to acidic residues within the first MSD alters the anion selectivity of the channel. The R domain regulates channel activity. Phosphorylation of the R domain at several different sites opens the channel. Regulation by phosphorylation with cAMP-dependent protein kinase (PKA) is complex: phosphorylation of multiple different PKA-consensus sequences regulates the channel. Moreover, deletion of part

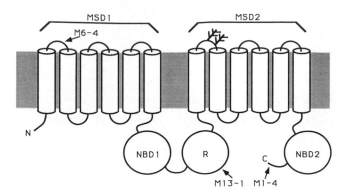

Fig. 1. Model showing the putative domains of CFTR. The glycosylation sites in MSD2 are indicated. The epitopes of antibodies M6-4, M13-1 and M1-4 are indicated.

of the R domain produces a channel that is open even without phosphorylation. The NBDs also control channel activity through an interaction with cytosolic nucleotides. ATP interacts with both NBDs and hydrolysis is probably required for channel opening. It is also possible that CFTR may have other activities in addition to being a regulated channel.

The NBDs and the R domain distinguish CFTR from the structure of known voltage- and ligand-gated ion channels, indicating that CFTR may represent the first identified member of a new family of ion channels. Recent work showing that expression of MDR is associated with volume-regulated Cl⁻ channels (Mostov et al., 1992; Gill et al., 1992) suggests that MDR may also be an ion channel and that other channels with this motif may be discovered.

TOPOLOGY OF CFTR

The topology of the model shown in Fig. 1 is not known with certainty, but the location, with reference to the membrane, of several sites is known (Denning et al., 1992b). The amino terminus is likely to be intracellular because of the lack of a signal sequence; the first predicted extracellular loop is likely to be so because it is recognized by antibodies directed to that epitope in nonpermeabilized cells; the NBD1 and R domains are intracellular, as assessed by the regulation of these two domains by ATP and phosphorylation, respectively, and because an antibody directed against the R domain only stains permeabilized cells; the third extracellular loop is extracellular because it contains sites that are glycosylated; NBD2 is intracellular, as assessed by the regulation of this domain by ATP; and finally, the C terminus is likely to be intracellular because it is recognized by antibodies directed against this epitope only after cells have been permeabilized.

CFTR IS LOCATED IN THE APICAL MEMBRANE OF SECRETORY EPITHELIA

For CFTR Cl⁻ channels to govern transepithelial Cl⁻ secretion, they must be located in the apical membrane. A

number of antibodies have been used to immunolocalize CFTR. CFTR has been found in the apical region of several epithelia including small pancreatic ducts, intestinal epithelia and Cl⁻-secreting epithelial cell lines (Marino et al., 1991; Crawford et al., 1991; Denning et al., 1992b,c; Kartner et al., 1992; Engelhardt and Wilson, 1992).

To directly determine whether CFTR is located in the apical membrane, we turned to intestinal epithelial cells that express high levels of endogenous CFTR and have cAMP-activated apical membrane Cl⁻ permeability (Denning et al., 1992b). We used T84 cells, CaCo2 cells, and HT29 clone 19A cells. In order to identify CFTR that is localized specifically in the apical membrane, the cells were grown on permeable filter supports so that they polarized, segregating apical from basolateral membrane proteins, and developed a transepithelial resistance and the ability to secrete Cl⁻ from the basal to the apical surface. We used monoclonal antibodies directed against different regions of the protein: the R domain (M13-1), the COOH terminus (M1-4) and a predicted extracellular domain (M6-4). All three antibodies immunoprecipitated and immunostained recombinant CFTR expressed in heterologous cells.

We immunostained the epithelial cells and examined the cellular distribution of CFTR using confocal laser-scanning microscopy. We found that the pattern of staining for CFTR resembled the staining pattern observed with several apical membrane markers. However, it differed from the staining pattern for basolateral membrane proteins. The majority of CFTR staining was observed at the apical pole. In thin sections of cell monolayers, we also observed staining specifically at the apical membrane.

However, such immunocytochemical studies cannot distinguish between CFTR that is located in the apical membrane and CFTR that is located in a vesicular pole just beneath the apical membrane. This distinction is important for understanding the function and regulation of CFTR. Evidence that CFTR is located in the apical membrane came from studies in nonpermeabilized cells. We found that antibody M6-4, directed against an extracellular epitope, stained nonpermeabilized epithelia. In contrast, antibodies directed against intracellular epitopes (M13-1 and M1-4) only stained permeabilized monolayers.

The conclusion that CFTR is a regulated Cl⁻ channel and the observation that it is located in the apical membrane, places it in a location where its activation by PKA-dependent phosphorylation would directly mediate Cl⁻ exit from the cell during Cl⁻ secretion. It is also, however, possible that CFTR is located beneath the apical membrane and functions on intracellular membranes (Barasch et al., 1991).

CFTRΔF508 IS INCOMPLETELY GLYCOSYLATED

Studies of the biosynthesis of CFTR in transfected cells identified a defect associated with the ΔF508 mutation (Cheng et al., 1990; Gregory et al., 1991). The progress of wild-type CFTR through the biosynthetic pathway can be followed by its state of glycosylation (Fig. 2). The nascent CFTR protein migrates at approximately 150 kDa on a polyacrylamide gel (this form is referred to as band A) (Gregory et al., 1990; De Jonge et al., 1989; Gregory et al.,

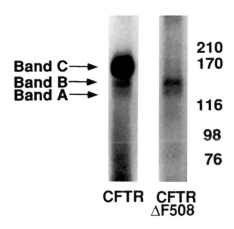

Fig. 2. Migration of CFTR on a polyacrylamide gel. Immunoprecipitates of CFTR and CFTRΔF508 were phosphorylated with PKA and [³²P]ATP and separated by gel electrophoresis. The unglycosylated protein is band A. The core glycosylated form is band B, and the fully glycosylated form is band C. The positions of marker proteins (kDa) are indicated.

1991). A more slowly migrating form is called band B. This form represents core glycosylated protein that is endoglycosidase H-sensitive, suggesting partial glycosylation in the endoplasmic reticulum. The mature form of the protein migrates as band C, a broad diffuse band of approximately 170 kDa. The band C form is endoglycosidase H-insensitive, but can be shifted to band A with N-Glycanase treatment.

In contrast to results with wild-type CFTR, when CFTRΔF508 was expressed in heterologous cells, it migrated only as bands A and B. Based on these results, Cheng and his coworkers (Cheng et al., 1990; Gregory et al., 1991) proposed that the ΔF508 mutant version of CFTR is misfolded. The abnormal glycosylation pattern of CFTRΔF508 suggested that the mutant protein did not reach the Golgi complex and was not delivered to the plasma membrane. Instead, it was recognized as abnormal and targeted for retention and degradation in the endoplasmic reticulum. Incomplete glycosylation does not in itself cause Cl⁻ impermeability, because protein that lacked glycosylation sites (constructed by site-directed mutagenesis) was present in the plasma membrane and had normal Cl⁻ channel activity.

CFTRΔF508 IS MISSING FROM THE APICAL MEMBRANE OF AIRWAY EPITHELIA

A direct test of the hypothesis that CFTRΔF508 is not at the apical membrane of CF epithelia requires several things. First, it requires the use of nonrecombinant normal and CF epithelia. Because the studies of protein glycosylation were done in recombinant cells, the results could have been an artifact of overexpressing CFTR, or of expressing it in nonpolarized cells. Second, it requires a method of assessing whether CFTR is actually in the apical membrane, because that is where the CF defect in Cl⁻ permeability resides (Quinton, 1990; Boat et al., 1989). Third, it requires a detec-

tion method, which is very sensitive and which clearly distinguishes signal from background. This is essential because CFTR is often present at low levels in nonrecombinant cells (Riordan et al., 1989; Trapnell et al., 1991). To assess the location of CFTR, we used primary cultures of CF airway epithelial cells because they are the main site of disease in patients with CF. We cultured the cells on permeable filter supports so that they developed a transepithelial resistance and polarized with a distinct apical membrane that expresses the CF Cl⁻ transport defect.

To localize CFTR that is in the apical membrane and provide a quantifiable method for assessing antibody binding, we developed a new technique (Denning et al., 1992c). We incubated nonpermeabilized airway epithelia with the antibody directed against the extracellular epitope (M6-4). We then incubated with a biotinylated secondary antibody followed by streptavidin. Finally, we incubated the cells with a suspension of biotinylated fluorescent beads. The beads were easy to count because of their large size (approximately 1 μm) and high fluorescence intensity. In principle, this method is similar to immunogold electron microscopy. As controls we used antibodies against intracellular epitopes (M13-1 or M1-4), nonspecific mouse IgG, or no primary antibody.

To verify the technique we tested it with T84 cells, which express CFTR in the apical membrane, and with NIH 3T3 fibroblasts expressing recombinant CFTR. The data showed that nonspecific binding was identical for all of the antibodies except antibody M6-4, directed against an extracellular epitope. That antibody showed at an increased number of beads bound per field in cells expressing wild-type CFTR, but not in cells expressing CFTRΔF508.

We used this technique to examine primary cultures of CF airway epithelial cells. Fig. 3A shows binding of antibody/bead complexes to the apical membrane of nonpermeabilized airway epithelia. In nonCF epithelia, the number of beads per field with antibody M6-4 was always greater than with control antibodies, including antibody M1-4, M13-1 and nonimmune mouse IgG. In contrast, in CF epithelia there was no difference in the number of beads per field when epithelia were exposed to antibody M6-4 or the various controls. This result suggests that CFTR is in the apical membrane of normal airway epithelia, but is missing from or present at a greatly reduced amount in the apical membrane of CF epithelia. The CF epithelia studied in Fig. 2 were derived from patients bearing the ΔF508 mutation, other mutations that are also misprocessed, nonsense mutations that would be expected to fail to produce a complete protein, or unidentified mutations.

The difference between normal and CF epithelia is illustrated more clearly in Fig. 3B, which shows the data from Fig. 3A normalized to the average number of beads/field observed with antibody M1-4. In normal epithelia, binding with antibody M6-4 averaged 4.65 ± 1.00 times the binding with antibody M1-4. In contrast in CF epithelia, binding with antibody M6-4 was 1.02 ± 0.03 times the binding with antibody M1-4.

We also studied permeabilized airway epithelial cells, immunostained them with antibodies against intracellular epitopes, and then used confocal laser scanning microscopy to localize CFTR. In normal airway epithelia, we found the

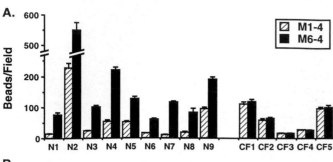

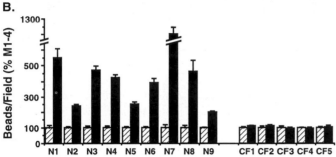

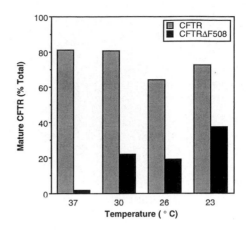

Fig. 4. Effect of temperature on processing of CFTR and CFTRΔF508. Data show the percent of total CFTR that is present in the mature, band C form. Cells were grown at the indicated temperatures for two days before immunoprecipitation of CFTR. From Denning et al. (1992a), with permission.

Fig. 3. (A) Binding of antibody/bead complex to the apical membrane of nonpermeabilized normal and CF airway epithelia. Data are from nine normal and five CF cultures, each from a different subject. Nonpermeabilized primary cultures of airway epithelia were incubated with antibodies M1-4 (crosshatch bars) or M6-4 (solid bars). (B) Data from (A) normalized to the average number of beads/field observed with antibody M1-4. From Denning et al. (1992c), with permission.

most intense staining in the area of the apical membrane. In contrast, in CF epithelia containing the ΔF508 mutation, the brightest staining was encountered beneath the apical membrane in a pattern spread throughout the cytoplasm. Because of the low level of immunostaining, we have not been able to localize mutant CFTR to a specific intracellular organelle: however, in some CF epithelia the pattern appeared to be primarily perinuclear.

PROCESSING OF CFTRΔF508 REVERTS TOWARD THAT OF WILD TYPE AT REDUCED TEMPERATURE

Our finding that CFTR containing the ΔF508 mutant is not present in the plasma membrane is consistent with earlier functional studies, which have failed to detect cAMP-stimulated Cl⁻ currents in the apical membrane of CF epithelial cells (Quinton, 1990), as well as with previous studies that have failed to detect cAMP-stimulated Cl⁻ channels in cells expressing CFTRΔF508 (Rich et al., 1990). Cl⁻ channel activity was detected, however, when CFTRΔF508 was expressed in Xenopus oocytes (Drumm et al., 1991), Vero cells (Dalemans et al., 1991) and Sf9 insect cells (Bear et al., 1992). Because oocytes and Sf9 cells are typically maintained at lower temperatures than mammalian cells, and because processing of nascent proteins can be sensitive to temperature, we tested the effect of temperature on the processing of CFTRΔF508.

As a marker of processing, we measured the amount of

CFTR that is present in the mature, fully glycosylated band C form (Denning et al., 1992a). We found that when temperature was reduced from 37°C to lower temperatures, processing of wild-type CFTR was not appreciably affected. However, in the ΔF508 mutant the reduction in temperature produced an increase in the amount of mature CFTR (Fig. 4). This observation is consistent with the finding in other systems that the conformation of nascent proteins and their subsequent processing and transport can be temperature-sensitive.

We found that the amount of mature, fully glycosylated band C CFTR increased in amount as the duration of incubation temperature increased and that the effect was reversible. When cells were incubated at a low temperature to allow CFTR to mature and then were switched back to the nonpermissive 37°C, the amount of CFTR progressively decreased with a half-time of approximately seven hours. Moreover, in pulse-chase experiments we found that if the protein was synthesized at 37°C and then the temperature was reduced to 26°C, mutant CFTR that had been synthesized at 37°C was chased into the mature form. This result shows that correct processing of the mutant is not the result of an effect of temperature on protein synthesis.

These results suggested that at a reduced temperature, CFTRΔF508 was delivered to the plasma membrane, where it could mediate Cl⁻ transport. To test that hypothesis, we used the whole-cell patch-clamp to measure cAMP-activated Cl⁻ currents in the plasma membrane of cells expressing CFTRΔF508. We found that after incubation at 30°C for two days, cAMP agonists stimulated large Cl⁻-selective currents. All of the properties of these currents were the same as those of wild-type, with the exception that when they were studied at the single channel level they had a reduced probability of being in the open state (P_o). In excised, cell-free patches addition of PKA and 1 mM ATP produced a P_o of 0.34 for wild-type CFTR and 0.13 for CFTRΔF508. The reduced P_o of CFTRΔF508 is similar to a value previously reported from CFTR expressed in Vero cells (Dalemans et al., 1991).

These data suggest that the defective processing of CFTR can be corrected when temperature is reduced. They also indicate that when the mutant CFTRΔF508 is correctly localized, it retains at least partial function. Thus, the possibility is raised that a therapeutic maneuver designed to deliver mutant protein to the plasma membrane could be of potential benefit in CF.

REFERENCES

Ames, G. F., Mimura, C. S. and Shyamala, V. (1990). Bacterial periplasmic permeases belong to a family of transport proteins operating from *Escherichia coli* to human: Traffic ATPases. *FEMS Microbiol. Rev.* **75**, 429-446.

Barasch, J., Kiss, B., Prince, A., Saiman, L., Gruenert, D. and Al-Awqati, Q. (1991). Defective acidification of intracellular organelles in cystic fibrosis. *Nature* **352**, 70-73.

Bear, C. E., Jensen, T. J. and Riordan, J. R. (1992). Functional capacity of the major mutant form of the cystic fibrosis transmembrane conductance regulator. *Biophys. J.* **61**, A127.

Boat, T. F., Welsh, M. J. and Beaudet, A. L. (1989). Cystic fibrosis. In *The Metabolic Basis of Inherited Disease* (ed. C. R. Scriver, A. L. Beaudet, W. S. Sly, and D. Valle), pp. 2649-2680. New York, NY: McGraw-Hill, Inc.

Cheng, S. H., Gregory, R. J., Marshall, J., Paul, S., Souza, D. W., White, G. A., O'Riordan, C. R. and Smith, A. E. (1990). Defective intracellular transport and processing of CFTR is the molecular basis of most cystic fibrosis. *Cell* **63**, 827-834.

Crawford, I., Maloney, P. C., Zeitlin, P. L., Guggino, W. B., Hyde, S. C., Turley, H., Gatter, K. C., Harris, A. and Higgins, C. F. (1991). Immunocytochemical localization of the cystic fibrosis gene product CFTR. *Proc. Nat. Acad. Sci. USA* **88**, 9262-9266.

Dalemans, W., Barbry, P., Champigny, G., Jallat, S., Dott, K., Dreyer, D., Crystal, R. G., Pavirani, A., Lecocq, J. P. and Lazdunski, M. (1991). Altered chloride ion channel kinetics associated with the delta F508 cystic fibrosis mutation. *Nature* **354**, 526-528.

De Jonge, H. R., Van Den Berghe, N., Tilly, B. C., Kansen, M. and Bijman, J. (1989). (Dys)regulation of epithelial chloride channels. *Biochem. Soc. Trans.* **17**, 816-818.

Denning, G. M., Anderson, M. P., Amara, J., Marshall, J., Smith, A. E. and Welsh, M. J. (1992a). Processing of mutant CFTR(Δ508) is temperature sensitive. *Nature* **358**, 761-764.

Denning, G. M., Ostedgaard, L. S., Cheng, S. H., Smith, A. E. and Welsh, M. J. (1992b). Localization of cystic fibrosis transmembrane conductance regulator in chloride secretory epithelia. *J. Clin. Invest.* **89**, 339-349.

Denning, G. M., Ostedgaard, L. S. and Welsh, M. J. (1992c). Abnormal localization of cystic fibrosis transmembrane conductance regulator in primary cultures of cystic fibrosis airway epithelia. *J. Cell Biol.* **118**, 551-559.

Drumm, M. L., Wilkinson, D. J., Smit, L. S., Worrell, R. T., Strong, T. V., Frizzell, R. A., Dawson, D. C. and Collins, F. S. (1991). Chloride conductance expressed by delta F508 and other mutant CFTRs in Xenopus oocytes. *Science* **254**, 1797-1799.

Engelhardt, J. F. and Wilson, J. M. (1992). Expression of normal and variant CFTR in human bronchus. *Pediatr. Pulmon.* **8**, 185-186.

Gill, D. R., Hyde, S. C., Higgins, C. F., Valverde, M. A., Mintenig, G. M. and Sepulveda, F. V. (1992). Separation of drug transport and chloride channel functions of the human multidrug resistance P-glycoprotein. *Cell* **71**, 23-32.

Gregory, R. J., Cheng, S. H., Rich, D. P., Marshall, J., Paul, S., Hehir, K., Ostedgaard, L., Klinger, K. W., Welsh, M. J. and Smith, A. E. (1990). Expression and characterization of the cystic fibrosis transmembrane conductance regulator. *Nature* **347**, 382-386.

Gregory, R. J., Rich, D. P., Cheng, S. H., Souza, D. W., Paul, S., Manavalan, P., Anderson, M. P., Welsh, M. J. and Smith, A. F. (1991). Maturation and function of cystic fibrosis transmembrane conductance regulator variants bearing mutations in putative nucleotide-binding domains 1 and 2. *Mol. Cell. Biol.* **11**, 3886-3893.

Hyde, S. C., Emsley, P., Hartshorn, M. J., Mimmack, M. M., Gileadi, U., Pearce, S. R., Gallagher, M. P., Gill, D. R., Hubbard, R. E. and Higgins, C. F. (1990). Structural model of ATP-binding proteins associated with cystic fibrosis, multidrug resistance and bacterial transport. *Nature* **346**, 362-365.

Kartner, N., Augustinas, O., Jensen, T. J., Naismith, A. L. and Riordan, J. R. (1992). Mislocalization of ΔF508 CFTR in cystic fibrosis sweat gland. *Nature Gen.* **1**, 321-327.

Kerem, B-S., Rommens, J. M., Buchanan, J. A., Markiewicz, D., Cox, T. K., Chakravarti, A., Buchwald, M. and Tsui, L-C. (1989). Identification of the cystic fibrosis gene: genetic analysis. *Science* **245**, 1073-1080.

Marino, C. R., Matovcik, L. M., Gorelick, F. S. and Cohn, J. A. (1991). Localization of the cystic fibrosis transmembrane conductance regulator in pancreas. *J. Clin. Invest.* **88**, 712-716.

Mostov, K., Apodaca, G., Aroeti, B. and Okamoto, C. (1992). Plasma membrane protein sorting in polarized epithelial cells. *J. Cell Biol.* **116**, 577-583.

Quinton, P. M. (1990). Cystic fibrosis: a disease in electrolyte transport. *FASEB J.* **4**, 2709-2717.

Rich, D. P., Anderson, M. P., Gregory, R. J., Cheng, S. H., Paul, S., Jefferson, D. M., McCann, J. D., Klinger, K. W., Smith, A. E. and Welsh, M. J. (1990). Expression of cystic fibrosis transmembrane conductance regulator corrects defective chloride channel regulation in cystic fibrosis airway epithelial cells. *Nature* **347**, 358-363.

Riordan, J. R., Rommens, J. M., Kerem, B-S., Alon, N., Rozmahel, R., Grzelczak, Z., Zielenski, J., Lok, S., Plavsic, N., Chou, J-L., Drumm, M. L., Iannuzzi, M. C., Collins, F. S. and Tsui, L-C. (1989). Identification of the cystic fibrosis gene: cloning and characterization of complementary DNA. *Science* **245**, 1066-1073.

Trapnell, B. C., Chu, C. S., Paakko, P. K., Banks, T. C., Yoshimura, K., Ferrans, V. J., Chernick, M. S. and Crystal, R. G. (1991). Expression of the cystic fibrosis transmembrane conductance regulator gene in the respiratory tract of normal individuals and individuals with cystic fibrosis. *Proc. Nat. Acad. Sci. USA* **88**, 6565-6569.

Tsui, L-C. (1992). Mutations and sequence variations detected in the cystic fibrosis transmembrane conductance regulator (CFTR) gene: A report from the cystic fibrosis genetic analysis consortium. *Human Mutation* **1**, 197-203.

Welsh, M. J., Anderson, M. P., Rich, D. P., Berger, H. A., Denning, G. M., Ostedgaard, L. S., Sheppard, D. N., Cheng, S. H., Gregory, R. J. and Smith, A. E. (1992). Cystic fibrosis transmembrane conductance regulator: a chloride channel with novel regulation. *Neuron* **8**, 821-829.

Index

Journal of Cell Science Supplements

No. 1 Higher Order Structure in the Nucleus
Edited by P. R. Cook and R. A. Laskey
ISBN: 0 9508709 4 3   234 pp.
Proceedings of 1st BSCB–COB Symposium
£8   U.S.$17   1984

No. 2 The Cell Surface in Plant Growth and Development
Edited by K. Roberts, A. W. B. Johnston, C. W. Lloyd, P. Shaw and H. W. Woolhouse
ISBN: 0 9508709 7 8   350 pp.
The 6th John Innes Symposium
£11   U.S.$24   1985

No. 3 Growth Factors: Structure and Function
Edited by C. R. Hopkins and R. C. Hughes
ISBN: 0 9508709 9 4   242 pp.
BSCB–COB Symposium
Sold out   1985

No. 4 Prospects in Cell Biology
Edited by A. V. Grimstone, Henry Harris and R. T. Johnson
ISBN: 0 948601 01 9   458 pp.
An essay volume to mark the journal's 20th anniversary
Sold out   1986

No. 5 The Cytoskeleton: Cell Function and Organization
Edited by C. W. Lloyd, J. S. Hyams and R. M. Warn
ISBN: 0 948601 04 3   360 pp.
BSCB–COB Symposium
Sold out   1986

No. 6 The Molecular Biology of DNA Repair
Edited by A. R. S. Collins, R. T. Johnson and J. M. Boyle
ISBN: 0 948601 06 X   353 pp.
£36   U.S.$64   1987

No. 7 Virus Replication and Genome Interactions
Edited by J. W. Davies et al.
ISBN: 0 948601 10 8   350 pp.
The 7th John Innes Symposium
£36   U.S.$64   1987

No. 8 Cell Behaviour: Shape, Adhesion and Motility
Edited by J. Heaysman, A. Middleton and F. Watts
ISBN: 0 948601 12 4   449 pp.
BSCB–COB Symposium
£31   U.S.$54   1987

No. 9 Macrophage Plasma Membrane Receptors: Structure and Function
Edited by S. Gordon
ISBN: 0 948601 13 2   200 pp.
£25   U.S.$44   1988

No. 10 Stem Cells
Edited by Brian I. Lord and T. Michael Dexter
ISBN: 0 948601 16 7   285 pp.
BSCB–COB Symposium
£31   U.S.$59   1988

No. 11 Protein Targeting
Edited by K. F. Chater et al.
ISBN: 0 948601 21 3   261 pp.
The 8th John Innes Symposium
£31   U.S.$59   1989

No. 12 The Cell Cycle
Edited by R. T. Hunt et al.
ISBN: 0 948601 23 X   300 pp.
BSCB–COB Symposium
Sold out   1989

No. 13 Growth Factors in Cell & Developmental Biology
Edited by M. Waterfield
ISBN: 0 948601 27 3   208 pp. + index
£26   U.S.$49   1990

No. 14 Motor Proteins
Edited by R. Cross and J. Kendrick Jones
ISBN: 0 948601 29 9   175 pp.
EMBO techniques workshop
£31   U.S.$54   1991

No. 15 Nerve Cell Biology
Edited by Dennis Bray and A. Lumsden et al.
ISBN: 0 948601 30 2   134 pp.
BSCB–COB Symposium
£34   U.S.$62   1991

No. 16 Transcriptional Regulation in Cell Differentiation and Development
Edited by Peter Rigby, Robb Krumlauf and Frank Grosveld
ISBN: 0 948601 37 X   130 pp.
BSCB–COB Symposium
£34   U.S.$52   1992

No. 17 Epithelial and Neuronal Cell Polarity and Differentiation
Edited by E. Rodriguez Boulan and W. J. Nelson
ISBN: 0 948601 40 X   245 pp.
Keystone Symposium
£49   U.S.$69   1993

> This series of supplementary casebound volumes deals with topics of outstanding interest to cell and molecular biologists

These are provided free to subscribers to *Journal of Cell Science*. They may be purchased separately from:
The Company of Biologists Limited, Bidder Building, 140 Cowley Road, Cambridge CB4 4DL, UK

ORDERING: Add £4 ($6) per book for postage and packaging
24-hour by FAX: Cambridge (0223) 423353/International +44 223 423353